American Minority Relations

Fourth Edition

James W. Vander Zanden

Ohio State University

Alfred A. Knopf   *New York*

THIS IS A BORZOI BOOK PUBLISHED BY
ALFRED A. KNOPF, INC.
Fourth Edition

987654321
Copyright © 1983 by Alfred A. Knopf, Inc.
Copyright © 1963, 1966, 1972 by The Ronald Press
Company
Library of Congress Cataloging in Publication Data

Vander Zanden, James Wilfrid.
American minority relations.

Includes bibliographical references and indexes.
1. Minorities —United States.   2. United States —Race
relations. 3. Racism —United States.
I. Title.
E184.A1V3 1983   305.8′00973   82-13958
ISBN 0-394-32954-6

Manufactured in the United States of America

Book designed by Karin Gerdes Kincheloe

Preface

*T*his fourth edition of a widely-used and successful textbook is designed for the course in minority relations. In the past two decades a deluge of new materials treating American minority relations has appeared. Indeed, it has reached a point where many a specialist in the area feels overwhelmed. Although in truth a good deal of the material has had a journalistic and impressionistic quality, it nonetheless has generally contained useful insights into various facets of minority-dominant relations. In addition, there has been a significant proliferation of sophisticated empirical studies, often encompassing and cutting across several disciplines—sociology, psychology, biology, anthropology, political science, and history.

Students in race relations courses should have access to the newly available knowledge in some convenient, manageable form—and in a form that is relevant to the contemporary world in which they live. And that is the purpose of this text. It aims to be home base for the student, providing a solid, sound foundation for exploring the field. While thorough and comprehensive, it is intentionally compact so that instructors can additionally, if they so choose, select from the large array of current supplementary titles.

In treating the vast amount of data and theory within the field, I have attempted to strike a judicious balance between theory and description. This approach avoids the disadvantages of a mere descriptive rundown of each of the minority groups, on the one hand, and a too ambitious theoretical and conceptual approach, on the other. The former, it seems to me, fails to provide a firm grounding in theory or to give the reader an understanding of the considerable dimensions and processes involved in intergroup relations, while the latter strikes me as presumptuous and unsatisfactory in terms of our understanding of human behavior in general and of religious, ethnic, and race relations in particular.

Part I of the book sets the stage for the consideration of American minority relations in treating a number of key concepts and analyzing some of the facts and myths revolving about race. Part II examines the sources of racism, considering a number of variables that typically come into play in the emergence and initial stabilization of racism. It shows how racism is maintained by becoming deeply embedded in the social and cultural fabric—indeed how it becomes institutionalized. The last chapter in Part II deals with the personality bulwarks of racism. Part III considers four processes of intergroup relations—conflict, stratification, segregation, and assimilation—particularly in terms of recent developments in these areas.

Part IV examines the reactions of minorities to their disadvantaged status. These are discussed primarily in terms of acceptance or aggression and avoidance or assimilation. This approach permits a study of assimilationist-oriented minorities and an extensive analytical consideration of the Black "Revolution," including a treatment of Black Power. Finally, Part V examines that body of sociological literature dealing with means by which democratic goals may be advanced and racism combated.

James W. Vander Zanden

Columbus, Ohio

Contents

American Minority Relations

Introduction

The Nature of Minority Relations 1

*D*ivisions among people along racial and ethnic lines are a central feature of contemporary life. Throughout the world people are killing each other over differences of color, facial features, language, dress, food habits, and religious faith. Consider the appalling outpourings of blood in recent decades between Arabs and Jews in the Middle East, Protestants and Catholics in Northern Ireland, Turks and Greeks in Cyprus, and among the Hausa, Yoruba, and Ibo in Nigeria, and the Laotians, Cambodians, and Vietnamese in Southeast Asia.

Likewise, anyone reading the newspapers or watching television today can hardly escape the conclusion that the United States confronts serious racial and ethnic difficulties. More than a decade ago a presidential panel formed to investigate racial outbreaks in American cities and known as the Kerner Commission (1968) warned: "Our nation is moving toward two societies, one black, one white—separate and unequal." A decade later the *New York Times,* surveying racial progress in the nation, concluded: "The division between white and black Americans still exists, and the prospects of healing the rift may be more dismal today than they were 10 years ago" (Herbers, 1978). Examining public opinion polls, the *Times* found that most whites believe either that the battle for racial justice has been won or that the endeavor is too costly in terms of the sacrifices that white people must make. Yet the problems of ghetto blacks continue to mount. Chronically high unemployment in black neighborhoods has raised fears that the United States may have acquired a permanent underclass. All this has contributed to a badly divided society.

Much the same holds true with respect to ethnicity (*see* Table 1.1). The United States now finds itself experiencing an enormous influx of aliens, many of them illegal. Large numbers of immigrants from Latin America arrive in poverty, poorly educated, and knowing only a few simple phrases of English. Bilingualism has become a fact of life in the Southwest, New York City, and Miami. Some social scientists say that in the decades ahead the United States can expect to encounter some

TABLE 1.1 RACIAL AND ETHNIC CATEGORIES, 1980 CENSUS

White	188,341,000
Black	26,488,000
Hispanics*	14,600,000
American Indian, Eskimo, Aleutian Islanders	1,418,177
Chinese	806,000
Filipino	775,000
Japanese	701,000
Asian Indian	362,000
Korean	355,000
Vietnamese	262,000
Hawaiian	167,000
Samoan	42,000
Guamanian	32,000

*Due to a peculiarity of the 1980 Census form, many Hispanics were additionally counted in the "white" or "black" categories.

Source: U.S. Bureau of the Census.

of the same forces of disunity that Canada has experienced between its French- and English-speaking populations.

Population projections show California, the nation's most populous state, becoming the first "Third World" state by the 1990s as whites of European ancestry become a numerical minority there. As New York's Ellis Island was the gateway for the great trans-Atlantic tide of immigration in the past, California's proximity to Latin America and the Pacific has made it the gateway for the majority of contemporary immigrants. Refugees from Southeast Asia and uncounted legal and illegal aliens from Latin America, Taiwan, Korea, and the Philippines have gravitated to California. At least eighty-five languages are currently spoken in California, complicating the task of the state's schools.

The Scientific Study of Minority Relations

Foreign observers often comment that Americans think they ought to live in a society that does not entail many conflicts. People tend to believe that a society is good when things are harmonious and people do not express dissatisfaction. But this is not always true. Where there are injustices and inequalities, conflict can contribute to social change and social health. Of course, conflict can also be of a harmful sort. It can result in death, suffering, destruction, and devastation. These then are matters that warrant scientific interest and study.

The Pursuit of Objectivity

Sociology examines minority relations with a scientific orientation characterized by *a rigorous, disciplined pursuit of objectivity.* Underlying this approach is the assumption that there is a "real world"—that something exists "out there," something that is divorced from individuals themselves, and that is knowable. Thus, whether calculated by an American, a Russian, or an Indonesian, or by a Communist, a Methodist, or a Hindu spiritualist, two plus two nonetheless equals four.

Put still another way, there are such things as *facts*—certain scientifically verifiable observations—and hence we can make reliable statements regarding what *is.* However, people do not necessarily regard "what is" as desirable, as the way things *ought* to be. Hence we find it useful to distinguish between facts and *values.* **Values** are conceptions regarding the desirability or undesirability of things, including their beauty, morality, merit, or worth—in brief, notions of what "ought" to be. Science, be it chemistry or sociology, can only ascertain facts. It cannot tell us whether these facts are good or bad—whether it is ethically desirable or undesirable that every chemical compound contains unvarying proportions of its constituent elements (the law of constant composition) or that black-white relations within the United States have been characterized by discrimination and segregation.

That science should concern itself only with "what is" is of course an ideal. In practice, things do not work out quite this way because science involves *human* activity. It is carried on by individual people and by groups of people. This element injects subjectivity into the picture. All human beings have values, and to the extent to which we are human, we cannot be completely objective. Even at our best, we find values subtly invading our work. Indeed, the very fact of studying human behavior reveals we have values that make us concerned about how people act, and the decision to focus upon social rather than biological, psychological, or other factors betrays an implicit belief that the social factor is somehow "more significant" than the others. Similarly, values shape our selection of research problems (i.e., race relations rather than the structure of business enterprise), our preference for certain hypotheses, and our neglect of others.

What we have been saying adds up to this. As a science, sociology is not characterized by the absolute absence of values but by *a rigorous, disciplined* attempt to look as objectively as is humanly possible upon the phenomena that it studies. As such, sociologists are enjoined to avoid such emotional involvement in their work that they cannot adopt a new approach or reject an old answer when their findings indicate that this is required. Further, sociologists are enjoined not to turn their backs on facts or to distort them simply because they do not like them (Shibutani and Kwan, 1965). Much of education in sociology beyond the bachelor's degree is oriented toward fostering this kind of commitment and developing those skills whereby valid, reliable knowledge can be realized. And there is the additional check—indeed, social pressure—provided by scientists' peers. Once they publish their work in professional publications, scientists must expect other scientists, not necessarily sharing their biases, to scrutinize and criticize what they have done.

Sociological Controversy

During the past few decades considerable controversy has been generated within sociological circles over the questions of "knowledge for what?" and "sociology for whom?" Let us consider these matters.

Knowledge for What? A good many nineteenth-century American sociologists were personally interested in social reform, and viewed sociology as a potentially powerful instrument for relieving human suffering and guiding people in the search for a better future. A surprising number launched their careers as Protestant ministers. In succeeding decades, despite changes in the philosophical and social climate, sociology has secured many of its recruits from among highly idealistic youth, those who hope for the solution of human problems in the scientific study of society.

During its formative years sociology struggled to gain respectability and acceptance within the scientific community (Harvard University, for instance, did not establish a department of sociology until 1930 and Princeton University did not have one until 1960). Partly as a response to this, a countertheme arose that asserted sociology should remain aloof from involvement with social problems and concern itself strictly with the enlargement of sociological knowledge. This was the dominant position of the profession during the 1940s, 1950s, and 1960s. It was associated with such individuals as Talcott Parsons and George A. Lundberg who advocated a neutral, amoral sociology—one in which sociologists were bound to the tenet "Thou shall not commit a value judgment." Robert Bierstedt (1963:12–13), a prominent sociologist of this period, expresses the view as follows:

> Sociology is a pure science, not an applied science. The immediate goal of sociology is the acquisition of knowledge about human society, not the utilization of that knowledge. Physicists do not build bridges, physiologists do not treat people afflicted with pneumonia, and chemists do not fill prescriptions at the corner drugstore. Similarly, sociologists do not determine questions of public policy, do not tell legislators what laws should be passed or repealed, and do not dispense relief to the ill, the lame, the blind, or the poor. . . . Sociology . . . stands in the same relation to administration, legislation, diplomacy, teaching, supervision, social work,

and citizenship, as physics does to engineering, physiology to medicine, jurisprudence to law, astronomy to navigation, chemistry to pharmacy, and biology to plant and animal husbandry.

Bierstedt concedes that sociological knowledge can be used for solving some of the world's problems, but insists that this application is not the job of sociologists. Rather, he maintains, a division of labor operates in which the individuals who acquire sociological knowledge are not necessarily the ones who undertake to apply it.

Brewton Berry outlines a somewhat similar position for the study of race relations. Responding to those who accuse sociologists of "fiddling about leisurely" studying race problems in the face of urgent calls for remedial social engineering, Berry (1965:18) writes:

> We fully appreciate the seriousness and urgency of the situation, but we believe that knowledge and understanding are prerequisites for wise and effective action. We are sympathetic, for instance, with the medical research scientists who work away in their laboratories while an epidemic rages in the community. Why, some will say, do they not do something immediately useful? Why not put into practical use such knowledge and skill as they have, imperfect though it be? Why waste their efforts on research when the times demand action? It is our opinion that, in the long run, the research scientists will relieve more suffering by their investigations than by abandoning their study and devoting themselves to therapy.

During the 1960s and 1970s a group of "new-breed" sociologists emerged who challenged the position advanced by Bierstedt and Berry. For these younger Ph.D.s, many of whom were student-power, civil-rights, and peace activists during the 1960s and early 1970s, the notion of a value-free and unbiased sociology is a myth. They stress that sociologists ought to concern themselves with the task of restructuring society so that all people, unimpeded by racism, can lead fuller, richer, and more fruitful lives. Indeed, these critics of the Bierstedt-Berry stance argue that the apostles of sociological "neutrality" are remiss in their public and civic responsibilities, that they come to champion moral insensitivity—a crass disregard for such things as the suffering of the poor and minority groups, the destructiveness of war, and the high social costs of crime and delinquency. To ignore values, they maintain, is to usher in an era of spiritless technicians, individuals capable of crippling mankind with a sociological atomic bomb—not a groundless fear in a world where already prisoners of war are systematically brainwashed and homemakers' buying habits are systematically molded through sophisticated advertising campaigns. Before Hiroshima, physicists also liked to talk about their value-free science but today many of them are no longer quite sure that this can or should be the case.

A value-free sociology, the critics assert, is a sterile, irrelevant sociology and they point an accusing finger at the established sociological journals for the "inconsequential trivia" that allegedly appear within their pages. They insist that the strong ethic of social concern that characterized many early sociologists must be resurrected and that sociology must concern itself with human suffering and its alleviation. They criticize as "inward-looking" those sociologists who relegate social betterment to a secondary place and accuse them of being more concerned with the betterment of their occupational group than with the larger society that they ultimately serve. Moreover, these "new-breed" sociologists ask why any sociologists' professional status should set them aside from other human beings. Accordingly, these sociologists seek to establish bridges between sociology and what they view as the larger hopes, aspirations, and purposes of humankind.

Sociology for Whom? Another question increasingly being raised, especially by younger sociologists, is: "Sociology for whom?" Those asking this question generally note that sociologists are as much social beings as the people they study, and they are not free of the social demands of colleagues, research organizations and government granting agencies, political systems, university administrators, students, or friends. In brief, a variety of individuals and groups act as influences on sociologists' conduct. Moreover, values do not exist in a vacuum or in the abstract. Values are found within groups and serve the interests of groups. Since a conflict of values and interests often characterizes differing groups, it is argued that the choice for sociologists becomes a choice of whose interests shall be served by their work.

Critics of contemporary American sociology contend that the ideology of ethical neutrality actually serves to mask a very definite commitment: ". . . the choice that has generally been made by sociologists is to put their skills at the service of the 'establishment,' that is to say, of groups who wield a great deal of economic and political power in the society" (Biblarz, 1969:4). They insist that a "noncommitted" sociology is the handmaiden of the status quo—"a gentleman's promise that boats will not be rocked." Indeed, "to do *nothing* in today's world is as political in its effect as to do something; to assent is as political as to dissent" (Berreman, 1971:19). Hence proponents of this view argue that the alternatives are not "neutrality" and "advocacy"; rather, "to be uncommitted is not to be neutral but to be committed—consciously or not—to the *status quo*" (Dowd, 1964:63). Accordingly, sociologists are increasingly being asked, "Which side are you on?"—the implication being, for example, that one stands either for or against a racist society.

Is a Resolution of the Divergent Views Possible? Much of the controversy that we have considered revolves about the uses of science, and in particular of sociology. Traditionally many scientists have assessed scientific work in terms of its contribution to knowledge, as opposed to its usefulness, on grounds that only in this manner can science remain fairly autonomous and free. Conversely, they argue, if practical utility becomes the sole measure of significance, then science becomes only a handmaiden—of business, the church, the state, the party, or the "movement." In truth there is a basic duality in science: It can provide greater understanding of how things operate and occur, and it can also provide understanding that enables people to change things and to move toward chosen goals. And as with most dualities in life, this one has given rise to ambivalent attitudes. Further, since people generally find ambivalence difficult to tolerate, scientists have historically dealt with their indecision by periodically swinging violently to one extreme position or the other—in the process tending to deny the worth of the other alternative.

Perhaps we can be a little more relaxed about these matters if we realize that we need not be addicted to either position—that sociology is *nothing but* self-contained knowledge, entirely insulated from the world of social action, or that sociology is *nothing but* a guide to action (Merton and Nisbet, 1976). In truth, sociology is both. Some sociologists no doubt—by temperament or capacity—are more comfortable or better suited in one or the other paths of inquiry, and some move back and forth between paths. In brief, then, we need not see a hard-and-fast boundary separating pure from applied science.

Finally, it needs to be understood that science does not call upon sociologists to give up their moral convictions or biases; indeed, such a demand would be humanly unrealistic and impossible. But by the same token our discussion should not be taken as a recommendation for license to offer value judgments at random, resulting in a "this I believe"-type sociology. Rather, regardless of the path sociologists take—either in the direction of pure or applied science—it is nonetheless incumbent upon them to cultivate rigorously a disciplined approach to the phenomena that they study so that they may determine facts as they are and not as they might wish them to be.

Minorities

We hear a good deal nowadays about **minority groups** (or simply *minorities*). In some respects the term is an unfortunate one for it has numerical connotations. Yet despite its literal meaning, a minority is *not* a statistical category. Although minority groups may be smaller in size than dominant groups, this need not be the case. Within the Union of South Africa and some areas of our southern states, blacks constitute a numerical majority of the population. Moreover, at least until recently, a limited number of Europeans dominated "minority" peoples in a colonial arrangement within Africa, Asia, and Latin America. Yet despite the fact that they are a numerical majority in such settings, members of minority groups occupy a disadvantaged position within the dominant culture and experience various disabilities because of it. Social subordination and disadvantage are the key elements in distinguishing a minority group from a **dominant group**—the group that is superordinate and advantaged in the social relationship.

Characteristics of Minority Groups

Sociologists commonly distinguish five features as characteristic of minority groups (Wagley and Harris, 1964). Let us consider each of these in turn:

1. *A minority is a social group whose members experience discrimination, segregation, oppression, or persecution at the hands of another social group.* Within human affairs minorities are disadvantaged groups. They enjoy less of the good things of society—wealth, power, status, and territory—than do members of the dominant group. Moreover, minority-group members carry more of the burdens of society, those tasks that are considered less pleasant in a particular society. But the minority not only suffers oppression at the hands of the dominant group. Most commonly the minority is a *source* of the dominant group's advantages, particularly its wealth and status. The oppression of one people confers privilege upon another.

2. *The disabilities experienced by minorities are related to special characteristics that its members share, either physical or cultural or both, which the dominant group holds in low esteem.* Groups that are identified primarily on cultural grounds—by such behaviors as language, religion, food habits, folk practices, dress, gestures, or mannerisms—are termed **ethnic groups.** Examples within the United States include Jews, Italian-Americans, and Hispanics. Groups identified chiefly on physical grounds—such hereditary characteristics as skin color, facial features, hair texture, or stature—are termed racial groups. Examples within the United States include blacks and whites. Usually the dominant group holds in low regard those cultural or racial characteristics that distinguish the members of the minority group from themselves. The disapproval ranges in strength from ridicule and suspicion to hate. But of even greater significance, the dominant group has the power to translate its preferences for behavior (its **norms** and values—its morality) into the operating standards of the society. "Law and order" within the society is primarily the "law and order" of the dominant group. Since the dominant group finds various practices and customs of the minority abhorrent, it may attempt to suppress the culture of the minority and label the behavior of its members deviant. When the minority's distinguish-

ing traits are also associated with racial characteristics, the dominant group may evolve a doctrine of racial superiority and inferiority. In their most virulent form such doctrines lead to **genocide** —policies aimed at the physical extermination of a people.

3. *Minorities are self-conscious social units; they are characterized by a consciousness of kind.* The individuals making up a minority recognize the fact of their membership and this recognition affects their behavior. Minority members are aware of something that they share in common with others like themselves. It is a sense that "I am one of them." And by the same token, "I am not one of those." The common traits that the members share form the basis of an esprit de corps, an ingroup feeling, a sense of belonging to a group distinct from the dominant group. In sum, the members of a minority derive a sense of *peoplehood.*

A consciousness of oneness is intensified by the members' common suffering and burden. Persecution accentuates a group's self-consciousness. In this manner, group boundaries are sharpened. Individuals come to know who is and who is not a member of their group. This awareness serves to encapsulate people so that the flow of their action is primarily focused and contained within the group. Barriers are erected to keep "outsiders" distant. It is sometimes said, "Jews have survived as a people *despite* the fact that they were persecuted." It would be more sociologically accurate to say, "Jews have survived as a people *because* they were persecuted." Persecution compelled Jews to cultivate and retain their distinctive heritage. It deepened Jewish self-consciousness and ingroup loyalties. Indeed, some Jewish leaders currently believe that assimilation is a greater threat to the group's survival within the United States than is anti-Semitism. These leaders note that on many college campuses more than 50 percent of the Jewish students marry non-Jews. In the process, Jewish self-consciousness and ingroup loyalties erode and Jews compromise traditional practices and come to identify with non-Jewish institutions.

4. *Generally a person does not become a member of a minority voluntarily; he or she is born into it.* Members of a minority usually (but not always) conceive of themselves as being alike by virtue of their common ancestry. At any rate, and this is critical, by virtue of their real or presumed ancestry, members of the dominant group ascribe minority group status to them. At times one parent alone (father or mother) is sufficient to ensure the membership of a child in a minority, and in certain cases, a single grandparent or great-grandparent suffices. Within the United States an individual who is physically indistinguishable from the dominant white group but who has a known black grandparent is commonly defined as a black. In Nazi Germany it was of no avail

that a "Jew" looked like German non-Jews, had been converted to Christianity, and had taken a Christian spouse—the person was still, according to the Nazis, a "Jew." In this sense, minority membership is an **ascribed status.**

5. *Members of a minority group, by choice or necessity, tend to marry within their own group (endogamy).* Ingroup marriage is enforced sometimes by the dominant group, sometimes by the minority, and frequently by both. Until the 1970s, white-black marriage was barred by whites through miscegenation laws in many areas of the United States. It was also informally discouraged by many blacks. This pattern of endogamy functions to perpetuate the physical and cultural differences between the dominant and minority groups as well as inequalities in status.

Robin M. Williams, Jr. (1964:304), captures the core of the above five features in this summary definition: *"Minorities . . . are any culturally or physically distinctive and self-conscious social aggregates, with hereditary membership and a high degree of endogamy, which are subject to political, or economic, or social discrimination by a dominant segment of an environing political society."*

The Relativity of Minority Membership

A racial, nationality, or religious group may be dominant in one area and a minority in another. Jews constitute the dominant group in Israel, while Arabs represent a minority group there. In the Arab nations the situation is reversed. Roman Catholics are a dominant group within Spain and Italy but a minority within Norway. Chinese exercise dominance over Tibetans and the various nationality groups within contemporary China but constitute a minority throughout most other areas of the world. In various historical periods the dominant-minority relationship may also be altered or, in fact in some instances, reversed. During the Nazi occupation of Czechoslovakia, the Sudeten Germans secured a position of dominance over the Czechs among whom they previously had been a minority.

Furthermore, dominant and minority group memberships are not necessarily mutually exclusive. It is possible for an individual to have dominant and minority roles simultaneously. This possibility derives from the fact that, within the United States for example, the dominant-minority group classification has a threefold basis: race, religion, and nationality. Traditionally Roman Catholics have been viewed as members of a prominent religious minority, yet many of their members are simultaneously whites and thus racially grouped with the dominant group. Blacks, on the other hand, are racially grouped with a minority, yet in terms of religion may be members of the dominant Protestant group. Norwegians in some areas of the Midwest, by virtue of their national descent and unique cultural traits, are accorded minority status, although they are members of the dominant white race and the dominant Protestant religion.

Minorities on the World Scene

Within the Western world we generally conceive of a *society* as a culturally distinctive and politically sovereign entity that enjoys specific geographical frontiers. We commonly think of *cultural distinctiveness* in terms of a population whose members possess a considerable degree of homogeneity in customs, often minimally taken to be a population whose members speak a common language. We usually take *political sovereignty* to mean self-sufficiency, a condition in which a population has original and definitive jurisdiction in the main spheres of social life (it enjoys functional autonomy in decision-making). And we view the matter of *geographical frontiers* in terms of territoriality—a population that occupies a definable piece of the earth's surface. In practice the most typical referent of society is taken to be the nation-state: "Mostly, then, when we look for a society we find the political unit, and when speaking of the former we mean in effect that latter" (Nadel, 1957:187). In this Westernized view all states are sovereign and every piece of the earth's surface can appropriately be divided up in terms of the legal possession of this or that people so that, at least in theory, there are not any blank spaces on the map or overlap between the territories of two states (Leach, 1960).

Western legal and constitutional definitions of society are one thing; practice is still another (Connor, 1978). We often mistakenly equate nationalism with a feeling of loyalty to the state (a political unit) rather than with loyalty to the nation (an ethnic entity). Take Europe. Almost every territory of Europe has combined at some time or other with almost every one of its neighbors. Indeed, the territories covered by European nation-states have never been, and could not possibly be, exactly the same as the territories inhabited by various ethnic nationality groups. Frequently such groups occupy small pieces of territory or are dispersed by residence and place of occupation throughout the territory of the dominant group. Hence political self-determination for one nationality has often been quite incompatible with political self-determination for another. Thus a large number of European nation-states contain multiple nationality groups, including Great Britain (Scotch, Welsh, and English), Belgium (Flemish and Walloons), Czechoslovakia (Czechs and Slovaks), and Switzerland (Germans, French, and Italians). Seldom do we find the formula "one nation, one state" realized within Europe.

The story was not too dissimilar in precolonial "Burma," where the "frontiers" that separated the petty political units were not clearly demarcated lines but zones of mutual interests in which there prevailed interpenetrating networks of relationships. "Frontier" zones were occupied by people who were not an integral part of some larger whole, although they may have been involved as tributaries, as raiders, or sometimes as furnishers of forest products. Local and regional groups politically and culturally graded into and overlapped with one another so that it was often impossible to state where the lines of cleavage ran; people at times even had recourse to more than one ethnic "identity"; and in some cases, as in highland "Burma," whole villages or communities shifted their ethnic or tribal "identity," for instance, where Kachin became Shan (Leach, 1954; Lehman, 1967).

In truth, "societies" in much of the world, whether they are called tribes, nations, national minorities, or ethnic groups, are in part the artificial constructs of Western social scientists and colonial administrators who carved up areas and drew boundaries with little regard for ethnic distributions. In many areas of the world we seldom find sharp boundaries but rather continuous variation and/or interpenetration so that it is next to impossible to say where one population begins and another ends. Two distinguished anthropologists note this situation for some areas of Africa (Fortes and Evans-Pritchard, 1940:23):

> This overlapping and interlocking of societies is largely due to the fact that the point at which political relations, narrowly defined in terms of military action and legal sanctions, end is not the point at which all social relations cease. The social structure of a people stretches beyond their political system, so defined, for there are always social relations of one kind or another between peoples of different autonomous political groups. Clans, age-sets, ritual associations, relations of affinity and of trade, and social relations of other kinds unite people of different political units. Common language or closely related languages, similar customs and beliefs, and so on, also unite them. Hence a strong feeling of community may exist between groups which do not acknowledge a single ruler or units for specific political purposes. Community of language and culture . . . does not necessarily give rise to political unity, any more than linguistic and cultural dissimilarity prevents political unity.

Even to use political terms for delimiting a "society" in some areas of Africa ignores the common phenomenon of intermediate zones in which relations between different political units are not covered by the formula "war without and law within." Such a formula is not applicable to the Nuba peoples of the African Sudan, and one gains a not too different picture from some other areas of Africa (Nadel, 1947; Goody, 1962; Turnbull, 1961, 1965). There are some 250 ethnic groups in Nigeria, 200 in Zaïre, and 130 in Tanzania. Cameroon's 200 tribes speak 24 languages; as many as 72 languages have been counted in Zambia, 50 in Ghana, and a staggering 700 languages and dialects in Zaïre. There are religious differences within countries as well. In recent years hundreds of people were killed in fighting between Nigeria's Moslem and Christian peoples.

In a very real sense, Western social scientists and colonial administrators often created "minority problems" by imposing European legal and constitutional definitions of a national state upon the peoples of much of Africa and Southeast Asia. The problem of national minorities arises from a conceptual scheme of what the most inclusive social unit *ought* to be—an ideal of *fashioning* a political entity or state that includes some and excludes others. Hence, national minority status is not a condition inherent in relationships—it is a property conferred on a relationship, a matter of social definition emanating from a conception of what a "society" (nation-state) is. Of equal significance, the dominant group, by virtue of its superior power, is able in considerable measure to translate its definition of "society" into actuality.

Put still another way, the sense of "society-ness" or "group-ness" derives from the level of "entity" awareness ("consciousness of kind"), or the popularity of mental images in which some are included and others are excluded from certain flows of social interaction. Thus "American Indian," "white," "black," "Irish," "Mexican," and the like are essentially subjective phenomena. But this does not mean that such "groups" are not real. They are real because people define them as real. People *attribute* to certain relationships the properties of "thinghood," that is, they define certain perceived regularities in social interaction in "entity" (group) terms. In brief, we order and classify the information we obtain from our sense organs and *impose* a structure upon it. The consequence of this fact for the subject matter of this book is, as we have noted, that humans create dominant-minority group "problems"—such "problems" themselves do not inhere in the mere existence of human or group differences.

Types of Minorities

As the sociologist Louis Wirth (1945) suggests, minorities can be classified in any number of ways. Among these are (1) the number and size of the minorities within the society, (2) the degree to which minority status involves friction and discrimination, (3) the nature of the social arrangements that govern the interaction between the minority and dominant groups, and (4) the goals toward which the minority and dominant groups are striving. In view of the contemporary world setting, Wirth feels that the last criterion is the most meaningful and satisfactory. Accordingly, he distinguishes among four types of minorities: (1) pluralistic, (2) assimilationist, (3) secessionist, and (4) militant.

A *pluralistic minority* desires to live peacefully side-by-side with the dominant group by seeking tolerance for its differences. But while craving tolerance for its various cultural idiosyncrasies, a pluralistic minority also seeks to maintain its cultural identity against dominant-group absorption. Switzerland provides an example of a culturally pluralistic nation. A majority of the Swiss speak a variety of German known as *Schwyzertütsch;* about 20 percent speak French; another 6 percent, Italian; and slightly more than 1 percent speak an ancient language known as Romansh. Within the various cantons, or provinces, there are notable differences in costume, dialect, and patterns of life. Although a majority of the people are Protestant, there is a sizable Catholic population. Within this setting, Switzerland recognizes all four languages, although only German, French, and Italian have been declared "official languages" into which all federal documents are translated. Although religious and ethnic prejudice is by no means nonexistent, the Swiss have learned to live harmoniously with their differences.

Whereas a pluralistic minority seeks to maintain its group integrity, an *assimilationist minority* expects to be absorbed within an emergent common culture that is the product of the blending of divergent racial and ethnic strains. Assimilation is viewed as a two-way process in which, through a fusion of the differing racial stocks and cultural traditions, a new people and culture emerge. This was the original expectation of most of the European immigrant groups coming to the United States.

The *secessionist minority* repudiates both assimilation and cultural pluralism. Although desiring to maintain their own cultural identity, they are not satisfied, as are the cultural pluralists, with mere toleration or cultural autonomy. The aim of the secessionists is statehood—full political self-determination. Frequently the secessionist minority enjoyed national sovereignty at an earlier period and cultivates among its members the romantic sentiments associated with it. No matter how archaic the cultural patterns, strong emphasis is placed upon the revival of the language, lore, literature, and ceremonial institutions associated with the group's prior independence. The Irish, Czech, Polish, Lithuanian, Estonian, Latvian, and Finnish nationalistic movements that culminated in the establishment of independent nations at the end of World War I are illustrative of secessionist movements. The Zionist movement among Jews and the Garveyite movement among blacks in the 1920s are other examples.

A *militant minority* goes far beyond the demand for equality, or even cultural and political autonomy, and insists upon reversing the prevailing group statuses. Domination over others is set as its goal. Such a group is frequently convinced of its own superiority. The Sudeten Germans, aided and abetted by the Nazis, made claims upon the Czechoslovakian republic that in effect would have reduced the Czechs to minority status.

Wirth's types have not gone without criticism. The fourth type, "militant," is not the same kind of concept as the others, dealing as it does with tactics. Similarly, there is no reason why some of the other types may not also be "militant" in their tactics. Still another effort to classify minorities has been undertaken by Oliver C. Cox (1948), who distinguishes among the different kinds of situations that characterize dominant-minority relations:

1. Situations in which the non-white is a stranger in a white society, such as a Hindu in the United States or a black in many parts of Canada and in Argentina—the stranger situation.

2. Situations of original white contact in which the culture of the colored group is very simple, such as the conquistadors and Indians in the West Indies, and the Dutch and Hottentots in South Africa—the original contact situation.

3. Situations of colored enslavement in which a small aristocracy of whites exploits large quantities of natural resources (as in plantation settings) with forced colored labor, raised or purchased like capital in a slave market, such as that in the pre-Civil War South and in Jamaica before 1834—the slavery situation.

4. Situations in which a small minority of whites in a colored society is bent upon maintaining a ruling-class status, such as the pre-World War II British in the West Indies or the Dutch in Indonesia—the ruling-class situation.

5. Situations in which there are large proportions of both colored and white persons seeking to live in the same area, with whites insisting that the society is a "white man's country," for instance, United States and South Africa—the bipartite situation.

6. Situations in which colored-and-white amalgamation is far advanced and in which a white ruling class is not established, as for example in Brazil—the amalgamative situation.

7. Situations in which a minority of whites has been subdued by a dominantly colored population, as that which occurred in Haiti during the turn of the eighteenth century, or the expulsion of the whites from Japan in 1638—the nationalistic situation.

It is not always clear, however, which variable Cox is using in his classificatory approach: the nature of the original contact, the degree of cultural contrast, the proportionate size of the minority, or some other.

Prejudice

People today are quick to disassociate themselves from prejudice, which has taken on so many unfavorable connotations. "I'm not prejudiced," is a frequently heard comment. "In fact, one of my best friends is a Jew. But, you know, I just can't stand most of 'em! They're just full of gall!" It is difficult to examine dispassionately and objectively something that is so widely condemned yet simultaneously so prevalent.

The term **prejudice** is used with somewhat differing meanings by various individuals. Prejudice is commonly taken to mean a "prejudgment" about a person or group without bothering to verify the opinion or to examine the merits of the judgment. Implicit in this definition is the assumption that prejudice involves a hasty or premature appraisal of individuals or groups. If this is the case, knowledge and experience should be all that is necessary to dispel prejudice. In truth, however, considerable evidence is available that suggests that knowledge and experience frequently have little impact upon prejudice. Thus a definition of prejudice as a "pre-judgment" is *not* adequate.

In recent years social scientists have come to view prejudice as an attitude—a state of mind. Like any other attitude, prejudice has three aspects: what people think—the *cognitive* level; what they feel—the *emotional* level; and how they are inclined to act—the *action-oriented* level. Let us consider each of these levels in turn.

The cognitive level consists of an individual's mental picture or image of a minority group. It deals with how individuals perceive a minority, what they believe about it, and what traits they attribute to its members. An individual's prejudiced "picture" of blacks may be that they fight and brawl, have criminal instincts, live like animals, and are mentally inferior, lazy, slow, unimaginative, and sloppy. Jews may be pictured as possessing unbounded power and control in money matters, as sticking together, as conniving to outwit Gentiles, and as pursuing unscrupulous, ruthless, and unpatriotic activities.

The emotional level refers to the feelings that the minority inspires within the individual. Fear, sympathy, pity, hate, anger, love, contempt, and envy are emotional responses. The idea of patronizing a rest room, of eating at the same restaurant, or of shaking hands with a Jew or black may excite horror or disgust in some individuals. Blacks moving into a previously all-white neighborhood may produce fear and anxiety among whites. The social standing of a prominent Jewish executive or doctor may elicit envy among some Gentiles. Identification with the persecuted may lead some whites to experience sympathy for blacks and to desire that a black win in a boxing match with a white. Although the emotional level of prejudice is distinct from the cognitive level, the two may appear together—one may overlay the other.

The action-oriented level refers to the tendency or disposition to act in certain ways toward a minority group. Here the emphasis is upon tendencies to act, *not* upon the actions themselves. Whites may desire to keep blacks out of their circle of friends and reject any direct personal relations with them. Similarly, whites may favor barring blacks from their social clubs, athletic organizations, and business and professional associations. They may prefer segregated schools, parks, buses, washrooms, lunch counters, and waiting rooms. Accordingly, they may be viewed as disposed toward discriminatory behavior.

We shall conceive of *prejudice as a system of negative conceptions, feeling, and action-orientations regarding the members of a particular group*. This definition reflects the three major levels of an attitude system: the cognitive, the emotional, and the action-oriented.

John B. McConahay and Joseph C. Hough, Jr. (1976), detect the emergence in recent years of a new form of prejudice toward blacks among relatively affluent, suburban whites. They term it **symbolic racism.** Symbolic racism is not the racism of the Old South with its doctrines of racial inferiority and legally mandated segregation. Rather, it is a new form of racism in which three elements converge. First, many whites believe that blacks have become too demanding, too pushy, and too angry, and that blacks are getting more than they merit. Second, many whites feel that blacks are not playing by "the rules of the game" typified by such traditional American values as hard work, individualism, and the delay of gratification. And third, many whites have formed a negative image of blacks associated with notions of welfare, urban riots, crime in the streets, affirmative-action programs, and quota systems. In brief, symbolic racism views blacks as violating cherished values and making illegitimate demands upon whites for social change. It leads whites to vote against black office seekers and candidates favorable to black programs (Kinder and Sears, 1981). "Racism" becomes "somebody else's" problem while white suburbanites focus upon their own private lives and needs.

Stereotypes

We have observed that prejudice is a state of mind. Further, we noted that one aspect of this state of mind is the cognitive level—the image or picture we carry in our heads concerning a people, for instance, the "fighting" Irish, the "inscrutable" Orientals, the "stolid" Swedes, the "grasping" Jews, the "emotional" Italians, and the "shiftless" blacks. Walter Lippmann, a distinguished American journalist and author, dubs "these pictures in our heads" **stereotypes** (1922:16). He indicates that the world is filled with "so much subtlety, so much variety, so many permutations and combinations . . . we have to reconstruct it on a simpler model before we can manage with it." In other words, we find it almost impossible to weigh every reaction of every person, minute-by-minute in terms of its individual meanings. Instead, we type individuals and groups in snap-judgment style. Without stereotypes we would find it necessary to interpret each new situation as if we had never met anything of the kind before. Stereotypes are convenient and have the virtue of efficiency although not always of accuracy.

We may define stereotypes as the unscientific and hence unreliable generalizations that people make about other people as persons or groups. They constitute *beliefs* about people. Such beliefs, however, overlook the differences found among a people with regard to a trait. Stereotypes would have us believe that all people in the group are identical—fighting, inscrutable, stolid, or grasping, for example. Moreover, they overlook the fact that people have a great many traits. In stereotypes, people are "sized up" in terms of only one or a limited number of characteristics. Stereotypes obscure a variety of characteristics by magnifying one attribute out of proportion to its significance.

It is often suggested that stereotypes are rigid, firm, and unchanging. Evidence, however, indicates that, while some stereotypes are relatively stable, others do change through time. Studies of stereotypes among Princeton University undergraduates are revealing. In 1932, in a pioneer investigation of stereotypes, two psychologists (Katz and Braly, 1933) asked Princeton undergraduates to select out of a list of eighty-four attributes five that they thought were most characteristic of each of the following: Americans, English, Germans, Jews, "Negroes," Japanese, Italians, Chinese, Irish, and Turks. After a lapse of nearly twenty years, another psychologist (Gilbert, 1951) repeated the study. Then, in 1967, Marvin Karlins, Thomas L. Coffman, and Gary Walters (1969) again replicated the work with a third generation of Princeton students.

Evidence for the *persistence* of ethnic and racial stereotypes is contained in the fact that the characteristics checked most frequently by the 1951 and 1967 students were, for the most part, the ones most frequently checked in 1932. But perhaps of greatest interest is that the apparent "fading" of stereotypes noted in the 1951 study is not confirmed in the 1967 study. Although many of the 1932 assignments declined in frequency, they were merely *replaced* by others, resulting again in 1967 in a high degree of stereotype uniformity. Further, the "new" stereotypes *resemble* earlier ones. For example, the hot-tempered image of the Italian is still reflected in the temperamental cluster—"passionate" (44 percent), "impulsive" (28 percent), and "quick-tempered" (28 percent)—and is supplemented by "pleasure loving" (33 percent) and "sensual" (26 percent). The findings of these studies are summarized in Table 1.2.

Also of significance is the reluctance of the 1951 and 1967 students to engage in stereotyping. Many expressed sentiments indicating they felt it was unreasonable to force them to make generalizations about people. Some were especially concerned with the fact that they were asked to characterize people with whom they had never been in contact. One wrote:

> I refuse to be a part of a childish game like this. It seems to me that the Psych. Dept. at Princeton, at least, ought to recognize the intelligence of students who choose courses in this department. As far as I have come into contact with these so-called ethnic groups I can think of no distinguishing characteristics which will apply to any group as a whole.

Stereotyping runs counter to the image of the "thinking American," who is not "supposed" to fall into stylized modes of thought. If people label, there is a tendency to think of them as prejudiced, as thinking irrationally and contrary to an American idealized way of making choices. Apparently the image of the "thinking American" took its toll of students who were prepared to stereotype, or at least to *admit* to stereotyping. Hence, caution is in order. Indeed, although the character of the new stereotypes is consistent with the more liberal attitudes found in most contemporary college communities, the most outstanding aspect of the recent stereotypes is nevertheless their uniformity. In brief, the students' protestations against being asked to classify various groups as an irrelevant task should not have been accompanied by such highly standardized impressions of the groups if indeed they were not prone to stereotyping.

Discrimination

Earlier in the chapter we observed that prejudice is an attitude—a state of mind. Attitudes are not to be equated with behavior, with what people actually do. They are merely predispositions or predilections for certain kinds of actions. As such, attitudes are not necessarily correlated with actual behavior. A student may feel considerable hostility toward a professor, yet he may take great pains to hide his feelings and act instead in a personable, friendly, and ingratiating manner. His failure to act out his genuine feelings in aggressive and antagonistic actions may result from fear that his professor will retaliate and lower his grade. By the same token, a student may bear warm, friendly, and sympathetic attitudes toward a professor and yet engage in cool, ritualistic, and formalized actions. The student's failure to translate her attitudes into action may be the product of her concern that other students will consider her an "oddball" or an "apple polisher."

Similarly with prejudice. White business managers may bear considerable prejudice toward blacks yet nevertheless display friendly responses toward black customers to gain their good will. Thus their negative sentiments are not translated into behavior. On the other hand, business managers who lack prejudice may refuse to accept black customers, because they believe their presence would injure their business. In this instance, the managers fail to translate their nonprejudiced outlook into overt action. Accordingly, it is necessary to distinguish between *prejudice,* which is a state of mind, and *discrimination.* **Discrimination** entails overt action in which members of an ethnic or a racial group are treated unequally and unfavorably by members of the dominant group. Members of the minority are arbitrarily denied various rights and privileges even when their qualifications are equal to those of dominant-group members.

TABLE 1.2 STEREOTYPES IN THREE GENERATIONS OF

Trait	% Checking Trait			Trait	% Checking Trait		
	1933	1951	1967		1933	1951	1967
Americans				**Germans**			
Industrious	48	30	23	Scientifically			
Intelligent	47	˙32	20	minded	78	62	47
Materialistic	33	37	67	Industrious	65	50	59
Ambitious	33	21	42	Stolid	44	10	9
Progressive	27	5	17	Intelligent	32	32	19
Pleasure loving	26	27	28	Methodical	31	20	21
Alert	23	7	7	Extremely			
Efficient	21	9	15	nationalistic	24	50	43
Aggressive	20	8	15	Progressive	16	3	13
Straightforward	19	—	9	Efficient	16	—	46
Practical	19	—	12	Jovial	15	—	5
Sportsmanlike	19	—	9	Musical	13	—	4
Individualistic[a]	—	26	15	Persistent	11	—	4
Conventional[b]	—	—	17	Practical	11	—	9
Scientifically				Aggressive[a]	—	27	30
minded[b]	—	—	15	Arrogant[a]	—	23	18
Ostentatious[b]	—	—	15	Ambitious[b]	—	—	15
Chinese				**Irish**			
Superstitious	34	18	8	Pugnacious	45	24	13
Sly	29	4	6	Quick tempered	39	35	43
Conservative	29	14	15	Witty	38	16	7
Tradition loving	26	26	32	Honest	32	11	17
Loyal to				Very religious	29	30	27
family ties	22	35	50	Industrious	21	8	8
Industrious	18	18	23	Extremely			
Meditative	19	—	21	nationalistic	21	20	41
Reserved	17	18	15	Superstitious	18	—	11
Very religious	15	—	6	Quarrelsome	14	—	5
Ignorant	15	—	7	Imaginative	13	—	3
Deceitful	14	—	5	Aggressive	13	—	5
Quiet	13	19	23	Stubborn	13	—	23
Courteous[b]	—	—	20	Tradition loving[b]	—	—	25
Extremely				Loyal to			
nationalistic[b]	—	—	19	family ties[b]	—	—	23
Humorless[b]	—	—	17	Argumentative[b]	—	—	20
Artistic[b]	—	—	15	Boastful[b]	—	—	17
English				**Italians**			
Sportsmanlike	53	21	22	Artistic	53	28	30
Intelligent	46	29	23	Impulsive	44	19	28
Conventional	34	25	19	Passionate	37	25	44
Tradition loving	31	42	21	Quick tempered	35	15	28
Conservative	30	22	53	Musical	32	22	9
Reserved	29	39	40	Imaginative	30	20	7
Sophisticated	27	37	47	Very religious	21	33	25
Courteous	21	17	17	Talkative	21	23	23
Honest	20	11	17	Revengeful	17	—	0
Industrious	18	—	17	Physically dirty	13	—	4
Extremely				Lazy	12	—	0
nationalistic	18	—	7	Unreliable	11	—	3
Humorless	17	—	11	Pleasure loving[a]	—	28	33
Practical[b]	—	—	25				

Trait	% Checking Trait			Trait	% Checking Trait		
	1933	1951	1967		1933	1951	1967
Italians				**Negroes[c]**			
Loyal to family ties[b]	—	—	26	Superstitious	84	41	13
Sensual[b]	—	—	23	Lazy	75	31	26
Argumentative[b]	—	—	19	Happy-go-lucky	38	17	27
Japanese				Ignorant	38	24	11
Intelligent	45	11	20	Musical	26	33	47
Industrious	43	12	57	Ostentatious	26	11	25
Progressive	24	2	17	Very religious	24	17	8
Shrewd	22	13	7	Stupid	22	10	4
Sly	20	21	3	Physically dirty	17	—	3
Quiet	19	—	14	Naive	14	—	4
Imitative	17	24	22	Slovenly	13	—	5
Alert	16	—	11	Unreliable	12	—	6
Suave	16	—	0	Pleasure loving[a]	—	19	26
Neat	16	—	7	Sensitive[b]	—	—	17
Treacherous	13	17	1	Gregarious[b]	—	—	17
Aggressive	13	—	19	Talkative[b]	—	—	14
Extremely nationalistic[a]	—	18	21	Imitative[b]	—	—	13
Ambitious[b]	—	—	33				
Efficient[b]	—	—	27				
Loyal to family ties[b]	—	—	23				
Courteous[b]	—	—	22	**Turks**			
Jews				Cruel	47	12	9
Shrewd	79	47	30	Very religious	26	6	7
Mercenary	49	28	15	Treacherous	21	3	13
Industrious	48	29	33	Sensual	20	4	9
Grasping	34	17	17	Ignorant	15	7	13
Intelligent	29	37	37	Physically dirty	15	7	14
Ambitious	21	28	48	Deceitful	13	—	7
Sly	20	14	7	Sly	12	7	7
Loyal to family ties	15	19	19	Quarrelsome	12	—	9
Persistent	13	—	9	Revengeful	12	—	6
Talkative	13	—	3	Conservative	12	—	11
Aggressive	12	—	23	Superstitious	11	—	5
Very religious	12	—	7	Aggressive[b]	—	—	17
Materialistic[b]	—	—	46	Quick tempered[b]	—	—	13
Practical[b]	—	—	19	Impulsive[b]	—	—	12
				Conventional[b]	—	—	10
				Pleasure loving[b]	—	—	11
				Slovenly[b]	—	—	10

[a]Indicates the additional traits reported by Gilbert (1951).

[b]Indicates the new traits needed in 1967 to account for the 10 most frequently selected traits today.

[c]The title "Negroes" is the word employed in the study.

Source: Marvin Karlins, Thomas L. Coffman, and Gary Walters, "On the Fading of Social Stereotypes: Studies in Three Generations of College Students," *Journal of Personality and Social Psychology* 13 (1969): Table 1, pp. 4–5. By permission.

The Relationship Between Prejudice and Discrimination

We noted above that discrimination is not simply the result—the acting-out—of prejudice. Discrimination occurs without prejudice and prejudice without discrimination. Overall, however, an association exists between prejudice and discrimination such that the more prejudiced people are the more likely they are to practice discrimination. Yet there are numerous occasions when there is far from a one-to-one relation between the two. In the 1930s, for instance, the sociologist Richard T. LaPiere (1934) traveled throughout the United States with a Chinese couple. In the course of the trip, LaPiere and the Chinese couple asked for service in hundreds of hotels, auto camps, tourist homes, and restaurants. They were refused service only once. Six months later, LaPiere wrote each of the establishments and asked if Chinese guests were welcome. Over 90 percent replied that they would *not* accommodate Chinese, clearly in contradiction to their actions. Here is a clear case of verbal prejudice that was not accompanied by face-to-face discrimination.

Melvin L. DeFleur and Frank R. Westie (1958) conducted a study that bears directly on this question of attitude versus action. They attempted to find out how willing a number of college students were to be photographed with members of another race. First, they gave the students a verbal test that measured their attitudes toward blacks. Then the students were asked to sign "releases" indicating that they were willing to be photographed with blacks and that they would allow these photographs to be widely publicized. DeFleur and Westie found that many of the students were inconsistent: one-third of those who had revealed liberal attitudes balked at signing the releases. Finally, the students were asked why they had signed, or refused to sign, the releases. From the answers it appeared that most of the students were greatly influenced by *social pressure*—by whether they thought that persons they respected, particularly parents and friends, would approve of their signing. This and other research suggests that a considerable gap often exists between what people say and what they do (Crosby et al., 1980).

During the past thirty-five years the National Opinion Research Center (NORC) has monitored racial attitudes within the United States (Taylor, Sheatsley, and Greeley, 1978). Throughout this period white Americans have shown a steady but gradual shift toward greater liberalism on racial matters. The sharpest change occurred between 1970 and 1972. Analysis of the data from successive surveys since 1963 reveals that much of the long-term change can be attributed to new age cohorts. Individuals born between 1940 and 1958 are less prejudiced, in general, than are individuals born earlier in the century. But despite these changes, strong currents of symbolic racism, noted earlier in the

chapter, have surfaced. Many whites resent the economic improve-
ments achieved by blacks in the 1960s and 1970s (Ross et al., 1976;
Farley et al., 1978).

All this suggests that contradictory forces are operative in American
life. Under these circumstances, *situational* factors play an especially
important part in shaping people's actual behaviors (*see* Figure 1.1). In
the contemporary United States a public show of blatantly racist and
discriminatory behavior is usually defined as counter to the nation's

**FIGURE 1.1 RACIAL ATTITUDES, SITUATIONAL
FACTORS, AND BEHAVIOR.**

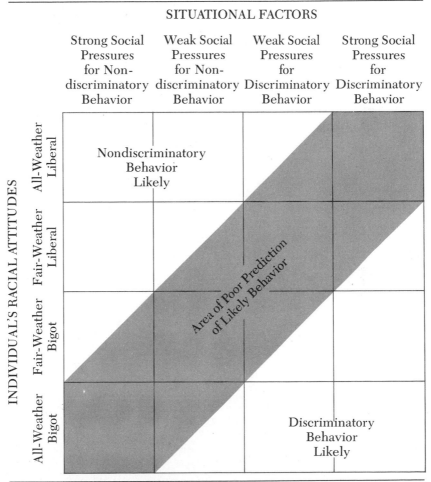

Situational factors account for a part of the divergence between
expressed racial attitudes and overt action.
Source: Adapted from L. G. Warner and M. L. de Fleur, "Attitude as an interactionist
concept." *American Sociological Review* 34 (1969): 168.

democratic ideals and as being "in poor taste." Yet simultaneously, many whites define interracial neighborhoods as unacceptable and "flee" from them to virtually all-white suburbs without social sanctions. Hence, the social setting in which individuals find themselves does much to determine their specific responses.

In sum, interracial behavior is a function of at least two attitudes— an attitude toward the *object* and an attitude toward the *situation.* More specifically, whites do not simply have attitudes toward blacks; they have attitudes toward living in a desegregated neighborhood, working with blacks, attending schools with blacks, marrying blacks, and participating in civil-rights demonstrations with blacks. Other factors besides the situational factor also play a part. For example, blacks differ from each other in age, education, occupation, sex, and marital status. Attitudes toward these characteristics affect white discriminatory behavior toward blacks (Liska, 1974; Smedley and Bayton, 1978).

Institutional Racism

Social scientists distinguish between two kinds of racism, *individual racism* and *institutional racism.* Prejudice and discrimination find expression in individual racism—a concept generally applied, for example, to the attitudes and behavior of whites toward blacks. It is of course useful to investigate prejudice and discrimination. However, the study of individual racism leaves much to be desired if we wish to understand the social arrangements whereby people of one racial group are systematically oppressed and exploited by the institutions of a society controlled by another racial group—that is, by **institutional racism.** Institutional racism involves *more than* simply prejudice and discrimination. It calls our attention to the fact that one or more of the institutions of a society functions to impose more burdens on and give less benefits to the members of one racial or ethnic group than another on an ongoing basis (Carmichael and Hamilton, 1967). Within the United States decisions are made, issues defined, commitments entered into, and resources allocated in such a manner that blacks are systematically deprived (Friedman, 1969).

The intentions of people are irrelevant to the question of whether a society operates in a structurally racist fashion. Indeed, privilege in a racist society cannot be avoided by dominant-group members, even by those who reject the society's institutions. The "iron law" of white privilege means that children of the upper-middle class who have "dropped out" to live in poverty still hold their racial rights in reserve should they decide to reenter the mainstream (Blauner, 1972). Of equal importance, institutional racism entails a kind of social and cultural imperialism in which the dominant group undertakes to impose its values, morality, and customs upon the minority. This orientation finds expression in white definitions of black ghetto life as "criminal," "deficient," and "pathological" and in white attempts to "whitewash" blacks so as to divest blacks of their unique cultural patterns.

Viewed from the perspective of institutional racism, prejudice is not a little demon that emerges in people simply because they are depraved (because they have some psychological "hang-up"). Rather, in large measure, prejudice derives from the racist manner in which the society is structured. Institutions shape and restrict the experiences that people will have. Consequently, prejudices are learned; they do not grow out of a social vacuum but out of the concrete social experiences people have in a racist social order. And it follows that discrimination is not primarily an expression of prejudice but rather a by-product of purposive striving to attain or hold social, economic, and political advantages and privileges. Hence, within the United States, whites and blacks for the most part are residentially, occupationally, and socially segregated; the two racial divisions frequently operate parallel but separate and distinctive organizations, and the black community characteristically remains economically depressed and dependent on the wealthier and more powerful white community.

In this book, we shall make periodic reference to **racism.** We shall employ the term as an inclusive concept that embraces the notions of prejudice, discrimination, and institutional racism.

Gatekeeping

One mechanism by which institutional racism is brought about is **gatekeeping**—the decision-making process whereby individuals are admitted to offices and positions of power, privilege, and status within the society (Erickson, 1975). Individuals usually exercise some degree of choice over their own future careers. However, given the scarcity of positions in various areas of the economy, some people evaluate the qualifications of job applicants to determine whether the candidates will achieve their wishes. Most generally gatekeepers are professionals with experience and credentials in the fields they monitor. Such individuals are found in schools, colleges, employment agencies, and business and government personnel offices.

Historically, most gatekeepers have been white and male. In theory they assess individuals on the basis of merit, skills, and talents and not in terms of race, ethnicity, class, family, community, or other group attributes. In point of fact, however, merit, skills, and talent are relative matters. In determining qualifications, which group's *values* will be used for judging who is "capable," "bright," "conscientious," and "resourceful"? Will the standards of excellence be those of the white middle class? the Puerto Rican community? the Jewish community? the

Chicano community? the black community? Further, which group's members will be the *judges* who determine the individuals meeting the qualifications? Will the judges who guard the gates be whites, Puerto Ricans, Jews, Chicanos, or blacks?

Within the United States a white power structure has traditionally tended the gates that regulate the flow of people into those positions that provide access to the society's good things. Whites have determined which individuals would be allowed to pass through entry portals to good jobs, good schools, good universities, good housing, and good health-care facilities. For the most part whites have admitted those who fit their own image and adhere to their values as expressed in family patterns; dress and hair codes; the ownership, use, and care of property; and personal behavior. To the extent to which black ghetto life or Chicano life in the Rio Grande valley, for example, has varied from that of middle-class whites, blacks and Chicanos have been "filtered" out of the "system." Wealth, power, status, and territory have been funneled toward privileged whites just as chips flow to those having a stacked deck of cards.

School and college counselors are one example of gatekeepers. They regulate the flow of students to courses and programs of higher rank. Research suggests that counselors do not operate in an unbiased manner (Erickson, 1975). They tend to be more effective in describing mobility channels for and more encouraging to students who are members of their own racial or ethnic group. And they are more prone to assist ingroup than outgroup students by writing letters, making telephone calls, and bending or overlooking organizational rules.

Real-estate agents are also gatekeepers. Although more Americans are exposed to token integration now than in the past, the predominant experience of most remains a relatively homogeneous racial neighborhood. Acting as community gatekeepers, realtors play an important part in perpetuating segregated patterns of housing. A good many studies have examined these matters. Typically, in such studies, couples of different races who are otherwise similar are sent to real-estate agents as prospective clients. This research reveals that agents do racially discriminate among the couples. The "clients' " race helps determine whether agents will show them homes, and determines where the homes they show them will be located (Pearce, 1979). Such racial steering is a mechanism of institutional racism.

SUMMARY

1. Sociology examines minority relations with a scientific orientation characterized by a rigorous, disciplined pursuit of objectivity. Sociologists are enjoined to avoid such emotional involvement in their work that they cannot adopt a new approach or reject an old answer when

their findings indicate that this is required. Further, sociologists are enjoined not to turn their back on facts or distort them simply because they do not like them.

2. During the past few decades considerable controversy has been generated within sociological circles over the quesions of "knowledge for what?" and "sociology for whom?" During its formative years, sociology sought to remain neutral on questions of social policy. However, during the 1960s and 1970s a group of "new-breed" sociologists emerged who challenged the view that sociologists should not commit value judgments. Much of the controversy has revolved about the uses of science. Many sociologists have come to appreciate that sociology is both a pure and applied science and that a sharp boundary does not separate these two aspects of the discipline.

3. A minority is not a statistical category but a social group. Sociologists characterize a minority in terms of five features: (a) A minority is a social group whose members experience discrimination, segregation, oppression, or persecution at the hands of another social group. (b) The disabilities experienced by minorities are related to special characteristics that its members share, either physical or cultural or both, which the dominant group holds in low esteem. (c) Minorities are self-conscious social units; they are characterized by a consciousness of kind. (d) Generally people do not become members of a minority voluntarily; they are born into it. (e) Members of a minority group, by choice or necessity, tend to marry within their own group.

4. A racial, nationality, or religious group may be dominant in one area and a minority in another. Furthermore, dominant and minority group memberships are not necessarily mutually exclusive. It is possible for an individual to have dominant and minority roles simultaneously. This possibility derives from the fact that within the United States (and some other nations) the dominant-minority group classification has a threefold basis: race, religion, and nationality. All this points to the relativity of minority membership.

5. "Societies" are humanly constructed entities. In the Western world a society is commonly equated with a nation-state. Yet this results in difficulties for we often mistakenly equate nationalism with a feeling of loyalty to the state (a political unit) rather than with loyalty to the nation (an ethnic entity). The fact that in the world we seldom find "one nation, one state" gives rise to problems of national minorities. The problems of national minorities arise from a conceptual scheme of what the most inclusive social unit ought to be—an ideal of fashioning a political entity or state that includes some and excludes others.

6. Louis Wirth distinguishes among four types of minorities on the basis of the goals toward which the minority and dominant groups are

striving. A pluralistic minority desires to live peacefully side-by-side with the dominant group. An assimilationist minority expects to be absorbed within an emergent common culture that is the product of the blending of divergent racial and ethnic strains. A secessionist minority repudiates both assimilation and cultural pluralism and takes as its goal full political self-determination. A militant minority insists upon reversing the statuses and sets domination over others as its goal.

7. The definition of prejudice as a "pre-judgment" is not adequate. Prejudice is a state of mind, an attitude. Like any other attitude, prejudice has three aspects. Social scientists distinguish between what people think—the cognitive level; what they feel—the emotional level; and how they are inclined to act—the action-oriented level.

8. Stereotypes are one dimension of the cognitive level of prejudice. They are the images or pictures we carry in our heads concerning a people. They derive from the fact that we find it impossible to weigh every reaction of every person, minute-by-minute in terms of its individual meanings. Instead, we type individuals and groups in snap-judgment style. However, stereotypes overlook the differences found among a people with regard to a trait. Moreover, they overlook the fact that people have a great many traits.

9. Whereas prejudice is a state of mind, discrimination is action— what people actually do. Under circumstances of discrimination, members of the minority are arbitrarily denied rights and privileges even when their qualifications are equal to those of dominant-group members.

10. Discrimination occurs without prejudice and prejudice without discrimination. Overall, however, an association exists between prejudice and discrimination such that the more prejudiced are also more likely to practice discrimination. Situational factors play an especially important part in determining whether people will translate their prejudices into overt actions.

11. The concepts of prejudice and discrimination primarily have an individual emphasis. For example, they focus upon a specific white's attitude or behavior toward a particular black or group of blacks. Institutional racism, in contrast, continually imposes burdens on and withholds benefits from the members of a racial or ethnic group through society's institutions. Privilege in a racist society cannot be avoided by dominant-group members, even by those who reject the society's institutions.

12. Gatekeeping is one mechanism by which institutional racism is brought about. Given the scarcity of positions in various areas of life, some people—gatekeepers—evaluate the qualifications of job applicants to determine whether the candidates will achieve their wishes. Historically, most gatekeepers have been white and male.

GLOSSARY

Ascribed Status   A position in the social structure assigned to an individual independent of his or her unique characteristics or talents.

Discrimination   Overt action in which members of an ethnic or racial group are treated unequally and unfavorably by members of the dominant group.

Dominant Group   Any culturally or physically distinctive and self-conscious social aggregate, with hereditary membership and a high degree of endogamy, which discriminates against a subordinate social group.

Ethnic Group   A social segment of a society identified primarily on cultural grounds by such behaviors as language, religion, food habits, folk practices, dress, gestures, or mannerisms.

Gatekeeping   The decision-making process whereby individuals are admitted to offices and positions of power, privilege, and high status within the society.

Genocide   A set of policies of a dominant group that are aimed at the physical extermination of the members of a minority group.

Institutional Racism   The social arrangements whereby people of one racial or ethnic group are systematically oppressed and exploited by the institutions of a society controlled by another racial group.

Minority Group   Any culturally or physically distinctive and self-conscious social aggregate, with hereditary membership and a high degree of endogamy, which is subject to political, economic, or social discrimination by a dominant segment of an environing political society.

Norms   Rules that specify appropriate and inappropriate behavior.

Prejudice   A system of negative conceptions, feelings, and action-orientations regarding the members of a particular group.

Racism   An inclusive concept that embraces the notions of prejudice, discrimination, and racism.

Stereotype   The unscientific and hence unreliable generalization that people make about other people as persons or groups.

Symbolic Racism   A new form of racism between whites and blacks in which three elements converge. First, many whites believe that blacks have become too demanding, too pushy, and too angry, and that blacks are getting more than they merit. Second, many whites feel that blacks are not playing by "the rules of the game." And third, many whites have formed a negative image of blacks associated with notions of welfare, urban riots, black mayors, crime in the streets, affirmative-action programs, and quota systems.

Values   Conceptions regarding the desirability or undesirability of things, including their beauty, morality, merit, or worth.

Race: Fact and Myth

No treatment of minority relations would be complete without a consideration of "race." By virtue of the ignorance, superstition, and prejudice that have surrounded the matter for generations, we have postponed consideration of the topic until we could thoroughly examine it. Various questions need to be dealt with: What is race? Are there "pure" races? Are Jews a "race"? Are there intellectually superior races? Are there "racial" personalities and temperaments? Is there a "racial" morality? Is racial interbreeding harmful? How are races formed? Although myths of one sort or another have clouded these basic human questions, scientific evidence can help to dispel some of the mystery and confusion.

What Is Race?

We of course all know—scientists and the public alike—that people in various parts of the world differ in certain hereditary features, in such things as skin color, hair texture, various facial features, stature, and head shape. It is equally true that the number of features that humankind everywhere shares in common is very much larger and of considerably greater importance than its divergent features. Nonetheless, differences do exist and are readily evident. We encounter little difficulty, for instance, distinguishing *groups* of Swedes, Japanese, and Ethiopians from one another. The concept of **race** has often been employed to refer to this fact. Races are populations differing in the incidence of certain hereditary traits. Considerable controversy, however, surrounds the concept of race.

Conceptions of Race

Three schools of thought exist regarding race: the "fixed type," the "breeding population," and the "no-race" traditions. Let us examine each of these more closely.

The Fixed Type School.   The fixed type approach to race enjoyed primacy in the period between 1850 and 1950, although it continues to appear in the writings of some East European scholars and shades of it periodically emerge in the works of the American anthropologist Carleton S. Coon (1962, 1965, 1967). And among the lay public in the United States the fixed type view still occupies a preeminent position. According to this notion, races are relatively fixed and immutable hereditary groupings that reach back into antiquity. Scholars of this tradition, such individuals as Joseph Deniker (1912), William Z. Ripley (1899), Egon von Eickstedt (1934), and Earnest A. Hooton (1946), typically began by distinguishing a number of more or less "pure," ancestral races and then in turn a number of "mixed" populations. The number three was popular for the identification of "pure" races ("Mongoloids," "Caucasoids," and "Negroids"), though a few scholars suggested that perhaps a fourth or fifth "oid" might advisedly also be added; and then there were also those who took a more microscopic view, and liked to talk about "Nordics," "Alpines," "Baltics," "Keltics," "Mediterraneans," and perhaps thirty or a hundred more "races." The typology of the late Earnest A. Hooton, Harvard University physical anthropologist, is illustrative and is summarized in Figure 2.1.

Scholars of the fixed type school saw the task of science as one of identifying and describing "original races" and in turn of *separating* present-day populations into the various ancestral components. Viewed in this fashion, race is a combination of characteristics that is discernible in *individuals.* Illustrative is a study of the population of Ireland undertaken by Harvard University anthropologists Earnest A. Hooton and C. Wesley Dupertuis (1955). The researchers secured a representative sample of Irish males and then made more than eighty measurements on each individual, for instance, the person's chest breadth, sitting height, cephalic index, nasal index, extent of lip eversion, and inner arm skin color. Using Hooton's subtypes of the "white" race, the researchers undertook to fish individuals out of the Irish sample and place them in one or another subtype (*see* Table 2.1). In essence, the "racial types" derived in this manner reflected the typological guesses that Hooton had made prior to the study and that he had arrived at largely through intuition.

The fixed type approach is now discredited. Scholars using this approach observed, for instance, that in Sweden there are a good many tall, blond, and blue-eyed people. Hence they inferred the existence of an ancestral "Nordic" race. What they failed to note was that there are also a good many short, dark-haired, and brown-eyed Swedes, and still more Swedes with various combinations of stature, hair shading, and eye color. Interestingly enough, if Swedish premilitary induction records are to be believed, only 11 percent of Swedish young men are of the "pure" Nordic type with tall stature, blond hair, blue eyes, and long skulls (Lundborg and Linders, 1926).

FIGURE 2.1 EARNEST A. HOOTON'S TYPOLOGY OF THE RACES OF MAN.

PRIMARY RACE (a great division of mankind)

	WHITE RACE	NEGROID RACE	MONGOLOID RACE
Primary Subraces (formed by evolutionary processes within a primary race)	Mediterranean Ainu Keltic Nordic Alpine East Baltic	African Negro Nilotic Negro Negrito	Classic Mongoloid Arctic Mongoloid
Composite Subraces (stabilized blends due to interbreeding of primary subraces of a primary race)	Armenoid Dinaric		
Residual Mixed Types (interbreeds)	Nordic-Alpine Nordic-Mediterranean		

COMPOSITE RACE (formed by stabilization of blends of two or more primary races)

	PREDOMINANTLY WHITE	PREDOMINANTLY NEGROID	PREDOMINANTLY MONGOLOID
Secondary Subraces (formed by evolutionary processes within a secondary race)	Australian Indo-Dravidian Polynesian	Tasmanian Melanesian-Papuan Bushman-Hottentot Melanesian Papuan Bushman Hottentot	American Indian Indonesian-Mongoloid Malay-Mongoloid Indonesian

Source: Adapted from Earnest A. Hooton, *Up from the Ape*, rev. ed. (New York: The Macmillan Co., 1946), part V.

TABLE 2.1 HOOTON'S TYPOLOGY OF IRISH
RACIAL TYPES

Sub-Racial Types	Sorting Criteria	Percentage of Total Series
Nordic Mediterranean	Long-headed; short stature; mixed hair; mixed eyes	28.9
Keltic	Long-headed; darkish or red hair; blue-eyed	25.3
Dinaric	Round-headed; long, hooked noses; mixed hair; mixed eyes	18.6
Nordic Alpine	Round-headed; mixed hair; mixed eyes	18.4
Predominantly Nordic	Long-headed; "near blonds"; either blue or mixed eyes	6.8
East Baltic	Round-headed; blond or red-headed; either light or mixed eyes	1.1
Pure Nordic	Long-headed; fair-haired; blue-eyed	0.6
Pure Mediterranean	Long-headed; brunet hair; dark eyes	0.3

Source: Adapted from Earnest A. Hooton and C. Wesley Dupertuis, *The Physical Anthropology of Ireland* (Cambridge, Mass.: Peabody Museum of Archaeology and Ethnology, Harvard University, 1955), 141–143.

Further, while individuals as "types" clearly exist—for instance, tall, blond, blue-eyed men and women—the inference that they recapitulate ancestral strains (a "Nordic" race) is nonsense. Individual "types" are merely chance combinations of genetically independent traits. Since traits are independent and "segregate" out separately, such types prove nothing about the appearance of ancestral groups. Blue eyes and blond hair are no more proof for an original "Nordic" race than are short hair and heavy beards evidence for an ancestral race of Trolls, or red hair and freckles for an original Rufous race. The search for racial types is premised upon the notion that traits are transmitted as complexes, that somehow they are linked together to constitute some sort of Caucasian, Nordic, or Mediterranean "package." Such a notion is pre-Mendelian and unscientific.

Scholars of the fixed type school commonly compounded their difficulties by viewing various contemporary populations as simply mixtures, in varying degrees, of a few "original races." It is not surprising that of the many racial classifications premised upon this mistaken notion, all found their nemesis in certain people who defied placement, such groups as the San of the Kalahari Desert, the Polynesians, the Veddas, the Lapps, the Australian aborigines, the Ainus of northern Japan, and many others.

Take the Polynesians. Their skin color ranges from almost white to dark brown; some are roundheads, others are longheads; their noses may be slender and high, or broad, short, and concave; their hair is prevailingly wavy but sometimes straight and even frizzly. Some scholars using the fixed type approach, in their search for simplicity, were inclined to label the Polynesians "Caucasians." Others were more cautious and like Hooton preferred to view the Polynesians as a "composite race." Yet, in truth, no possible combination of "Caucasoid," "Negroid" and Mongoloid" (ill-defined as these terms are) could produce the Polynesian. The blood group distributions in Polynesia could hardly be explained in terms of some sort of Caucasoid-Negroid-Mongoloid admixture. Still other scholars of this school preferred to add another "oid." But this really did not help matters for it simply shifted the problem to a lower level—in turn there were some "Polynesian" groups that did not quite fit, and so where was the multiplication of races to stop?

The Breeding Population School. A more recent view conceives of race as a "breeding population" within a species. This view is identified with such individuals as William C. Boyd (1950), Theodosius Dobzhansky (1962), Stanley M. Garn (1963, 1964, 1965), and Marshall T. Newman (1963). While still searching for "types," these scholars focus their attention upon *groups* characterized by sets of average tendencies—the frequencies of given genes within particular groups (e.g., the relative prevalence of genes for such blood types as ABO, MNS, Diego, Duffy, and sickle-cell anemia) and the "commonness" of particular phenotypic traits (e.g., the prevalence of "inner-eye folds," body hair, and male pattern balding). This school generally provides us with an abbreviated statement of average tendencies within various populations ("races").

Breeding population scholars typically seek to identify and describe "natural units" of humankind that constitute taxonomic units below the species level—geographically delimited populations that have more or less finite and known breeding limits. They stress the view that social barriers (associated with language, religion, caste, and class) and geographical barriers (associated with mountain ranges, deserts, oceans, and territorial distance) operate as reproductive barriers. Viewed from this perspective, humankind is divided into mating groups or reproductive communities—termed **"demes"** or **"Mendelian populations"**—the members of which are more likely to interbreed among themselves than with other populations. In brief, there arise through such mechanisms as isolation, mutation, natural selection, and genetic drift more or less stable, differentiated gene pools among humankind—people who have a common genetic heritage.

There is a difference of opinion among the scholars commonly identified with this school as to just how finite "races" are. Garn (1964:316) —who recognizes nine major "geographical races" and thirty-two "local races"—speaks of races as "discrete groupings" and "natural units, reproductively isolated from each other and with separate evolutionary histories through time." The impression unmistakably conveyed by Garn (1963, 1964) is that he views his taxonomic races as mirroring nature in being more or less discretely delimited divisions of humankind.

In contrast with Garn, Theodosius Dobzhansky (1962, 1963), a distinguished geneticist, argues that "if races have to be 'discrete units,' then there are no races" and that racial classification "is a matter of convenience and hence of judgment"—even a matter of "common sense." But he also insists:

> . . . it does not follow that races are arbitrary and "mere" inventions of the classifiers; some authors have talked themselves into denying that the human species has any races at all! Let us make very clear what is and what is not arbitrary about races. Race *differences* are facts of nature which can, given sufficient study, be ascertained objectively: Mendelian populations of any kind, from small tribes to inhabitants of countries and continents, may differ in frequencies of some genetic variants or they may not. If they so differ, they are racially distinct (Dobzhansky, 1962:367).

According to this view, race is both a real biological phenomenon and a category of classification (Dobzhansky, 1968).

The No-Race School.   The "no-race" school denies that "races" are real if viewed as relatively discrete biological entities "out there" in nature and as units of evolution. Ashley Montagu (1963, 1964) and Frank B. Livingstone (1962) take this position. For the most part proponents of the no-race position build their case on two premises:

1. *Racial differences are continuous.* Most of us recognize that Scandinavian peoples such as the Swedes exhibit a series of physical characteristics that distinguish them from Mediterranean peoples such as the Italians. Swedes are often classed within the Caucasian subrace of Nordics; Italians within the Caucasian subrace of Mediterraneans. Between the Nordics and the Mediterraneans in the central zone of Europe are the Alpine subrace. Yet proponents of the no-race position ask, "Among what people or where geographically in Europe can one say with definitive authority, 'Here Nordics end and Alpines start' "? Or, "Here Alpines

end and Mediterraneans begin"? Or, for that matter, why distinguish among merely Nordics, Alpines, and Mediterraneans? Why not five or nine or some other number of subraces? Might not one classificatory system have as much merit as another? Moreover, if we study, district by district, the inhabitants of Germany, France, or northern and central Italy, we find Nordic, Alpine, and Mediterranean types and every conceivable intermediate type.

On a larger scale members of the no-race school ask, "Where and among what people in Africa can one with justice to the evidence indicate that here and among these people Caucasians cease and there and among those people Negroids start?" The problem is readily seen. It stems from the fact that most racial differences are *continuous* rather than *discrete.* With regard to skin color, hair form, stature, and head shape, populations often show no sharp distinctions. Variations on the contrary are gradual and continuous. Blood types, however, are discrete. An individual's blood is either A, B, AB, or O, not a mixture or a shading of all four. Yet here too populations generally differ not so much in the presence or absence of a given gene for blood type, but in its frequency—for instance, most populations merely differ in the relative prevalence of the ABO blood groups (although there are a few exceptions including the apparent absence of blood group B among a number of American Indian tribes and certain groups of Australian aborigines; *see* Table 2.2). In sum, "races" are not characterized by fixed clear-cut differences but by fluid, continuous differences. It is next to impossible to say where one population ends and another begins.

2. *Trait distributions tend to be discordant.* Peoples throughout the world differ in a great many traits. However, variations among the traits occur independently of one another (i.e., they do not necessarily vary together). Since the inheritance of blood-group systems follows Mendelian rules (e.g., the ABO, MSN, Rh, Duffy, Kidd, and Diego systems), they constitute some of our best material for studying population divergence at the genetic level. Maps showing the patterns of distribution of various blood-group types reveal no more than partial coincidence and sometimes striking discordance within populations. Moreover, considerable juggling is necessary to make taxonomies of blood systems coincide with "natural populations."

Perhaps a number of illustrations may help to clarify the matter. If we take blood groups to be a valid guide to overall genetic similarities, it is unlikely that "African Negroids" and "Oceanic Negroids" (populations in Melanesia) are at all closely related. Consequently, to place the two populations taxonomically together by virtue of their similar hair form may be a serious error. On the

TABLE 2.2 PERCENTAGE OF INDIVIDUALS OF
THE FOUR BLOOD GROUPS AMONG CERTAIN
POPULATIONS

	O	A	B	AB
AMERICA				
Utes (Montana)	97.4	2.6	—	—
Navaho (New Mexico)	77.7	22.5	—	—
Blackfeet (Montana)	23.5	76.5	—	—
Eskimos (Cape Farewell)	41.1	53.8	3.5	1.4
Toba (Argentina)	98.5	1.5	—	—
Bororo (Brazil)	100.0	—	—	—
AUSTRALIA				
Aborigines (West Australia)	48.1	51.9	—	—
Aborigines (South Australia)	42.6	57.4	—	—
Aborigines (Queensland)	58.6	37.8	3.6	—
ASIA				
Kirghiz (USSR)	31.6	27.4	32.2	8.8
Hindu (Bombay)	31.8	29.2	28.3	10.8
Chinese (Peking)	30.7	25.1	34.2	10.0
Japanese (Tokyo)	30.1	38.4	21.9	9.7
Bogobos (Philippines)	53.6	16.9	26.5	3.0
Micronesians (Saipan)	50.5	33.8	14.0	1.7
AFRICA				
Egyptians (Cairo)	27.3	38.5	25.5	8.8
Kikuyu (Kenya)	60.4	18.7	19.8	1.1
Bembe (Brazzaville)	50.0	25.7	20.3	4.1
Bushman (Kun-Bechuanaland)	37.0	53.4	5.5	4.1
Bushman (Magon-Bechuanaland)	61.1	34.7	4.2	—
Hottentot (Vaal River)	26.4	44.8	24.7	4.0
Zulu (South Africa)	51.8	24.6	21.6	2.0
EUROPE				
Irish (Dublin)	55.2	31.1	12.1	1.7
English (London)	47.9	42.4	8.3	1.4
Swedes (Stockholm)	37.9	46.1	9.5	6.5
French (Paris)	39.8	42.3	11.8	6.1
Hungarians (Budapest)	36.1	41.8	15.9	6.2
Russian (Moscow)	33.3	37.4	22.8	6.5

other hand "Mongoloid" peoples, commonly grouped together by
virtue of their straight hair and inner-eye fold, may indeed be
closely related. Yet even in this case we find considerable regional
variation with respect to numerous other characteristics. This variation is most apparent in the major blood systems. Consequently
what is really meant by the category "Mongoloid" is by no means
clear.

Likewise, contrary to many popular myths, classifications based on skin color do not yield the same results as those based on some other characteristic. There is not even a necessary direct correlation between skin color and hair form. For instance, extremely kinky hair is found among the moderately pigmented San of the Kalahari Desert of South Africa and straight or wavy hair among some otherwise dark-pigmented peoples of southern India.

Conceptions of Race: Conclusion. Humans do not lend themselves easily to cut-and-dried "racial" classifications and neat labels. Where two or more people come into contact, populations are usually found that are intermediate or that combine the traits of the different stocks. The longer the time over which such contacts occur, the more widely spread are the intermediate populations and the more blurred the "divisions." In time there unfolds a situation, like that in contemporary Europe, in which one or a multiple number of "subraces" can be identified according to one's own predilections.

The world "racial" panorama is complex and varied, and no two people would probably classify "races" in the same way. Here we will not attempt the task at all. As we have noted, present-day scientists are far from agreement in making a division of human "races." Indeed, the number of "races" one identifies depends upon the purpose of the classification. As such, it is a matter of convenience and judgment. By necessity any classification of "races" is almost entirely arbitrary and depends upon the particular characteristics on which one chooses to base it. Any number of "racial" classifications of the same populations but based on different gene frequencies may be equally valid and useful. The concept "race" merely enables us to place a "handle" on a phenomenon, to look at, to describe, and to analyze it. Classification and systematization are tools employed to make diversity intelligible and manageable. But this need not bar us from recognizing the shortcomings or relative value of our tools.

In itself color (or some other trait) is meaningless. It is not important in itself as an optical event but rather as a bearer of a message. In brief, it stands as a "sign" or "mark" of a social status or role. Hence, whether races are real in a biological sense is not the chief issue for this book. Race *is* real in a social sense. As W. I. Thomas (1931:189) once observed, "If men [and women] define situations as real, they are real in their consequences." In other words, what people believe affects their behavior, whether the beliefs are true or not. For instance, although there are no such things as elves, some people have a firm image as to what elves are like and what they do. If people believe in elves—and the notion is not an uncommon one in folklore—people then are likely to take them into account in their behavior. And if people believe there are races, then they too act on the basis of their beliefs—the results often being prejudice, discrimination, and institutional racism. And it is these latter matters that are the focus of this book.

Are Jews a Race?

There are a good many people who assert that Jews constitute a "race." They go on to claim that they can identify a Jew from other people simply on the basis of appearance: short to medium stature; black hair; a long, hooked nose; greasy skin; a dark complexion; and a tendency for the women to be somewhat hefty. In testing the validity of this stereotype we confront the question, "Do Jews possess a complex of physical characteristics that makes them a distinct racial group?" Science answers the question with an unequivocal "No." In fact even the Nazis implicitly answered the question negatively, as they required Jews to display on their clothing the Star of David or yellow armbands so that "Aryans" might identify them. Apparently, in the absence of such insignia, the "Aryans" were having difficulty distinguishing the Jews.

Jews are widely distributed throughout the world. During the Babylonian captivity in the sixth century B.C., they intermingled and intermixed with the Mesopotamian peoples. During the Hellenistic period they followed Alexander the Great into Egypt, Syria, Asia Minor, and other regions. At the time of the Maccabees, in the second century B.C., the Jews moved to the farthest corners of the Roman Empire, including Spain, Italy, France, and the Rhineland of Germany. With the coming of the First Crusade in the eleventh century and the persecution of the Jews by Christian knights, Rhineland Jews migrated to present-day Poland, Russia, and the Ukraine (Montagu, 1942). Likewise, there are Chinese Jews who are identical in "Mongoloid" features with other Chinese; there are Abyssinian and American blacks who are Jews; and in Italy there is a Jewish community of former Catholics. Jewish settlements are found in Transcaucasia, Syria, Turkistan, Persia, Afghanistan, Morocco, and Algeria.

Obviously it is not possible here to present the detailed statistics demonstrating the considerable variability in physical characteristics among the misnamed Jewish race. The type usually regarded as typically "Jewish" is actually prevalent among the peoples of the eastern Mediterranean area, most of whom are not Jews and never have been. Thus Turks, Greeks, Syrians, and others are often mistaken for Jews by those who claim to be able to identify Jews by their appearance. Actually the Jews involved in the widespread migrations just described tended through time to interbreed with the inhabitants of the new lands. Accordingly, they often became indistinguishable from the aboriginal groups. By way of illustration, it is calculated that in Germany, between 1921 and 1925, for every 100 Jewish marriages, there were 58 all-Jewish and 42 mixed marriages. In 1926, in Berlin, there were 861 all-Jewish and 554 Jewish-Gentile marriages (Comas, 1951). In the light of such evidence it is not surprising to note that a census of schoolchildren taken in Germany during the nineteenth century revealed that among 75,000 Jewish children, 32 percent had light hair and 46 percent light eyes.

Other evidence likewise points to the fact that different populations of Jews at one time or another have intermixed with the various populations among whom they were living. Among Jews in Yemen 100 percent had dark eyes and dark hair. But among Jews in Baden (part of Germany), the dark-eyed Jews were in the minority (48.8 percent), although nearly 85 percent had dark hair, while 2.3 percent had red hair. Some 51.2 percent had light eyes and 12.8 percent had fair or blond hair. Consequently, a significant number of Baden Jews, accordingly, had the so-called Aryan traits. Similarly, in Lithuania 34.8 percent of the Jews had light eyes and 29.0 percent had fair or blond hair. When head shape is considered, Jews in different regions of the world show considerable differences from one another. Jews residing in the Daghestan Caucasus are predominantly round-headed; those in North Africa and especially those in Yemen are predominantly long-headed; and those in Europe tend to be of all varieties with the intermediate types predominating.

Quite clearly Jews are not of a uniform physical type. Even the hooked nose, ostensibly so characteristic of Jews, was shown by one study to be prevalent among only 44 percent of the Jews of one group, while straight noses were found among 40 percent, the "Roman" nose among 9 percent, and the tip-tilted nose among 7 percent. A trip to the new nation of Israel testifies to the absence of a Jewish "race." The flow of Jews into Israel, more than a million and a half during the last thirty years, has come in two main streams, the first ("Western" or "European" Jews) from eastern and central Europe, the second ("Eastern" or "Oriental" Jews) from the West Asian or North African countries—Yemen, Egypt, Tunisia, Iraq, Morocco, Algeria. In fact these two disparate traditions have been termed "the two Israels." This ingathering of the long-wandering tribes of Israel dramatically reveals the extent to which Jews have become not only the cultural but also the physical products of the cultures and peoples among whom they lived as "outsiders" for so long. Jews seeking to regain homogeneity in Israel now not only have to bridge all the great differences of culture that separate peoples of industrialized and nonindustrialized societies, but also have to close the gap of color.

In summary, the existence among Jews of "Caucasian," "Mongoloid," and "Negroid" types, the presence of blonds and brunets, of hooked and Roman noses, and of round, long, and intermediate heads is demonstrable evidence of the nonexistence of a Jewish "race." Those emotional and temperamental reactions that may characterize some Jews, such as distinctive facial expressions, bodily posturings and mannerisms, styles of speaking and intonation can be traced to Jewish cultural traditions and to the treatment Jews received at the hands of the non-Jews.

Who then is a Jew? We need to resort to a *social* definition. A Jew is an individual who is defined as a Jew by the community-at-large or by Jews or both.

How Are Races Formed?

We have observed that people in various parts of the world differ in certain hereditary characteristics including skin color, hair texture, facial features, stature, and head shape. This raises the question: "How did the various people get the way they are?" or "How are races formed?" A statement on race prepared by distinguished scientists from nations throughout the world and issued under the auspices of UNESCO has answered the question in these terms:

> Scientists have reached general agreement in recognizing that mankind is one: that all men belong to the same species, *Homo sapiens.* It is further generally agreed among scientists that all men are probably derived from the same common stock; and that such differences as exist between different groups of mankind are due to the operation of evolutionary factors of differentiation such as isolation, the drift and random fixation of the material particles which control heredity (the genes), changes in the structure of these particles, hybridization, and natural selection. In these ways groups have arisen of varying stability and degree of differentiation which have been classified in different ways for different purposes.

Mutations

If human beings are of a common stock, we must look at the mechanism by which they become differentiated. In short, how do new genes appear? The process is termed **mutation.** Mutation involves physical change in the chemical structure of a gene or in its position in relation to other genes. The exact cause or causes of mutation are not known. Various hair forms, for instance, have been the product of mutation. It is known that among swine, mice, rats, and rabbits curly hair has appeared spontaneously through mutation. Similarly, although kinky hair is usually found among blacks and not among whites, kinky hair has occurred as a mutation among whites who were apparently of exclusively white ancestry. On record are three Norwegian families in which such a mutation appeared.

Mutations constitute the raw materials of evolutionary change and racial differentiation. Some authorities assert that at least one mutation occurs in every human being sometime between conception and death. Most mutations, perhaps as many as 99 percent, are harmful. Hemophilia (also called "bleeder's disease" because it is characterized by a defect in the clotting power of blood) is a case in point. It is estimated that one in every 100,000 individuals in the English-speaking world today has a hemophilia gene that came into being spontaneously. England's Queen Victoria apparently inherited such a gene. In any event, she transmitted the trait through her daughters and granddaughters to the royalty of Russia and Spain.

Natural Selection

Occasionally a mutation appears that has a selective survival value. Among rabbits, for example, in a territory where the ground is covered with snow half the year, mutations in favor of a seasonal shift of coat color to white would be of adaptive value in lessening their chance of being killed by natural enemies. They would possess an advantage over brown rabbits whose coats remained unchanged. Through the action of environment, the mutant rabbits would be preserved so that they would tend to leave more offspring behind than the unchanging brown rabbits. And, through time, as would be expected, the mutant rabbits would flourish in comparison with the brown rabbits. Consequently those varieties within a species that are best suited to a particular environment have a survival advantage over other members of the species and they are the ones more likely to reproduce. This process is termed **natural selection.**

It appears that some distinctive traits among human populations may have arisen in this manner. A case in point is the sickle-cell gene, which in its heterozygous state (where the gene is present in one but not the other parent) confers immunity to malaria (in the homozygous state— where the gene is inherited from both parents—it produces serious symptoms and often fatal anemia). The heterozygous carriers of the gene possess the greatest fitness in a population living in localities where malaria is prevalent. Another gene, which when homozygous produces thalassemia (Mediterranean anemia), also confers immunity to malaria in the heterozygous state. It appears that the combined distribution of the sickle-cell and the thalassemia genes in the tropics of the Old World resembles that of fasciparum malaria (there are exceptions associated with migrations and population mixtures).

Carleton S. Coon, Stanley M. Garn, and Joseph B. Birdsell (1950) argue that natural selection has produced distinct races among humankind. They illustrate their point with body build. Desert people, including the Tuareg of the Sahara and the Somalis of the Horn of Africa, are tall, lean people, with long arms and legs, shallow bodies, and narrow hands and feet. According to Coon, Garn, and Birdsell such a build is adaptive to dry desert heat. The skin surface area among such people is great in proportion to their volume and weight. The crucial factor seems to be that the build presents the maximum skin surface area (in proportion to mass and weight) to the external environment, thus permitting a maximum evaporation surface for cooling. Since roughly 50 percent of the body's blood is inside the legs at any one time, a long, pipelike leg is an excellent radiator. It exposes much more cooling surface than a short, barrel-like one.

On the other hand, among people of the Arctic Circle, the opposite condition prevails. In contrast to the inhabitants of desert areas, Arctic people present the least possible skin surface area to the environment in proportion to volume and weight. The Eskimo and Chukchi peoples are built to radiate as little heat as possible. Their bodies are thickset and chunky, their chests thick and wide, their legs short and thick, their fingers and toes short, and their wrists and ankles small. Likewise, Arctic-dwelling peoples often are at the door of starvation. Selection would favor those who could store and utilize fat, or in other words "obesity" would have survival value where food is scarce.

Coon, Garn, and Birdsell view the "Mongoloid face" as a piece of adaptive thermal "engineering." They argue that the presence of the world's most Mongoloid people in the coldest inhabited parts of the world, in Siberia and the Yukon, suggests that Mongoloids are adapted to cold. A person with thin, bony features, especially a narrow, prominent nose, would be in danger of freezing the face. On the other hand, a person with a flat face padded with fat, and with a sparse beard, would be well adapted. This is the Mongoloid face in its extreme form. Likewise, epicanthic folds (giving the appearance of slanting eyes) protect the eyeball with fatty layers of padding, bringing the lids close to one another. Whiskers are also a disadvantage, as moisture from the individual's breath freezes on the hair, and soon the face underneath freezes too.

Such theories, however, are quite speculative. We lack experimental evidence for testing their validity. Indeed, the critics have dealt rather harshly with Coon, Garn, and Birdsell. For instance, the distinguished physical anthropologist Sherwood L. Washburn observes that large numbers of Mongoloids currently live in the hot, moist tropics, and many of them have lived for thousands of years under conditions that have been anything but cold. Moreover, Washburn (1963:51) fails to find the types of correlations that would support the Coon, Garn, and Birdsell position:

> If one follows the form of the nose, in Europe, as one moves north, narrow noses are correlated with cold climate; in Eastern Asia low noses are correlated with cold climate. In neither case is there the slightest evidence that the difference in the form of the nose has anything whatsoever to do with warming the air that comes into the face.

Washburn insists that the Mongoloid face has nothing to do with adaptation to the cold. He argues that it constitutes a complex structural pattern related to the teeth and hence is primarily the result of large masseter (chewing) muscles and the bones from which these muscles arise. Superficially a very similar pattern is observed among the San of the Kalahari Desert, whose facial form can hardly be attributed to thermal engineering. Caution, then, is called for in attempting to ascertain the role played by natural selection in race formation.

Isolation

Mutations possessing adaptive value would have been established among early humans because the populations were characteristically small. The land mass of Asia, Africa, and Europe is considerable. Consequently, early groups of humans were frequently isolated from other groups of humans over considerable periods of history. Of necessity breeding took place largely or entirely within isolated groups. Such natural factors as mountain ranges, rivers, forests, deserts, seas, and distance served to reinforce isolation. Thus, in time, no matter how much alike all peoples had initially been, groups isolated from one another would soon become different by virtue of the differing mutations among them. Isolation, then, is another factor contributing to racial differentiation.

Genetic Drift

Changes in gene frequencies within a population may be due to chance alone. This is termed **genetic drift.** It is responsible for random evolutionary change in small breeding populations. Early humans were commonly found in relatively isolated bands or tribes, groups characterized by small numbers. Under these circumstances abrupt and unpredictable shifts of gene frequencies might occur by *chance* over several generations. The principle of genetic drift can readily be understood by analogy. Suppose that a person with a name as rare and unusual as the author's raises a family with five sons. If this family lives in New York City the name will still be rare, but if the family happens to live in a country hamlet, in a few generations the name may become relatively frequent. Now consider families with a common name like Smith. One family by the name of Smith, by moving out of the hamlet, may eliminate the name from the community. In contrast, one Smith family leaving New York would make no appreciable difference in the frequency of Smiths in that city.

Small populations may also come to differ from the populations of their origin for still another reason, the "founder effect." When a new colony is established by a few individuals, it cannot be fully and proportionately representative of the gene pool from which it is drawn. In short, the new colony comes to differ because it *initially* received a somewhat different genetic repertory.

Hybridization

Hybridization involves crossings between populations that differ in genetic characteristics. Such interbreeding increases the range of genetic recombinations. Members of two different races may interbreed to produce yet a third race. Some physical anthropologists say that new "races" are emerging in Latin America (alloys of Native Americans, Mediterranean whites, and blacks); in Hawaii (Polynesians, whites, and Mongoloids); and in the continental United States (blacks and whites).

Are There Superior Races?

In the field of minority relations probably few other aspects have attracted as much attention as the question of whether certain racial or ethnic groups are innately superior or inferior. Notions of this sort have had wide currency in the modern age. They formed a cornerstone of official government policy in Nazi Germany, and they historically provided the ideological foundation for segregated institutions in the United States. According to racist views, populations differ in their hereditary endowments and this factor produces social inequality. Even on American college campuses it is not uncommon to hear students currently express the view that some groups are "naturally" superior to other groups: blacks in athletics, whites in intelligence, Jews in business pursuits, and Asians in mathematics, engineering, and computer science. Obviously a consideration of all these beliefs would take us far afield and would require volumes of scientific data. Consequently, we shall limit our discussion to the subject of intelligence and a number of related matters.

Notions of Racial Intellectual Superiority

With the development in 1905 of the first tests to quantitatively measure intelligence, developed by Alfred Binet, a noted French psychologist, seemingly a scientific instrument was at hand to substantiate the doctrine of white intellectual superiority. Early authorities alleged that the Binet scale was a true test of inborn intelligence, relatively free of the disturbing influences of environment. Investigations based upon the Binet and related tests suggested that racial and ethnic groups differ markedly from one another in innate intelligence. In the various studies of black children employing the Binet test, the intelligence quotient (IQ) ranged from 83 to 99, with an average around 90. A score of about 100 was considered normal for the population at large. Consequently, blacks were said to perform at a lower-than-average level. With Native Americans (who have usually been called "Indians" by other Americans in the past), IQ performance was also low, the scores ranging between 70 and 90. Mexicans did only slightly better. However, the scores of Chinese and Japanese approximated those of whites, ranging from 85 to 114, with an average only slightly below 100. Among European immigrant groups, Italians ranged from 76 to 100, with an average about 87, and the Poles did equally poorly. On the other hand, immigrants from Great Britain, Holland, Germany, and the Scandinavian countries were superior to others in test performance.

Contemporary intelligence and achievement testing, employing a variety of tests, tends to corroborate the earlier findings of performance differences among racial and ethnic groups on IQ tests. As part of the Civil Rights Act of 1964, Congress ordered the United States commissioner of education to conduct a survey of educational opportunities in the nation. The result was the "Coleman Report," named after James S. Coleman (1966), a prominent sociologist who had the prime responsibility for planning and carrying out the survey. The report was based on a sample of some 4,000 schools, 605,000 students, and 60,000 teachers. As part of the survey, achievement tests were administered to students at various grade levels. Attention was paid to six racial and ethnic groups: blacks, Native Americans, Oriental-Americans, Puerto Ricans living in the continental United States, Mexican-Americans, and whites other than Mexican-Americans and Puerto Ricans. Coleman and his associates used these terms of identification not in a biological or genetic sense, but as reflecting social categories by which people identified themselves and were identified by others. The results for twelfth grade students, indicated in Figure 2.2, are representative, and reveal sharp difference among the various racial and ethnic groups. The whites' average score tended to be above those of the other groups, followed in order by Oriental-Americans, Native Americans, Mexican-Americans, Puerto Ricans, and blacks.

A number of scholars have interpreted these and other findings as indicating white intellectual superiority and black inferiority. In recent years, a group of "new hereditarians," such people as Dwight J. Ingle, a professor of physiology at the University of Chicago, William Shockley, a Nobel Prize-winning physicist at Stanford University, and Arthur R. Jensen, a University of California (Berkeley) educational psychologist, have argued that hereditary factors have a major influence on "racial" differences in intelligence. Ingle and Shockley go so far as to imply that genetic research aimed at "positive eugenics" might be needed if blacks are to achieve "true equality" (indeed, Shockley calls for a "voluntary, sterilization bonus" plan for blacks with low IQ's).

Jensen's work (1969, 1973) in particular has commanded a good deal of interest and generated considerable controversy, in part because his paper appeared in the prestigious *Harvard Educational Review.* Jensen

FIGURE 2.2 ACHIEVEMENT SCORES, NATIONAL SAMPLE OF 12TH GRADE STUDENTS, 1965.

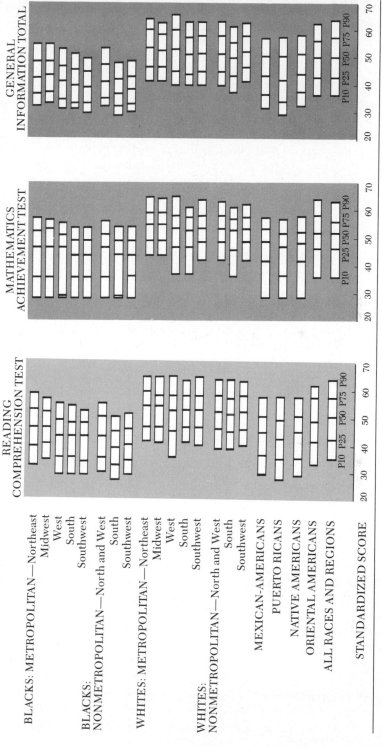

Each bar indicates the distribution of test scores having its endpoints at the first and last deciles (10 and 90 percentage points) and showing also the location of the median and the first and third quartiles (25 and 75 percentage points).
Source: James S. Coleman, *Equality of Educational Opportunity* (Washington, D.C.: U.S. Government Printing Office, 1966), Figs. 3.11.24, 3.11.25, and 3.11.31, pp. 244, 245, and 251.

believes that hereditary factors are primarily responsible for the fact that blacks average fifteen points below whites on IQ tests. Blacks, he argues, are disadvantaged when it comes to "cognitive" or "conceptual" learning—the capacity for abstract reasoning and problem-solving (the key to higher mental functions) while tending to do well in tasks involving rote learning—memorizing mainly through repetition. He views the influence of environment as limited by the "threshold" effect—below a certain threshold of environmental adequacy, deprivation does have a marked depressing effect on IQ, but above that threshold, remedial action does little to raise intelligence. Hence, "compensatory" education programs, such as Head Start, are doomed to failure for black children so long as the emphasis falls upon "cognitive" learning. Rather, Jensen insists, education needs to gear itself to accord with different and unequal racial patterns of native ability.

What assessment can we make of the view that racial and ethnic groups differ in native intelligence? How might we appraise the position of Jensen and other "new hereditarians"? In coming to grips with these matters, we need to ask, "How valid are intelligence tests?" It is to this issue that we now turn our attention.

How Valid Are Intelligence Tests?

During the first two decades of the twentieth century, most authorities tended to conclude that blacks were the intellectual inferiors of whites. Robert M. Yerkes (1921:870), chairperson of a committee of psychologists that designed intelligence and aptitude tests for the U.S. Army during World War I, concluded that intelligence tests "brought into clear relief . . . the intellectual inferiority of the negro [sic]. Quite apart from educational status, which is utterly unsatisfactory, the negro soldier is of relatively low grade intelligence." This discovery was "in the nature of a lesson, for it suggests that education alone will not place the negro race on a par with its Caucasian competitors."

By the 1930s, however, authorities were beginning to question the adequacy of intelligence tests as measures of innate, native intelligence. Social and cultural factors were shown to influence test results. Social scientists came to recognize that membership in a particular culture influences what the individual is likely to learn or fails to learn. This is reflected in the following illustration: In one portion of the National Intelligence Test, a psychological test in wide use at the time in the United States, individuals are presented with a series of incomplete sentences in which they are asked to supply the missing word. One such sentence reads, "_____ should prevail in churches and libraries"; the correct answer is "silence." But in the southern black church, silence is neither the rule nor the ideal. The worshipers are expected to participate actively and audibly. In fact, a church service characterized by silence might well be considered a failure. Accordingly, many southern black children might be expected to answer this question "incorrectly."

Contemporary intelligence tests are not immune to similar problems of cultural bias. The cultural distance between suburb and ghetto is not zero (Loehlin, Lindzey, and Spuhler, 1975). Psychologist Jane R. Mercer (1972:47,95) notes: "IQ tests are Anglocentric [based on the experience of white Anglo-Saxon Americans]; they measure the extent to which an individual's background matches the average cultural pattern of American society. . . . The more 'Anglicized' a non-Anglo child is, the better he does on the IQ test."

The effect of environmental changes on intelligence test performance also led educators to take a second look at the tests. During World War I, more than a million recruits including blacks were given psychological tests. The results showed that blacks from the South, where economic and educational handicaps were greater than in the North, did more poorly than northern blacks. But most striking perhaps of all was that blacks from some *northern* states turned out scores averaging higher than *whites* from some *southern* states. Skeptics said that the superior performance of northern blacks was due to **selective migration:** Blacks with superior intelligence, energy, and initiative left the South, leaving behind blacks with less intelligence. To test the theory of selective migration, the psychologist Otto Klineberg (1935) carefully searched school records in several southern cities and provided a detailed statistical comparison of the school marks obtained by the migrants and nonmigrants. He could find no differences between the two groups. He concluded that the environmental opportunities of northern blacks were responsible for their higher IQ scores.

Other research supported the environmentalist conclusion. In another study, in which he used New York City school records, Klineberg (1935) found that IQ scores of blacks in that city increased with length of residence. The sociologist Everett S. Lee (1951) undertook a parallel study in Philadelphia. He too found a steady upward trend in the average IQ scores of the black migrants, so that, by the time all were in the ninth grade, those who had come in at the first grade were less than a point below those born in the city. Findings such as these do not square with the notion that IQ tests only measure innate intelligence.

By the 1940s evidence also pointed to the cultural bias of intelligence tests as tools for assessing the intelligence of Native Americans. As noted earlier, the test scores of Native Americans generally fall below those of white groups. But John H. Rohrer (1942) found that the performance of the Osage Indians was comparable to that of whites. The noteworthy point here, however, is that these Indians were exceptional in that they live under conditions that are similar to those of the whites with whom they were compared. Oil had been discovered on their reservation, enabling them to acquire an economic position and a social and environmental condition far superior to those of most Native-American communities. On two different tests—one a nonlanguage test, the second depending on language—they obtained average IQ scores of 104 and 100, respectively.

The net result of continuing research on intelligence testing indicates that as yet a "noncultural" and "nonenvironmental" test has not been devised. Indeed, a "noncultural (culture-free)" test is a misnomer. There is no more reason to expect a culture-free intelligence than to expect a body-build and weight that do not reflect the influence of diet. It is known that environmental factors account for large differences in measured intelligence performance and that minority groups are usually disadvantaged in favorable environmental conditions. Thus studies have repeatedly shown that black children taken as a group, especially those who come from ghetto schools, do not enjoy educational and related opportunities commensurate with those of suburban whites. And recently the psychologists Sandra Scarr-Salapatek and Richard A. Weinberg (1975, 1976) found that most of the IQ gap between blacks and whites is closed among black children who are adopted as infants by white middle-class foster parents.

Moreover, it is not sufficient to divide the variance with respect to a behavioral trait into genetic and environmental variance, for in this way we lose what in many cases is the most important part of the variance, the *interaction* between genetic and environmental factors. In truth, the issue posed by the "new hereditarians" (Ingle, Shockley, Jensen)—the relationship between "racial" hereditary factors and intelligence—has its roots in the old nature-nurture controversy; the kinds of questions they ask reveal a preoccupation with "either/or" and "how much of which" formulations. They give no or insufficient attention to development and process, to the dynamic interplay between nature and environment (Vander Zanden, 1981a). Indeed, in learning, *the human organism modifies itself by responding* (consider, for instance, some of the work currently in progress in neurobiology that suggests that ribonucleic acid [RNA] may weave the molecular memory structure of the brain in accordance with social experience).

Still other questions have been raised regarding racist interpretations of differences in black and white IQ scores. Any research that seriously attempts to make comparisons between or among "races" must sooner or later grapple with the questions: "What constitutes a race?" and "How do we go about classifying an individual or a group of people in terms of race?" Yet as we have already observed, these remain unsettled matters. Most racial comparisons rest upon *social* definitions of race. The distinctive genetic background of the individuals being tested is generally assumed rather than demonstrated; in a scientific sense, it is uncontrolled. Curiously, "racial" studies of intelligence revert to lay conceptions of race. Most commonly the racial sorting is done on the basis of the subject's self-classification or by the opinion of the researcher. The sole or dominant criterion is usually skin color. Nor do racial comparisons allow for the considerable penetration of "Caucasian" genes among blacks within the United States, a penetration that renders any discussion of pure races invalid and any suspicion of massive genetic distinctions between black and white Americans unlikely.

In conclusion, any claims regarding innate differences between blacks and whites with regard to intelligence cannot be substantiated unless three conditions are met:

1. Adequate tests of native intelligence, uncontaminated by environmental influences, and with proved reliability and validity will have to be developed.

2. The environment—the social and cultural backgrounds—of the blacks and whites being tested must be fully equal.

3. The distinctive *genetic* homogeneity of the black group being tested, as well as that of the white group, must be *demonstrated,* not assumed (Tumin, 1963:9).

To date, none of these conditions has been met. Hence, it cannot be definitively asserted that innate, native differences in intelligence exist between racial and ethnic groups. Nor, on the other hand, can it be definitively stated that *no* differences exist between racial and ethnic groups in innate, native intelligence. On the basis of what evidence is currently available, however, most contemporary authorities are of the opinion that notions of appreciable inborn differences in intelligence between various racial and ethnic groups simply cannot be supported. Moreover, should such differences be found in the future, they are unlikely to be of major consequence or to have any great importance for social participation.

Uses and Misuses of Intelligence Tests

Intelligence tests have been used by the public schools for many years. Many educators and psychologists take intelligence tests to be reasonably good measures of scholastic aptitude. Proponents of intelligence testing say that knowledge of students' aptitude scores can help a teacher in making decisions about the kind and level of material with which to provide each student. They insist that good teaching requires teachers to design instructional strategies in accordance with the differing aptitudes of their students. When combined with other test results and classroom observations, an IQ score may be a helpful tool. But even the staunchest advocates of intelligence testing recognize that teachers should view a single IQ score only as an exceedingly tentative estimate of a student's scholastic aptitude.

Although IQ scores may in theory constitute helpful educational tools, critics point out that far too many teachers use low IQ scores as an excuse for not attempting to teach some students. Using IQ scores, teachers often form fatalistic expectations regarding students' academic abilities. The greatest danger lurks for youngsters from minority backgrounds. Indeed, black, Chicano, and poor children are more likely to be labeled as mentally retarded and be placed in programs for the educable retarded than are Anglo or upper-status children (Beeghley and Butler, 1974). This labeling process has resulted in a form of institutional racism in many special education programs.

As noted earlier in the chapter, most IQ tests contain a good deal of culturally loaded material, especially in verbal content like vocabulary. The tests reflect white, urban, middle-class culture and linguistic usage. Critics of intelligence testing say that for ghetto-black and Hispanic children, standard English vocabulary and middle-class "wisdom" are often relatively unfamiliar. Consequently, children from different ethnic backgrounds may not understand a question in the same way (i.e., the same question may have different meanings in different environments). Further, ghetto-black and Spanish-speaking children are frequently fearful of the testing process and expect to do poorly. Yet, goodly numbers of these same children are competent problem-solvers outside of school. They have mastered the skills, knowledge, and strategies essential for successful adjustment.

All this has led psychologists and educators like Leon J. Kamin (1974) to charge that IQ tests have been used by elites within the United States to justify privilege and to define inequality, exploitation, and racism as natural and moral. If intelligence is largely inherited, then little can be done to improve children's abilities through education. And if children's abilities cannot be improved, then differences in privilege and power, being largely inherited, are permanent.

Developing the argument further, some critics of intelligence testing say that if IQ tests do not measure intelligence, but merely the mastery of white middle-class values and language skills, then the tests serve as tools to guarantee the continued advantage of white elites. Although various occupational positions are theoretically open to all Americans on the basis of ability and merit, the use of IQ tests for educational and job placement ensures that the sons and daughters of the white privileged classes—having acquired the "proper" credentials as measured by IQ tests—are able to secure the best positions.

Are There Distinct Racial Personalities and Behaviors?

Many Americans believe that people of differing racial and ethnic groups differ fundamentally in ways rooted in their biology. Jews are alleged to be shrewd, sly, and mercenary; blacks, criminal, lazy, and irresponsible; Italians, impulsive, passionate, and quick-tempered; Native Americans, unshrinking, stalwart, and brave. Such traits are supposedly the products of inborn, genetic programming. Here we have much the same situation and much the same scientific support that we found regarding innate intellectual differences. Often, the alleged traits are fictitious and change with the times. In 1935 most Americans thought of the Japanese as progressive, intelligent, and industrious; by 1942 they were thought to be cunning and treacherous; by 1950 they were considered loyal friends and allies; but by 1980 they had become unethical and ruthless competitors in the popular mind. When there was a need for Chinese laborers in California in the 1850s, they were portrayed as frugal, sober, and law-abiding; when labor was plentiful and they competed with white workers, they were considered to be dirty, repulsive, unassimilable, and dangerous. Much the same situation existed in India during World War II, where American troops found the people dirty and uncivilized and Hindu intellectuals found the Americans boorish, materialistic, unintellectual, and uncivilized. Accordingly, such appraisals often rest on subjective evaluation. This is not to deny that peoples may differ, but such differences are inconsistent and appear related to social and environmental factors, not to biology.

Are There "Racial" Personalities?

One useful technique for determining personality characteristics is the Rorschach test. Subjects are shown an inkblot and are asked what they "see" in the configuration. Individuals give their responses to each of ten inkblots. Psychologists assume that subjects portray a "total action" picture of their psychological condition without realizing that they are revealing their innermost frustrations, hostilities, and emotions. No matter what their interpretations—whether they see a volcano, a bear, individuals bowing to each other, a genital organ, or a woman's face in the shadows—the subjects are believed to be projecting their basic personality patterns.

Psychologists (Klineberg, 1951) have administered the Rorschach test to a group of Chinese born in China and a group of Chinese who lived their entire life in the United States. Had the basic personalities of the Chinese been genetic, one would expect their responses to be similar. Yet the study revealed some striking differences in the personality patterns of the two groups. The psychologists concluded that the reason for the differences was the assimilation of the Chinese-Americans into the American way of life. In a word, environmental factors were responsible.

Such findings are supported by other evidence. As Ashley Montagu (1951) points out, the alleged "expansive and rhythm-loving" black reared in England becomes as composed, phlegmatic, and awkward rhythmically as English culture deems desirable. And, despite the fact that between the sixteenth and nineteenth centuries there were no new invasions of England nor any major genetic infusions from the outside, the boisterous joy of life of the Elizabethan period gave way to the prudish Victorian age, while the rationalism of the eighteenth century gave way to the romanticism of the nineteenth century. Clearly such phenomena would seem incapable of interpretation in strictly biological terms.

Is There a "Racial" Morality?

Closely related to other racial myths is the notion that there is an association between racial membership and morality. At times a nationality group is erroneously equated with a race. Thus blanket assertions are sometimes heard that Italians are "racially" disposed toward crime, racketeering, and acts of violence. Questioned, the proponent of this viewpoint may indignantly recite a list of Italian names including Capone, Luciano, Costello, Fischetti, and various Cosa Nostra criminals. It is interesting that such infamous "bad men" of the 1930s as Dillinger, Van Meter, Floyd, Nelson, Barker, and Kelly—all with traditional "old-American" names—are conveniently forgotten. Actually the rate of criminal convictions among foreign-born Italians during the first half of this century was approximately the same as that for other foreign-born language groups and less than that for native-born whites. Although the incidence of crimes against the person was higher among Italians, their crime rates for drunkenness, forgery, and disorderly conduct were lower than those of other groups. It is also worth noting that Italian-American crime syndicates have thrived because a large number of non-Italians demand the illicit goods and services they sell.

At the present time many whites view blacks as an embodiment of crime and danger and therefore law-and-order campaigns often connote racist motives. Blacks, who are 13 percent of the nation's population, do account for about 32 percent of all arrests tabulated in the Uniform Crime Index of the Federal Bureau of Investigation (FBI). More specifically, blacks are substantially overrepresented among those arrested for murder and nonnegligent homicide (54 percent), forcible rape (45 percent), robbery (59 percent), aggravated assault (40 percent), burglary (28 percent), larceny and theft (31 percent), and motor vehicle theft (26 percent). More than 40 percent of the inmates in federal prisons and 48 percent of those in state prisons are black. Other minorities, notably Hispanics and Native Americans, also have rates of arrest and incarceration that are higher than those for whites. But their rates are lower than those of blacks.

Many criminologists believe, however, that the Uniform Crime Index does not reflect the true crime rates for various racial and ethnic groups. For instance, they argue that black and white crime rates are not appreciably different. They point out that blacks are more likely to be arrested than are whites. After arrest, blacks are less likely to secure bail, and consequently they are more likely to be counted in jail statistics. They are more likely to be indicted and less likely to have their cases dismissed. If tried, blacks are more likely than whites to be convicted. If convicted, they are less likely to be granted probation.

Further, these criminologists argue that *detected* crime does not accurately reflect *undetected* criminal behavior. Sociologists have undertaken a number of studies in which white and black teenagers complete questionnaires reporting on their own delinquent behavior. The sociologists then canvass juvenile court records to ascertain the official delinquency status of the adolescents. This research confirms that blacks have an official delinquency rate that is substantially higher than that for whites. But when self-reported delinquency is used as the criterion, whites are found to have rates equal to or slightly higher than those for blacks (Chambliss and Nagasawa, 1969; Gould, 1969; Williams and Gold, 1972).

It should also be stressed that official crime statistics underreport white-collar crime, which is considerably more prevalent among whites than among blacks. White-collar crime is crime committed by persons of respectability and high social status in the course of their occupational activities. Among the white-collar crimes committed by executives of large corporations are price fixing, misrepresentation in advertising, infringements of patents, unfair labor practices, financial fraud, stock manipulation, and dumping toxic wastes in rivers. White-collar criminals are not prosecuted as frequently as other criminals. Sentences handed out to them are usually relatively light in relation to the damage these criminals do. For instance, embezzlers at banks steal an average of $23,000 each, but only 17 percent of them go to jail. Bank robbers, by comparison, steal only one-eighth as much, but 91 percent of them end up in prison.

Other criminologists believe that official reports that reveal high crime rates among blacks are accurate and do not reflect selection bias (Hindelang, 1978, 1981). A number of household surveys have been undertaken to discover how many families have been the victims of major crimes. These data constitute what sociologists term the "victimization rate." Social scientists then compare the victimization rate with the "crime rate" reported by citizens to local police departments and through them to the FBI. This research reveals that about half again as many robberies, twice as many serious assaults and thefts, three times as many burglaries, and four times as many rapes occur as FBI reports indicate. Rates for murder and auto theft are highly accurate. In a number of victimization surveys, individuals are asked to report the race of the criminal. The results show a much higher rate of involvement for blacks as perpetrators of crime than for whites in crimes of rape, robbery, assault, and burglary.

Some criminologists, although they believe that blacks have higher rates for homicide and other assaultive crimes than do whites, look to social rather than genetic factors for the explanation. One point of view attributes the high incidence of homicide and assault by blacks to frustrations engendered by racism. Unequal opportunity and discrimination, overcrowding and blight within urban ghettos, and demoralizing conditions within a racist social order breed anger and hostility, which find expression in explosive assaults or in repeated acts of predatory crime. Another point of view suggests that laws are enacted to protect the interests of white elites, and consequently many of the activities criminalized by society are activities in which less powerful persons (blacks, the poor, and the young) are disproportionately involved. In this sense crime is part of the "Catch 22" of unemployment among black youth. Without employment, youths drift into crime, making future employment in the legitimate sphere even more difficult to obtain. The middle class in turn abandons crime areas, taking away businesses that had provided some employment.

To conclude our discussion of facts and myths about black criminality, it should be stressed that the overwhelming majority of black people in the United States, like the majority of Americans in general, conform to societal norms in their behavior. They are not criminals or deviants. They are law-abiding citizens engaged in the daily business of life.

SUMMARY

1. Three schools of thought exist regarding race: the "fixed type," the "breeding population," and the "no-race" traditions. Scholars of the fixed type school view races as established and immutable hereditary groupings that reach back into antiquity. They view the task of science as one of identifying and describing "original races" and in turn of separating present-day populations into the various ancestral components.

2. Scholars interested in breeding populations seek to identify and describe "natural units" of humankind that constitute taxonomic units below the species level. They stress the view that social and geographical barriers operate as barriers to reproductive intermingling. As a consequence there arise through such mechanisms as isolation, mutation, natural selection, and genetic drift more or less stable, differentiated gene pools among humankind.

3. The no-race school denies that races are real if viewed as relatively discrete biological entities "out there" in nature and as units of evolu-

tion. They build their case upon two premises. First, racial differences are continuous so that it is next to impossible to say where one population begins and another ends. Second, trait distributions tend to be discordant.

4. Humans do not lend themselves easily to cut-and-dried "racial" classifications. Whether races are real in a biological sense is not the chief issue of this book. Race is real in a social sense. What people believe affects their behavior, whether the beliefs are true or not. And if people believe that there are races, then they act on the basis of such beliefs.

5. The existence among Jews of "Caucasian," "Mongoloid," and "Negroid" types, the presence of blonds and brunets, of hooked and Roman noses, and of round, long, and intermediate heads is demonstrable evidence of the nonexistence of a Jewish "race." Who then is a Jew? We need to resort to a social definition. A Jew is an individual who is defined as a Jew by the community-at-large or by Jews or both.

6. Scientists have reached general agreement in recognizing that humankind is one and that all individuals belong to the same species, *Homo sapiens.* It is generally agreed that all human groups are derived from the same common stock. Such differences as exist between different groups are due to the operation of evolutionary factors associated with isolation, mutations, natural selection, genetic drift, and hybridization.

7. Many authorities allege that IQ tests measure innate intelligence. Since racial and ethnic groups differ in their average scores on such tests, some have concluded that there are intellectually superior and inferior races.

8. Many social scientists now question the adequacy of intelligence tests as measures of innate, native intelligence. They say that intelligence tests are not immune to problems of cultural bias. Further, it is not sufficient to divide the variance with respect to a behavioral trait into genetic and environmental variance, for in this way we lose what in many cases is the most important part of the variance, the interaction between genetic and environmental factors. And finally, most racial comparisons rest upon social rather than genetic definitions of race.

9. Intelligence tests have been used by the public schools for many years. Many educators and psychologists take intelligence tests to be reasonably good measures of scholastic aptitude and helpful educational tools. Critics point out that far too many teachers use low IQ scores as an excuse for not attempting to teach some students. The greatest danger exists for youngsters from minority backgrounds. Some psychologists charge that IQ tests have been used by elites within the United States to justify privilege and to perpetuate inequality.

10. There appears little foundation to the view that racial and ethnic

groups differ in personality characteristics that are rooted in differing genetic constitutions. Likewise, there are not "racial moralities."

11. There is some question as to whether the crime rate of blacks is higher than the crime rate of whites. Some criminologists cite evidence to show that the crime rates of blacks and whites are not appreciably different. Other criminologists believe that official reports that reveal high crime rates of blacks are accurate. Although these latter criminologists take the view that blacks have higher rates for homicide and other assaultive crimes than do whites, they look to social rather than genetic factors for the explanation.

GLOSSARY

Demes (also termed **Mendelian Populations**) The groups formed by the division of humankind into mating groups or reproductive communities.

Genetic Drift Changes in gene frequencies within a population that are due to chance alone.

Hybridization Crossings between populations differing in genetic characteristics. Such interbreeding increases the range of genetic recombinations.

Mutation Physical change in the chemical structure or position of a gene in relation to other genes.

Natural Selection The process by which those varieties within a species that are best suited to a particular environment have a survival advantage over other members of the species and are the ones more likely to reproduce biologically successful offspring.

Race Populations differing in the incidence of certain hereditary traits.

Selective Migration The theory that some segments of a population or community are more susceptible to geographical mobility or movement than are other segments.

II

Sources of Racism

Origins of Racism 3

*H*ow does racism arise? Admittedly, our knowledge on this matter is limited, although there is no shortage of theories that purport to supply us with explanations. Available evidence suggests that the processes involved are complex and that no single sequence of processes holds for all cases. Nonetheless, we do encounter a number of ingredients that typically come into play in the emergence and initial stabilization of racism: (1) contact, (2) social visibility, (3) ethnocentrism, (4) competition, and (5) unequal power (Noel, 1972). Let us examine each of these variables in turn.

Contact

Contact between differing racial and ethnic groups is probably a development that is as old as humankind itself. Skeletal fossils from the third interglacial epoch—estimated to be between 30,000 and 150,000 years ago—suggest that Homo sapiens and Neanderthals coexisted and interbred in the Israeli caves of Mount Carmel (Howells, 1973). Archaeological data also affords indisputable evidence that, long before the dawn of history, human beings were often on the move, invading the territory of others and borrowing ideas from their enemies and from strangers. Similarly, ancient folklore recounts such migrations—the Aztecs, for instance, told stories of their origin "in the North," of their invasion of Mexico, and of their conquest of the native tribes they found there; and the Bible recounts the migrations of the early Hebrews. And as philologists have amply demonstrated, languages provide considerable evidence for the prevalence of population movements (Berry, 1965).

If migration were not a common practice, if people were content to live among their own kind in communities that were more or less isolated from one another, racial and ethnic prejudice would be virtually unknown. In considering migration, it is useful to distinguish among a number of different types of movement (Petersen, 1958).

Primitive Migration

The movement of nonindustrial peoples appears related to their inability to cope with forces of nature. By virtue of their limited technological level, nonindustrial people exercise little control over their subsistence. The resources available within one locality are generally inadequate to support a food-gathering or hunting people. Instead they must range over a wider area, frequently moving haphazardly or back and forth over their traditional territory. Although a herding people usually have greater control over their food supply than do gathering and hunting peoples, they too need to migrate for new grazing lands. Similarly an agrarian people may migrate when there is a sharp disparity between the produce from the land and the number of people subsisting upon it. The disparity may come about suddenly, as by drought or an attack of locusts, or by the steady Malthusian pressure of an increasing population on land that is limited in extent or fertility. Within their new settings, the migrants typically seek to resume their previous way of life. During the modern period, however, the more usual destination for migrants has been the city, where new ways of thinking and behaving are demanded of them.

Forced and Impelled Migrations

In forced migrations it is the state or a functionally similar institution that serves as the activating agent for the migration. Sociologists distinguish between impelled migration, in which the migrants retain some power to decide whether to leave, and forced migration, in which they lack this power. The early Nazi policy of encouraging Jewish emigration by various anti-Semitic measures is illustrative of impelled migration, whereas their later policy of herding Jews into cattle trains and transporting them to concentration camps is an example of forced migration.

Impelled migration frequently takes the form of flight. As a new people moves into a territory, it may drive before it the weaker occupants of that territory. This apparently was the case during the early centuries of the Christian era, when invaders from the East made their way into Europe. During the modern period, the mass flight of East Germans to West Germany had so undermined the East German Communist regime that in the summer of 1961 the Soviet Union precipitated the Berlin crisis and unilaterally closed the border between East and West Berlin. More recently Afghans have fled to Pakistan and Cambodians to Thailand in the face of respective Russian and Vietnamese invasions of their homelands.

Forced migration has assumed considerable importance since the turn of the twentieth century, with millions of people uprooted from their homelands. The separation of Pakistan from India was accompanied by the migration of more than 12 million Moslems and Hindus, in part induced by terrorism and in part arranged under government auspices. During World War II, the Soviet Union, claiming that they were "disloyal nationalities," resorted to the forced deportation from their homelands of the Volga Germans, the Chechen-Ingush, the Crimean Tartars, and the Kalmuks, a movement involving more than 2 million people. The overseas shipment of Africans during the mercantile age—involving some 10 to 20 million blacks—similarly constituted a forcible movement of people.

Free Migration

In primitive migration the chief activating force is the lack of means to satisfy physiological needs, and in forced migration the migrants are largely passive. In free migration, on the other hand, the decisive element is the will of the migrants. The overseas migration of Europeans to the New World during the nineteenth century affords an illustration of this type of migration. The numbers involved in the free migration were not large—they were pioneers who helped to break the ice and clear the way for later mass migrations. The pioneers were often adventurers or intellectuals who were motivated by their ideals. Their letters home and their accounts in European newspapers encouraged others to follow them to the New World.

Mass Migration

The pioneers blazed the trails that others followed. Migration soon became the style. Once it began, it stimulated still further migration. Emigration became a *social* pattern, and it can be largely understood in term of the mechanisms of collective behavior. In various parts of Europe there developed what became known as "America fever": Emigration became an important aspect in the atmosphere of the times. In Sweden, children were "educated to emigrate"; they followed a tradition that made emigration the "natural" thing to do. In fact, the failure to emigrate may actually have posed difficulties for individuals with respect to the expectations that had been set for them.

Whatever the motivating factors, migration brings people of differing racial or ethnic backgrounds into contact with one another. But racial or cultural differences in and of themselves do not ipso facto set people apart. Various features become factors for group differentiation only through *social definition.* For example, within the United States, we ignore moles, circumcision, and ear lobe contour as features having broad "social" significance. In brief, group differences provide a convenient peg on which to hang the argument of deeper inferiority—to activate and sanction prejudice, discrimination, and institutional racism. It is to this matter of social differentiation and visibility that we now turn our attention.

Social Visibility

Categories are necessary to social life. They enable us to group things into "classes" or "pigeonholes" and to respond to them in terms of this placement rather than in terms of their uniqueness. In this manner we reduce the complexity of our world through subsuming the diverse under the general. In life, we not only have categories for such things as animals, plants, and minerals, but also for people. Hence, by virtue of any number of historical circumstances, people evolve categories for classifying their fellows. For instance, they are slaves, newcomers, foreigners, or heathens. Certain traits with high social visibility serve as identifying symbols of the category (Williams, 1964).

At times we distinguish among groups of people on the basis of certain hereditary physical traits: for instance, Japanese, Native-Americans, blacks, and whites within the United States. Cultural traits likewise provide identifying clues. Names, language, accents, mannerisms, dress, gestures, typical facial expressions, food habits, religious practices, and various types of folk behavior supply "marks," or "signs," of ethnic membership. The evidence of ethnic membership may be apparent in dress: for instance, among many Amish and Hasidic Jews. Then again, the identifying traits may be less readily apparent. In most respects, Catholics are undifferentiated from the great mass of Protestant Americans. Yet clues to Catholic membership are frequently discernible. Individuals who attach statues of the Virgin Mary to their automobile dashboards, who indicate that they go to Mass, or who have attended and whose children attend Catholic parochial schools are customarily identified as Roman Catholics.

The identifying "marks," or "signs," of group membership are sometimes perceptible by senses other than sight. Language and accent involve audibility. Odors, the product of differing hygienic or dietary practices, may provide evidence of ethnic membership. Yet olfactory hallucinations are not uncommon. Individuals may associate garlic with Italians, and accordingly, even in the objective absence of the particular odor, "smell" garlic when they meet Italians. Association may also provide clues of group membership; individuals who are frequently found in the company of known Jews are often identified as Jews; similarly, with individuals in frequent association with blacks.

Individuals who decide to escape from their membership in particular racial or ethnic groups may undertake to diminish or to eliminate their "visibility." Blacks may employ hair straighteners and bleach; Jews may change their names from "Cohen," "Blumberg," and "Finkelstein" to Anglicized names and display crosses as jewelry. When visible signs are so insignificant as to make it impossible to detect minority-group and dominant-group membership by simple observation, the minority may be compelled to display some identifying symbol. In Nazi Germany, Jews were required to wear the Star of David or a yellow armband. Pope Innocent III, unable to distinguish Christian from heretics, decreed that the latter dress in a distinctive manner. Such evidence points to the fact that a dominant-minority relationship requires some visible and conspicuous feature or features by which the members of the two groups can be differentiated and identified. In the absence of such traits, the boundaries between the ingroup and the outgroup could not be maintained.

By employing cues deriving from racial or cultural traits we are able to sort individuals into the relevant categories of social life ("white," "black," "Jew," "Gentile," "Native American")—to "place" or "locate" them within one or more institutional structures. On the basis of such information we come to define the situation. We activate within our minds a map, so to speak, that guides us in identifying the mutual set of expectations that will operate within the relationship. We establish what we can expect of another person and what that person can expect of us; for instance, what a "white" can expect of a "black" and what a "black" can expect of a "white."

By virtue of categories, we "size up" people in terms of only one or a limited number of characteristics (Gergen, 1967). One consequence of categorization is that it can deter "personalistic" encounters; it tends to foster *object* relations as opposed to *person-centered* relations. Rather than being viewed as a unique individual, the person who is marked as an exemplar of a group becomes an object. The individual is identified first of all as a Jew, a black, or a white. The person so typed becomes an *It* rather than a *Thou.* Hence, in a very real sense categories not only serve to systematize our experiences, but they influence what we experience as well.

Ethnocentrism

Contact and social visibility are indispensable elements for racism, but they are equally indispensable elements for equalitarian intergroup relations (Brewer and Campbell, 1976). Ethnic and racial groups can interact and form stable patterns of relations without racism. The anthropologist Ethel John Lindgren (1938) provides us with an illustration (*see* chapter 6). She undertook anthropological field work in northwestern Manchuria among the Tungus and Cossacks. These two racially and culturally unlike peoples have lived together, traded, and associated with each other for generations. Nonetheless, they have managed to avoid conflict and racist notions. Indeed, they have maintained harmonious and cooperative relationships. Lindgren's research highlights for us that contact and social visibility merely set the stage on which other variables may or may not come into play. Other variables are necessary if racism is to develop. One of these variables is **ethnocentrism.**

The Nature of Ethnocentrism

William Graham Sumner (1906:13), who coined the word, described ethnocentrism as "this view of things in which one's own group is the center of everything, and all others are scaled and rated with reference to it." In other words, ethnocentrism means the tendency of group members to appraise peoples of other cultures by the standards of judgment prevailing in their own culture. Individuals assume that in *the nature of things* other people should be organized according to the same assumptions as prevail within their own group. Ethnocentrism entails strong *positive* feelings toward an ingroup, even ingroup glorification. It is often, although not inevitably, accompanied by prejudice —*negative* conceptions, feelings, and action-orientations regarding the members of an outgroup.

Notions that one's own group is superior to other groups are not new to humankind. It is not uncommon for individuals anywhere in the world to believe that they, and they alone, belong to the "best people." As the anthropologist Ruth Benedict (1940:155) points out, "The formula 'I belong to the Elect' has a far longer history than has modern racism." Among even the most nonindustrial, non-Western peoples this formula is an integral part of their whole life experience. Prior to mass contact with outside groups, they were prone to look upon themselves grandiosely as "*the* human beings," as "People." The designation applied exclusively to their own group. Zuñi, Déné, and Kiowa among others were tribal designations by which individuals knew themselves, and these names were equated with "humankind." Outside of their own closed group, human beings in the true sense did not exist. Other peoples were seen within this highly provincial outlook:

> They were not people with whom my own tribe had common cause. God did not create them of the same clay, or they did not spring out of the same water jar, or they did not come up through the same hole in the ground. But my own little group was under the special providence of God; he gave it the middle place in the "world" and he foretold that if ever it was wiped out, the world would perish. To my tribe alone he gave the ceremonies which preserve the world (Benedict, 1940:156).

Ethnocentrism and Assumptions of Belief Dissimilarity

One factor that apparently fosters ethnocentrism is the tendency of people to be attracted to others who hold beliefs and attitudes similar to their own; conversely, they tend to experience an aversion toward people with dissimilar beliefs and attitudes. On the basis of his research, the social psychologist Milton Rokeach (1960) maintains that whites are motivated to reject blacks less by racism than by assumed belief and value differences. He says that whites generally perceive blacks as holding contrasting beliefs, and it is this perception and not race per se that leads to rejection. Indeed, a variety of studies (Byrne and Wong, 1962; Hendrick et al., 1971; Mezei, 1971; Moe et al., 1981) have revealed that in a social situation, whites typically accept a black whose beliefs are similar to their own more easily than a white with different beliefs.

An illustration of this principle is a study undertaken by Milton Rokeach and Louis Mezei (1966) using twenty-four white and twenty-six black subjects. The study was carried out in the setting of the personnel offices of two state mental hospitals near Detroit. The subjects were applying for jobs as janitors, attendants, and laundry workers. Each subject completed an application and provided a statement regarding his opinions on how to deal with difficult mental patients. These opinions were classified as "harsh" or "permissive." The subject was then sent to a waiting room occupied by four other "interviewees," in reality confederates of the experimenter. Two of the four men already in the waiting room were white, and two were black. These four men initiated a discussion with each of the subjects as to how to handle mental patients, two advocating a "harsh" solution and two a "permissive" one. Later each subject was asked which one of these four men he would like to work with in his future job. The fifty subjects overwhelmingly selected as co-workers those individuals who held the same kind of opinions they did—"harsh" or "permissive"—about handling patients, *regardless* of the race of the co-worker. This tendency of people to organize the world of human beings in terms of the principle of *belief congruence* appears to be an important factor feeding ethnocentric tendencies. Further, ethnocentrism, once established in one group, tends to beget ethnocentrism (indeed, even hostility) in other groups with which it interacts (Catton and Hong, 1962; Doise, 1969).

The Outgroup Viewed as Deviant

Where people are strongly ethnocentric, it is not difficult for them to perceive the outgroup as an object for loathing. The outgroup is "a symbol of strangeness, evil, and danger to the community as a whole"

(Speier, 1941:445). Their existence disturbs the order of life in the sense in which order is understood and experienced by the ingroup. Their customs are viewed as scandalous and their rites as sacrilegious. Their laws seem incomprehensible and consequently the people themselves appear to be lawless. Their gods are false gods. In brief, *the outgroup often appears to be engaged in deviant acts.*

It is not difficult, then, for the ingroup to perceive the outgroup—when judged by ingroup standards—as somehow ridiculous, evil, scandalous, and sacrilegious. We find numerous illustrations of this principle. The Gusii of East Africa ridicule uncircumcised males for their childishness and accuse a still uncircumcised older boy of cowardice. This view provides the basis for an unfavorable image of their uncircumcising Luo neighbors. By the same token, the Luo and the Kipsigis (the latter also neighbors of the Gusii) ridicule the Gusii for the emphasis the Gusii place on modesty surrounding nudity and elimination (LeVine and LeVine, 1966). The anthropologist Edward M. Bruner (1956) describes a parallel situation in the Dakotas. The Hidatsa Indians hold sharing among tribal members to be an important moral value. In contrast, white ranchers view individual thrift and providence as high moral virtues. Both the Hidatsa and the whites view one another as deviant groups with defective moralities.

Ingroup Virtues Become Outgroup Vices

The above discussion deals with characteristics on which groups differ. We note similar effects for certain traits on which groups are similar, but in which the behavior of the outgroup is *perceived* in a *different* context than comparable behavior within the ingroup. It is often alleged, for instance, that Jews are disliked because they are ambitious, aggressive, and materialistic, a view that rests on the assumption that these traits are viewed as undesirable, regardless of the group to which they are applied. Yet a study by Gerhart Saenger and Samuel Flowerman (1954) of 292 college students reveals that this is not the case. Only 28 percent of the students viewed materialistic behavior as undesirable; 25 percent disapproved of aggressiveness; 17 percent, of emotionality; and 3 percent, of ambitiousness, the trait most frequently ascribed to Jews. Further, the students described *both* Americans and Jews as aggressive, ambitious, industrious, materialistic, efficient, practical, and intelligent. And interestingly enough, there was one group to whom the students ascribed an even greater proportion of "typically" Jewish characteristics: business people.

The sociologist Robert K. Merton (1957:428) also notes how the very same behavior may undergo a complete change of evaluation in its transition from the ingroup to the outgroup:

Did Lincoln work far into the night? This testifies that he was industrious, resolute, perseverant, and eager to realize his capacities to the full. Do the outgroup Jews or Japanese keep these same hours? This only bears witness to their sweatshop mentality, their ruthless undercutting of American standards, their unfair competitive practices. Is the in-group hero frugal, thrifty, and sparing? Then the out-group villain is stingy, miserly and penny-pinching. All honor is due to the in-group Abe for his having been smart, shrewd, and intelligent and, by the same token, all contempt is owing the out-group Abes for their being sharp, cunning, crafty, and too clever by far.

Connotative Meanings of Color Names

In considering the part ethnocentrism played in the rise of racism, it is instructive to consider the initial English confrontation with and impressions of Africans (Jordan, 1968). Apparently English voyagers did not touch upon the shores of West Africa until after 1550, virtually a century after Prince Henry the Navigator had launched a sustained Portuguese thrust southward around Africa en route to the Orient. The English found the peoples of Africa very different from themselves, differences that they viewed in an ethnocentric fashion: their religion was un-Christian ("heathen"); their manner of living was anything but English ("savage"); and they seemed to be a sexually "lustful" and "uninhibited" people.

Color, however, was for the English the most arresting characteristic of the Africans. The English actually described Africans as *black,* an exaggerated term itself suggesting that the African's complexion had a powerful impact upon English perceptions. In England prior to African contacts, perhaps more than among southern European nations, the concept of blackness was already loaded with intense ethnocentric meaning. The *Oxford English Dictionary* describes the meaning of "black" before the sixteenth century in these terms:

> Deeply stained with dirt; soiled, dirty, foul. . . . Having dark or deadly purposes, malignant; pertaining to or involving death, deadly; baneful, disastrous, sinister. . . . Foul, iniquitous, atrocious, horrible, wicked. . . . Indicating disgrace, censure, liability to punishment, etc.

Black, then, was an emotionally partisan color, denoting baseness, evil, danger, and repulsion. In direct contrast was the concept of "whiteness." No other colors were so frequently employed to denote polarization: White and black implied purity and filthiness, virginity and sin, virtue and baseness, beauty and ugliness, beneficence and evil, God and the devil.

These early connotative meanings of color names persist into the modern period. A cursory examination of *Webster's New Collegiate*

Dictionary reveals the adverse implications attached to the word *black:* blackball, blackbook, blackguard, black-letter, blacklist, blackmail, black dog, black sheep, and so on. Moreover, the psychologist John E. Williams (1964) found that the connotative meanings of the color names "black" and "white" (presented in a nonracial context) are strikingly different and that they are relatively stable across both regional and racial lines: The connotative meaning of the color name *white* is "good," "active," and "weak," while the color name *black* is "bad," "passive," and "strong." In another study among white college students from both the South and Midwest, Williams (1966) discovered that the racial terms "Negro" and "Caucasian" have connotative meanings similar to the color names with which they are linked by the color-coding custom. He suggests that such color connotations are learned early in childhood and may influence the subsequent development of racial attitudes (*see* chapter 4). More recently, Williams and his associates (1971) have found a reversal of the traditional connotations of the colors "white" and "black" among black college students. This development appears related to the Black Power and the "Black Is Beautiful" movements.

But are the emotional reactions and associations triggered by various colors generalized to people? Will, for instance, individuals who have a negative emotional reaction to black also experience negative feelings for people whose skins are dark? In theory, such a possibility seems highly plausible. Artists, for instance, have long used to advantage the assumption that colors have the capacity to directly elicit certain types of feelings or emotions. Further, research reveals that emotions generated by color can be generalized to objects continuously paired with color (Williams and Morland, 1976).

Competition

By itself ethnocentrism need not lead to intergroup conflict or racism (Noel, 1972). As noted earlier in the chapter, the Cossacks (a "Caucasian," agricultural, and sedentary people) and the Tungus (a "Mongoloid," reindeer-herding, nomadic people) lived in peace for several generations in northwestern Manchuria as independent but economically interdependent societies (Lindgren, 1938). Each group had an ethnocentric preference for the ingroup and its customs. Apparently the conflict potential was neutralized by low population density, outside foreign pressures that drew the two peoples together, economies and cultures that complemented one another, and the absence of competition between the two groups. It is this last matter, competition, to which we now turn our attention.

Scarce, Divisible Resources

Within any society people act in relation to certain "good things" or resources that can be shared by everyone (Williams, 1947). These resources are not scarce in the sense that one individual's sharing in them reduces or interferes with others' enjoyment of them. Religious salvation and national prestige are conspicuous illustrations of this. The adherents of a religious faith can all participate in a great many of its values, for example, salvation, without detracting from the participation of others. By the same token, all Americans share in any increase or decrease in national prestige. National prestige as such is "participated in" rather than "divided up." On the other hand, there are some resources within any society that are scarce and divisible, such resources as wealth, power, and status. In each instance (all other things being equal), the more there is for the one, the less there is for others (Labovitz and Hagedorn, 1975).

People typically seek to improve their outcome with regard to those things that they define as good, worthwhile, and desirable. Where the outcomes of two distinct groups are perceived to be mutually exclusive and legitimate, so that each can realize what it defines as a rightful outcome only at the expense of the other, competition will ensue. In other words, if two groups both believe they have a just claim upon the same scarce, divisible "good things," their relationship will be characterized by competition—even conflict. Generally speaking, the attitudes that the members of a group evolve toward an outgroup tend to be consistent with their perceptions of the relationships they have with the outgroup. Hence *where the relations between two groups are perceived as competitive, negative attitudes—prejudice—will be generated toward the outgroup.*

The hypothesis that intergroup competition for scarce values begets prejudice, discrimination, and racism is one that abounds in race relations literature. Several studies lend support to this hypothesis. For instance, experiments by Muzafer Sherif and his associates (1961) have shown that in the absence of institutional controls, boys' groups normally develop very hostile, discriminatory relationships after a relatively short period of competition in sports and games (*see* chapter 6 for a lengthy review of this study). Similarly, Robert R. Blake and Jane S. Manton (1961), on the basis of their experiments dealing with competition, suggest that a loss in competition leads to hostility toward the winning group. Even though members of competing groups report that they understand the competitor's view as well as they understand those of their own group, they in fact do not. In all groups, the members know their own group's position best and distort the other group's position. Further, research suggests that winners and losers in competition feel uncomfortable in one another's presence and that the resulting difficulties in interpersonal encounters can contribute to intergroup prejudice (Rabbie and Horowitz, 1969). Finally, research reveals that the fear of equal status competition with blacks (the prospect of *future* competition) is associated with the tendency of whites to discriminate against blacks (Hamblin, 1962).

Thus far in our consideration of competition we have not distinguished among the factors of wealth, power, and status. It has probably occurred to some readers that a favorable position with regard to either wealth, power, or status tends to be associated with a favorable position with regard to the other two. Although often true, however, it is not always the case. By way of illustration, the sheriff of many rural counties may possess considerable political power but be ranked low in economic wealth or status. Similarly, a member of one of the aristocratic "old" families of the South may enjoy considerable status but have little in the way of power or wealth. And the "new rich" may have wealth but lack comparable power or status, as in the case of some Texas oil barons. Since some social scientists stress the role of one factor over the others, let us consider each factor in turn.

Economic Competition and Gains

We have noted that groups in competition for scarce values often develop prejudice toward one another. Some writers argue that economic competition plays a particularly critical role. Donald Young (1937) notes that within American history there is a direct correlation between peaks of agitation against minorities and the valleys of economic depression. The major "anti-foreign" movements—the Native American Party in the 1830s, the Know-Nothing Party of the 1850s, the American Protective Association of the late nineteenth century, and the post-World War I Ku Klux Klan—won their largest following during hard times. Various regional movements—against Chinese, Japanese, and Filipinos on the West Coast, Italians in Louisiana, and French Canadians in New England—have similarly coincided with economic difficulties in these areas. At least two forces appear to operate in such settings. First, hard times have been associated with widespread unemployment that has intensified intergroup competition for jobs. Second, the frustrations associated with unemployment may breed hostile and aggressive impulses that are vented upon minority groups.

Race riots and violence have often been associated with intense intergroup competition. The 1919 Chicago race riot was centered in two areas: the area around the stockyards, where blacks had entered the meat packing industry in thousands and were accused of taking white men's jobs while the whites were away in the army; and the Hyde Park area, where the chief grievance was the financial loss to white owners in black residence areas, allegedly through depreciation of property values. In the Atlanta riot of 1906 one of the chief incitements to violence was the circulation of cards showing black carpenters and bricklayers building houses, thus menacing the economic security of white craftsmen (Johnson, 1939). And in the 1943 Detroit riot blacks were in sharp competition with whites for housing accommodations in the areas surrounding the black ghetto of Paradise Valley, while competition for other goods and services, already scarce in the wartime economy, intensified antagonisms (Lee and Humphrey, 1943; Grimshaw, 1960).

Split Labor Markets.   The sociologist Edna Bonacich (1972, 1975) says that economic competition within a **split labor market** underlies the development of antagonism among ethnic groups. A split labor market is an economic arena in which large differences exist in the price of labor at the same occupational level. Bonacich focuses upon the divergent interests of three key groups: employers (usually white), higher-paid labor (usually white), and cheaper labor (usually nonwhite). Employers desire a labor supply that is cheap and docile so that they might compete effectively with other employers and maximize profits. Historically employers have attempted to replace higher-paid labor with cheaper labor through importing overseas groups (the importation of slaves from Africa and later immigrants from Ireland, Italy, and Southeast Europe) or using indigenous conquered peoples (Native-American populations throughout Latin America).

When a group sells its labor at rates substantially lower than the prevailing ones, higher-paid labor faces severe competition to maintain its economic advantage. If the cheaper labor is of a differing racial or ethnic group, the resulting class antagonism typically takes the form of racism. The antagonism focuses upon ethnic or racial issues although at root the conflict is one of class. The more expensive labor resists displacement through either *exclusion* or a **caste system.** Both approaches secure victory for the higher-paid workers by preventing further undercutting of their jobs and wages.

The anti-Chinese movement, which flourished in California in the 1870s, provides a good illustration of an exclusion strategy. When the established Democratic and Republican parties failed to heed the demands of white workers, the latter organized the Workingmen's party and swept state and local offices with the slogan "The Chinese must go." In San Francisco whites assaulted, harassed, and tormented Chinese. Chinese homes and shops were looted and burned. The anti-Chinese agitation led Congress to enact a law in 1882 that prohibited Chinese from entering the United States except for a small group of scholars, ministers, and merchants. Hence, white workers undertook to drive the Chinese from their communities and to shut off the entry of new immigrants.

A racial caste system is a second strategy by which more expensive labor sustains its privileged jobs and wages. Unable to exclude blacks from the work force in the United States, white labor erected social and legal barriers to avoid competition from black workers. White labor monopolized vital skills, excluded blacks from education and training programs, and disfranchised black voters. Segregation allows an aristocracy of labor to entrench itself. The higher-paid workers resort to exclusiveness rather than exclusion. The net result is that blacks are relegated to low-paying jobs. One estimate is that the cost of being black in the early 1970s was in excess of $1,647 annually (Johnson and Sell, 1976).

Marxist Interpretations.   Bonacich (1972, 1975) blames higher-paid white workers for the fate of the Chinese and of black people in this country. In contrast, more traditional Marxists hold capitalists responsible for germinating racism within the white working class (Cox, 1948; Szymaski, 1976, 1978; Geschwender, 1978). Marxists say that racial prejudice and exploitation developed in the Western world with the rise of capitalism. They trace racial and ethnic antagonisms to the policies and attitudes of the leading capitalist people, the white people of Europe and North America (Cox, 1948:322). Essentially racism is said to serve the economic interests of the capitalist class in four ways:

1. By viewing another people as inferior—as mental, moral, and physical inferiors—capitalists find it easier to exploit, oppress, and ill-treat these people in good conscience. Simultaneously, capitalists make colonialism and racist practices palatable and acceptable to the white masses.

2. Racism is financially advantageous since the white capitalists can pay minority workers less in wages and realize greater profits for themselves.

3. Racism divides the working class by pitting white workers and minority workers against each other. In this manner capitalists drive down wages and divert discontent away from themselves. It is a tactic of "divide and conquer." Albert Szymaski (1978:781) characterizes this dynamic as follows:

Since the early days of industrial capitalism in the U.S., one ethnic group has been played off against the other; first the native-born against the Irish, then the English-speaking against the new immigrants from Southern and Eastern Europe, then, especially since World War I, whites against blacks, and more recently, Anglophones against Latins. . . . Meanwhile, the poorer and ethnically distinct sections of the working class have borne resentments against the slightly more privileged white, the native-born or the English-speaking. The net result of this mutual antagonism is an especially low level of working-class consciousness, weak unions, little class solidarity or effective class action.

4. Capitalism has difficulty sustaining full employment for an extended period. During "good times" there is high demand for labor and workers become more assertive and demand higher wages and benefits. Capitalists therefore hold some people in reserve—out of the labor force—as the unemployed. Such individuals can be hired during "good times" or during labor strife. When the economy contracts, these workers are readily released to rejoin the ranks of the unemployed with few unsettling effects. Capitalists consider minority individuals like blacks to be ideal persons for the reserved labor force.

It goes without saying that the Marxist viewpoint is exceedingly controversial. As pointed out above, Bonacich places the responsibility for racism on higher-paid white workers rather than on capitalists. Whereas both Bonacich and the Marxists look to a link between class and racism, there are some social scientists who claim that racial conflict and class conflict are quite independent of each other (Katznelson, 1971; Allen, 1973, 1975; Blauner, 1973). They point out that racism cuts across class lines and prevails among whites regardless of their material interests. All these differing schools of thought have marshaled considerable statistical data to support their respective positions (Reich, 1972; Szymaski, 1976, 1978; Villemez, 1978; Beck, 1980). A cynic might be moved to conclude that on the issue of the relationship between class and race, statistics are frequently used to "prove" whatever a person wishes to prove.

The sociologist Sidney M. Willhelm (1971, 1980) takes still another tack. He says that Marxists remain locked within nineteenth-century conceptions of the economic system. Willhelm argues that "mature" capitalism of the postindustrial period has made black labor expendable, irrelevant to the capitalist drive for profits; automation and computer technologies have rendered the great mass of unskilled black workers unemployable. "White America," says Willhelm, "employs the new technology not with thoughts of incorporating but, rather, of doing away with the colored race" (1971:211). The black ghetto is "the equivalent" of the Indian reservation. Just as the people of the one reservation were incapacitated and destroyed with whiskey sold by whites, so the people of the other reservation are ravaged by drugs. Willhelm concludes that white racism has brought blacks to "the identical, ultimate fate of the American Indian."

Power Gains

Power may be broadly defined as the ability to control or influence the behavior of others, even when they are inclined to act in some other fashion. Striving for power can be quite normal. In normal people feelings of power may be born of the realization of their own superior strength—their physical strength, mental capacities, maturity, or wisdom. Striving for power, however, may also involve compensation for what are experienced as psychological shortcomings—the product of anxiety, hatred, and feelings of inferiority. In a word, normal striving for power is born of strength; the compensatory, of weakness. Many Americans choose to seek power precisely because power is associated with security in our society. The striving for power can also serve a number of functions for the individual. First, it functions as a protection against helplessness, which is one of the basic elements in anxiety. Second, it functions as a protection against the danger of feeling, or being regarded as, insignificant. Power-striving, then, may derive from both cultural and personality sources.

Evidence points to the fact that high levels of prejudice may be associated with power-seeking personalities (Adorno, 1950). Power may be sought as an end in itself. Since power is commonly equated with the dominant racial or ethnic group, weakness—the absence of power—can be overcome through gaining a sense of participation in the dominant group. The power that individuals lack, but strive for, apparently can be realized from identification with a powerful group such as "the white race." The minority group is seen as weak and ineffective. Its weakness "invites" attack from the would-be powerful, who by attack assert "I am powerful." But, being weak—helpless and insignificant—individuals realize by this means a power that is not genuine in that it is not rooted in the personality itself. Accordingly individuals have to repeatedly assert and demonstrate power in hopes of proving to themselves and the world that they actually are powerful. But the constant and excessive reassertion of prejudicial attitudes and racist behavior betrays the precarious status of the individual's sense of adequacy and strength. On the other hand, the weakness of the minority serves to outrage the would-be powerful by reminding individuals of their own weakness. Thus, the minority must be attacked, even destroyed.

Racism, anti-Semitism, and prejudice may also be used and exploited by political leaders in the pursuit of power. By attributing evils and difficulties to an outgroup, members of the ingroup can escape feelings of blame for their own failures or for failures in cherished institutions. It is painful to admit and to recognize such failure. How much more convenient and comforting it is to place the responsibility upon another! Thus political leaders throughout history have found it expedient to divert the hostility and aggressiveness of the ingroup to outgroups. Hitler and Goebbels were masters at the art. The German people—frustrated by defeat in World War I, plagued by economic chaos, disgruntled by the problems of life in general—were given the Jews, communists and international bankers as targets on which to vent their rage. Russians and Cubans—restless under the failure of dreams for a "new world" and a "new life" to materialize and by the inevitable frustrations of life—are presented with "Yankees," "foreign imperialists," and "Wall Street capitalists" as permissible targets for hate and aggression. In ancient Rome, it was the Christian minority that was used as the target to divert attention from the problems, failures, and corruption within the Roman state. Tertullian observed,

> If the Tiber rose to the walls of the city, if the inundation of the Nile failed to give the fields enough water, if the heavens did not send rain, if an earthquake occurred, if famine threatened, if pestilence raged, the cry resounded: "Throw the Christians to the lions."

Political leaders need not create racial or ethnic prejudices; there is no hard evidence to suggest that they do. They may, however, capitalize upon incipient or marked tendencies toward prejudice among the ingroup and exploit and intensify these tendencies. The late V.O. Key, Jr. (1950), an authority on southern politics, stressed the view that for decades whites of the "Black Belt" counties constituted the core and backbone of the political South. Historically the Black Belt made up only a small part of the area of the South, although it was here that large-scale-plantation or multiple-unit agriculture prevailed. And it was here that were located most of the large agricultural operators who oversaw the work of many tenants, sharecroppers, and laborers, most of whom were black. Although the Black Belt whites were few in number (blacks constituted a majority of the population of the Black Belt), Key argued that their unity and political skill enabled them "to run a shoestring into decisive power at critical junctures in southern political history." It was this group of whites who were the prime movers in the fight to protect slave property and in the establishment of the Confederate States. Later, with conservative allies in the cities, they put down the reformist Populist movement. And through the propagation of the racist position, they impressed on the entire South a philosophy agreeable to their needs and succeeded for decades in maintaining a regional unity in national politics to defend these necessities. Their major vehicle for decades was the southern Democratic party.

In recent years some politicians have resorted to campaign "code words" with racial implications. The Fair Campaign Practices Committee has noted that new forms of racial smear have developed that are much more difficult to handle than earlier more blatant appeals to racism. Among the suspect euphemisms are "crime in the streets" and "law and order."

Status Gains

Most of us enjoy the feeling that we are not just average but perhaps, at least to some degree, special and important. We like to identify with a winning football team, the "best" school, fraternity, or community, and so it goes. Indeed, our American culture places considerable emphasis upon status. Yet not all Americans are able to realize the status that they desire. For members of the dominant group, however, status is acquired simply through the fact that they are a white or a Gentile. By virtue of their dominant-group membership, individuals can acquire a sense of status that their own achievements might not command. **Status** is our sense of worth and respect, especially our feeling that we are admired and well thought of.

Membership in the dominant group can take on enormous emotional significance for status-starved individuals. Thus southern "Jim Crow" (segregation) laws historically provided numerous functions for whites, especially those whose statuses were comparable to those of minority blacks. As the historian C. Vann Woodward (1966) has carefully documented, the passage of most "Jim Crow" legislation took place at the turn of the twentieth century when poor whites were gaining political leverage in the South, while remaining economically little better off than blacks. The symbolic value of these various forms of segregation are highest for those whose status claims are otherwise negligible. By the same token, whites may refuse to interact socially with blacks because they fear they would *lose* status merely by associating with a "low-status" person (Blalock, 1967).

Status concerns have played a part in the slow, at times imperceptible, progress made in eliminating de facto school segregation. Middle-class parents seek to pass on to their children a status at least as good as their own. Some college professors are a case in point. Although often strong advocates of equality, they nonetheless want for their children "equality-plus." They generally attempt to give their children an elite education of the sort required by their own occupation. This proves difficult in class-heterogeneous schools. They prefer token integration of students, but not enough to interfere with the skills essential to an educational elite. It is not so much that they are anti-black as pro-middle class. Moreover, people learn fashionable circumlocutions far faster than they change their racist habits. Some New York parents recite liberal platitudes in one breath and in the next declare that "New York City schools are impossible," which is the reason they give for moving to Scarsdale. Yet they remain tactfully vague about *why* the schools are impossible.

Vested Interests

Closely associated with the hypothesis that intergroup competition breeds racism is another hypothesis: A racial or ethnic group that commands a disproportionate advantage over another group in access to wealth, power, and status evolves and employs prejudice, discrimination, and racism as instruments for defending its position of privilege and advantage. One of the clearest formulations of a vested interest approach is suggested by the sociologist Herbert Blumer (1961). Blumer views prejudice and discrimination as weapons employed by groups in social conflict and hence as arising from a sense of "group position." The dominant group, Blumer asserts, comes to view itself as being entitled to certain rights and privileges. These rights and privileges may include the ownership of choice property, the right to certain jobs, occupations, and professions, the claim to certain positions of power, the right to exclusive membership in particular institutions including schools, churches, and recreation facilities, the claim to certain positions of social prestige and to the display of the symbols associated with these positions, and the claim to certain areas of intimacy and privacy (Smith, 1981).

In Blumer's view, race prejudice arises from a fear that the minority threatens or will threaten the advantaged position of the dominant group:

> The source of race prejudice lies in a felt challenge to this sense of group position. The challenge, one must recognize, may come in many different ways. It may be in the form of an affront to feelings of group superiority; it may be in the form of attempts at familiarity or transgressing the boundary line of group exclusiveness; it may be in the form of encroachment at countless points of proprietary claim; it may be a challenge to power and privilege; it may take the form of economic competition. Race prejudice is a defensive reaction to such challenging of the sense of group position. It consists of the disturbed feelings, usually of marked hostility, that are thereby aroused. As such, race prejudice is a protective device. It functions, however shortsightedly, to preserve the integrity and the position of the dominant group (Blumer, 1961:222).

Prejudice arises, Blumer asserts, through a collective process in which spokesmen for a racial or ethnic group—prominent public figures, leaders of powerful organizations, and intellectual and social elites—operating chiefly through the mass media publicly characterize another group. Such spokesmen foster feelings of racial superiority, racial distance, and a claim to certain rights and privileges. Other members of the dominant group, although often having different views and feelings, fall into line fearing ingroup ostracism. The sense of group position serves as a special kind of social norm, especially for individuals who strongly identify with the ingroup. In this fashion a sense of group position—with its encompassing matrix of prejudice—becomes a general kind of orientation. It is a hypothesis, then, that views the dominant group as having a vested interest in another group's subordination; the dominant group has a stake in preserving an order characterized by privilege and advantage. Prejudice becomes an instrument for defending this privilege and advantage.

In keeping with this hypothesis, some writers (Jenkins, 1935; Degler, 1959; Jordon, 1968; Genovese, 1974) emphasize the part that the economic factor played in the appearance of racism. The emergence and elaboration of racist ideas were closely associated in time with the advent and development of black slavery. An integral aspect of slavery was the economic gain realized by white slaveowners. Accordingly, some have concluded that the racist dogma evolved primarily as a means to excuse and sanction the institution of slavery in general and the economic exploitation of slaves in particular.

Initially, black slavery in America was explained primarily on religious grounds: The black was a heathen and a barbarian, a descendant of Noah's son Ham, cursed by God and doomed to be a servant forever as the price of an ancient sin. With the passing of time and the conversion of blacks to Christianity, this position no longer constituted a satisfactory defense of slavery. Gradually, then, the biological argument came into prominence. Physical appearance was increasingly made the foundation for the assignment to blacks of a fundamental physical, mental, and moral inferiority.

There is evidence that at the present time some whites benefit occupationally from the presence and low status of blacks. The primary beneficiaries apparently are white workers in proprietary, managerial, sales, and upper-level manual occupations. Many whites in these occupations enjoy what have been termed "white bonus jobs"—positions filled by whites that would be filled by blacks if blacks were not subordinated and that would not exist if blacks were not present. The Kerner Commission (1968) estimates, for instance, that 1.3 million non-white men would have to be upgraded occupationally to make the black job distribution roughly equal to that of whites. This would in turn jeopardize the privileged position of 1.3 million white workers. Other beneficiaries of black subordination are white housewives who employ black domestic workers. And there are those white professionals who carry out the "dirty work" of administering the lives of the ghetto poor: social workers, school teachers, urban development people, and police. These whites, then, have a stake—a vested interest—in black subordination; the racist ideology is congruent with their economic interests.

The Ku Klux Klan: A Case Study of Status Anxieties

Intergroup competition and the vested interests of whites have figured in the rise of the various Ku Klux Klan (KKK) movements in the United States. The Ku Klux Klan was born on Christmas Eve, 1865. A group of Confederate veterans assembled to form an organization that would undertake to reverse the course of Reconstruction. Defeated, ragged, half-starved, enfeebled by want and wounds, many Confederate veterans had returned to their homes to find the South broken and charred. Vast changes threatened the traditional stratification system.

Old elites were challenged by new groups whom they derogatively called "scalawags" and "carpetbaggers." In five states former slaves constituted the majority of the electorate, while in the Black Belt whites felt themselves humilitated by slaves seemingly turned rulers.

In this situation it is not surprising that an organization such as the Klan should arise. With most legal avenues barred by which to effect their aims, whites turned to the secret society, terror, and intimidation. Klansmen, riding at night, robed and hooded in white and mounted on white-sheeted horses, threatened, flogged, mutilated, and murdered blacks, scalawags, and carpetbaggers and burned their homes, farms, and stores. The Confederate general Nathan Bedford Forrest III became the Klan's first imperial wizard. The "Invisible Empire" grew to a half-million members in four years. But with the passing of Reconstruction in the 1870s and its threat to the white elite, the KKK faded into oblivion.

Then, in 1915, the Klan was revived by William J. Simmons, a former revivalist and traveling salesman. The organization found it slow going until 1920, when the Klan was taken over by Edward Young Clarke, an able promoter. Interestingly enough, it wielded its greatest power not in the Old South, but in parts of the Midwest, Southwest, and Far West. This reborn Klan was not a legitimate descendant of the Klan of the Reconstruction period, it was rather an offspring of the old Know-Nothing party which had a "hate-the-foreigner-and-Catholic" program. The Klan, primarily representing a xenophobic response to the massive immigration of Catholics, Jews, and socialists from Southern and Eastern Europe to the United States, added blacks, Jews, and "communists" to its hate list. At its peak in the 1920s the organization gained some 5 million members and became a political force in Oregon, Texas, Oklahoma, and Indiana. But Klan outrages and scandals soon turned the tide against it. The conviction of the Indiana grand dragon for rape and the revelation of the Mer Rouge murders, whippings in Texas, and other atrocities resulted in the virtual extinction of the rejuvenated Klan by 1930.

Revived again following World War II, the hooded order lasted only a few embattled years. From one end of the South to the other the KKK found itself despised and discredited, denounced and prosecuted. Southern lawmakers legislated against mask-wearing and cross-burning, while state and federal agencies prosecuted a number of Klan leaders and activists. The Klan's fate seemed sealed when, in the 1950s, the U.S. attorney general placed it on the list of subversive organizations.

With the Supreme Court's school-desegregation ruling in *Brown* v. *Board of Education* (1954), the racial climate of the South changed. Many whites again felt threatened. White Citizens' Councils spread across the South and drastic, stringent sanctions fell upon black advocates of integration. Deep-South politicians raced to outdo one another in segregationist militancy. At the University of Alabama a mob rioted when a black woman, Autherine Lucy, enrolled under court order. Increasingly, whites acted as if they believed that they could defeat desegregation.

In this atmosphere of mounting tension and resistance, the Klan made its reappearance. It quickly entrenched itself in South Carolina, Georgia, Alabama, and Florida. Elsewhere it found little support. The KKK, as contrasted to the Citizens' Councils, did not find its strength in the rural Black Belt of the South. The Klan was primarily an urban phenomenon, with the preponderance of its strength located in the Piedmont of the Southeast. But it was not a united movement. Internal factionalism led to splintering. There were at least sixteen Klans, all bitter rivals of one another.

During the 1960s, in the wake of the civil-rights movement, Klan strength rose to some 10,000 to 15,000 members and spread to other areas of the South. Klan organizations harassed and occasionally murdered blacks and civil-rights workers. By the late 1960s, membership sagged once more. In 1975 the FBI estimated that no more than 2,200 individuals were members of the various Klan groups (the Anti-Defamation League of B'nai B'rith put the figure at 6,500).

In the 1980s there has again been an upswing in the Klan, which, it is estimated, has 10,500 active members and 100,000 sympathizers. A number of the Klans have links to the American Nazi party, and Klan organizations are spreading beyond their bastion in the South. To achieve wider acceptance, some of the Klans now accept women and Roman Catholics, individuals previously shunned. In states across the nation Klans are operating paramilitary camps at which members are learning to shoot guns and handle other weaponry. In addition, some groups are organizing Klan Youth Corps camps.

One reason for the revival of the Klan may be seen in a central theme stressed by contemporary Klan members: The United States is headed toward a violent race war and the Klan Special Forces are needed to prepare white people for survival. Says thirty-five-year-old Roger Handley, who serves as Alabama grand dragon and the imperial klaliff in one Klan: "We are going into revolution in this country. The Klan is not going to bring it on. It will be a war between the races" (W. King, 1980:159). In addition, white resistance to school busing for desegregation and affirmative-action programs, reaction against the influx of Spanish-speaking and Asian immigrants to the United States, and concern with the faltering economy at home and the specter of American powerlessness abroad have found expression in the Klan.

A study of the Klan (Vander Zanden, 1965), locating the names and occupations of 153 Klan members, reveals four occupational groupings: (1) skilled workers (e.g., garage mechanics, machinists, carpenters, and stonemasons); (2) marginal business operators (e.g., small building-trade contractors and proprietors of food markets, luncheonettes and grills, mon culture and from kinship and other kinds of personal ties, state societies are held together largely by the existence of a central political authority which claims a monopoly of coercive power over all persons within a given territory. Theoretically, with a sufficiently strong development of the apparatus of government, a state society can extend law and order over limitless subgroups of strangers who neither speak the same language, worship the same gods, nor strive for the same values.

Contemporary South Africa provides a good illustration of this principle.

Factors Influencing the Outcome of Intergroup Contacts

European "expansion" began in the fifteenth and sixteenth centuries and rested largely upon force deriving from superior weaponry. Contact between differing racial and ethnic groups brought about a variety of outcomes. Where the native population consisted of small, sparsely settled, nomadic groups (e.g., in Brazil, the United States, and the Western Cape in South Africa), the characteristic pattern of contact was frontier expansion of the whites punctuated by sporadic skirmishes, raids, and guerrilla warfare. Generally the outcome was virtual genocide of the natives or encapsulation of their scattered remnants on reservations. Where, in contrast, the European conquerors encountered large, densely settled, politically centralized, agricultural, and even urbanized nation-states (e.g., Mexico), the outcome was quite different—one of subjugation:

> Military conquest was not accompanied by extermination but by subjugation. The dominant group established its control either by "beheading" the indigenous societies and substituting itself as a new aristocracy, or by using the ruling class of the defeated peoples and ruling through it. In both situations the native masses became politically subordinate and economically exploited through some form of serfdom, forced or "contract" labor, debt peonage, or share-cropping tenancy (van den Berghe, 1967:125.).

The sociologist Stanley Lieberson (1961) finds that power differences also play a part in determining whether conflict or assimilation ensue when groups come into contact. Most situations of intergroup contact involve at least one indigenous group (a group native to and already established in an area) and at least one group migrating to the area. Either the indigenous or the migrant group may enjoy the power advantage, and hence Lieberson distinguishes between *migrant superordination* and *indigenous superordination.*

Migrant superordination generally occurs when the population migrating to a new contact situation is superior in technology (especially in weaponry) and is more tightly organized than the indigenous group.

and service stations); (3) marginal white-collar workers (e.g., grocery-store clerks, service-station attendants, police officers, and salespeople); (4) transportation workers (primarily truck drivers); and unskilled and semiskilled workers in the textile, construction, automotive, aircraft, coal, and steel industries. The sample is of unknown representativeness, and it is undoubtedly biased, yet it probably reflects the occupational breadth of the Klan's membership.

Two-thirds of the Klan members were found to be in the first three categories. These positions—skilled workers, marginal business proprietors and marginal white-collar workers—are commonly ranked within the status hierarchy in the upper rungs of the working class and the lower rungs of the middle class. They occupy an intermediate position in the social structure between clear-cut "blue-collar" manual jobs and "white-collar" jobs—between the "working class" and the "middle class"—positions that are somewhat hazy and vague in their placement in one or the other of the socioeconomic class divisions. American society, with its emphasis upon success, its belief in an open class system, and its high valuation of middle-class status, places such individuals in a difficult position. Their status ranking tends to be nebulous and ambiguous. At best, they have a toehold in the middle class; at worst, middle-class status seems just beyond their grasp. As a consequence their status tends to be insecure, causing them anxiety. Torn between the status America says they *ought* to have and what they in fact *actually* have, they feel disgruntled, discontented, and frustrated. Such people tend to be "status-starved." John Paul Rogers, a thirty-nine-year-old barber from Lake Wales, Florida, is a grand wizard of the United Klans. At white rallies he declares: "Black is beautiful, tan is grand. But white's still the color of the big boss man" (Langford, 1980).

Society gives such status-starved people a way out. They are still white and they are still Americans: two things that are important in our society. They seize upon those status elements that are available to them, but elevate and magnify them out of proportion to their place in the social order. They *overconform* to racist patterns and to patriotic identification with the United States. Judged by white dominant-group standards, their adherence to white racial values and Americanism is excessive. This leads to conflict with other values, most particularly the sanctity of the individual and of private property.

This exaggeration of values commonly esteemed in America is reflected in this statement appearing in the handbook of the U.S. Klans, Knights of the Ku Klux Klan:

> We invite all men who can qualify to become citizens of the Invisible Empire, to approach the portal of our beneficent domain, join us in our noble work of extending its boundaries, and in disseminating the gospel of Klankraft, thereby encouraging, conserving, protecting and making vital the fraternal relationship in the presence of an honorable clannishness; to share with us the sacred duty of protecting womanhood; to main-

tain forever the God-given supremacy of the White Race; to commemo-
rate the holy and chivalric achievement of our fathers; to safeguard the
sacred rights, privileges and institutions of our civil government; to bless
mankind and to keep eternally ablaze the sacred fire of a fervent devotion
to a pure Americanism.

Secrecy plays a role similar to exaggerated conformity. The strongly
emphasized exclusion of all outsiders creates a highly tangible and
explicit group identification, setting Klan members apart from the
amorphous mass of humanity. That which is secret and mysterious has
a quality of importance and essentiality. By the possession of such se-
crets, the Klan members secure prestige.

Lacking prestige-giving symbols in the world at large, Klan members
establish their own world, an "Invisible Empire." It is a world with its
own esteemed symbols: its grotesque, differentially valued purple, red,
green, and white gowns; its elaborate honorific insignia; and its exaggerated status-exalting nomenclature—Imperial Wizard, Grand Dragon, Grand Titan, Grand Giant, and Exalted Cyclops. Without secure
anchorage in the class structure of the larger society, Klan members
compensate by finding security harbored in the Klan itself.

Unequal Power

As pointed out in chapter 1, unequal power is a defining property of
dominant-minority group relationships. Power implies that in human
affairs one party is able to realize its will over and against the will of
another party. Whereas competition provides the motivation for systems of social inequality and ethnocentrism channels competition along
racial and ethnic lines, power determines which group will subordinate
the other (Noel, 1972). Without power, prejudices cannot be translated
into discrimination and groups cannot turn their claims upon scarce
values into institutional racism. Power is the vehicle by which subordination and superordination are effected (Baker, 1978).

Power in Intergroup Relationships

When groups disagree as to which group will enjoy the good things
and which group will bear the burdens of the society, power supplies
the answer. Power allows one racial or ethnic group to impose limits on
the ability of others to compete. The dominant group can screen others
off from access to knowledge, skills, and resources. By dictating the
terms by which the game of life is played, the dominant group fashions
the flow of good things to itself. To play the game "by the rules" means
that there is no game at all because "the deck is stacked"—the outcome
is a foregone conclusion. By defining what is possible, what is rational,

what is real, and what is right, the dominant group guarantees that its
members will be advantaged and the members of the minority disadvantaged. Power, then, provides an answer to the distributive question:
"Who shall get what, when, and how?"

And when groups disagree as to which group will translate its preferences for behavior (its norms and values—its morality) into the operating standards of society, once again power supplies the answer. Power
allows the dominant group to translate its social values into "law and
order" by manipulating rewards and imposing penalties. Perhaps most
devastating of all, a powerful dominant group can undertake to eradicate the distinctive customs of a people—and even the people themselves. The policies pursued by whites toward Native Americans
provide good illustrations of such practices. Power, then, decides whose
social values and norms shall govern human affairs—who will define
whose behavior is deviant, pathological, abhorrent, "barbaric," and
"uncivilized," and who will make their definitions stick.

Within human affairs force constitutes the final court of appeals.
There is no appeal from force except the exercise of superior force.
Clearly the ability to take life—to effect physical violence—can constitute an important instrument of social control as well as an instrument
for challenging that same social control.

To be effective, however, force need not be implemented. It need
merely remain in the wings, so to speak, ready at any moment to make
its appearance. Many sociologists, in recognition of this fact, distinguish
between force and power. **Force** refers to the *application* of sanctions;
it is the implementation of coercive remedies. *Power,* in contrast, entails the *capacity* or *ability* to introduce force within a social situation;
it is the potential for instituting force but *not* the actual implementation
of force itself.

The **state** is an arrangement that consists of people who exercise an
effective monopoly in the use of physical coercion within a given territory. The sociologist Randall Collins (1975) points out that the state may
be many things, but above all, it is the military and the police. We
sometimes hear that the state is merely a kind of grade-school assembly
in which individuals get together to operate for the common good. This
is often true. But when vital interests are at stake—when "push comes
to shove"—the issue becomes: Who will threaten whom, who will fight
whom, and who will win? It is in this context that we speak of the state;
it is the dominant apparatus of violence.

The state has important consequences for dominant-minority relations. The anthropologists Charles Wagley and Marvin Harris (1964:-
242) observe:

Only with the development of the state did human societies become
equipped with a form of social organization which could bind masses of
culturally and physically heterogeneous "strangers" in a single social entity. Whereas primitive peoples derive their cohesion largely from a com-

These conditions enable the migrant group to impose its political and economic institutions upon the indigenous population. Through its political and economic dominance, the migrant group can effectively cultivate its own cultural practices and maintain its distinct social institutions (educational, family, religious, and so on). In this setting warfare often accompanies the early contacts between the two groups. Even where the initial contact is friendly, conflict is generated as the migrants begin to interfere with the natives' established order. A. Grenfell Price (1950:1) notes the consequences of white invasion and subordination of the indigenous populations of Australia, Canada, New Zealand, and the United States:

> During an opening period of pioneer invasion on moving frontiers the whites decimated the natives with their diseases; occupied their lands by seizure or pseudo-purchase; slaughtered those who resisted; intensified tribal warfare by supplying white weapons; ridiculed and disrupted native religions, society and culture, and generally reduced the unhappy peoples to a state of despondency under which they neither desired to live, nor to have children to undergo similar conditions.

With the passage of time the subordinated indigenous people begins to participate in the economy introduced by the migrant group, a fact that often accentuates the disruption of their native institutions. This development, in turn, has frequently fostered both nationalism and a greater sense of racial unity. In many African states, where blacks were subdivided in tribal groups prior to contact with whites, racial consciousness and unity among Africans were actually created by European colonialism. Contact characterized by migrant superordination is especially likely to breed a high incidence of racial and ethnic turmoil—in brief, *conflict.*

In contrast to migrant superordination, **indigenous superordination** entails the political and economic domination of the migrants by the indigenous population. When a population migrates to a subordinate position, Lieberson (1961) argues, considerably less conflict results. The movement of many European and Oriental populations to the United States, for example, did not give rise to warfare, nationalism, or long-term conflict. The occasional labor and racial strife marking the history of immigration to the United States is not on the same level as efforts to eliminate or revolutionize a particular social order.

In appraising differences in the effects of migrant and indigenous subordination, it is necessary to consider the options available to the migrants:

> Irish migrants to the United States in the 1840's, for example, although clearly subordinate to native whites of other origins, fared better economically than if they had remained in their mother country. Further, the option of returning to the homeland often exists for populations migrating to subordinate situations. . . . Finally, when contacts between

racial and ethnic groups are under the control of the indigenous population, threats of demographic and institutional imbalance are reduced since the superordinate populations can limit the numbers and groups entering. For example, when Oriental migration to the United States threatened whites, sharp cuts were executed in the quotas (Lieberson, 1961:905–906).

In indigenous superordination, then, conflict is likely to be limited and sporadic, while considerable emphasis is placed upon the *assimilation* of migrants. The history of migration to the United States provides a classic example. Hence, the consequences ensuing from indigenous superordination are in marked contrast to those of migrant superordination.

SUMMARY

1. Contact between differing racial and ethnic groups sets the stage for racism. If migration were not a common practice, if people were content to live among their own kind in communities that were more or less isolated from one another, racial and ethnic prejudice would be virtually unknown. Migration commonly takes one of four forms: primitive migration, forced and impelled migration, free migration, and mass migration.

2. Categories are necessary to social life. They enable us to group things into "classes" or "pigeonholes," and to respond to them in terms of this placement rather than in terms of their uniqueness. We also evolve categories for people. Certain traits with high social visibility serve as identifying symbols of the category. The traits may be physical or cultural or both. One consequence of categorization is that it fosters object relations as opposed to person-centered relations.

3. Ethnocentrism entails strong positive feelings toward an ingroup, even ingroup glorification. One factor that apparently fosters ethnocentrism is the tendency of people to be attracted to others who hold beliefs and attitudes similar to their own; likewise they tend to experience an aversion toward people with dissimilar beliefs and attitudes. Once established in one group, ethnocentrism tends to beget ethnocentrism in other groups with which the first group interacts.

4. Where people are strongly ethnocentric, it is not difficult for them to perceive the outgroup as an object for loathing. In fact, the outgroup often appears to be engaged in deviant acts. Even where the behavior of the outgroup resembles the behavior of the ingroup, the ingroup may perceive the behavior of the outgroup to be different. In this manner ingroup virtues become outgroup vices.

5. Among the English, black is an emotionally partisan color, denoting baseness, evil, danger, and repulsion. When English voyagers touched

upon the shores of West Africa after 1550, the negative connotations associated with the word "black" were transferred to people whom the English described as black in skin color.

6. There are some good things within any society that are scarce and divisible including wealth, power, and status. The more there is for the one, the less there is for others. People typically seek to improve their outcome with regard to those things that they define as good, worthwhile, and desirable. Where the outcomes of two distinct groups are perceived to be mutually exclusive and legitimate, so that each can realize what it defines as a rightful outcome only at the expense of the other, competition will ensue. The attitudes that the members of a group evolve toward an outgroup tend to be consistent with their perceptions of the relationships they have with the outgroup. Hence where the relations between two groups are perceived as competitive, negative attitudes—prejudice—will be generated toward the outgroup.

7. Economic competition plays a particularly critical role in the emergence of racism. Within American history there is a direct correlation between peaks of agitation against minorities and the valleys of economic depression. Race riots and violence have also been associated with intense intergroup competition. The sociologist Edna Bonacich views economic competition within a split labor market as a particularly fertile setting for the development of antagonism among ethnic groups. Whereas Bonacich blames higher-paid workers for racism, Marxists hold capitalists responsible for germinating racism within the white working class.

8. Striving for power can be quite normal. However, it may also involve compensation for what are experienced as psychological shortcomings. High levels of prejudice are often associated with power-seeking personalities. Apparently prejudice functions as a psychological mechanism by which some individuals cope with their insecurities and inadequacies. Racism may also be used and exploited by political leaders in the pursuit of power.

9. By virtue of their dominant-group membership, individuals can acquire a sense of status that their own achievements might not command. Membership in the dominant group can take on enormous emotional significance for status-starved individuals. The passage of most "Jim Crow" legislation took place at the turn of the twentieth century, when poor whites were gaining political leverage in the South, while economically remaining little better off than blacks.

10. The sociologist Herbert Blumer views prejudice and discrimination as weapons employed by groups in social conflict and hence as arising from a sense of "group position." The sense of group position serves as a special kind of social norm, especially for individuals who strongly

identify with the ingroup. Thus in the last analysis prejudice becomes an instrument for defending privilege and advantage. Intergroup competition and white vested interests have figured in the rise of the various Ku Klux Klan movements.

11. When groups disagree as to which group will enjoy the good things and which group will bear the burdens of the society, power supplies the answer. And when groups disagree as to which group will translate its preferences for behavior (its norms and values—its morality) into the operating standards of society, once again power supplies the answer. The group that controls the state apparatus is able to translate its wishes into the patterns whereby people carry out their daily lives.

12. European expansion brought about a variety of outcomes. Where the native population consisted of small, sparsely settled nomadic groups, the characteristic pattern of contact was frontier expansion of the whites accompanied by the killing of the natives or their encapsulation on reservations. Where, in contrast, the European conquerors encountered large, densely settled, politically centralized, agricultural groups, and even urbanized nation-states, the outcome was one of subjugation.

13. Power differences play a part in determining whether conflict or assimilation will ensue when groups come into contact. Contact characterized by migrant superordination is especially likely to breed a high incidence of racial and ethnic conflict. In indigenous superordination, conflict is likely to be limited and the emphasis falls upon the assimilation of migrants.

GLOSSARY

Caste System An arrangement of stratification based on inherited inequality.

Ethnocentrism The tendency of group members to appraise peoples of other cultures by the standards of judgment prevailing in their own culture.

Force The application of sanctions; the implementation of coercive remedies.

Indigenous Superordination The political and economic domination of migrant peoples by the aboriginal or native population.

Migrant Superordination The political and economic domination of the aboriginal or native population by a migrant people.

Power The ability to control or influence the behavior of others.

Split Labor Market An economic arena in which large differences exist in the price of labor at the same occupational level.

State An arrangement that consists of people who exercise an effective monopoly in the use of physical coercion within a given territory.

Status Our sense of worth and respect, especially our feeling that we are admired and thought well of.

Maintenance of Racism

*I*ntergroup contact and social visibility set the stage for racism. Competition provides the motivation for systems of social inequality. Ethnocentrism channels the competition along racial and ethnic lines. Power determines which group will subordinate the other. As discussed in chapter 3, these five factors typically come into play in the emergence and initial stabilization of racism.

Once racism has arisen within a society, it may continue even when the originating sources wane or disappear. Racism becomes embedded within the social and cultural fabric of a society. In this sense it is *institutionalized* in the manner of other social patterns. This matter—the maintenance of racism—is the focus of the chapter.

The Role of Culture

Peoples throughout the world exhibit markedly different patterns of behavior. Part of the explanation for this diversity is **culture.** Culture is a set of ready-made definitions of the situation that individuals only slightly retail in their own unique manner (Kluckhohn and Kelly, 1945). It is a set of blueprints for action. Thus culture provides us with guideposts or a kind of map for life's activities. It tells us how to think, feel, and act. It provides us with our standards for determining what is "good" and what is "bad," what is "right" and what is "wrong."

The pervasive influence that culture has on us is vividly captured in the following illustration by the anthropologist Clyde Kluckhohn (1960:21–22):

> Some years ago I met in New York City a young man who did not speak a word of English and was obviously bewildered by American ways. By "blood" he was as American as you and I, for his parents had gone from Indiana to China as missionaries. Orphaned in infancy, he was reared by a Chinese family in a remote village. All who met him found him more Chinese than American. The facts of his blue eyes and light hair were less

impressive than a Chinese style of gait, Chinese arm and hand movements, Chinese facial expression, and Chinese modes of thought. The
biological heritage was American, but the cultural training had been
Chinese. He returned to China.

Social Conformity and Intergroup Relations

Culture provides guideposts for intergroup relations. The interaction
between members of the dominant and minority groups is mapped out
or patterned by culture. The guideposts of a culture are norms. Norms
are generally accepted, sanctioned prescriptions for, or prohibitions
against, various types of behavior. They tell us what we *should, ought,*
and *must* do, as well as what we *should not, ought not,* and *must not*
do. They are expectations shared by the members of the society-at-large
or by the members of particular groups within the society. A large part
of our behavior can be understood in terms of the operation of the
norms of our society or of groups of which we are members. This does
not mean, however, that we are necessarily conscious of our cultural
norms. The anthropologist Ralph Linton (1945:125) notes:

> It has been said that the last thing which a dweller in the deep sea would
> be likely to discover would be water. He would become conscious of its
> existence only if some accident brought him to the surface and introduced
> him to air. Man, throughout most of his history, has been only vaguely
> conscious of the existence of culture and has owed even this consciousness
> to contrasts between the customs of his own society and those of some
> other with which he happened to be brought into contact.

Hence, we tend to take our culture for granted; it is more or less second
nature to us.

Norms tell dominant-group members how they are expected to
think, act, and feel toward minority-group members. Simultaneously,
they tell minority-group members how they are expected to think, act,
and feel toward dominant-group members. They may spell out, for
example, the "proper" racial etiquette. Until relatively recently in rural
areas of the South a black male was "supposed" to go to the back door
of a white's home, knock on the door, retreat down the steps to the
ground level, and, at the appearance of the white, remove his hat. He
was "expected" to speak with deference and to intersperse his speech
with frequent expressions of "sir" and "sho 'nuff." Whites were "expected" to call blacks by their first name and to instruct, not ask, blacks
what to do.

Discrimination may be a response to social norms. Racist behavior
comes to be a "learned-by-rote" set of definitions and rules by which
dominant-group members relate to minority-group members. Just as
members of a society learn that they are to respect and salute their

nation's flag or that they should eat with forks rather than with chopsticks, so they also learn bigotry. They learn that outgroup members are not to be included among their intimate associates as neighbors and friends.

Evidence supporting this interpretation is provided by the social psychologist Thomas F. Pettigrew (1958). He studied anti-black prejudice among whites in the southern United States and South Africa. Pettigrew first measured the degree of prejudice against blacks by an attitude scale. He then administered another questionnaire scaled to measure conformity to norms independent of prejudice (the items differed for the two nations and were selected with a view toward each nation's distinct cultural heritage). In both South Africa and the southern United States, where prejudice and discrimination against blacks is a norm, those who showed the most conformity to norms were also the most prejudiced.

The part that norms play in discriminatory behavior was also revealed by the sociologists Lyle G. Warner and Melvin L. DeFleur (1969) in a study conducted among students in a border-state university. They found that even the least prejudiced students became vulnerable to participation in discriminatory behavior when asked to behave favorably toward blacks in situations where their behavior would be in violation of norms and open to surveillance by others.

Social Distance

One index of the role of culture in patterning prejudice is the degree of *similarity* that exists in the responses of a society's members to various racial and ethnic groups. If members rank the various groups within a society in a similar fashion, one concludes that this is the product of the operation of norms. A familiar technique, devised by Emory S. Bogardus (1959), seeks to measure the **social distance** at which members of one group hold another group and its members. Bogardus formulated a list of statements representing varying degrees of social intimacy or distance. He asked his subjects to mark those classifications to which they would willingly admit members of a given group. The scale of statements is

> To close kinship by marriage (1 point)
> To my club as personal chums (2 points)
> To my street as neighbors (3 points)
> To employment in my occupation (4 points)
> To citizenship in my country (5 points)
> As visitors only to my country (6 points)
> Would exclude from my country (7 points)

In 1926, Bogardus secured the responses of 1,725 Americans to forty racial and ethnic groups. The individuals were between the ages of eighteen to thirty-five. Approximately half were college students and half were college graduates who were employed but were taking one or more postgraduate courses. The study was conducted among respondents from thirty-two well-distributed areas in the United States and included blacks, who constituted 10 percent of the participants. Bogardus obtained a racial distance score for each racial and ethnic group employing a scale from 1.00 (the lowest possible distance score) to 7.00 (the highest possible distance score). The results of the 1926 study and similar studies in 1946 (with 1,950 subjects), 1956 (with 2,053 subjects), and 1966 (with 2,605 subjects) are indicated in Table 4.1. Near the top of the preference-ranking scale (i.e., those persons with whom the respondents would like to associate) are English, native-born white Americans, and other northern Europeans; then Spaniards, Italians, and generally southern and eastern Europeans; near the bottom, Orientals and blacks. It is of interest to note that through the years an overall decline occurred in distance reactions (Bogardus, 1959, 1968).

Social scientists within the United States have been checking the social distance positions of various groups by this means for more than fifty years. The most striking of their findings is that a similar pattern of preference is found across the nation, varying little with income, region, education, occupation, or even with ethnic group. With a few minor shifts, the relative positions of the groups remain substantially constant.

To a considerable extent the social-distance rankings of minority-group members are quite similar to those of dominant-group members. There is, however, one important difference. While the minority-group members retain the standardized pattern, they move their own group up from its lower position to one near the top of the scale. Thus Bogardus (1959, 1968) found that blacks placed blacks at the top of their racial preferences, while Jews similarly put their own group on top. In summary, evidence suggests that the distances at which various ethnic and racial groups are held is relatively consistent within the United States. This consistency suggests that culture, more particularly norms, is a crucial factor in understanding prejudice, discrimination, and racism.

Culture and the Perception of Groups

We never really "see" the physical world about us. Rather the world we "see" is the product of the interaction between our anatomy, the physical aspects of the universe, and what we have learned from our past experience. Thus our perception is never a photographic image of the physical world. People differ considerably in the world they "see." Many factors enter into our perception of the world about us, one of which is culture. The anthropologist A. Irving Hallowell (1951) gives an interesting example of the relation of culture to perception. He was

TABLE 4.1 CHANGES IN RACIAL DISTANCE INDICES

	I — Racial Distance Indices Given Racial Groups in 1926 by 1,725 Selected Persons throughout the U.S.		II — Racial Distance Indices Given Racial Groups in 1946 by 1,950 Selected Persons throughout the U.S.		III — Racial Distance Indices Given Racial Groups in 1956 by 2,053 Selected Persons throughout the U.S.		IV — Racial Distance Indices Given Racial Groups in 1966 by 2,605 Selected Persons throughout the U.S.	
1	English	1.06	Americans (U.S. white)	1.04	Americans (U.S. white)	1.08	Americans (U.S. white)	1.07
2	Americans (U.S. white)	1.10	Canadians	1.11	Canadians	1.16	English	1.14
3	Canadians	1.13	English	1.13	English	1.23	Canadians	1.15
4	Scots	1.13	Irish	1.24	French	1.47	French	1.36
5	Irish	1.30	Scots	1.26	Irish	1.56	Irish	1.40
6	French	1.32	French	1.31	Swedish	1.57	Swedish	1.42
7	Germans	1.46	Norwegians	1.35	Scots	1.60	Norwegians	1.50
8	Swedish	1.54	Hollanders	1.37	Germans	1.61	Italians	1.51
9	Hollanders	1.56	Swedish	1.40	Hollanders	1.63	Scots	1.53
10	Norwegians	1.59	Germans	1.59	Norwegians	1.66	Germans	1.54
11	Spanish	1.72	Finns	1.63	Finns	1.80	Hollanders	1.54
12	Finns	1.83	Czechs	1.76	Italians	1.89	Finns	1.67
13	Russians	1.88	Russians	1.83	Poles	2.07	Greeks	1.82
14	Italians	1.94	Poles	1.84	Spanish	2.08	Spanish	1.93
15	Poles	2.01	Spanish	1.94	Greeks	2.09	Jews	1.97
16	Armenians	2.06	Italians	2.28	Jews	2.15	Poles	1.98
17	Czechs	2.08	Armenians	2.29	Czechs	2.22	Czechs	2.02
18	Indians (American)	2.38	Greeks	2.29	Armenians	2.33	Indians (American)	2.12
19	Jews	2.39	Jews	2.32	Japanese Americans	2.34	Japanese Americans	2.14
20	Greeks	2.47	Indians (American)	2.45	Indians (American)	2.35	Armenians	2.18
21	Mexicans	2.69	Chinese	2.50	Filipinos	2.46	Filipinos	2.31
22	Mexican Americans	—	Mexican Americans	2.52	Mexican Americans	2.51	Chinese	2.34
23	Japanese	2.80	Filipinos	2.76	Turks	2.52	Mexican Americans	2.37
24	Japanese Americans	—	Mexicans	2.89	Russians	2.56	Russians	2.38
25	Filipinos	3.00	Turks	2.89	Chinese	2.68	Japanese	2.41
26	Negroes	3.28	Japanese Americans	2.90	Japanese	2.70	Turks	2.48
27	Turks	3.30	Koreans	3.05	Negroes	2.74	Koreans	2.51
28	Chinese	3.36	Indians (from India)	3.43	Mexicans	2.79	Mexicans	2.56
29	Koreans	3.60	Negroes	3.60	Indians (from India)	2.80	Negroes	2.56
30	Indians (from India)	3.91	Japanese	3.61	Koreans	2.83	Indians (from India)	2.62
	Arithmetic Mean of 48,300 Racial Reactions	2.14	Arithmetic Mean of 58,500 Racial Reactions	2.12	Arithmetic Mean of 61,590 Racial Reactions	2.08	Arithmetic Mean of 78,150 Racial Reactions	1.92
	Spread in Distance	2.85	Spread in Distance	2.57	Spread in Distance	1.75	Spread in Distance	1.56

Source: Emory S. Bogardus, "Comparing Racial Distance in Ethiopia, South, and the United States," *Sociology and Social Research* 52 (1968): 152.

discussing with a group of students the differing names that various peoples have given to the constellation Ursa Major (for instance, *dipper, bear, otter,* or *plow*) and the influence that the assignment of such names has had upon the perception of these stars. When he finished, feeling he had made the point, one student spoke up, asserting, "But it *does* look like a dipper." As Hallowell's remarks indicate, it probably *does* look like a plow to those who use that label, rather than a dipper.

The social psychologist James W. Bagby (1957) formulated an interesting experiment that demonstrates the part culture plays in our perception of the world about us. Mexicans and Americans constituted the subjects in the study. Bagby set up ten pairs of slides to be viewed through a stereoscope. On one side he mounted pictures of objects familiar to most Mexicans (e.g., a matador, a dark-haired girl, and a peon). On the other side he mounted a similar picture of objects familiar to most Americans, (e.g., a baseball player, a blonde girl, and a farmer). The corresponding photographs resembled one another in contour, texture, and the distribution of light and shadows. Most Americans saw only those objects that were already familiar to them (e.g., the baseball player rather than the matador), and most Mexicans likewise saw only those objects placed within the context of their culture (e.g., the matador rather than the baseball player). To a surprising extent, then, our selection and interpretation of the sensory cues reaching us from our environment rest upon cultural definitions and standards. The world we see is a world heavily colored and impregnated with cultural connotations.

Perception is not merely selective; it may also be distorted by cultural definitions. The psychologists Eugene and Ruth Horowitz (1938) demonstrated this fact more than forty years ago in an experiment involving southern white children. They briefly showed the children a picture of a large apartment building fronted by a well-kept lawn, taken in brilliant sunlight. After the picture was removed, they asked the children: "Who was at the window?," "What was she or he doing?," "Who was cleaning up the grounds?" Actually, no figures of people had been in the picture. Nevertheless, most of the children readily described some individual in answer to each of the questions calling for such a response. When the children responded that they had seen a black woman at the window, they almost invariably attributed to her a menial activity (e.g., cleaning the window). The answer to the question "Who was cleaning up the grounds?" was usually "A colored man."

Another interesting study revealing how cultural definitions can affect perceptions was made by the psychologist Gregory Razran (1950). One hundred college students and fifty noncollege men were shown pictures of thirty young women, all strangers to them. They were asked to rank each photograph on a five-point scale that would indicate their general liking for the young woman, her beauty, her character, her intelligence, her ambition, and her "entertainingness."

Two months later the same group was again shown the identical photographs but with surnames added. For some of the photographs Jewish names were given, such as Finkelstein and Cohen; to others, Irish surnames such as O'Shaughnessy and McGillicuddy; to others, Italian surnames such as Valenti and Scadano; and to others, old-American surnames such as Davis and Clark. The labeling of the photographs with the surnames had a definite effect upon the manner in which the women were perceived. The addition of Jewish and Italian names resulted in a substantial drop in general liking and a smaller drop in the judgment of beauty and character. The falling of likability of the "Jewish women" was twice as great as for "Italians" and five times as great as for "Irish." On the other hand, it also resulted in a rise in the ambition and intelligence ratings for the young women with Jewish surnames. Clearly, cultural definitions had a marked effect on the perception of the photographs and on the judgment of the characteristics assigned to the women.

The influence of cultural definitions on perception can be seen in other contexts. If we meet people of Irish ancestry at a social event and do not know their ethnic membership, we look at them with a more or less open mind. When someone tells us that they are Irish, our perception is altered. We may expect them to be witty, quick-tempered, and quick to use their fists. If their anger flares, we say, "Aha! How like the Irish!" But, if a non-Irish person shows the same traits, we say "Things have gone hard with him recently," "He has had one too many drinks," or "His health has been bothering him lately." We remember those Irish who are witty and quick-tempered; we tend to overlook and forget those who are not. Similarly with Jews. If we are in the supermarket and someone nearby is quite loud, we may turn and see it is a Jewish acquaintance. "Aha," we say to ourselves, "a typical Jew." But, if the individual were non-Jewish, we would say, "Has that person got a loud mouth! How irritating!" The attribute is merely associated with the individual as an individual, and no larger ethnic category is involved. We tend to overlook subdued and quiet Jews. They simply do not "register." But let a Jew speak loudly and act aggressively, and we conclude, "You might know, a Jew!" That person registers!

Prejudice and superstition resemble each other in some respects. Take, for instance, the superstition that if a black cat crosses our path, some misfortune will befall us. The consequence of this superstition is that it makes black cats, *but only black cats,* highly visible. We hardly notice cats of another color, since the superstition implies that they do not pose a danger. Indeed, the very logic of a superstitious belief discourages disconfirmation. We overlook the fact that misfortune sometimes occurs when a cat of another color crosses our path. But when a black cat crosses our path, we find it easy to find some instance of misfortune, no matter how slight or delayed in time (Selznick and Steinberg, 1969).

Reference Groups and Racism

More than a century ago the American writer Henry Thoreau observed, "If a man does not keep pace with his companions, perhaps it is because he hears a different drummer." Implicit in Thoreau's observation is the social psychological concept of the **reference group.** A reference group is a social unit with which individuals identify. It is that group that provides the standards and anchorage regulating people's behavior within a particular context. Individuals may be members of the group, relating themselves psychologically to it, or they may be nonmembers who aspire to membership, achieving the relation through mental identification. In any event, individuals use the group as a model for their behavior.

Reference Groups and Attitudes

Social scientists have undertaken considerable research on the relationship between the attitudes individuals hold and the reference groups of which they are members. The research has ranged from attitude studies of the American soldier to studies of attitude shifts occurring with changing reference groups among Roman Catholic students and Bennington College students. These studies demonstrate the close relationship between individuals' attitudes and their reference group. This general finding has been confirmed in studies dealing with attitudes toward racial and ethnic minorities.

Lawrence E. Schlesinger (1955), for instance, devised an experimental situation in which college students were exposed to information that they believed to represent the opinions of their fellow students regarding Jews (but information that in fact had been designed by Schlesinger). After exposure to the "peer" information, the students were asked individually to answer a variety of questions regarding their attitudes toward Jews. The answers to these questions were compared with the results of an anti-Semitism attitude test that the students had completed two weeks before the experiment. Schlesinger found that as a result of exposure to "peer" information, the students' expression of agreement or disagreement with favorable or unfavorable assertions about Jews changed in the direction of conformity with perceived peer opinion. Schlesinger concluded that most of the students were highly suggestible, tending to conform to supposed peer opinion, whether this was pro- or anti-Semitic, and almost regardless of their prior levels of prejudice.

The sociologist Leonard Pearlin (1954) also conducted a study that investigated the role of reference groups among students at a white southern women's college. The study is particularly significant because it was undertaken at a time when southern colleges were racially segregated. The majority of the students experienced at the college a climate of opinion that was more favorable toward blacks than that to which they had been exposed prior to their coming to college. Thus many of the students came into contact with attitudes that were in conflict with those they had previously experienced in segregated southern communities.

The data from the Pearlin study indicate that the least prejudiced students were those who had experienced a weakening of ties to precollege membership groups, while the more prejudiced were those who had retained firm affiliations with such groups. Likewise, the least prejudiced students were those who most strongly referred themselves to college groups, while the more prejudiced were those who referred themselves less strongly to campus groups. Thus the shift toward favorable attitudes toward blacks was in part the product of a double-edged process. On the one hand, there occurred a weakening of ties to precollege groups. This weakening of ties was accompanied by a decrease in the effectiveness of the precollege groups in regulating the individual's attitudes unfavorablely toward blacks. On the other hand, it was not sufficient that one simply "drift away" from previously established social relationships. Of equal importance in the modification of attitudes was the establishment of strong identification with those groups possessing attitudes favorable toward blacks. By virtue of identifying with new reference groups, individuals shift their attitudes in accordance with those harbored by the new groups.

The process of acquiring more favorable attitudes toward blacks, then, involves both *disattachment* and *attachment:* disattachment from previous reference groups unfavorable to blacks and attachment to new reference groups favorable to blacks. Attitude changes cannot be reckoned solely in terms of exposure to new attitudes. Not all the students underwent a modification of their attitudes toward blacks, although they had been exposed to the new ideas. Whether individuals undergo a modification of their attitudes depends to a considerable extent on their relationship to groups holding the opposing sentiments. Generally, where a shift in attitudes occurs, there will be found a detachment from those groups from which they initially derived and found support for their attitudes. Correspondingly, the shift in attitude will be in the direction of the sentiments of those groups with which they develop the firmest attachments and identifications.

In summary, stereotypes of and attitudes toward minorities are anchored in the group. Individuals view themselves as being members in good standing within certain groups or as wishing to become members in good standing. Individuals tend to accept a group's attitudes as part of their acceptance of the group. Further, they identify themselves with these same attitudes so as to be accepted by the group. Consequently, the group's views become their own views.

Reference Groups and Behavior

Attitudes are one thing; behavior another. Attitudes involve a *predisposition* to think, feel, and act in particular ways. They do not constitute the actual response or series of responses that individuals make. This distinction between attitudes and behavior is also the distinction that social scientists make between prejudice and discrimination (*see* chapter 1). Our discussion in the section above dealt with attitudes (prejudice). We now turn our attention to actions (discrimination) and more particularly to the relationship between behavior and reference groups.

We are members of a large number of groups, many of which possess subcultures and even countercultures that may conflict or clash with the dominant culture in which we live. The differing groups often make conflicting demands upon us and, as a consequence, our behavior periodically appears to be inconsistent. Such inconsistencies in behavior can be understood within a reference-group framework. When operating within the context of one reference group we may behave one way; we may behave quite differently when operating under the influence of another reference group.

The literature of race relations contains many illustrations of inconsistencies in people's behavior that is rooted in their conflicting reference groups. Consider the case of white union members during the Detroit race riots in 1943 (Sherif, 1949). The workers were members of unions like the United Auto Workers, which had black members. Union norms called for interracial solidarity and equal job opportunities for blacks. Had these union members been *nothing but* good union members, they would not have participated in the race riots. But they were also members of other groups, especially neighborhood and ethnic groups, that constantly reminded them of their racial membership. In these nonwork settings they acted contrary to the equalitarian dictates of their union roles.

The inconsistency in the union members' behavior can be partially understood in terms of the differing reference groups that operated within the differing contexts. As good union members they participated in campaigns for equal job rights for blacks. But, they had conflicting loyalties. As participants in a race riot, they acted in conformity with their neighborhood and ethnic loyalties. Still, on the job they could behave in a nondiscriminatory fashion on the basis of their union loyalties.

New reference groups may also bring about conformity to new norms despite contrary and well-established practices and attitudes. Take the case of southern rural and small-town white migrants to Chicago who harbor considerable antipathy toward blacks. They express strong preferences for a segregated arrangement and in their daily talk they deplore the fact that blacks are "taking over Chicago." Nonetheless, in most of their behavior they make a peaceful, if reluctant, accommodation to Chicago's pluralist patterns. The sociologist Lewis Killian (1953) finds that while the old segregated South continues to be the reference group for white migrant attitudes, Chicago functions as the reference group for their behavior. Similarly, as patrons of a "hillbilly" tavern these white migrants would be more likely to beat up blacks than permit them to be served. But within the context of a different reference group—the nonsegregated "greasy-spoon" restaurant next door, where they are regular patrons—they eat lunch on a nonsegregated basis. And many of them not only work in plants with blacks, but share the same restrooms and dressing rooms.

Hence, a good deal of accumulating research points to the fact that individuals' attitudes and feelings toward various racial and ethnic groups are not simple and straightforward, but rather diverse, complex, and often *contradictory*. It appears that the *situation* in which individuals find themselves does much to determine which of their *heterogeneous* attitudes and feelings about a minority will be brought into open play. Individuals, then, come into situations of contact with minority groups prepared to respond to them in a number of different ways, some favorable, others unfavorable. *Which responses individuals in fact bring forth depends to a considerable extent upon which of their many reference groups is functioning within the situation to provide them with behavioral standards.*

Some sociologists, among them Joseph D. Lohman and Dietrich C. Reitzes (1952:242), go so far as to suggest that "individual behavior is, for all practical purposes, made a fiction." They believe that the individuals' personal attitude toward minorities is of little consequence in explaining their actual behavior. "The reality is the social fact: the key to the situation and the individual's action is the collectivity. . . ." Most social scientists would probably not concur in such an extreme statement of group determinism. Nevertheless, the role of reference groups in patterning behavior toward minorities is undoubtedly considerable and accepted by most social scientists.

Conformity to the norms of a group is the product of both external and internal forces. The group itself exerts pressure for conformity to its norms by positive and negative means. Conformity is rewarded, encouraged, and approved. Nonconformity is punished by ridicule, scorn, warnings, ostracism, rejection, and even physical assault. Conformity may also be the product of internal forces operating within individuals. In accepting the group's definition of the situation, individuals develop self-conceptions that in effect regulate their conduct in accordance with the norms of the group. Individuals may not see conformity as an act of external coercion. Rather, through conformity, individuals achieve pride, self-identity, a sense of security—products of belonging to a group. It is *their* group, *their* norms. They conform because they have internalized roles that are consistent with the group's norms.

The Thomas Theorem

More than a half-century ago, the sociologist W. I. Thomas (1931:189) noted, "If men [and women] define situations as real, they are real in their consequences." Thomas was pointing to the fact that people respond not only to the objective features of a situation, but also to the *meaning* the situation has for them. Once the meaning has been assigned, it serves to determine not only people's behavior, but also some of the consequences of their behavior.

The Self-fulfilling Prophecy

The Thomas theorem is the foundation of the **self-fulfilling prophecy**. The self-fulfilling prophecy is a false definition of a situation that leads people to engage in behavior that turns the false definition into reality. Accordingly, the act of making a definition is also an act of making a prophecy. The fact that the definition is made creates conditions whereby the prophecy is realized.

Daily life provides numerous illustrations of the workings of the self-fulfilling prophecy. A woman possessing the skills and ability to pass a mathematics examination is convinced that she is destined to fail because "girls don't do well in math." Anxious, she devotes more time to worry than to study, her mind preoccupied with thoughts of failing the examination. In turn she takes the examination and fails. What has happened? Initially she was in a situation in which she was objectively capable of passing the examination. But she defined the examination as one that she could not pass. She defined the situation as real, and accordingly the situation was real in its consequences. She made a definition and then acted in terms of the definition, bringing about the anticipated result.

In the beginning the self-fulfilling prophecy is a *false* definition of the situation. The consequences never would have come about in its absence. But by accepting the false definition, people undertake behavior that makes the initially false state of affairs come true. One of the most difficult points to grasp is that there is no conspiracy to make the definition come true. Rather the fulfillment of the prophecy occurs unintentionally because individuals act as if it were true—in accordance with their beliefs.

The operation of the self-fulfilling prophecy can be observed in the realm of race relations. Many whites define blacks as inferior—as defective in one way or another. The definition is accepted as gospel. The definition is not necessarily intended to accomplish black inferiority; it is simply accepted as fact. But flowing from the definition are a series of consequences. Whites, through their control of social resources and their gatekeeping positions, allocate to blacks a lesser share of the privileges and opportunities of the society. They believe it would be senseless to provide blacks with more because it would be of no avail. But in so doing whites do not give blacks a chance to prove or disprove the definition. Rather the consequences are built into whites' behavior. The very inferiority that was alleged in the initial definition results. Whites then see blacks in menial jobs, with limited education, in poor housing, and with various health problems, and find it easy to conclude that blacks *are* inferior, or at the very least, "different." Although there is no scientific support for the notion of innate black inferiority, whites, believing blacks to be deficient, bring about a disadvantaged state for the great mass of blacks. The prophecy is self-fulfilling. The fact of having made the definition creates the conditions whereby the prophecy is realized. And through time the scars of racism come to feed and justify continued racism.

A study by the social psychologists Pamela C. Rubovits and Martin L. Maehr (1973) points to the part that self-fulfilling expectations play in learning and education. The subjects were sixty-six white female undergraduates enrolled in a teacher-training course. Each student-teacher met with four students, two of whom were black and two of whom were white. The student-teacher was provided the children's names, their IQ scores, and a lesson plan dealing with television. Unknown to the student-teachers, Rubovits and Maehr had rigged the IQ scores by randomly assigning a high IQ (between 130 and 135) to one black student and one white student, each of whom they identified as "gifted." The other black student and the other white student were assigned lower IQ scores (between 98 and 102) and identified as "non-gifted."

Rubovits and Maehr found that the student-teachers gave the greatest amount of attention to the gifted white student. As Table 4.2 reveals, the gifted white student was encouraged more, praised more, and criticized less than the other three students. Further, in informal interviews the student-teachers selected the gifted white student most frequently as the most-liked student, the brightest student, and the student most likely to emerge as a class leader.

Distressingly, the study revealed the prevalence of racist behavior among young, idealistic student-teachers, most of whom expressed liberal sentiments on racial issues. As demonstrated in Table 4.2, both black students received less attention, less encouragement, less praise, and more criticism than both white students. Most startling was the fact that the "gifted" black student was given the least attention, was praised the least, and was criticized the most. Generalizations from these data should be made cautiously. Nonetheless, they do suggest why teachers are often able to do little to equalize the performance levels of blacks and whites.

TABLE 4.2 MEAN NUMBER OF STUDENT-TEACHER RESPONSES TO "GIFTED" AND "NONGIFTED" WHITE AND BLACK STUDENTS

Type of Interaction	White	Black
Total attention		
Gifted	36.1	29.6
Nongifted	32.3	30.3
Encouragement		
Gifted	6.2	5.5
Nongifted	6.3	5.3
Ignoring		
Gifted	5.1	6.9
Nongifted	4.6	6.9
Praise		
Gifted	2.0	0.6
Nongifted	1.3	1.6
Criticism		
Gifted	0.8	1.9
Nongifted	0.7	0.9

Source: Adapted from Pamela C. Rubovits and Martin L. Maehr, "Pygmalion Black and White," *Journal of Personality and Social Psychology* 25 (1973): 212.

The Vicious Circle

The self-fulfilling prophecy may or may not be circular in character. If a self-fulfilling prophecy is circular, *the end is again the beginning,* the reassertion of the beginning, perhaps in a strengthened form. The student who failed the mathematics examination is a case in point. Having failed one examination, the student's self-confidence may be further undermined, her anxiety intensified, to the extent that her studying for subsequent examinations may be further impaired. Accordingly, she fails those examinations as well. Once set in motion the vicious-circle process goes on and on of its own momentum. This is seen historically in the typical case of international armament: armament in country A → fear in country B → armament in country B → fear in country A → armament in country A, and so on.

Gunnar Myrdal (1944), in his classic study of American race relations, speaks of the "self-perpetuating color bar" and concludes that "discrimination breeds discrimination." White prejudice and discrimination maintain low standards of living and poor health and education for blacks. Black disadvantage in turn gives support to white prejudice. White prejudice and black standards thus mutually "cause" each other. In this sense, discrimination begets discrimination. This sequence can

be depicted as follows: discrimination→lower income level→lower
standard of living→lower education→lower earning capacity→dis-
crimination.

The discriminating group begins with an advantage. Through discrimination it cuts the other group off from a wide range of economic
and social privileges and opportunities. The process of discriminating
gives the privileged group a new sense of its superiority, reinforcing its
discriminatory tendencies. Prejudice is in turn ratified by the factual
evidences of inferiority that accompany the lack of opportunity charac-
terizing those who live in poverty, who suffer repeated frustration, who
have little incentive to improve their lot, and who feel themselves to
be social outcasts. In this manner discrimination elicits attitudes and
behaviors favorable to its perpetuation.

Myrdal suggests that by this means a vicious circle can ensue. On the
one hand, the blacks' standard of living is kept down by discrimination
on the part of the whites. On the other hand, the whites' reason for
discrimination is partly dependent on the blacks' quality of life. The
blacks' poverty and problems stimulate and feed white antipathies. And
with their antipathies toward blacks intensified, whites discriminate
against blacks all the more. As a consequence, the blacks' standard of
living suffers and white prejudice mounts. Thus, through time, prejudice and discrimination progressively worsen.

Such formulations, however, must be carefully interpreted or they
may mislead. Social systems are not indefinitely plastic. There are limits
to the variation that occurs within them. The endless cumulation of
effects is checked by such factors as the need for a certain amount of
order, beyond which a system cannot proceed without disruption. Likewise, each variable in the situation is sustained by the others. If one is
changed, there will be the pull and push of the others to bring it back into
line. Furthermore, a given line of development may have one series of
consequences at one stage and different or even opposite effects at later
stages. Thus, whites may go along with black advancement in employment so long as the advancement is limited. But should white jobs be
endangered, whites may mount a devastating counterattack. There is
still another limitation to the vicious-circle interpretation. The support
of "the facts" is not essential to prejudice, as has been shown by the
elaborate cultural equipment for prejudice that most Americans share
even when they know no facts or when they have had no contact with
the people in question.

Acquiring Racist Attitudes and Practices

Socialization is an important mechanism through which racist attitudes and practices are transmitted. However, socialization does not

explain how or why racism emerges in the first place. In this sense, socialization *maintains* but does not *cause* racism. **Socialization** is that process whereby people develop through interaction with others those ways of thinking, feeling, and acting that characterize the members of their society.

Socialization is a lifetime process, one in which individuals learn what to expect and value and how to act in various situations. Through socialization children are inducted into society and acquire its cultural ways. They gain "socially approved knowledge" and "a taken-for-granted" perspective toward existing social arrangements. Consequently, the social world becomes second nature to them. An aura of inevitability comes to surround the fact that some people are advantaged and others disadvantaged. People forget that they create the social world. Alternative social arrangements simply do not come to mind (Newman, 1973).

Racial Awareness

The development of children's racial attitudes and behaviors is a lengthy and complex process. Before children acquire racial beliefs, they must be aware of physical differences among people and categorize individuals with respect to the relevant physical cues (Katz, 1973). Research reveals that children as young as three can correctly identify racial differences between blacks and whites. By the age of five, the vast majority of children can make such identifications accurately (Goodman, 1952; Porter, 1971; Katz, 1976; Williams and Morland, 1976).

A study by J. Kenneth Morland (1958) of 454 nursery-school children in Lynchburg, Virginia, is representative of racial awareness studies. The measuring instrument consisted of a set of eight pictures about which the children were asked to make racial identifications. The ability to recognize racial differences was scored in terms of "high," "medium," or "low," depending on how many times the pictures of blacks and whites were identified correctly. Each child had sixteen chances to do this, two for each picture. They were scored "high" if they missed none or one of the sixteen; "medium," if they missed two or three; and "low," if they missed more than three. Among the three-year-olds tested, fewer than two of ten scored "high," while among the six-year-olds, more than nine of ten scored "high." A regular progression in racial recognition ability takes place with age, with the most rapid spurt occurring during the fourth year.

Research by Phyllis A. Katz and her associates (1975) suggests that during the preschool period, white children attend less to distinguishing characteristics among blacks than they do among whites. For example, the presence of eyeglasses or a smile on black faces is a less important differentiating feature than the same cue is for white faces. During middle childhood, white children explore racial cues more actively and attend more closely to the considerable range of individual differences that exist among both blacks and whites. But as the children advance into adolescence, they once more give less attention to individual differences among blacks, suggesting more stereotyped patterns of perception and thinking.

During the past twenty years the psychologist John E. Williams and his associates have studied racial awareness and attitudes in children (Williams and Morland, 1976). This research suggests that both white and black children show a preference for the color white over the color black when presented with objects colored either white or black. Williams speculates that young children have a preference for white because of their early experiences with light and darkness. Human beings, he argues, require reasonably high levels of illumination to interact effectively with their environment. Williams concludes that children find darkness inherently aversive and that this predisposition translates into a preference for the color white over the color black. This association is reinforced by cultural symbolism that equates white with purity, virginity, virtue, and God and black with filthiness, sin, evil, and the devil. More importantly, the practice of color coding racial groups as "whites" and "blacks" encourages children to generalize color meanings to racial groups. Consequently, the children of both races acquire a pro-Euro-American and an anti-Afro-American bias.

Williams and his associates claim that a pro-white bias persists among both white and black children into the early school years. For instance, black preschoolers display a preference for white children in their choice of playmates. But when black children enter desegregated public schools, they gradually shift to a black racial preference. However, much of the Williams research was undertaken before the full impact of the Black Power movement, with its strong emphasis on black standards of beauty and black cultural heritage, was felt in black communities. Further, some evidence suggests that the association between color bias and racial bias proceeds from racial bias to color bias rather than the reverse as claimed by Williams. Finally, some question exists as to whether skin color is the chief determinant of racial prejudice (Dent, 1978; Sorce, 1979; Steinberg and Hall, 1981). Hair and eye features may play an equally important or an even more important role.

In other research the sociologist Frank R. Westie (1964) studied racial awareness and prejudice among a sample of Indianapolis elementary-school children. He found that the children were relatively unprejudiced and, in general, incapable of coherent, consistent stereotyping. He concludes:

> The vast majority of the 232 grade school children . . . were as incoherent about their out-group preferences and images as children are about almost any other social phenomenon. It is one thing to demonstrate that

prejudice and stereotyping *can,* in some cases, develop in young children; it is quite another to say that they are characteristic of children (Westie, 1964:591).

In conclusion, it appears that children develop racial awareness at an early age. Prejudice, however, seems to be a later development, but at just what age children commonly develop prejudice is not clear. More research is clearly needed on this matter.

The Transmission of Racial Attitudes

Learning that one is a "white" or a "black" is part of the process of acquiring one's self-identity. Children learn their racial role in much the same manner in which they learn other roles. They acquire the symbols and expectations appropriate to their racial role and in the process come to answer the question: "Who am I?" Society provides them with the answer through the experience of everyday life. In answering this question children also need to answer its corollary: "And who are all those?" The answers to these questions are already contained in the culture of the society and are transmitted to children by parents and peers.

Olive Westbrooke Quinn's (1954) study of the transmission of racial attitudes among southern whites sheds additional light on the process. She interviewed high-school and college youths in Tennessee, Arkansas, and Mississippi. Direct instruction played a relatively unimportant role in the transmission to them of racial attitudes. Even the most perceptive and self-analytical of the young people had difficulty producing any memories of the direct teaching of such attitudes. For the most part, verbal instruction had been avoided.

Racial attitudes were largely "caught, rather than taught." When verbal instructions were given, they were generally preceded by some incident in which the child violated the racial norms:

> One time when I was leaving to go to kindergarten, I kissed my nurse. Father waited until I was in the car with him, and then he told me not to. I asked why, but Father was very domineering, and he told me I was too young to understand and that I'd just have to do as he said (Quinn, 1954:42).

While direct verbal instruction was seldom used, indirect verbal instruction was not avoided. Indirect verbal instruction, given by the simple expedient of letting the child "overhear" adult conversation, constituted a major means of transmitting racial attitudes. As Quinn suggests, it is probably not accidental, except in a few cases, when parents permit their children to overhear adult conversation. Ordinarily, parents exercise care that their children will not hear things about which they are considered "too young" to know. However, when adults freely discuss sexual "looseness" and "immorality" among blacks in the presence of children but maintain a strict silence on the subject of white sexual irregularities, it is difficult to escape the conclusion that they are not averse to their children hearing such talk:

> I knew Alma [a black] lived with men. It's funny, I never heard much talk about the morals of white people; it came to me as a decided shock that white people are often sexually immoral, but I have always known—or nearly always—that colored people are not hampered by morals. I never heard any tales of sexual immorality involving white people until I was considered grown (Quinn, 1954:43).

The shortcomings and deficiences of black employees are freely paraded before children, and stereotyped images of black behavior are related. The following excerpts from a diary kept by Quinn is revealing on this point:

> Tonight I went to Bea's for the evening. She and her mother were very much elated that at last they had found a Negro woman who had agreed to come to the house and do the laundry. All of us were sitting on the front porch, Bea, her mother, Sue and I. Mrs. White was laying plans for the morrow. "Bea," she said, "remind me to lock up the silver tomorrow. We don't know a thing about this nigger." Then she turned to me, "You know, you can't trust any of them. I always lock up my good silver" (Quinn, 1954:44).

These remarks of Mrs. White were not addressed to her granddaughter, Sue, but they did not escape her. By listening to the casual conversation of adults, she had again had the lesson driven home that blacks were untrustworthy. In the process of growing up, children identify with their parents. Children "try on" the behavior of adults. In this manner, they assimilate and internalize the norms in the world about them.

Another indirect means by which racial attitudes are communicated to children is through instructing them not to make disparaging remarks about blacks; rather, they are told that they must not let the black know their genuine feelings. But implicit within such instruction rests the assumption of black inferiority, the underlying premise of which appears as an unquestioned fact within this context. The child may be instructed to respect black feelings and rights, yet the overtone is unmistakable that the black is helpless, servile, and inferior. Further, such instruction may have an additional impact as reflected in this observation by one youth: "You know, I think from the fact that I was told so often that I must treat colored people with consideration, I got the idea that I could mistreat them if I wanted to" (Quinn, 1954:43). In short, this youth had come to view his parent's admonitions as an invitation to engage in the contrary behavior. When parents seem excessive in their warnings, the fact may not escape the child. The child interprets the parents' words as in effect saying: *I don't really believe this myself. That is why I keep repeating it. I keep saying it over and over to convince* both *you and myself that I genuinely mean it. But I really have considerable inner doubt. That is why I can't be satisfied with just saying it once or twice. I need to constantly assert it. So don't take me seriously.*

Children take on their society's "people habits" in much the same fashion that they take on its food habits. Just as all foods are not regarded as equally palatable, all peoples are not regarded as equally acceptable. Children soon learn which foods are "good" and which foods are "not so good." By similar mechanisms they learn which people are "good" and which people are "not so good."

There are numerous indirect means by which attitudes toward minorities are communicated to children. Cues are constantly given the children as to appropriate and inappropriate behavior. A general atmosphere may prevail of racial or ethnic antagonism, an atmosphere of which the child is not unaware. From parental actions and inactions—big and small—their gestures, facial expressions, tone of voice, rapidity of speech, muscular movement, speed and rhythm of breathing, and other cues, sentiments are communicated. Parents are usually under the impression that they are not the ones responsible for teaching their children prejudice. Often they are not doing so consciously, but unconsciously cues are being emitted by them. Parents may actually seek to avoid the topic: "We don't discuss race in front of him." But the very failure to openly discuss race suggests to the child that perhaps the parents feel "uncomfortable" on the subject, itself a significant cue.

SUMMARY

1. Once racism has arisen within a society, it may continue even when the originating sources wane or disappear. Racism becomes embedded within the social and cultural fabric of society. In this sense it is institutionalized in the manner of other social patterns.

2. Culture provides guideposts for intergroup relations. The interaction between members of the dominant and minority groups is mapped out or patterned by culture. The guideposts of a culture are norms. Conformity is demanded to racial norms just as to the other norms of a society.

3. One index of the role of culture in patterning prejudice is the degree of similarity that exists in the responses of a society's members to various racial and ethnic groups. A familiar technique, devised by Emory S. Bogardus, seeks to measure the social distance at which members of one group hold another group and its members. A similar pattern of preference is found across the nation, varying little with income, region, education, occupation, and ethnic membership.

4. Our perception of the physical world is never a photographic

image. People differ considerably in the world they "see." Many factors enter into our perception of the world, one of which is culture. Cultural definitions affect individuals' perceptions of racial and ethnic groups.

5. A close relationship holds between individuals' attitudes and their reference group. Research by Leonard Pearlin shows that the process of acquiring more favorable attitudes toward blacks involves both disattachment and attachment: disattachment from previous reference groups unfavorable to blacks and attachment to new reference groups favorable to blacks. Stereotypes and attitudes are anchored in group experience.

6. We are members of a large number of groups, many of which possess contrasting subcultures and even clashing countercultures. The differing groups often make conflicting demands upon us and as a consequence our behavior periodically appears to be inconsistent. Individuals come into situations of contact with minority groups prepared to respond to them in a number of different ways, some favorable, others unfavorable. Which responses individuals in fact bring forth depends to a considerable extent upon which of their many reference groups is functioning within the situation to provide them with behavioral standards.

7. A number of decades ago, the sociologist W.I. Thomas noted, "If men [and women] define situations as real, they are real in their consequences." The Thomas theorem is the foundation of the self-fulfilling prophecy. In the beginning the self-fulfilling prophecy is a false definition of the situation. The fulfillment of a prophecy occurs unintentionally because individuals act as if it were true. The self-fulfilling prophecy results in whites, believing blacks to be inferior and deficient, bringing about a disadvantaged state for the great mass of blacks.

8. The self-fulfilling prophecy may become caught up in a vicious circle. The self-fulfilling prophecy is circular, the end becoming again the beginning. As a consequence, discrimination breeds discrimination. White prejudice and discrimination keep black living, health, and education standards low. Black disadvantage in turn gives support to white prejudice. White prejudice and black standards thus mutually "cause" each other.

9. The development of children's racial attitudes and behaviors is a lengthy and complex process. Before children acquire racial beliefs, they must be aware of physical differences among people and categorize individuals with respect to relevant physical cues. Research reveals that children as young as three years can correctly identify racial differences between blacks and whites. By the age of five, the vast majority of children can make such identifications accurately.

10. Racial attitudes are largely "caught, rather than taught." Parents provide children with indirect verbal instruction by letting children

"overhear" adult conversations. Further, the shortcomings and deficiencies of blacks may be freely paraded before children. Children may acquire racist attitudes when their parents instruct them not to make racist statements, yet the admonition constitutes an invitation to engage in the contrary behavior. Children take on their society's "people habits" in much the same fashion that they take on its food habits.

GLOSSARY

Culture   A set of ready-made definitions of the situation which each person only slightly retailors in his or her own unique manner. It is a set of blueprints for action.

Reference Group   A social unit with which individuals identify. It is that group that provides the standards and anchorage regulating people's behavior within a particular context.

Self-fulfilling Prophecy   A false definition of a situation that leads people to engage in behavior that turns the false definition into reality.

Social Distance   A subjective sense of being set apart from (as opposed to being near to) members of a particular group.

Socialization   The process whereby people develop through interaction with others those ways of thinking, feeling, and acting that characterize the members of their society.

Personality Bulwarks of Racism 5

*R*acism may satisfy a variety of personal needs, so that racist attitudes and behaviors therefore may become rooted in the basic personality structures of some individuals. Chapters 3 and 4 considered how the interpersonal dynamics of prejudice and discrimination among the members of differing ethnic and racial groups foster and maintain racist institutions. Since these factors have to do with social interaction among people, they are termed "group-centered" orientations. Other approaches are "personality centered." Rather than emphasizing what occurs *between* people, personality-centered theories stress what goes on *within* people. These latter theories interpret dominant-minority relations primarily in terms of personalities. Since prejudice is a state of mind, and as such is "carried" in specific individuals, some social scientists insist that we look for the sources of prejudice within the individual personality. These social scientists are often quite critical of "group-centered" social scientists, who they feel view individuals as "interchangeable specimens of gutless creatures" (Newcomb, 1954: 237). In turn, "group-centered" social scientists accuse their "personality-centered" counterparts of depicting prejudice as some sort of individual disorder, ignoring the fact that society is organized in such a manner as to manufacture and stimulate intergroup hostility.

For the most part, personality-centered theories tell us little about the origins of racism—how and why one group to be disdained is singled out while others are not. They are helpful, however, in understanding how racism may be maintained and even intensified. They particularly provide us with insights into the personality bulwarks of racism.

Frustration and Aggression

During the 1930s and 1940s the personality theories of Sigmund Freud came to occupy a major place in the work of American psychologists. Freud stressed the part that unconscious motivation—stemming from impulses buried below the level of awareness—plays in individuals' behavior. According to Freud, human behavior arises out of the struggle that takes place between instinctual drives associated with sex and aggression and societal prohibitions. As a consequence of being forbidden and punished, many of these impulses are driven out of our awareness. Nonetheless, they still affect the our behavior, finding new expression in slips of the tongue, dreams, religion, art, literature, myth, and symptoms of mental pathology. When Freudian concepts were applied to the realm of race relations by psychologists like John Dollard (1939), the result was the scapegoat theory of prejudice.

The Scapegoat Theory of Prejudice

During the past forty years the scapegoat theory has provided a popular explanation of prejudice. The major postulates of the theory are the following:

1. *Needs.* All individuals experience a variety of needs. Some of these needs are biologically induced, like hunger, thirst, sex, and sleep, and others are socially induced, like a desire for social rewards, rights, and privileges.

2. *Frustration.* For one reason or another individuals often find themselves *blocked* from realizing their needs or desires. In a word, individuals are *frustrated.*

3. *Aggression.* Frustrated individuals experience anger, which disposes them toward aggressive actions. Blocked in realizing their needs or desires (especially where the blockage is repeated and persistent), they become enraged, boiling cauldrons of anger. They want to strike out, to destroy, to tear to pieces.

4. *Displacement.* Enraged people need to vent their emotions and it makes little or no difference against whom they direct their aggressive feelings. If some specific person is guilty of contributing to their frustration, they will direct their aggression against that person. But at times this is not possible. It may be dangerous to attack another, especially if the person is a powerful figure. Thus children frustrated by parents or students thwarted by a professor cannot generally strike back at the source; it would be too dangerous. Similarly frustration may stem not only from identifiable persons but from some impersonal events, "fate," pervasive source, or even one's own acts or thoughts of commission and omission. In such circumstances, there is no direct external source against whom one can retaliate. Nevertheless, the impulse to vent anger persists. Under such circumstances people unconsciously, at times consciously, seek out a person, group, or object on which to "take out" their feelings; they find a "scapegoat." When hostilities are

removed from the source or sources of frustration and discharged upon a scapegoat, the process is referred to as **displacement.** Displacement appears to be a common practice. More than one person has complained to a frustrated friend after receiving an unwarranted attack, "Don't take it out on me."

5. *Weak Victims.* Hostile aggression is more conveniently displaced on those people who are too weak or defenseless to strike back with retaliatory aggression. They become the innocent victims of aggression. The student enraged by a poor grade, unable to retaliate against the professor, responds to a trivial remark by a roommate with harsh, angry, and abusive words. The husband who encounters difficulties and irritations at work comes home in the evening ready, upon the slightest provocation, to snap at family members and vent his anger. Family members learn to watch for cues of such feelings, to "soft-pedal" requests, and to behave at these times as unobtrusively as possible.

Aggression may also be deflected toward minorities, because they are often portrayed as too weak or defenseless to strike back. The southern white reaction to blacks following the Civil War is taken by Dollard (1957) to be a case in point. He attributes the postwar upsurge in racism to displaced hostility that arose from southern social disorganization and resentment toward the victorious North. In brief, after the bloody Civil War, the South turned its spent and fruitless hostility to the blacks. Since white southerners could not avenge themselves directly against the North, they turned their aggression against the blacks for whom the North had fought. To punish the blacks represented a kind of deflected expression of hostility toward the victors, who had won the actual war but who could not win the fight for black freedom. Blacks and Yankees became associated in the mind of white southerners.

6. *Rationalization.* Generally the expression of hostile impulses toward one's fellows is discouraged, even prohibited by moral and ethical considerations, by norms. To "take out" one's feelings upon an *innocent* individual or group would conflict even more with such norms. Given the democratic creed of America, such behavior would bespeak rank injustice, hatred, and irrationality. It would tend to offend one's feelings of self-pride, morality, and intelligence. If one is to avoid feelings of self-condemnation, of guilt, it is essential that some excuse be available to sanction such behavior. In brief, the behavior, otherwise immoral, must be made to appear both rational and morally acceptable. Humans are quite ingenious in coming up with excuses for their behavior. This process is referred to as **rationalization.** Individuals justify their behavior by finding some convincing reason why they can hate and discriminate against a minority group. Accordingly, a racist ideology tends

to be evolved. Whites can then rationalize: "I hate blacks because they are criminally inclined, dirty, immoral, lazy, and irresponsible." In this manner they can feel justified for their feelings.

Experimental Evidence of Scapegoating

Any number of studies have been conducted in an attempt to test the scapegoating hypothesis experimentally. One of the earliest of these projects was undertaken by Neal E. Miller and Richard Bugelski (1948). The subjects of the experiment were thirty-one young men between the ages of eighteen and twenty, working at a government camp. The researchers learned that the young men were about to experience a frustrating situation. As part of the educational program of the camp, they were going to be required to take a long, uninteresting test, a test promising to be so difficult that everyone was bound to fail miserably. Furthermore, the test would run far overtime so that the young men would miss what they had looked forward to as the most interesting event of the otherwise dull week: bank night at the local theater. This event was awaited with special eagerness, as the previous week one member of the group had won $200 at a similar event.

Accordingly, two frustrating experiences were awaiting the men. To the extent to which they were motivated to succeed on the tests, they were bound to experience frustration by virtue of failure. To the extent to which they were motivated to attend bank night, they were bound to experience frustration by the interference of the testing program. The frustration and aggressive feelings that the experimenters anticipated under these circumstances were confirmed. Before and after the frustrating situation, the young men were tested as to their attitudes toward a number of minority groups. It was found that after the frustrating situations there was a definite decrease in the number of favorable items checked. The experimenters concluded that aggression aroused by the ingroup authorities in blocking the desires of these young men were generalized and displaced to the outgroup minorities. Apparently the production of generalized feelings of hostility is particularly great when the frustration is experienced as unreasonable, unjust, and unnecessary.

Limitations of the Scapegoat Theory

Although a number of studies have tended to confirm the scapegoat hypothesis, still others have contradicted it (Vander Zanden, 1981). Apparently the predictive value of the hypothesis has been limited by its focus on the motivational states of individuals, while overlooking a number of other relevant factors or variables. Let us examine a few of these.

The Personality of the Displacer.   Leonard Berkowitz (1962) holds that highly prejudiced individuals will displace aggression more than nonprejudiced individuals when confronted with equally frustrating situations. In other words, whether displacement occurs depends not merely upon the objective fact of frustration or upon the availability of objects for displacement, but also upon the personality of the individual. Berkowitz's experiment involved female college students who had scored either very high or very low on an anti-Semitism attitude scale. These students were individually subjected either to an annoying, frustrating treatment by the experimenter or to a more neutral, nonfrustrating experience with him. After this treatment, the students were given a topic to discuss with another young woman, but unknown to them this person was actually the experimenter's confederate. A questionnaire rating by the confederate immediately after the conclusion of the discussion constituted the hostility index. In comparison with the nonfrustrated, highly anti-Semitic students, the frustrated highly anti-Semitic students gave evidence of increased unfriendliness toward their peer (in reality, the confederate). On the other hand, tolerant students who received the harsh treatment displayed greater friendliness to the other students. For the highly anti-Semitic students, then, the hostility engendered by the frustrating experimenter presumably displaced to the neutral bystander. This displacement did not occur in the less prejudiced group. Similar results were obtained when the confederate was given a "Jewish" name. Hence, Berkowitz concludes that highly prejudiced individuals are more prone to seek scapegoats than less prejudiced individuals.

Similarly individuals differ in how they handle frustration. Not all people respond to frustration by aggression. Individuals may respond with some new or added effort by which to realize their goal. Or they may substitute a different goal. Then, again, they may respond by regression, a lowering of their level of performance, evasion of the situation by leaving it, or by apathy and resignation. The reaction to frustration varies according to the circumstances and an individual's perception of them.

Even should frustration foster aggressive impulses, aggression need not be displaced. Some individuals are intrapunitive—they direct their aggressive impulses inward against themselves rather than outward against the world. Such individuals tend to "bottle up" their rage—to take their rage out on themselves—a fact that symptomatically may express itself in headaches, ulcers, or psychological depression. Nathan W. Ackerman and Marie Jahoda (1950) indicate that among their anti-Semitic patients they failed to find any cases of deep depression, a fact that they attribute to the tendency of anti-Semites to handle rage through attacks upon others (extrapunitiveness) rather than through intrapunitive reactions.

The Kind of Frustration Involved. A number of social scientists have suggested that people are more likely to seek scapegoats in response to some kinds of frustration than to others. The psychologists Seymour Feshbach and Robert Singer (1957) investigated this possibility in differing responses to personal and shared threats. While a personal threat poses a danger primarily to individuals themselves, a shared threat constitutes a danger to the larger society of which individuals are a part. Feshbach and Singer randomly assigned the members of introductory psychology classes to six groups: three personal threat groups (marital failure, mental illness, and severe personal injury); two shared threat groups (the danger of flood and hurricane and the possibility of atomic war); and a control group (a group that was exposed to none of the threats and to which the other five groups were later compared).

Tests measuring attitudes toward blacks were administered to the students. Four weeks later five of the groups (but not the control group) were asked to discuss mimeographed statements about one of the five threats (each group receiving statements concerning a different threat). After the discussions, attitudes toward blacks were again measured in each of the five groups and the control group. All three personal threat groups gained significantly in prejudice beyond the change in the control group. On the other hand, the flood and hurricane group experienced an appreciable decline in prejudice toward blacks. Feshbach and Singer suggest that this was perhaps a result of a sense of shared fate. The group discussing the threat of an atomic war, however, displayed a gain in prejudice. It is conceivable that the frequent linkage of atomic war with the Soviet Union resulted in hostility to Russians, which the students then displaced upon blacks. In conclusion, the study by Feshbach and Singer suggests that some kinds of frustration are more likely to produce hostility directed at scapegoats than others.

The Perceived Qualities of Potential Targets. Critics of the scapegoat hypothesis have noted that aggression is not always displaced upon an innocent victim or upon the safest available target. The hypothesis fails to explain, for instance, why at times minorities displace their hostilities against dominant groups. For some minorities the dominant group is not a defenseless target; in fact, it may be quite powerful. Further, individuals of the political "left" may look for scapegoats among groups that are economically privileged or powerful. The scapegoat, then, may not always be a "safe goat" as the theory would lead us to believe.

The fact that aggression is not always displaced upon an innocent victim or upon the safest available target has led some social scientists to raise this question: Are some groups commonly perceived in such a fashion that they constitute particularly vulnerable or susceptible targets for the displacement of aggression? Leonard Berkowitz (1962) answers the question in the affirmative. Experimentally he has demonstrated that hostility will be displaced from the frustrater to another individual in direct ratio to the degree of dislike for this latter person.

In his experiments Berkowitz administered shocks to individuals who were working as partners on a common task. The subjects believed the shocks were applied by their partner and hence they acquired a dislike for the partner. Later the subjects were frustrated by one of the experimenters. The frustrated subjects were then presented with a task involving two potential targets for their hostility: the person they had been trained to dislike and a neutral individual. The study revealed that the frustrated subjects directed considerably more aggression against the disliked person than against the neutral person. Berkowitz concludes that groups used as scapegoats are groups that individuals for one reason or another have *already* learned to dislike.

Berkowitz suggests still another point. A disliked group can be associated with an immediate frustrater, permitting the transfer of hostility aroused by the latter to the former. Hence, industrial workers may become more hostile to Jews in their community after receiving a cut in pay if they associate the disliked Jews with the non-Jewish factory owners. The workers may regard both the factory owners and Jews as rich and unscrupulous. Frustrated, they identify Jews with the immediate frustrater (the factory owners) and displace their rage from the factory owners to Jews.

The Role of Culture.   Whether individuals display open aggression depends in part on the degree to which their culture or subculture *permits* aggression. In some societies, aggressive behavior may be viewed as the mark of a "real man" and hence be encouraged and rewarded. The Kwakiutl of the Pacific Northwest are a people who have integrated their lives around a pattern of intense rivalry. In other societies aggression may be regarded as an evil force that disrupts group harmony. This latter view characterized the Zuñi of the American Southwest, who placed cooperation at the center of their social organization. Among some occupational groups within the United States— sailors, marines, soldiers, lumberjacks, longshoremen, and oil field workers—a "he-man" subgroup actively fosters violent interpersonal aggression. The man who exclaims, "I don't believe in fighting" wins no popularity contests. Similarly, W. J. Cash (1954) describes the "one-hell-of-a-fellow" complex among southern males. Such males, more rare today than in former times, idealize violence and interpersonal aggression. In contrast, some groups define overt aggression and fighting as sinful or at least ungentlemanly and uncivilized. Many Christians define Christ's Sermon on the Mount as suggesting that aggression in any form is evil:

In brief, there are varieties of cultural settings in which aggression is expressed and even encouraged and others in which aggression is defined as improper or immoral. Whether or not one expresses his aggressions is not simply a consequence of the degree of psychological frustration. The definitions of appropriate behavior provided by the groups in which one acts are equally important in determining the outcome of frustration (Westie, 1964:610).

Our observations suggest that directing hostility against scapegoats is a more complex phenomenon than early formulations of the theory led us to believe. We need to take into account a variety of other factors. It is also important to note that the scapegoat model overlooks the possibility of realistic social conflict. What may appear to be displacement in some instances may be aggression directed against the true source of the frustration. In circumstances of economic, power, or status competition, aggression breeds counteraggression.

Projection

Projection involves the tendency of people to attribute to others motives or traits that they sense within themselves but that would be painful to acknowledge. It is a mechanism by which attitudes and behavior that cannot be accepted in the self are attributed to others. In brief, we see others as we are ourselves. To the alcoholic it may be the other fellow who drinks too much; to the failing student it may be the teacher who is incompetent; to the football player making a stupid play it may be the quarterback who was in error; to the hostile and aggressive boy it may be the other lad who started the fight. For the business manager the thought that "I'm going to ruin this Jew and run him out of business" is one that generally evokes feelings of guilt and shame. In projection it becomes, "The Jews are trying to ruin me and run me out of business." Aggression against the Jew then becomes justified self-defense. Jews are portrayed as "deserving" to be ruined for their "unethical" practices. Projection is a prevalent mechanism in dominant-minority relations.

Projection and the Cultural Heritage

Whites in the United States and South Africa have stereotyped the members of a number of minorities, especially blacks, as consumed by inordinate sexual desire. The prevalence of these notions has led some social scientists to seek an answer in psychological mechanisms of projection. These social scientists note that both American and South African whites have had long cultural traditions that have defined sex in rather negative terms: "dirty," "filthy," "nasty," and even "sinful."

According to this view, the Fathers of the Christian Church contributed in no small way to Western hostility toward sex. Celibacy as an ideal state, superior to marriage, was developed. Saint Paul declared, "But I say to the unmarried and to widows, it is good for them if they abide even as I. But if they have not continency, let them marry: For it is better to marry than to burn" (Bible, 1 Cor. 7:8–9). The mother of Christ, the Virgin Mary, was honored in part for her virginity, a cornerstone of her purity, since sex was seen as defiling and degrading. With time came the ascetic cults, the founding of monasteries, and the establishment of celibacy as a requirement for the clergy. Saint Augustine in his *City of God* drew a distinction between the city of God and the city of the devil, implying a dichotomy and an antithesis between the spirit and the flesh. Christian leaders frequently commented on fleshly lust as being intrinsically evil.

Projection psychologists say that these teachings have had social consequences. Given a cultural heritage that sexual desire is wrong, the feeling of such desire is often experienced as a terrible thing, to be shunned at all costs. Yet it is an inevitable aspect of physical functioning. It cannot be entirely avoided for sexual desire makes itself felt. Many individuals are thus placed in a dilemma. On the one hand, they cannot deny the existence of the feeling. On the other hand, they cannot admit that they themselves harbor such feelings, feelings that by definition are "lustful" and "sinful." Unable to repress awareness of sexual desire, they instead repress the recognition of its origin within themselves, and the lustfulness is projected outside of themselves on others. The mechanism can be stated in these terms: "I may feel sexual desire, but I am not responsible for it. You are. I am aware of lustful feelings. But it is *your* lust, *not mine,* that I am seeing."

Projection and Notions of Inordinate Black Sexuality

Some psychologists say that the projection of sexual desire is of considerable aid in helping us to understand the preoccupation that southern whites historically have had with black sexuality and the fear of black sexual attack. Discussions of the race issue with racists and southern segregationists often boil down to the question: "Would you want your sister (or daughter) to marry a black?" But why such concern with this issue? Since it takes two to make a legal marriage, supposedly the white sister or daughter could refuse a black suitor. Freudian psychologists insist that the question does not make sense on the conscious level. But it does make sense, they say, if there is a repressed or unconscious feeling of sexual attraction among whites for blacks (Dollard, 1957; MacCrone, 1937; Hernton, 1965). A clear implication of the question is that a white woman would have no hesitation in marrying a black, and, in fact, would readily do so once there is genuine social equality between whites and blacks.

Freudian psychologists reason as follows. Prejudiced whites often call nonbigoted whites "nigger-lovers." The choice of the word suggests that the racists are fighting a feeling of attraction for blacks within themselves (Allport, 1954). Further, white racist stereotypes depict blacks as uninhibited, rhythmic, and passionate. In a word, the black becomes an image—a symbol—for free and passionate sex. Experiencing sexual desire, white Americans, by virtue of their puritanical traditions (traditions that are particularly prevalent within the South), are often required to repress their feelings. But, in repressing them, it becomes easy to externalize them—to project these feelings upon the black. It is the black who is uninhibited, rhythmic, and passionate—the very qualities many whites would themselves like to express. Such projection is facilitated by the less stringent sex codes found among lower-socioeconomic-class blacks. Accordingly, many whites do not find it difficult to embellish upon the theme of black sexuality.

By virtue of this projection, say Freudian psychologists (Hernton, 1965; West, 1965; Fanon, 1967), the black becomes sexually tempting and attractive. The black has sex appeal, *plus*—even a good many whites agree to this! Black women are commonly depicted in racist jokes, stories, and folklore as especially voluptuous, sensual, and passionate, and, accordingly, implicitly desirable as sexual partners. Dollard (1957) indicates that the image of the black woman in the talk and fantasy of southern racists was that of a seducing, accessible person dominated by sexual feeling and, so far as straight-out sexual gratification goes, desirable. In jokes the black woman was represented as a crude, direct person, with little suppression or veiling of her sexual interest. The remark was current in "Southerntown" (a pseudonym for a Mississippi community) that a man did not know what sexual experience was until he had had an experience with a black woman.

Likewise, white racists portray the black male as especially virile and capable. Dollard (1957) reports that the idea was prevalent that black males are more like savages than humans and that their sexual appetites are more vigorous and ungoverned than those of white men. And the belief was prevalent in "Southerntown" that the genitals of black men are larger than those of white men. Consequently, it is not difficult for racists to conclude, at least on an unconscious level, that one's daughter or sister may actually find black men attractive as husbands. Do not women generally find virile, capable men attractive? Simultaneously such projection permits vicarious gratification of forbidden desires. By focusing thoughts on and telling stories of black immorality, whites can compensate in part for their inability or failure to implement their own desires.

The white image of the black, then, makes the black sexually attractive. But such sentiments cannot be reckoned with openly—they are "disgraceful" and even "sinful." Although repressed—unconscious— they make their presence known in the preoccupation that many whites have with black sexuality, betraying sexual attraction. Thus, Freudian psychologists note what many laypeople have also observed, namely, those people who make vehement but unnecessary protestations of their innocence of, or of their horror at, certain types of behavior reveal their own attraction to the behavior. It is not unusual to find in life the former prostitute who is a militant, fanatical crusader against vice or the former Communist who is a militant leader in the fight against Communism. A similar principle is said to operate with the white racist who constantly asks, "Would you want your daughter (or sister) to marry a black?"

The psychoanalyst Robert Seidenberg (1952) provides an interesting case illustrating this general principle. One of his white patients inquired of him, "Is it true that Negroes have extra long penises and that they are erect all the time? Wouldn't it be disgusting to have intercourse with a Negro?" Later in therapy it was revealed that this woman could experience sexual pleasure with her husband only when she fantasized that a "large black Negro" was trying to rape her. In a word, her preoccupation with the issue and disavowal of it betrayed her own attraction to black males.

The matter is intensified by the fact that historically it was white males, not black males, who most frequently transgressed the caste line and sexually engaged women of the other racial group. If white men can find black women so titillating, why then may not white women find black men exciting? And if black men are especially accomplished copulators—indeed sexual athletes—white women may like them especially well. This final blow to the white man's pride in his masculinity has to be avoided at all costs. And it has been avoided at the cost of all blacks who have ever been lynched under the faintest suspicion of intercourse with a white woman. Even at the present time, compared to other defendants, black men who assault white women are more likely to have their cases filed as felonies, receive sentences, and be incarcerated in state penitentiaries (LaFree, 1980). Finally, since white men feel sexually threatened by the presumed attraction of black men for white women and white women for black men, white men seek to thwart integration (Stember, 1976).

The sociologist Gary I. Schulman (1974) says that circumstances that make salient the sexuality of black males can activate the potential for racist violence among white men. He investigated this view in a controlled laboratory experiment. His subjects were white male college students from relatively stable homes whose self-identification and political attitudes were decidedly liberal. By no stretch of the imagination could the subjects be considered bigots, nor were they mentally troubled, southern-reared, or economically competitive with blacks.

Each subject was placed in a conflict situation: he had to choose between cheating at a task (assigned him by the experimenter) to prevent someone else from being given electric shocks and not cheating and thus allowing an innocent victim to experience pain. The number of times that the subjects failed to cheat was compared under four experimental conditions: (1) when the victim was a white male, (2) when the victim was a white male known to be sexually involved with a black female, (3) when the victim was a black male, and (4) when the victim was a black male known to be sexually involved with a white female. The subjects were led to believe that the study dealt with intuition, empathy, and extrasensory perception.

All comparisons of the pain given to a white versus a black victim showed the black victim receiving significantly more pain: an 80 percent rate in condition four (the black male-white female situation); 70 percent in condition three (the lone black male situation); 48 percent in condition one (the lone white male situation); and 36 percent in condition two (the white male-black female situation). The data support the hypothesis that liberal-minded white males are capable of violent racial behavior. The results also support the sexual-threat hypothesis since the black victim known to be sexually involved with a white female received more electric shocks than victims under any other condition.

Notions of Inordinate Sexuality among Other Minorities

Dominant-group whites have also attributed inordinate sexuality to minorities other than blacks. Freudian psychologists suggest that here too the explanation is to be sought in projection mechanisms. During the decades preceding the Civil War a rash of anti-Catholic books appeared as "convent disclosures." Later evidence exposed these "disclosures" as frauds, but not before intense anti-Catholic sentiment had been aroused by them. Nuns and priests were vividly depicted as engaging in licentious practices and infanticide (Meyers, 1960). Dark tales of sexual debauchery have long been a staple of Catholic-haters' propaganda.

Among the more scurrilous of these attacks were those launched against the Catholic clergy after the turn of the twentieth century by the former Populist leader and United States senator from Georgia, Tom Watson. In Watson's widely circulated magazine, the confessional was depicted as a place "in which a lewd priest sows the minds of girls and married women with lascivious suggestions." It was "an open way to damnation along which untold thousands of our sisters have traveled to hell." The Catholic confessional was pictured as a snare where there were made "secret confessions to unmarried Lotharios, parading as priests and enjoying themselves carnally with the choicest women of the earth." Watson betrays his own probable subconscious projection of debauchery to priests in his assertion that in the confessional "the priest finds out what girls and married women he can seduce. Having discovered the trail, *he wouldn't be human,* if he did not take advantage of the opportunity." Watson assumed—projected—that what was "human" for him held true for others as well.

Not dissimilar charges have been directed against Jews and rabbis. Watson, fanning the flames of hate against Leo Frank, a Jew framed in the rape-murder of a white fourteen-year-old Georgia girl, wrote, "Leo Frank was a typical young Jewish man of business who lives for pleasure *and runs after Gentile girls.* Every student of sociology knows that the black man's lust after the white woman *is not much fiercer than the lust of the licentious Jew for the Gentile.*" Frank was subsequently hanged by an armed mob of twenty-five or thirty men grandiosely styling themselves "a vigilance committee." In Europe it also has been a common practice to accuse Jews of gross sexual immorality. In Hitler's Germany in particular, Jews were depicted as given to overindulgence, rape, and perversion. A special newspaper was formed for the purpose of warning the "chaste and innocent" Germans against alleged Jewish sexual perverts who ostensibly derived diabolical pleasure from raping "Aryan" women (Loewenstein, 1951). Yet it was precisely the Elite Guard of "Aryan" masculinity, the S.S., who were infamous for, among other things, raping Jewish women.

Jews as Living Inkblots

Historically Jews have represented a particularly suitable projection screen for people's conflicts. It is easy to project one's own unacceptable feelings on an external object that lacks a clear, sharp structure of its own. Psychologists employ this principle in various "projective tests" of which the Rorschach test is the best known. In the formless inkblot, people are capable of "seeing" an extraordinary number of things. In the process of interpreting inkblots, individuals project their intimate fantasy life and general personality pattern. Thus, projective tests are useful tools in psychology. Ackerman and Jahoda (1950:58) note that for the anti-Semite "the Jew is a living Rorschach inkblot." The Jew is portrayed culturally as many things: as "successful" and as "low class," as "capitalist" and as "Communist," as "clannish" and as "intruder into other people's society," as "oversexed" and as "impotent," and as "strong" and as "weak." Thus the image of the Jew is unstructured. Jews might be almost anything. As such, Jews have constituted an especially suitable "inkblot" for the projection of traits and motives that one cannot acknowledge within oneself.

On the basis of a study of forty patients exhibiting anti-Semitism in psychoanalytic treatment, Ackerman and Jahoda concluded that not only do different people attribute different and mutually contradictory characteristics to Jews, but the same individual may make quite inconsistent accusations against them. One man asserted that Jews were degraded robbers and at another time that they were too ethical. One woman contended that Jews are the incarnation of vulgarity but simultaneously they represented to her the symbol of a God figure. Accordingly, Jews might represent almost anything and as such become a projection screen for inner conflict. One woman patient accused Jews of being shams and fakers, capable of realizing high positions by unfair means. She herself was a highly successful businesswoman. Psychiatric analysis indicated that the woman continuously accused herself of having secured success without merit, by being a "faker" who "bluffed" her way into positions of prestige.

Bruno Bettelheim and Morris Janowitz (1950) suggest that prejudiced individuals are prone to project onto Jews those tendencies represented by the demands of the person's own conscience or superego. Within the United States, failure to realize success goals is generally attributed to one's own shortcomings. Such alleged traits of Jews as "ambitious," "hard working," "cooperative" (clannish), "resolute," "perseverant," "shrewd," and "intelligent" remind some individuals of their own failure to live up to societal expectations, expectations that have become an integral part of their consciences. But finding it too painful to admit their own shortcomings, individuals excuse them by blaming Jews for their failures.

Limitations of Projection Theories

Projection theories suffer many of the same shortcomings as frustration-aggression theories. For instance, they fail to explain why only one minority is selected for the projection of certain traits when there are several minorities to choose from. Nor do projection theories tell us why the stereotypes of various minorities differ from one another.

Yet there is an even more severe problem with projection theories. They are premised upon inferences from observable facts, not upon the facts themselves. In short, the evidence for them is at best circumstantial. The theories need to be subjected to rigid experimental testing, but testing poses severe methodological difficulties. Unconscious motivation is, by definition, not in the conscious mind. Consequently, scientists lack the means by which to observe and study it objectively. Therapy may give partial confirmation to such notions. But the rigid experimental testing so essential to science has been lacking. One theory could be substituted for another, and there could be any number of theories to explain the same phenomenon. Consider the interpretation of anti-Semitism provided by Arnold M. Rose (1944), a sociologist elected to the presidency of the American Sociological Association. Rose suggests that Jews are hated primarily because they serve for Gentiles as a symbol of city life and because Gentiles project their hatred of city life on Jews. Many social scientists find Rose's explanation rather farfetched. Yet how can either party demonstrate the correctness of their position when unconscious mechanisms are held to be at work?

Further, other explanations are available for the stereotypes that some whites hold regarding the inordinate sexuality of blacks. One explanation has to do with status and the defense of group position. If an advantaged group permits outgroup members to enter into intimate relationships with its ingroup members, the advantaged group runs the risk that the boundaries dividing the two groups will erode and ultimately will be breached. Moreover, interracial marriage would mean that one's nephews or grandchildren would be members of the outgroup (where a black parent ensures the placement of a child in the black group). This "demeaning" placement of one's "blood kin" is threatening to a person's self-image as a member of an elite group.

Do these criticisms mean that projection theories are of little value? Of course not. As was noted, psychiatric work gives some confirmation of them. Similarly, for some time the virus theory of disease was generally accepted even though the evidence for it was at best circumstantial. Later, more powerful microscopes lent support to the theory. Thus, merely because a theory lacks experimental support, in the absence of contrary evidence, it need not be rejected. *Caution* needs, however, to be reserved in relation to it.

The Prejudiced Personality

A number of researchers have advanced the hypothesis that prejudice constitutes an ingredient that is closely and intricately bound to an *entire* personality structure. They say that prejudice is a property or symptom of a basic personality organization. This view runs counter to the argument that prejudice represents a more or less *isolated* trait to be found in almost any kind of personality. This latter position suggests that prejudice is an independent tendency that merely manifests itself as a specific response to a specific stimulus.

According to prejudiced-personality theorists, individuals differ in their susceptibility to antidemocratic propaganda and in their readiness to act in an undemocratic fashion. The crucial factor determining susceptibility and readiness is the personality organization. The personality structure contains both contradictions and consistencies, but all the aspects are ultimately integrated and organized within a larger whole.

To understand prejudice, these social scientists insist, one must examine the total personality. They view personality as a more or less enduring organization of forces contained within individuals. These enduring patterns channel the responses that individuals make in a situation. It is the personality that gives consistency to behavior. Although it arises through interaction in a social environment, the personality does not, once developed, simply respond as a passive object to the environment. A basic structure exists within individuals that then initiates action upon and within the social environment.

The Authoritarian Personality

Perhaps the most ambitious and comprehensive effort to define a prejudiced-personality type was undertaken by a group of University of California psychologists at Berkeley led by T. W. Adorno (1950). Considerable attention has since been focused upon their findings, which appeared in a book entitled *The Authoritarian Personality.* The work represents a milestone in research in the field of dominant-minority relations. Particularly impressive were their efforts to develop a series of scales for the measurement of anti-Semitism (the A-S scale); ethnocentrism (the E scale, concerned with attitudes toward "Japs," "Okies," Filipinos, foreigners, criminals, and others); political and economic conservatism (the PEC scale); and basic personality patterns (the F scale). Together with these tests they employed detailed clinical interviews and projective tests on subjects who ranked among the highest 25 percent and the lowest 25 percent on the scale measuring antiminority attitudes. The clinical interviews and projective tests were used to gain access to the conscious as well as unconscious aspects of the personalities of their subjects. The great majority of the subjects lived within the San Francisco Bay area and were drawn from the middle class. In addition, smaller groups of working-class men and women, inmates at San Quentin State Prison, and patients at a psychiatric clinic were studied.

The Berkeley group state the major premise upon which they based their theory and research in these terms: ". . . the political, economic, and social convictions of an individual often form a broad and coherent pattern, as if bound together by a "mentality" or "spirit," and . . . this pattern is an expression of deep-lying trends in his personality" (Adorno, 1950:1).

By employing the questionnaire associated with the F Scale (referred to as the Implicit Antidemocratic Trends or Potentiality of Fascism Scale and by many subsequent researchers as the Authoritarian Scale), the Berkeley group believed they could measure an individual's basic personality patterns. They grouped the thirty-eight items composing the F Scale under nine general characteristics. These characteristics define the antidemocratic or potentially fascistic syndrome. *Syndrome* is a word commonly used medically to refer to a collection of concurrent symptoms associated with a disorder or disease. Let us examine these nine characteristics, defining each and then illustrating each with two statements found in the questionnaire:

1. Conventionalism. Conventionalism involves a rigid adherence to conventional, middle-class values.

> *Example:* "Obedience and respect for authority are the most important virtues children should learn."
> *Example:* "If people would talk less and work more, everybody would be better off."

2. Authoritarian Submission. Authoritarian submission entails a submissive, uncritical attitude toward idealized moral authorities of the ingroup.

> *Example:* "Young people sometimes get rebellious ideas, but as they grow up they ought to get over them and settle down."
> *Example:* "Science has its place, but there are many important things that can never possibly be understood by the human mind."

3. Authoritarian Aggression. Authoritarian aggression involves a tendency to be on the lookout for, and to condemn, reject, and punish people who violate conventional values.

> *Example:* "An insult to our honor should always be punished."
> *Example:* "Homosexuals are hardly better than criminals and ought to be severely punished."

4. Anti-Intraception. Anti-intraception is an opposition to the subjective, the imaginative, and the tender-minded.

> *Example:* "The businessman and the manufacturer are much more important to society than the artist and the professor."
> *Example:* "Nowadays more and more people are prying into matters that should remain personal and private."

5. Superstition and Stereotypy. Superstition and stereotypy entail a belief that mystical determinants influence an individual's fate and a tendency to think in rigid categories.

> *Example:* "Some day it will probably be shown that astrology can explain a lot."
> *Example:* "Some people are born with an urge to jump from high places."

6. Power and "Toughness." Power and "toughness" are viewed as a preoccupation with the dominance-submission, strong-weak, leader-follower dimension, an identification with power figures, an overemphasis upon conventional morality, and an exaggerated assertion of strength and toughness.

Example: "No weakness or difficulty can hold us back if we have enough will power."

Example: "Most people don't realize how much our lives are controlled by plots hatched in secret places."

7. Destructiveness and Cynicism. Destructiveness and cynicism are a generalized hostility toward and a vilification of humans.

Example: "Human nature being what it is, there will always be war and conflict."

Example: "Familiarity breeds contempt."

8. Projectivity. Projectivity entails a disposition to believe that wild and dangerous things go on in the world and more generally the projection outward of unconscious emotional impulses.

Example: "Wars and social troubles may someday be ended by an earthquake or flood that will destroy the whole world."

Example: "Nowadays when so many different kinds of people move around and mix together so much, a person has to protect himself especially carefully against catching an infection or disease from them."

9. Sex. Sex entails an exaggerated concern with sexual "goings-on."

Example: "The wild sex life of the old Greeks and Romans was tame compared to some of the goings-on in this country, even in places where people might least expect it."

Example: "Sex crimes, such as rape and attacks on children, deserve more than mere imprisonment; such criminals ought to be publicly whipped, or worse."

With the F Scale the Berkeley group hoped to identify a personality type that was potentially undemocratic and fascistic. Consequently, they expected F Scale scores to correlate with scores from the Anti-Semitism, Ethnocentrism, and the Political and Economic Conservatism Scales. This outcome indeed proved to be the case. For the first version of the F scale the mean correlation with A-S (the Anti-Semitism Scale) was .53; with E (the Ethnocentrism Scale) it was .65; and with PEC (the Political and Economic Conservatism Scales), .54. (A correlation coefficient can range from -1.00 to $+1.00$. If it is $+1.00$, there is a perfect positive relationship between two variables—meaning that as one of the variables increases, the other also increases. If it is -1.00, there is a perfect negative relationship between two variables—meaning that as one of the variables increases, the other decreases. If the correlation coefficient is .00, there is no relationship between the variables.)

The Berkeley researchers revised the F Scale several times by dropping items that did not correlate with total scores or that were not predictive of A-S and E scores. On the final version of the F Scale, the mean correlation with an E Scale that included anti-Semitic items was .75. Hence the Berkeley group felt that its work convincingly demonstrated that prejudice and authoritarianism (as defined by the F Scale) often constitute closely interrelated personality characteristics.

Origins of the Authoritarian Personality in Childhood

The Berkeley researchers did not limit themselves to defining the personality patterns of those ranking high in prejudice. They were also concerned with the early childhood interrelationships within the family that they believed had fostered these patterns. In keeping with a predominantly Freudian approach, the Berkeley group viewed early relationships with parents and siblings as of paramount importance in determining the basic personality organization. Hence the researchers undertook to identify a composite picture of the family patterns of the highly prejudiced. This picture emerged as an overview or abstraction taken from the total group. Accordingly, exceptions and variations existed in specific cases.

The home discipline of the prejudiced subjects was relatively harsh, arbitrary, and threatening. One subject reported that his father "did not believe in sparing the rod for stealing candy or someone's peaches off the tree." Another stated, "But mother had a way of punishing me —lock me in a closet—or threaten to give me to a neighborhood woman who she said was a witch." Within these families, relationships tended to be rather clearly defined in roles of dominance and submission as opposed to equalitarianism. As a result, the child developed an image of the parents as somewhat distant and forbidding. The child fearfully submitted to the demands of the parents and felt constrained to suppress impulses that were not acceptable to them. On the other hand, those low in prejudice tended to come from families placing less emphasis on obedience and greater emphasis on the unconditional giving of love and affection.

In a related study (Frenkel-Brunswik, 1948), children high in prejudice and children low in prejudice were asked to define the perfect boy. The highly prejudiced tended to define the perfect boy as being "polite," "having good manners," "being clean," whereas those low in prejudice tended to define the perfect boy in terms of "companionship" and "being fun." The tendency toward conformity in the prejudiced child found expression in frequent endorsement of such statements as

"There is only one right way to do anything" and "Appearances are usually the best test." The prejudiced children accepted the parental emphasis upon discipline, describing the perfect father in punitive and restrictive terms rather than in terms of love and understanding. Describing the perfect father, one child indicated, "He spanks you when you are bad and does not give you too much money. . . ." Another reported, "When you ask for something he ought not to give it to you right away. Not soft on you, strict." In contrast, the children low in prejudice were more likely to be treated as an equal and given the opportunity to express feelings of disagreement.

The goals that the parents of the highly prejudiced sought to instill were highly conventional in nature. The parents encouraged their children to adopt a rigid, status-centered set of values: "That which is socially accepted and helpful in climbing the social ladder is 'good,' and that which deviates and is socially inferior is 'bad.' " Prejudiced subjects tended to feel themselves "forgotten," the victims of injustice who did not "get" enough of the things they deserved from parents. The parents of the nonprejudiced were less status ridden; they showed less anxiety about conformity and less intolerance toward deviant behavior. Rather than recurrently condemning their children, they provided them with guidance and support and helped them to work out their problems.

Criticism of *The Authoritarian Personality*

Probably no other research in the field of race and ethnic relations has received greater attention than that of *The Authoritarian Personality*. Scores of studies have appeared criticizing, testing, refining, and qualifying the findings of the Berkeley group. Obviously, we cannot consider all of the many criticisms of *The Authoritarian Personality*. Here we will single out a number of the more important ones.

1. Many of the criticisms focus on research methods (Christie and Jahoda, 1954; Kirscht and Dillehay, 1967). Critics note that the sample of persons studied was not necessarily representative of the larger population. The subjects were primarily drawn from among the middle class and members of formal organizations like veterans' groups, labor unions, and Kiwanis clubs. Yet middle-class people and members of formal organizations differ in many respects from other segments of the population. Similarly some critics suggest that the study's scales are inadequate, in fact faulty, and that many items are ambiguous. The psychologist Solomon E. Asch (1952:545) goes even a step further and rejects "the assumption that one can deduct the content of psychological processes from the content of attitude items."

2. Some social scientists say that a tendency toward "acquiescence" accounts for some of the apparent relationship between an authoritarian personality type and prejudice. The items in the F Scale are all "agree" items. A number of researchers have discovered that some people have a marked tendency to agree with almost any proposition, not only on the F Scale but on any and all scales, regardless of content. Conversely, other people disagree with practically every proposition, regardless of its nature. Psychologists christen these types "Yea-sayers" and "Nay-sayers":

The difficulty lies in the fact that every time you agree with an item on the F-scale you chalk up a credit toward authoritarianism. If you agree that "obedience and respect for authority are the most important virtues children should learn," ping! you score one! If you agree that "to a greater extent than most people realize, our lives are governed by plots hatched in secret by politicians," ping! you score another point for authoritarianism. In other words, all the items are unidirectional, so worded that agreement always signifies authoritarianism. Only by disagreeing with every item can you obtain a completely "democratic" score (Allport, 1962:131).

3. The Berkeley group held that the association between authoritarianism (as measured by the F Scale) and a variety of the other attitudes (including prejudice) argues for the existence of a unified personality configuration. Not so, argue some critics. These writers note that authoritarian tendencies increase as intelligence, education, and socioeconomic class status go down (Hyman and Sheatsley, 1954; MacKinnon and Centers, 1956). Hence, some insist, the numerous components of authoritarianism are found together in a person simply because they are the norms of people with little education and with low-socioeconomic-class status:

. . . there is the real possibility that *both* authoritarian beliefs and prejudices may be learned in the same way that we learn that the world is round (or flat, or held up on the back of a giant turtle). The association of both prejudices and personality items with formal education forces us to take seriously the possibility that widespread indoctrination, relatively independent of individual psychological needs, may account for at least a considerable part of the correlation of authoritarianism and prejudice. Thus, *both* authoritarianism and prejudice may tend to be characteristic of persons in economically and socially deprived positions in the social structure (Williams, 1964:90).

Gertrude J. Selznick and Stephen Steinberg (1969) take this criticism a step further. They argue that the authors of the *The Authoritarian Personality* were led astray by asking: Why do people *accept* anti-Semitic beliefs? In a society that culturally embodies anti-Semitism, an elaborate theory is not necessary: People acquire anti-Semitism through the normal processes of socialization. Rather we need to ask: Why in such a society do some people *reject* anti-Semitic beliefs? Phrasing the question in this manner directs our attention to the forces that run counter to the attitudes of the mass culture. These forces include the attitudes of science, democracy, and humanitarianism that are transmitted chiefly through the educational system. Hence, it is the educated—especially the more highly educated—who reject not only anti-Semitism but also anti-intellectualism and antidemocratic attitudes.

4. Some critics allege that authoritarianism is only indirectly related to prejudice. Walter C. Kaufman (1957) suggests, for example, on the basis of his study of 213 non-Jewish college undergraduates, that status is more closely related to anti-Semitism than is authoritarianism. By employing statistical measures, Kaufman undertook to determine the association between both authoritarianism and status and scores on the anti-Semitism scale. He attempted to discover through the use of partial correlations (statistical measures) the degree to which authoritarianism and status were each *independently* correlated with the anti-Semitism score. In other words, he measured the degree to which authoritarianism was correlated with anti-Semitism when the effect of status was allowed for, or to put it another way, was held constant. Similarly, he measured the degree to which status was correlated with prejudice when the effect of authoritarianism was allowed for. Since status and authoritarianism might go hand-in-hand, Kaufman wanted to look at the separate effect of each. The partial correlation of status and anti-Semitism was .48 (moderately high), while that of authoritarianism and anti-Semitism was .12 (quite low). Kaufman concluded that concern with status is the dominant dimension related to anti-Semitism and that the correlation he found of .53 between authoritarianism and anti-Semitism could be largely explained by their mutual relationship and concern with status. Thus, when the effect of status was held constant, the correlation between authoritarianism and anti-Semitism dropped to .12.

5. A recurring criticism of *The Authoritarian Personality* deals with its tendency to equate authoritarianism tendencies with a right-wing (fascistic) political orientation. May we not find, suggest some critics, intemperate and exaggerated love-prejudice just as we find intemperate and exaggerated hate-prejudice? They ask: what about communistic authoritarianism of the left? Indeed, can one be authoritarian even if one's attitudes are "on the side of the angels"?

Rokeach takes this kind of position. He criticizes the F Scale as being a measure of right-wing authoritarianism rather than a measure of authoritarianism in general (Roberts and Rokeach, 1956;

Rokeach, 1960). Authoritarianism as described by the Berkeley group, Rokeach argues, is a subspecies of a more general personality syndrome, which he calls "dogmatism." Whereas Communists score relatively low on the Berkeley F and prejudice scales, they score higher on Rokeach's Dogmatism Scale than most other political groups. Rokeach stresses that authoritarianism should be viewed as a mode of thought (a structure characterized by a "closed mind," dependence upon some absolute authority, and patterns of intolerance toward certain groups) rather than as a set of beliefs (i.e., the favorableness or unfavorableness of attitudes toward certain minorities). Hence what is crucial, according to Rokeach, is the tenacity with which beliefs are held, not the beliefs themselves; he views dogmatism as a stylistic personality attribute, relatively free from specific beliefs.

6. Finally, critics have often observed that the Berkeley group failed to give sufficient recognition to the role culture plays in prejudice. Where a society evolves elaborate definitions and norms governing interracial behavior, the mere presence of prejudice in people tells us very little about their distinctive modes of personality. Under these circumstances prejudice and discrimination may constitute the characteristics of "normal" personalities. The matter is emphasized by comparative studies of prejudice in the southern and northern United States. Evidence abounds to support the fact that white southerners are typically more intolerant of blacks than white northerners. Yet Thomas F. Pettigrew (1959) could not find any higher incidence of authoritarianism in four small southern towns in Georgia and North Carolina than in four communities in New England that were roughly matched to them. From his data, which included a study of various sociocultural variables, Pettigrew concluded that it was the sociocultural and social adjustment factors that accounted for the sharp differences between the North and the South, not differences in personality. Nor does the authoritarian personality theory take into account inconsistency in prejudice and discrimination (e.g., tolerance of blacks in one's union but not in one's neighborhood).

After reviewing *The Authoritarian Personality* and various criticisms of it, what can we conclude? Perhaps Robin M. Williams, Jr. (1964:94), summarizes the situation best in this appraisal:

> . . . there is every reason to accept the contention that authoritarianism, of the kind that is indexed by the F-scale, tends to enhance the likelihood of ethnic prejudice. But neither the authoritarian syndrome nor other related personality tendencies invariably constitute either a necessary or sufficient set of conditions for prejudice, much less discriminatory behavior.

Hence, despite the lack of overall consensus on the study, the Berkeley research commands considerable respect.

SUMMARY

1. Racism may satisfy a variety of personal needs, and racist attitudes and behaviors therefore may become rooted in the basic personality structure of some individuals. Group-centered orientations stress what goes on between people, whereas personality-centered orientations emphasize what goes on within people. Since prejudice is a state of mind, and as such is "carried" in specific individuals, personality-centered theorists look for the sources of prejudice within the individual personality.

2. The scapegoat theory has provided a popular explanation of prejudice. Its major postulates are: (a) All individuals experience a variety of needs. (b) Individuals are frustrated in realizing their needs. (c) Frustrated individuals experience anger, which disposes them toward aggressive actions. (d) Individuals cannot always discharge their anger toward the frustrating agent and consequently displace it on a scapegoat. (e) People who are too weak or defenseless to strike back are ideal scapegoats. (f) Individuals justify their seeking scapegoats by finding some convincing reason why they can hate and discriminate against a minority group.

3. Using scapegoats is a more complex phenomenon than early formulations of the theory led us to believe. We need to take into account a number of other factors. Among these factors are the personality of the displacer, the kind of frustration involved, the perceived qualities of the potential target, and the cultural norms operating in an intergroup situation.

4. Whites in the United States and South Africa have stereotyped blacks as consumed by inordinate sexual desire. Projection psychologists say that this notion is rooted in projection mechanisms. Within Western societies sex is defined in rather negative terms. Yet it is an inevitable aspect of physical functioning. Many individuals thus find themselves in a dilemma. Unable to repress awareness of sexual desire, they instead respond by repressing the recognition of its origin within themselves, and the lustfulness is projected outside of themselves on others.

5. White racist stereotypes depict blacks as uninhibited, rhythmic, and passionate. Black women are portrayed as excellent sexual partners and black men as especially virile and capable. Consequently, Freudian psychologists say blacks become sexually attractive to whites. But this prospect is especially threatening to white men who fear sexual attraction between black men and white women. Circumstances that make salient the sexuality of black males can activate the potential for racist violence among white men.

6. Historically, Jews have represented a particularly suitable projection screen for people's conflicts. It is easy to project one's own unac-

ceptable feelings upon an external object that lacks a clear, sharp structure of its own. For anti-Semites, the Jew is a living Rorschach inkblot. The Jew is portrayed culturally as many things: as "successful" and as "low class," as "capitalist" and as "Communist," as "clannish" and as "intruder into other people's society," as "oversexed" and as "impotent," and as "strong" and as "weak."

7. There are severe problems with projection theories. They are premised on inferences from observable facts, not on the facts themselves. The evidence for them is at best circumstantial. The theories need to be subjected to rigid experimental testing, but testing poses severe methodological difficulties. Unconscious motivation is, by definition, not in the conscious mind. Consequently, scientists lack the means by which to observe and study it objectively.

8. A number of researchers at Berkeley have advanced the hypothesis that prejudice constitutes an ingredient that is closely and intricately bound to an entire personality structure. The study, *The Authoritarian Personality,* represents the best illustration of this approach. Prejudice is portrayed as part of a syndrome consisting of a variety of other traits: conventionalism, authoritarian submission, authoritarian aggression, anti-intraception, superstition and stereotypy, power and "toughness," destructiveness and cynicism, projectivity, and exaggerated concern with sexuality.

9. In keeping with a predominantly Freudian approach, the Berkeley group viewed early relationships with parents and siblings as of paramount importance in determining the basic personality organization. The home discipline of the prejudiced tends to be relatively harsh, arbitrary, and threatening. Relationships tend to be rather clearly defined in roles of dominance and submission as opposed to equalitarian policies. The parents encourage their children to adopt a rigid, status-centered set of values. In contrast, the parents of the unprejudiced are less status ridden. They show less anxiety regarding conformity. Rather than recurrently condemning their children, they provide them with guidance and support.

10. Scores of studies have appeared criticizing, testing, refining, and qualifying the findings of the Berkeley group. A number of these criticisms are the following: (a) The sample of persons studied was not necessarily representative of the larger population. (b) A tendency toward "acquiescence" accounts for some aspects of the apparent relationship between an authoritarian personality type and prejudice. (c) The components of authoritarianism may be found together in a person simply because they are the norms of people with little education and with low-socioeconomic-class status. (d) Authoritarianism is only indirectly related to prejudice. (e) Authoritarian tendencies are not limited to those with a right-wing political orientation for we also find authoritarianism of the left. (f) Where a society evolves elaborate defini-

tions and norms governing interracial behavior, the mere presence of prejudice in people tells us very little about their distinctive modes of personality.

GLOSSARY

Displacement   A process by which hostilities are removed from the source or sources of frustration and discharged upon a scapegoat.

Projection   The tendency of people to attribute to others motives or traits that they sense within themselves but that would be painful to acknowledge.

Rationalization   Coming up with excuses or justifications for behavior that would otherwise be viewed as unacceptable.

# III

Intergroup
Relations

Conflict **6**

For the most part members of dominant and minority groups do not interact in a random or haphazard fashion. Rather, when people of differing racial and ethnic groups live together within the same or neighboring communities, they develop patterned ways of dealing with one another. Certain regularities and recurrences come to characterize their relationships. Continuities in intergroup behavior typically take the form of conflict, stratification, segregation, and assimilation. In this and the four chapters that follow we will consider each of these processes. The chapters will depict the flow of action as it is organized and mapped within the lives of dominant and minority peoples.

Conflict in Intergroup Relations

We commonly associate racial and ethnic relations with "social problems." The fact that conflict is often an important element in such relations contributes to this viewpoint. And the feeling is compounded by our tendency to equate conflict with violence. While it is true that wars, riots, terrorist acts, and lynchings periodically emerge in contact settings, conflict need not be expressed in violent terms. Boycotts, strikes, wade-ins, sit-ins, passive resistance, legal litigation, and racist humor represent forms of conflict in which violence may be absent. **Conflict** entails a struggle over values and claims to wealth, power, and status in which the opponents attempt to neutralize, injure, or eliminate their rivals. At times it results in genocide, the annihilation of a people—the fate of a number of Native American tribes.

Sources of Social Conflict

As noted in chapters 1 and 3, one of the principal sources of conflict among people is their mutual claim upon the same scarce, divisible "good things," especially wealth, power, and status. Not uncommonly the more there is for one group the less there is for the other. Nor does a once-and-for-all solution exist to the problem of distributing scarce resources among the members of a society. Some groups are advantaged and other groups are disadvantaged. Those who are privileged have an interest in conserving, consolidating, and expanding their share. Those who are less well off seek to acquire a larger proportion of the scarce resources. The same social arrangements that contribute to the suffering and misery of some foster a sense of security and freedom in others. Seldom do privileged groups voluntarily relinquish their advantaged position. The result of the clash between opposing interest groups is conflict (Oberschall, 1973).

A second important source of social conflict is value differences. Values are ethical principles to which people feel a strong emotional attachment and which they employ in judging behavior (Vander Zanden, 1981a). Values tell people what is good and what is bad, what is commendable and what is deplorable, and what is important and what is unimportant. People invest themselves emotionally in their values. They do not simply experience the world; they "feel" about it. Often individuals consider their values to be sacred, immortal truths revealed to them by their gods or their wise ancestors. (National values are often attributed to a leader with a pivotal position in a country's history. In this way, Americans look to Washington, Russians to Lenin, and the Chinese to Mao.) Consider such contemporary issues in the United States as abortion and gun control. Does abortion constitute murder or does it represent a woman's right to control her own body and destiny? Are handguns a social menace or the foundation of a people's liberty and right to self-defense? Which group will be able to transform its morality into the operating standards for a society and define the behavior of the other group as deviant? Such questions involve value clashes that are a source of social conflict. Since each minority group constitutes a "subsociety" possessing a distinct "subculture," a dominant group may seek to suppress the unique customs of a minority.

Conflict and Social Stability

We often conclude that if conflict is absent from a relationship, the relationship is highly integrated, stable, and secure. Some married couples pride themselves on "never once having had a quarrel"—a statement taken to be a testimonial to their love and happiness. But most marriage counselors and psychiatrists come to a contrary conclusion. In any deep, intimate relationship such as marriage, some bickering is inevitable and its absence suggests that the relationship may have failed. If people are to resolve their differences, some quarreling must take place. Where all conflict is absent, family stagnation is the likely outcome. The crucial issue in relating conflict to marital success is not the absence of conflict but how the couple quarrel, how often, over what issues, and with what degree of intensity.

Similarly, the absence of racial and ethnic conflict does not necessarily signify the existence of stable, nonstressful relationships. It may merely mean that a dominant group has more or less successfully coerced and intimidated a minority. We find it easy to confuse peace with satisfaction and silence with consent. Where a relationship is stable, where people feel that it will not be endangered by disagreements, conflicts are likely to emerge. In fact, under some conditions, conflicts in intergroup relations may represent an index of a better integration of the minority within the community. A minority group that feels that the bonds uniting it to the dominant group are unstable may lack the security that is needed to display hostility and engage in conflict. On the other hand, overt conflict may be an indication that the minority feels sufficiently secure in its relationship with the dominant group to risk expression of conflict. The members feel that the consensual bond between the groups is sufficiently strong to withstand antagonistic action (Coser, 1956, 1968).

Also, the more the parties to conflict feel themselves integrated within society, the less likely is their conflict to take a violent form. Their disputes find expression in conflict *within* the system as opposed to conflict *about* the system. The adversaries choose weapons that will not permanently menace their common bonds. Violent class or ethnic wars are likely to give way to less militant means of conflict resolution (including institutionalized strikes, demonstrations, or boycotts) in those societies that permit the integration of the underclasses and minorities within the social order.

The civil-rights movement provides an illustration of socially bounded conflict. The dominant technique of the movement during the 1960s was to achieve change through the courts and through legislative social reform. Even when the Reverend Martin Luther King, Jr., and his associates violated the law, they subsequently accepted punishment under the law. They thereby reaffirmed their willingness to fight within the system and by its rules (Newman, 1973).

On the other hand, when the members of a group feel themselves more or less permanently excluded from participation in the society's benefits, they may reject the assumptions on which the society is built. If they no longer accord legitimacy to the prevailing social order, they may attack it through revolutionary violence. This latter orientation found expression during the 1960s and 1970s in the rhetoric of some blacks who lashed out against "racism," "oppression," and "colonization" and championed "black liberation." Their language contrasted with that of Reverend King, who spoke against "discrimination" and fought for "equality of opportunity" and "equality before the law."

Social Consequences of Racial and Ethnic Conflict

The emphasis placed upon peace and harmony within the United States contributes to the popular notion that conflict is harmful. According to this view, any expression of conflict within a society or between groups is to be condemned. Where a value system defines most forms of human conflict as harmful and morally wrong, attention is riveted upon conflict's negative aspects. Now it is true that conflict may reach a frequency and intensity whereby the social system is imperiled or undermined. Undeniably hostility is a potentially destructive and disruptive force within human interaction. Racial and ethnic conflicts often drain and dissipate energies and resources that might otherwise find direction within more productive channels and cooperative activities. Similarly, fears and expectations of friction may lead to an inefficient and ineffective employment of labor resources and individual talents. And conflict may imperil institutional functioning. This has occurred in several American cities where school desegregation and busing controversies have imperiled the functioning of the educational system. It is not surprising, then, that societies usually take considerable care to regulate, suppress, and rechannel aggressive impulses.

Yet it is easy to overlook other consequences of ethnic and racial conflict as well. First, a society that is riddled by a good many divisions that run in every direction is in less danger of being torn apart by violence than one split along just one line. Where individuals are affiliated with numerous groups having differing interests and values, they find themselves caught up in a variety of intergroup conflicts: racial group versus racial group, religious denomination versus religious denomination, nationality versus nationality, class versus class, business versus business, labor versus business, and so on. Consequently, those who are antagonists in one conflict (e.g., class) are allies in another (e.g., religion). Thus the individual's segmental participation in numerous groups, rather than total absorption by one group, results in a kind of balancing mechanism and prevents deep cleavages along one axis.

Second, conflict may prevent social systems from ossifying by exerting pressure for change and innovation. Conflict prevents habitual arrangements from freezing into rigid molds. It challenges people and compels them to search for new solutions to altered circumstances. In this sense, conflict may contribute to social vitality.

Third, conflict quickens group allegiances and loyalties and thus provides a social glue that binds people together. Humans are social beings. Consequently, their social identities are anchored in groups. One way a person answers the question "Who am I?" is through acknowledging a racial or ethnic membership. Conflict highlights racial and ethnic boundaries and ingroup-outgroup distinctions. Within the United States racial conflict has enabled many blacks to achieve a substantial measure of identity (Himes, 1973). The Black Power movement afforded blacks a sense of dignity, belonging, self-worth, and pride in a society in which blacks were otherwise relegated to menial and marginal statuses. Although our discussion does not exhaust the social consequences of conflict, it does point up the fact that the impact of conflict is not necessarily or entirely negative.

Social Violence in the United States

We like to imagine ourselves as a democratic, peace-loving, and rational people, yet in truth the United States has been a violent nation. Indeed, we prefer to forget that from the earliest settlement period whites systematically subjected the indigenous population to repeated assault. We also conveniently forget about Shays' Rebellion in Massachusetts in 1787 and Pennsylvania's Whiskey Rebellion in 1794 or about our frontier and vigilante tradition of violence. Similarly, we have forgotten about the Draft Riots of the Civil War in which, during a span of five days, nearly 2,000 people were killed. And again we like to forget that economic strife erupted countless times in various agrarian revolts and in such bloody affairs as the railroad strikes of 1877, the Homestead and Pullman strikes of the 1890s, and the steel strikes of the 1930s.

We also tend to forget our record of social violence—assaults upon individuals or their property solely or primarily because of their ethnic, religious, or racial affiliations. We are prone to forget the anti-Catholic riots—the anti-Irish riots—of the 1840s and 1850s, with an especially bloody outbreak in Philadelphia, the City of Brotherly Love, in 1844. We forget about the anti-Chinese riots in the closing decades of the nineteenth century that were extraordinarily cruel. And we forget the 1940s with the wartime attacks not only on the civil rights of, but also against the persons and property of Chicanos and Japanese-Americans. The American tradition of violence has likewise enshrouded white-black relations, finding expression in at least six broad patterns of action (Masotti et al., 1969): suppression-insurrection; lynchings; white-dominated, person-oriented rioting; racial warfare, person-oriented rioting; black-dominated, property-oriented rioting; and black-dominated, person-oriented violence. Let us consider each of these patterns of violence in turn.

Suppression-Insurrection

The suppression-insurrection pattern of racial violence derived from the dominant-subservient or master-slave relationship. Underlying this arrangement was the assumption that masters had the "right" to resort to violence in dealing with their slaves. Physical force was a means for maintaining white dominance. Slavery so completely disrupted black institutions, culture, and communication that it was virtually impossible for blacks to mount a serious challenge to their subjugation. Nonetheless, during the eighteenth and nineteenth centuries a number of slave rebellions occurred, including the insurrections of Gabriel in Virginia (1800), Denmark Vesey in South Carolina (1822), and Nat Turner in Southhampton County, Virginia (1831). Hundreds of other less well-known slave rebellions also took place, but they were universally suppressed.

Lynchings

Lynching is a mob action—usually a hanging—that summarily and illegally takes an individual's life. In lynching the action is one-sided and directed against specific individuals. In this way, lynchings differ from race riots, in which the mob action involves a two-way encounter. Before the Civil War, the lynching of blacks was relatively rare except in cases of insurrection conspiracies. The financial investment in slaves restrained mob action. But with the coming of Reconstruction, the disfranchisement of the white elite, and "scalawag" and "carpetbagger" rule, lynching became a major instrument for "keeping blacks in their place."

It is possible to gain an estimate of the number of lynchings from an annual summary made by the Chicago *Tribune* between 1882 and 1917 and from the statistics kept by Tuskegee Institute from 1889 until 1953. The largest number of lynchings occurred during the 1890s, when 420 whites and 1,111 blacks met death at the hands of lynch mobs. After the 1890s, lynchings progressively decreased. In the 1900s there were 885 lynchings (94 whites and 791 blacks); in the 1910s, 616 (53 whites and 563 blacks); in the 1920s, 315 (34 whites and 281 blacks); and in the 1930s, 131 (11 whites and 120 blacks). By the 1940s the figure had fallen to 32, and by the 1950s the practice became virtually extinct. Except for New England, lynchings have occurred in all sections of the United States but were most frequent in the South.

Contrary to popular opinion, most black lynch victims were not charged with rape. However, southern efforts to justify lynchings traditionally revolved about the assertion that such fearsome tactics were essential to control and frighten blacks, who would otherwise undertake wholesale sexual attacks upon white women. South Carolina Sena-

tor Cole L. Blease, defending lynching, told a political rally in 1930, "Whenever the Constitution comes between me and the virtue of the white women of the South, I say, to hell with the Constitution." Various studies have suggested that no more than 25 percent of the blacks lynched since 1882 were accused of rape or attempted rape. The Tuskegee statistics reveal that accusations of homicide were responsible for slightly better than 40 percent of the lynchings. Robbery, theft, insulting white people, attempting to vote, not knowing "a black's place," and related charges were of lesser significance in the total picture. In some instances the lynched victim was mistaken for another person or was completely innocent of the alleged crime.

Lynchings often involved torture, mutilation, and immolation. The Southern Commission on the Study of Lynching (1931:40) cites the following case having marked sadistic overtones:

> The sheriff along with the accused Negro was seized by the mob, and the two were carried to the scene of the crime. Here quickly assembled a thousand or more men, women, and children. The accused Negro was hung up in a sweet-gum tree by his arms, just high enough to keep his feet off the ground. Members of the mob tortured him for more than an hour. A pole was jabbed in his mouth. His toes were cut off joint by joint. His fingers were similarly removed, and members of the mob extracted his teeth with wire pliers. After further unmentionable mutilations, the Negro's still living body was saturated with gasoline and a lighted match was applied. As the flames leaped up, hundreds of shots were fired into the dying victim. During the day, thousands of people from miles around rode out to see the sight. Not till nightfall did the officers remove the body and bury it.

Since lynchings involved strong elements of popular excitement, they offered otherwise disgruntled whites an opportunity to express pent-up emotions and feelings. The hard core of most lynch mobs was drawn predominantly from young, propertyless, unemployed whites, some of whom had court records (Cantril, 1941).

White-Dominated, Person-Oriented Rioting

In contrast with lynching, white-dominated, person-oriented rioting is not an attack on particular individuals. Rather, the violence typically takes the following course: The attackers are white; their victims are black; the violence originates with and is directed and controlled by whites; the whites seek to inflict personal injury more-or-less indiscriminately on the blacks; the blacks, as victims, do little seriously to defend themselves. Traditionally racial violence of this sort resulted not from conscious policy decisions of whites, but rather from white reactions to real or perceived assaults by blacks upon the existing racial structure.

In brief, if blacks were seen as "staying in their place," there was little likelihood of violence (G. B. Johnson, 1939; Lieberson and Silverman, 1965).

The model for this form of violence is the Springfield, Illinois, race riot of 1908 (Crouthamel, 1969). Feeling against blacks had been running high in Illinois during this period because of the influx of blacks to Chicago, Peoria, East St. Louis, and Springfield. In mid-August, 1908, the white community became enraged at the alleged rape of two white women by blacks. On Friday afternoon, August 15, a crowd of some 4,000 white persons gathered outside the jail where the two arrested black suspects were being held. Many were merely curious bystanders, others shoppers in town for the evening, and still others youthful thrill-seekers. Many, however, were motivated by race hatred and, in the case of immigrant white laborers, anxious to put the competing blacks "in their place." The crowd's mood became progressively ugly. When the crowd learned that the two black suspects had been secretly removed from the jail and taken to the state prison in Bloomington, two days of rioting, burning, and lynching were unloosed. Some 3,700 militiamen were called into Springfield and subsequently restored order. The black response to this outbreak was one of terror and flight. Such terrorizing of a black community also occurred in the South during Reconstruction—indeed, "Reconstruction was in a sense a prolonged race riot" (G. B. Johnson, 1939). The pattern continued in the 1890s and on into the first two decades of the 1900s in a number of cities: Wilmington, North Carolina (1896); East St. Louis, Illinois (1917); Washington, D.C. (1919); and Tulsa, Oklahoma (1921).

Racial Warfare, Person-Oriented Rioting

Blacks have not always remained passive victims during riots. In this fourth pattern both blacks and whites engage in attacks upon members of the other group. The model for this type of violence is the 1943 riot in Detroit, Michigan (Lee and Humphrey, 1943). Within Detroit, a climate of racial tension had been building up for some years. Two years earlier, in the spring of 1941, blacks and whites were pitted against each other during a strike in Ford Motor's large River Rouge plant. Furthermore, Detroit abounded in white, extreme right-wing, hate groups.

During the early war years, a considerable influx of blacks and whites from the South had supplied smoldering embers that contributed to racial tension. Whites from Kentucky, Tennessee, Oklahoma, and Arkansas, many of them former sharecroppers, brought with them racist notions of blacks. Within Detroit southern blacks were able to secure jobs that gave them a wage and a sense of freedom that they had previously not known. Among southern white immigrants, for that matter many northerners as well, Detroit blacks were seen as becoming too

"uppity." The situation was compounded by Detroit's severe housing shortage that condemned thousands of both whites and blacks to live in slums, tents, and trailers.

Such were the setting and the diverse currents that provided the backdrop for the Detroit riot. The initial outbreak flared Sunday evening, June 20, at Belle Isle, Detroit's 985-acre playground and beach. Versions differ regarding the chief incident that precipitated the riot. Whatever the triggering event, the riot began on the bridge leading to the island, and within a short time some 200 white sailors were fighting with blacks. A number of blacks were severely kicked and beaten. Rumors quickly spread through the black and white communities.

Within Paradise Valley, the congested black ghetto, rioting broke out in the early morning hours of Monday, June 21. By 2:00 A.M. a white man had been stabbed in the chest, a police officer had suffered a possible skull fracture, and injured people were being taken into Detroit's Municipal Receiving Hospital at a rate of one a minute. Blacks stoned white workers inside a streetcar and attacked whites coming off from work at the Chevrolet Gear and Axle Plant. Large groups of blacks started looting stores and destroying white property in Black districts. By 3:00 A.M. the situation appeared to be out of control, especially in Paradise Valley. An hour later whites began ganging up on isolated blacks along Woodward Avenue.

During the day the rioting continued. Gangs of whites stopped and burned black cars on Woodward Avenue, the city's main north-south thoroughfare. Although police took action against black looters, there were numerous reports of their failure to protect blacks from white attack. The sociologist Norman D. Humphrey gives this account of one such incident:

> There was an automobile burning on Woodward and up a side street a Negro was being horribly beaten. Eventually the mob let the Negro go, and he staggered down to the car tracks, and he tried to get on a streetcar. But the car wouldn't stop for him.
>
> The Negro was punch-drunk. There were policemen down the street, but they didn't pay any attention to him.
>
> I started shouting, "Hey, copper. Hey, copper." And I pointed to the Negro in the middle of the street. The policeman finally took notice of me, but instead of going in the direction in which I was pointing he walked over to his parked scout car. Then two huge hoodlums began to slug the Negro, and he hung there on the side of the safety zone, taking the punches as if he were a bag of sand. . . . (Lee and Humphrey, 1943:32–33.)

In the black community, groups of blacks looted white-owned or -operated stores.

By early evening, 10,000 surging, angry whites had jammed the City Hall area. As the evening wore on, violence increased. Whites stopped streetcars and removed and beat black passengers. Automobiles were overturned in the street, and some of them were set on fire. A large white mob attempted to invade the black ghetto, but it was momentarily stopped by police near the Frazer Hotel, a black hostelry. Black snipers in the hotel opened fire on the police, and a pitched battle between the snipers and the police ensued. Police were peppered with bullets from hotel windows. They returned the fire, blazing away at windows and hurling tear-gas bombs.

Later that evening Governor Harry F. Kelly made a formal, official request for federal troops. Shortly before midnight, President Franklin D. Roosevelt signed the proclamation requested by the governor, calling upon the "military forces of the United States" to put down the "domestic violence" in Michigan. The U.S. Army quickly restored order within Detroit and dispersed the mobs. Nevertheless, tension continued to prevail in Detroit for days thereafter.

In the rioting, 34 people had lost their lives (25 blacks and 9 whites). Twelve blacks were shot to death by police while looting stores and three others after they reportedly had fired shots at the police. The City Receiving Hospital treated 433 riot victims of whom 222 were whites and 211 blacks. At least 101 riot victims were hospitalized.

Black-Dominated, Property-Oriented Rioting

In black-dominated, property-oriented rioting, blacks initiate the violence and direct their hostilities toward property rather than toward persons. Most of the property is white owned but located within the black ghetto. The violence seldom spreads outside black neighborhoods to white residential areas or to "neutral" downtown locations. The first major occurrence of this type of violence occurred in Harlem in 1935. On March 19, a black youth was caught stealing a knife from a Harlem dimestore. The crowd that gathered outside the store gained the impression that white store personnel had murdered the youth. The rumor spread and blacks roamed the streets of Harlem, breaking store windows and looting. With the exception of confrontations between police and looters, incidents between blacks and whites were at a minimum. The looting continued through the next day, but was finally brought under control through the efforts of police and local black leaders.

During the summer of 1964, the 1935 Harlem-riot pattern reappeared in outbreaks in Philadelphia, Rochester, and Harlem. By 1970, most major American cities had also experienced "long, hot summers." The most serious ghetto outbreaks were as follows:

1. *New York City, July 1964.* Harlem blacks held a rally to protest the killing of a black youth by an off-duty white police officer. Rally

speakers denounced the police and called for community action. At the conclusion of the rally, crowd members marched to a Harlem police station. Along the route of the march, scuffles broke out with the police that then erupted into six days of rioting. In the Bedford-Stuyvesant section of Brooklyn, rioting also occurred. The final toll was 1 person dead, 143 injured, and 461 arrested.

2. *Los Angeles, August 1965.* On August 11 white police officers arrested a black man for driving under the influence of alcohol in the Watts section of Los Angeles. The man resisted arrest. Scuffling broke out between police officers and a number of onlookers. The disorder rapidly spread throughout the area and turned into six days of rioting, arson, and looting. Of the thirty-four people killed, twenty-eight were black. By the sixth day, 15,000 National Guard troops and 1,000 city and county police officers were patrolling forty-six square miles and had arrested 3,952 adults and juveniles.

3. *Cleveland, July 1966.* A minor incident in a neighborhood bar in the black section of Hough turned into widespread looting and fire-bombing. A so-called shoot-out was probably the most significant development. During a five-hour gun battle on the evening of July 23, ten persons were killed, including three police officers and three black militants.

4. *Newark, July 1967.* Violence erupted when blacks heard and believed a false rumor that police officers had killed a black taxi driver. As the rioting, looting, and fire-bombing spread, exaggerated reports of black snipers prompted state officials to call up National Guard units for duty in Newark. In six days of rioting, 26 people were killed and 1,500 injured.

5. *Detroit, July 1967.* Probably the worst riot of the decade erupted in Detroit on a muggy night in response to a police raid on an after-hours drinking club. During eight days of rioting, 43 people were killed, 2,000 injured, 7,000 arrested, and 5,000 left homeless. Army and National Guard units were sent into the city. Troops fired machine guns from Sherman tanks at suspected black snipers.

6. *Washington, D.C., April 1968.* The Washington outbreak was a response to the killing of Reverend Martin Luther King, Jr., in Memphis. Stokely Carmichael (a leader of the Student Nonviolent Coordinating Committee—SNCC) led a march of protesters down 14th Street. The march swelled into a riot. During four days, 9 died, 1,000 were injured, and 6,000 arrested.

The National Advisory Committee on Civil Disorders (the Kerner Commission, 1968) provided the following insights on the rioting:

In the 75 disorders studied by a Senate subcommittee, 83 deaths were reported. Eighty-two percent of the deaths and more than half the injuries occurred in Newark and Detroit. About 10 percent of the dead and 38 percent of the injured were public employees, primarily law officers and firemen. The overwhelming majority of the persons killed or injured in all the disorders were Negro civilians.

Violence usually occurred almost immediately following the occurrence of the final precipitating incident, and then escalated rapidly. With but few exceptions, violence subsided during the day, and flared rapidly again at night. The night-day cycles continued through the early period of the major disorders.

Disorder generally began with rock and bottle throwing and window breaking. Once store windows were broken, looting usually followed.

Disorder did not erupt as a result of a single "triggering" or "precipitation" incident. Instead, it was generated out of an increasingly disturbed social atmosphere, in which typically a series of tension-heightening incidents over a period of weeks or months became linked in the minds of many in the Negro community with a reservoir of underlying grievances. At some point in the mounting tension, a further incident—in itself often routine or trivial—became the breaking point and the tension spilled over into violence.

"Prior" incidents, which increased tensions and ultimately led to violence, were police actions in almost half the cases; police actions were "final" incidents before the outbreak of violence in 12 of the 24 surveyed disorders.

The typical rioter was a teenager or young adult, a lifelong resident of the city in which he rioted, a high school dropout; he was, nevertheless, somewhat better educated than his nonrioting Negro neighbor, and was usually underemployed or employed in a menial job. He was proud of his race, extremely hostile to both whites and middle-class Negroes and, although informed about politics, highly distrustful of the political system.

A Detroit survey revealed that approximately 11 percent of the total residents of two riot areas admitted participation in the rioting, 20 to 25 percent identified themselves as "bystanders," over 16 percent identified themselves as "counter-rioters" who urged rioters to "cool it," and the remaining 48 to 53 percent said they were at home or elsewhere and did not participate. In a survey of Negro males between the ages of 15 and 35 residing in the disturbance area in Newark, about 45 percent identified themselves as rioters, and about 55 percent as "noninvolved."

What the rioters appeared to be seeking was fuller participation in the social order and the material benefits enjoyed by the majority of American citizens. Rather than rejecting the American system, they were anxious to obtain a place for themselves in it.

Although specific grievances varied from city to city, at least twelve deeply held grievances can be identified and ranked into three levels of relative intensity:

First Level of Intensity
  1. Police practices
  2. Unemployment and underemployment
  3. Inadequate housing

Second Level of Intensity
  4. Inadequate education
  5. Poor recreation facilities and programs
  6. Ineffectiveness of the political structure and grievance mechanisms

Third Level of Intensity
  7. Disrespectful white attitudes
  8. Discriminatory administration of justice
  9. Inadequacy of federal programs
  10. Inadequacy of municipal services
  11. Discriminatory consumer and credit practices
  12. Inadequate welfare programs

Social and economic conditions in the riot cities constituted a clear pattern of severe disadvantage for Negroes compared with whites, whether the Negroes lived in the area where the riot took place or outside it. Negroes had completed fewer years of education and fewer had attended high school. Negroes were twice as likely to be unemployed and three times as likely to be in unskilled and service jobs. Negroes averaged 70 percent of the income earned by whites and were more than twice as likely to be living in poverty. Although housing cost Negroes relatively more, they had worse housing—three times as likely to be overcrowded and substandard. When compared to white suburbs, the relative disadvantage is even more pronounced. (Kerner Commission, 1968:6–8)

Black-Dominated, Person-Oriented Violence

During the late 1960s and early 1970s, the nation's press carried a number of stories telling of premeditated shoot-outs, snipings, and attacks by black militants and teen-agers on police. The Lemberg Center for the Study of Violence at Brandeis University found these reports to be largely inaccurate and sensational. Nonetheless, the potential for outbreaks of black-dominated, person-oriented violence did and continues to reside within the nation's black ghettos.

The ideological basis for violent attacks on police officers and whites in positions of power rests on the view that the black ghettos are colonies of white America. The two-nation metaphor of "colony" and "colonizer" has suggested to some militant blacks the need of freeing one from the other—a conflict of interest best handled by making the separation more complete and violent. Viewed from this perspective the police and other armed agents of the state constitute "an army of occupation" protecting the interests of outside exploiters and maintaining white domination over the ghetto. Some black militants have called for "a war of independence" and identify sympathetically with guerrilla warfare of the sort waged in the Third World.

The importance of such tactics is made clear in a statement by Reverend Albert B. Cleage, Jr., a militant black minister from Detroit:

In terms of the realities of the situation, we have got to evolve a strategy of chaos. Deliberately we have got to tear up everything that doesn't give us an equal shake. They say that Negroes have always had a genius for tearing up things. I'm not talking about the natural ability that we have to tear up things. I'm talking about a deliberately conceived plan to tear up those things from which we are excluded, those things that do not give us equality of opportunity, anything that exists in these United States— either accept us in it, or—we'll do everything possible to tear it up (Franklin, 1971:220).

The ominous nature of such warnings has taken on new meaning with the Miami riot of May 1980. The riot was triggered by the acquittal of four white police officers accused of bludgeoning to death Arthur McDuffie, a black insurance agent. Angry blacks attended a downtown protest rally. After the rally protesters broke into the Justice Building and vandalized the first floor. Others set fire to the nearby State Office Building and smashed and burned dozens of cars in the parking lot. Uptown in Liberty City, the black ghetto, rioting broke out in full force. Three young whites who were driving home from a fishing trip were pulled from their car and beaten to death. Along some streets rioters set up roadblocks and lay in wait for whites. Regarding the violence one young black said, "It was payback. Payback for all the stuff Whitey has done to us."

As the riot wore on, attacks on whites gave way to looting and fire-bombing. Snipers deterred fire fighters from combating the blazes. By the second day, blacks became the chief victims of violence. In some cases, white police officers went on sprees of their own, attacking blacks and vandalizing cars. During the course of the three-day riot, eighteen people were killed and damage to property exceeded $200 million. Some 3,600 National Guard troops were sent to Miami and ended the rioting.

Many factors fed the violence in Miami. Large numbers of blacks had come to believe that the criminal justice system was not working for them. Miami blacks, especially the youth, had encountered increasingly high levels of unemployment. As a consequence, a growing proportion of the city's black population was being rendered a permanent under-class. The Miami situation was exacerbated by the city's being an entry point for refugees, especially Cubans. During the previous two decades, Cubans had displaced blacks from the hotel service jobs that blacks had held for years. From 1968 to 1978, the percentage of blacks holding jobs as machine operators fell from 10.3 percent of the black population to 2.2 percent; conversely, the number of unskilled black laborers rose from 12.4 percent to 25 percent. For many blacks it seemed as if the engine of social progress had been thrown into reverse. Similarly, in 1960 blacks owned 25 percent of Miami's gasoline stations. By 1979, the figure stood at 9 percent while the Hispanic-owned stations rose from 12 percent to 18 percent. Blacks increasingly had come to feel that they were third-class citizens behind whites and Hispanics (Porter and Dunn, 1981).

Sources of Black Militancy

The upsurge in black militancy during the 1960s and early 1970s was associated with a broad crisis of **legitimacy** within American life. Draft resisters, student protesters, and liberated women also came to question the legitimacy of the authority exercised by the military, college administrators, and males—authority that the last group had come to regard as being historically, if not biologically, under their jurisdiction. Indeed this denial of legitimacy has come to encompass traditional authorities in the family, the school, the church, the army, and even the national political system. Among the factors underlying the decline in legitimacy were the nation's involvement in the unpopular war in Vietnam, the widespread loss of credibility associated with the style and nature of the Johnson and Nixon administrations, the traumatic impact of the political assassinations of a number of charismatic leaders, including the Kennedy brothers and the Reverend Martin Luther King, Jr. (individuals who enjoyed the trust of the excluded and disaffected), and the appeal to youth of a more humanist, experimental, and relativistic world outlook.

Although black unrest was closely tied to the broader crisis of legitimacy within American society, sociologists and psychologists suggested that a variety of other factors were also at work. Many of these factors are once more coming to the forefront in the 1980s. These factors are captured and portrayed by the interpretations (i.e., hypotheses) discussed below.

The Relative Deprivation Thesis

Relative deprivation refers to the gap between what people actually have and what they have come to expect and feel to be their just due. The discrepancy between the rapid escalation of black expectations and what in fact blacks have been able to attain has contributed to black militancy and rioting. During the 1960s, civil-rights leaders and top government officials promised a lot—a new day for blacks that would be achieved through civil-rights legislation and the war on poverty (a Great Society). However, they delivered little. Blacks were led to believe that they would be much better off, but little dramatic improvement occurred. At the same time television penetrated—indeed invaded—the black ghettos, feeding discontent among blacks with trite depictions of white middle-class life styles.

Other forces also fed a sense of relative deprivation. With the migration of blacks from rural areas to urban centers, the educational, occupational, and income gap between blacks and whites became exaggerated and magnified. Further, the early gains of the civil-rights movement made credible the notion that blacks would rapidly gain a fair share of America's good things. Yet many blacks found themselves much in the position of underprivileged urchins who have their noses pressed against the store window, longing for the goodies inside; in the past, segregation and discrimination barred them from entering the door—now they could enter the store, but they lacked the economic resources for securing the goodies. Hence, new expectations went unfulfilled, or in any event were fulfilled too slowly. Such circumstances gave rise to frustration, which then found expression in aggressive and violent outbursts (a variant of the frustration-aggression theory). We shall consider the matter of relative deprivation at greater length in chapter 13.

Social Disorganization Thesis

Black rioting and militancy have also been associated with a breakdown of consensual norms within society and with the inability or unwillingness of the agencies of social control to effect their restoration. Such circumstances derive from massive social change—from such trends as industrialization, urbanization, and modernization that give birth to new classes and groups with new social perceptions and life styles. Accompanying these changes are **anomie** and **alienation,** conditions in which individuals no longer feel attached to or part of the existing social and political order. When large numbers of people experience frustration and stress over an extended period, they become susceptible to courses of action not otherwise considered. As the black population became increasingly urbanized, traditional patterns of racial subordination were no longer deemed appropriate.

Part of the larger breakdown of traditional patterns is the disintegration of ruling elites: Traditional elites find their cohesiveness undermined, their ruling effectiveness impaired, and their legitimacy questioned. The historian Crane Brinton (1938) found this sort of disintegration underlying the four revolutions he studied, including the breakdown in Tzarist Russia of March, 1917. Something of this sort occurred in the United States. In prior decades the low incidence of black violence in the South was partly the product of the well-founded fear by blacks that severe retribution would be visited upon them. But as black strength increased sufficiently in urban centers and whites became troubled by brutal retaliation, it became safer for blacks to translate their rage against white oppression into violence. Indeed, the faint stirrings of white conscience concerning their racist behavior may have had the paradoxical effect of legitimizing black violence without

simultaneously leading to actions that dramatically alter racist institutions. During the past several decades American society has widely
disseminated the message that blacks were and are being treated badly.
This in turn has suggested that blacks are justified in taking strong, even
violent, actions to eradicate racism.

Group Conflict Thesis

Civil violence has also been viewed as a product of a struggle for
power among various groups within a society. As we observed in chapter 3, some things defined as "good" are scarce and divisible, so that the
more there is for the one, the less there is for the other. By virtue of
their control of critical institutions, whites have been able to effect
black subordination and hence to lay claim to an unequal and larger
share of the socially defined "good" things. The slogan—Black Power
—reflects a demand by blacks that the "good" things of American life
be reallocated. Viewed from this perspective, rioting represents a
"Black Revolt," a renunciation of allegiance and subjection to the white
"Establishment."

Any number of sociologists have suggested that the looting accompanying racial outbreaks has constituted a bid for a redistribution of property: "It is a message that certain deprived sectors of the population
want what they consider their fair share—and that they will resort to
violence to get it" (Dynes and Quarantilli, 1968:14). In Watts, Newark,
Detroit, and Miami, the main businesses affected were groceries, supermarkets, pawn shops, and furniture and liquor stores, while banks,
utility stations, industrial plants, schools, hospitals, and private residences (except where the latter were burned as a by-product of being
in or near vulnerable business establishments) were usually ignored.
The looters generally received support from many people in their community and often worked together in pairs, as family units, or in small
groups. Property redefinition typically passed through three stages: In
the first stage, looting was initially a symbolic act of defiance—an assault
upon the "white man's" reverence for property; in the second stage, a
more conscious, deliberate plundering developed, at times spurred on
by delinquent gangs; and, in the third stage, looting became the socially
expected thing to do, on occasion becoming transformed into a "carni-
val spirit." Widespread looting may then constitute a kind of mass
protest against white establishment conceptions of property.

Psychology of Violence Thesis

"At the level of individuals, violence is a cleansing force. It frees the
native from his inferiority complex and from his despair and inaction;
it makes him fearless and restores his self-respect." These words were

written by Frantz Fanon (1966:73), a black psychoanalyst from Martinique who served with the Algerian rebels. In his book, *The Wretched of the Earth,* he argued that violence is not only a political necessity for colonial peoples seeking their independence but a personal necessity for "colored natives" striving to be "men." Because the systematic violence of colonialism deadened and degraded the natives, Fanon insisted, they could achieve psychic wholeness only by committing acts of violence against the white rulers and masters whom they wish to supplant.

Kenneth B. Clark makes a somewhat similar point. Discussing black youth engaged in urban rioting, Clark (1967:22), a black psychologist, writes:

> Direct observation of the young Negroes reveals that they are not only destructive, but in the process of destroying are seeking to affirm. They are affirming their power to destroy. In the act of rebelling they appear to be asserting the ability to rebel. Beneath the random and clearly destructive and irrational behavior, there remains the pathetic logic of asserting self-esteem and searching for a positive identity by exposing oneself to danger and even inviting death. This is the quest for the self-esteem of the truly desperate human being. This is the way those who have absolutely nothing to lose seek a pathetic affirmation of self even if it is obtained moments before death.

Robert W. Friedrichs (1968) also argues that blacks need to pass through a period of emotional catharsis characterized by aggression and social withdrawal if they are later to move on to full participation in American society. Thus ghetto rioting is seen as a search for self-esteem and a positive group identity.

Riot Ideology Thesis

T. M. Tomlinson (1968) suggests that in recent decades a "riot ideology" has become fashionable in black communities and that a significant minority of blacks have come to view civil violence as a legitimate and productive mode of protest. It is of interest that the idea that ghetto "riots" are "weapons" and "rebellions" only began to be publicized and to gain popular acceptance during the spring of 1966. The kind of behavior exhibited in these later "riots," including those following Reverend Martin Luther King Jr.'s assassination in the spring of 1968, was practically indistinguishable from that typical of the 1964 "riots" or the 1965 Watts "riot." What changed were the accompanying attitudes and interpretations.

Hence, the California McCone Commission report was probably correct in denying a political or revolutionary basis to the Watts disturbance. Further proof of this verdict is reflected in the lead article in the September, 1965, issue of the *Liberator,* a militant black publication.

The postriot article, headlined "Watts, L.A.: A First Hand Report, Rebellion Without Ideology," stated that the riots lacked purpose, ideology, and organization. It took roughly a year-and-a-half after the 1964 "riots" for militant black intellectuals, including Stokely Carmichael and Rap Brown, to formulate the interpretation that the riots had a revolutionary message and were conscious political acts. It took another two years for this conclusion to be taken over by a significant number of rank-and-file blacks.

According to the riot ideology thesis, civil violence among blacks is a response to frustrations experienced within a racist society and to *shared interpretations* of these frustrations. The sociologist Seymour Spilerman (1970) points out that television provided the media vehicle that stimulated the development of heightened racial consciousness among blacks. Television has portrayed the desperation and plight of ghetto blacks and the ineffectiveness of government programs in combating black disadvantage. Simultaneously, television has carried the speeches and commentaries of black militants and film tape of ghetto rioting, looting, and fire-bombing. Spilerman says that factors such as these lay the groundwork for the mass dissemination of an ideology of violence.

Intergroup Cooperation

With conflict so rampant within the world, it may seem that conflict among differing racial and ethnic groups is inevitable. But is conflict inevitable? And should conflict arise between groups, is it inevitable that the turbulence continuously escalate in intensity? Or are there mechanisms whereby conflict may be contained and even resolved? It is to these matters that we now turn our attention. (Chapter 15 also deals with strategies for combating racism.)

Harmonious Intergroup Relations: A Case Study

Racism and conflict is not an inevitable outcome of intergroup contact. The anthropologist Ethel John Lindgren (1938) provides us with an example of a harmonious relationship that is particularly insightful because it involves two peoples with quite different racial and cultural backgrounds: the Tungus and the Cossacks. For a time during the 1930s, Lindgren lived in northwestern Manchuria among the two groups and observed their relationship.

Racially the Reindeer Tungus are a "Mongoloid" people while the Russian Cossacks are a stocky, burly "Caucasoid" people. The Tungus maintain a nomadic existence. They dwell in tents and depend upon their domesticated reindeer, hunting, and trade with the Cossacks for subsistence. The Cossacks dwell in village homes and derive their subsistence from farming, stock-raising, and trading with the Tungus. Religiously, the Tungus are nominal Christians who continue to abide by their ancient religious practices. They place great reliance on shamans, individuals adept at curing the sick, predicting the future, and communicating with spirits. The Cossacks are zealous Christians who simultaneously manage an elaborate repertoire of superstition and folk belief.

Despite these considerable differences, Lindgren reports:

> I heard no Tungus or Cossack express fear, contempt, or hatred in relation to the other group as a whole or any individual composing it. A few traits of the opposite group are habitually criticized, and a few praised on the basis of a comparison with the corresponding traits of the speaker's culture (p. 607).

In brief, each group harbors ethnocentric attitudes.

The Tungus criticize the Cossacks for the prevalence of thefts in their community, a crime unknown among the Tungus. For their part, the Cossacks acknowledge the scrupulous honesty of the Tungus, a trait the Cossacks find quite praiseworthy. However, the Cossacks criticize the Tungus for their acts of random violence, which occur while the Tungus are under the influence of alcohol, behavior the Tungus themselves deplore. But despite these criticisms of the other's behavior, Lindgren notes: "Expressions of dislike and distrust with regard to individuals in the other group are of exactly the same type as those applied within the group itself, and admiration seems to predominate over criticism" (p. 607). Nor was Lindgren able to discover any tradition of unfriendly relations between the two groups, although she inquired of the elderly about previous hostility.

The two groups come in contact on a regular basis. Markets provide one opportunity. Two or three times during the winter, when the Tungus are busy hunting, the Cossacks travel with horse-drawn sledges up the frozen rivers and meet the Tungus at a forest rendezvous. Likewise during the summer, when the Cossacks are occupied with farming, the Tungus make several trips to the Cossack village. The markets last a number of days. The Tungus trade furs to the Cossacks in exchange for needles, thread, axes, iron pots, copper kettles, gunpowder, flour, and clothing. The trade takes place between trading partners who call each other *andak* or "friend." A Tungus commonly boasts about the wealth and superior products of his Cossack *andak*, who in turn boasts about his Tungus *andak*'s hunting prowess.

The Tungus and Cossacks also encounter one another when on hunting excursions. The two peoples do not divide the hunting grounds. Nonetheless, the first to arrive in a valley, Tungus or Cossack, is left undisturbed. Later in the evening, members of the two groups seek out the other's camp for the sake of company. Longer visits also take place.

Lindgren attributes the good relationships between the Tungus and the Cossacks to a number of factors. First, the two peoples have always had small populations so that individuals were able to establish primary-type relationships with one another. Second, the groups were not in competition for land or other scarce resources. The Tungus herded more than a 7000-square-mile territory while the Cossacks cultivated a relatively small tract. Third, both groups bore hostility toward the Chinese, who had imposed a tax on their fur trade, a shared resentment that strengthened the bonds between them. And fourth, both groups benefited economically from mutual trade. Their cultures also closely complemented one another. Both peoples shared Christian beliefs while the Cossacks took delight in praising the insights and successful prophecies of the Tungus shamans.

Conditions since the 1930s have not permitted Western social scientists to return to northwestern Manchuria to update material on the Tungus and the Cossacks. Their amicable relationships may have continued. On the other hand, it is possible that a depletion of game, population changes, or trading disagreements may have fostered discord and conflict.

Arousal and Resolution of Conflict: Case Studies

Muzafer Sherif and his associates (1961) have conducted a number of classic experiments designed to show how conflict typically arises between two groups, and how, occasionally at least, hostility gives way to cordial relationships. For experimental purposes they employed an isolated summer camp as the setting. For their subjects they chose boys eleven or twelve years old, all of whom were healthy, socially well-adjusted, somewhat above average in intelligence, and from stable, white, Protestant, middle-class homes—in brief, boys with a homogeneous background. This procedure was designed to rule out from the beginning explanations of hostility or friendly intergroup attitudes in terms of differences in socioeconomic, ethnic, religious, or family backgrounds. The several stages of one experiment were as follows:

For the first six days of their stay in the camp (stage one), the boys were paired into two groups, neither of which was aware of the other group's existence. Although the two campsites were not far apart, they were out of sight and earshot of each other. Each group had its own facilities for swimming, boating, campfires, and the like. The researchers fostered group cohesion through common and interdependent activities characterized by goals integral to actual situations—cookouts, preparing campfires, improving swimming facilities, treasure hunts, and so on. Before the end of the first stage each group had adopted a name ("Eagles" and "Rattlers"), had developed a recognized status hierarchy among its members, had formulated individual role assignments, and had evolved various norms concerning "toughness" and cursing.

The second six days (stage two) consisted of experimental efforts to create friction between the Eagles and the Rattlers. The experimenters brought the two groups into competitive contact with one another through games and tournaments (baseball, touch football, a tug-of-war, and a treasure-hunt) in which cumulative scores were kept for each group (not for individuals). The experimenters also devised situations designed to be frustrating to one group and perceived by it as caused by the other group. For instance, Sherif arranged for the Eagles to preempt a ball field that the Rattlers considered to be their "turf." Friction became commonplace. The Eagles, after a defeat in a tournament game, burned a banner left behind by the Rattlers. The next morning the Rattlers seized the Eagles' flag when they arrived on the athletic field. Other incidents—name-calling, scuffling, and raiding—developed.

The third six-day period (stage three) was designed as an integration phase. Sherif and his associates first undertook to test the hypothesis that pleasant social contacts between members of conflicting groups would reduce friction between them. The hostile Rattlers and Eagles were brought together for social events: going to the movies, eating in the same dining hall, shooting off firecrackers, and so on. But far from reducing conflict, these situations only provided new opportunities for the rival groups to berate and attack each other. For instance, in the dining hall, they would hurl paper, food, and vile names at each other.

Sherif and his associates then returned to a corollary of their initial assumption about the creation of conflict. They reasoned that just as competition generates friction, working in common on a project should promote harmony. To test this hypothesis experimentally, they created a series of urgent and natural situations that challenged the boys. In this way superordinate-goal activities were introduced. One of these followed the shutting off of the common water supply by the experimenters, a development explained by the experimenters as the work of "vandals." A plan was formulated whereby the damage was repaired through a good deal of work on everyone's part. As the boys began to complain of thirst, Eagles and Rattlers found themselves working side by side. A similar opportunity offered itself when the boys requested a movie. The experimenters told them that the camp could not afford to rent one. The two groups then got together, chose the film by a vote, jointly financed the venture, and enjoyed the showing together. In due course, intergroup frictions were virtually eliminated, new friendships developed between individuals across group lines, and the groups actively sought opportunities to mingle, entertain, and "treat" each other.

The Sherif experiments demonstrate the role that competition plays in generating hostility and prejudice. It also shows that the possibilities for achieving harmony are greatly enhanced when groups are brought together to work toward *common goals.* Hostility gives way when groups pull together to achieve overriding goals that are real and compelling to all concerned. This often occurs, for instance, in real life situations during wartime when various racial and ethnic groups rally together to pursue the war effort against a common national enemy.

SUMMARY

1. One of the principal sources of conflict among people is their mutual claim upon the same scarce, divisible "good things," especially wealth, power, and status. Not uncommonly the more there is for one group the less there is for the other. A second important source of social conflict is value differences. Groups are divided on the matter of which group will be able to transform its morality into the operating standards for a society.

2. The absence of racial and ethnic conflict does not necessarily signify the existence of stable, nonstressful relationships. It may merely mean that a dominant group has more or less successfully coerced and intimidated the subservient group. Also, the more the parties to conflict feel themselves integrated within society, the less likely is their conflict to take a violent form.

3. Conflict is a potentially destructive and disruptive force within human interaction. Racial and ethnic conflicts often drain and dissipate energies and resources that might otherwise find direction within more productive channels and cooperative activities. And conflict may imperil institutional functioning. Yet racial conflict also has other consequences. A society that is ridden by a good many divisions that run in every direction is in less danger of being torn apart by violence than one split along just one line. Conflict may prevent social systems from ossifying by exerting pressure for change and innovation. And conflict quickens group allegiances and loyalties and thus provides a social glue that binds people together.

4. The suppression-insurrection pattern of racial violence was derived from the dominant-subservient or master-slave relationship. Underlying this arrangement was the assumption that masters had the "right" to resort to violence in dealing with their slaves. Physical force was a means for maintaining white dominance.

5. In lynching the action is one-sided and directed against specific individuals. Before the Civil War, the lynching of blacks was relatively rare except in cases of insurrection conspiracies. The largest number of lynchings occurred during the 1890s and early 1900s.

6. In white-dominated, person-oriented rioting, violence typically takes the following course: The attackers are white; their victims are black; the violence originates with and is directed and controlled by whites; the whites seek to inflict personal injury more-or-less indiscriminately upon the blacks; the blacks, as victims, do little seriously to fight back or to defend themselves. The model for this form of violence is the Springfield, Illinois, race riot of 1908.

7. Blacks have not always remained passive victims during riots. In racial warfare, person-oriented rioting, both blacks and whites engage in attacks upon members of the other group. The model for this type of violence is the 1943 riot in Detroit. In the riot blacks attacked whites on streetcars and assaulted whites leaving work at various auto plants. Whites attempted to invade the black ghetto and to assault blacks.

8. In black-dominated, property-oriented rioting, blacks initiate the violence and direct their hostilities toward property rather than toward persons. The 1935 Harlem riot was of this sort. The ghetto outbreaks of the 1960s and early 1970s also centered about looting and fire-bombing.

9. During the late 1960s and early 1970s, the nation's press carried a number of stories telling of premeditated shoot-outs, snipings, and attacks by blacks on whites and the police. These reports turned out to be largely inaccurate and sensational. Nonetheless, the potential for outbreaks of black-dominated, person-oriented violence did and continues to reside within the nation's black ghettos.

10. The discrepancy between the rapid escalation of black expectations and what in fact blacks have been able to attain has contributed to black militancy and rioting. This formulation is the relative deprivation thesis. During the 1960s, civil-rights leaders and top government officials promised a lot but delivered little. Further, the early gains of the civil-rights movement made credible the notion that blacks would rapidly gain a fair share of America's good things.

11. The social disorganization thesis suggests that black rioting and militancy have resulted from a breakdown of consensual norms within society and from the inability or unwillingness of the agencies of social control to effect their restoration. Such circumstances derive from massive social change. Anomie and alienation accompany these changes. When large numbers of people experience frustration and stress over an extended period, they become susceptible to courses of action not otherwise considered.

12. The group conflict thesis views civil violence as a product of a struggle for power among various groups within a society. By virtue of their control of critical institutions, whites have been able to effect black subordination and hence to lay claim to an unequal and larger share of the socially defined "good" things. Black militancy entails a

demand by blacks that the "good" things of American life be real-located.

13. According to the psychology of violence thesis, blacks need to pass through a period of emotional catharsis characterized by aggression and social withdrawal if they are later to move on to full participation in American society. Thus ghetto rioting is seen as a search for self-esteem and a positive group identity.

14. The riot ideology thesis holds that in recent decades it has become fashionable in black communities to view civil violence as a legitimate and productive mode of protest. Violence is seen as a response to frustrations experienced within a racist society and to shared interpretations of these frustrations. Television provided the media vehicle that stimulated the development of heightened racial consciousness among blacks.

15. Racial and ethnic conflict is not an inevitable outcome of inter-group contact. This point is demonstrated by the harmonious relation-ships that prevail among the Tungus and the Cossacks. Research by Muzafer Sherif also demonstrates that the possibilities for achieving harmony are greatly enhanced when groups are brought together to work toward common goals. Hostility gives way when groups pull to-gether to achieve overriding goals that are real and compelling to all concerned.

GLOSSARY

Alienation   A pervasive sense of powerlessness, meaninglessness, isola-tion, and self-estrangement.

Anomie   A condition within a society or group in which there exists a weakened respect for some of the norms.

Conflict   A struggle over values and claims to wealth, power, and status in which the opponents attempt to neutralize, injure, or elimi-nate their rivals.

Legitimacy   Exercise of power that people accept because the formu-lation of policies and orders follows rules to which they subscribe.

Lynching   Mob action that summarily and illegally takes an individ-ual's life, especially by hanging.

Relative Deprivation   The gap between what people actually have and what they have come to expect and feel to be their just due.

Stratification 7

*W*ithin a society, people are ranked in a hierarchy—a social ladder—that differentiates them as superior or inferior, higher or lower. We refer to this differential ranking of people as **social stratification**. Broadly considered, it is questionable whether any society, even the simplest, lacks some form of social inequality. In this sense, social stratification is universal. In certain socially important respects, all societies differentiate among and rank people.

Social Inequality

Stratification contains the answer to the distributive problem of *who gets what, when, and how.* As a consequence, a society's "good" things —especially wealth, status, and power—are allocated in an uneven manner. Simultaneously, the burdens and unpleasant chores are unequally distributed among the members of the society. In sum, stratification represents institutionalized inequality in the allocation of social rewards and burdens. Individuals are locked within an arena of social relationships in which they sharply differ in their life-chances and styles of living.

Dimensions of Stratification

The sociologist Max Weber (1946, 1947) profoundly influenced sociological considerations of social stratification. He pointed out that people are ranked along three dimensions: privilege, status, and power. The privilege hierarchy (Weber used the term "class") has to do with people's ability to command access to various goods and services. People of similar rank share roughly comparable incomes and consequently have kindred *life-chances.* By **life-chances** Weber meant the typical probability that people will enjoy those goods and services that contribute to physical survival and comfort and to a feeling of psychological well-being. In modern societies the most meaningful measure of individuals' life-chances is their income. Personal or family income is the foundation of a person's standard of living or socioeconomic level.

Status has to do with people's sense of worth and respect, especially the feeling that they are admired and thought well of. Specific units of prestige do not show up on a yearly balance sheet. Rather, status is intangible—something that people carry in their heads. It provides an expansive feeling of being important and special. All this is not to say that human beings neglect opportunities to give status a tangible form in their daily lives. They do so through titles, seats of honor, badges and ribbons, trophies, honorary degrees, and, in general, rituals that reveal respect, awe, and deference.

Power entails the ability to control or influence the behavior of others, even when they are disposed to act in some other fashion. As a consequence of inequalities in power, there are those who rule and lead and those who yield and follow. Power allows some individuals to make the world work on their behalf. By gaining mastery of skills, knowledge, and critical resources, a person is able to gain control over the behavior of other people. To interpose oneself between people and the means whereby people meet their subsistence and social needs is to effect mastery over people.

Wherever we turn in life we encounter power (e.g., who will decide when a phone conversation will be terminated, which party will sleep on which side of the bed, and how a task will be "properly" performed?). The ubiquity of power has led the sociologist Amos Hawley (1963:422) to remark: "Every social act is an exercise of power, every social relationship is a power equation, and every social group or system is an organization of power."

Privilege, status, and power constitute analytically distinct dimensions of stratification. Clearly they are not identical nor do they necessarily overlap. Hangmen, prostitutes, and professional criminals often receive relatively high economic returns but enjoy little status or power. University faculty members rank comparatively low in income and power yet public opinion polls show them ranking high in status. Some public officials enjoy considerable power yet receive low salaries and little status. Nonetheless, these three dimensions tend to hang together, feeding and supporting each other.

Conflict and Stratification

Weber's dimensions of stratification allow us to distinguish among the principal components of social inequality. As pointed out in chapters 3 and 6, clashes over wealth (i.e., privilege), status, and power underlie much human conflict. The other major source of friction is clashing social values. Given the prevalence of differing interests and values among human beings, the potential for aggression is ever-present in intergroup relations. But aggression given full rein in a constant war of all against all would imperil the survival of the species. Consequently, aggression must be regulated and contained.

Two primary means exist by which human beings can manage aggression: stratification and territoriality. In stratification, people establish a hierarchy or order of preference in the distribution of such good things as wealth, status, and power. Additionally, the high-ranking people impose their values on others by translating their morality into law. Stratification limits aggression because people interact in ways that conform to their advantaged or disadvantaged roles. They fit their actions together in ways that reflect their superior or inferior ranks.

In territoriality people effect monopoly rights over the scarce resources in an area and impose their set of values upon the inhabitants of the area. Territoriality limits aggression to the extent to which people refrain from going where they are likely to be involved in unpleasant or violent encounters. Segregation is an important mechanism of territoriality (*see* chapters 8 and 9).

Territory is an instrument by which elites appropriate privilege. Not only are their homes, resorts, and offices located in the most desirable places, their command of territory—factories, mines, and plantations—makes them gatekeepers in the distribution of good things. Within the United States, racial and ethnic minorities, women, institutional inmates, and the aged and youth are especially deprived of society's good things. Additionally, territory is a vehicle for effecting control over people. The disadvantaged can be placed on "reservations"—blacks and Chicanos in ghettos, women in kitchens, "deviants" in prisons and mental institutions, the aged in nursing homes, and youth on campuses (where growing numbers of young people are diverted without threatening the jobs of the working population). Consequently subject peoples, besides forfeiting the full fruits of territory, are controlled by territorial arrangements (Vander Zanden, 1981b).

But stratification and territoriality contain a fundamental contradiction. They not only serve to control aggression; they also breed counteraggression (van den Berghe, 1974). The disadvantages imposed by the haves are not suffered gladly by the have-nots. Hierarchical and territorial benefits are both aggressively defended and challenged. Consequently a social order is not fixed for all time.

Systems of Stratification

Human beings discovered early in their history that role differentiation was necessary. Among other things, a division of labor results in greater efficiency. The earliest and simplest expressions of specialization were the divisions of labor between the sexes and among age groups. With the growth in technological specialties, the division of labor became increasingly complex. To these differing divisions of labor human beings have linked various systems of stratification. As a result, rewards and burdens are unequally distributed among the various roles or positions making up the divisions of labor. Within the United States the most critical and fundamental systems of stratification are class, gender, age, and race and/or ethnicity.

Class Stratification. In our daily conversations we make reference to the "lower class," the "middle class," and the "upper class." We commonly think of these social classes as constituting rather distinct groups. Sociologists study social classes in a variety of ways, each of which renders a somewhat different image of class. One approach considers class to be a statistical category. As such it seeks an "objective" measure of rank, most commonly income, occupation, or education (or some combination of these characteristics). A second method views class as a social category. It employs a "subjective" measure of class. Sociologists ask individuals, "Which would you say you belong to: the middle class, lower class, upper-middle class, working class, or upper class?" A third approach defines class as a social group. Rather than asking people to rank *themselves* (as in the subjective approach), sociologists ask them how they rank *others.* This "reputational" approach rests on people's knowledge of who associates with whom.

The sociologists Richard D. Coleman and Lee Rainwater (1978) provide us with one picture of the class structure of urban America. They brought together the subjective and reputational methods in a survey of Boston and Kansas City residents. Interviewers asked individuals about levels of contemporary living. The urbanites ranked each other and themselves in the following manner:

1. *People who have really made it.* At the very top of the American class structure is an elite class of wealthy individuals. Some of these are old rich (the Rockefellers); others the celebrity rich (Paul Newman); still others the anonymous rich (a millionaire shopping center developer); and yet another group made up of the run-of-the-mill rich (a well-heeled physician).

2. *People who are doing very well.* Corporate executives and professional people make up this class. These individuals reside in large, comfortable homes, belong to relatively exclusive country clubs, occasionally vacation in Europe and places known for their elite clientele, and send their children to private colleges or reputable, large state universities.

3. *People who have achieved the middle-class dream.* These individuals enjoy the "good life" as defined in material terms but they lack the luxuries of those in the higher classes. More often

than not they are suburbanites who reside in a three-bedroom home with a family-TV room.

4. *People who have a comfortable life.* While enjoying a "comfortable" life, the members of this class have less money at their disposal than the individuals of the upper and upper-middle classes and they live in less fashionable suburbs.

5. *People who are just getting by.* Some Americans enjoy "respectable" jobs but "the pay is not the greatest." The husband may be employed as a blue-collar worker and the wife typically works as a waitress or store clerk. The couple may own or rent a small home but they find that "getting by" puts a strain on their joint income.

6. *People who are having a really difficult time.* Members of this stratum find "the going tough." Both the husband and the wife work but their income is low. Much of their leisure time is spent viewing television. They do, however, have one consolation: they "aren't on welfare."

7. *People who are poor.* At the "bottom of the heap" are "people who are down and out." Many of them receive government assistance.

Within the United States there is a tendency for privileged positions, or at any rate the opportunities whereby the positions are secured, to be passed on from one generation to the next. By virtue of family and kinship loyalties, one generation attempts to pass on to future generations its advantaged position. Consequently, people's social positions at birth tend to parallel their adult social positions. The net result is that society is composed of relatively enduring classes that monopolize certain positions. In this manner some degree of stability and permanence comes to characterize the class system. This continuity contributes to a common life style and common values and sentiments among members of the same social class.

Gender Stratification.   Men and women differ in their access to privilege, status, and power. The distribution problem of who gets what, when, and how has traditionally been answered in favor of males. It is males who get the best jobs, who are usually relieved of menial household chores, who enjoy the top political offices, who schedule sexual intercourse, and who get most of the orgasms. Gender stratification is an element of *sexism*. **Sexism** entails those social arrangements and enduring patterns by which members of one gender group dominate and oppress the members of the other gender group. *Male chauvinism* denotes sexism practiced by men.

Sexism pervades the social fabric. The sociologist Jessie Bernard observes:

[Sexism is] the unconscious, taken-for-granted, assumed, unquestioned, unexamined, unchallenged acceptance of the belief that the world as it looks to men is the only world, that the way of dealing with it which men have created is the only way, that the values which men have evolved are the only ones, that the way sex looks to men is the only way it can look to anyone, that what men think about what women are like is the only way to think about what women are like (Gornick and Moran, 1971: xxv).

Women who work in the wage economy often find themselves relegated to low-paying or part-time jobs, especially secretarial and clerical work. For full-time, year-round workers, the "pay gap" in median earnings has widened between women and men. Women's pay as a percentage of men's has declined from 64 percent in 1955 to 61 percent in 1960, to 60 percent in 1965, to 59 percent in 1970, to 57 percent in 1975, to 56 percent in 1980. The sociologists David L. Featherman and Robert M. Hauser (1976) calculate that discrimination accounts for about 84 percent of the gap in earnings. Historically the earnings in female-typed occupations like nurse, elementary-school teacher, social worker, secretary, and clerk have been considerably lower than those in comparable male-dominated occupations (McLaughlin, 1978; Wolf and Fligstein, 1979).

Age Stratification. All societies employ age as a central reference point for the ascription of certain roles (Dowd, 1981). For example, within the United States, age operates directly as a criterion for driving a car (age sixteen), voting (age eighteen), becoming president (age thirty-five), and retiring from a job (age sixty-five or seventy). Indeed, most changes in role during an individual's life span are accompanied by a change in chronological age—entering school, completing school, getting one's first job, marrying, having children, being promoted at work, seeing one's youngest child married, becoming a grandparent, and retiring.

Societies divide their members into **age grades**—social layers that are based upon periods in life. Like other forms of stratification, age grading involves the differentiation and ranking of people as superior or inferior, higher or lower. However, unlike movement up or down the class ladder, the mobility of people from one age grade to the next is biologically determined and consequently irreversible (Riley, Johnson, and Foner, 1972).

Within the United States the favored age status is youth. Americans typically define adulthood as a period of responsibility. In contrast, adolescence is portrayed as an irresponsible and carefree period, a time when young people should "have a good time." The elderly have a more restricted position and considerably less prestige. In proportion to their chronological age, Americans stereotype the elderly as mentally enfeebled and senile; unemployable because they are said to be in their second childhood; asexual because older people are viewed as physically unattractive; troublesome since older people are thought to be cranky; and boring because they are believed to live shallow, empty lives. In many respects the elderly, particularly the very old, are America's lepers. **Ageism** entails the systematic negative stereotyping of and discrimination against people because of their age.

Racial and Ethnic Stratification. Chapter 1 examined the nature of dominant-minority group relationships. From this treatment it should be clear that racial and ethnic stratification differs appreciably from systems of stratification premised on class, gender, and age. Its most distinguishing characteristic is that only racial and ethnic groups have the *potential* to carve their own autonomous nation from the existing state. Political separatism offers a solution to disadvantaged racial or ethnic groups that is not possible for disadvantaged class, gender, or age groups. The reason for this is that class, gender, and age groups normally lack the potential for becoming self-sufficient political states because they do not function as self-sufficient social or economic groups.

Although the probability of a separatist movement and its chances for success vary enormously among nations, the underlying potential for such movements exists in most nations with diverse racial and ethnic groups. The issue, then, unlike class stratification, is not replacement of one party or elite by another or even a revolutionary change in the political system. Rather, the question is one of whether the racial or ethnic segments of the society will be willing to participate within the existing nation-state arrangement (Lieberson, 1970). The new states of Africa and Asia provide a good illustration of this. Although there are many competing nonethnic loyalties in the new states—ties to class, party, business, union, profession, or whatever—groups formed of these ties are seldom considered as possible self-standing, maximal social units (i.e., candidates for nationhood). In contrast, competing religious, linguistic, racial, cultural, and related loyalties often threaten the state's very existence, as in the case of Nigeria (i.e., the secessionist Ibo state of Biafra) and Zaïre (i.e., the secessionist Katanga province).

In sum, class conflicts threaten governments and forms of government. They rarely threaten to destroy the nation itself because they do not have alternative definitions of the territorial boundaries of the nation. The sociologist Glifford Geertz (1963:111) observes: "Economic or class or intellectual disaffection threatens revolution, but disaffection based on race, language, or culture threatens partition, irredentism, or merger, a redrawing of the very limits of the state, a new definition of its domain."

The Relationship Between Class and Racial-Ethnic Systems

Within the United States the class and the racial-ethnic systems criss-cross. A general formulation of this principle is found in August B. Hollingshead's statement (1952:680) that a social structure may be "differentiated *vertically* along racial, ethnic and religious lines, and each of these vertical cleavages, in turn, is differentiated *horizontally* by a series of strata or classes that are encompassed within it." Thus religious, ethnic, and racial groups are not arranged in a simple higher and lower ranking with respect to the class stratification system. Each of the religious, ethnic, and racial groups tends to span a range of higher and lower positions within the class structure, sometimes from the top to the bottom, sometimes within a narrower range. The most critical consequence of these two stratification structures is that members of a minority group who achieve mobility into a higher class are not accorded many of the benefits bestowed upon members of the dominant group of the equivalent class.

The two systems need to be kept conceptually separate to discover the nature of their interrelationships. An illustration will help to clarify the matter. How does A, member of the old-American group and the "working class," articulate his or her attitude toward B, a member of the black (or Chicano or Haitian or Italian) group who has an "upper-middle-class" status? In terms of the class hierarchy, the minority-group member would outrank the member of the old-American group. But, in terms of the ethnic or racial structure, the reverse situation would hold true. Reciprocally, the question becomes: How does B articulate his or her attitude in relation to A? Do the attitudes of one stratification structure, either the ethnic and racial or class structure, tend to prevail? Do confusion and tension ensue from the crisscrossing of the two sets of expectations within specific situations?

The answers to these questions partially depend upon whether individual B is a member of the black, Chicano, Haitian, or Italian group. Quite possibly the matter would be resolved somewhat differently in the case of an Italian, in the one instance, and a black, in the other (the attitudes of the class structure tending to prevail in the former case, the attitudes of the racial and ethnic system in the latter).

The importance of keeping these two systems conceptually separate is seen in still another connection. It is known that family, clique, associational, and social relationships tend to be confined to members of one's own or closely adjoining classes. To what extent does the ethnic or racial factor divide the intimate group life of members of the same social class? By way of illustration, do middle-class Jews have more intimate social contacts with middle-class Gentiles or with lower-class

Jews? The same question can be asked of Cubans, Poles, and blacks in relation to the old-American group. The matter again depends to a considerable extent upon the ranking of the ethnic or racial minority on the social-distance scale (Gordon, 1958).

The distinction between the two systems is similarly of importance in considering social mobility (i.e., the movement of people up and down the stratification hierarchy). In situations where the accent falls on democratic relations, status ideally is determined by what individuals can *do,* not by what they *are.* A distinction can be made between these two types of status: achieved status and ascribed status. *Ascribed statuses* are assigned to individuals, without reference to ability, on the basis of such characteristics as sex, age, and family membership. **Achieved statuses** are acquired by individuals through competition and individual effort. Within the ethnic and racial structure of stratification, status is ascribed to individuals by the society; it is not rooted in their own competitive or individual effort. On the other hand, within the class structure, there is greater room for achieving high status, although one's achievement is often limited by inheritance and unequal access to opportunities, both of which are linked to family membership. To the extent to which status is ascribed (e.g., on the basis of religious, ethnic, and racial membership), social mobility within a social order is impaired. To the extent to which status is achieved, social mobility is facilitated.

Black Plight: Class or Race

The civil-rights and Black Power movements of the 1960s and 1970s sought to correct the plight of blacks and other minorities within the United States. New civil-rights legislation and federal programs were enacted to remedy the nation's social ills. Despite these developments, large numbers of blacks remain in a world of poverty and despair. Social scientists have usually explained black disadvantage as the result of white racism. However, a number of them, including some black sociologists, have recently been arguing that this traditional explanation is too simple. They say that current black difficulties can better be understood as the product of class factors and economic trends. The ensuing controversy has come to occupy center stage in the sociology of racial and ethnic minorities.

The Class Argument

William J. Wilson, a black sociologist, argues that economic opportunities for blacks now are shaped more by their class than by their race. In *The Declining Significance of Race* (1978), Wilson contends that race can no longer be considered as important as it once was in determining the life-chances of blacks. He says that access to higher-paying jobs is increasingly based on education. Within this context educated blacks are experiencing unprecedented job opportunities equivalent to those of whites with comparable qualifications.

Following publication of the book, the American Sociological Association awarded Wilson its prestigious Sydney Spivack Award. Among other things, the award recognizes "significant sociological work that has appeared during the past five years." Simultaneously, the Association of Black Sociologists, an organization with several hundred members, issued a statement condemning the book's thesis and expressing concern that Wilson had received the award.

Wilson contends that relations between racial groups are shaped largely by the character of the economic system of production. Moreover, the internal differences and divisions that characterize the members of a group—the social, status, and class distinctions—hinge upon the type of economic order and the position individuals occupy within it. According to Wilson, American society has undergone three stages in black-white relations. Each stage embodies a different form of stratification. Stage one—the period of plantation economy and racial-caste oppression—coincided with antebellum slavery. Stage two—the period of industrial expansion, class conflict, and racial oppression—begins in the last quarter of the nineteenth century and ends at roughly the New Deal era. Stage three—the period of progressive transition from racial inequalities to class inequalities—is associated with the modern industrial era, which flowered during the 1960s and 1970s.

In stage one, the preindustrial period, the slave-based plantation economy of the South permitted a small white elite to achieve enormous regional power. The system virtually excluded free white labor. As a consequence, both blacks and nonslaveholding whites lacked meaningful input in the operation of the South's political and economic life. A slaveholding elite shaped a social order that relegated blacks to indefinite servitude and that reflected and promoted its class interests.

Stage two, the industrial period, brought about new patterns of race relations. A rapidly growing industrial system drew whites from rural America and peasant communities of Europe to work in the new factories and mines. Wilson says that these white laborers viewed free blacks as rivals. In the South white workers succeeded in walling off black competition during the late nineteenth century by helping to produce and elaborate a system of Jim Crow segregation laws. In the North the majority of blacks were trapped in menial positions and were victimized by the hostilities of lower-class whites and European immigrant ethnics. At times racial tension exploded in bloody riots such as those in East St. Louis in 1917 and Chicago in 1919. Management exploited racial antagonisms by using blacks as strikebreakers and permanent replacements to undercut white labor and unions.

Stage three, the modern industrial period, brought with it another new pattern of race relations, one in which class came to replace race as the most important factor influencing black life-chances. As the black populations of the nation's ghettos grew, blacks evolved their own institutions and organizations. This development contributed to internal class differentiation within black communities. Simultaneously the nation's productive system became increasingly automated. Better-paying jobs came to require complex, technical skills with access to them dependent upon educational criteria. And for the first time in the nation's history the state apparatus, rather than being an instrument for oppressing blacks, became an agency promoting racial equality. Responding to the pressures of increased black political resources and to the racial protest movement, government removed barriers to municipal, state, and federal jobs and fought job discrimination in the private sector.

Wilson says that these combined economic and political changes created a pattern of black occupational upgrading. Talented and educated blacks now enjoy unprecedented job opportunities in both the private and public sectors. But the demands of a high technology society threaten to solidify the position of the black underclass. According to Wilson, disadvantaged ghetto blacks owe their plight less to the efforts of whites to keep them subjugated than to the job requirements of a technological age. Economic class is now the principal factor holding blacks back. Blacks have moved historically from a situation in which virtually all of them experienced racial oppression to one in which only the black underclass experiences economic subordination.

All this is not to say that race is now an insignificant aspect of American life or that middle-class blacks escape fully the burdens of racism. Instead, Wilson argues that race is less determinative of fortunes and destinies than it once was. Blacks with the requisite skills can now advance economically while the black underclass without the skills cannot. Consequently the black poor have been left behind. And Wilson believes that the economic gap among blacks is likely to widen due to the vulnerability of low-skilled blacks to unemployment fostered by automation, the loss of central-city jobs, the movement of labor-intensive industries to Taiwan and Southeast Asia, and other changes in the economy. These trends tend to polarize blacks, with a growing and secure middle class at one pole and an increasingly alienated underclass at the other.

Wilson says that under circumstances such as these an emphasis on race obscures the significant differences that exist in the experience and suffering of blacks. More importantly, a preoccupation with race and racial discrimination prevents Americans of all races from addressing the special needs of the most disadvantaged blacks. Policies of affirmative action do not go far enough to meet the "hopeless state" of poor blacks. He claims that affirmative action is a program that assists middle-class blacks. Instead the challenge of the modern period requires public policies that attack inequality on a broad front. Such policies would go beyond ethnic and racial discrimination to confront the destructive features of class subordination. In the absence of such programs, underclass blacks can only become more dependent upon welfare grants and illegal hustles in the black ghettos.

The Race Argument

Many social scientists do not accept Wilson's view that class, not race, is the primary factor underlying the plight of poor blacks. They claim that there is "a unified black experience" within the United States that transcends class. Consequently, the starting point of any analysis of the black situation has to be the recognition that race is the most pervasive fact in the black experience. For instance, Charles V. Willie (1979), a black sociologist, says that the economic sphere cannot be isolated from the other institutions of society. He suggests that, contrary to Wilson's rosy picture of an equalized opportunity structure for blacks and whites, large gaps still persist between the two races in employment, education, housing, and other vital areas. Willie points out that, with respect to employment and earnings, blacks and whites with similar characteristics are not treated alike in the marketplace. As evidence, he cites a study by the U.S. Commission on Civil Rights, which found that in 1975 black males with the same characteristics as white males could be expected to earn 85 percent of the amount that white males earned. Those who favor race as an explanation stress the part that institutional racism plays in American life (*see* chapter 1). They say that white racism is the central force confronting blacks. White elites have shaped institutional life so that good things like wealth, status, and power flow to the advantaged white group. Further, whites have translated their value preferences into law. Consequently, the United States has always been a white nation and has always operated for the benefit of whites.

Viewed from this perspective racism shapes the lives of all Americans from the cradle to the grave. No aspect of life escapes its insidious and devastating touch. White gatekeepers control the entry points to desirable positions. Some blacks may be permitted token entry, but whites never jeopardize their command of the social order. Proponents of the race argument say that even when whites operate in a seemingly color-blind fashion, they never truly relinquish control. Intelligence, certification, and other testing programs that govern entry to schools and professions are culturally biased instruments that function to protect and advance white interests. Blacks can "make it" in the United States only by surrendering their blackness—by abandoning black culture and black identifications—for an artificial "whiteness." Nonetheless, blacks remain "black" and suffer the oppression of all blacks because the world in which they live is a white world. Thus achieving middle-class status and moving to white suburbs hardly free blacks from the psychological shackles of racism.

Kenneth B. Clark (1978, 1980), a black psychologist, calls the notion of black progress seductive and enticing. But, he insists, the conclusion is premature. The number of blacks in executive, managerial, and policy-making positions remains minuscule. Tokenism, not genuine compliance with equal-opportunity and affirmative-action programs, is the rule rather than the exception. Whites do not accept as individuals like themselves those few blacks who do gain entry to better positions. Instead, token blacks have become superficial symbols, so much fraudulent window dressing, that all is well with America. Middle-class blacks rarely are admitted to the informal social cliques and clubs within which people come to know, evaluate, and respect one another. It is in these person-to-person networks that the contacts are made and the liaisons established that lead to the centers of power in business, education, and government.

Clark does not deny that class plays a part in America's system of racial inequality. But he gives a quite different interpretation to class than does Wilson. Clark says that within the United States class and race merge in such a way that blacks are at the bottom of society and whites at the top. Consequently, whites tend to regard people of color as lower-class without distinguishing among them in terms of their educational or occupational status. Nowhere is this convergence of racial and class definitions more clear than in school-busing controversies (Giles, Gatlin, and Cataldo, 1976). Schools are perceived to be either "white" and "middle class" or "black" and "lower class." Thus the insidious view takes hold that middle-class white children must be protected from the "contamination" that would result by busing them to "lower-class black" schools.

Some sociologists like Thomas F. Pettigrew (1980) argue that race remains as important as ever in determining the life-chances of blacks. He says that the black poor are far worse off than the white poor and that the black middle class still has a long way to go before it catches up with the white middle class in economic security, status, and wealth. And Pettigrew notes that the gap in median family income between blacks and whites is not closing.

Critics of Wilson's class argument are skeptical that the gains achieved by middle-class blacks will hold. Harry Edwards (1979), a black sociologist, says that the *Bakke* case and hundreds of suits by whites against affirmative-action programs are hardly grounds for black optimism. Simultaneously, a growing neglect of affirmative-action compliance, federal budget cutting, "tax revolts," and economic "hard times" do not bode well for blacks. Edwards concludes that these factors have already halted and even *reversed* economic gains at all levels of black society.

Clark (1978, 1980) makes the same point. He notes that whites continue to control corporate, university, and government life and hence blacks always remain vulnerable to white racism. Further, black upward mobility remains dependent upon the benevolence of whites, who can give or withhold and who determine the pace and effectiveness of uplift programs. Clark sees "busing," "quotas," "reverse discrimination," "meritocracy," and "maintaining standards" as racial code words for continuing racist practices. Even some former white civil-rights activists, he says:

> ... present arguments against further racial progress on the ground that any attempt to remedy past racism, such as programs to insure black representation in college classes, is itself a form of racism because it treats blacks as a special, separate group. Thus, in the name of an attack on racism, they would perpetuate racism (Clark, 1980:26).

Finally, Clark argues that white unwillingness to come to grips with the plight of ghetto blacks and the failure of whites to see the racial dehumanization in the United States is a symptom of the depth and severity of the racist disease.

The Social Significance of the Class-Race Controversy

The class-race controversy has profound social implications. Each view leads to a somewhat different approach for dealing with the plight of blacks. Consequently, the benefits that would flow to various groups within the black community would differ if one or the other interpretation were translated into social policy. It is hardly surprising, therefore, that the protagonists have carried on their debate in a highly charged, bitter, and vituperative manner.

Wilson's thesis has significant consequences (Record, 1980). He suggests that patterns of black mobility are now coming to resemble those of the Irish and other European immigrant ethnics. These groups also started on the lower rungs of the class ladder and moved upward in response to political and economic opportunities. Wilson believes that the gains made by large numbers of blacks are too often obscured by discussions that focus on the plight of the black underclass. The message Wilson sends blacks is that the American Dream is a realistic hope for them as well as for whites. Blacks too can make it in the United States. Education is the principal escalator in mobility, providing ascent not only in the economic sphere but also in the social and political spheres. In sum, middle-class blacks have arrived. They are a viable, dynamic, and growing group capable of sustaining themselves and socializing their young to participate fully in all realms of American life.

By the same token, Wilson underscores the increasingly difficult circumstances confronting ghetto blacks. He emphasizes that technological developments, industrial relocations, and new job requirements are rendering poor blacks a permanent underclass. His work suggests that existing public programs have failed to draw members of this group into the mainstream. In some instances welfare programs have only worsened the plight of poor blacks by undermining mobility aspirations and promoting dependence upon government handouts. Wilson suggests that in the absence of fundamental structural changes, especially in the economy, the black underclass will be unable to improve its circumstances. Poor blacks are currently caught up in a vicious circle with no major points at which the cumulative and enduring effects of their economic subordination can be broken. Consequently, their life of disadvantage becomes self-perpetuating.

As noted earlier in the chapter, Wilson believes that affirmative-action programs have primarily assisted middle-class blacks and have failed to address the needs of poor blacks. Many black leaders and intellectuals have used figures showing a widening gap between blacks and whites in median family income as the basis for arguing for more affirmative-action programs (the ratio of black-white median family income fell from 61 percent in 1969 to 59 percent in 1978). But in the epilogue to the paperback edition of his book, Wilson says that such figures are misleading. The figures obscure the sharply divergent trends "within" the black population. Wilson shows that the black-white ratio of median family income in male-headed families *increased* from 72 percent in 1969 to 80 percent in 1978. Simultaneously, the large increase in the number of black female-headed families, with median family incomes about one-third of male-headed families, lowered the overall income ratio.

All this leads Wilson to reject as a myth the notion that all blacks, regardless of their station in life, have a uniform experience in a racist society. At a University of Pennsylvania symposium, he argued that the uniform-experience thesis has been advanced by middle-class blacks who have stood to gain the most from antidiscrimination programs. And Wilson accused black intellectuals and leaders of having a vested interest in projecting race, rather than class, as the central issue in developing policies to promote black progress. It allows advantaged blacks to gain leverage from the black community for their own personal advancement in corporations, universities, and government. Moreover, the notion of a uniform black experience downplays growing class hostilities in the black community. These hostilities threaten the positions of middle-class blacks as spokespersons for the entire black community. But Wilson asserts that affirmative-action programs, since they focus upon race and not class, fail to come to grips with the special problems of the black underclass (Gershman, 1980).

Needless to say, Wilson's arguments have provoked a heated counterattack. Many black intellectuals and leaders have charged that

Wilson "misinterprets" the current status of blacks and that his work justifies a retreat from policies designed to overcome the negative effects of racial discrimination. In criticizing *The Declining Significance of Race,* the Association of Black Sociologists said that it was "outraged over the misrepresentation of the black experience. We are also extremely disturbed over the policy implications that may derive from this work and that, given the nature of American society, are likely to set in motion equally objectionable trends in funding, research, and training" (Scully, 1978:7).

Similarly, Vernon E. Jordan, until recently leader of the National Urban League, has termed the "illusion of black progress" as "one of the most dangerous myths in America today," and adds, "It is dangerous because it is false and provides the rationale for former friends to back away from affirmation action, from full-employment policies and from implementing school desegregation" (Johnson, 1979:11). Black leaders like Jesse Jackson and Richard Hatcher have demanded special government assistance for black businesses and programs. They have justified such demands as "reparations" owed blacks for past and present injustices (Gershman, 1980).

Critics of Wilson's position argue that since race is the most pervasive fact in the experience of all blacks, racism must be the central focus of attack. Blacks must unite, regardless of class, to combat their common foe—an unjust social system. Clark (1978, 1980) says that the United States cannot hope to solve its other domestic problems until it comes to terms with racial injustice. The fiscal stability of American cities will continue to erode so long as deteriorating ghettos inhabited by undereducated and unemployed blacks are permitted to proliferate. The nation's economy will remain precarious so long as a tenth of the nation is held in a condition of economic underdevelopment. And domestic peace is continuously endangered where large numbers of blacks are relegated to "the stigmatized status of tax consumers on welfare rolls." Clark insists that continuing racial injustice and cruelty cannot be excused by stating the problem in such a way that the *victims*—poor blacks—are blamed for failing to improve their economic and social positions.

Social Mobility

An integral element in the "American dream" has been the belief that any American who so wills can get ahead and make good. The saga of "from rags to riches" has contributed to an underlying faith in America and its capitalist democracy. The upward mobility of immigrant stock in the American status system has reinforced the belief. Since the Civil War, there has been a great excess in upward over downward mobility in American life. Immigrant groups have benefited from this fact and generally have been able to improve their circumstances.

Experiences as "Middleman" Minorities

Racial and ethnic groups have displayed dissimilar rates of upward mobility. For example, any number of social scientists have noted that American Jews have climbed the social-status ladder more quickly and achieved middle-class status more widely than any other American ethnic group (Strodtbeck, McDonald, and Rosen, 1957; Hurvitz, 1958; Greeley, 1976). In the Northeast, Greeks have similarly tended to attain middle-class status more rapidly than most other groups.

The factors responsible for differing rates of upward mobility have varied with the group in question. For one thing, immigrant groups have differed in the extent to which they have possessed those skills that are adaptive within a commercial-industrial setting. Many Jews and Greeks came to the United States with occupational skills better suited to urban living than those of their fellow immigrants. By the same token, ethnic and racial groups whose cultures were rooted within rural, peasant surroundings were less likely to possess the cultural values appropriate to achievement in America. While most of the Roman Catholic immigrants from eastern and southern Europe and blacks from the South came from rural communities, many Jews and Levantine Greeks came from small towns or cities.

Upward mobility has likewise been related to the ability of ethnic and racial groups to organize effectively to protect and further their interests. Where the ethnic group had previous Old World experience in facing the problem of minority-group adaptation, it was often prepared, as were the Jews and Greeks, to develop more quickly effective community organization in the United States. The Jews had confronted a hostile Gentile world for centuries in Europe, and the Greeks had faced Turkish persecution.

The sociologist Edna Bonacich (1973) highlights the adaptive mechanisms evolved by "middleman minorities" over a prolonged period. Such minorities are commonly trading peoples who assume special occupational niches by virtue of their historical circumstances (Blalock, 1967). Among these groups are the Jews in Europe, Greeks in the United States, the Chinese in Southeast Asia, Asians in East Africa, Armenians in Turkey, Syrians in West Africa, and Parsis in India. In contrast to most ethnic minorities, "middleman minorities" occupy an intermediate rather than a low-status position.

The experience of European Jews is a case in point. By A.D. 313 Christianity had become the official religion of Rome. Full citizenship rights were dependent upon religion and Jews were labeled "nonbelievers." Later the Crusades fanned the flames of fanatical religious intolerance. By virtue of medieval bigotry and persecution, a relatively higher proportion of Jews than Christians turned to trade and commerce, activities that at first enjoyed a marginal place in a predominantly agrarian age. Some Jews prospered. With the growth of cities in Italy in the tenth century and Germany in the eleventh century, commerce and its associated money economy blossomed. But the Catholic church prohibited as a cardinal sin a central ingredient of the new commercial order—the lending of money at interest. Jews, being non-Christians, could lend to non-Jews. The temptation to make interest on money is considerable to most people. Money can beget money. And Jewish merchants were no exception. But the money lender is hardly a popular person. Debtors not uncommonly harbor considerable antagonism for their creditors.

Although during the medieval period only a minority of Jews were moneylenders, the entire Jewish group came to be identified as such and hated. Since the Jews lived isolated in their own ghetto communities, the Jews known by the Gentile populace tended to be the hated moneylenders whom the Church labeled "usurers," and this became their image—one that found expression in the character Shylock in Shakespeare's *Merchant of Venice.* At times, by virtue of lending money to princes and the wealthy (which they were often compelled to do), the Jews became identified with the ruling classes during a period when the aristocracy was under growing fire. This identification fanned the flames of hostility toward the Jews. Similarly, as in Spain in the thirteenth, fourteenth, and fifteenth centuries, and in Austria and other German states in the seventeenth and nineteenth centuries, the most prominent Jews were appointed councilors of the crown and served as tax gatherers and commercial monopolists. Tax collectors are not popular people, and the Jews reaped new antagonism. These hardships fostered Jewish ingroup solidarity. Simultaneously, many Jews acquired the values and skills that are most adaptive in an urban and commercial environment. Some social scientists say that their European experiences later gave many Jews within the United States a "head start" in the competitive race for status and achievement.

Group Characteristics Affecting Mobility

The sociologist Bernard C. Rosen (1959) suggests that a crucial factor influencing people's mobility is their orientation toward achievement. Individuals differ in their psychological need to excel, their willingness to compete for social status, and their levels of educational and vocational aspiration. Rosen examines the differences in (1) motivation, (2) values, and (3) aspirations among a number of ethnic groups to determine the part these three factors play in the dissimilar rates of social mobility experienced by these groups. Employing ethnographic, attitudinal, and personality data, he asserts that the groups do differ in their orientation toward achievement.

1. *Motivation.* Motivation is generated by a least two kinds of socialization practices: achievement training that teaches children to do things well and independence training that teaches them to do things for themselves.

Achievement training encourages individuals to set high goals and to strive to realize these goals. Independent training fosters self-reliant attitudes within children and prepares them for independent decision-making. Rosen found that various ethnic groups place different emphases upon these sorts of training in the rearing of children. As a result, achievement motivation has been more prevalent among Greeks, Jews, and white Protestants than among Italians, French Canadians, and blacks. The Italians, French Canadians, and blacks came from agrarian societies or regions in which opportunities for achievement were severely curtailed by the social structure and where habits of resignation and fatalism prevailed. Under these conditions children were not typically encouraged to be achievers.

2. *Values.* By itself the achievement motive is not a sufficient source of upward mobility. It provides the inner impetus to excel, but it does not impel individuals to take the steps essential for advancement. In addition, individuals must be prepared to plan, work hard, make sacrifices, and leave their home communities in search of opportunity. Whether individuals will understand the importance of these factors depends in part upon the values transmitted to them by their group. The cultures of white Protestants, Jews, and Greeks stand out as equipping their members with these values considerably more than do the cultures of Italians and French Canadians. However, Rosen's hypothesis that blacks would score low in values favorable to success proved incorrect. The black score was not significantly different from those for white Protestants and Greeks, although it was significantly lower than the Jewish score.

3. *Aspirations.* Still a third ingredient is necessary for social mobility: high educational and vocational aspirations. Achievement motivation and success-oriented values can find expression in many areas that have little to do with upward mobility. For instance, excellence and effort can be directed into deviant, recreational, or religious behavior. Consequently, individuals also need to set high vocational goals and prepare themselves appropriately to move up the social ladder. Again the ethnic groups differed in orienting their members toward vocational and educational preparation—the white Protestants, Jews, and Greeks enjoyed

considerable advantage over Italians and French Canadians. In terms of educational aspirations, the black score was comparable to those of Jews, white Protestants, and Greeks, although the vocational aspiration score of blacks was the lowest of any of the six groups.

Religion and Worldly Success

In an essay that has become a sociological classic, *The Protestant Ethic and the Spirit of Capitalism* (1905/1930), Max Weber held that during the feudal era Protestantism contributed to the rise of modern capitalism. According to Weber, the newly emerging Protestant denominations liberated their members from tradition and provided a stimulus to rational economic activity. These effects were most evident in the religious beliefs popularized by religious reformers like John Calvin and propagated by the Congregationalists (Puritans) and Presbyterians. Weber saw the spirit (or ideology) of capitalism in the Protestant ethic. He thought that the Calvinist denominations encouraged individuals to work hard and to save their money as ways to glorify God. They fostered sobriety, thrift, restraint, industry, and the avoidance of fleshly pleasure. And they stressed that daily and worldly affairs should be carried on in a rational and methodical manner. But such beliefs and practices were also the engine of capitalism. They had the unintended result of contributing to economic growth and prosperity among Protestants.

In the decades since Weber published his study, his thesis has been investigated and debated by numerous scholars. Many of them have found his work wanting (Robertson, 1933; Samuelsson, 1961; Stokes, 1975). But in one way or another the idea that there may be some relationship between religious affiliation and worldly success has always intrigued sociologists. During the past forty years, American sociologists have found a rather consistent pattern in the rankings of various religious groups on measures of socioeconomic achievement (Cantril, 1943; Bogue, 1959; Mayer and Sharp, 1963; Glenn and Hyland, 1967; Roof, 1979). With respect to income, occupational status, and educational attainment, Jews, Episcopalians, Presbyterians, and Congregationalists have commonly occupied the top ranks; Catholics, Lutherans, and Methodists the middle positions; and Baptists the bottom. Explanations for this distribution have varied. Most usually sociologists have looked to group differences in motivation, values, and aspirations (the factors cited by Rosen). These factors parallel the ingredients highlighted by Weber in his discussion of the Protestant ethic.

Today religious affiliation no longer provides a measure of the Protestant ethic, if indeed it ever did. The beliefs embedded in the Protestant ethic are widely diffused throughout American life (Kim, 1977). Further, there are some Protestant messages that, rather than fostering upward social mobility, render groups susceptible to exploitation. For instance, the Beatitudes ("Blessed are. . . ."), subscribed to by some black denominations, depict all miseries and deprivations as God's test for an eternal Heavenly reward. Finally, in the post-World War II period, Catholics have been rapidly catching up with Protestants and Jews. Indeed, the issue is no longer whether a gap exists between Catholics and Protestants, but whether the situation has reversed: Have Catholics now pulled ahead of Protestants in their status attainments?

The sociologist Andrew M. Greeley (1976, 1977) argues that Catholics now surpass Protestants and are part of the nation's elite. He finds that while Catholics may educationally and occupationally still lag behind some Protestant groups, in income they now rank at the top (even above Episcopalians and Presbyterians, and second only to Jews). Among Catholics of European heritage, Irish Catholics rank first in income, followed in order by Italian Catholics, German Catholics, and Polish Catholics. Greeley bases his conclusions on a composite sample compiled between 1972 and 1976 by the National Opinion Research Center (the sample does not include Spanish-speaking Catholics). However, not all sociologists (Roof, 1979, 1981) accept Greeley's analysis and cite data to show that Catholics have not surpassed Episcopalians and Presbyterians in income. Nonetheless, there is little doubt that the gains made by Catholic ethnics since 1945 are truly phenomenal.

Greeley (1976:20)—himself a proud Irish Catholic—contends that Catholic ethnics have turned out quite well relative to so-called Protestant and American traits:

> The neighborhood is a 10-square-block area with almost 14,000 people, an average of 39.8 inhabitants per acre—three times that of the most crowded portions of Tokyo, Calcutta, and many other Asian cities. One block contains 1,349 children. . . . Garbage disposal is a chronic problem —usually trash is simply dumped in the narrow passageways between buildings. . . .
>
> These are the poorest of the poor people, making less than three quarters of the income of nonminority-group members in the same jobs. The rates of desertion, juvenile delinquency, mental disorder, and prostitution are the highest in the city here. Social disorganization in this neighborhood, according to all outside observers—even the sympathetic ones—is practically total and irredeemable.
>
> Blacks? Latinos? Inhabitants of some Third World city? No—Poles in Chicago in 1920.

Today, in what Greeley terms the "ethnic miracle," Poles and other European Catholics have for the most part made it in the United States. At the turn of the century Polish immigrants were despised and condemned. They were stereotyped and joked about. And Congress, in response to popular pressures (from Americans already naturalized) passed discriminatory immigration legislation in the 1920s to bar other

Poles from entering the United States. Greeley says that hard work, sacrifice, and savings made the ethnic miracle possible. But Greeley notes that Poles (and Italians) who have attended college are under-represented in the higher-prestige occupations. He calculates that for those who attended college, the "cost" of being Polish (or Italian) is about one-third as high as the cost of being black, and more than half that of being Spanish speaking. Thus Greeley believes that the question of continuing discrimination against Poles (and Italians) must remain an open issue.

Mobility Aspirations of Ghetto Blacks

Despite civil-rights legislation and the aura of racial progress, a sense of desperation and futility continues to pervade the nation's black ghettos. Many youths are functional illiterates, school dropouts, unemployed, and unprepared for better-paying jobs. Residents live in deteriorated housing, having inadequate sanitation and health services. Crime, drug abuse, and other social ills abound.

Not untypical of black ghettos is the government-built Cabrini-Green housing project on Chicago's Near North Side (Blum, 1981). The 13,500 residents are all poor and mostly black. Nine of ten residents receive public assistance and only four of ten have telephones. Seventy-eight towering structures, some nineteen stories high, make up the project. The buildings are laid out in rows across seventy acres. The Cabrini-Green project is much like big-city projects elsewhere. Critics have termed them "America's dumping grounds for the poor."

At Cabrini-Green, the elevators seldom work and the stairs are usually dark, smelly, and filled with graffiti. Almost 70 percent of the residents are children who have access to a few scattered swings and basketball hoops but little else. Crime is rampant with shootings, murders, rapes, robberies, and even gang warfare not uncommon occurrences. Fear haunts the residents, who remain in their apartments much of the time—even during the day. Inside their apartments blacks confront the huge rodent and cockroach populations that infest the buildings.

Youth often join area gangs out of boredom. At the root of the gang structure is drug-trafficking. By pooling their funds, youngsters can purchase enough marijuana and other substances to go around. Liquor is to the adults what drugs are to the younger people. The streets surrounding the project are lined with liquor stores, with patrons milling about their doorways.

During the past twenty years or so social scientists have debated whether the values of ghetto blacks like those living at Cabrini-Green differ substantially from the values of the mainstream of American society (Della-Fave, 1974; Kilson, 1981). Proponents of the *culture-of-*

poverty thesis subscribe to the following premises: (1) Among the poor there exists a set of unique values; (2) these values derive from the experience of living in poverty; (3) the day-to-day behavior of the poor is governed by these values; (4) viewed from the perspective of middle-class "respectability" much of the behavior of the poor is deviant; (5) the behavior of the poor works against their rising out of poverty; (6) the values of the poor are passed on from one generation to the next through socialization; and (7) because of the self-perpetuating nature of the values, the poor fail to take advantage of opportunities for upward mobility even when they are available to them. Hence, according to the culture-of-poverty thesis, poor blacks are locked within a self-perpetuating cycle of disadvantage by values that undermine their mobility aspirations.

The culture-of-poverty thesis seemingly found government sponsorship with the publication in 1965 of the "Moynihan report," a document named after its author, Daniel P. Moynihan, later a U.S. Senator from New York. Titled *The Negro Family* and circulated in government circles by the Office of Policy Planning and Research (Department of Labor), the report was confidential (labeled "for official use only"). However, its contents soon leaked to the press and the document was subsequently "declassified." The report aroused a storm of controversy, angering many civil-rights workers, blacks, professionals, and social workers (Rainwater and Yancey, 1967).

In the document, Moynihan argued:

> The evidence . . . is that the Negro family in the urban ghettos is crumbling. A middle-class group has managed to save itself, but for vast numbers of the unskilled, poorly educated city working class the fabric of conventional social relationships has all but disintegrated. . . .
>
> At the heart of the deterioration of the fabric of Negro society is the deterioration of the Negro family.
>
> It is the fundamental source of the weakness of the Negro community at the present time (Moynihan, 1965: p. 5).

The Moynihan report was widely interpreted as saying that black family instability (rather than white society) was a basic cause of black inequality and of "the tangle of pathology" found in black illegitimacy, welfare dependency, poor school performance, unemployment, drug addiction, alcoholism, and delinquency. Consequently, some labeled the document "racist." This interpretation ran counter to the theme of the report, namely a call for a bold change in federal policy in which the government would identify itself with the black movement and shift its programs (after the enactment of civil-rights legislation) to the achievement of equal opportunity for blacks. In this manner, it was reasoned, the good things of American life might come to be distributed among blacks in a manner roughly equivalent to that found among whites.

Moynihan said a vicious cycle operates in which black men lack a stable place in the economic system. As a consequence, they cannot be strong husbands and fathers. Therefore black families break up, and women must assume the task of rearing children without male assistance. Often the women must also assume the task of bringing in income so that a matriarchal arrangement emerges. Since children do not grow up in a stable home environment and hence learn that they cannot look forward to a stable life, they are not able to achieve in school; they leave school early and therefore are in a very poor position to qualify for jobs that will produce a decent income. And so the cycle starts again. In this manner poverty has taken on a life of its own so that the elimination of formal discrimination in the United States will not bring about a cure. Perhaps not surprisingly, some read the report as locating the source of the black plight within the weaknesses and defects of blacks themselves rather than in external conditions of economic and social discrimination. In other words, Moynihan portrayed poverty as breeding a distinct social ethos—a unique system of values and norms—that in turn is transmitted to successive generations (Lewis, 1965). Moynihan's thesis was hardly a new one. E. Franklin Frazier, a black sociologist, among others, had advanced a somewhat similar view as early as 1932.

Any number of social scientists, however, have challenged the culture-of-poverty thesis. Illustrative is the position of the social anthropologist Elliot Liebow (1967) who employed the participant-observer technique in studying a black street corner men's group in Washington, D.C. Liebow portrays the black man, not as a carrier of an independent cultural tradition, but as very much immersed in and accepting of the broad culture of American life. He differs from other American men not in goals, Liebow argues—he too wants a stable marriage and job—but in his ability to realize these goals. Although he wants marriage, he fears his own ability to carry out the responsibilities of husband and father. His own father failed—had to "cut out"—and he has no evidence he will fare any better. Although he has attended school, he is illiterate (or almost so) and he is essentially unskilled: "Armed with models who have failed, convinced of his own worthlessness, illiterate and unskilled, he enters marriage and the job market with the smell of failure all around him" (p. 211).

Liebow concludes that the similarities between black father and son do *"not* result from 'cultural transmission' but from the fact that the son goes out and *independently* experiences the same failures, in the same areas, and for much the same reasons as his father" (p. 223). The process only *appears* to be a self-sustaining cultural process. Consequently, Liebow rejects the notion that the poor have a distinctive set of values.

Charles A. Valentine (1968) takes a position similar to that of Liebow. He too denies that lower-class people are socialized in a separate culture. Many of the elements used to depict the poor (resignation, fatalism, low aspiration, and hopelessness) are simply "secondary" attitudes *adaptive* to the circumstances of lower-class life. In brief, a distinction exists between people being poor and being individuals with a unique cultural tradition.

Likewise, Barbara E. Coward and her associates (1974) were unable to document a bonafide "culture of poverty" among blacks in a ghetto in a large Southwestern city. Nor could Alan S. Berger and William Simon (1974) find any evidence that the black family is drastically different from the white family in the ways its treats its children and in the results it produces. The study employed data collected from a random sample of teen-agers in Illinois.

Any number of social scientists have found a great many strengths in black families (Billingsley, 1968; Hill, 1972). Family units extending across several generations and family structures headed by capable and emotionally strong women foster a positive environment rather than family instability. And there is no firm evidence that the absence of a father contributes directly to pathological conditions, delinquency, or confused sexual identifications (Blackwell, 1975).

Discussions of the family patterns of ghetto blacks often overlook the part played by public policy in discouraging many black men from living with their families in a husband-father role. A mother's eligibility for public assistance to support her children (Aid to Families with Dependent Children, or ADC) is linked to the presence of an "able-bodied" man in the household. ADC procedures have often compelled low-income black families to choose between a father and money in the home. Many take the pragmatic course and opt for money.

It may appear to the reader that this controversy is a trivial matter, just another illustration of academic backbiting. Yet it has major policy consequences. If the alleged culture patterns of the lower classes are more important in their lives than the condition of being poor, then it is more important for the power-holders of society to do away with these lifeways than to do away with poverty. Federal funds, then, should be diverted from the creation of more jobs, better housing, and good schools to programs focusing upon individuals and employing psychiatric techniques and self-improvement strategies. Further, if black ghettos are "sick" and "disorganized," permitting blacks a voice in community and social programs would be foolhardy. The net effect of a culture-of-poverty orientation is to divert attention from implementation of civil-rights legislation and affirmative-action programs. It shifts the spotlight from the dominant institutions of American life to the poor blacks themselves and portrays a "defective culture" as the source of black ills.

Is a reconciliation between the divergent positions possible? Some sociologists, like L. Richard Della-Fave (1974), believe so. He proposes a framework based upon Hyman Rodman's (1963) concept of the "value stretch." Rodman suggests that all classes within the United States share a common commitment to the nation's success values. However, lower-class members "stretch" the values so that lesser degrees of success become acceptable. Consequently, they come to tolerate and eventually to evaluate favorably deviations from the attainments mandated by middle-class values. Della-Fave says that the values of ghetto blacks resemble those of the middle class in a preference for success. But the values of poor blacks differ from middle-class values in terms of success expectations and tolerance of lower levels of achievement.

The anthropologist Ulf Hannerz (1969) also says that the "culture-of-poverty" and "economic-determinist" positions can be reconciled. He observes, "The socio-economic conditions impose limits on the kinds of life ghetto dwellers may have, but these kinds of life are culturally transmitted and shared as many individuals in the present, and many in the past, live or have lived under the same premises" (p. 21). In brief, ghetto members share certain experiences in common deriving from the fact of their common poverty. But they do not exist in social vacuums or cultural limbos. The adjustments they make occur in interaction with one another—"it is hardly possible to invent new adaptations again and again, as men are always observing each other and interacting with each other" (p. 21).

Race and the Status Attainment Process

In recent years sociologists have shown considerable interest in the factors underlying status transmission and attainment. They have searched for the factors that lead to social mobility and the causal relationships that exist among the factors. Most typically sociologists begin with a person's family of origin. They then identify the links that intervene between this status and the individual's later placement in the status hierarchy (Blau and Duncan, 1967, 1972; Sewell and Hauser, 1976; Jencks, 1979). The emphasis falls upon stages in the life span: first, birth into a family with an already established status ranking; second, a period of formal schooling; and third, adult life as the bearer of a particular occupational status. Sociologists ask: How and to what degree do the circumstances of birth determine subsequent status? And, how does status attained at one stage of the life span affect the prospects for a later stage?

Most of the research has centered upon samples of white males. This work reveals that education has the primary influence upon the occupational level that an individual attains. The main importance of the status of an individual's parents lies in its influence on the adolescent's aspirations. Sociological studies suggest that these aspirations contribute to the individual's educational attainment, which in turn influences the individual's first occupational placement and, through it, later occupational attainment. Pictured in this fashion, occupational attainment is a function of a large number of mediating links in a chain extending from birth across the life span.

Recently, a number of sociologists have undertaken studies comparing the status-attainment process for black and white males (Portes and Wilson, 1976; Kerckhoff and Campbell, 1977a, 1977b; Howell and Frese, 1979). This research reveals that important differences exist between the two groups. A youth's views of the opportunity structure and his feelings of fatalism toward advancement has greater importance for blacks than for whites. Further, the father's education has considerable predictive value for the ambitions of white youths but little for those of black youths, even in families where the father is present. In contrast, the mother is the chief source of influence in goal setting for black males. Overall, the socioeconomic status of the parents plays a greater part in the attainment process for whites than for blacks. On the other hand, doing well in high school is a stronger predictor of attainment for blacks than for whites.

Sociological research in the 1960s suggested that blacks encountered a "double handicap" (Blau and Duncan, 1967; Duncan, 1968). Black parents were unable to pass on to their children whatever status advantages they enjoyed. And educational investments did not have the same payoffs in occupational and income advantages for blacks that they had for whites. Consequently, blacks suffered unequal opportunities in pursuit of socioeconomic achievement.

During the past decade young blacks with college educations have made remarkable progress in achieving economic equality with whites. These gains have been documented by Richard B. Freeman in a report for the Carnegie Commission on Higher Education entitled *Black Elite: The New Market for Highly Educated Blacks* (1977). As recently as 1959, the typical black male *college* graduate earned less than the typical white male *high school* graduate. By 1973 the young black male graduate (age twenty-five to twenty-nine) was earning *more* than the comparable white college graduate. Black women had achieved income parity with white women much earlier. Black and white female college graduates received roughly similar incomes in 1959. By 1973, black women college graduates were also earning more than their white peers. Overall, Freeman found that in the 1970s blacks received a significantly higher return on their investment in higher education than whites did. It is important to emphasize, however, that these advances were not the result of the natural operation of social and economic factors. Rather, they derived from governmental intervention to change discriminatory patterns in response to the civil-rights movement and black political pressure.

The sociologist Christopher Jencks and his colleagues at the Harvard Center for Educational Policy Research similarly find that black youths now find good payoffs from a college education. In *Who Gets Ahead? —The Determinants of Economic Success* (1979), Jencks provides data containing the following messages. If you are black and think that finishing high school will help you in getting a better job, forget it. For both blacks and whites a high-school diploma counts next to nothing. If you are black and want money and a good job, go to college, buckle down, and graduate. It does not particularly matter what you major in or which college you attend, the credential is worth more than almost anything else. For whites, much the same advice holds (Yankelovich, 1979).

SUMMARY

1. Stratification contains the answer to the distributive problem of who gets what, when, and how. As a consequence, a society's "good" things—especially wealth, status, and power—are allocated in an uneven manner. Simultaneously, the burdens and unpleasant chores are unequally distributed among the members of the society. In sum, stratification represents institutionalized inequality in the allocation of social rewards and burdens.

2. The sociologist Max Weber profoundly influenced sociological considerations of social stratification. He pointed out that people are ranked along three dimensions: privilege (wealth), status, and power. The privilege hierarchy has to do with people's ability to command access to various goods and services. Status has to do with people's sense of worth and respect, especially the feeling that they are admired and thought well of. Power entails the ability to control or influence the behavior of others, even when they are disposed to act in some other fashion.

3. Clashes over wealth, status, and power underlie much human conflict. Given the prevalence of differing interests and values among human beings, aggression is an ever-present potential in intergroup relations. But aggression given full rein in a constant war of all against all would imperil the survival of the species. Consequently, aggression must be regulated. Two primary means exist by which human beings can manage aggression: stratification and territoriality. In stratification, people establish a hierarchy or order of preference in the distribution of a society's scarce, divisible good things. Stratification limits aggression because people interact in ways that conform to their advantaged and disadvantaged roles. In territoriality, people effect monopoly rights over the scarce resources in an area. Territoriality limits aggression to the extent to which people refrain from going where they are likely to be involved in unpleasant or violent encounters.

4. Within the United States the most critical and fundamental systems of stratification are class, gender, age, and race-ethnicity. Racial and ethnic stratification differs from the other systems in that only racial and

ethnic groups have the potential to carve their own autonomous nation from the existing state. Political separatism offers a solution to disadvantaged racial or ethnic groups that is not possible for disadvantaged class, gender, or age groups.

5. Hollingshead pointed out that a social structure may be "differentiated *vertically* along racial, ethnic and religious lines, and each of these vertical cleavages, in turn, is differentiated *horizontally* by a series of strata or classes that are encompassed within it." Each of the religious, ethnic, and racial groups tends to span a range of higher and lower positions within the class structure, sometimes from the top to the bottom, sometimes within a narrower range.

6. W. J. Wilson argues that economic opportunities for blacks now are shaped more by their class than by their race. He contends that race can no longer be considered as important as it once was in determining the life-chances of blacks. Educated blacks are now experiencing unprecedented job opportunities equivalent to those of whites with comparable qualifications. However, the demands of a high technology society threaten to solidify the position of the black underclass. Economic class is now the principal factor holding ghetto blacks back.

7. Many social scientists do not accept Wilson's view that class, not race, underlies the plight of blacks. They claim that there is "a unified black experience" within the United States that transcends class. Consequently, the starting point of any analysis of the black situation has to be the recognition that race is the most pervasive fact in the black experience. Those who favor a race explanation stress the part that institutional racism plays in American life. Critics of Wilson's class argument are also skeptical that the gains achieved by middle-class blacks will hold during economic recessions.

8. The class-race controversy has profound social implications. Each view leads to a somewhat different approach for dealing with the plight of blacks. The message Wilson sends blacks is that the American Dream is a realistic hope for them as well as for whites. By the same token, Wilson underscores the increasingly difficult circumstances confronting ghetto blacks. He suggests that existing public programs have failed to draw members of the black underclass into the mainstream. Critics of Wilson say that the illusion of black progress is a dangerous myth. They contend that racism must be the central focus of attack. Blacks must unite, regardless of class, to combat an unjust social system.

9. Racial and ethnic groups have displayed dissimilar rates of upward mobility. American Jews have climbed the social-status ladder more quickly and achieved middle-class status more widely than any other American ethnic group. In the Northeast, Greeks have similarly tended to attain middle-class status more rapidly than most other groups. The factors responsible for differing rates of upward mobility have varied with the group in question. For one thing, many Jews and Greeks came

to the United States with occupational skills better suited to urban living than those of their fellow immigrants. Upward mobility has likewise been related to the ability of ethnic and racial groups to organize effectively in order to protect and further their interests. Where the ethnic group had previous Old World experience in facing the problem of minority-group adaptation, it was often prepared, as were the Jews and Greeks, to develop more quickly effective community organization in America.

10. A crucial factor influencing people's mobility is their orientation toward achievement. Individuals differ in their psychological need to excel, their willingness to compete for social status, and their levels of educational and vocational aspiration. Rosen examines the differences in (1) motivation, (2) values, and (3) aspirations among a number of ethnic groups to determine the part these three factors play in the dissimilar rates of social mobility of these groups.

11. In an essay that has become a sociological classic, *The Protestant Ethic and the Spirit of Capitalism,* Weber held that during the feudal era Protestantism contributed to the rise of modern capitalism. Although his work has been found wanting, sociologists have been intrigued by the idea that a relationship may exist between religious affiliation and worldly success. During the past forty years, American sociologists have found a rather consistent pattern in the rankings of various religious groups on measures of socioeconomic achievement. With respect to income, occupational status, and educational attainment, Jews, Episcopalians, Presbyterians, and Congregationalists have commonly occupied the top ranks; Catholics, Lutherans, and Methodists the middle positions; and Baptists the bottom. Explanations for this distribution have varied. Most usually sociologists have looked to group differences in motivation, values, and aspirations. However, since 1945 the gains made by Catholic ethnics have been extraordinary, in some cases Catholics overtaking some Protestant groups in income, occupation, and education.

12. During the past twenty years or so social scientists have debated whether the values of ghetto blacks differ substantially from the values of the mainstream of American society. Proponents of the culture-of-poverty thesis say that a basic cause of black inequality is black family instability. Because of the self-perpetuating nature of their values, poor blacks fail to take advantage of opportunities for upward mobility, even when they are available to them. However, critics deny that lower-class people are socialized in a separate culture. They point out that a distinction exists between people being poor and being individuals with a unique cultural tradition. Any number of social scientists have found a great many strengths in black families.

13. Recently sociologists have shown considerable interest in the factors underlying status transmission and attainment. Most typically they begin with a person's family of origin. They then identify the links that

intervene between this status and the individual's later placement in the status hierarchy. Most of the research has centered upon samples of white males. This work reveals that education has the primary influence upon the occupational level that an individual attains. The main importance of the status of an individual's parents lies in its influence on the adolescent's aspirations. Recently, a number of sociologists have undertaken studies comparing the status-attainment process for black and white males. This research reveals that important differences exist between the two groups. A youth's views of the opportunity structure and his feelings of fatalism toward advancement has greater importance for blacks than for whites. Further, the father's education has considerable predictive value for the ambitions of white youths but little for those of black youths.

GLOSSARY

Achieved Status   A postiton in the social structure allocated to an individual on the basis of his or her unique talents or characteristics.

Age Grades   Social layers that are based upon periods in life.

Ageism   The systematic negative stereotyping of and discrimination against people because of their age.

Life-chance   The typical probability that people will enjoy those goods and services that contribute to physical survival and comfort and to a feeling of psychological well-being.

Sexism   Those social arrangements and enduring patterns by which members of one gender group dominate and oppress the members of the other gender group.

Social Stratification   The social hierarchy—or social ladder—along which people are ranked that differentiates them as superior or inferior, higher or lower.

Segregation: Native Americans and Blacks

Segregation is the process or state whereby people are separated or set apart. As such, it places limits on social interaction among individuals of differing racial and ethnic groups. One form of segregation is physical or spatial separation. As pointed out in chapter 7, territoriality is one means by which human beings manage aggression. By virtue of territoriality, one people establish monopoly rights over the scarce resources in an area and impose their set of values upon the other inhabitants of the area. Territoriality limits aggression to the extent to which individuals do not go where they will have unpleasant or violent encounters. But by the same token, territory is also an instrument by which elites establish, maintain, and appropriate privilege. In this sense, territorial segregation—as expressed in black and Chicano ghettos—is a mechanism by which dominant groups control minority groups.

Of course individuals and groups are also sifted and sorted out in space for reasons other than victimization. Clustering may occur voluntarily when individuals or groups find close spatial proximity an advantage. Thus members of some racial and ethnic groups prefer to live near one another. Close proximity facilitates communication, understanding, and rapport among like-minded individuals. And it allows people jointly to carry on those activities that contribute and support their sense of oneness or peoplehood. By living together in common neighborhoods, the members of a group can support their special religious institutions, schools, fraternal orders, and ethnic food and clothing stores. Chinatowns, Little Italys, Jewish neighborhoods, and Little Havanas are examples of such clustering. Further, segregated neighborhoods afford protection against the intrusion of strange beliefs, values, and norms, while giving a group political leverage at City Hall through bloc-voting and political organization. Thus ethnic groups may prefer to maintain cultures and communities of their own and resist absorption into the dominant society for a variety of reasons. In sum, both voluntary and involuntary factors produce territorial segregation.

Segregation may also find expression in discrimination. As noted in chapter 1, discrimination entails overt action in which members of a group are treated unequally and unfavorably on the basis of their ethnic or racial membership by members of the dominant group. By virtue of discrimination, minorities are arbitrarily denied certain rights and privileges even when their qualifications are equal to those of dominant-group members. But discrimination should not be viewed as a practice limited to members of the dominant group. Racial and ethnic minorities may discriminate against members of the dominant group as well. However, the difference between the two groups is one of clout. The ability of the dominant group to carry out discriminatory behavior is generally considerably greater than that of the minority.

Native Americans

There are within the United States 1.4 million American Indians, Eskimos, and Aleuts. No definition of American Indian, or Native American, is universally accepted. The 1980 census assumes that a person who can identify with a specific tribe is an Indian. Similarly, the Indian Self-Determination Act of 1975 defines an Indian as a person who is a member of a federally recognized Indian tribe. However, as pointed out in chapter 1, sociologists prefer a social definition of group membership. Viewed from this perspective Indians are individuals who are defined by the members of their community as Indians and who so identify themselves. Indeed, many non-Indians are surprised to find blond-haired, blue-eyed individuals and black people—sometimes named Smith, Jones, or Callahan—who are known as reservation Indians.

More than 500 Native American tribes or nations are found in the United States. Another fifty or more tribes have become extinct through massacres by whites, disease, destruction of their economic base, or absorption by other groups. Native American tribes vary in size from those with less than 100 members (the Chumash of California and the Modocs of Oklahoma) to those with more than 160,000 members (the Navajos of Arizona, New Mexico, and Utah). Anglo-Americans typically have a stereotyped image of how Native Americans look, how they behave, how they live, and even how they think. In truth, of course, Native American peoples vary substantially in their history, customs, language, government, religion, economy, wealth, location, and identities.

Background

In 1492 there were between 700 thousand and 1.2 million Native Americans in the area that now comprises the United States. Contrary to popular belief, most Native American nations did not consist of nomadic hunting peoples. Most Native Americans were farming and fishing peoples with relatively stable communities. For the most part they were thinly scattered throughout the territory in hundreds of tribes, with numerous distinctive cultures, some of which were as different from each other as were the cultures of England and China of that period. In some cases the Native American groups were treated as alien nations that could be either enemies or allies against competing European powers. Yet in due course, in the regions of earliest contact with Europeans—the area along the Atlantic seaboard and the Gulf of Mexico—the tribal territories of the Native Americans were appropriated and the aborigines were either annihilated or driven inland. Some made their way into the swamps, coves, and wooded mountains of these regions.

Period of Genocide and Separation. Following the American Revolution, the new government followed a policy of negotiating treaties of land cession with the Indians. Where the Native Americans failed to agree, they were confronted with military force. Local groups of whites often moved on their own against the Native Americans. When the Native Americans resisted white encroachments upon their lands, warfare ensued, the Seminole War in Florida and the Black Hawk War in the Illinois Territory being among the better known of the wars fought east of the Mississippi. Eventually, with the exception of portions of the Iroquois nations, the tribes "signed" treaties of cession and moved westward. Some went resignedly, others at bayonet point. At least 70,000 Native Americans were removed in the 1830s from southeastern states. Of these some 20,000 died en route westward. Most were Creeks, Choctaws, Cherokees, Chickasaws, and Seminoles.

West of the Mississippi, the tragedies of defeat and expropriation were repeated. With the discovery of gold in California, wagon trains of gold seekers and emigrants began to rumble across the Plains. Native American lands were expropriated and granted to the railroads, mining corporations, ranchers, speculators, and profiteers. The U.S. military was dispatched to the West to protect and promote commerce by means of outposts. Native American peoples were settled on reservations and issued rations in compensation for their loss of lands and hunting opportunities. At times bands of dissatisfied warriors rebelled —the uprisings in the Southern Plains in 1874, of the Sioux in 1876, the Nez Perce in 1877, the Cheyenne and the Bannock in 1878, the Utes in 1879, the Apache any number of times in the 1870s and 1880s, and farther west in northeast California the Modocs in 1872–1873. As in the East the aim of the frontiersmen was to get rid of the Native Americans, even to the point of massacring them. At Sand Creek in Colorado in 1864 militiamen descended upon an encampment of Cheyenne who had been guaranteed safe conduct and slaughtered most of them. And in the frigid Plains winter of 1890, U.S. forces armed with Hotchkiss machine guns mowed down nearly 300 Sioux at Wounded Knee, South

Dakota. Yet it proved impossible to exterminate the Indians (in 1870 it was estimated that it cost the federal government about $1 million for every dead Indian), and the stage was set for the formulation of a new policy.

Period of Coerced Assimilation. Until 1871, the federal government treated the tribes as sovereign yet dependent domestic nations with whom it entered into "treaty" arrangements, a practice ended that year by Congress. The 1870s marked the beginning of a new phase in Anglo-Native American relations. Native Americans were considered "wards" of the government. No longer was the aim one of extermination. In any event, it appeared at the time that Native Americans were a "vanishing race." The new policy was directed at "forced assimilation." Strenuous efforts were undertaken to eliminate Native American cultures. Native Americans were to be "civilized" by taking on Anglo-American ways, learning English, wearing hair and clothing in the manner of whites, working six days a week, and attending Christian services on Sunday. Native American children were forcibly indoctrinated at boarding schools far removed from reservation homes. Traditional leaders were replaced by "paper chiefs," who were placed in positions of authority by whites to implement federal policy.

Under the Dawes Act of 1887, tribal lands were broken up and divided among individual Native Americans with the aim of making them small freehold farmers. The remaining tribal holdings were declared "surplus" and opened to non-Indian settlement. White officials believed that breaking up Indian lands into individual parcels would foster patterns and practices similar to those then prevalent among white settlers while eliminating the economic basis for tribal organization. The net result was that within sixty years, 86 million acres of the best Indian lands were lost through purchase and fraudulent deals by whites. Some 90,000 Native Americans were made landless. The effect of individualizing the tribal estate was the creation of massive poverty and poor health conditions, with Native Americans often existing in a slough of despondency.

On the surface it appeared that a federal bureaucracy—the Bureau of Indian Affairs—succeeded in replacing Native American ways with those of the "civilized" nation. The majority of Native Americans spoke English and adopted clothing and houses similar to those of whites. Only a few nations, including the Pueblos and Navajos of the Southwest, maintained their traditional dress and housing. And by 1930 the great majority of Native Americans professed Christian-church affiliations. But a more detailed look reveals that less than a dozen Native American languages had died out, many forms of religion and ceremonialism remained strong, new Indian religions had emerged, and the vast majority of Native Americans adhered to traditional values (Spicer, 1980).

Period of Tribal Restoration. In 1929 a new policy in Indian affairs was inaugurated and later strengthened during the Roosevelt New Deal years. It reversed previous policy and encouraged Indians to retain their tribal identifications and cultures. The new program stopped all allotment of remaining Native American lands and sought to rebuild a land base for Native American communities. Tribes were encouraged to adopt tribal councils patterned after constitutional, representative democracies. Day schools were established on a number of reservations and children were no longer sent away to boarding schools. In both kinds of schools, however, the government encouraged efforts to deal positively with Indian cultures rather than to ignore and disparage them. The new policies sought to improve Indian health, promote native arts and crafts, and provide Native Americans with the constitutional right of religious freedom.

Period of Termination. During the post-World War II period a good many white Americans were troubled by reservations that they believed were a kind of concentration camp. So in the 1950s government policy was once more reversed. The Eisenhower administration aimed to get the federal government "out of the Indian business." This liquidation of the government's responsibility meant that Native Americans peoples in effect lost the special standing they had under federal law as "dual citizens" of their tribe and the United States (Indians were granted American citizenship in 1924). Likewise, Native Americans lost tax-exempt status for their land.

The Eisenhower administration also placed a new emphasis upon relocation—removing Native Americans from the reservations and setting them up in employment in urban areas. The federal government viewed the reservations as economic dead ends and sought a solution to high rates of Native-American unemployment by moving Indians into the mainstream of urban life. But Native Americans were all too often taken to the cities, given brief training, found a job, and then abandoned (Svensson, 1978). Perhaps most drastic of all, certain tribes were "freed" from federal supervision, a policy called "termination." The two tribes most affected by this latter policy were the Menominees in Wisconsin and the Klamaths in Oregon. Both reservations contained important stands of timber. Termination led to the dissipation of tribal capital and the undermining of the Indian communities. But termination fitted with the integrationist and civil-rights spirit of the times, so to many Americans it seemed the right thing to do. The program was slowed during the Kennedy-Johnson administrations and then reversed by the Nixon administration. In 1973 the Menominees were successful in reestablishing their federal relationship, although the Klamaths' relationship remained terminated.

Period of "Self-Determination." During the 1970s the goal of national policy reversed once more. The government sought to strengthen Native-American control over Indian affairs without cutting Native Americans off from federal concern and support. Self-determination among Indian peoples was encouraged and the threat of termination was removed. The spearhead for many of the efforts has been the Indian Self–Determination Act of 1975, which encouraged Native Americans to take over supervision of most public services on the reservations. However, self-determination programs conceal the fact that reservation communities typically lack an economic base and depend largely on federal monies. Federal priorities in land use, competition with state and local interest groups (e.g., for water rights and mineral resources), and limited managerial and technical expertise have frustrated economic development (Guillemin, 1978). As many Native Americans see it, the issue confronting them continues to be survival. They wish to keep their traditional cultures and their distinctive identities. To do so, they must first hold on to their land base and develop some measure of economic independence. As the nation moved into the 1980s, Indian policy remained a dynamic and unresolved political issue.

Contemporary Situation. As depicted in the discussion above, the course of governmental policy toward Native Americans has repeatedly oscillated between separatist and assimilationist extremes. Native Americans have paid the price for the inconsistencies and vacillations in federal programs. Today the overwhelming majority of Native Americans live west of the Mississippi River, with the largest populations in Oklahoma, Arizona, and California. The problems of Indian peoples abound. Thirty-eight percent of the more than 1 million Native Americans live on incomes below the poverty line. On reservations 48 percent live below the poverty line; 55 percent of reservation housing is substandard; 58 percent of reservation children drop out of school before finishing eighth grade; and unemployment on reservations exceeds 40 percent.

The life expectancy of Native Americans is ten years shorter than that of whites. Rates of tuberculosis, dysentery, enteritis, trachoma, pneumonia, and alcoholism are high. The majority of Indian health problems are related to inadequate diet, shelter, and sanitation. More than 70 percent of reservation Indians haul their drinking water a mile or more, often from unsanitary sources (and only the smallest fraction have indoor plumbing). In Dallas 40 percent of the Native Americans have never had dental care of any kind. In Minnesota 40 percent of the Indian population is estimated to have a serious alcohol problem. In the states with large Native American populations, between a quarter and a third of all Indian children are removed from their families and placed in foster homes, adoptive homes, or institutions (Sorkin, 1978).

Since the 1950s, there has been a steady migration of Native American people from reservations to cities. More than half of the nation's

Indian population now resides in urban areas. Cities with the largest Native American concentrations are Los Angeles, San Francisco-Oakland, Tulsa, Minneapolis-St. Paul, Chicago, and Phoenix. As immigrants to urban centers, Native Americans often remain marginal relative to the integration of other minorities. For the most part, Indian families do not live near one another and Indian neighborhoods have not developed (an exception is a Brooklyn enclave of Mohawks). Many are excluded from federal assistance although they are still enrolled as tribal members. However, most cities do have "Indian bars," where Native Americans congregate. And there are numerous Urban Indian centers, which conduct pow-wows and traditional ceremonies.

The status of Native Americans as a racial and cultural minority results in discrimination in most off-reservation contexts. Prejudice and discrimination tend to be strongest in the areas surrounding the reservations, where the frontier conception of Native Americans as shiftless and drunken inferiors tends to persist. Not infrequently, Native Americans are subject to Jim-Crow behavior, if not laws, in towns near reservations and at times are subject to police abuse. Further, surrounding cities and corporations have commonly used reservations for garbage dumps and toxic wastes. And Native Americans continue to be victimized through the leasing of Indian lands by white farmers and various corporate interests.

As with any minority, Native Americans have exhibited different responses to their disadvantaged circumstances (*see* chapters 12 and 14). Some have "spun-off" into the larger community, becoming more or less assimilated. Others have chosen to stress their tribal identity and to undertake the development of effective self-governing communities. And still others have found appeal in "Pan-Indianism," the coming together of Native Americans regardless of tribal affiliation to realize common ends and to develop "an ethnic Indian" derived from a synthesis of diverse Indian cultures.

Blacks

In 1980, the Bureau of the Census reported that there were 26.5 million blacks in the United States, 11.7 percent of the total population (*see* Tables 8.1 and 8.2). In 1970, the figure stood at 22.6 million (11.1 percent). The nation's total population as reported in the 1980 census was about 225.5 million, up from 203.2 million in 1970. Consequently, the black population grew by 17.0 percent during the decade, faster than the 11.0 percent overall increase in the total population. Census officials said that the figures were the result of both an actual increase among blacks, whose birth rate exceeded that of whites, and improved counting procedures in black communities.

TABLE 8.1 BLACK POPULATION, 1980

Blacks: Top Ten States: Percent of Total Population		Blacks: Top Ten States: Total Population	
1. Mississippi	35.2	1. New York	2,402,000
2. South Carolina	30.4	2. California	1,819,000
3. Louisiana	29.4	3. Texas	1,710,000
4. Georgia	26.8	4. Illinois	1,675,000
5. Alabama	25.6	5. Georgia	1,465,000
6. Maryland	22.7	6. Florida	1,342,000
7. North Carolina	22.4	7. North Carolina	1,316,000
8. Virginia	18.9	8. Louisiana	1,237,000
9. Arkansas	16.3	9. Michigan	1,199,000
10. Delaware	16.1	10. Ohio	1,077,000

Source: U.S. Bureau of the Census

TABLE 8.2 BLACKS IN THE TOP FIFTY METROPOLITAN AREAS, 1980

Metropolitan Area	Total Population	Black	% Black
1. New York	9,119,737	1,940,415	21.3
2. Los Angeles-Long Beach	7,477,657	944,009	12.6
3. Chicago	7,102,328	1,427,827	20.1
4. Philadelphia	4,716,818	884,405	18.8
5. Detroit	4,352,762	890,417	20.5
6. San Francisco-Oakland	3,252,721	391,214	12.0
7. Washington, D.C.	3,060,240	853,043	27.9
8. Dallas-Fort Worth	2,974,878	419,272	14.1
9. Houston	2,905,350	528,513	18.2
10. Boston	2,763,357	160,434	5.8
11. Nassau-Suffolk	2,605,813	162,484	6.2
12. St. Louis	2,355,276	407,734	17.3
13. Pittsburgh	2,263,894	175,603	7.8
14. Baltimore	2,174,023	556,872	25.6
15. Minneapolis-St. Paul	2,114,256	50,046	2.4
16. Atlanta	2,029,618	498,821	24.6
17. Newark	1,965,304	417,513	21.2
18. Anaheim-Santa Anna-Gdn Grove	1,931,570	25,285	1.3
19. Cleveland	1,898,720	345,632	18.2
20. San Diego	1,861,846	104,452	5.6
21. Miami	1,625,979	280,379	17.2
22. Denver-Boulder	1,619,921	77,779	4.8
23. Seattle-Everett	1,606,765	58,140	3.6
24. Tampa	1,569,492	145,701	9.3
25. Riverside-San Bernardino-Ont.	1,557,080	78,597	5.0
26. Phoenix	1,508,030	48,112	3.2

Background

It is quite likely that the first black came to the New World with Columbus. During the period of exploration, Spain was a racial melting pot: the Moors had a considerable admixture of black ancestry and black slaves had also been brought to the country from central Africa. Hence, there is every reason to believe that some blacks were among the Spanish explorers and colonists.

In 1619 English colonists at Jamestown, Virginia, purchased from a Dutch man-of-war twenty blacks. Since there was no precedent in English law regarding slaves, it appears the blacks initially assumed the status of indentured servants, much in the fashion of whites. However, the blacks' distinctive physical characteristics doubtless furthered their differential treatment from the beginning, and in time facilitated their

TABLE 8.2 BLACKS IN THE TOP FIFTY METROPOLITAN AREAS, 1980 (Continued)

Metropolitan Area	Total Population	Black	% Black
27. Cincinnati	1,401,403	173,656	12.4
28. Milwaukee	1,397,143	150,677	10.8
29. Kansas City	1,327,020	173,184	13.1
30. San Jose	1,295,071	43,715	3.4
31. Buffalo	1,242,573	113,975	9.2
32. Portland	1,242,187	33,384	2.7
33. New Orleans	1,186,725	387,393	32.6
34. Indianapolis	1,166,929	157,258	13.5
35. Columbus, Ohio	1,093,293	134,686	12.3
36. San Antonio	1,071,954	72,739	6.8
37. Ft. Lauderdale-Hollywood	1,014,043	113,582	11.2
38. Sacramento	1,014,002	61,298	6.0
39. Rochester	971,879	77,930	8.0
40. Salt Lake City-Ogden	936,255	8,684	0.9
41. Providence-Warwick-Pawtucket	919,216	24,928	2.7
42. Memphis	912,887	363,944	39.9
43. Louisville	906,240	117,845	13.0
44. Nashville-Davidson	850,505	137,348	16.1
45. Birmingham	847,360	239,673	28.3
46. Oklahoma City	834,088	74,960	9.0
47. Dayton	830,070	105,261	12.7
48. Greensboro-Winst. Salem-High Pt.	827,385	159,578	19.3
49. Norfolk-Va. Beach-Portsmouth	806,691	223,413	27.7
50. Albany-Schenectady-Troy	795,019	29,309	3.7

Source: U.S. Bureau of the Census.

enslavement. In the 1660s legal recognition was given to the enslavement of blacks for life and the first law was passed penalizing interracial sexual relations.

The growth of black slavery was closely tied with the development of the plantation system of agriculture that evolved within the South. Prior to the invention in 1793 of the cotton gin, slaves were primarily used in commercial agriculture based on tobacco, rice, indigo, and naval stores. To supply the considerable demand for slaves, an elaborate trade system emerged. The voyage of the slaves from Africa to America, often referred to as the "Middle Passage," was a veritable nightmare, with overcrowding and epidemics common. About 10 million slaves were brought to the Western Hemisphere, most destined for the sugar plantations of Brazil and the Caribbean. British North America and French Louisiana received less than one of every twenty slaves. Some slaves were brought from the West Indies, but most came from a narrow strip along the West African coast and from central Africa.

At the time of the first federal census, taken in 1790, there were 757,208 blacks in the country (about 20 percent of the total population), of which more than 90 percent were concentrated in the South. However, it was not until Eli Whitney solved the problem of separating the cotton seed from the close-adhering lint that cotton became the major crop of the South. By 1815 the production of cotton had increased at a phenomenal rate. This expansion of the cotton economy was accompanied by the growth of the slave population, which reached 1,771,656 in 1820.

In any event, and this is our primary concern here, even at the time of the Declaration of Independence, black slavery was deeply entrenched and the idea of black inferiority was well established. This fact was underlined when Southerners succeeded at the Constitutional Convention of 1787 in winning additional representation on the basis of slavery, in securing federal support for the capture and rendition of fugitive slaves, and in preventing the closing of the slave trade before 1808. In truth the New Nation arose as a Greek-style democracy, where democracy was accepted, but only for a segment of the population. Indeed, until the last several decades whites for the most part did not see democracy as extending to blacks anymore than Americans generally see democracy as extending to children (e.g., in the realm of voting rights). The doctrine of black inferiority or "differences" served to place the black beyond the pale of the American democratic creed.

Yet the dilemmas posed by racism within an egalitarian society have been a source of constant embarrassment. "It always appeared a most iniquitous scheme to me," Abigail Adams wrote her husband (John Adams) in 1774, "to fight ourselves for what we are daily robbing and plundering from those who have as good a right to freedom as we have." Hence, from its earliest days a conflict has been inherent in the

American system between the dictates of its creed and its racial practice (Myrdal, 1944). The main norms of the American creed are centered in the belief in the common brotherhood and sisterhood of humanity as found in Christian teaching and the belief in equality and in the rights of liberty as found in the Declaration of Independence. It is a creed that "all men [and women] are created equal." The contradiction between the American value system and the way in which blacks have been treated has, if anything, forced many whites to think even more harshly of the black than they might if they lived in a more explicitly ascriptive culture.

There is little justification, then, to repress a group such as blacks within an egalitarian society unless they are defined as a congenitally inferior race. Consequently, whites have been under pressure either to deny blacks the right to participate in the society, because they are "inferior," or to ignore their existence, to make them an "invisible" people. Whites in the South historically insisted on the first alternative. The North tried for many decades to take the second path (Lipset, 1963).

Historians agree that the political struggle that unfolded between the North and the South prior to the Civil War was more a contest over the role of the plantation elite and economy in the American republic than a disagreement over the social position of blacks. Later, confronted with southern insurrection, President Lincoln issued the Emancipation Proclamation chiefly as a military measure. In August 1862, Horace Greeley, in a famous letter to the president known as the "Prayer of 20 Millions," complained "that the Union cause has suffered and is now suffering immensely from your mistaken deference to slavery." Lincoln replied:

> My paramount object in this struggle *is* to save the Union, and is *not* either to save or destroy Slavery. If I could save the Union without freeing *any* slave, I would do it; and if I could save it by freeing *all* the slaves, I would also do that. What I do about Slavery and the colored race, I do because I believe it helps to save this Union; and what I forbear, I forbear, because I do *not* believe it would help to save the Union.

When Lincoln did issue the proclamation, it did not free a single slave. It applied *only* to Confederate states not yet conquered. The proclamation exempted areas occupied by federal troops and Union slave states.

During Reconstruction the Radical Republicans were partially motivated by the abolitionist argument that a legalized caste system was incompatible with American institutions. However, a more pressing concern for them was the fear that the southern states would return to the Union with the old planter elite still in control. The North's lack of commitment to black rights doomed Reconstruction. By employing illegal methods, intimidating newly enfranchised black voters, and using their dominant social and economic positions, privileged southern whites were able to reestablish white supremacy. The fate of blacks was sealed for nearly a century by the "Compromise of 1877." Southern Democrats threw their political support to Rutherford B. Hayes, the Republican candidate, in the disputed presidential election of 1876. In exchange the southerners won a Republican commitment for "home rule." "Home rule" meant many things, but above all it meant that white supremacists would be free to nullify black constitutional rights and govern the South without northern "interference."

The Origins of "Jim Crow"

It has not been uncommon for white southerners and many other Americans to assume the "Jim Crow" system in the South—legalized segregation—always was that way. Or at any rate, if not always, then "since slavery times" or "since the Civil War" or "since Reconstruction." Such notions are part of a prevalent myth that has viewed southern race patterns as having been virtually immune to change for more than three hundred years, as having remained untouched by the passage of time until the past decade or so.

The myth persists despite the fact that southerners have probably been more familiar with the shifting fortunes of history than other Americans have been. Their own history has amply demonstrated that an old order and its institutions can perish quite quickly and rather completely. Following the Civil War, a new order was instituted that had behind it all the authority and confidence of a victorious North; and then again, within a span of ten years, this new order was to give way to still a third. Each successive regime in the South—slavery and secession, emancipation and reconstruction, redemption and reunion—had its characteristic economic organization, its system of politics, and its social arrangements. And in each the race patterns were quite distinct.

The noted American historian C. Vann Woodward (1966) convincingly demonstrates the changing character of the southern racial structure in his study of the rise of Jim Crowism. He suggests that the assumption is often incorrectly made that Reconstruction constituted an interruption of normal relations between the races in the South. According to this view, once the white southerners had overthrown the carpetbagger and scalawag regimes and established "home rule," they proceeded to restore to normalcy the disturbed relations between the two racial groups. This view overlooks the fact that segregation would have been impractical under slavery, as black domestic servants participated quite extensively in the life and households of the white upper classes. Furthermore, the institution of Jim Crowism did not follow automatically upon the overthrow of Reconstruction but was largely a later development.

Accounts written by both critics and friends of the South during the two decades following Reconstruction give ample testimony to the fact that Jim Crow was virtually absent from the region. Blacks generally received equality of treatment on common carriers, trains, and street-cars; were freely admitted to theaters, lectures, and exhibitions; and were served at the bars, restaurants, soda fountains, and ice-cream saloons patronized by whites. However, when there was sufficient room, whites avoided sitting with blacks, and within restaurants were usually served at separate tables. Similarly, blacks were not disfranchised immediately after the overthrow of Reconstruction. Although blacks were often coerced and defrauded, they continued to vote in large numbers in most parts of the South for more than two decades after Reconstruction.

In South Carolina in 1898, when the movement for the institution of Jim Crow separation on railway cars was gathering momentum, the *Charleston News and Courier,* the oldest newspaper in the South, editorialized against the measure in these terms:

> As we have got-on fairly well for a third of a century, including a long period of reconstruction, without such a measure, we can probably get on as well hereafter without it, and certainly so extreme a measure should not be adopted and enforced without added and urgent cause.

The editor then called attention to what he considered the *absurd* consequences to which such a law might lead:

> If there must be Jim Crow cars on the railroads, there should be Jim Crow cars on the street railways. Also on all passenger boats. . . . If there are to be Jim Crow cars, moreover, there should be Jim Crow waiting saloons at all stations, and Jim Crow eating houses. . . . There should be Jim Crow sections of the jury box, and a separate Jim Crow dock and witness stand in every court—and a Jim Crow Bible for colored witnesses to kiss. It would be advisable also to have a Jim Crow section in county auditors' and treasurers' offices for the accommodation of colored taxpayers.

What the editor of the Charleston papers obviously regarded as an absurdity became in a very short time a reality.

It should not be assumed that a golden age of race relations prevailed in the period between Reconstruction and the institution of the Jim Crow laws. It was precisely in the eighties and nineties that lynching attained its most staggering proportions. The absence of formalized segregation did not mean that blacks were accepted as social equals by whites. Such acceptance was no more frequent before the introduction of the Jim Crow era than it was at the height of that era. Segregation probably entailed a lowering of the black's status, but it did not imply a fall from full equality. Evidence indicates that blacks were often denied their civil rights and discriminated against before the era of genuine segregation, which was introduced in the 1890s. In education custom dictated the separate education of blacks and whites. But after the 1890s the principle of segregation became a hard-and-fast dogma of southern life. Legalized Jim Crow came to reinforce the informal mechanisms of social distance that regulated white-black interaction.

During the decades immediately following Reconstruction, the southern Bourbon regimes had a conservative philosophy on the race question. Blacks were viewed as subordinate. However, the conservatives denied that this necessitated their being ostracized. Similarly, they believed blacks were inferior. But they denied that segregation must be the result. The conservatives looked with disapproval on whites who championed the cause of the black. They saw such individuals as false friends, who pretended friendship for the black to advance selfish ends of party advantage and private gain. At the same time, they disapproved of the Negrophobe fanatics who proposed an aggressive war against blacks and a program of virulent racism. And then too the old Bourbon aristocracy sought to maintain power by manipulating the black vote against the poor whites.

In contrast with the conservative philosophy, there arose in the 1890s another approach, worked out and expressed by the Populists. The Populists fancied themselves exponents of a new realism on the race issue. They saw their realism as neither the product of a liberal conscience nor a *noblesse oblige* paternalism. Many Populist leaders hoped that the great mass of southern white farmers and sharecroppers would join hands with their black counterparts in a fight against want, poverty, and large business and landed interests. A Texas Populist expressed the position in these terms: "They [blacks] are in the ditch just like we are." Populist leaders such as Tom Watson, before he became a virulent racist, preached that the identity of interests of the farming groups of both races transcended differences in race. Eventually disillusioned, the Populists assumed a leading role in promoting a strong Jim Crow program.

Prior to 1900, the only law of a Jim Crow type adopted by the majority of southern states was that applying to passengers aboard trains. South Carolina did not adopt such a measure until 1898, North Carolina not until 1899, and Virginia not until 1900. During the decade that followed, the application of mandatory segregation in new areas of life unfolded in fadlike fashion, each wave bringing additional laws. Across the South, law and custom dictated that "White Only" or "Colored" signs appear over entrances, exits, toilets, water fountains, waiting rooms, and ticket windows. Segregation was formally instituted in wide areas of life. Some southern communities even went to the extreme of enacting laws requiring the residential segregation of blacks. Similarly, various measures were adopted to disfranchise blacks. Mississippi was the first state to move in this direction, with South Carolina following in 1895, Louisiana in 1898, North Carolina in 1900, Alabama in 1901, Virginia in 1902, Georgia in 1908, and Oklahoma in 1910. These laws were aimed at nullifying the effect of the Fifteenth Amendment. Since blacks could not be deprived of the right to vote on grounds of race, a whole battery of poll taxes, educational and literacy tests, white primaries, and grandfather clauses were evolved to achieve the same end.

Woodward suggests that the South's adoption of extreme racism was due not so much to a conversion as it was to a relaxation of the opposition. By the 1890s and early 1900s, there developed a general weakening and discrediting of the numerous forces that had hitherto kept racism in check. As the years passed, opinion in the North shifted away from liberalism and conceded one point after another, so that at no time were the sections very far apart on race policy. Within the South the position of the conservatives was undermined, and their willingness and ability to hold the Negrophobe fanatics in check were diminished. Although the conservatives had reaped enormous prestige by their overthrow of the Reconstruction regimes, an accumulation of grievances, financial scandals, and alliances with northeastern capital served to undercut their popularity in the South. Simultaneously, the Populists found their biracial partnership dissolving in frustration and bitterness as their opponents raised the cry of white supremacy against them. For a good many of the Populists it became easy to blame the blacks for their defeat, to make them the scapegoat, and to vent their bitterness and hostility on them. It was not long before former Populists were found in the forefront of many rabid anti-black movements. With the capitulation of northern liberalism, the decline in the strength of the southern conservatives, and the flight of the Populists from biracialism, racism triumphed.

The rise of the Jim Crow statutes in the South had the effect of tightening and freezing segregationist arrangements. In some instances these statutes actually served to instigate such practices. Prior to the enactment of these laws the blacks could and did do many things in the South that they were subsequently prevented from doing. It is clear, then, that formalized segregation is relatively new in the South and that the southern race patterns have not been immune to social change.

The Second Reconstruction

By the early years of the twentieth century, the Jim Crow order was well established in the South. The sanction of law was lent to racial ostracism that extended to churches and schools, to housing and jobs, to eating and drinking establishments, to public transportation, sports, hospitals, prisons, asylums, and even to funeral homes and cemeteries. As Woodward (1966:7–8) observes:

The new Southern system was regarded as the "final settlement," the "return to sanity," the "permanent system." Few stopped to reflect that previous systems had also been regarded as final, sane, and permanent by their supporters. The illusion of permanency was encouraged by the complacency of a long-critical North, the propaganda of reconciliation, and the resigned compliance of the Negro. The illusion was strengthened further by the passage of several decades during which change was averted or minimized.

Beginning with World War II, a new era of change set upon the South. Major assaults were directed against segregation from a great many quarters, with demands that the South institute immediate reform. The stage was set for the new era with the May 17, 1954, school desegregation ruling. On that date, the Supreme Court, consolidating cases arising in Delaware, Kansas, South Carolina, and Virginia, unanimously ruled that the "separate but equal" doctrine, which had been used to bar black children from white public schools, was unconstitutional. Mandatory school segregation was thus struck down. In so doing, the Supreme Court again demonstrated that it could change its mind. Fifty-eight years earlier, in the case of *Plessy* v. *Ferguson,* it held the contrary. In the years that followed the 1954 ruling, the Supreme Court moved toward outlawing legalized segregation in all areas of American life. In addition to the Supreme Court, pressures increased in other quarters. Demands mounted across the United States for congressional enactment of new civil rights legislation. Similarly, executive orders of presidents, policy decisions of federal agencies and the military, and actions by labor unions, professional groups, churches and others contributed to the assault upon Jim Crow. This new era of change is sometimes referred to as the "Second Reconstruction."

Movement and Countermovement.   Social change need not "just happen." It may occur because people undertake to *make* it take place. When people feel dissatisfied with the institutions of their society, they may initiate social change. Through organized effort—a social movement—they attempt to change an unsatisfactory situation. And as we discuss elsewhere in the book, this is precisely what a good many blacks have undertaken to do (*see* chapters 11 to 14).

Yet social movements do not initiate social change simply because they arise. Cultural persistence poses one formidable impediment to social reform. Once a pattern of social relationships has been established, it tends to carry on unchanged, except as the dynamics of other social forces operate to undermine it. Generally people find comfort, security, and a sense of well-being in old, familiar, and established ways. New forms of behavior, adjustments, and definitions often confront people with ambiguities and contradictions. For many individuals, efforts to resolve such ambiguities and contradictions would set up disturbing tensions that would in turn involve serious difficulties. Accordingly, it is frequently easier to go along with the old way of doing things, especially when no incentive for inaugurating the new way is seen. The situation is compounded when people assign strong emotional qualities to the old way, such as many whites assign to traditional race patterns. Thus the fact of cultural tenacity has proved a major obstacle to the integrationist movement.

Another impediment to social reform may be the emergence of a countermovement—a resistance movement. Movement frequently begets countermovement. Between the two movements a dynamic interaction may ensue, involving a more or less prolonged struggle. Thus integrationist efforts to topple the Jim Crow order stimulated the rise of a large-scale resistance movement. This movement attempted to minimize the consequences of the various assaults on the South's racial system, and to save the existing system intact. Let us turn to an examination of the southern resistance movement and the progressive accommodation of whites to desegregation.

Accommodation to "Undesired" Change.   The Supreme Court's decision of May 17, 1954, holding segregated public schools unconstitutional, confronted the South with the demand that mandatory school segregation be ended. Three more or less distinct phases can be noted in the resistance that unfolded within the region to this new demand for change. Here we will focus our attention upon Virginia, South Carolina, Georgia, Alabama, Mississippi, Louisiana, and Arkansas, where the resistance was most intense.

The first phase, from May 17, 1954, through May 31, 1955, was generally characterized by two co-existing themes. The first theme was a prevailing disbelief, "It won't happen!" For the great mass of southern whites the whole matter of desegregation appeared obtuse, one far off in Washington. It did not appear to them that desegregation could actually happen. Since the prospect of desegregation was a threatening, discomforting development, many southern whites responded by magically denying the reality of the new situation. They reassured themselves that desegregation was unthinkable and thus would simply not take place. The second theme involved an attitude of "buying time." This orientation was most prevalent among state government leaders. It was widely believed among them that some desegregation would be inescapable. But if it were inescapable, they nevertheless hoped to delay it, and delay became their major tactic. Overall, the southern scene was generally quiet and calm during the first year, with the region's leaders and newspapers reacting with restraint. Although new segregationist laws were added to the legal arsenal in hopes of delaying and circumventing the high court's ruling, their number was limited.

Then, on May 31, 1955, the Supreme Court handed down its decree *implementing* the ruling of the previous year. It declared that the federal district courts would have jurisdiction over lawsuits to enforce the ruling. It told the lower courts to be guided by "equitable principles" characterized by a "practical flexibility," but it warned that "constitutional principles cannot be allowed to yield simply because of disagreement with them." Defendant school districts were instructed that "a prompt and reasonable start toward full compliance" would be required and that admissions on a racially nondiscriminatory basis must be made with "all deliberate speed."

The high court's 1955 decree initiated the second phase of the resistance, characterized by a marked tightening of sentiment throughout the Deep and mid-South. The National Association for the Advancement of Colored People immediately followed the decree with a new offensive. Some 170 school boards in seventeen states were confronted with petitions signed by local blacks demanding immediate school desegregation. The fiction "It can't happen" was exploded. Angered, whites inaugurated a policy of adamant resistance in which compromise was ruled out. Methods of resistance grew bolder. Within the heavily black populated Black Belt areas, the White Citizens' Councils mushroomed. Although these organizations had previously been limited to a handful of chapters, thousands now signed council membership cards, and council rallies were well attended. Newspapers published the names of blacks who signed the petitions, and whites applied sanctions and social pressures against them. On the government level, state leaders rushed into law more than 200 new acts, in a desperate effort to find some legal mechanism through which to circumvent the Supreme Court's ruling.

By the fall of 1956 the school-desegregation battle appeared stalemated, with the segregationists in the saddle. For integrationists the situation was bleak. Congressman Charles C. Diggs of Michigan, himself a black man, lamented,

> We cannot point to one instance of submission by Mississippi, Georgia, South Carolina, or Alabama to the Supreme Court's three-year-old decision outlawing school segregation. There is little question that the Deep South has won the first round in the battle for compliance with the decision of May 17, 1954.

It was within this context that the Little Rock drama unfolded in late 1957, setting the basis for the third phase in the southern resistance—a phase of progressive accommodation to desegregation.

History will very likely show that Little Rock represented the key battle between school integrationists and segregationists, the turning point of the struggle. Arkansas Governor Orval Faubus had called out the National Guard in an effort to block the desegregation of Little Rock Central High School. As a result, a historic precedent was inevitable.

The issue posed by Faubus was whether a state could use the National Guard, the ultimate coercive weapon at its command, to enforce segregation. The issue could not be compromised, since a state either could or could not use armed forces to defy the federal courts. As developments unfolded, President Eisenhower decisively intervened, broke the stalemate, and turned the tide in favor of desegregation.

Confronted by the new situation posed by the developments at Little Rock, segregationists could have taken one of two courses: Either they could have intensified their resistance efforts and searched for new weapons or they could have begun the process of accommodation to school desegregation. The first course would have involved a continuation of the second phase, namely, adamant resistance and the rejection of compromise. Yet legal avenues for a permanent blocking of desegregation had been effectively closed. Extralegal methods including violence and armed resistance would have offered still another means of blocking desegregation. But rioting, chaos, and violence would have jeopardized still other values. And Little Rock demonstrated that force would be met with force. If the South needed a reminder, memories of the Civil War still haunted the region, a war that demonstrated the folly of such an approach.

The South, accordingly, moved in the direction of the second alternative and began the process of accommodation to school desegregation. Virginia is a case in point. In Virginia, James Lindsay Almond, Jr., a fire-and-brimstone orator of the old school, became governor in January, 1958. Before his election as governor, Almond had served eight years as Virginia's Attorney General, and had been in the forefront of the fight to maintain the segregated order. It was a self-labeled program of "massive resistance" to desegregation. Campaigning for governor, Almond told Virginians, "There can be no surrender. . . . I am willing to continue the fight to the last ditch, and then to dig another ditch. . . . If we yield one inch we are lost forever. . . . There can be no middle ground that will provide an avenue of escape. . . ."

Yet within thirteen months Almond stood before his 100-member House of Delegates and the 40-member Senate of Virginia, called into emergency session by him. "Massive resistance" had collapsed in the courts. Seven Virginia public schools had opened early in 1959 on a desegregated basis. Although his speech was elaborately embellished, paying homage to the cause of "massive resistance," Almond essentially declared that (1) the maintenance of completely segregated public schools was no longer possible in Virginia, (2) all legal avenues had been closed, and (3) the choice had become some integration if public schools were to be maintained or no public schools if total segregation was the goal. Significantly Almond cast his lot with the public schools and carried the state legislature with him. In subsequent speeches he explained, "I tell you now that we cannot overthrow the federal government, and we cannot reverse a final decree of a federal court."

No mistake could be more costly than to "succumb to the blandishments of those who would have Virginia abandon public education and thereby consign a generation of children to the darkness of illiteracy, the pits of indolence and dependency and the dungeons of delinquency."

Defeated in their efforts to block school desegregation, southern leaders began to tell their constituents, "We have done everything possible to prevent desegregation. We can do no more. We are now in a situation where we will have to accept some blacks in our white public schools. But we will do all in our power to see to it that the number of black children is held to a bare minimum. We will maintain our southern way of life!" Although school desegregation was often little more than "token," involving small numbers of blacks, the walls of school segregation were breached.

Southern leaders such as Virginia's James Lindsay Almond, Jr., served to make school desegregation palatable to the white citizenry. Their loyalty to "southern institutions" could not generally be questioned. They functioned to redefine school desegregation in terms that made it no longer equivalent to social equality. They reassured whites that southern traditions would carry on, that they need not feel alarmed or threatened. And, simultaneously, social change continued.

Yet despite signs that white southerners were progressively accommodating themselves to school desegregation, it was not until the introduction, debate, and enactment of the Civil Rights Act of 1964 that significant gains took place along the road toward ending formal segregation. The failure of southern whites to block school desegregation and the passage of new civil-rights legislation led many southern leaders to take the course of still further accommodation to desegregation. The late Senator Richard B. Russell, a longtime Senate power and leader of Senate anti-civil-rights forces, called upon his fellow Georgians to live with the new law:

> Violence and law violation will only compound our difficulties and increase our troubles. It is the understatement of the year to say that I do not like this statute [the 1964 Civil Rights Act]. However, it is now on the books. All good citizens will learn to live with the statute and abide by its final adjudication even though we reserve the right to advocate by legal means its repeal or modification. We put everything we had into the fight, but the odds against us mounted from day to day until we were finally gagged and overwhelmed.

Within four months of the passage of the Civil Rights Act of 1964, a U.S. government survey of public accommodations in fifty-three cities in the nineteen states that had no anti-Jim Crow public facilities' laws revealed that desegregation had been accomplished in two-thirds of the hotels in fifty-one cities and more than two-thirds of the motels in forty-six cities; more than two-thirds of theaters in forty-nine cities;

more than two-thirds of sports facilities in forty-eight cities; more than two-thirds of public parks in fifty cities; more than two-thirds of libraries in fifty-two cities; and more than two-thirds of chain restaurants in fifty cities (the largest downtown restaurants in major cities generally desegregated although neighborhood luncheonettes and taverns often remained segregated). All this did not mean that all southern whites were bowing gracefully to desegregation, but that instances of accommodation more than offset instances of whites who chose the course of continuing resistance. Nor did it mean that the use of public facilities once restricted to whites had as yet become the pattern among southern blacks.

In addition to the traditional judicial approach for ending formal school segregation, Title VI of the Civil Rights Acts of 1964 provided for an administrative remedy; federal officials were authorized to cut off funds to school districts practicing segregation. Under the Johnson administration, school desegregation was pushed largely in this fashion, with the courts playing a complementary role in the process. The Nixon administration, however, relied less on cut-off actions, deferring more to the courts and acting as an "adviser" to the courts in drafting desegregation plans.

By October, 1970, some 94 percent of the South's 2,702 school districts were estimated by the Justice Department to be in compliance with constitutional and legal requirements for school desegregation. And on August 31, 1970, in Virginia, eleven years after Governor Almond had started the state down the path of accommodation to desegregation, another governor, Linwood Holton, personally escorted his white 13-year-old daughter to a predominantly black public school in Richmond to dramatize the duty of white people to act lawfully and constructively to make desegregation work. On the same day in Georgia, longtime arch-segregationist and U.S. senator, Herman E. Talmadge, was interviewed on television. Rather abruptly, he was asked whether he was a segregationist. "Well sir," Talmadge replied, "no sir, I'm not." After the program he mused, "It's just a *fait accompli.* There's nothing left to defend." Indeed, in sixteen years the South had changed!

The Fate of the Second Reconstruction. By 1970, if not earlier, concern was increasingly being expressed among blacks and civil-rights supporters that the Second Reconstruction was endangered—that the nation was again confronted with the betrayal of black rights much in the fashion of 1877 (if one takes the "Compromise" and the withdrawal of federal troops from the last of the former Confederate states as the close of the First Reconstruction). Ominously, in March 1970, Daniel P. Moynihan—at that time serving as President Nixon's "liberal-in-residence" and later a U.S. senator from New York—suggested that with respect to the race issue the nation could best benefit from "a period of 'benign neglect.'" By October 1970, Reverend Theodore M. Hesburgh, president of the University of Notre Dame, could issue the following statement as chairperson of the U.S. Commission on Civil Rights:

> Our examination of various laws, executive orders, and judicial decisions has disclosed that there is indeed an impressive array of civil rights guarantees that provide protection against discrimination in virtually every aspect of life. . . . There is, however, a gap between what these guarantees have promised and what has actually been delivered. . . .
>
> The commission has examined the Federal civil rights enforcement effort and found it wanting.

A similar failure had occurred after the First Reconstruction—a failure to enforce basic laws and decrees.

Noting developments such as these, some recalled the thesis advanced by the historian Arthur Schlesinger, Sr., in which he argues that from its earliest days the United States has been dominated by alternating political attitudes: the conservative (Tory or Hamiltonian) philosophy and the liberal (Whig or Jeffersonian) philosophy. Liberal periods witness the accent on popular rights, programs of reform, and efforts to share power with the unrepresented, as contrasted with the accent in conservative periods on property rights, safety first for the commercial classes, and efforts to perpetuate the power of the status quo. Schlesinger points out that liberal gains generally remain on the statute books even after the conservatives recover power. They acquiesce in the new status quo. However, they try to sabotage the reform measures by halfhearted enforcement and reduced appropriations. It was not difficult for supporters of this pendulum theory to conclude that America had entered a new conservative era, especially in the realm of black rights.

As the decade of the seventies was launched, many whites in the North pulled back in a conservative direction, much as their counterparts had ninety years earlier. Some felt that integration was made impractical by the flight of whites to the suburbs, that to pursue it was only to "fuel the politics of George Wallace," and that it was not worth the cost anyway. Others, including several national columnists, had adopted the view that forced integration was either disruptive or accomplished little and that more was to be gained by channeling energies into a drive to improve the quality of schools, whatever their racial composition. Many educators, North and South, became skeptical about the benefits of integration and were inclined to look with disfavor on plans that required the extentive reshuffling of students. And too, the decline of northern interest in desegregation coincided with an attack upon segregation in northern schools, a tendency reinforced by the fears aroused by ghetto rioting and racial friction that occasionally occurred in desegregated school settings.

As the nation entered the 1980s, it was clear that in many respects the United States still remained two nations—one white and the other black. Although whites and blacks mix on the streets, in stores, in schools, and on the job, these surface manifestations of equality are misleading. Members of each group more or less live their personal and intimate lives independently of each other. The primary beneficiaries of the civil-rights movement have been middle-class and well-educated blacks. Social and economic barriers to full integration have proven more difficult to crack than formal and legal obstacles. And some blacks, frustrated and disillusioned by the slow progress of integration, have concluded that other issues, such as jobs, are more important to them. These blacks find integration less appealing than they once did and prefer "a go-it-alone" strategy.

At the beginning of the 1980s the nation has begun moving down a road that involves the dismantling of the War on Poverty and other federal programs for minorities and the poor. Budget-cutting and budget-balancing have taken a severe toll in social programs. Since blacks are disproportionately represented in these programs, many whites perceive them as being "black programs" and thus expendable. More and more blacks are finding themselves up against the wall. They consider themselves scapegoats and believe that whites do not care what happens to them. They come to experience apathy, despair, numbness, or rage as they live in urban islands of poverty with squalid streets, dilapidated and abandoned housing, rampant unemployment, and high rates of crime, alcoholism, and drug abuse while around them the nation seemingly enjoys great affluence.

During recent years the attitudes of whites have shifted. The notion is gaining prevalence among whites that blacks have had enough help, that black progress should now be the product of "black sweat," that the problems blacks have are of their own making, and that white people have their own problems. Whites profess a willingness to "give blacks a chance," but they are not willing to penalize themselves should this be necessary to assist blacks to get ahead.

The idea that the "pendulum has swung a little bit too far" in favor of blacks is often heard among whites. Many whites believe that blacks now enjoy equality of opportunity and that there is little need for special programs targeted toward black people. Whites speak negatively about "reverse discrimination," "racial preference," and "quotas." Global attitudes on racial justice have become increasingly favorable, especially among younger whites. For instance, a 1978 Louis Harris poll showed that 54 percent of whites would *not* be upset if blacks moved into their neighborhood, up from 32 percent in 1963. Yet simultaneously, white attitudes on implementation programs have become less favorable. Although whites seem increasingly committed to integration as an ideal, they are increasingly reluctant to support the mechanisms whereby integration can be achieved, including busing, affirmative-action programs, and public housing in the suburbs (Raines, 1979).

More and more whites seem sympathetic toward politicians who reject the argument that blacks should receive special treatment to make up for past racial injustices. And white liberals have increasingly shifted their interest and attention from civil-rights issues to other concerns including peace, the rights of women, and economic justice. In some respects race relations have more sharply polarized in recent years. Blacks view whites as the enemy and whites see blacks as a threat. The perception of whites that many ghetto blacks are criminals has intensified racial antagonisms. Remarkable parallels, then, can be found between the First and Second Reconstructions. Yet it is easy to overlook the changes that have occurred during the past several decades, matters to which we now turn our attention.

Income

During the 1950s, the incomes of both black and white families rose at about the same rate. Consequently, the black-white gap in purchasing power persisted. Shortly before the passage of the 1964 Civil Rights Act (forbidding racial discrimination in many areas of American life), the median income of black families was 54 percent of that of white families. After the law was passed, the percentage steadily rose, reaching 61 percent by the early 1970s. This was the one period since the end of World War II during which black families began to close the gap in income with white families. The median income of black families fell to 58 percent of that of white families during the recession of 1971 to 1973, but then reached a new high of 62 percent in 1976. However, by 1980, the median income of blacks had fallen back to 58 percent of that of whites.

Whereas black families accounted for 22 percent of all low-income families during the 1970s, in 1981 they made up 28 percent. In large measure this increase in low-income black families is associated with changing family patterns. Among both blacks and whites the families with the highest incomes are those that include both a husband and a wife. Families headed by women tend to have low incomes. During the 1970s the number of black single-parent families headed by women increased by 65 percent (the comparable rise for whites was 40 percent). It was the addition of nearly a million such households, most at the lowest income level, that cancelled out the gains made by black two-spouse families. Thus for every black family that moved into the middle class, three others were added to the bottom positions of the economic ladder.

Although black *families* did not improve their status relative to white families during the 1970s, the earnings of black *workers* rose more rapidly than did those of whites during the same period. A 1978 study prepared by the RAND Corporation (Lindsey, 1978) reveals that the wage gap between black and white women has nearly disappeared (black women now earn 95 percent of the salaries of white women, up from 64 percent in 1959). A primary factor in the income gains of black women has been the substantial reduction of black women engaged in domestic work. However, the average earnings of black men still lag behind those of white men. Black men now earn 73 percent as much as do white men, up from 58 percent in 1959. The gains have occurred because blacks and whites are becoming more alike in those attributes producing higher wages, especially education. However, should black men continue to gain ground at their recent pace, it will take thirty to forty years before their earnings reach parity with those of white men. The study concludes that government-mandated affirmative-action programs have played only a minor role in raising black earnings.

Jobs

Blacks have typically worked at less prestigious and lower-paying jobs than whites (Farley, 1980). There are many reasons for this. Until recent decades, the black population was concentrated in the rural South rather than in the more highly industrialized North (farm laborers typically earn considerably less than industrial workers). Employers and labor unions discriminated against blacks. And blacks completed fewer years of schooling than did whites. But as these factors changed —as blacks migrated to the cities, formal discrimination declined, and blacks stayed in school longer—blacks have made some job gains. In 1950, about 33 percent of white men and 8 percent of black men held white-collar jobs—a racial gap of 25 percent. The proportion of white men in these jobs is now 42 percent, but the proportion of black men has more than tripled, closing the racial gap somewhat to 16 percent. During the same period the racial gap between black and white women has closed substantially.

There are some 9,300 black physicians in the United States, double the figure of twenty years ago. However, in some cities and sections of the nation black physicians find it difficult to gain access to hospitals and other medical facilities. The proportion of black medical students increased from 3.8 percent of total enrollment in 1970 to 6.3 percent in 1974. But by 1980, the proportion slipped to 5.7 percent. The number of black lawyers has also grown. There are now nearly 12,000 black lawyers in the United States, six times the 1960 figure. Yet private practice holds so little promise for black lawyers that the vast majority work for government agencies.

Employed blacks continue to lag behind whites in job benefits. One aspect of work is job authority—one's position in an organizational hierarchy. On the whole, the average job authority of black men is markedly lower than that of white men. Further, black men in authority receive lower income returns, especially at higher occupational levels, than do whites. The exclusion of blacks from authority positions is costly. One study finds that on the average it accounts for about one-third of the total black-white income gap (Kluegel, 1978).

Unemployment

The plight of poor blacks has worsened in recent years, especially as black unemployment has mounted (Reinhold, 1979). Black unemployment has been running at double the rate it did in the 1960s. Official government figures reveal that at least 40 percent of all black teen-age job-seekers are unemployed. In some cities, like Detroit and Oakland, the percentage is considerably higher. However, official statistics understate black youth unemployment. Many youths are not counted because they have "disappeared" from the system—they are not employed or in school but are on the streets. The gap between black and white teen-age unemployment has widened from 1.3 times the white rate in the 1950s to more than 2.6 times in the 1980s.

Population experts expect that the problem of youth unemployment will increasingly become a problem of *black* youth unemployment. Black fertility has not fallen as sharply as that for whites. Whereas black teen-agers made up 11 percent of the youth labor force in 1970, they are expected to account for 15 percent by 1985 and about 20 percent in 1990.

Youth unemployment has serious consequences, touching many areas of American life. M. Henry Brenner, an economist at Johns Hopkins University, calculates that every rise of 1.0 percentage point in the unemployment rate is likely to lead to increases of 8.7 percentage points in narcotics arrests, 5.7 percentage points in robberies, and 3.8 percentage points in homicides for all unemployed youth (Kaufman, 1980).

Millions of black youths pass into adulthood handicapped by not having had experience in the work force. A "hangover" effect carries into adulthood so that unemployment feeds on itself. The young people fail to acquire those attitudes, behaviors, and skills conducive to securing and maintaining gainful employment.

Discrimination also plays a part. Blacks are still losing out on jobs because of racism. The unemployment rate among blacks with a *college* education is higher (27.2 percent) than that of whites who are *high-school dropouts* (22.3 percent). Blacks are also disadvantaged in government service. They have 3.4 percent of the highest-paying federal jobs (GS-16 to GS-18) although they make up 13.0 percent of the white-collar work force. And when blacks reach top positions in government, the jobs frequently center on equal employment and social services or are outside the mainstream of their agency's work.

The outlook for black employment is clouded by changes in the economy. Technological developments have eliminated many unskilled and semiskilled jobs. The Labor Department projects that by 1985 two out of every three jobs will be in white-collar and service occupations. During the 1970s 44 percent of black youth in contrast to 36 percent of white youth were in slow-growth, blue-collar jobs. Consequently, a serious problem is posed for those who have to work with their hands in a society that has less and less work for people with primarily manual skills.

The location of jobs in the nation continues to shift away from central cities toward the suburbs, smaller cities, and the Sun Belt, all distant from current black population centers (economists estimate that the average black inner-city youth who holds a job spends 2.5 more hours a week getting to and from work than the average white youth). Some labor-intensive industries, traditional employers of minority workers, have migrated to Taiwan, Korea, and Southeast Asia. Further, an influx of both legal and illegal aliens are taking jobs once held by blacks. And the emergence of a large underground economy of illegal activities, including drugs, running numbers, prostitution, mugging, and robbery, has opened avenues by which young people can make more money with less effort than in the legitimate economy. Compounding black problems has been the concentration of blacks within unskilled and semiskilled jobs, which are usually hard hit when the economy slumps. Since black workers typically have less seniority than white workers, they are the first to be furloughed during recessions. All these developments have contributed to the growth of a permanent black underclass.

Housing

Perhaps in no area of American life have segregated patterns hung on so tenaciously as in housing. Residential segregation contributes to segregation in other spheres of life, including the schools, government, and employment, and hinders black status attainment (Erbe, 1975; Parcel, 1979; Villemez, 1980). Three-fourths of all black families now live in metropolitan areas, and 55 percent of all blacks live in inner cities. Of those who live in cities, 56 percent live in the most impoverished and dilapidated sections. In many cities of the nation, residential segregation increased during the 1970s (Fly and Reinhart, 1980). Consequently, the trend during recent decades has been toward a growing concentration of the black poor in the cities. In fact, some social scientists and black leaders have charged that the nation's cities have become "reservations" for the minority poor.

The U.S. Bureau of the Census reports that from 1960 to 1979 the number of blacks living in suburbs grew by 72 percent to about 5 million, compared with a 38 percent growth in the white suburban population (*see* Table 8.3). For example, East Cleveland had few black residents in 1960. But by 1970 the Cleveland suburb was 60 percent black and by 1980 the figure reached 82 percent.

Black movement to the suburbs occurs largely between black city neighborhoods and suburbs that are primarily black or rapidly becoming so. For instance, of the 200 or so suburbs that ring Chicago, only 15 have sizeable black populations. Most black suburbanites settle in formerly white neighborhoods where housing has deteriorated in physical condition and market value (Clay, 1979). Suburbs with high proportions of blacks are characterized by lower income, higher unemployment, and lower educational levels than neighboring predominantly white suburbs. Black suburbanization often occurs through "leapfrogging" neighborhoods or communities rather than through "spillover" (moving from one adjacent neighborhood to another).

Blockbusting still remains a problem in many communities across the nation. It is a technique by which real-estate agents increase their profits by selling a house to a black family in a white neighborhood with the expectation that other whites will then sell their houses quickly and cheaply. The houses are later sold to blacks at inflated prices. In blockbusting real-estate agents attempt to prey on white fears that black entry into their neighborhoods will result in an increase in the crime rate, will lower the quality of the schools, will increase expenditures for public services, and will lower property values. Accordingly, when blacks begin to integrate a neighborhood, some real-estate interests attempt to stampede whites into flight.

Discrimination continues to play a part in determining black residential patterns. Although Congress outlawed racial discrimination in the sale or rental of housing (Title VIII of the Civil Rights Act of 1968), the ban is widely circumvented by real-estate agents and mortgage lenders. Surveys of mortgage-lending practices reveal that, in relation to whites of comparable income, black applicants are more likely to be denied mortgages and to pay higher interest rates when they get mortgages.

Other forces are also at work in influencing black residential patterns. Ethnic communities, especially cohesive ones, are usually difficult for blacks to penetrate (Logan and Stearns, 1981). In contrast blacks generally find it easier to enter communities with no ethnic identity and significant housing turnover. The high price of housing in white suburbs also looms as a major obstacle confronting blacks.

When middle-class blacks enter white suburbs they frequently find that the attitude of their neighbors is one of "resigned acceptance." But in some circumstances they encounter racism. Private clubs are not inclined to accept blacks and whites communicate to blacks that they are "unwelcome" in various stores. In some instances employees are instructed to "keep an eye" on black shoppers, especially black teenagers. And many white suburbanites refuse to vote for federal grants that would assist or attract minorities to their communities. Rental

TABLE 8.3   PERCENT OF BLACKS IN SUBURBS OF THE FIFTY LARGEST U.S. METROPOLITAN AREAS

	1970	1980
Norfolk-Virginia Beach	31.9%	32.4%
Memphis	32.4%	21.1%
Washington	8.3%	16.7%
Miami	12.2%	15.1%
Birmingham	20.4%	14.5%
Newark	8.8%	13.8%
Atlanta	8.4%	13.5%
New Orleans	12.5%	12.6%
St. Louis	7.0%	10.6%
Fort Lauderdale area	14.2%	10.3%
Los Angeles area	6.2%	9.6%
Baltimore	6.0%	9.1%
Philadelphia	6.7%	8.1%
Nashville	10.7%	8.0%
Greensboro-Winston-Salem-High Point	7.8%	7.9%
New York	5.9%	7.6%
Cleveland	3.4%	7.1%
Houston	9.6%	6.7%
San Francisco area	5.4%	6.5%
Nassau-Suffolk, N.Y.	4.7%	6.2%
Chicago	3.6%	5.6%
Louisville	3.3%	5.6%
San Antonio	4.2%	5.3%
Dayton	3.2%	4.8%
Cincinnati	2.9%	4.3%
Pittsburgh	3.5%	4.0%
Dallas-Fort Worth	3.6%	3.9%
Tampa-St. Petersburg	4.5%	3.9%
Riverside-Ontario-San Bernardino	3.3%	3.9%
Oklahoma City	1.7%	3.8%
Detroit	3.4%	4.2%
Sacramento	2.0%	3.3%
San Diego	1.4%	2.7%
San Jose	1.2%	2.2%
Buffalo	1.6%	2.1%
Rochester, N.Y.	1.4%	2.1%
Columbus, Ohio	1.9%	1.9%
Denver	0.4%	1.7%
Boston	1.0%	1.6%
Phoenix	1.3%	1.4%
Kansas City	0.9%	1.3%
Anaheim-Santa Ana	0.3%	1.0%
Seattle	0.4%	1.0%
Indianapolis	0.8%	1.0%
Albany, N.Y., area	0.7%	1.0%
Providence	0.8%	0.8%
Minneapolis-St. Paul	0.2%	0.6%
Portland, Oreg.	0.2%	0.6%
Salt Lake City	0.5%	0.6%
Milwaukee	0.2%	0.5%

Source: U.S. Bureau of the Census.

housing is especially difficult for blacks to obtain in white suburbs. In some cases apartment owners fix their own black-white ratio.

Any number of northern cities are troubled by deep-seated racial tensions. Boston is a case in point (Knight, 1979). Despite its desire for a progressive and liberal reputation, Boston is a sharply segregated city. A strong sense of "turf" marks the city's Irish and Italian neighborhoods. Blacks complain of feeling unwanted in downtown Boston and unwelcome at tourist attractions, sporting events, restaurants, and nightclubs. Discrimination is so pervasive that even the lowest-paying and most menial city jobs are reserved for whites. In recent years the city's racial tensions have boiled over in incidents ranging from verbal abuse to street brawls, stonings, and fire-bombings. Racial hostility is so high that blacks fear to walk into South Boston, the citadel of the city's Irish, and whites fear going into Roxbury, a black neighborhood.

Health

Black children are four times more likely than white children to be born in poverty, twice as likely to die during the first year of life, twice as likely to have no regular source of medical care, and 25 percent more likely to die from illness during childhood (Barden, 1981). Further, many black children feel that they have no place to go and consequently turn to crime. Black children are arrested at almost seven times the rate of white children for more serious, violent crime. In fact, murder is the number one cause of death among young adult black males. Overall, the life expectancy of blacks lags six years behind that of whites.

A 1978 Social Security Administration report found that black workers are 50 percent more likely than whites to be severely disabled from job injuries or illnesses. The higher incidence is explained by the concentration of blacks in more dangerous occupations and their greater reluctance to seek early medical care for health problems. Likewise, blacks are less likely to survive cancer five years after the disease has been detected. Apparently blacks are less likely to get the most up-to-date treatment and follow-up care.

Education

Since public-school enrollments closely parallel housing patterns, desegregation of the schools has constituted a formidable task. At the time of the Supreme Court's 1954 school desegregation ruling in *Brown* v. *Board of Education*, blacks were segregated from whites in southern schools by law, termed de jure segregation. In northern cities segregation has been de facto. Although not explicitly created by law, de facto segregation derives from a system of neighborhood schools in combination with residential concentrations of minority groups. Public officials, boards of education, and sociologists have debated the relative evils of de jure and de facto segregation. But to the black children who encounter segregation, there is no difference. Segregation is segregation whatever it is called.

During the three decades since the Supreme Court ruled against segregated schools, sweeping changes have taken place in education. Racially separate school systems, once legally mandated in seventeen southern states, have now been outlawed. For the most part, blacks are no longer denied admission to public schools or colleges because of formal racial barriers. During the 1970s a nationwide drive was launched to get more blacks and whites into desegregated schools (*see* chapter 15). In many cities, the courts have ordered the busing of children to achieve racial balance. But the approach has been bitterly fought by many whites, and opposition to busing has mounted in the 1980s. Likewise, colleges have been under government pressure to enroll more blacks.

Despite the progress in school desegregation, most of the nation's black children remain in segregated classes. Nearly two-thirds are still in predominantly minority schools. In the South the figure is down from 79 percent a decade ago to 59 percent today, better than in the other regions of the nation. In contrast, the number of black children in the Northeast attending schools at which at least half of the student enrollment was black rose from 68 percent to 71 percent during the 1970s.

In major cities across the nation the enrollment of white children in central-city schools is dropping precipitously as whites move to the suburbs or send their children to private schools. In Atlanta, the public-school system is now 90 percent black as against 45 percent black two decades ago. Some school systems like that in New York City have abandoned thoughts of systemwide desegregation, although encouraging integration through open enrollment programs, zoning, busing, specialized schools, and "magnet" programs.

Blacks now stay in school longer and go on to college more frequently than was the case in the 1970s. Census data shows that during the 1970s the number of blacks age eighteen to twenty-four who dropped out of high school fell from 35 to 24 percent (the dropout rate of whites went down from 18 to 15 percent). Further, among high-school graduates, blacks and whites are now entering college at roughly the same rate. However, about one-eighth of all black youths complete a college education as against one-quarter of all white youths.

During the 1970s black enrollment in the nation's colleges more than doubled (reaching 1.1 million in 1980). In 1981 blacks constituted about 11 percent of undergraduates, against 7 percent in 1970 and 6 percent in 1960. At the graduate- and professional-school level, blacks accounted for 6 percent of the students, up from 4 percent in 1970. Yet it is easy to overestimate racial progress on the nation's campuses. Many fraternities and sororities still discriminate against minority students. And often black and white students go their separate ways. Cliques and friendships mostly follow racial lines. Black students commonly eat together in dining halls and have little interaction with white students outside the classrooms.

Blacks colleges are also experiencing deepening problems. The schools have trained many of today's black leaders and enroll some 200,000 students. Coupled with the financial difficulties confronting most institutions of higher learning, black colleges have faced mounting competition from traditionally white colleges in recruiting black students, especially the "cream" of the nation's black high-school graduates. Black colleges have attempted to improve their curricula and upgrade their faculties, while offering good remedial programs.

Voting and Officeholding

The Voting Rights Act of 1965 opened the way for black participation in southern politics. Among other things, the act forbids poll taxes and literacy tests, outlaws the stuffing of ballot boxes, and establishes criminal penalties for anyone who intimidates a person trying to vote. As the Supreme Court once observed, the right to vote is the most fundamental right because it is "preservative" of all other rights. Prior to congressional passage of the 1965 law, blacks were disenfranchised in many areas of the South. The Voting Rights Act dramatically elevated the level of black political participation (*see* Table 8.4). However, black voting strength has occasionally been diluted through various forms of subtle discrimination, including the gerrymandering of districts, the annexation of territory to change a city's racial composition, and the election of representatives on a citywide or countrywide basis rather than on a districtwide basis.

Politics involves the counting of heads. By voting their interests and shifting their alliances, blacks have been able to increase the number of their public officeholders and defeat candidates who oppose their

TABLE 8.4 BLACK VOTER REGISTRATION (IN THOUSANDS)

	1964	1966	1980
Alabama	111	250	350
Georgia	270	300	450
Louisiana	165	243	465
Mississippi	29	175	330
South Carolina	144	191	320
Texas	375	400	620
Virginia	200	205	360

Source: Voter Education Project.

aims. But many observers agree that black representation would be considerably greater if blacks would use their voting potential to the fullest extent. One problem is that some 9 million eligible blacks are not registered to vote.

The black vote has made a difference where blacks have registered to vote and vote in significant numbers. Consider Selma, Alabama, where on March 25, 1965, the violence-plagued march to Montgomery by black and white demonstrators began. In 1981 the Reverend F. D. Reese and three other blacks who were involved in the civil-rights movement served on the city council. They worked alongside Mayor Joe Smitherman, a white. Smitherman was also mayor when Reverend Reese and other marchers were bombarded with tear gas at Edmund Pettus Bridge in the "Bloody Sunday" episode that focused world attention on Selma. Speaking of Mayor Smitherman, Reverend Reese says, "Of course we tamed him. He is actually engaged now in looking after the rights of blacks in the town, because of the voting strength that we have. Sometimes that vote can make them smile when they want to frown" (Raines, 1978:16).

In 1980 the United States had 4,912 elected officials who were blacks, including 182 mayors, in contrast to only 1,469 such officials in 1969. Southern states and states with large urban populations have the largest number: 387 in Mississippi, 363 in Louisiana, 298 in Illinois, 284 in Michigan, and 261 in the District of Columbia. Most black officeholders are found at the municipal level and their numbers thin out as the level of office rises. Of the elected officials who were black, 1,214 were in education-related posts, 526 in judicial or law-enforcement positions, 451 at the county level, 323 in state legislatures, and 18 in Congress. (There were also 27 blacks among the 678 presidentially appointed federal judges.) Despite black gains since the 1960s, blacks constitute only 1 percent of all elected public officials (there are 490,200 total elected offices in the United States).

Since the nation's black population is so highly centered in metropolitan areas, the circumstances of blacks are largely determined by conditions in the nation's cities. Federal aid to the cities has assumed enormous significance. In 1967, direct federal aid to St. Louis made up only 1 percent of the city's general revenue. By 1978, the figure reached 54 percent. During the same period aid to Newark went from less than 2 percent to 55 percent, in Buffalo from 2 percent to 69 percent, and in Cleveland from 8 percent to 68 percent.

Federal budget-cutting in the 1980s has imperiled the extent of assistance that the cities can expect from the federal government. Simultaneously, the loss by the central cities of major industries and the progressive movement of the middle class of all races to the suburbs have resulted in a steadily shrinking tax base for the revenues necessary to provide basic services. Further, as the proportion of black city dwellers grow, blacks are finding that many of the former powers of the city have been ceded to county governments and outside agencies in the hands of whites. These factors raise ominous clouds for ghetto blacks in the 1980s.

SUMMARY

1. Segregation places limits on social interaction among individuals of differing racial and ethnic groups. One form of segregation is physical or spatial separation. As pointed out in chapter 7, territoriality is one means by which human beings manage aggression. In this respect, spatial segregation may be involuntary, imposed on a minority people by a dominant group. But individuals and groups are also sifted and sorted out in space for voluntary reasons. Clustering offers advantages to an ethnic group. Close proximity facilitates communication, understanding, and rapport among like-minded individuals. Segregated communities also afford protection against the intrusion of strange beliefs, values, and norms. Another form of segregation is discrimination. Here members of a group, based upon their ethnic or racial membership, are treated unequally and unfavorably by members of the dominant group.

2. There are currently in the United States nearly 1 million Native Americans. Government policy toward Native Americans has passed through five phases. Following the American Revolution, genocide and separation dominated federal policy. Native Americans were murdered and their lands were expropriated. Indian peoples were settled on reservations. In the 1870s new policies were instituted in which Native Americans were considered "wards" of the government. The program was aimed at "forced assimilation." Under the Dawes Act of 1887 tribal lands were broken up and divided among individual Indians. The remaining tribal holdings were declared "surplus" and opened to non-Indian settlement. In 1929 a new policy was inaugurated that had as its goal tribal restoration. It reversed previous policy and encouraged the Native Americans to retain their tribal identifications and cultures. During the post-World War II period the government reversed itself once again. The Eisenhower administration attempted to get the federal government "out of the Indian business." Perhaps the most drastic policy was "termination," under which certain tribes were freed from federal supervision. During the 1970s the goal of national policy shifted again to one of "self-determination." The government sought to strengthen Native American control over Indian affairs without cutting off Native Americans from federal concern and support.

3. Today the overwhelming majority of Indians live west of the Mississippi River. The problems of Indian peoples abound. Thirty-eight percent of the more than 1 million Native Americans live on incomes below the poverty line. The life expectancy of American Indians is ten

years shorter than that of whites. During the past three decades, there has been a steady migration of Indians from reservations to cities. More than half of the nation's Indian population now resides in urban areas. The status of Indians as a racial and cultural minority results in discrimination in most off-reservation contexts.

4. In 1980, the Bureau of the Census reported that there were 26.5 million blacks in the United States, 11.7 percent of the total population. The first slaves in English North America were in Jamestown, Virginia. Since there was no precedent in English law regarding slaves, it appears that the blacks initially assumed the status of indentured servants. However, the blacks' distinctive physical characteristics doubtless furthered their differential treatment from the beginning and in time facilitated their enslavement. The New Nation arose as a Greek-style democracy, where democracy was extended only to a segment of the population. Yet the problems posed by racism within an egalitarian society have been a source of constant embarrassment.

5. The historian C. Vann Woodward maintains that the assumption is often incorrectly made that the institution of Jim Crowism (legalized segregation) followed automatically upon the overthrow of Reconstruction. Instead, Jim Crow was largely a later development. It should not be assumed that a golden age of race relations prevailed in the period between Reconstruction and the institution of the Jim Crow laws. Rather legalized Jim Crow came to reinforce the informal mechanisms of social distance that regulated white-black interaction.

6. Beginning with World War II, a new era of change set upon the South. Major assaults were directed against segregation from a great many quarters. This new era of change is sometimes referred to as the "Second Reconstruction." The Supreme Court's decision of May 17, 1954, holding segregated public schools unconstitutional, confronted the South with the demand that mandatory school segregation be ended. At first white southerners attempted to block school desegregation by "buying time." But when the Supreme Court handed down its May 31, 1955, implementing decree, white southerners mounted an assault upon black petitioners who called for school desegregation. Little Rock represented the key battle between school integrationists and segregationists. The federal government intervened in the Little Rock desegregation case to enforce a court-ordered school-desegregation ruling. During the next decade the South began the process of accommodation to school desegregation.

7. By 1970, if not earlier, concern was increasingly being expressed among blacks and civil-rights supporters that the Second Reconstruction was endangered. As the decade of the 1970s progressed, many whites reverted to conservatism. Consequently, in many respects the United States still remains two nations—one white and the other black. During recent years attitudes have shifted. The notion is gaining preva-

lence among whites that blacks have had enough help, that black progress should now be the product of "black sweat," that the problems blacks have are of their own making, and that white people have their own problems. Although whites seem increasingly committed to integration as an ideal, they are increasingly reluctant to support the mechanisms whereby integration can be achieved, including busing, affirmative-action programs, and public housing in the suburbs.

8. During the 1950s, the incomes of both black and white families rose at about the same rate. After the passage of the 1964 Civil Rights Act black families began to close the gap with white families in income. But in recent years the gap has once again widened. Although black families have not improved their status relative to white families during the 1970s, the earnings of black workers rose more rapidly than did those of whites during the same period.

9. Blacks have typically worked at less prestigious and lower-paying jobs than whites. Black men have been able to close the gap somewhat between themselves and white men but the racial gap still remains considerable. However, the racial gap between black and white women has closed substantially. Employed blacks continue to lag behind whites in job benefits.

10. The plight of poor blacks has worsened in recent years, especially as black unemployment has mounted. In recent years black unemployment has been running at double the rate it did in the 1960s. The outlook for black employment is clouded by changes in the economy. Technological developments have eliminated many unskilled and semiskilled jobs. The location of jobs in the nation continues to shift away from central cities toward the suburbs, smaller cities, and the Sun Belt, all distant from current black population centers.

11. Perhaps in no area of American life have segregated patterns hung on so tenaciously as in housing. Residential segregation contributes to segregation in other spheres of life, including the schools, government, and employment, and hinders black status attainment. In many cities of the nation, residential segregation increased during the 1970s. Consequently, the trend in recent decades has been toward a growing concentration of the black poor in the cities.

12. Black children are four times more likely than white children to be born in poverty, twice as likely to die during the first year of life, twice as likely to have no regular source of medical care, and 25 percent more likely to die from illness during childhood. A 1978 Social Security Administration report found that black workers are 50 percent more likely than whites to be severely disabled from job injuries or illnesses.

13. Since public-school enrollments closely parallel housing patterns, desegregation of the schools has constituted a formidable task. As opposed to the situation during the 1950s, blacks are no longer typically

denied admission to public schools or colleges because of formal racial barriers. During the 1970s a nationwide drive was launched to get more blacks and whites into desegregated schools. Despite the progress in school desegregation, most of the nation's black children remain in segregated classes.

14. The Voting Rights Act of 1965 opened the way for black participation in southern politics. The law dramatically elevated the level of black political participation. The number of elected officials who are black has increased. However, despite black gains during the past two decades, blacks constitute only 1 percent of all elected public officials.

GLOSSARY

Segregation   The process or state whereby people are separated or set apart.

Segregation: Hispanics, Asians, and Jews 9

A s noted in chapter 8, segregation is the process by which people are separated or set apart. One form of segregation consists of physical or spatial separation. Another form finds expression in discrimination. In either form, segregation places limits upon social interaction among individuals of differing racial and ethnic groups and contributes to disadvantage among some peoples. Chapter 8 examined patterns of segregation as they have applied within the United States to Native Americans and blacks. This chapter continues the discussion by focusing on Chicanos, Puerto Ricans, Cubans, Chinese, Japanese, Indochinese, and Jews.

Chicanos

What Americans of Mexican ancestry call themselves or prefer to be called is a matter of considerable sensitivity. The term "Chicano" has gained widespread acceptance in recent years among the members of this ethnic group. The reason in part stems from its popular origin and the fact that it has been chosen by members of the group itself. As such it has not been imposed on the group by Anglo-Americans, as was the term "Mexican–American" (a parallel exists between the differing uses and connotations of "black" versus "Negro"). "Brown" and "La Raza" are other terms also denoting peoplehood—ethnic pride, identity, and solidarity. However, some descendants of Spanish settlers in the Southwest prefer to be known as "Hispanos," "Californios," or "Tejanos."

The Bureau of the Census reports that 14.6 million persons, or about 6.4 percent of the population, listed themselves as of Spanish origin in the 1980 census. An estimated two-thirds of Spanish-speaking Americans are of Mexican ancestry. The 1980 census (*see* Table 9.1) showed that in New Mexico Hispanics were 36.6 percent of the population; in Texas, 21 percent; in California, 19.2 percent; in Arizona, 16.2; and in

TABLE 9.1 HISPANICS IN THE TOP FIFTY
METROPOLITAN AREAS, 1980

SMSA	Total Population	Hispanic Population	Hispanics as Percentage of Population
1. New York	9,119,737	1,493,081	16.4
2. Los Angeles-Long Beach	7,477,657	2,065,727	27.6
3. Chicago	7,102,328	580,592	8.2
4. Philadelphia	4,716,818	116,280	2.5
5. Detroit	4,352,762	71,589	1.6
6. San Francisco-Oakland	3,252,721	351,915	10.8
7. Washington, D.C.	3,060,240	93,353	3.1
8. Dallas-Fort Worth	2,974,878	249,613	8.4
9. Houston	2,905,350	424,901	14.6
10. Boston	2,763,357	66,417	2.4
11. Nassau-Suffolk	2,605,813	101,975	3.9
12. St. Louis	2,355,276	22,284	0.9
13. Pittsburgh	2,263,894	11,881	0.5
14. Baltimore	2,174,023	21,410	1.0
15. Minneapolis-St. Paul	2,114,256	22,271	1.1
16. Atlanta	2,029,618	23,383	1.2
17. Newark	1,965,304	132,356	6.7
18. Anaheim-Santa Anna- Gdn Grove	1,931,570	286,331	14.8
19. Cleveland	1,898,720	25,920	1.4
20. San Diego	1,861,846	275,176	14.8
21. Miami	1,625,979	581,030	35.7
22. Denver-Boulder	1,619,921	173,362	10.7
23. Seattle-Everett	1,606,765	32,057	2.0
24. Tampa	1,569,492	79,429	5.1
25. Riverside-San Bernardino-Ont.	1,557,080	289,791	18.6
26. Phoenix	1,508,030	198,999	13.2
27. Cincinnati	1,401,403	7,877	0.6
28. Milwaukee	1,397,143	34,343	2.5
29. Kansas City	1,327,020	31,820	2.4
30. San Jose	1,295,071	226,611	17.5
31. Buffalo	1,242,573	16,206	1.3
32. Portland	1,242,187	24,327	2.0
33. New Orleans	1,186,725	48,407	4.1
34. Indianapolis	1,166,929	8,845	0.8
35. Columbus, Ohio	1,093,293	7,572	0.7
36. San Antonio	1,071,954	481,511	44.9

continued on page 240

TABLE 9.1   HISPANICS IN THE TOP FIFTY METROPOLITAN AREAS, 1980 (Continued)

SMSA	Total Population	Hispanic Population	Hispanics as Percentage of Population
37. Ft. Lauderdale-Hollywood	1,014,043	40,252	4.0
38. Sacramento	1,014,002	101,692	10.0
39. Rochester	971,879	19,342	2.0
40. Salt Lake City-Ogden	936,255	47,268	5.0
41. Providence-Warwick-Pawtucket	919,216	19,333	2.1
42. Memphis	912,887	8,139	0.9
43. Louisville	906,240	5,472	0.6
44. Nashville-Davidson	850,505	5,973	0.7
45. Birmingham	847,360	5,531	0.7
46. Oklahoma City	834,088	18,522	2.2
47. Dayton	830,070	5,653	0.7
48. Greensboro-Winston Salem-High Pt.	827,385	5,574	0.7
49. Norfolk-Va. Beach-Portsmouth	806,691	13,779	1.7
50. Albany-Schenectady-Troy	795,019	8,146	1.0

Source: Bureau of the Census.

Colorado, 11.7 percent. Los Angeles is the world's second largest Latin city, surpassed only by Mexico City. Other cities with large Chicano populations are San Francisco, Chicago, Detroit, Denver, and Seattle. However, no one knows exactly how many Chicanos there are in the United States. Some are in the country "illegally" and hence try to avoid detection. Population experts also question the accuracy of the count made by the census of the Hispanic population.* And Chicano leaders likewise claim that the Bureau of the Census has consistently under-

---

*The 1980 census form produced confusion among people of Hispanic origin as to which categories they were to check in listing their racial and ethnic memberships. In 1970 the Bureau of the Census had counted 93 percent of Mexicans, Cubans, and other Hispanic people as "white." But in the most recent census Hispanics classed themselves, with 40 percent checking "other" on question number four, the race question. Farther down the questionnaire, question number seven asked Spanish respondents to check their ethnic group. Some Hispanics, having checked "other" for number four, concluded that this was all that was necessary and failed to complete number seven.

counted their population, and consequently diluted Chicano political strength.

Background

The Southwest became a part of the United States between 1845 and 1854 as the result of the annexation of Texas, the conquest of northern Mexico, and the Gadsden Purchase. In 1846 President James K. Polk ordered United States forces into Mexico after a border clash between military units of the two nations. Abraham Lincoln, then a freshman member of Congress, accused Polk of provoking the Mexican-American War by sending troops "into the midst of a peaceful Mexican settlement." And Henry David Thoreau went to jail rather than pay taxes to support the war.

Following the conclusion of the war in 1848, Mexico ceded to the United States a vast territory that encompassed California, Arizona, New Mexico, Nevada, Utah, and portions of a number of other states, and also approved the prior annexation of Texas. The area was greater in extent than Germany and France combined, and represented one-half of the territory that in 1821 constituted Mexico. The settlement still rankles in Mexico. Under the terms of the Treaty of Guadalupe Hidalgo, all Mexican citizens in the territory were to become United States citizens if they did not leave the territory within one year. Very few returned to Mexico. At the time of the treaty, approximately 75,000 Spanish-speaking people lived in the Southwest: about 7,500 in California, roughly 1,000 in Arizona, perhaps 5,000 in Texas, and 60,000 in New Mexico. The overwhelming majority of these people were of mixed Spanish-Indian ancestry (McWilliams, 1949). Many of them bear some of the proudest names of the Spanish explorers-soldiers-settlers who made this territory a part of New Spain in the 1500s and whose ancestors, mixing with the Indians, were third generation before the Pilgrims landed in Massachusetts. Although the Treaty of Guadalupe Hidalgo theoretically protected the holders of Spanish and Mexican land grants, the inhabitants commonly lost their landholdings through legal chicanery and physical intimidation.

North from Mexico

During the early 1900s, a new group of Mexican nationals began to enter the United States, migrating to work from their homes, during the cotton harvest, to the old cotton-producing sections of East Texas and then, after the harvest, returning to their homes. East Texas had long been a cotton-growing section in contrast with the cattle areas of South and West Texas. Although blacks supplied the primary source of labor, Mexicans constituted a secondary source. About the turn of the twentieth century, cotton production started advancing into Central Texas and between 1910 and 1930 into West Texas, replacing cattle raising in wide areas. In these new cotton-producing areas, landlords and overseers relied primarily upon transient Mexican labor. As the years passed, many of the immigrants remained in the United States and became ancestral to much of the contemporary Spanish-speaking population of the Southwest (McWilliams, 1949).

By 1940 nearly 400,000 transient workers, two-thirds of whom were Mexicans, were engaged in following the "big swing" through the cotton-producing regions of Texas. Each year a vast army of migratory workers started harvesting cotton in the southern part of the state, moved northward into eastern Texas, and then proceeded into the central and western cotton-growing areas. The workers were organized by labor contractors and truckers. These latter individuals usually spoke English, knew the routes, dealt with the employers, and organized the expedition. They transported the workers in open or stake trucks, hired the crews out to employers, and oversaw the work (McWilliams, 1949).

The conditions of life for transient workers were difficult. Writing in 1946, Pauline R. Kibbe (1946:176) observed:

> Generally speaking, the Latin American migratory worker going into West Texas is regarded as a necessary evil, nothing more nor less than an unavoidable adjunct to the harvest season. Judging by the treatment accorded him in that section of the State, one might assume that he is not a human being at all, but a species of farm implement that comes mysteriously and spontaneously into being coincident with the maturing of the cotton, that requires no upkeep or special consideration during the period of its usefulness, needs no protection from the elements, and when the crop has been harvested, vanishes into the limbo of forgotten things— until the next harvest season rolls around. He has no past, no future, only a brief and anonymous present.

Sanitary facilities were especially inadequate and hygienic conditions were poor.

Beginning in 1942 Mexican nationals came to this country for migrant farm work under agreements entered into by the governments of Mexico and the United States. Prior to the program's termination in 1964, as many as 450,000 Mexicans annually entered the United States for this purpose. Another source of Mexican labor has been commuters (numbering about 50,000) who daily cross the border to work in and near nine border cities.

Historically employment opportunities for Chicanos have resided overwhelmingly in unskilled jobs. In agriculture, ranching, and mining, early industries of the Southwest, these were the people who served as laborers. And as we have noted, as crops needed cultivation or harvesting, Chicanos made up the majority of field hands doing the chopping, thinning, and picking. When the railroads were laid, they were the section hands, and they still serve today as maintenance-of-ways workers. When irrigation works spread in the Southwest, Chicanos were the ditch diggers and irrigators; when fruits and vegetables needed sorting and packing, it was the Chicanos who manned the canning plants and packing sheds; when smelters were built, they handled the ore; and when construction boomed, they were the hod carriers and common laborers.

The disparity between economic conditions and opportunities in Mexico and the United States encourages Mexican nationals to seek employment in the United States. More than half of Mexico's work force is unemployed or underemployed. A high birth rate in Mexico yields a population growth that far outstrips Mexico's capacity to create jobs. Consequently, immigration to the United States has functioned in part as Mexico's social and economic safety valve. Simultaneously, employers in the United States yearn for labor that will work hard and "scared" for low wages.

Large numbers of Mexican nationals enter the United States "illegally." However, "undocumented workers" do not feel that they are committing a crime by entering the United States. They refer to it as going to *el norte*. Many view the Southwest as Mexican territory and consider the Anglos to be the "illegals." By virtue of the large Chicano population in the Southwest, the United States does not seem to be a totally foreign country, but more like a politically detached cultural homeland.

Some Mexican nationals swim or wade across the Rio Grande River. Others cross the border with the aid of paid smugglers, called "coyotes." The smuggling of aliens is becoming highly organized, with a network extending from smugglers through labor contractors to growers and urban manufacturers. Once in the United States, Mexican workers are provided bogus documents, including resident alien identification cards, birth certificates, and Social Security cards. Most large Hispanic communities have a flourishing trade in these documents. Still other Mexicans enter the United States with passes or short-term visas.

The typical immigrant is a male in his twenties with an elementary-school education. Most come from the central region of Mexico. They commonly are in search of subsistence for their families and they usually plan to return to Mexico with their earnings. However, once in the United States, some change their minds (Stevens, 1979).

Mexican aliens are increasingly by-passing the nation's farms and ranches, their traditional sources of employment, for better-paying urban jobs in construction, manufacturing, and service industries (Crewdson, 1980c). Unlike those in agriculture, who often return to Mexico at the end of the harvest season, those who work in urban jobs tend to stay in the United States unless they are apprehended by immigration agents. Many employers prefer foreign workers because they work for lower wages and are among their most reliable and enthusiastic employees. In the case of the garment industry and many light industries, employers say that illegal aliens offer them their only means for staying in business and meeting determined foreign competition. Chicanos also constitute a major labor source for service businesses such as hotels and restaurants.

The government admits that it is impossible to count illegal aliens accurately. In fact, some federal officials claim that the government does a better job of counting its migratory birds than its migratory workers. Official estimates place the number of illegal aliens between 2 and 12 million. However, some population experts believe that government estimates of Mexican aliens in the United States are much too high and that they number between 1 and 3 million (Crewdson, 1980a). While many Mexican nationals illegally cross into the United States, much of the traffic is offset by movement in the opposite direction. New arrivals often work several months, accumulate a certain amount of money, and return home. Heading south across the border, the Mexicans are usually not stopped by immigration agents.

The reverse flow of Mexican nationals generally begins in the fall and reaches its peak in December, when thousands of Mexicans return to their home villages in Mexico for the holidays (Sterba, 1977b). Toward the end of January, the workers begin once again the trek northward. Mexicans who go back and forth each year generally know the ropes—where to cross and how to use fraudulent identity cards. If they are caught, they are simply bused across the border into Mexico and released, and they try again. Immigration officials say that effective policing of the 1,945-mile border is impossible, short of building a Berlin Wall. Border patrol agents acknowledge that they are lucky to catch one of every five or more persons who surreptitiously enter the United States. During some years, the immigration service has apprehended more than a million Mexican nationals who have illegally entered the United States.

Mexican nationals are subject to many forms of abuse. Bandits rove the Mexican-American border beating up aliens and stealing whatever money or possessions they have. Some employers hire illegal aliens and then turn them in to immigration agents shortly before payday. Or they pay the workers by check. Later, when the deported workers attempt to cash their paychecks in Mexico, they discover that their employers have issued stop-payment orders (Sterba, 1977a). At times employers withhold Social Security taxes from an immigrant's pay and then pocket the money because there is no record that the Chicano was ever hired. Similarly, some supervisors extort from the workers a percentage of their pay under threat of firing.

Alien workers are very vulnerable to exploitation since they are

afraid that they will be apprehended by law-enforcement officers, returned to Mexico, or fired. In 1979 a Department of Labor team in
Houston found that forty of sixty-three employers it checked were
short-changing alien workers by paying them less than the federal minimal wage, by not paying them overtime, and by not paying them fully
for all hours worked. The most frequent violators were employers in the
construction trades, hotels, and restaurants.

In some instances, migrant laborers are held in involuntary servitude
(Crewdson, 1980b). They are transported in trucks by labor contractors
who supply them to growers for work in the tomato fields of Arkansas,
the apple orchards of Virginia, the vegetable fields and orange groves of
Florida, the tobacco farms of North Carolina and Virginia, the potato
fields of Idaho, and the cotton fields of North Texas. Not uncommonly the
Chicano workers are held in debt peonage, compelled to work off inflated debts. Employers enforce servitude through intimidation. Workers fear that if they attempt to leave, the contractor will turn them in to
the immigration service for illegal entry. They may be locked up by
night and guarded by day, beaten or threatened with death should they
incur the displeasure of an employer, and their children may be held
hostage to ensure the continued servitude of the parents. Further,
employers frequently withhold their workers' pay until the end of the
season.

Peonage is less frequent in the Southwest because of the proximity
of the Mexican border. California, Texas, and Arizona have large numbers of illegal workers who are capable of meeting the labor demands
of farmers and ranchers. In this region employers usually find that the
aliens' fear of detection by immigration authorities suffices to produce
a submissive labor force.

The impact of illegal aliens on the American economy is difficult to
determine. Some labor leaders express concern that illegal aliens displace American workers, especially taking jobs from young people just
starting out. This fear has stimulated a wave of neonativism among
some workers with citizenship. But any number of economists say that
the matter is hardly so simple. Aliens not only take jobs, they also make
jobs. For instance, the job of a worker in a vegetable-processing plant
is "supported" by the alien worker who picks the vegetables. Illegal
workers spend their salaries and generate demand for American goods
and services. But some of these funds also flow from the United States
to Mexico as the immigrants send money back home.

In any event, alien workers seldom displace American workers in
agriculture, where the work is arduous and the wages low. Further,
most illegal aliens are concentrated in the Southwest, a Sun Belt region
enjoying the nation's greatest prosperity. Finally, a 1976 Department
of Labor sampling found that illegal aliens paid more in taxes than they
received in government services. Migrants make reasonably little use

of social welfare programs. Most of those who come to the United States are young men and not the elderly or other groups most likely to need a variety of social services.

As many policy makers see the issue of alien workers, the United States confronts the following decisions if it wishes to curb illegal immigration: Should the nation in effect concede its lower-paying, less attractive jobs to those immigrants willing to take them and legalize their presence with a "guest worker" permit along the lines of the worker exchanges between member nations of the European Economic Community? Or should the United States enact legislation barring employers from hiring illegal aliens (placing the primary burden for enforcement on the private sector)? Both approaches have aroused considerable opposition. And some public officials admit that the problem may not be solvable. These leaders say that Americans, accustomed to believing that every problem has a solution, must face the reality that some of their problems simply cannot be solved.

The Current Situation

In recent years, Chicanos, long ignored by the news media, have been catapulted into the national limelight as a result of such developments as the organization of California farm workers by Cesar Chavez and Reies Tijerina's crusade to regain the land indigenous Tejanos of New Mexico claim was illegally taken from them. Yet news reports have served to reinforce nationally a false image of the Chicanos as a rural people (Grebler, Moore, and Guzman, 1970). While this was the case prior to World War II, today an estimated 80 percent are urban (although some who reside in urban areas have agricultural jobs). Moreover, Chicanos do not form a homogeneous group with identical values, customs, or aspirations. They are divided along socioeconomic-class lines from the affluent rancher, businessman, or public official to the migrant worker or relatively isolated farmer in the mountains of New Mexico. And they also differ in the extent to which they have become Anglicized and integrated into the larger society.

In southwestern towns and cities with any sizeable Chicano population, separate Chicano ghettos are prevalent. In smaller towns the Chicano section is usually set apart from the rest of the town by a railroad track, a highway, or a river. In larger communities, there is usually at least one section made up of Chicanos. Informal patterns of discrimination generally operate to maintain residential segregation and to bar Chicanos as renters or property owners from other neighborhoods. Nevertheless, the restrictions on Chicanos have been rarely as strict as those on blacks in the United States, especially in higher-income areas, where the assumption frequently has been that if people can afford to buy, they probably are "Spanish" and hence "white," and if they are poor they are "Mexican" and hence "nonwhite," and cannot buy anyhow. Within Chicano ghettos poor housing and overcrowding are the rule.

Education. The level of formal education found among Chicanos tends to be low in terms of American standards. Thus they find themselves at a considerable disadvantage in the larger American society, where a premium is placed upon formal schooling and academic achievement. Their life, especially in the past, was geared by their cultural heritage to an agricultural environment, so conflicts between rural and urban values have served to complicate their adjustment to American life. Poor school attendance, limited average grade completion, and frequent school failures contribute to the situation.

Until relatively recently, Chicano children were often segregated for purposes of instruction, either in separate buildings or in segregated classes within the same building. Nevertheless, there was no overall pattern for the segregation. Throughout most of the Southwest, segregation of Chicanos was considered desirable but not absolutely essential, and in this way differed from the attitude of southern whites toward the segregation of blacks. In some communities segregation was strict and complete, in others there was a "Mexican" school, but a few favored children with Spanish surnames who came from the top socioeconomic level of the Chicano subcommunity would attend the white school. Still other communities, lacking separate segregated schools, maintained segregated classrooms in the "white" school. Some communities even fluctuated between segregation and non-segregation depending upon the current number of Chicano students. In many schools the speaking of Spanish was forbidden both in the classrooms and on the playground and not infrequently students were punished for lapsing into Spanish. During the past decade there has been a growing recognition among educators and public officials that cultural diversity and cultural pluralism are legitimate concerns of the public schools. In 1980 the Department of Education estimated that there were 3.5 million children in the United States who could speak little or no English, 70 percent of them Hispanic. In Los Angeles, Hispanics are the largest ethnic group in the school system. Yet in Los Angeles, of the 25,710 teachers in the system, it is estimated that only 2,000 can speak Spanish.

Chicano youngsters often confront another problem, too, in adapting successfully to school, in addition to lack of instruction they can understand. They may be told in the public schools that they do not speak "Spanish." Although Chicano speech is perfectly adequate for the needs of the community, because "Chicano Spanish" typically contains a mixture of words from English and Spanish academic linguists do not consider it to be "true Spanish" (Peñalosa, 1979). For similar reasons a recent survey reported that none of the 136 bilingual teachers in New

Mexico could pass a fourth-grade-level "Spanish" examination. Those who graded their exams did not consider their answers "correct."

Chicanos view their language as a badge of ethnic solidarity (Lopez, 1976). It is a binding factor that strengthens the ties of Chicano to Chicano. Indeed, Chicanos often test one another (although not necessarily consciously) on linguistic criteria, especially if the other person seems in some ways marginal in other aspects of Chicano ethnicity. But a child who has mastered the subtleties of language that Chicano culture values will probably be seen as linguistically incompetent and considered uneducable by the public school authorities.

In a recent national poll of Hispanics conducted by the New York-based Hispanic Opinion and Preference Research, Spanish-speaking respondents were divided on the issue of bilingual education. Most support went for teaching mainly English, with supplementary Spanish. Others favored transitional teaching in Spanish while students learn English. And about the same proportion of respondents said that they favored an English-only school (19 percent) as those who preferred an all-Spanish program (18 percent). Underlying much of the disagreement about bilingual education is a basic dilemma: If Spanish-speaking children are taught in English, they do not learn and the disadvantage they suffer in the early grades becomes permanent; if they are taught in Spanish, they do not become fluent in English in a nation in which the command of English is essential for full incorporation within American life and economic activity.

There is strong opposition to bilingual education among segments of the Anglo population. Critics contend that programs incorporating the use of Spanish pose obstacles to the long-term goal of having Hispanics enter the social and economic mainstream. They fear that unless Hispanic children learn English, the United States may drift toward a separate Spanish-speaking minority and one day confront the sort of problem posed for Canadian unity by the French-speaking minority in the province of Quebec.

In the present educational system, however, as Chicano children advance in age, they drop out from schools at progressively increasing rates. Further, schools with large Chicano enrollments tend to be characterized by overcrowding, inferior equipment and plant facilities, and less competent teachers. On the college level, the number of students of Spanish origin increased from 242,000 in 1972 (the first year for which statistics are available) to 443,000 in 1980. Although Hispanics account for about 7 percent of the total population, they make up only 4.8 percent of college enrollment.

Voting and Political Rights. During the 1970s Chicanos were unable to translate their growing population into a proportionate political clout. For instance, the Southwest Voter Registration and Education Project estimates that only 3.4 million Hispanics (59 percent of those eligible to vote) were registered in the 1980 presidential election. Of these, only 2.1 million actually cast votes. Yet the number of Hispanic voters who cast ballots in the 1980 election was 20 percent higher than in 1976.

Partly as a result of low voter registration and turnouts, Hispanics are vastly underrepresented at all levels of government. In 1981 only six Hispanics were members of Congress and no Hispanics held statewide offices anywhere in the nation except in New Mexico. In Texas, where one of five residents is of Mexican ancestry, only 12 percent of the state legislators are Hispanic and Hispanics constitute less than 10 percent of the members of city councils and school boards. A major obstacle to electing Hispanic officials has been citywide or at-large elections rather than elections by district or ward (Crewdson, 1981).

Most commonly U.S. citizens of Mexican ancestry have acquired the status of citizens by birth rather than naturalization. Many factors have contributed to the reluctance of Chicanos to become citizens and thus to obtain voting rights: (1) language problems, (2) an inability to furnish adequate proof of legal entry, and the possibility of deportation once naturalization proceedings are initiated, (3) a continuing loyalty to Mexico, and (4) a failure to ascertain any advantages in being an American citizen.

In 1975 Congress extended the Voting Rights Act to protect the rights of Hispanic voters. The provision requires that bilingual ballots, voting machines, and other assistance be made available in those areas of the nation where residents who do not speak English make up more than 5 percent of the population and where illiteracy rates are high and voting turnouts low. The bilingual provision has had a substantial impact in some areas of the nation, including the Rio Grande Valley of Texas. Nonetheless, a 1979 Federal Election Commission report asserted that the nation has been "quite reluctant" as a whole to face up to the problem of non-English-speaking voters. In some areas of Texas, for instance, local election officials acknowledged that they had never read the law.

Two issues in particular have tended to galvanize the Chicano population. Chicanos have insisted that their children be provided a bilingual education. And they have attempted to curb police abuse of Hispanic people. The problem of police abuse has been commonplace. One case that has attracted considerable attention took place in Houston on May 6, 1977 (Huey, 1977). Six white police officers took a Chicano prisoner, Joe Campos Torres, to a downtown parking lot and began to beat him. "Let's see if this wetback can swim," said one officer. Not long afterwards the drowned body of the battered prisoner was found floating in Buffalo Bayou, which flows behind the parking lot.

Brought to trial, the white police officers were convicted of negligent homicide (a misdemeanor usually reserved for fatal traffic accidents). The jury then suspended the sentences and placed the police officers on probation. The verdict and sentences sparked Chicano demonstrations. The U.S. Justice Department entered the case and charged the officers with engaging in a conspiracy to violate civil rights that resulted in a person's death. The mayor of Houston, Fred Hofheinz, observed, "Our police department is white supremacist. There is an illness afoot here—a frontier mentality—that has condoned police excess for years, especially to keep minorities in their place."

Puerto Ricans

In 1898, Spain ceded Puerto Rico, a Caribbean island, 35 miles wide, 100 miles long, to the United States. Despite the rapid economic and political changes that followed, Puerto Rico retains in language, religion, and many other aspects its Latin character. Since 1917, Puerto Ricans have been U.S. citizens, but until 1948 they did not elect their own governor. Although sending delegates to national party conventions, they do not vote for the president of the United States nor are they represented in Congress by voting members. Racial intermixture has been going on in Puerto Rico since the sixteenth century, and the people range from light-skinned whites to dark-skinned blacks. While the blacks were for the most part not discriminated against during Spanish occupancy, Spanish whites enjoyed a higher status, and whenever it was possible to do so, they denied black ancestry. Since 1898, Puerto Ricans have adopted in some measure American patterns of race consciousness, making distinctions on the basis of skin color and physical appearance. Nevertheless, discrimination is only subtly apparent in social affairs and is infrequent in other spheres of life, including employment (Mills, Senior, and Goldsen, 1950).

Puerto Ricans have been migrating to the mainland of the United States for more than a hundred years, but it is only since the end of World War II that the migration has taken on mass dimensions. There are some 1.8 million Puerto Ricans on the mainland (and 3.2 million in Puerto Rico). Of these an estimated 1.2 million reside in New York City, giving it the largest Puerto Rican population of any city in the world. Other mainland cities with sizeable Puerto Rican populations are Chicago, Philadelphia, Cleveland, Newark, Hartford, and Boston. Since 1972 the flow of Puerto Ricans to the mainland has reversed. Every year, 30,000 more Puerto Ricans return to the Caribbean Island than leave it for the mainland United States. Many of those who return have gained skills that allow them to assume middle-class status in Puerto Rico.

A number of special institutions have grown up in mainland Puerto Rican communities, most notably food shops, storefront churches, and travel agencies. The *bodegas* (the Latin food shops) owe their existence in part to the great difference between the island's food habits and those prevailing within the United States. The storefront churches have a strong evangelical, puritanical, and even Holy Roller cast and are making inroads on the traditional Roman Catholicism of the Puerto Ricans. The travel agencies can be spotted by the sign "PASAJES" ("passages") on their fronts and deal mainly in "thrift"-class plane tickets to Puerto Rico (Rand, 1958).

Self-improvement and economic and family reasons are the most common explanations that Puerto Ricans give for coming to the mainland (Vidal, 1980d). Population pressure on the island (the island is more densely populated than any Latin American country) has contributed to low living standards and a lack of jobs, which, when coupled with New York City's reputation for economic opportunity, have served to stimulate out-migration. Many of the migrants also respond to the pull of relatives already settled in New York. In recent decades, however, automation and the loss of hundreds of thousands of manufacturing jobs have made it harder for Puerto Ricans to find entry-level jobs of the kind that gave earlier migrants their start (Vidal, 1980d).

For many Puerto Ricans, coming to the mainland is not a "once-and-for-all" decision. As citizens of the United States they do not encounter difficulties experienced by other aliens in moving back and forth between their homeland and mainland communities. Travel is so important to Puerto Ricans that air fare increases are sometimes deemed an issue by Puerto Rican political leaders. And travel agents often play leadership roles in Puerto Rican community affairs. Travel between the mainland and Puerto Rico is heaviest between Christmas and January 6, Three Kings Day, the traditional gift-giving day on the island (Vidal, 1980d).

Language is one of the main problems confronting the migrants. Spanish is the language of the island, and at least three-fifths of Puerto Ricans arrive in New York City without a mastery of English adequate to make their way inconspicuously. Yet, to travel on subways or buses and to function in many other areas of life, some familiarity with English is necessary. Most Puerto Ricans say that a command of English is essential if they hope to get ahead on the mainland. Yet they also want to retain Spanish and the cultural links associated with it (Vidal, 1980c). Many Puerto Ricans experience ambivalence as to whether they will eventually settle on the mainland or return to their homeland. The jet age has made it possible to retain close ties with relatives in Puerto Rico and strong identities as Puerto Ricans. On the island itself the population is deeply divided over the question of statehood, independence, or commonwealth status.

Puerto Rican migrants cluster primarily in the manufacturing and processing industries of New York City, where some 50 to 60 percent of those working find employment. Another 30 percent are found in the service trades and domestic service. Puerto Ricans are restricted mainly to semiskilled and unskilled jobs in the city's factories, hotels, restaurants, and other service trades. Some white-collar jobs opened during the 1960s and even before in banking. Although many migrants experience downward mobility in terms of their job level, their average earnings in New York City are considerably higher than they enjoyed within Puerto Rico. Only a small proportion of the women go into domestic work, while a considerable number find employment within the garment industry.

A 1980 study by the National Puerto Rican Forum, a nonprofit Puerto Rican organization operating with federal, state, local, and private funds, revealed that Puerto Ricans on the mainland were worse off relative to other Americans than they had been a decade earlier (Kihss, 1980; Smothers, 1981). Puerto Rican families had an income that was 71 percent of the national average in 1959. By 1970, the figure had fallen to only 59 percent and by 1979 to 47 percent. The 1979 average family income of Puerto Ricans was $8,282. The national average for all American families was $17,640 and for black families, $10,879.

Of mainland Puerto Rican families, 41 percent were headed by women and nearly 40 percent of the Puerto Rican population lived below the poverty line. Overall, the incidence of poverty and unemployment is more severe among Puerto Ricans than among members of virtually any ethnic group in the United States.

Puerto Ricans in New York are concentrated in slum areas, finding housing in pre-World War I tenement buildings when they can get apartments at all. Vacancies in any New York City rental housing are almost nonexistent, so apartments can rarely be obtained legitimately. At the very least, bribes are demanded for answering questions about apartments; at worst, a large "purchase price" or "key money" is demanded for an apartment the tenants will not own, and must pay monthly rent on. As a rule the apartments are self-contained, having several rooms, including a closet toilet. In some slum areas, however, a whole family may occupy only one room. The slum buildings are often in a poor state of repair, but tenants are frequently afraid to report violations lest the whole building be abandoned or condemned. If this happens, new housing is difficult to come by. As a result a continuous deterioration of the buildings occurs. Further, the dwellings are frequently infested with vermin: rats, mice, cockroaches, and bedbugs. Leaking roofs, broken windows, and splintered steps are common. Alleys and streets are strewn with litter, which remains to rot and decay. In winter, apartments that are equipped with central heating are often as cold as those without it. In summer, the sticky weather and the warmth exuded by hot-water pipes in the apartments combine with the smell of garbage and defective plumbing to push the residents into the streets, where the atmosphere is likely to be cooler and more fragrant. In areas like the South Bronx landlords have stopped repairing the buildings and paying their taxes. When they are sued for tax delinquency, the landlords abandon the buildings. Likewise, landlords have been known to arrange for mysterious arson fires and then collect insurance on the gutted buildings.

Crime and drug abuse are major concerns of New York City's Puerto Rican population (Vidal, 1980b). Further, Puerto Rican inhabitants of the city have higher death rates from cirrhosis of the liver, drug addiction, accidents, murder, and diabetes than the city's population as a whole. And Puerto Rican children have higher death rates from accidents, murders, bronchitis, influenza, and pneumonia than most other children (Kihss, 1980).

The schooling of Puerto Rican children has been a concern to both parents and educators in New York City. A significant proportion (about 40 percent) of the children are Spanish-speaking, possessing little or no facility in English. The number of teachers who are bilingual does not begin to approximate the need of the school system. As a result children often learn little in school, although kept there and promoted. Even as late as 1968, little more than 1 percent of Puerto Rican high-school graduates received academic diplomas, about 8 percent received vocational certificates, while 90 percent were given general diplomas (attesting to a student's class attendance). As of 1980 only 31.9 percent of New York City's Puerto Rican population over fourteen years of age were high-school graduates (Kihss, 1980). The academic difficulties of Puerto Rican children are often compounded by a considerable turnover of students during the school year, as their parents shift residences. In the schools, Puerto Ricans are diagnosed as severely or profoundly retarded at a rate 60 percent greater than that for blacks and four times that for whites (Vidal, 1980c). Many social scientists attribute the high rates of "retardation" to racial bias and linguistic and cultural differences between teachers and students.

In Puerto Rico, race is subordinate to social class; in New York City it is made central to Puerto Rican life. As viewed by American culture, the Puerto Ricans are not a single racial type. A third of them are perceived as having "black" characteristics. The world into which these "black" Puerto Ricans move within the city is largely a black world, with all the restrictions commonly imposed upon it by the dominant white group. It is particularly difficult for this group of Puerto Ricans, by virtue of racial barriers, to move out of the slums in Spanish Harlem, the South Bronx, and the Lower East Side.

The fair-skinned Puerto Ricans, if they so choose, can generally find their way into the larger white world. Similarly, dark-skinned Puerto Ricans can often find their way into the black group. But for those in the intermediate racial group the situation is more difficult. The intermediate group distinguishes between itself and blacks, a distinction that is recognized on the island. Within Puerto Rico the personal aspirations and achievements of this group's members determined their positions within the social order. But in New York City this margin of privilege is no longer acknowledged. To many mainland whites such individuals are blacks. Traditionally this intermediate group tended to emphasize the desirability of whiteness in a society in which they were not considered white. They found they could hold only certain jobs, mix socially only with certain people, and for the most part live only in Puerto Rican or black neighborhoods. Still, in truth, Puerto Ricans have managed to maintain the pattern of a single ethnic community in which people mingle in social events of all kinds in disregard of the color marks that affect American behavior. Recently, a Puerto Rican identity has been stressed and the alternative of becoming either white or black has been increasingly rejected. On the whole Puerto Ricans have had an ambivalent attitude toward blacks—sometimes seeing them as allies, sometimes as rivals.

Cubans

Cubans are the smallest of the three major Spanish-speaking ethnic minorities in the United States. Few Cubans lived in the United States prior to the 1959 Castro-led revolution. Whereas Mexicans and Puerto Ricans have entered the United States chiefly for economic reasons, many Cubans have been political refugees. In large measure the Cubans have settled in Miami and have maintained a close-knit ethnic community.

During the last years of the Batista dictatorship in the late 1950s, some 10,000 to 15,000 Cubans entered the United States each year. Some, although from the privileged classes, were out of favor with the Batista regime, others were politically or socially alienated individuals, and still others were unemployed workers seeking economic opportunity (Pérez, 1980). However, Cuban migration did not start in earnest until after Batista's overthrow and Castro made it clear that his government would seek the complete restructuring of Cuban society. Commercial air traffic between Cuba and the United States remained in effect until the missile crisis of October 1962. During the period between the revolution and the suspension of air traffic, some 155,000 Cubans entered the United States, By virtue of U.S. hostility to the Castro regime, the Cubans were granted refugee status (allowing them to enter the nation in unlimited number).

Between 1962 and 1965 another 30,000 Cubans managed to flee from Cuba in small boats or through a third country from which they made their way to the United States. In 1965 the Johnson administration reached an agreement with the Castro government establishing an airlift between Cuba and Miami. The airlift was ended in 1973. But during its eight-year existence, 257,000 Cubans entered the United States. Until 1980, Cuban immigration was limited to Cubans who could reach some third nation and then make application for admission to the United States. In 1980 a flood of 124,789 new refugees crossed to the United States in small boats from Mariel, Cuba (a fishing port west of Havana).

The socioeconomic characteristics of the Cuban immigrants have shifted over time. In the period from 1959 to 1962, the Castro regime undertook to replace a capitalist order with a state-run system. As a consequence, many Cuban professionals, managers, landowners, and entrepreneurial and commercial people left Cuba for the United States. These people were drawn predominantly from the middle and privileged classes. In fact, some had been quite wealthy and had taken the precaution of sending their money abroad, much of it finding its way into Florida real estate. Later the composition of the migrants diversified, drawing people from the lower-middle and blue-collar classes (Pérez, 1980; Wilson and Portes, 1980).

The Mariel refugees consisted of three groups (Montgomery, 1981): 10,800 dissidents who crowded into the Peruvian embassy to seek political asylum; relatives of Cubans who had previously fled Cuba; and individuals banished by Cuban authorities. In this last group were convicts, mental patients, homosexuals, and others considered undesirable by the Castro regime. According to the Immigration and Naturalization Service, 23,970 of the Mariel group admitted that they had spent time in Cuban jails (and presumably there were others who also had been in jail but who failed to make the admission). By virtue of their criminal backgrounds, 1,800 Cubans were placed in the federal penitentiary in Atlanta. Many of the Mariel refugees possessed limited education and lacked skills needed in the United States. Consequently, high rates of unemployment have prevailed among this group. Also, whereas most of the earlier entries were white, 20 percent of those in the Mariel group were black (Ramirez, 1980).

Many Cubans have enjoyed upward social mobility within the United States. Cuban-owned enterprises increased in the Miami area from 919 in 1967 to more than 8,000 a decade later. Most are centered in textiles, leather, furniture, cigar making, construction, finance, and service areas (restaurants, supermarkets, and funeral parlors). An estimated 40 percent of the construction companies are Cuban owned and Cubans are believed to control 20 percent of the local banks (Wilson and Portes, 1980). In recent years Miami has become the hub of a flourishing trade with Latin America and a center of Latin American tourism. This development has owed much to Cuban fluency in Spanish and to the entrepreneurial initiative of many of the Cubans.

Within the Miami area, Cubans have been able to retain much of their culture and meet most of their needs within the ethnic community. They can work, shop, bank, and find entertainment in Cuban establishments where only Spanish is spoken (Pérez, 1980). Likewise, Cuban private and Catholic parochial schools have proliferated. Various federal agencies have attempted to resettle some of the Cubans outside the Miami area. However, more than a quarter of these have relocated in the city. Acculturation and assimilation have proceeded slowly among Miami Cubans. The Cubans have also tended to maintain their social distance from other Hispanic groups in the United States.

Chinese

It was during the gold-rush period in California that the first large-scale immigration of the Chinese to the United States occurred. Initially, the Chinese were welcomed as a source of cheap labor. The American fortune seekers who expected to find gold had no intention of performing menial or laborious tasks, or of earning their money as common laborers. Under these circumstances, the Chinese were readily sought. Governor John MacDougall, in addressing the California legislature in 1852, referred to the Chinese as the "most desirable of our adopted citizens" and recommended "a system of land grants to induce further immigration and settlement of that race" (McKenzie, 1928:-25–26). Chinese were employed in building the Union Pacific, Northern Pacific, and Southern Pacific railroads; reclaiming swamplands; building levees and roads; mining borax, quicksilver, and coal in western states; and making cigars, shoes, and garments in San Francisco factories (Schrieke, 1936; Miller, 1974; Lyman, 1974). Chinese men were also hired to do cooking, washing, and gardening.

It was not long, however, before the speculative bubble of gold burst and whites were thrown into the employment market. Increasingly, American labor began feeling the competitive economic pinch of the cheap Chinese labor. From a total of 758 Chinese in the continental United States in 1850, the number rose to 105,465 in 1880, most of whom resided in California. The competitive impact was intensified by the fact that the Chinese population in America was overwhelmingly male (between 1860 and 1900 the ratio of Chinese males per 100 Chinese females was exceedingly high: 1,858 in 1860; 1,284 in 1870; 2,106 in 1880; 2,678 in 1890; and 1,887 in 1900). Numerical equality between the sexes was not achieved until the middle of the twentieth century.

The Chinese constituted a highly visible group. The newly arrived immigrants often made their way along the street in a sort of dogtrot, displayed food habits different from those of the dominant Americans, dressed in Chinese clothes, wore their hair in a queue, spoke a quite different language, and frequently believed in omens, good-luck signs, and practices that dominant Americans viewed as superstitious. Out of this situation involving economic competition and high social visibility there arose the cry "The Chinese must go." These factors were compounded by the search for scapegoats following the business crash of

1876: business houses failed; banks and mines closed; and a drought hit agriculture. The Chinese were severely persecuted and subject to violence, bloodshed, pillage, and incendiarism. In 1871 a riot in Los Angeles resulted in the murder of nineteen Chinese. Frequent riots occurred elsewhere in the West in the 1880s and 1890s. During one outbreak in 1885 in Rock Springs, Wyoming, a mob killed twenty-eight Chinese. In San Francisco it was not uncommon to see the Chinese pelted with stones or mud, beaten or kicked, harassed on the streets, and tormented by having their queues cut. Under the leadership of Denis Kearney, an Irish labor leader, the Workingmen's party was founded on a militant anti-Chinese program. It succeeded in electing candidates to major local and state offices.

Some Chinese responded to this persecution by returning to China, but most dispersed eastward throughout the United States. In 1880, some 22 percent of the Chinese were in cities with a population of 25,000 and over, whereas 78 percent were in less populated areas. But hand-in-hand with the dispersion of the Chinese went a trend toward greater urbanization. By 1890, 42.7 percent were concentrated in urban centers having a population of 25,000 or more; by 1920, the figure had risen to 66 percent (Lee, 1949, 1960). Today at least 99 percent of the Chinese are urbanites (U.S. Census Bureau, 1970, 1980.)

With the urbanization of the Chinese, Chinatowns appeared in various American cities. A Chinatown is a "ghetto" made up of Chinese, "a community within a non-Chinese community, having no independent economic structure but attached symbiotically to the larger economic, political, and social base" (Lee, 1949: 148). Chinatowns arose both as voluntary and involuntary responses to common problems. The dominant group often erected barriers to Chinese entry into white neighborhoods. And meeting rebuffs in the larger society, many Chinese preferred to insulate themselves defensively from further rebuffs by residing in their own ethnic community. Kinship and clan ties, a desire to preserve meaningful and cherished Chinese cultural traditions and practices, and an inability to afford housing in other than low-rent areas also operated to attract Chinese to common urban settlements (Yuan, 1963).

The Chinatown of Philadelphia was perhaps not untypical of Chinatowns within the United States forty or so years ago (Cheng, 1948). In 1940, it occupied one square block in a blighted area of Philadelphia. The stores abounded with all kinds of decorations: Signs were made of wooden boards with Chinese characters; neon signs lit up the fronts of most restaurants; and the store windows were full of big Chinese vases, porcelain statues of "Milo," and strips of red paper announcing the merchandise inside. Within Chinatown proper, there were eighteen stores, a curio shop, one needle manufacturing company, one barbershop, and ten or twelve gambling and opium houses and brothels (providing recreation and respite from the day's toil for single Chinese men).

In 1940, some 922 Chinese resided in Philadelphia, of which about one-third lived in Chinatown proper. The occupational range of the Chinese in Philadelphia was very limited. In 1945, it was estimated that 400 were employed as laundry operatives, 100 in restaurants, 18 in grocery stores, 2 in art-goods and curio shops, 12 in engineering, 4 as typists, and 11 in other divers occupations. Outside Chinatown, Chinese laundries were more or less evenly scattered throughout the city and were typically operated by unmarried men who made their residence within the laundry building. The laundryman functioned as an "intimate stranger" within the white community—intimate since he lived within the community and was known derogatorily as "Charley Chinaman," yet a stranger since he tended to be culturally and socially isolated from the larger community. As such, he was often a lonely soul. Chinese restaurants were found in a number of sections of Philadelphia: The majority were concentrated in South Philadelphia, where the black population predominated; a number in West and North Philadelphia catered exclusively to white customers; and a few in Chinatown proper catered to the customers in the Chinese gambling houses.

Since World War II, except for those in a few large cities, Chinatowns have largely disappeared from the American scene. Rose Hum Lee (1960) says that for a Chinatown to survive, at least 360 Chinese must either live in it itself or live within the same city or state where it is located. Although theoretically the ghetto is considered the "home" for the Chinese, many live outside it for work or personal reasons. Once the Chinese population falls below 360, the Chinatown struggles vainly to survive—the population is not large enough to support separate economic and other institutions.

Further, Chinatowns most often are located near central business districts. Urban expansion—with its attendant demolition of buildings, rezoning of land use, and widening of transportation arteries—together with the invasion of new immigrant groups have proved devastating to the continued maintenance of many American Chinatowns. In Pittsburgh, for instance, the Chinatown was totally obliterated by the building of a modern expressway. A population once dispersed seldom relocates, in toto, at a new site. Many Chinese utilize the opportunity to resettle elsewhere. The assimilation of second- and third-generation Chinese and the lowering of dominant group barriers have hastened the process. With education, many younger Chinese have been able to acquire those skills that have enabled them to escape from the limited range of occupations previously open to Chinese—launderers, waiters, cooks, domestic workers, restaurateurs, and seamstresses—and to find their way into American middle-class life.

The Chinatowns of New York City, San Francisco, and a few other large cities, however, have obtained a new lease on life and have actually expanded in recent years as a result of sharp increases in immigration from Hong Kong and Taiwan (made possible by the passage of new immigration legislation in 1965 that did away with the old quota system under which only 105 Chinese were allowed entry a year). Outsiders often view Chinatowns as exotic tourist areas. But in fact problems abound in them. A good many of the some 25,000 yearly immigrants have settled in the New York City and San Francisco Chinatowns, contributing to even greater overcrowding. Above the gaudy storefronts four or more families are often jammed into tiny flats. Toilet facilities are shared and families arrange cooking hours in shifts. Rents are typically quite high. Widespread poverty complicates the problems of the Chinese (e.g., in San Francisco more than a quarter of the residents of Chinatown live below the poverty level). And the incidence of tuberculosis among Chinese-Americans is the second highest among ethnic groups in the United States (American Indians have the highest incidence). In New York City, the Chinese population has spilled from lower Manhattan into other parts of the city, including a number of "little Chinatowns" that have sprung up in Queens.

Contrary to the popular image of New York City's Chinatown as purely a tourist center, in recent years its garment industry has become the center of the city's apparel industry. It is second only to the restaurant business as the chief source of employment for Chinese immigrants. There are an estimated 500 garment factories in Chinatown, employing 20,000 to 22,000 people (Wang, 1981). In New York City the Department of Labor has filed civil actions against eighty-five employers, most of them garment manufacturers in Chinatown. It has accused the firms of employing aliens, in some cases children as young as ten, at substandard wages (Crewdson, 1979). Since many of the aliens have entered the United States illegally, they fear being turned over to immigration officials and consequently are compelled to accept the low wages offered by unscrupulous employers. Seven-day weeks and ten-hour days with no overtime pay are common.

During World War II and the four decades since it ended, employment and housing opportunities have increased for people of Chinese ancestry. Many have moved beyond the Chinatown boundaries, socially, economically, and geographically. They have acquired a college education and, together with college-educated Chinese immigrants from Hong Kong and Taiwan, have found their way into universities, laboratories, hospitals, and architectural and engineering firms. However, few Chinese have entered law, education, the social sciences, or the arts (Kang-Ning, 1981).

Within the Chinese community, cultural and social differences between American-born Chinese and recent immigrants have created new tensions (Light and Wong, 1977). And though still a low-crime area, Chinatowns have a growing teen-age problem. Many immigrant youths have encountered the problems of language handicap, unemployment, low-paying jobs that require long hours, a high cost of living, and social estrangement from the white society as well as from the old established

Chinatown communities. Likewise, some American-born Chinese who are school dropouts and unemployed have turned to crime (Kang-Ning, 1981). Chinese youth gangs have plagued a number of Chinatowns, extorting, robbing, burglarizing, and killing (Wong, 1977).

Within the United States, the Chinese have experienced a long tradition of discrimination. In 1882 Congress passed the first Chinese Exclusion Act suspending for ten years all Chinese immigration, save for a small group of scholars, ministers, and merchants. In 1892 the act was extended another ten years, and in 1902 the suspension of Chinese immigration was extended indefinitely. In 1943, under the impact of war conditions, President Franklin D. Roosevelt signed a law that provided for an annual Chinese quota of 105 individuals and made Chinese aliens eligible for citizenship. Exclusion legislation contributed to the decline of the Chinese population in the United States from a high of 107,488 in 1890 to a low of 61,639 in 1920. Other factors contributing to the decline were the excess of departures from the United States over admissions, and the marked disproportion in the sex ratio of the Chinese within the United States (Lyman, 1974). Since 1920, the Chinese population has increased through internal growth and immigration and is now estimated to be in excess of 806,000.

California early enacted a series of anti-Chinese laws. Lawmakers successfully drove Chinese from mining activity within the state by a foreign miners' tax. An early legal decision prevented the Chinese from testifying against a white person in court, a decision that often placed them at the mercy of their persecutors. For a time, Chinese children were excluded from some public schools. San Francisco enacted various ordinances harassing Chinese laundries, including an act that made it a misdemeanor for any person on a sidewalk to carry baskets suspended on a pole across the shoulders, a typical Chinese practice. As late as 1952 the California constitution provided that corporations could neither directly nor indirectly employ Chinese; forbade the employment of Chinese in any state, county, municipal or public job; and empowered cities and towns to remove Chinese from within city limits. This discriminatory legislation has either been repealed or declared unconstitutional.

Japanese

At the peak of the anti-Chinese agitation during the late 1870s and early 1880s, the Japanese population of the continental United States was virtually nil—the 1880 census recorded only 148 Japanese. By 1890 their number had risen to 2,039; by 1900, to 24,326; and by 1910, to 72,157 (in 1980 the figure was more than 700,000, 40 percent of whom resided in Hawaii). The immigrants moved through the port cities of

Seattle and San Francisco into the surrounding areas and cities. As late as 1940 nearly 90 percent of the non-Hawaiian Japanese population was concentrated in the Pacific Coast states—74 percent in California and 39 percent in Los Angeles County. As with the Chinese, much of the initial impetus in anti-Japanese feelings came from workingmen's groups: in Seattle, the Western Central Labor Union; and in San Francisco, the Labor Council. The anti-Japanese movement gained momentum in 1900, and, as a result of the previous decades of agitation against the Chinese, mounted quickly. Pressure came from labor and patriotic groups for legislation to exclude the Japanese in much the manner as the Chinese had been excluded earlier.

The first formal step taken against the Japanese was the action taken by the San Francisco School Board in 1906, which attempted to segregate Oriental students in separate schools. By virtue of protests from the Japanese government, President Theodore Roosevelt prevailed on San Francisco authorities to rescind the measure. As a sequel to this settlement, Roosevelt took steps to check Japanese immigration through the "Gentleman's Agreement" of 1907. Under the agreement Japan undertook to refuse laborers passports to the United States unless they were coming to join a husband, parent, or child; to resume a formerly acquired domicile; or to assume control of a previously owned farming enterprise. The agreement did not end immigration or check the agitation against the Japanese, but it did serve to change the nature of the immigration and to relieve tension between the United States and Japan (La Violette, 1946). Prior to the agreement most Japanese immigrants were males, but, following 1907, a considerable number of Japanese women entered to become wives of the men who had preceded them. Many of these were arranged marriages. Some 38,000 brides entered the United States until the "Ladies Agreement" was reached in 1920 (the product of stepped-up American agitation against the "Yellow Peril"), by which Japan agreed to end the migration. By 1920 the Japanese population within the United States stood at 111,010. Then in 1924 Congress enacted legislation barring Japanese immigration.

Prior to the attack on Pearl Harbor in 1941, 55 percent of the Japanese within the United States were urban inhabitants. Within the cities they were largely concentrated in "little Tokyos," the result of various social and economic forces and restrictive covenants that prevented them from buying or renting housing outside these areas. Similarly, informal restrictions served to bar them from occupations and professions for which their education had fitted them. Within Los Angeles, the Japanese established groceries, hotels, restaurants, fruit stands, barbershops, flower shops, nurseries, cleaning and dyeing shops, and similar establishments, most of which were small businesses run by a single family. Along the West Coast, the Japanese were an important source of labor in lumber mills and fish canneries. They were also heavily concentrated in agriculture, often working on truck farms near urban centers. Immediately prior to American entry into World War II, the Japanese were raising about 42 percent of the produce crops in California, including berries, onions, asparagus, celery, lettuce, peppers, tomatoes, cucumbers, spinach, and cauliflower. The bulk of the farmers operated as tenants, since state legislation forbade alien Japanese from owning land. In addition, there were about 1,600 Japanese-owned farms, the titles of which were vested in American-born Japanese (American citizens) to circumvent the proscription against alien Japanese.

While some ethnic minorities reacted to oppression with passivity, the Japanese tended to respond with assertiveness. They demanded better employment and housing conditions, violated contracts, struck when the strike would be least opportune for the farmers, and were eager to become landowners. E. K. Strong, Jr. (1933), in a sample of 1,457 first-generation newcomers, found that during their first five years in the United States 80.7 percent were common laborers. Twenty years later only 46.1 percent of first generation Japanese were in this group, the rest becoming owners, managers, or tradesmen. As the sociologist William Petersen (1966, 1971) observes, even in a country whose patron saint is the Horatio Alger hero, there is no parallel to the Japanese success story. It is little wonder that the Caucasian stereotype of the Japanese came to be that of an aggressive, cunning, and conniving individual, a stereotype in some respects similar to that of the Jew. It was a stereotype in sharp contrast with that of the Chinese, who were commonly depicted as humble and ignorant.

The Japanese success in establishing themselves in small-scale farming resulted in demands of the dominant white group for the restriction of Japanese landownership and tenure. In 1913, California enacted the first antialien landownership law barring aliens who were ineligible for citizenship from owning agricultural land or from leasing land for periods longer than three years. In 1920, and again in 1923, the law was revised, each time being made more severe. The ingenious feature of the act was that the prohibition ran against "aliens ineligible to citizenship." Until 1870, American naturalization laws had defined aliens eligible to citizenship as "free white persons." In 1870 the word "white" was removed, but it was added again in 1875, largely through the impact of the anti-Chinese agitation in California (McWilliams, 1944; Kitano, 1980). On this basis the Japanese as alien "non-whites" were barred from citizenship. In 1922 the U.S. Supreme Court upheld this interpretation in the *Ozawa* case, declaring that a Japanese was not a "white" person and hence was ineligible for citizenship. However, American-born Japanese still automatically became citizens by birth.

Prior to World War II, West Coast Japanese were commonly denied free access to many places of public recreation, including swimming pools and dance halls, although in Los Angeles movie theaters did not discriminate against them. Intermarriage with Caucasians was forbidden in most western states. In restaurants the Japanese often received less courteous treatment than white patrons. On the other hand, store clerks (with some exceptions) usually treated the Japanese in a courteous manner, they were permitted to use the public libraries, and there was no discrimination against them at public schools. Since World War II, the discriminatory and repressive measures aimed at the Japanese have been either repealed or declared unconstitutional. In 1952 the Supreme Court declared that citizenship could not be denied anyone on the basis of race. Similarly, the alien land laws have been declared unconstitutional, and the Japanese are now eligible for admission to the United States under new immigration legislation.

With the Japanese attack upon Pearl Harbor on December 7, 1941, there occurred an intense upsurge in anti-Japanese feelings on the West Coast. Rumors (later proved false) circulated of Japanese sabotage and "fifth-column" activities. Suspicions were aroused by the facts that the Japanese sometimes lived near airfields and some of them engaged in coastwise fishing (to columnist Walter Lippmann the very lack of sabotage and espionage on the West Coast was cause for alarm; he warned that such innocuous behavior was merely a ploy to disarm American suspicions). The Japanese suspected of having strong loyalties to their mother country were quickly rounded up by the FBI. Out of the war hysteria that followed the early months of the war, a decision was made by military leaders to evacuate the Japanese from the Pacific Coast states and place them in internment centers (interestingly enough, Hawaii's Japanese population—one-third of the total population of the island and 3,000 miles closer to Japan—was generally allowed to go about its business). Ten centers were established in the West and Middle West, to which, beginning in the spring of 1942, some 100,000 Japanese were sent (*see* chapter 11). Nearly two-thirds of these were American citizens. This action by the government was racial rather than political, since none of America's other so-called enemies-in-residence (Germans and Italians) were subjected to relocation.

The relocation caused the Japanese considerable hardship. Businesspeople and merchants, within the space of a few weeks, had to sell or liquidate their business interests and properties. Buyers, as a rule, were unwilling to pay reasonable prices when fully aware of the commercial disadvantage of the Japanese in having to make quick sales. Farmers were in the worst bargaining position possible, as evacuation came after planting and fertilizing but before harvesting. Unable to harvest their crops, they had to make the best bargain available (Thomas and Nichimoto, 1946). Leonard Bloom and Ruth Riemer (1949) estimate that the evacuated Japanese suffered an economic loss of $367.5 million (in terms of the 1941 value of the dollar). A sample survey of 206 families showed the median loss per family to be $9,870.

Soon after the evacuation, some of the interned Japanese were resettled in non-western parts of the United States. Students were often given permission to attend college; employment permits were given for some agricultural and industrial workers; and church groups (through the establishment of hostels) aided those unable to find employment. In December 1944, the military ban on returning to the West Coast area was lifted. Although the wartime resettlement patterns entailed some dispersion of the Japanese through non-western portions of the United States, by 1950 some 80 percent of the persons of Japanese descent within the continental United States were living in western states. Initially, there was some opposition to the return of the Japanese to California and some serious incidents occurred. But the new storm raised a counterreaction among Americans for fair play, and this became the dominant response. By virtue of the wartime evacuation, many formerly independent Japanese business establishments were disrupted and lost. Japanese farmers found it extremely difficult to reestablish themselves. The net result was the emergence of a new employment pattern, represented by a major shift from independent employment or employment by other Japanese to employment by non-Japanese employers.

The Japanese have taken a pragmatic attitude toward American life. In this respect they resemble earlier Japanese in the homeland who adopted elements of Chinese and Indian culture, reconciled Buddhist and Confucian tenets with their native Shintoism, and then adopted various Western patterns. They have woven American values and behavior into the fabric of their culture and seized opportunities to advance economically (Kitano, 1980; Woodrum, 1981). The large majority no longer live in Japanese neighborhoods but are dispersed among Americans of other racial and ethnic origins. The higher the educational level of the Japanese-Americans, the more close friendships they are likely to have outside their ethnic group. Only Native Americans marry outside their ethnic group more frequently than Japanese-Americans. The first-generation immigrants (*Issei*) married outside the group only 1 percent of the time; the second-generation (*Nisei*), 10 percent; and the third-generation (*Sansei*), 40 percent. Some sociologists like Darrel Montero (1978) wonder if the japanese-American community can survive to the fourth generation—the *Yonsei.*

Indochinese

The collapse of the South Vietnamese government in 1975 and political upheavals in Cambodia and Laos led by 1982 to the admission of more than 500,000 Indochinese refugees to the United States. Vietnamese have accounted for at least 80 percent of the entries. In April

1975, as rebel forces advanced on Saigon, the American embassy helped arrange for the departure of more than 60,000 Vietnamese who had been associated with the Thieu government or who had been employed by the Americans. Another 70,000 arranged for their own transportation (Wright, 1980). Still other refugees fled to Hong Kong and Thailand. As a result of the abruptness of the evacuation, many Vietnamese came to the United States psychologically unprepared to start life anew (Montero, 1979).

The U.S. government set up receiving stations in Guam and the Philippines for these refugees. From these stations, the Vietnamese were brought to reception centers at Camp Pendleton, California, Fort Chaffee, Arkansas, Elgin Air Force Base, Florida, and Fort Indiantown Gap, Pennsylvania. The centers were designed to facilitate the rapid assimilation of the refugees into American life. Nine private social service agencies, including the U.S. Catholic Conference, the International Rescue Committee, and the Church World Service, undertook to find sponsors and jobs for the refugees to hasten the absorption process and to keep them off the public welfare rolls.

A sample of the Indochinese refugees revealed that 55 percent of the arrivals were male; 82 percent were under thirty-five years of age and 65 percent were under age twenty-five; and nearly 50 percent indicated that they were Catholic (although less than 10 percent of the South Vietnam population is Catholic, many of the Catholics had been born in North Vietnam and had fled to the South in 1954). Of the refugees who were more than eighteen years of age, 20 percent had some college education; another 38 percent, some secondary schooling; still another 18 percent some elementary schooling (2 percent had no schooling and 23 percent did not report their education). Nearly a third of the heads of households (31.2 percent) had been employed in professional, managerial, and technical areas in Vietnam. Although 64.7 percent of the refugees had no English-speaking skills, 13.9 percent had good skills and 21 percent some skills in English usage (Liu, Lamanna, and Murata, 1979).

Refugee children were sent to classrooms set up in the centers. Since the students were forbidden to speak in their native language, many did not learn effectively and appeared to be unresponsive. The values taught by the schools stressed assertiveness and independence, which clashed sharply with the expectations that the parents held for their children's behavior. Consequently, many parents tried to keep their children out of the schools. Adult programs prepared the refugees for jobs in the lowest rungs of the occupational ladder, whereas many of the Vietnamese anticipated middle-class jobs more in keeping with their positions in Vietnam.

The refugees found themselves particularly at odds with government and private-agency efforts to split up their extended families into smaller units for resettlement purposes. The traditional Vietnamese family often consisted of more than twenty-five members, including grandparents, parents, children, and other relatives. As a result, many refugees declined sponsorship offers that entailed the breakup of the family. Sponsors provided food, clothing, and shelter for a refugee family until it became self-supporting. They also helped members find jobs and enroll their children in school (Wright, 1980).

The jobs open to the refugees usually required little skill, paid low wages, and offered few opportunities for advancement. A 1975 survey revealed that 85 percent of those Vietnamese who had held white-collar jobs in Vietnam had blue-collar jobs in the United States. By 1977, however, the figure had dropped to 61 percent. Like other alien groups, the Vietnamese have encountered many obstacles to the transfer of their foreign-acquired skills to the American setting (educational degrees and licensing procedures are often not recognized, and language difficulties are encountered). Some of the refugees shifted to public assistance rather than continuing to work in low-paying, dead-end employment. Further, within several months of resettlement, the refugees tended to regroup on their own within Vietnamese communities in Los Angeles, San Francisco, New Orleans, and Dallas (Stein, 1979; Wright, 1980).

During recent years a new wave of Vietnamese refugees have made their way to compounds in Thailand, Malaysia, and Hong Kong. Some escaped from Vietnam by small unseaworthy boats. Others fled from Cambodia in response to the mass killings and atrocities in that nation. This group of refugees has presented a different picture than the 1975 wave of refugees. They are primarily peasants, boatpeople, and fishing people. Their educational levels are low and their English-speaking skills poor. Hence, the migration pattern from Indochina has paralleled that from other nations like Cuba where new regimes have been installed. During the early period of the flight from new Communist regimes, the exodus consists of individuals disproportionately from the upper educational, occupational, and status levels. Later the refugee group becomes more representative of the population of the society (Stein, 1979; Montero, 1979).

The Vietnamese have encountered some hostility within the United States. A 1975 Gallup Poll revealed that 54 percent of Americans felt that the Vietnamese should not be permitted to stay in this country (Montero, 1979). In some sections of the nation like Manitowoc, Wisconsin, and the Houston-Galveston area of Texas, the Vietnamese have been subject to harassment. For instance, in the 1980s, American shrimpers and Vietnamese newcomers have engaged in a rancorous territorial competition over the limited resources of Galveston Bay. In a federal court case, the Vietnamese accused the American fishermen of conspiring with the Ku Klux Klan to frighten them into leaving the bay area.

Jews

The American Jewish Committee places the world Jewish population at about 14.3 million. The United States, with about 5.8 million Jews, has the largest Jewish population, outstripping Israel, which counts a Jewish population of 3.1 million, and the Soviet Union, with 2.7 million Jews. In the United States, the New York metropolitan area contains the largest concentration of Jews—2.0 million. Other areas with sizeable Jewish populations are Los Angeles, 455,000; Philadelphia, 350,000; Chicago, 253,000; Miami, 225,000; and Boston, 170,000.

Since 1654, when a group of twenty-three Jews arrived at New Amsterdam, Jewish migration has been continual, ebbing and rising in response to economic factors and the persecution of Jews in various parts of the world. The earliest settlements were established by Spanish- and Portuguese-speaking Jews (i.e., Sephardim). Later they were joined by Jews from the German-speaking areas of Europe and from Poland (i.e., Ashkenazim), who spoke Yiddish (a language derived from Middle High German, Hebrew, and Aramaic). The 1880s began a great migration of Jews from Eastern Europe, including Russia. In 1880 perhaps no more than one-sixth of the nation's 250,000 Jews were from Eastern Europe. Forty years later, they and their children made up about five-sixths of the 4 million Jews in the United States (Goren, 1980). During the 1930s, some 150,000 Jewish refugees fleeing Nazism arrived from Germany.

Jewish-Americans have maintained strong sympathies with world Jewry. The mass murder of European Jews during Hitlerism, the establishment in the post-World War II period of the nation of Israel, and the plight of Soviet Jews have produced an outpouring of support. However, since the founding of Israel in 1948, some 350,000 Jews have emigrated from it to the United States. The immigrants have posed a problem for the Jewish community since they have chosen to leave the Jewish homeland. A high proportion of the immigrants are well-educated, skilled, and young. They have left Israel for a variety of reasons: economic opportunity in the United States, the burden of Israeli security in a nation surrounded by hostile Arab nations, and lengthy military reserve duty that periodically disrupts people's personal lives (Kass and Lipset, 1980).

Israeli leaders express concern over the outflow of Israelis. For one thing, it has posed a serious brain drain. But it also has constituted a challenge to the hope and idealism that led to the establishment of the Jewish state. Those who have settled in Israel have fulfilled the ultimate Zionist injunction and are called *olim* ("those who go up"). In contrast, those who leave the Jewish state are *yordim* ("those who go down"). Many Israelis look upon the emigrants as deserters and renegades, individuals who are abandoning and forsaking their motherland. And some intensely pro-Israeli American Jews have been reluctant to welcome the Israeli immigrants.

Close to 70 percent of Russian Jewish émigrés have chosen to come to the United States rather than go to Israel. This development has posed a severe blow to the Zionist dream that a Jewish state would serve as a refuge and homeland for persecuted Jews. Some Jews have also felt that the Soviet Jews are not really all that "Jewish." Since the Soviets have long suppressed Jewish religious and cultural activities, only a small minority of the Russian émigrés have Jewish interests or identifications. Many simply seek a haven from Soviet hostility toward Jews and a life of normalcy. More than half the arrivals from the Soviet Union have made their home in New York City. Brighton Beach in Brooklyn, dubbed "Little Odessa," has been a center for newly arrived Soviet Jews (Kass and Lipset, 1980).

There has been a long history of anti-Semitism—prejudice and discrimination directed against Jews—within the United States. The first Jewish refugees to arrive at New Amsterdam were threatened with expulsion. They petitioned their brethren in Amsterdam to assist them and Jewish shareholders of the Dutch West India Company used their influence to secure a more acceptable immigration policy (Goren, 1980).

Jews have long encountered discriminatory barriers in employment. Even as late as the 1950s, the job market for Jews was "tight." In a study conducted by Jewish organizations in Chicago between 1952 and 1955 (Weiss, 1958), it was found that, of 40,000 job orders placed with Chicago's commercial employment agencies, 8,800, or 22 percent, were restrictive against Jews. Of the 5,500 firms covered by the survey, 1,500, or 27 percent, specified restrictions against Jews, including such statements as "Protestants only, no Jews or Orientals"; "We have no religious preference as long as they are of the Nordic race"; "We're desperate, but not desperate enough to hire Jews"; and "We only employ high type Anglo-Saxons." In 1956, the Institute of Industrial Relations of the University of California undertook a survey of job discrimination against Jews in the San Francisco Bay area. It reported that, of the 340 private employers in major industries interviewed, 75, or 22 percent, acknowledged that they either barred Jews completely or limited their employment on a quota system.

It was not uncommon prior to 1948 to find "restrictive covenant" clauses in title deeds to property in fashionable sections of American cities. Restrictive covenants serve as instruments to bar particular religious and racial groups, usually specifying that the property could not be sold to any but "White Gentiles." These agreements were enforceable within the courts and were a means by which Jews were excluded from many neighborhoods. In 1948, the U.S. Supreme Court ruled that such covenants were no longer enforceable in the courts, as they violated the "equal protection" guaranty of the Fourteenth Amendment.

However, discriminatory practices persisted, largely achieved through "gentlemen's agreements" and informal means.

A 1960 case in Greenwich, Connecticut, is illustrative. A prominent real-estate broker in that community acknowledged to the Connecticut Commission on Civil Rights that she had written a memorandum to her sales staff warning against selling property to Jews. A part of the memorandum follows:

> From this date on when anyone telephones us in answer to an ad in any newspaper and their name is, or appears to be, Jewish, do not meet them anywhere!
>
> If it happens on Sunday, tell them we do not show on Sunday, take a phone number and throw it away!
>
> If they walk into the office in answer to an ad we are running, screen them carefully . . .
>
> We can do only one thing by cooperating with them [Jews] and that is to be liable to severe criticism by the board [Greenwich Real Estate Board] and our fellow brokers, as these people are everywhere and just roam from one broker to another hoping to get into Greenwich (*New York Times*, September 15, 1961:35).

Until the mid-1960s or even more recently some colleges and universities discriminated against Jews in their admission policies. At times "quota systems" were maintained in which a specified number of Jewish students were accepted, despite the fact that other Jewish applicants may have been more qualified than many of the accepted Gentile students. Medical schools in particular had a long tradition of imposing quotas on the number of Jewish admissions.

Country clubs, luncheon clubs, and similar social clubs have represented an important area of discrimination directed against Jews. Even today exclusive clubs and informal gatherings of the "prestige classes" constitute strongholds of discrimination. While the influence of such clubs may be waning somewhat, they nonetheless are valuable centers where ideas are presented and major business transactions are informally handled. Hence, the failure of Jews to acquire social club membership seriously hampers their climb up the executive ladder in the world of business.

A 1981 Gallup Poll revealed that positive attitudes toward Jews have increased in recent years. Of the polled Americans 40 percent reported "highly favorable" opinions of Jews, as against 33 percent in 1975. Only 2 percent of the sample indicated they had highly unfavorable opinions of Jews. Likewise, in 1978, 82 percent of interviewed Americans said they would vote for a Jewish presidential candidate in contrast with 46 percent in 1937. And the proportion of Americans who said they approved of marriages between Jews and non-Jews rose from 59 percent in 1968 to 69 percent in 1978. Some aspects of political anti-Semitism —defined as a preoccupation with alleged Jewish power—have declined almost to the vanishing point. (In 1938 as many as 41 percent of Americans agreed with the statement that Jews have too much power in the United States; in 1945 it reached a peak of 58 percent, but declined to 17 percent in 1962, 11 percent in 1964, and 8 percent by 1980.) "Conventional" anti-Semitism—belief in Jewish clannishness and unethical business practices—has declined less radically. Recent polls show that a third of Americans still view Jews as pushy, clannish, and unethical, and about the same proportion suspect Jews of being more loyal to Israel than to the United States (*New York Times*, 1981). For 1981 the Anti-Defamation League of B'nai Brith reported 974 episodes of anti-Semitic vandalism against private and public property and 350 bodily assaults against individual Jews and Jewish institutions. The comparable figures for 1980 were 377 episodes of vandalism and 112 cases of bodily assaults or harassments. The overwhelming majority of the vandalism incidents consisted of swastika daubings and anti-Jewish graffiti. Less than 3 percent involved arson and bombings (Blair, 1982). Most of the episodes were believed to be the work of hostile individuals acting without organizational direction. In 1981, the American Jewish Committee took note of these incidents but nonetheless concluded that it would be a "mistake" to interpret the trouble as signaling "a new and dangerous wave of anti-Semitism in the United States." While noting the existence of Ku Klux Klan and neo-Nazi groups, the Jewish organization said that "they receive media attention far beyond what their numbers and strength warrant." Further, "there is no individual of stature on the political scene today who is an overt anti-Semite." It concluded that "on balance" the Jewish position within the United States remains "secure." Nonetheless, some Jewish leaders, while cautioning against panic, felt that the rise in anti-Semitic incidents "is something to be vigilant about."

SUMMARY

1. What Americans of Mexican ancestry call themselves or prefer to be called is a matter of considerable sensitivity. The term "Chicano" has gained considerable acceptance during recent years. No one knows exactly how many Chicanos there are in the United States. The Bureau of the Census reports that 14.6 million persons, or about 6.4 percent of the population, listed themselves as of Spanish origin in the 1980 census. An estimated two-thirds of Spanish-speaking Americans are of Mexican ancestry.

2. The Southwest became a part of the United States between 1845 and 1854 as the result of the annexation of Texas, the conquest of northern Mexico, and the Gadsden Purchase. The outcome of the

Treaty of Guadalupe Hidalgo still rankles in Mexico. Although the treaty theoretically protected the holders of Spanish and Mexican land grants, the inhabitants commonly lost their landholdings through legal chicanery and physical intimidation.

3. During the early 1900s, a group of Mexican nationals began to enter the United States, migrating to work from their homes, during the cotton harvest, to the old cotton-producing sections of East Texas and then, after the harvest, returning to their homes. About the turn of the twentieth century, cotton production started advancing into Central Texas and between 1910 and 1930 into West Texas. In these new cotton-producing areas, landlords and overseers relied primarily upon transient Mexican labor. Between 1942 and 1964 Mexican nationals came to this country for migrant farm work under agreements entered into by the governments of Mexico and the United States.

4. The disparity between economic conditions and opportunities in Mexico and the United States encourages Mexican nationals to seek employment in the United States. Large numbers of Mexican nationals enter the United States "illegally." However, "undocumented workers" do not feel that they are committing a crime by entering the United States. The typical immigrant is a male in his twenties with an elementary-school education. Mexican nationals are subject to many forms of abuse. Alien workers are very vulnerable to exploitation since they are afraid that they will be apprehended by law-enforcement officers, returned to Mexico, or fired. In some instances, migrant laborers are held in involuntary servitude.

5. Today an estimated 80 percent of the Chicano population are urban (although some who reside in urban areas have agricultural jobs). Chicanos do not form a homogeneous group with identical values, customs, or aspirations. In southwestern towns and cities with any sizeable Chicano population, separate Chicano ghettos are prevalent. The level of formal education found among Chicanos tends to be low in terms of American standards. Partly as a result of low voter registration and turnouts, Hispanics are vastly underrepresented at all levels of government.

6. Puerto Ricans have been migrating to the mainland of the United States for more than a hundred years, but it is only since the end of World War II that the migration took on mass dimensions. There are some 1.8 million Puerto Ricans on the mainland. For many Puerto Ricans, coming to the mainland is not a "once-and-for-all" decision. Language is one of the main problems confronting the migrants. A 1980 study revealed that Puerto Ricans on the mainland were worse off relative to other Americans than they had been a decade earlier. Crime and drug abuse are major concerns of New York City's Puerto Rican population.

7. Whereas Mexicans and Puerto Ricans have entered the United States chiefly for economic reasons, many Cubans have been political refugees. The socioeconomic characteristics of the Cuban immigrants have shifted over time. In the period from 1959 to 1962, the Castro regime undertook to replace a capitalist order with a state-run system. As a consequence, many Cubans who left their homeland were from the middle and privileged classes. Later the composition of the migrants diversified, drawing people from the lower-middle and blue-collar classes. Within the Miami area, Cubans have been able to retain much of their culture and meet most of their needs within the ethnic community.

8. Initially the Chinese were welcomed in the western United States as a source of cheap labor. But as the United States moved into the post-Civil War period, American labor began feeling the competitive economic pinch of Chinese labor. Out of a situation involving competition for jobs and high social visibility there arose the cry "The Chinese must go." The Chinese were severely persecuted, subject to violence, riots, bloodshed, and incendiarism. Some Chinese responded to this persecution by dispersing throughout the country and settling in Chinatowns within urban areas. Today Chinatowns remain only in a few large cities like San Francisco and New York. These Chinatowns have obtained a new lease on life as a result of sharp increases in immigration from Hong Kong and Taiwan.

9. At the peak of the anti-Chinese agitation in the late 1870s and early 1880s, the Japanese population in the United States was extremely small. But as Japanese immigration increased, a campaign against the Japanese mounted on the West Coast. The "Gentleman's Agreement" of 1907 restricted the entry of Japanese to the United States. Immediately prior to American entry into World War II, the Japanese were found as small business people and farmers. During the war, some 100,000 Japanese were interned in camps as potential enemies. The relocation worked a considerable hardship upon them. After the war Japanese farmers found it extremely difficult to reestablish themselves. The net result was the emergence of a new employment pattern, represented by a major shift from independent employment or employment by other Japanese to employment by non-Japanese employers.

10. The collapse of the South Vietnamese government in 1975 and political upheavals in Cambodia and Laos led by 1982 to the admission of more than 500,000 Indochinese refugees to the United States. Vietnamese have accounted for at least 80 percent of the entries. During the early period of the flight, the exodus disproportionately consisted of individuals from the upper educational, occupational, and status levels of Vietnamese society. Later the refugee group became more representative of the overall Vietnamese population. The Vietnamese have encountered some hostility within the United States. Many middle-class

Vietnamese have had to assume blue-collar jobs on coming to the United States.

11. Since 1654, when a group of twenty-three Jews arrived at New Amsterdam, Jewish migration has been continual, ebbing and rising in response to economic factors and the persecution of Jews in various parts of the world. Jews have experienced a long history of anti-Semitism—prejudice and discrimination against them—within the United States. Through the years discrimination has been severe in employment and housing. Since World War II attitudes toward Jews have become more positive within the United States and discrimination has lessened.

Patterns of
Assimilation
10

*T*he fact that the United States is a nation composed of different ethnic and racial groups directs our attention to group diversity and change. Some processes lead to greater similarity or homogeneity among groups. Sociologists term these forces *assimilation*. We may view **assimilation** as those processes whereby groups with distinctive identities become culturally and socially fused together. Other processes sustain or produce diversity or heterogeneity among groups. These forces are termed *pluralism*. **Pluralism** involves those processes whereby groups evolve or maintain their distinctive identities within a society, neither culturally nor socially fusing together.

The Nature of Assimilation

Sociologists find it useful to distinguish between *culture* and *social structure*. Culture has to do with the customs of a people. It supplies individuals with a set of common understandings by which they map their behavior. Culture provides people with shared guidelines by which they interpret their experience and guide their action. **Social structure** has to do with the relatively stable interpersonal relationships that emerge among the people practicing customs. It entails social interaction among people, especially the social ties that people evolve as they organize, direct, and execute the essential tasks of social living. Culture constitutes the more or less standardized solutions that serve to direct people in meeting the problems of social life. Social structure involves the relationships that characterize people in actually carrying out these solutions.

Sociologists carry over the distinction between culture and social structure to the study of assimilation. They distinguish between *cultural assimilation* and *social assimilation*. Cultural assimilation, also termed **acculturation,** refers to the process whereby people with divergent customs come to share common modes of action, norms, language, and dress. Social assimilation, commonly termed **integration,** refers to the process whereby people with divergent institutions (social structures) become fused within a common institutional life.

Acculturation

Culture is not static, but undergoes continuous change. Some changes in custom (i.e., those standardized ways of thinking, feeling, and acting that people acquire as members of society) result from intergroup contact. Acculturation is set in motion as people with differing traditions come together in such a way that they take into account the behavior of the other group. Acculturation occurs in a number of forms:

Intercultural Transmission. Intercultural transmission involves the diffusion of elements or parts of culture from one group to another. It is a matter of historical fact that each culture contains a minimum of traits and patterns unique to it or actually invented by it. It is easy, for example, to minimize America's debt to other cultures. As an illustration, consider the following account of the cultural content of a "one hundred per cent" American written as satire by a distinguished anthropologist, Ralph Linton (1937: 428).

> If our patriot is old-fashioned enough to adhere to the so-called American breakfast, his coffee will be accompanied by an orange, domesticated in the Mediterranean region, a cantaloupe domesticated in Persia, or grapes, domesticated in Asia Minor. He will follow this with a bowl of cereal made from grain domesticated in the Near East and prepared by methods also invented there. From this he will go on to waffles, a Scandinavian invention, with plenty of butter, originally a Near-Eastern cosmetic. As a side dish he may have the egg of a bird domesticated in Southeastern Asia or strips of the flesh of an animal domesticated in the same region, which have been salted and smoked by a process invented in Northern Europe.

Cultural Creativity. Contact situations entail not only the borrowing or mixing of cultural traits. Many early anthropologists made the error of viewing culture as so loosely knit together that the main theoretical task of cultural analysis consisted in disentangling the various elements from their matrix and showing whence they came. Culture was seen as just so many patches and shreds. Increasingly, we have come to realize that the parts comprising culture are often closely interwoven in such a fashion that a change in one part has consequences for other parts and for the whole. Hence in considering acculturation it is essential that we view it not merely as a culture-receiving process but as a *culture-producing* process as well.

Illustrative is the following case of the Malagasy of Madagascar, who had to convert Christian saints into the ancestor-idols of their own religion before they could accept them:

> When Catholic missionaries first began to work in Madagascar the natives were much puzzled by the phenomenon of saints. Supernatural associations were at once established, partly by the missionaries' observed attitudes and behavior toward the saintly images, partly because the Malagasy themselves had images which were associated with their ancestor worship. However, the Christian concept of the nature and function of saints had no native parallel. The Malagasy finally concluded that the new figures represented the ancestors of the Europeans. These ancestors were, of course, primarily interested in the well-being of their descendants, but would help non-relatives in return for a suitable fee. Having thus rationalized and brought within the scope of native concepts of the supernatural, their worship was taken up with considerable enthusiasm (Linton, 1940:477).

Cultural creativity may also contribute to the emergence of an entirely new culture. This process can be seen in the fusion of the Indian and Spanish cultures to produce the Mestizo culture of Latin America and in the fusion of the Norman and Saxon cultures to produce the English culture.

Cultural Disintegration. As a result of culture contact, rapid cultural change may be initiated that cannot be managed by the cultural system. The system may find itself overtaxed and disintegrate. This condition may be induced by the dominant culture forcing changes upon a people unprepared for them, an especially devastating development when accompanied by drastic shifts in demographic and ecological conditions—for instance, by virtue of massacres, the introduction of deadly new diseases, the depletion of wild life (as in the case of the buffalo), and the like. Similarly it may be the product of a people taking over great quantities of alien cultural material that their cultural system is unable to ingest and integrate into the whole. Vast disorganization has been particularly evident in situations where small, nonliterate societies have come into extensive contact with Western peoples, a condition reflected among some Native American peoples.

Integration

Integration entails alterations in the *relationships* among people (in the flow of interaction that characterizes people's daily lives). As we noted earlier in the chapter, the focus of acculturation is upon the customs of a people; the focus of integration is upon the people who are practicing the customs. Typically a racial or ethnic group develops a network of organizations and informal social relationships that permit and encourage its members to remain within its confines for the meeting of a wide variety of needs. Social cliques, ingroup dating and marriage, common residential patterns—even common occupations, schools, and religious affiliations—may characterize the group's members (Gordon, 1964).

Integration involves the fusion of groups in the sense that social interaction is no longer predicated on one's racial or ethnic identity. The descendants of the former dominant group and the former minority group no longer make "dominant-minority" group distinctions. Individuals thus find their place within the community without reference to ethnic or racial origins. Hence, integration embraces the elimination of prejudice, discrimination, and institutional racism. As the sociologists Lewis Killian and Charles Grigg (1964:108) observe, the solution to America's racial problems has usually been phrased in ways that would lead blacks to foreswear their identity as blacks: "But for a lasting solution, the meaning of 'American' must lose its implicit racial modifier, 'white.' Even without biological amalgamation, integration requires a sincere acceptance by all Americans that it is just as good to be a black American as to be a white American."

Acculturation without Integration

Institutional duplication is characteristic of a society containing differing cultures. The society is compartmentalized into quasi-independent units, each of which has a set of homologous institutions and limited points of contact with the other units (e.g., individuals of the differing groups have dealings with one another only in their participation in a common money economy and through their subjection to a common political body). Put still another way, *where there is cultural pluralism, there is also social pluralism.* Hence, not only do the people of the society experience different cultural worlds but they move in different social worlds as well. In such a society, we cannot take a social phenomenon and trace its ramifications throughout the entire society (van den Berghe, 1964, 1976). If this is the case, then we can see that *acculturation is a necessary precondition to integration.* In other words, people must come to share a relatively common cultural map or blueprint for life (common guideposts that serve to channel their life activities). Only under such circumstances does the possibility exist of their coming to interact within the *same* institutional order so that the flow of their social actions (their social relationships) will be unimpeded by sharp boundaries and distinctions.

The reverse proposition, however, does not hold. Acculturation can occur in the absence of integration. Blacks within the United States present a good illustration. Although sharing with whites in the larger American culture, blacks still experience much white prejudice and discrimination—barriers to the free flow of social interaction. American

Judaism provides still another illustration of this (Lazerwitz and Harrison, 1979). For many American Jews, traditional Judaism has been "de-Judaized." In the realm of religion, there are congregations of the Orthodox, Conservative, and Reform varieties, named in order of their degree of adherence to traditional rituals and practices. Synagogues and temples, particularly those of the Conservative and Reform persuasions, have made major acculturating adjustments to the standards of American life—for example, Conservative Judaism has introduced English into portions of the service and into the synagogue's business affairs, has altered the function of the rabbi, has abolished the segregation of the sexes in worship, has emphasized "decorum," and has cultivated the "multifunctional" synagogue with age- and sex-graded recreational and educational programs. Yet with the shift away from Orthodox Jewish cultural practices (acculturation), there has simultaneously occurred a strong desire for the preservation of a Jewish ethnic identity (opposition to complete integration). Herbert Gans (1956) refers to this development as the emergence of "symbolic Judaism"—a kind of minimal adherence to specifically Jewish cultural patterns, in which emphasis is placed on a selection of nostalgic items of "Yiddish" background (e.g., Yiddish culinary delicacies or Yiddish phrases); the possession in the home of tangible objects denoting Jewishness (e.g., books or pictures with Jewish themes); a concern with "Jewish" problems; and a selection of festive religious traditions that help socialize the children into an awareness of and affection for a Jewish identity. Hence we find acculturation taking place in the absence of total integration.

Some Related Concepts

Assimilation is a social and cultural process that is to be distinguished from the biological process of *amalgamation*. **Amalgamation** involves the biological fusion of differing "racial" and "subracial" groups. Assimilation does not necessarily imply the absence of physical visibility between groups; populations differing in the incidence of genetically transmitted racial characteristics may persist. Assimilation does imply, however, the eventual elimination of cultural and social distinctions based on racial membership. Individuals, when assimilated, would no longer exhibit the cultural or social marks that identify them as members of an outgroup, nor would any racial characteristics that they possess function as the foundation for group prejudice or discrimination. Although for analytical purposes assimilation and amalgamation are two separate concepts, it should be noted that they usually go hand-in-hand. Assimilation promotes intermarriage and intermarriage promotes assimilation.

Assimilation also differs from *naturalization* and *absorption*. **Naturalization** denotes the acquisition of legal citizenship. **Absorption** refers to the immigrant's ability to secure and sustain economic employment within the new country. The immigrant may adopt the occupational pattern of the new country or add to this pattern through the introduction of new economic activities and occupations. On the whole, absorption proceeds more rapidly than acculturation or integration, because fewer changes in roles and institutions are required in the former than in the latter case (Borrie, 1959).

Minimum Assimilation: The Amish

Contact among groups does not inevitably result in assimilation. Groups may be in contact during a considerable period yet assimilation may be held to a bare minimum. The Old Order Amish of Pennsylvania are a case in point. The Amish are a religious sect, an offshoot of the Mennonites. The group originated in Alsace and the upper Rhineland of Germany and Switzerland during the Reformation conflicts of the sixteenth century. A schism occurred in the Mennonite movement in 1693, and Jacob Amman led his conservative followers, in time known as the Amish, from the larger group. The Amish were recruited from the peasantry and were both rural and lower class in background. The basic tenet of the group is that all practices and activities must be based upon a literal interpretation of the Bible, regardless of the laws or customs of the larger society. It appears that the movement originated as a revolt by a disadvantaged people against the culture of its day, a culture that had proved too punishing and too devoid of satisfactions to be followed longer. Because of religious persecution, the Amish migrated to Pennsylvania in the early 1700s. The group residing in Lancaster County is the oldest and most conservative of the Amish settlements in the United States (Gillin: 1948; Redekop, 1969; Hostetler, 1980).

The Amish are a kin-oriented, rural-dwelling, religion-centered people. Although frequently living adjacent to non-Amish farm neighbors, all Amish households in a geographic area form a "church district." The Amish are highly successful as farmers, and their farms are acknowledged to be among the best in the world. Although generally very conservative, the Amish are not conservative in their farming techniques. They have adopted the new methods of rotating crops, applying fertilizer, and introducing new commercial agricultural products. While prohibiting the use of the tractor, they do employ some modern farm equipment including cultivators, sprayers, binders, and balers.

The Amish are oriented toward two major goals: (1) "the Christian way of life" as defined by the sect's interpretation of the Bible and (2) successful farming as defined by agricultural abundance rather than financial success. Their main objective in farming is to accumulate sufficient means to buy enough land to keep all the children on farms.

To this end the Amish work hard, produce abundantly, and save extensively.

The Amish, far from being ashamed of their nonconformity, pride themselves on being a "peculiar people" who do not conform to the standards of the world. Nonconformity is mandatory in those areas in which "worldly" standards are in conflict with those of the Bible. The sect members eschew the bearing of arms, going to war, holding public office, owning life insurance, and participating in Social Security. Education beyond the eighth grade is opposed. They believe that higher education is both unnecessary and a danger in that it draws the children away from the farm and the Amish way of life. They approve of elementary education in the "three R's," since literacy is required for reading the Bible. The fact that the Amish are trilingual contributes to their social isolation: Pennsylvania Dutch is the familiar tongue at home and in informal conversation; High German is used exclusively for services and ceremonials; and English (acquired in school) is employed with the non-Amish.

Amish attire is distinctive. Men wear their hair long, cut in bangs, with low-crown, wide-brim hats on their heads. Their coats lack collars, lapels, pockets, and buttons (they are fastened with hooks and eyes). Trousers are plain and worn with homemade suspenders. Shirts are plain and worn without neckties. Married men wear a beard, but a mustache (considered the mark of a military man) is forbidden; unmarried men shave. Amish women wear plain, solid-color dresses with near-ankle-length skirts. Their stockings are of black cotton; their shoes are of a high-laced, low-heeled type; and their head covering is a homemade bonnet ("store hats" are forbidden). Within Amish society styles of dress become very important symbols of group identity. The symbols indicate whether people are fulfilling the expectations of the group (e.g., a young man who wears a hat with a brim that is too narrow is subject to punishment).

Amish conservatism extends widely to many areas of life. Telephones, radios, television sets, automobiles, washing machines, and electric lights are all forbidden. The Amish eschew all forms of "worldly" amusement including attendance at sporting events, movies, dance halls, and bars. Ornaments and jewelry are prohibited.

Marriage to outsiders is not permitted. Their marriages are very stable; divorces are unknown; and their families are large. All religious services are held in the homes of the members (the meetings rotate among the homes in each district). They lack a paid clergy and a formal bureaucratic church organization. They select their bishops, ministers, and deacons by election from among the married men. After the Sunday service (which may last for four hours), a large dinner is served for all members in the home in which the service was held.

A number of factors have operated to keep Amish assimilation at a bare minimum. First, competing customs have had little opportunity to be presented and tried out. The Amish are kept from contact with those from whom they might learn other customs and practices. Second, the group supplies plentiful rewards for following Amish practices. In time of difficulty or when starting a new farm, the community comes to the individual's aid. The group also satisfies various personal needs, including ego-satisfaction, affection, companionship, and security. In a word, the Amish community provides for all or most of the activities and needs of the people in it. Third, the fear of punishment is considerable. The members are taught that transgressions of God's will result, after death, in certain punishment in the fires of Hell. The group also excommunicates and "shuns" violators of its norms, withdrawing from all social intercourse with the wrongdoer. No member may knowingly eat at the table with an expelled member or have normal work or domestic relations with the person. If the case involves husband or wife, they are to suspend their usual marital relations. Shunning constitutes a powerful instrument for keeping the church intact and for preventing members from involvement in the wider society. Similarly it keeps the Old Order Amish socially isolated from innovators within their own group.

Yet Amish society has not been able to shut the door entirely on social change. Indeed, the Amish search for improvement and innovation in the sphere of production contrasts with a tradition of resistance to change in the sphere of religion. This underlying contradiction generates considerable internal stress within the Amish social order, for innovations in production do not necessarily meet the test of religious criteria. As such, pressure continuously exists to compromise religious doctrine and accommodate religion to the demand for excellence in farming. This element has been a major source of schism within Amish groups. On occasion entire congregations break with Old Order orthodoxy. The members of break-away groups typically adopt tractors, automobiles, and meeting houses, trim their hair and beards, secure clothing which resembles that of other Americans, and shift to non-farm occupations (Yutzy, 1968).

Among those who retain their Old Order allegiance, the individuals may still eschew electric lights, rubber-tired farm implements, and telephones. Yet they may install propane gas on their farms, secure the latest style gas-ranges, kerosene-burning refrigerators, and automatic, gas water-heaters with gasoline engines to keep up the water pressure. Their homes may be lit with gasoline mantle lanterns. And although they do not have their own telephones, they may use those of neighbors or pay phones. While not buying a car, they may ride in a cab or in the automobile of a non-Amish neighbor. To sell Grade A milk, they may alter their barns, milk houses, water supply, and habits of working with farm animals. Hence, the Amish society is hardly static.

The Rate of Assimilation

The rate of a group's assimilation within American society is a function of many factors. While social scientists are generally in agreement that assimilation is a complex phenomenon, they are not necessarily in agreement as to just what factors tend to be most crucial in influencing the speed with which a group is assimilated. The evidence relating to the various variables is incomplete and controversial. Here we will outline a number of propositions that represent as good an "educated guess" as one can currently make.

1. *The greater the difference between the host and the immigrant cultures, the greater will be the subordination, the greater the strength of the ethnic social systems, and the longer the period necessary for the assimilation of the ethnic group* (Warner and Srole, 1945). Most of the peoples from the British Isles have experienced slight subordination within the United States, developed weak subsystems, and gone through very short periods of assimilation. And whereas Irish Catholics have taken several generations to assimilate, the Protestant Irish have almost immediately assimilated.

2. *The larger the ratio of the incoming group to the resident population, the slower the rate of assimilation* (Williams, 1947). Where the ratio of the immigrant group to the native population is small, the natives tend to view the immigrants with both a disinterested aloofness and a patronizing air ("those quaint people"). But, as the ratio increases, the native population generally becomes more aware of the immigrant group's presence, often begins defining it as a threat, and to one degree or another erects barriers against the new group's assimilation. One or two Chinese families within a community may for most purposes be overlooked, yet nonetheless represent a passing focus for conversation ("those strange and interesting people"). The old-American stock may even derive considerable satisfaction and pride from their "open-minded," "tolerant," and "big-hearted" attitudes toward a few minority-groups members. It is not uncommon to hear the individual who feels guilty about his anti-Semitism declare, "Look! I don't hate Jews. Why one of my best friends is a Jew!" Similarly, a few Chinese or members of another minority may serve for the community much the same function as the "one Jewish friend": "Look! We don't hate Chinese or minorities. See what a tolerant community we are!" But as the Chinese increase in number, they are likely to be increasingly regarded as a threat and set off from the dominant group.

3. *The more rapid the influx of the incoming group, the slower the rate of assimilation* (Williams, 1947). A rapid influx of immigrants is likely to arouse among the natives a fear of engulfment—a feeling that they are going to be overpowered, overwhelmed, and swallowed up. Accordingly, they are likely both to intensify their resistance to immigrant assimilation and to erect various segregating barriers to it. By the same token, the immigrants are likely to respond by taking refuge in an intensified ingroup coalescence.

4. *The greater the dispersion of the immigrant group, especially in the same territorial pattern as the dominant group, the more rapid the immigrants' assimilation* (Schermerhorn, 1949). Where groups are concentrated in large numbers they tend to coalesce and perpetuate their native cultures. Where they are scattered, they are less capable of insulating themselves from the larger community and of preserving their native institutions, customs, and in-marriage patterns. Further, residential segregation has the effect of accenting the differences between groups by heightening their visibility.

5. *The higher the educational, income, and occupational levels of the incoming group, the more rapid its assimilation* (Weinstock, 1964). To the extent to which a group's members are concentrated on the lowest rungs of the class hierarchy, they suffer the additional disadvantage of incurring various class prejudices and discrimination. In time an entire group may come to be stereotyped as menial workers and laborers. Similarly, the higher the immigrant's former occupational status, the more transferable tends to be the skill within an urban industrial environment, and hence the greater the likelihood that the immigrant will be more rapidly assimilated.

6. *The greater the predisposition of the incoming group to change, the more rapid the rate of assimilation* (Borrie, 1959). Groups differ in the premium they assign to their traditional patterns as well as the premium they place upon admittance to the old-American group.

7. *The greater the predisposition of the receiving community to recognize differences, the more rapid the rate of assimilation.* Campaigns such as that of the "Americanization" movement following World War I often contribute to a "boomerang" effect in which assimilation, rather than being promoted, is actually delayed. Where group differences are accepted, people interact in a "matter-of-course" fashion and are less resistant to taking on new ways of behavior. But where differences are not accepted and where demands are raised that people divest them-

selves of particular traits, accentuated "consciousness of kind" and group cohesion tend to emerge, together with an intensified resistance to change. To attack group values is likely to strengthen them.

8. *The greater the degree of economic competition between the native and immigrant groups, the slower the rate of assimilation.* Economic competition is likely to contribute to hostile feelings, an intolerance of differences, an accentuated "consciousness of kind," and group cohesion.

9. *The greater the proximity and access to the homeland, the slower the rate of assimilation.* French-Canadian assimilation in New England and Mexican assimilation in the Southwest have been slowed by their respective geographical proximities to Quebec and Mexico. Proximity makes it relatively easy for immigrants to return to their original homes for periodic visits. Such visits may enable the immigrants to avoid deeply rooted ties and commitments within the new homeland. It also enables them to experience a reinforcement of previous cultural traditions and life patterns.

10. *In situations of continuous intergroup contact, subordinate migrants (newcomers who are politically and economically dominated by an established indigenous population) tend to be more rapidly assimilated than subordinate indigenous populations (native peoples who are subjected to political and economic domination by a migrant group).* On the other hand, conflict is more likely to occur in situations of migrant superordination (for a discussion of these matters, *see* chapter 3).

Marginality

Individuals often find the process of assimilation turbulent, stressful, and emotionally disruptive. As early as 1928, the sociologist Robert E. Park called attention to the individual who is torn between the conflicting demands of two cultural traditions, a person he termed "the marginal man." As viewed by Park **marginal persons** are people "whom fate has condemned to live in two societies and in two, not merely different but antagonistic, cultures" (Stonequist, 1937:xv). They are individuals caught in the conflict of cultures, people who live in two worlds, yet actually belong to neither. As an Amish student at a non-Amish college observed, "I feel I am a man without a country. I don't fit in at home too well, and I don't fit in at school."

Daniel Okimoto (1971:48) captures the identity confusion that often typifies marginal people when he writes about his dual American and Japanese ancestry:

In adapting to American society, we have had to face the persistent and perplexing problem of how to look upon our dual heritage. The difficulty of reconciling these twin aspects of our lives is often revealed in that moment of hesitation many experience when asked, "What are you?" In my own life there have been times when I have been frankly at a loss how to reply. Depending on my mood and the circumstances, my answers have vacillated between "American," "Japanese," and "Japanese American." Whatever the response, it usually felt somehow unnatural. I never considered myself 100-per cent American because of obvious physical differences. Nor did I think of myself as Japanese. The social opprobrium associated with being a member of a minority also made me slightly uncomfortable about declaring myself a Japanese American.

The following conditions are likely to foster marginality (Kerckhoff and McCormack, 1955):

1. Where two groups with differing cultures or subcultures are in intensive and continuous contact

2. Where some of the members of one group for one reason or another come under the influence of another group or come to place a premium upon membership in the other group

3. Where the barriers between the two groups are sufficiently permeable for members of one group to internalize the patterns of the other

4. Where for one reason or another the patterns between the two groups cannot be easily harmonized or where cultural and/or racial barriers serve to block full and legitimate membership within another group.

Marginal persons are confronted with numerous situations in which their role is ill-defined. But individuals differ in their definitions of situations and in their adjustments to them. There are a number of differing responses to marginal situations. Aaron Antonovsky (1956), on the basis of a study of fifty-eight Jewish men in New Haven, suggests a number of these responses:

1. *Active Jewish orientation.* These Jews identified themselves with things Jewish, were opposed to assimilation, tended to reject non-Jewish patterns and identifications, and felt strong solidarity with Jewish groups. One remarked, "If you're not Jewish, then you can't understand anyway. And if you are, you don't have to ask questions; you already know what we feel. And all Jews feel alike, there's no need to go around studying them." Another observed, "You say hello, goodbye, to the *goyim* [Gentiles], but don't mix."

2. *Passive Jewish orientation.* This group, although its reactions were in some ways similar to that of the first, was not quite as involved in, or as enthusiastic about, being Jewish. Nevertheless,

its members were oriented toward the Jewish group and accepted their membership within it as fundamental. They were not, however, characterized by a clear, articulate desire to see Jews continue and survive as a distinct group. One remarked, "I see little point to being Jewish, but that's what I am. And there's little point in trying to be something else."

3. *Ambivalent orientation.* This group's relationship to both Jewish and non-Jewish groups was fundamentally unsatisfying and conflicting. It was reflected in this statement by a Jewish man, a statement that reflects his ambivalent identification by his references to Jews as "the Jewish people," "they," and "we": *"The Jewish people* can be their own worst enemy, by the so-called ghetto idea. I grant you that sometimes *they* have to band together in a so-called ghetto to have strength. But I feel that *we* must get along with our fellow beings; this means taking both the good and bad of the gentiles."

4. *Dual orientation.* This group looked toward a slow but steady integration within the larger society and saw no insurmountable obstacles to it. They felt that the rewards to be gained from integration were substantial.

5. *Passive general orientation.* This group of Jews were indifferent to, and in the process of drifting away from, Jewish culture; yet they did not actively seek to shut themselves off from Jewish life. Their solidarity with the Jewish group was nominal; they were completely indifferent to Jewish group survival; yet they were also indifferent to assimilation. One remarked, "Being Jewish is the least of my worries."

6. *Active general orientation.* This group felt no solidarity with the Jewish group and came as close to assimilation as possible without hiding or denying their Jewishness.

Shuttling Between Social and Cultural Worlds

We have observed that the concept of the marginal person draws our attention to the fact that people may experience assimilation as a turbulent, stressful, and emotionally disruptive process. It provides us with a valuable theoretical advance over two simplified categories: those people who are assimilated and those who are not. But we need to take our analysis a step further and tackle the notion of "levels of assimilation." According to this view there exists a continuum of change wherein a given amount of "tribal (or immigrant) loss" is *replaced* through time by a comparative amount of "Westernized (or Americanized) gain." Consequently, at some point along the continuum, people invariably become "hung-up" or "lost" between two social and cultural worlds.

While the notion of levels of assimilation or a continuum of change is useful for analyzing the adjustment of some individuals, it fails to encompass another type of adaptation in which individuals shuttle between social and cultural worlds. In considering this matter an illustration may prove helpful, that of the Blackfeet Indians of Montana. The anthropologist Malcolm McFee (1968) studied the assimilation process among the Blackfeet. McFee found that all the Blackfeet live in houses, most drive cars, watch television, dress in Western clothes, attend regional schools and churches, and all but a few of the old people speak English. Indeed, in many respects they are similar to their non-Indian, rural Montana neighbors. Broadly speaking the Blackfeet can be divided into two contrasting *social* groups—the Indian-oriented group and the white-oriented group. The former are Blackfeet who *want to be Indian*—individuals who participate in such activities as bundle openings, Indian dances, song services, encampments, and visiting and who measure worth in terms of helpfulness and generosity to others, even to the point of self-impoverishment. In contrast the white-oriented group measures social worth by economic standards, scheduled work hours, formal education, and accumulated capital and feel that, while generosity in theory is fine, in practice it should not lead to the point where a family undermines its economic position. The population, then, is socially and culturally bifurcated. Yet, strictly speaking, neither group is made up of "marginal persons."

There are in addition some individuals who are Indian-oriented—they live with and want to be accepted by the Indian group and to maintain their Indian identity—yet who have received a good education in white schools and have had a wide range of experiences in various aspects of white culture. Such individuals seemingly would be "marginal persons." Yet they are not. They "shuttle" or "commute" between the two social and cultural worlds. Indeed, the bifurcated nature of the Blackfeet milieu has actually created a need for such individuals—mediators to mesh the forces of the two social and cultural worlds. In brief, such individuals have learned new ways without abandoning the old. They are, to use McFee's conception, "the 150% man." Such individuals seemingly are well adjusted, They simply commute or shuttle between systems and are not "marginal persons" in the classical sense. It is not inevitable, then, that people become "hung-up" or "lost" between two social and cultural worlds.

Controversial Issues

Considerable controversy has surrounded sociological interpretations of various aspects of the assimilation process. One issue has to do with theoretical schemes that depict intergroup relations as developing through a series of evolutionary stages. Another matter revolves about the nature of the ethnic revival that has taken place in the United States since the 1960s. Still another issue has concerned the suitability of an assimilation model as opposed to a colonial model for studying the circumstances of blacks and Chicanos within the United States. Admittedly, students and sociologists would prefer hard-and-fast answers to their questions. Yet controversy offers opportunities for arriving at more satisfactory answers through the resulting intellectual give-and-take and the research that it stimulates.

The Cycle of Robert E. Park

The late Robert E. Park (1949), one of America's outstanding students of race relations, suggested that, whenever and wherever different racial and ethnic groups continuously meet, they inevitably pass through a series of irreversible stages: The groups come into *contact;* invariably contact produces *competition;* from this competition some kind of adjustment or *accommodation* is realized; and, finally, there is *assimilation.* Within the United States, Park saw the process unfolding in somewhat this fashion:

The newcomers typically came to America poor, the product of European peasant stock. They were mostly uneducated, often ignorant of the English language, disillusioned by harsh treatment received at the hands of immigration officials, and bewildered by the strangeness, complexity, and tempo of urban America. Accordingly, they found themselves isolated from the mainstream of American life. Condescendingly viewed as "greenhorns," they were exploited as cheap labor by natives, taken advantage of by loan sharks, and swindled by some of their own countrymen who already "knew the ropes." Within the labor market they were the victims of the business cycle—welcomed in the upturn, discharged and abused in the downturn. Ghettos arose—Little Italys, Chinatowns, Little Bohemias, and Black Belts—the product of a number of forces: First, the immigrants were poor and hence were forced by rentals into the least desirable areas of the city—the slums. Second, they huddled together in spatially compact areas because their cultural likeness in language and traditions gave them a sense of comfort, belonging, and security. And third, the hostility and antagonism of the native population barred them from other areas and reinforced their desire to reside with their "own kind."

Within the labor force the newcomers found themselves in competition for jobs with the natives and earlier arrivals. Conspicuous by virtue of their speech, traditions, customs, and manners, they became a convenient foil for attacks by politicians searching for publicity and fame. Professional patriots, special interests, and anxious nationalists joined in the attacks. Sensational newspapers depicted a few crimes committed by immigrants as a "crime wave." In periods of economic depression their unpopularity was intensified by their disproportionate representation among the unemployed. Their continuing migration to the United States and their tendency to have large families served to accentuate native fears of engulfment.

Although contact first contributed to competition and conflict, it eventually resulted in a division of labor and the establishment of a *modus vivendi*. Thus, in time, competition and conflict increasingly gave way to accommodation. English more and more replaced the mother tongue; some of the immigrants attended night school to learn English, the new customs, and new skills. Various "German-American," "Italian-American," "Polish-American," and other nationality newspapers grew up, bringing a wider knowledge of American affairs to those who could not read English. City political machines with their neighborhood ward bosses quickly gained an appreciation for the potential of the newcomers' votes. These party machines, often corrupt, contributed to the integration of newcomers within American political and civic life. Party functionaries were quite adept at performing personal favors, providing relief in hard times, "fixing up" matters when immigrants got in trouble with the law, providing "Christmas baskets," and in general displaying personal interest in the immigrants. The children of the foreign-born functioned as carriers of the English language and American customs from the schools to the homes. And with time the birth rate of the ethnic groups began to decline. As they learned new skills, they started to climb up the occupational hierarchy; simultaneously, more recently arrived ethnic groups "pushed" them up the status ladder. Increasingly they gained acceptance and in due course became assimilated.

Park's natural-history model has won considerable acceptance, and the theory has been applied in a number of well-known studies including Louis Wirth's *The Ghetto* (1928). The scheme, however, has been criticized on several points. The sociologist Amitai Etzioni (1959) suggests that, like many natural-history theories, Park's theory is not sufficiently specified to be tested. He argues that Park formulated his theory in such a manner that different and even contradictory data can be interpreted to support it. Etzioni in particular criticizes Park's frequent use of the term "eventually":

> When an ethnic group is assimilating, it is suggested that the hypothesis is supported; if an ethnic group is not assimilating, it is suggested that it has not yet reached the stage of assimilation. "Eventually," one can still hold, every ethnic group will be assimilated. As no time interval is mentioned and the sociological conditions under which the process of assimilation will take place are not spelled out, the whole scheme becomes unscientific (1959: 255).

Park has also been criticized for his assumption that there is an inevitable and irreversible unilinear progression toward assimilation among differing groups. It appears that under some circumstances this does not occur. By way of illustration, some children of Jewish parents who have been converted to Christianity or who are of mixed Jewish-Christian marriages return to Judaism. Similarly, the Nazi program in Germany served to reverse the long-run trend toward Jewish assimilation in that nation.

The interaction between different racial and cultural groups takes many forms, and assimilation need not necessarily be the last stage. Indeed, the processes of competition, conflict, accommodation, and assimilation may more appropriately be viewed not as stages in a fixed sequence but as alternative situations. In addition to assimilation, there are at least four other possible stable outcomes of intergroup contact (Barth and Noel, 1972): exclusion (including expulsion and annihilation); symbiosis (a mutually beneficial exchange and interdependence); stratification (an arrangement of superordination and subordination); and pluralism (maintenance of distinct institutional arrangements within a common political and economic order).

Ethnic Revival

One of the most notable changes within the United States since the 1960s has been the renewed interest in ethnicity. Some observers have termed it an "ethnic revival." New organizations have been formed and old ones revitalized by Italian-Americans, Lithuanian-Americans, Slovakian-Americans, Polish-Americans, and many others. Television programs and slogans printed on T-shirts and bumper stickers herald a new ethnic awareness and pride. Prior to the 1960s it had been considered poor form to highlight ethnic membership, except on approved days of the year like St. Patrick's Day or Columbus Day. But as black consciousness and militance grew through the 1960s, the attitude toward ethnicity changed. The emphasis upon "black roots" accentuated and forged a black ethnicity (Taylor, 1979). And as whites came to recognize and accept the right of blacks to proclaim and celebrate their blackness, many other ethnic Americans saw no reason to continue hiding their own group pride. Hence, the black movement legitimated ethnic self-consciousness (Greeley, 1971; McLemore, 1980).

Some question exists, however, as to the depth and commitment of the ethnic revival. The sociologist Herbert J. Gans (1979) denies that a genuine revival has taken place and argues that assimilation continues to occur. He says that among third- and fourth-generation "ethnics" (the grand- and great-grand children of European immigrants) the focus falls on ethnic symbols that foster a sense of identity but that breed neither cultures nor organizations. Consequently, ethnicity has taken on the properties of a leisure-time activity and has lost its relevance in the earning of a living or the regulating of family life. He terms this development *symbolic ethnicity*. **Symbolic ethnicity** represents a nostalgic search for an exotic tradition that can occasionally be savored in a museum or at an ethnic festival. But today the ethnic role is no longer an ascriptive one but primarily a voluntary role that people choose.

William Yancey and his colleagues (1976) also suggest that contemporary ethnicity bears little relation to the ancestral European heritage. They see ethnicity not as some sort of fixed cultural quotient that simply survives from other times and places. Rather they conceive of ethnicity as arising and developing anew in response to conditions within the United States. It is crystallized under conditions that reinforce the maintenance of kinship and friendship networks. Among the favoring conditions are a concentration in similar occupations and industries (Jews in the garment industry, Italians in construction, and the Polish in steel); common residential neighborhoods (ethnic ghettos); and dependence on common institutions and services (the tendency of the Irish to participate in the urban political bureaucracy).

Another view, expressed by the sociologist Andrew M. Greeley (1974), the political commentator Michael Novak (1971), and others, argues that the extent of assimilation has been overestimated. These individuals call attention to studies that reveal that ethnic cultures and organizations are still viable and functioning. They note that ethnic differences in behavior patterns and attitudes still set Poles, Italians, Irish, and Jews apart from one another. Many ethnic groups continue to act and vote as political interest groups. And ethnic pride remains strong.

Some years ago the historian Marcus Hansen (1952) gave a somewhat different twist to the thesis that ethnicity has always been strong. He said that assimilation is but a temporary process and that ethnicity reemerges as third-generation nationalism. The second generation— the children of the immigrants—often felt keenly the discrimination directed against those who adhered to the "foreign" ways of their parents. Many sought to shed as quickly as possible the marks of ethnic identification. But whereas the second generation attempted to forget their foreign ways and the trauma of the Americanization process, the third generation could afford to remember an ancestral culture. Of equal significance, the third generation no longer could take its ethnic identity for granted. Individuals can relinquish their identity, but if they wish to experience it, they must make it more explicit than in the past and cultivate their association with it. Consequently, the ethnic identity rejected by the second generation is revived by the third generation.

Some sociologists interpret the Irish experience in the United States in terms of the Hansen thesis. The Irish came to the United States in large numbers following the potato famine in Ireland in the 1840s. They suffered a good deal of hardship in America, being victimized by prejudice and discrimination. But now, when they have "made" it—when for the first time it is legitimate for the Irish to act like Irish—they have forgotten how (Greeley, 1972). Seduced by the possibilities of respectability, they have become like "all other Americans." Many members of the third generation compensate by cultivating an Irish identity. Yet parades on St. Patrick's Day have become simply monuments to a cultural tradition of which few people in the parade are fully aware.

Still other researchers have interpreted the ethnic revival as a defensive political protest (Bergesen, 1977). They note that oftentimes the political activities of the working and lower-middle class white ethnics have constituted *pan-ethnic* rather than ethnic movements since they have involved coalitions of ethnic groups (Gans, 1979). Although at one time they considered one another enemies, they now unite around common economic and class interests. Many ethnics feel that they have to work harder and make more sacrifices to achieve a decent life in the United States than blacks, Chicanos, Vietnamese, and other more recent arrivals within American urban centers. And they are angry because they believe that they have been made to bear a disproportionate burden of contemporary social change. Many have become disillusioned with a strong central government, which they see as the champion of deprived minorities and the poor (Patterson, 1977; Stein and Hill, 1977).

The fact that white ethnics have at times rallied together in response to racial issues suggests that ethnic rhetoric may serve as a convenient euphemism for anti-black sentiments. The ethnics have entered the political arena in response to black militancy, expanding black ghettos that have encroached upon ethnic neighborhoods, and government welfare and affirmative-action programs. For instance, the Irish of South Boston have heightened their ethnic solidarity as a defensive reaction to what they perceive to be an external threat—an attack upon their control of the schools in their neighborhoods (Bergesen, 1977).

However, it should also be pointed out that for some people ethnicity represents a search for community in an impersonal urban world. It is one tool people use to shield themselves from the sharp edges of alienation. Ethnicity provides a basis for close, meaningful relationships that involve a high degree of personal intimacy, emotional depth, moral commitment, social acceptance, and continuity in time. During periods of crisis and confusion, such ties can be most reassuring.

Assimilation versus Colonial Models

There are two sociological schools of thought with respect to the experience of blacks and Hispanics in the United States. The one position argues that blacks and Hispanics are like European immigrant groups and that in due course they too will become assimilated. The other claims that blacks and Hispanics are like Third World colonized groups and are victims of special oppression and exploitation. Those who argue the merits of one or the other position tend to talk past one another as if speaking different languages.

The assimilationist perspective depicts groups in accordance with the Park model. Intergroup adaptation is portrayed as evolutionary, moving in the direction of less diversity and toward eventual fusion. European immigrant groups are deemed classic examples. Through time they became immersed within American life as they took over the essentials of the dominant Anglo-Saxon core culture. Political conservatives say that blacks and Hispanics are simply the last migrant groups to reach American cities. Viewed from this perspective, blacks and Hispanics, like the European arrivals of earlier periods, will achieve equality in the course of several generations (Kristol, 1969; Sowell, 1975, 1980). They are expected to repeat the cycle by which earlier immigrants gained skills, moved up the occupational ladder, and dispersed from ethnic neighborhoods. On the whole political conservatives see no need for special programs to assist blacks or Hispanics. Consequently, they have led the fight against special admission of minorities to colleges and professional schools, efforts to achieve greater desegregation through busing, and curriculum changes that would stress racial and ethnic identity.

In contrast, many political liberals and radicals say that the experiences of blacks and Hispanics in relation to whites resemble those of "colonial" peoples in relation to a "mother country" (Blackwell, 1975; Barrera, 1979). For instance, some Hispanics claim that dominant "Anglos" have followed a policy of *internal colonialism* and treated them as a captive people. The historian Rodolfo Acuña (1972) details the conditions that he believes defines a policy of internal colonialism:

1. The land of one people is seized by people from another nation who use military means to maintain control.

2. The original inhabitants become subjects of the conquerors.

3. The conquerors impose an alien culture and government on the subject people.

4. The conquered people become the victims of racism and cultural genocide.

5. The subject people are rendered politically and economically powerless.

6. The conquerors believe that they have a "mission" in occupying the territory and "civilizing" the people in question.

Likewise, Kenneth Clark (1964:10–11), a distinguished black psychologist, argues that the position of blacks in the United States is one of internal colonialism:

Ghettos are the consequence of the imposition of external power and the institutionalization of powerlessness. In this respect, they are in fact social, political, educational, and above all—economic—colonies. Those confined within the ghetto walls are subject peoples. They are victims of the greed, cruelty, insensitivity, guilt and fear of their masters.

Some sociologists like Robert Blauner (1969) and James A. Geschwender (1978) argue that a number of special features make black ghettos an expression of colonized status and distinguish them from the white ethnic communities of an earlier period. First, Poles, Italians, and Jews came to the United States voluntarily. In contrast, nonwhite peoples were brought into a situation of internal colonialism involuntarily. Second, the immigrant ghettos lasted only for one or two generations. They were merely brief way-stations on the road to assimilation. In contrast, black ghettos have had a long-term existence. Third, European ethnic groups experienced only a few decades during which their residential buildings, commercial stores, and other enterprises were owned by outsiders. In contrast, blacks own comparatively little of the property in black ghettos. Fourth, discrimination against European immigrants was never as intense as that against blacks. And finally, European immigrants arrived at a time of an expanding economy, which allowed the newcomers to move up the social ladder. But blacks have arrived in the cities at a time when the economy is less vigorous and the number of unskilled jobs is contracting. Thus proponents of the internal colonialism model argue that black problems within the United States are unique and old answers are irrelevant to the improvement of the black situation.

Intergroup Marriage

Intergroup marriage represents an important means through which both assimilation and racial amalgamation are realized. In the United States, intermarriage between peoples of differing nationality groups is a frequent occurrence; religious intermarriage is somewhat less common; while racial intermarriage is infrequent. Many sociologists view intergroup marriage as a particularly sensitive barometer of ethnic and racial antipathies—the higher the rate of intergroup marriage, the less intense the ethnocentrism and prejudice; the lower the rate of intergroup marriage, the more intense the ethnocentrism and prejudice.

Interethnic Marriage

Although evidence suggests that nationality is not as binding a force as race or religion in mate selection, it nevertheless operates as a restrictive-selective factor. Most evidence suggests that outgroup marriage is on the rise. The rates of intermarriage are highest among the earliest immigrant groups from Northern and Western Europe (Abramson, 1973; Alba, 1976). Among individuals of English ancestry, only about one in ten marriages is an ingroup marriage. For the Irish and Germans, it is about three, perhaps even four, in ten. For more recent arrivals from Southern and Eastern Europe, the rates of intermarriage are lower— among Poles about five in ten marriages are outgroup marriages and among Italians the figure is about four in ten. The rates of intergroup marriage among Hispanics are particularly low, less than two marriages of ten.

The sociologist B. R. Bugelski (1961) studied the rate of ingroup and outgroup marriage for Poles and Italians in Buffalo, New York, a city with sizable Polish and Italian populations. In 1930, ingroup marriages were the common practice with more than two-thirds of the marriages involving partners of the same group. By 1960, Bugelski found the pattern virtually reversed with more than two-thirds of the marriages involving partners from different ethnic groups.

Studies of mate selection in New Haven show similar patterns (Peach, 1980), while B. B. Wessel (1931), in a study of ethnicity in Woonsocket, Rhode Island, found that the rate of outgroup marriage for the first generation was 9.6 percent, for the second 20.9 percent, and for the third 40.4 percent. And Frank G. Mittelbach and Joan W. Moore (1968), in a study of marriages involving Chicanos in Los Angeles, found that the group's exogamy rate is roughly the same as that of the Italian and Polish ethnic populations in Buffalo a generation before—indeed, second- and third-generation Chicanos are more likely to marry "Anglos" than to marry immigrants from Mexico. A not dissimilar picture of outgroup marriage emerges among Puerto Ricans in New York City (Fitzpatrick, 1966).

Interreligious Marriage

In the United States, intermarriage among the various Protestant denominations—Baptists, Methodists, Lutherans, Episcopalians, and Congregationalists—is not uncommon, although it is probably not as common as is frequently assumed (Greeley, 1970). When the matter of religious intermarriage is raised, however, reference is usually made to the pattern involving Protestants, Catholics, and Jews. All three of these major religious groups encourage their members to marry within the fold, but their attitudes vary considerably. Protestant churches tend to be the most flexible, Jews the most rigid, and the Catholic church falls somewhere in between. A study involving 42,624 marriages in Indiana revealed that interfaith marriages (Protestants, Catholic, Jewish, and "other"), in comparison with intrafaith marriages, tend to be by civil ceremony. They tend to involve individuals who are members of religious minority groups, who have been previously married, who are older, who are in high-status occupations, and who reside in urban areas. Among interfaith couples, it is also more common for pregnancy to occur before marriage (Christensen and Barber, 1967).

Marriages between Catholics and Protestants represent the most significant interreligious marital pattern within the United States. Unfortunately there are insufficient data on the number of interfaith marriages not sanctioned by the Catholic church. A study by John L. Thomas (1951) revealed that, during the decade from 1940 to 1950, interfaith marriages sanctioned by Catholic nuptials represented 30 percent of all Catholic marriages in the United States. He further investigated interfaith marriages in 132 parishes distributed throughout the East and Midwest. Of 29,581 such marriages, 11,710, or 39.6 percent, were not sanctioned by Catholic nuptials. A sample survey of the American population made by the Bureau of the Census in 1957 (based on 35,000 households) found a rate of *existing* Catholic interfaith marriages of 21.6 percent. The comparable figure for Protestants was 8.6 percent. These figures, however, underestimate the rate of interreligious marriage as they fail to include the rate of conversion of one spouse to the faith of the other. In fact, data on Detroit white Protestants and white Catholics indicate how frequent the conversion process may be and how it may be trending. Of the combined Protestant-Catholic white sample, 85 percent reported that they and their spouses were of the same major faith, but only 68 percent had been reared in the same religion. Furthermore, among the members of the third generation, who had been born in the North and who had contracted a marriage with a person of another major faith, there appeared to be a greater tendency toward conversion of one spouse to the faith of the other than among the comparable first- and second-generation members of the sample (Lenski, 1963).

Some of the most accurate figures available on interreligious marriage are to be found for the state of Iowa (Chancellor and Monahan, 1955). Iowa marriage-application forms request individuals to cite their religious preference. In 1953, some 42 percent of all Iowa marriages involving a Catholic party were interfaith. For the same year, the Catholic Directory lists 30 percent of all Iowa marriages that were sanctioned by the church as being interfaith alliances. The state records reveal a much higher rate of Catholic-Protestant intermarriage, since the figures of the Catholic church do not include other-church and civil-ceremony marriages.

Thomas (1951) suggests that three major factors influence the rate of Catholic interfaith marriage. First, where Catholics represent a relatively small proportion of the total population, rates of interfaith marriage tend to be high (provided that ethnic or other differences do not bar contracts between Catholics and non-Catholics). Thus, he found that interfaith marriages sanctioned by the Catholic church constituted 70 percent of the Catholic marriages in the dioceses of Raleigh, Charleston, and Savannah-Atlanta (dioceses with a small proportion of Catholics to the total population), but that they represented only 10 percent of the marriages in the dioceses of El Paso, Corpus Christi, and Santa Fe (dioceses with a large proportion of Catholics to the total population). Second, the presence of cohesive ethnic groups within the community serve to check interreligious marriage. Third, the higher the socioeconomic class, the higher the proportion of marriages between Catholics and non-Catholics.

Recent studies of marriage between Jews and non-Jews reveal that the rate of such marriages is increasing and that Jews are accepting the marriages much more readily than in the past (Briggs, 1979). A 1976 survey sample of Jewish households in Kansas City found that 70 percent of Jewish males and 45 percent of Jewish females, ages twenty to twenty-four, had married non-Jews (Farber, Gordon, and Mayer, 1979). However, the rate of interfaith marriage was considerably lower for those age twenty-five to twenty-nine (38.7 percent for Jewish men and 22.9 percent for Jewish women) and those age thirty to thirty-four (31.7 percent and 27.1 percent respectively). Of the interfaith couples in Kansas City, 21.8 percent of the non-Jewish partners converted to Judaism whereas 20.3 percent of the Jewish partners no longer regarded themselves as Jewish. Other research shows that when individuals of different religions marry, they tend to be remarkably alike in educational and professional achievement (Briggs, 1979).

Based upon her study of intergroup marriage in New Haven, the sociologist Ruby Jo Kennedy (1944) advanced the hypothesis that the United States has developed not a single but a *triple melting pot*. She says that the sharpest increase in intergroup marriage has occurred *within* each of the three major religious groupings: Protestant, Catholic, and Jewish. For instance, the barriers have been lowered to marriages between Irish Catholics and Italian Catholics, between German Jews and Russian Jews, and between English Protestants and Swedish Protestants. Nonetheless, Protestants still marry Protestants, Catholics marry Catholics, and Jews marry Jews. However, other researchers have been unable to confirm Kennedy's thesis. And Ceri Peach (1980), who reexamined the marriage-license records of New Haven, could not substantiate Kennedy's conclusion even for New Haven. Rather than finding Kennedy's Protestant, Catholic, and Jewish melting pots, Peach found a racial-ethnic division of society into blacks, Jews, and white Gentiles.

Interracial Marriage

In 1979 the Bureau of the Census reported that interracial marriages continue to increase, but still make up less than 1 percent of the 48 million married couples within the United States. Between the 1960 and 1970 censuses, the number of married couples consisting of partners of different races increased by 108 percent, from 148,000 to 310,000. The corresponding increase between 1970 and 1977 was 36 percent—from 310,000 to 421,000. Black-white couples accounted for 125,000 of the marriages, an increase of 60,000 or 92 percent over the 1970 figure of 65,000. In about seven of ten marriages of blacks and whites, the male is black (Monahan, 1976). In different kinds of interracial marriages that also involved one white partner, the male is more often white (many servicemen married women of Asian ancestry). Interracial marriages were barred by many states prior to a 1967 Supreme Court decision prohibiting such statutes.

Our knowledge of interracial marriage in the United States is fragmentary and inadequate. However, Ernest Porterfield (1978) recently completed a study of forty black-white married couples in two midwestern and two southern cities. Thirty-three of the marriages consisted of a black male and a white female. On the whole Porterfield found that the couples were motivated by the same forces as persons in racially homogenous marriages. And for the most part the partners were of relatively like socioeconomic status. Seventy percent of the eighty individuals had not told their parents that they were dating a person of another race. Only 22.5 percent had one or both parents present at the wedding. Whereas 65.0 percent of the white parents rejected their child's marriage, only 27.5 percent of the black families did likewise. About half of the couples said that the white community had a negative reaction to the marriage and a quarter felt a negative reaction from the black community. Most of the couples had children and believed that their children would not encounter serious problems of discrimination. Of interest, Porterfield argues that white opposition to interracial marriage has stemmed less from a concern with racial "purity" than from a desire to ensure the "orderly replacement" of white power through ingroup marriage.

Immigration and Immigration Policies

During the nearly four centuries since the English settlement of Jamestown in 1607, more than 45 million people have migrated to the territory that now comprises the United States. Americans have both encouraged and discouraged the flow of newcomers. And today, as in the past, the issue of alien migrants remains a focal point of controversy.

Immigration to the United States

The government did not begin maintaining a record of immigration until 1820, and until 1907 the enumerations suffered from serious limitations. Overall the volume of immigration increased each decade, until the passage of restrictive legislation in the 1920s. Many immigrants also eventually returned home. Between 1907 and 1930 the ratios of out-flow to inflow for total alien migration ranged from 23.7 to 32.0 percent, with the exception of the World War I period, when it rose to 55 percent. During the depression years of the 1930s emigration exceeded immigration, but, since World War II, outflow relative to inflow has sharply declined.

The Period from 1783 to 1830.   In 1790 the white population of the United States was predominantly of English stock. There were com-paratively few Germans, Irish, and Dutch, and even fewer French, Canadians, Belgians, Swiss, Mexicans, and Swedes. Between 1783 and 1830 about 10,000 immigrants came to the United States each year. At the time of the first federal census in 1790, there were 757,208 blacks in the country. By 1820, the figure had reached 1,771,656.

The Period from 1830 to 1882.   The next period, from 1830 until 1882, was marked by a sharp increase in immigration. The great land areas beyond the Mississippi River served to induce many foreigners to come to the United States. Rapid industrialization created a demand for unskilled labor to build canals, railroads, and roads, to work in factories, and to carry out many manual tasks. During these fifty-two years, Eng-lish, Irish, Germans, and Scandinavians predominated among the mi-grants. The Irish came in especially large numbers after 1840, when the failure of their one crop, the potato, caused famine and resultant wide-spread suffering throughout Ireland. More than 1,350,000 Irish were recorded as having arrived in the United States during the eight years from 1847 to 1854. For the most part the Irish settled in the tenements of American cities, under slum conditions similar to those found among the Southern and Eastern Europeans of later date. In contrast with the Irish, the Germans and Scandinavians clung less tenaciously to the cities, many of them settling on farms in the Midwest. The German immigration reached its peak between 1880 and 1892, when more than 1,770,000 Germans were admitted; the Scandinavian immigration peaked between 1881 and 1890, with more than 656,000 arrivals.

The period from 1830 to 1882 was characterized by varied attitudes toward immigrants. Since organized labor was still struggling to secure recognition as an integral ingredient within the American industrial system, opposition from the trade unions on economic grounds had as yet not reached its full strength. Generally, manufacturers eagerly sought the cheap labor provided by successive waves of immigrant groups and were not anxious to see this flow impaired. However, consid-erable objection was raised to the admission of paupers, criminals, and other "undesirables" among the aliens, as well as to the increase of Catholics within the population. In particular, considerable opposition was directed against the Irish. Prior to the Civil War, the Know-Nothing movement gained widespread support, as nativistic sentiment was spurred on by economic competition and apprehension over the increasing number of culturally different Irish and German immigrants. The party blossomed from a splinter group into a political force that elected nine governors and displayed striking strength in state legislatures and Congress.

1882—A Turning Point.   The year 1882 represents a turning point in the history of American immigration. It marked the climax of the movement of migrants from Northern and Western Europe to the United States and the beginning of the large-scale movement of migrants from Southern and Eastern Europe. It was also the time of the passage of the Chinese Exclusion Act, and it inaugurated the beginning of federal control of immigration in general. Included in the so-called new migration (as opposed to the "old" migration from England, Germany, Scandinavia, France, and Holland) were the Italians, Poles, Jews, Greeks, Portuguese, Russians, and a varied assortment of other Slavs. Within the span of some twenty years there was a complete reversal in the proportions of immigrants from Northern and Western, and Southern and Eastern Europe. Whereas, in 1882, 87 percent came from the former area and only 13 percent from the latter, by 1907 the corresponding figures were 13 percent and 81 percent, respectively. In the decade from 1901 to 1910 Italy's 2 million immigrants alone exceeded the 1.9 million from all the countries of Northern and Western Europe combined. By virtue of significant cultural differences between the "new" immigrants and the rest of the American population, the "new immigrants were considered less "desirable" than the "old." Whereas the "old" migration had been predominately Protestant except for Irish Catholics and some German Catholics, an overwhelming percentage of the new immigrants were Catholic, Jewish, or Greek Orthodox in religion.

With the turn of the twentieth century, public sentiment in favor of restricting immigration became intense and widespread. The farmlands of the Midwest had all been homesteaded, and the settlement of the West and Southwest was well underway. The great railroads had been built, and great industries were flourishing. The "new" migration flowed into the large cities, where ethnic islands emerged. Within these separate neighborhoods and communities, native languages and customs were kept alive.

With the influx of the large-scale immigration from Eastern and Southern Europe and a marked increase in ethnic antipathies, Congress in 1907 authorized an immigration commission to make "full inquiry, examination, and investigation of immigration." Clearly, the United States was moving in the direction of a policy aimed at regulating and restricting immigration. As early as 1882, Congress had enacted a law prohibiting the Chinese from entry, save for a small group of scholars, ministers, and merchants. In the same year, legislation was also passed excluding paupers, criminals, "lunatics," and other undesirables, and imposing a head tax. In 1884, contract labor was outlawed; in 1903, insane persons, beggars, and anarchists were added to the exclusion lists; between 1907 and 1910, new types of mental "defectives" and persons involved in crimes of "moral turpitude" were included; and in 1917, a literacy test was added. The inflow of Japanese was curtailed in 1907 by an agreement between Japan and the United States.

Numerical Restriction of Immigration. Following World War I there occurred an upsurge in American isolationist sentiment, a wave of antipathy for immigrants and foreigners, and a mass fear of aliens as "Reds" and "radicals." Within this context Congress was finally persuaded to take direct action toward the numerical restriction of immigration, the result being the Emergency Quota Act of 1921. The purpose of the act was to curtail the total volume of immigration and to favor migrants from Western and Northern Europe. It provided for a quota system under which each nation was allocated an annual immigration allowance equal to 3 percent of the number of its foreign-born in the United States as reported by the 1910 census. As the quotas of 1921 still gave to the nations of the "new" migration a large share of the persons to be admitted each year, the law was revised in 1924. The Immigration Act of 1924, established a new formula for computing a country's quota, based on 2 percent of the number of people born in that country who were residing in the United States in 1890. In 1890 the flow of "new" immigrants had not been large enough to build up a large foreign-born population of Southern- and Eastern-European origin. The 1924 act also provided that beginning July 1, 1929, the quota of any country would have the same ratio to 150,000 as the number of persons of that national origin living in the United States had to the total population living in the United States, as determined by the 1920 census. Under the quota system, an estimated 84 percent of the quotas went to Northern and Western Europe and only 14 percent to Southern and Eastern Europe. The act of 1924 also barred Orientals from migrating to the United States. However, these restrictions were largely removed during World War II, and under the act of 1952 Orientals were assigned a token quota.

Post-World War II Legislation. A more recent step in legislation was the passage of the Immigration and Nationality (McCarran-Walter) Act of 1952. The act simplified the national-origins formula of the 1924 act by basing the annual quota on a flat ⅙ percent of the population according to the 1920 census. By presidential action, new quotas were established in 1953 for each quota area, totaling 154,657. These quotas were then periodically revised. Congress also passed a number of acts relating to the admission of displaced persons and refugees. The Displaced Persons Act of 1948 authorized the entry of certain displaced persons and refugees, without regard to the availability of quotas, but subject to charges against future quotas. The act expired in 1952, but in 1953 Congress authorized the issuance of 214,000 special nonquota visas until the end of 1956 to refugees from Communist-dominated nations. Similarly, special legislation was enacted in 1958 that permitted Hungarian refugees from the abortive 1956 revolution to enter the United States. It is important to note that the quota system actually provides only one-third of the yearly immigration into the United States. These supplementary laws have authorized the entry of hundreds of thousands of displaced persons, political refugees, and others without regard to the quota system. In addition, Congress yearly approves thousands of individual "private" laws to permit the entry and naturalization of named individuals.

Recent Legislation.   Critics have charged that U.S. immigration laws judge persons by race and place of birth rather than personal worth to society. In response to this criticism Congress enacted the Hart-Celler Act in 1965, which provided for the abolishment of the old national-origins quota system after June 30, 1968. It raised the ceiling on total annual immigration to 290,000 people. The countries of the Western Hemisphere had 120,000 visas available annually without limit for any one country. The Eastern Hemisphere had 170,000 visas, of which no one nation could use more than 20,000. This was the first time that a restriction had been placed on immigration from Canada and Latin America. The new legislation gave preference to applicants chiefly on the basis of (1) family ties to Americans and (2) occupational skills in short supply in the United States. Whereas the Statue of Liberty bears the inscription "Give me your tired, your poor, your huddled masses yearning to breathe," the pattern fostered by the new legislation was "Give me primarily your skilled workers and trained professionals."

The absence of preferential treatment for the nations of the Western Hemisphere resulted in considerable complaint. Some immigrants wishing to join relatives who had already immigrated had to wait a number of years before they were eligible for admission. Consequently, the Western Hemisphere Act of 1976, which distributed preferences equally to Eastern and Western Hemisphere nations, was passed. Further, Western Hemisphere immigrants with family ties or special skills were given priority over other immigrants. The 20,000-visa limit for nations in the Eastern Hemisphere was also made applicable to the West (*see* Table 10.1).

The "Melting Pot" Orientation

Americans are by no means unanimous in their conception of how assimilation may "best" proceed or what constitutes the most "desirable" immigration policy. Prior to World War I, the "melting pot"

TABLE 10.1 CHIEF BIRTHPLACES OF IMMIGRANTS

1969	Number	1979	Number
1. Mexico	44,623	1. Mexico	52,096
2. Italy	23,617	2. Philippines	41,300
3. Philippines	20,744	3. South Korea	29,248
4. Canada	18,582	4. China, Taiwan	24,264
5. Greece	17,724	5. Vietnam	22,546
6. Jamaica	16,947	6. Jamaica	19,714
7. Portugal	16,528	7. India	19,708
8. China, Taiwan	15,440	8. Dominican Republic	17,519
9. Britain	15,014	9. Cuba	15,585
10. Cuba	13,751	10. Britain	13,907

Source: U.S. Immigration and Naturalization Service

notion achieved considerable popularity, and it still enjoys currency in some quarters. According to this view, the multitude of whites from various European nations (blacks and Asians were not included) would fuse together within America, producing a new people and a new civilization—a people and a civilization that would achieve unparalleled glory in the annals of human history. Israel Zangwill (1921:33), a proponent of this thinking, declared with considerable enthusiasm:

> America is God's Crucible, the great Melting Pot where all the races of Europe are melting and reforming!—Here you stand good folk, think I, when I see you at Ellis Island, here you stand, in your fifty groups, with your fifty languages and histories, and your fifty hatreds and rivalries. But you won't be long like that, brothers, for these are the fires of God you come to—these are the fires of God. . . . Germans and Frenchmen, Irishmen and English, Jews and Russians, into the Crucible with you all! God is making the American! . . . The real American has not yet arrived. . . . He will be the fusion of all races, perhaps the coming superman. . . . Ah, Vera, what is the glory of Rome and Jerusalem, where all races and nations come to worship and look back, compared with the glory of America. . . .

Following World War I, the "melting pot" theory lost favor. There developed a growing awareness of the persistence of the cultural traits that the immigrants brought with them. For many native Americans, the great "crucible" of assimilation, the "melting pot," was not working fast enough. Initially, Northern Europeans had heavily predominated among the immigrants to the United States, peoples whose cultures were quite similar to that of the earlier settlers. But, by the turn of the twentieth century, the tide had shifted—migrants from Southern and Eastern Europe predominated. Native-born Americans were inclined to view the new arrivals as "different," in some respects even as "unassimilable." This sentiment was coupled with a postwar intensification of the fear of aliens and an abject terror after the Bolshevik Revolution of the alien as a "radical" and "Red." As pointed out above, a host of passions, prides, and prejudices surged to the foreground, and in 1921 Congress responded by passing the Emergency Quota Act of 1921 and later the Immigration Act of 1924.

The "Americanization" Orientation

Within the context of the post-World War I situation, the "Americanization" movement gained momentum. Whereas the "melting pot" theory had viewed the United States as evolving a new cultural way of life through a fusion of European cultures, the "Americanization" viewpoint saw American culture as an essentially finished product on the Anglo-Saxon pattern. It insisted that the immigrants promptly give up their cultural traits and take over those of the dominant American group. Differences were not to be long tolerated. Public schools, patriotic societies, and business organizations turned their attention to "Americanizing" the immigrants. All evidences of foreign heritage were to be quickly stamped out—aliens were to cease being "aliens" and to become "Americans." Other cultures were seen as "foreign"— as "peculiar," "inferior," and "a source of trouble."

The "Americanization" notion found its reflection in academic circles and was popularized by the sociologist Henry Pratt Fairchild. Fairchild (1925, 1947) viewed assimilation as similar to the physiological process whereby an organism secures nourishment. Foodstuffs are consumed by the organism. Ultimately the ingested food becomes an integral part of the physical organism and in this sense is assimilated. Fairchild (1947:109–112) saw the process as a one-way street in which no reciprocal exchange occurs; between human cultures, as between the body and food, no blending of consequence occurs: ". . . it appears that in social assimilation, as in physiological, . . . the receiving body sets the pattern. . . . And the process of assimilation does require that all foreigners . . . must be adapted to fit into an integrated whole without friction or disturbance."

The Theory of "Cultural Pluralism"

Adherents of both the "melting pot" and "Americanization" concepts look toward the evolution of a single cultural system. The former thinks that this can be achieved through "melting down" the immigrants and natives into a common whole; the latter, through divesting the immigrants of their "foreign ways" and remaking them into Anglicized Americans. Opposed to these notions is "cultural pluralism," a view that has won considerable favor since World War II among sociologists, demographers, and social scientists generally. It seeks uniformity through immigrant conformity in those areas where this is felt to be necessary to the national well-being. Yet simultaneously it permits immigrants to maintain their own cultural traits in other areas that are felt to be less essential. It implies an imperfect fusion of a number of diverse cultural ingredients within the framework of the larger society (Borrie, 1959). Through time many of the foreign-born, as well as succeeding generations, would come to share increasingly in the common core of American life, while simultaneously retaining certain cultural characteristics of their own groups. The retention of various religious preferences constitutes the classic example of this type of phenomenon. In brief, pluralism involves a continuation of the minority as a distinct unit within the larger society.

The proponents of this viewpoint suggest that cultural traits are quite persistent. This persistence, they argue, is an inescapable reality. In fact, to attack group values—to undertake their suppression—is likely to strengthen them. In addition, a number of advantages may flow from a cultural pluralistic approach. First, immigrants' retention of many of the traits of their original culture may constitute a stabilizing link between their old way of life and the new. Second, it avoids some of the dangers of social and personal disorganization that may follow from forcing immigrants into a world that they do not understand and that oversimplifies the complexities of American society. Cultural pluralism, then, enables the immigrant to incorporate elements of the American culture at a pace that muffles and makes bearable the shock of cultural collision. Third, ethnic groups that cut across other social groups—the most important of which are social classes—are an important factor in the maintenance of social solidarity and in the avoidance of class consciousness and class conflict. The pluralistic nature of American society functions to provide various sources for the consolidation of competing centers of power, a condition vital to the maintenance of the democratic process. Where there is a maximum concentration of power in one institution, for example, the monolithic totalitarian state, there is a minimum degree of freedom. Where there are competing groups, institutions, and voluntary associations—competing centers of power— democracy can flourish. Thus America's diversity in ethnic groups may contribute to the maintenance of the American democratic order.

Cultural pluralists put less emphasis than do proponents of the other viewpoints on conformity in all social and cultural areas. They would accept cultural differences between immigrants and native-born Americans in certain areas and would insist on the right of groups and individuals to be different so long as the differences do not lead to national disunity. The adjustment between the groups is viewed not as a one-way street but as a reciprocal process in which the immigrant stock and the native-born Americans would each integrate with the other. This orientation differs from the "melting pot" approach in its inclusion of non-European cultures in the process and in its willingness to tolerate—in fact, to welcome—differences through an extended period.

SUMMARY

1. Some social and cultural processes lead to greater similarity or homogeneity among groups—assimilation. Other processes sustain or produce diversity or heterogeneity among groups—pluralism. Sociologists distinguish between culture and social structure. Culture has to do with the customs of a people. Social structure involves the relatively stable interpersonal relationships that emerge among the people practicing the customs. Sociologists carry over the distinction between culture and social structure to the study of assimilation. They distinguish between cultural assimilation (acculturation) and social assimilation (integration).

2. Acculturation is set in motion as people with differing traditions come together in such a way that they take into account the behavior of the other group. Acculturation occurs in a number of forms. One form is intercultural transmission—the diffusion of elements or parts of culture from one group to another. Another form of acculturation is cultural creativity—the production of new or merged elements of culture. Still another form is cultural disintegration—cultural contact overtaxes an existing arrangement.

3. Integration entails alterations in the relationships among people. It involves the fusion of groups in the sense that social interaction is no longer predicated upon one's racial or ethnic identity. The descendants of the former minority group and the former dominant group no longer make "dominant-minority" group distinctions. Individuals thus find their place within the community without reference to ethnic or racial origins.

4. Institutional duplication is characteristic of a society containing differing cultures. The society is compartmentalized into quasi-independent units, each of which has a set of homologous institutions and limited points of contact with the other units. Put still another way, where there is cultural pluralism, there is also social pluralism. Acculturation is thus a necessary precondition to integration. The reverse proposition, however, does not hold. Acculturation can occur in the absence of integration.

5. The rate of a group's assimilation within American society is a function of many factors. These factors include the difference between the host and the immigrant cultures, the size of the incoming group, the rapidness of entry, the dispersion of the incoming group, the social status of the immigrants, the predisposition of both groups to change, the degree of economic competition between the groups, and the proximity of the immigrant group to its homeland.

6. Individuals often find the process of assimilation turbulent, stressful, and emotionally disruptive. Park has called attention to the individ-

ual who is torn between the conflicting demands of two cultural traditions. Marginal persons are individuals caught in the conflict of cultures, people who live in two worlds, yet actually belong to none.

7. While the notion of marginal persons is useful for analyzing the adjustment of some individuals, it fails to encompass another type of adaptation in which individuals shuttle between social and cultural worlds. Some Blackfeet Indians live in both Indian and white worlds, yet they are not marginal individuals. In the one world they act one way; in the other world still another way. They are able to compartmentalize their lives and commute between the two worlds.

8. Park suggested that, whenever and wherever different racial and ethnic groups continuously meet, they inevitably pass through a series of irreversible states: The groups come into contact; invariably contact produces competition; from this competition some kind of adjustment or accommodation is realized; and, finally, there is assimilation. Park's natural-history model has been criticized, particularly for his assumption that there is an inevitable and irreversible unilinear progression toward assimilation among differing groups.

9. One of the most notable changes within the United States since the 1960s has been the renewed interest in ethnicity. Some observers have termed it an "ethnic revival." Some question exists, however, as to the depth of the ethnic revival and commitment. Other sociologists take the opposite position and argue that the extent of assimilation has been overestimated. Still others have interpreted the ethnic revival as a defensive political protest.

10. There are two sociological schools of thought with respect to the experience of blacks and Hispanics in the United States. The one position argues that blacks and Hispanics are like European immigrant groups and that in due course they too will become assimilated. The other claims that blacks and Hispanics are like Third World colonized groups and are victims of special oppression and exploitation.

11. Intergroup marriage represents an important means through which both assimilation and racial amalgamation are realized. In the United States, marriage between peoples of different nationality groups is a frequent occurrence; interreligious marriage is somewhat less common; while interracial marriage is infrequent. Intergroup marriage is on the increase within the United States.

12. Americans have both encouraged and discouraged the flow of newcomers to the United States. The year 1882 represents a turning point in the history of American immigration. It marked the climax of the movement of migrants from Northern and Western Europe to the United States and the beginning of the large-scale movement of migrants from Southern and Eastern Europe. It also inaugurated the beginning of federal control of immigration. Following World War I there

occurred an upsurge in American opposition to various immigrant groups, and Congress responded by the passage of restrictive legislation. The old national-origins quota system was abandoned in 1968.

13. Americans are by no means unanimous in their concept of how assimilation may "best" proceed or what constitutes the most "desirable" immigration policy. Prior to World War I, the melting pot notion achieved considerable popularity. According to this view, the multitude of whites from various European nations would fuse together within the United States, producing a new people and a new civilization.

14. The Americanization orientation differs from that of the melting pot. Whereas the melting pot approach views the United States as evolving a new cultural way of life through the fusion of European cultures, the Americanization viewpoint sees American culture as an essentially finished product based on the Anglo-Saxon pattern. It insists that the immigrants promptly give up their cultural traits and take over those of the dominant American group.

15. Adherents of both the melting pot and Americanization concepts look toward the evolution of a single cultural system. The former thinks this can be achieved through "melting down" the immigrants and host population into a common whole; the latter, through divesting the immigrants of their "foreign ways" and remaking them into Anglicized Americans. Opposed to these notions is that of cultural pluralism. It seeks uniformity through immigrant conformity in those areas where this is felt to be necessary to the national well-being. Yet simultaneously it permits immigrants to maintain their own cultural traits in other areas that are felt to be less essential.

GLOSSARY

Absorption   The immigrant's ability to secure and sustain economic employment within the new country.

Acculturation   The process whereby people with divergent customs come to share common modes of action, norms, language, and dress.

Amalgamation   The biological fusion of differing "racial" and "subracial" groups.

Assimilation   Those processes whereby groups with distinctive identities become culturally and socially fused together.

Integration   The process whereby people with divergent institutions (social structures) become fused within a common institutional life.

Marginal Persons   People "whom fate has condemned to live in two societies and in two, not merely different but antagonistic, cultures."

Naturalization The acquisition of legal citizenship.

Pluralism Those processes whereby groups evolve or maintain their distinctive identities, neither culturally nor socially fusing together.

Social Structure A configuration in which different categories of people are bound together within a network of relationships.

Symbolic Ethnicity A nostalgic search for an exotic tradition that can occasionally be savored in a museum or at an ethnic festival.

IV

Minority Reactions to Dominance

Responding by Acceptance

*H*ow do minority group members think and feel about their subordinate status? How do they react to segregation, discrimination, disadvantaged conditions, and disparagement? What are their sentiments toward members of the dominant group? The answers to these questions are by no means simple. Any number of sociologists and anthropologists have attempted to classify minority reactions to dominance (Johnson, 1943; Davie, 1949; Noel, 1969). Yet none of these classificatory efforts has been entirely satisfactory. From these various approaches, however, we can identify four common patterns of reaction to dominance:

1. **Acceptance.** Minority-group members may come to acquiesce in—to accommodate themselves to—their disadvantaged and subordinate status.

2. **Aggression.** Minority-group members may respond to dominance by striking out against—engaging in hostile acts against— a status that is subordinate and disadvantaged.

3. **Avoidance.** Minority-group members may attempt to shun—to escape from—situations in which they are likely to experience prejudice and discrimination.

4. **Assimilation.** Minority-group members may attempt to become socially and culturally fused with the dominant group.

We may view avoidance and assimilation as opposites, each constituting a pole on a continuum (Noel, 1969). Each pole establishes an "outer

Avoidance	Assimilation

limit" or standard between which transitional or intermediate reactions can be located. Confronted with a potential intergroup situation, mi-

311

nority individuals may either avoid contact with the dominant group or merge themselves socially and culturally with it. The continuum reflects the fact that there are different degrees of avoidance and assimilation. A specific reaction is distributed somewhere along the continuum, depending on the degree to which it constitutes avoiding or assimilating tendencies.

Similarly, we may view acceptance and aggression as opposites, each constituting a pole on a continuum. Confronted with an intergroup situation—with contact with dominant-group members— minority individuals may either acquiesce in their disadvantaged and subordinate status or strike out against it.

These two continua pose choices that confront minority-group individuals within an intergroup situation (Noel, 1969). First, they must allow intergroup contact to take place or they must avoid (or, at least, minimize) such contact. Second, once in the contact situation, they must acquiesce in their subordinate status or strike out against it. In some situations, however, one or both decisions may remain latent. Hence, if a minority undertakes to assimilate and succeeds, it need not choose between aggression and acceptance; conversely, where contact is unavoidable and the dominant group imposes inequality, the minority's only choice revolves about the aggression-acceptance dimension.

Minorities never follow one pattern of response exclusively. Intergroup relations are much too complex for any one pattern to be always operative. Rather, at times one pattern may come into play, at other times another, and frequently some combination of responses may predominate. In this latter regard, based upon our two continua, we can identify four mixed response patterns: acceptance-avoidance, acceptance-assimilation, aggression-avoidance, and aggression-assimilation:

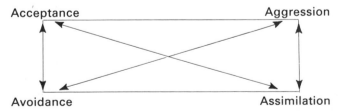

To gain a clear picture of minority reactions to dominance, we shall devote one chapter each to acceptance, aggression, avoidance, and assimilation. In this chapter we shall be concerned with acceptance.

Expressions of Acceptance

Acceptance involves the renunciation of protest against the circumstances of minority status and the organization of responses so that instead accommodation appears. Daily life requires that humans accommodate themselves to various unpleasant situations. It is necessary to accept, and make the best of, disagreeable aspects of work, disagreeable traits in associates, disagreeable elements in the weather, and disagreeable facts of disease and death, in fact all the aspects of life that are limiting. Thus acceptance is not an adaptive mechanism found exclusively among minority peoples. However, they may be required to employ it to an unusual degree. Here we shall examine some of the more typical manifestations of acceptance as it is reflected in minority-group adjustment to dominance. We shall draw heavily upon the work of two distinguished black sociologists, E. Franklin Frazier and Charles S. Johnson, who independently studied the circumstances of blacks during the pre-World War II period.

Resignation

Some minority-group members feel that the wisest course is to accept what cannot be changed or avoided: "You don't like it, but what can you do?" Although minority-group status may be disliked, there is a conscious resignation to it or a sense of futility about changing one's lot. The minority-group members accept their fate out of a feeling that there is nothing else to do. And some people feel that resignation reduces the wear and tear on their personalities.

This response was a common pattern of survival for blacks during slavery and continues to be followed by some, especially the older generation. A black lower-class woman with six children said she instructed her children as her mother had instructed her: "When white folks don't treat you right, don't try to hit back. The Negro is weak— that what he is, and the white man is power. Vengeance is mine, says the Lord, and we gotta leave to Him to vengeance us. We are the underdogs" (Frazier, 1940:49). These attitudes are rooted in the black experience of the rural hinterlands of Georgia, Alabama, and Mississippi and are increasingly anachronistic in the urban centers to which blacks have migrated in large numbers during the past seventy years (Aberbach and Walker, 1973).

The Case of the Rural South:
1865 to 1955

Within the rural areas of the South a social system of white dominance and black subordination survived the Civil War and the abolition of slavery. In this arrangement there was little room for blacks as large landowners or professionals. For the most part, a black tenant population predominated, dependent upon white owners and planters. Farming was often carried on in large-scale units, plantations, that were subdivided into smaller units worked by tenants. The system operated in such a manner as to control practically the entire life of the families living within it. Work was seasonal and highly dependent upon such externally controlled factors as flood, drought, pests, and market prices. During the year, tenants were advanced credit by the landlords for living needs. By virtue of costly credit advances, low returns on labor, and dishonest bookkeeping, tenants realized little if anything in the way of a cash surplus. Following World War II, with the shift of southern agriculture from cotton to other crops, the large-scale introduction of cattle, the mechanization of agriculture, the un-willingness of landlords to share federal subsidy payments with tenants, the purging of blacks who registered and voted—factors that were coupled with the increasing attraction of northern cities—blacks left the rural South in large numbers. Today the sharecropping system is largely dead. Some of the older sharecroppers still farm, but as day laborers. Others now depend on welfare and rent the shacks that dot the farm areas of the South.

The tenants under the sharecropping system had no stake in the land and no voice in determining what or how much would be planted or when and where the crop would be sold. By virtue of their position, the tenants were dependent upon the white landlords. As a result of this dependence and the southern racial structure of white dominance, the landlord could exercise considerable control over the lives of the black tenants. Such control—reinforced by lynchings, harassment, and ex-tralegal violence—constituted a potent weapon in the hands of whites seeking to cope with any militant sentiment among tenants. Even as late as 1957, at the time of the Little Rock school desegregation disorders, a white Arkansas plantation manager pointed to the role of black dependence when asked if blacks on his plantation might seek integration: "I can take care of things out here. It gets down to this—in winter time, when the groceries run out, they come to me."

Poverty prevailed among the black tenants to a degree equal to, if not greater than, almost any other segment of the American population (Native Americans being another blatant case). The houses were usually unpainted, small frame units of the "shotgun" type, typically resting on stones at each of the four corners. Underneath the house, a hound or two, a half-dozen chickens, and a few pigs not uncommonly found a sheltered place. Many of the houses were not equipped with glass windows; instead rough wooden shutters served as window coverings. The privy was standard equipment.

Where education was minimal and where there was little communi-cation with the "outside" world, traditional patterns of accommodation tended to prevail. Within the isolated, paternalistic, and oppressive context of the rural South, blacks went about their daily lives. Resisting their poverty only when it became acute, they developed a subculture with its own values and satisfactions, and adjusted to life and the racial system as they found it. In this setting, the racial situation was usually discussed in terms of personal relationships with "good" or "bad" landlords. A typical response encountered by Johnson (1943: 245) was "We get along fine with our white folks—but the poor whites make a lot of trouble."

Among rural blacks there was widespread unfamiliarity with developments in the antisegregation movement. In the contemporary world —where militancy is commonplace—it is often difficult to comprehend the devastating impact of a repressive, exploitative social order upon a subject people. Reverend Martin Luther King, Jr. (1958: 29) clearly noted this when he observed:

> Their minds and souls were so conditioned to the system of segregation that they submissively adjusted themselves to things as they were. This is the ultimate tragedy of segregation. It not only harms one physically but injures one spiritually. It sears the soul and degrades the personality.

Within the setting of the sharecropping South, a black explains how he instructed his son:

> When I goes to a white man's house I stands in the yard and yells, and he comes to the door. If he tells me to come then I goes up to the door to talk to him, and I don't go in unless he tell me. If he tell me, then I goes in, but I don't set down lessen he tell me. And I don't talk to white folks direct like I does to colored. I lets him do the talking, let him take the lead. That's what he wants, and if he says something to me that I don't like, I says, "Now, Mr. ———, don't you think I oughta do such and such a thing," and then mos' likely he say "yes," but you better not go straight at the thing with a white man, he'll think you're smart. Yes, suh, I tells my chillen to do lak that. That's the way to get along (Johnson, 1943: 247).

The civil-rights movement among blacks during the 1950s and 1960s did not typically stem from blacks in the rural communities. Relatively isolated on the plantations through cultural and educational factors, and intimidated by the dominant whites, they were generally removed from the mainstream of integrationist efforts. This outcome is not untypical. It is difficult to organize masses at the very lowest socioeconomic rungs of the society. It is among the urban and the more advantaged blacks that the integrationist appeal found its initial and greatest reception. College students in particular, propelled into the mainstream of American life and into currents of social mobility, were often in the forefront of such endeavors. On the other hand, rural blacks typically accommodated themselves to the prevalent racial and class structure or migrated from the countryside (Pinard et al., 1969).

Black Religion: Opiate or Inspiration?

Religion is often depicted as a preoccupation with otherworldly concerns and thus as an institution that draws people's attention away from the problems of the world. Viewed from this perspective, religious organizations do not attempt to change social conditions but to make them more bearable. It was this presumed aspect of the church that lead Karl Marx to comment in 1844 that religion is the "opium of the people." He believed that religion is a tool by which a ruling class keeps the oppressed in check by offering them salvation in the next world in return for subservience in this world.

The historian Kenneth Stampp (1956:158) says that most slaveowners viewed supervised religion as an effective means of controlling blacks:

> ... through religious instruction the bondsmen learned that slavery had divine sanction, that insolence was as much an offense against God as against the temporal master. They received the Biblical command that servants should obey their masters, and they heard of the punishments awaiting the disobedient slave in the hereafter. They heard, too, that eternal salvation would be their reward for faithful service. . . .

Many sociologists have also portrayed religion as a vehicle by which blacks sublimated their frustration into emotionalism and fixed their hopes on the afterworld (Johnson, 1941; Myrdal, 1944; Dollard, 1957).

Yet, as the sociologist Gary T. Marx (1967) points out, the effect of religion on racial protest has by no means been only in one direction. Although many blacks did turn to religion as a solace during slavery, black preachers such as Denmark Vesey and Nat Turner (leaders of slave revolts) and the religiously inspired abolitionists actively fought slavery. Black churches served as meeting places where protest strategy was planned and as stations on the underground railroad. And black spirituals and sermons were rich in protest symbolism.

More recently, black religion made a significant contribution to the mobilization of the civil-rights movement, which was identified with the leadership of Reverend Martin Luther King, Jr. Participation in the church of one of the established black denominations, especially those that emphasized black activism, increased militancy (Nelsen et al., 1975; Hunt and Hunt, 1977). In contrast, where membership was in a sectlike religious group, militancy was less likely. Thus black religion has produced both activism and quietism. Indeed, some have argued that had there been no black church, there would not have been a civil-rights movement in the 1960s. Many of the established black denominations functioned as "spearheads of reform" (Marx, 1967). Likewise, the anthropologist Bryan R. Wilson (1973) finds that religious movements have often had a strong protest theme among tribal and Third World peoples, including the Delaware Prophet movement (associated with the Pontiac Indian uprising), the Ghost Dances of 1870 and 1890 (among Pacific Coast and Plains Indians), and the Mau Mau (an anticolonial movement in Kenya during the 1950s).

Vested Interests in Minority Status

In his studies of the black middle class during the 1920s and 1930s, Frazier (1951) found that a sizeable proportion of upper- and middle-class blacks had secured their positions by virtue of racially separate institutions. Behind the walls of segregation that barred blacks from full participation in American life, institutions duplicating those in the white community had grown up. These institutions, largely the product of segregation, were believed to be imperiled by full-scale desegregation.

Prior to the Supreme Court's 1954 ruling in *Brown* v. *Board of Education* outlawing mandatory school segregation, the existence of a dual school system in the South gave black educators an exclusive monopoly in the education of black children and guaranteed them positions that since have often been endangered by desegregation. Likewise, many black entertainers benefited from whites who stereotyped blacks as being unusually rhythmic and accordingly demand their services. Owing to their vested interests, some blacks were placed in an ambivalent position with regard to segregation. On the one hand, they were anxious to do away with their disadvantaged minority status. On the other hand, they realized that success in the battle against segregation would wipe out certain of the benefits that they derived from it.

Some black institutions, such as the separate church, have a long history. The segregated church has provided a field in which black leaders could realize social and economic security. Many black pastors feel a vested interest in ministering to the spiritual needs of blacks. Consequently, some have been resistant to even moderate proposals to foster church integration. Frazier (1951: 334) cites an illustration:

> . . . it was suggested in a midwestern city that as a means of breaking down segregation in churches, a white church might take on an assistant Negro minister. The suggestion was immediately opposed by the Negro ministers in the city. Seemingly, they feared that if the plan were carried out members of the segregated Negro churches would be drawn away, into the white church.

A number of studies undertaken in the 1960s reveal that many black professionals experienced ambivalent feelings toward various aspects of desegregation. For instance, some black physicians preferred to take advantage of a segregated practice and to have a primarily black clientele (Back and Simpson, 1964). Indeed, some advocated separate hospitals on grounds that in them they would have more opportunities to develop their skills and to serve their "own people." Similarly, David H. Howard (1966), in a study of 100 male black physicians, dentists, lawyers, and public-school teachers, found uncertainty among them toward open competition with whites. While the professionals generally preferred the idea of open competition, they were hardly enthusiastic about it.

Frazier (1951, 1957) describes the class structure that arose in segregated black communities during the first half of the twentieth century as the product of discrimination against blacks in employment and the isolation of blacks from mainstream society. Consequently, occupations and incomes in the black community did not have the same relation to social status as they did in the white community. Blacks whose jobs and resources would have placed them in the middle class or even the lower-middle class in the white community often found themselves in the upper class in the social pyramid of the black community. Within the black communities prior to the 1960s, many black professionals and white-collar workers were able to assume an upper-class style of life.

Desegregation has had particular consequences for small black businesses. Take Birmingham, Alabama (Stuart, 1981). During the 1950s, before segregation laws were invalidated and black shoppers were welcomed in downtown stores, the black business district anchored by Fourth Avenue and Eighteenth Street was flourishing. There were dozens of small service shops, four movie theaters, and several restaurants and small hotels. Today the area consists of abandoned storefronts, cleared lots, boarded buildings, and only a few businesses. There are fewer than 500 black-owned businesses operating in Birmingham as against more than 1,000 during the late 1950s. The story is not too different elsewhere in the nation. The surviving enterprises have been primarily small banks and insurance companies catering to a black clientele. Joining these surviving institutions have been a number of new generation black-owned businesses, including automobile dealerships and a few companies that market goods and services whose appeal reaches to the purchasing agents of large corporations.

The ambivalent position that many middle- and upper-class blacks found themselves in with respect to desegregation is part of a more general problem of minority-group leadership. The social psychologist Kurt Lewin (1948), in his observations about Jews, noted the weakness of "leadership from the periphery." He was referring to leadership from minority-group members who are economically successful and who gain a degree of acceptance by the dominant group. These upper-class minority members can protect themselves to a certain extent from discrimination and prejudice. For example, they can often afford good housing and avoid slum living. Their incomes are relatively high, enabling them to avoid discrimination in employment. They enjoy material comforts, prestige, and security. And they are commonly sheltered from harsh day-to-day contact with members of the dominant group. Such individuals are frequently called upon for leadership by the minority group because of their status and power. But under these circumstances the minority is led by leaders who are lukewarm toward the group, who may, under a thin cover of loyalty, be fundamentally eager to leave it. Minority upper-class leaders often seek to soft-pedal any action that arouses the antagonism of the dominant group.

Displacement of Accommodating Leadership

The changes in American life following on the heels of the desegregation decision of the Supreme Court in 1954 contributed to new patterns of black leadership. High Court decisions withdrew legal support from the traditional framework of segregation and gave impetus to various civil-rights movements. Prior to these decisions, black leadership within the South was predominantly of the "accommodating" or "compromise" type. These compromise leaders held their position primarily because they were acceptable to white leaders. Blacks tended to go along with the leaders because accommodation appeared to be the most practical and effective type of adjustment within a setting where segregation had legal and extralegal sanction (Killian and Smith, 1960).

Booker T. Washington (1856–1915) enjoys a preeminent position among accommodating black leaders. Washington, president of Tuskegee Institute, gained instantaneous and nationwide recognition following his espousal in 1895 of a doctrine that came to be known as the "Atlanta Compromise." In a speech that year at the opening of the Atlanta Cotton States and International Exposition, Washington set forth the following position:"In all things that are purely social we can be as separate as the five fingers [in brief, segregated], yet one as the hand in all things essential to mutual progress." It was a doctrine that called upon blacks to make their peace with a segregated social order. As the noted historian C. Vann Woodward (1951:356) observes:

> It was a time when the hope born of Reconstruction had all but died for the Negro, when disfranchisement blocked his political advance and the caste system closed the door to integration in the white world, when the North had abandoned him to the South and the South was yielding to the clamor of her extremists.

Yet it would be a mistake to characterize Washington as an all-out accommodating leader. He never relinquished the right to full equality as an ultimate goal. However, for the time being he gave up on social and political equality and soft-pedaled the protest against inequalities in justice. He was quite willing to flatter southern whites *if* blacks were allowed to work undisturbed with their white friends for education and business. But in both fields he accepted the white doctrine of the blacks' "place." In education he pleaded for vocational training, a position that comforted whites in their beliefs about where blacks should be held in the occupation hierarchy. Washington believed that through patience, thrift, skill, industry, and good morals blacks would gradually improve their economic circumstances so much that, at a later stage, a discussion of equal rights could be taken up (Myrdal, 1944).

Although Washington achieved a position of national fame by virtue of the acclaim afforded him by whites, we should not overlook a long line of black protest leaders—the leaders of local slave insurrections (Gabriel Prosser, Denmark Vesey, Nat Turner, and others); black abolitionists (Sojourner Truth, Henry Highland Garnet, David Ruggles, Harriet Tubman, Frederick Douglass, and many others); and twentieth-century militants. (W.E.B. DuBois, Stokely Carmichael, H. Rap Brown, Eldridge Cleaver, and others). Frederick Douglas (1817–1895) is a case in point. He was an outstanding black abolitionist and one of this nation's best known orators—indeed, few antislavery leaders did so much to carry the case of the slave to the people of the United States and Europe (Franklin, 1952). In 1903, Kelly Miller contrasted the leadership afforded by Douglass and Washington for the readers of the *Boston Evening Transcript* (September 18 and 19, 1903):

> The two men are in part products of their times, but are also natural antipodes. Douglass lived in the day of moral giants; Washington in the era of merchant princes. The contemporaries of Douglass emphasized the rights of man; those of Washington his productive capacity. The age of Douglass acknowledged the sanction of the Golden Rule; that of Washington worships the Rule of Gold. The equality of men was constantly dinned into Douglass's ears; Washington hears nothing but the inferiority of the Negro and the dominance of the Saxon. Douglass could hardly receive a hearing today; Washington would have been hooted off the stage a generation ago. Thus all truly useful men must be, in a measure, timeservers; for unless they serve their time, they can scarcely serve at all. But great as was the diversity of formative influences that shaped these two great lives, there is no less opposability in their innate bias of souls. Douglass was like a lion, bold and fearless; Washington is lamblike, meek and submissive. Douglass escaped from personal bondage, which his soul abhorred; but for Lincoln's proclamation, Washington would probably have arisen to esteem and favor in the eyes of his master as a good and faithful servant. Douglass insisted upon rights; Washington upon duty. Douglass held up to public scorn the sins of the white man; Washington portrays the faults of his own race. Douglass spoke what he thought the world should hear; Washington only what he feels it is disposed to listen to. Douglass's conduct was actuated by principle; Washington's by prudence. Douglass had no limited, copyrighted programme for his race, but appealed to the decalogue, the golden rule, the declaration of independence, the constitution of the United States; Washington, holding these great principles in the shadowy background, presents a practical expedient applicable to

present needs. Douglass was a moralist, insisting upon the application of righteousness to public affairs; Washington is a practical statesman, accepting the best terms which he thinks it possible to secure.

The type of leader represented by Washington tended to dominate the black American scene during the first half of the twentieth century (with a few notable exceptions, including W.E.B. DuBois and Paul Robeson). Following 1954, militant black leaders, reflecting the protest motive instead of the theme of patience and accommodation, emerged on the southern horizon and gained considerable recognition. The late Reverend Martin Luther King, Jr., symbolized this new type of leadership. Whereas compromise leadership had typically operated in a noncontroversial and often clandestine manner, militant leadership has been characterized by its controversial, public, and activist techniques.

The sociologist Daniel C. Thompson (1963), in his study of black leadership in New Orleans during the early 1960s, distinguished between three types of black leaders:

1. *The Uncle Tom.* The most characteristic feature of Uncle Tom leaders is their acceptance of the subordinate status assigned blacks by white supremacists. They never make demands in terms of "black rights," but rather beg for favors. A New Orleans white lawyer describes one Uncle Tom leader whom he regards as a "great Negro leader": he came "hat in hand, stood at my desk, waiting for an invitation to be seated, as was his custom . . . as an humble, but great supplicant for the friendship of the white man for his race." Uncle Tom leaders have tended to stress to other blacks that they should "appreciate" what whites have done for "our people."

2. *The Racial Diplomat.* Unlike the Uncle Toms, the racial diplomat leaders do not accept segregation as right, but as effective diplomats, they display an astute understanding of the "ways of the South." They generally have a strong feeling of belonging in the local community and a keen sense of community pride. They identify with the problems of the total community and, as one racial diplomat put it, talk about the welfare of human beings, not just about "what is good for the Negro." They undertake to interpret the peculiar needs of blacks in terms of general community well-being.

3. *Race Man.* The race man provides militant leadership. Such leaders see the world through race-colored glasses and they give a racial interpretation to a good many community events. They harbor a good deal of bitterness toward whites and accommodating black leaders—in short, any who are able and qualified to help the black struggle but refuse to do so.

Within New Orleans and other American cities, blacks increasingly turned to militant black leaders as the 1960s unfolded. Harold W.

Pfautz and his colleagues (1975) have traced the changes that occurred in the black leadership of Providence, Rhode Island, during the 1960s and early 1970s. By the 1970s there had been a complete turnover in the black leadership from those who dominated the scene between 1939 and 1962. The new leaders are younger, more often local in origin, more likely to reside in the black working-class neighborhood, and more oriented toward the black community. This new generation of leaders has employed a considerably more militant style than did the previous generation.

The rise since the 1960s of black expectations, skills, and political power (based on black registration and voting), has made possible a black leadership whose effectiveness rests not on white support or tolerance, but on support within the black community. The new leadership is issue oriented, and the dominant issues are race and the economic circumstances of black people. The sociologist Everett C. Ladd, Jr. (1966:115), observes:

> The sharper the competition and the greater the estrangement, rejection, and isolation of the ethnic group in the political system, the more firmly will such leadership be identified with the interests of the ethnic group *as* ethnic group. The experience in the United States has been that as ethnic groups are accepted, they have increasingly few interests ethnically defined, and their leaders become differentiated by nonethnic considerations: they become Republican and Democratic leaders; upper-class, middle-class, and lower-class leaders; business, social welfare, labor, and intellectual leaders.

Ladd notes that blacks who are political leaders are *black* political leaders. But Paul J. King (1980:5), director of the National Association of Minority Contractors, disapproves of this pattern. He says:

> The notion of black leadership is an anachronism. It's just over. Black "leaders" should realize this. Those large institutions and Government should realize this.
>
> Now is the time to have leaders the way that white people have leaders, in particular areas—educators who are recognized (as experts), doctors to speak to health care. . . . Look at the white community. You have the A.F.L.-C.I.O. speaking for labor; and the national lawyers group with input on who becomes judges. Now, you can have ministers continuing to raise the moral issue. But there's got to be a way for a black who is in a position of so-called leadership to open the door and then turn it over to the specialist.

The Case of Evacuated West Coast Japanese

Soon after the American entry into World War II, the United States undertook to remove all Japanese residents from the three West Coast states. Between March 2 and June 8, 1942, some 100,000 Japanese were moved into ten temporary relocation centers in the West and Middle West. The mass evacuation was undertaken as a wartime measure in what was alleged to be the interest of national security. In the years intervening since this action, considerable controversy has stirred within the United States as to the wisdom, legitimacy, and fairness of the expulsion of the Japanese from their homes. The relocation centers were largely arranged in army camp style. The inmates—men, women, and children (both citizens and aliens)—were housed in barracks. The camps were surrounded by barbed wire.

An excellent study is available on the relocation center at Poston, Arizona, where nearly 10,000 of the evacuees were retained. Alexander H. Leighton (1945) discusses the reactions of the Japanese to the difficult and stressful situation they found themselves in there. He classifies these reactions as (1) cooperation, (2) withdrawal, and (3) aggressiveness. Here we are concerned with the cooperative and accommodative responses, although there were also strong overtones of withdrawal and aggressiveness.

Reactions to life in the camp were not the same for all the evacuees. One factor playing a major role in influencing their responses was their membership in the *Issei* and *Nisei* groups. The *Issei*s were first-generation immigrants who had come to the United States at about the turn of the century. They had not intended to make America their home but had hoped to acquire a little money and return to Japan. As a result they made no particular effort to learn English or to become part of the American community. Nevertheless, they did have contact with Americans through teachers of school-aged children, employers, and those ministers who took an interest in them. The *Issei*s were reluctant to give up their dream of returning to Japan, although they had gradually come to realize that its realization was unlikely. The war found them imbued with strong positive sentiments toward their native land, of which they still were legally citizens. Yet, by the same token, they had lived a good portion of their lives in the United States and were tied to the fortunes of this nation. In this dilemma, the *Issei*s wanted Japan to win the war but simultaneously wanted no harm to come to America.

The *Issei*s came to Poston feeling that their lives' work had been wasted; they experienced bitterness, apathy, and fear. They felt that American declarations about equal rights and equal opportunity were pure fiction. They tended to mistrust and misinterpret much of what the officials of the relocation center did and said. They were not in the least interested in building a model community within the center. Nevertheless, for the most part, they obeyed the rules of the camp. They adjusted themselves to life in Poston, more or less resigned to their fate. They assisted their neighbors with odd jobs to promote mutual comfort, but they withheld themselves from more active participation in hard work.

The *Nisei*s were the American-born and American-raised children of the *Issei*s. As such, they were American citizens. Many of them spoke Japanese as their first language, but, from the age of six, when they entered school, they had become increasingly assimilated within American life. Many had become Christians, while others who remained Buddhists took on many characteristics of American religious behavior. Despite social barriers, the *Niseis* had developed a fairly wide circle of American friends, and it was largely from these that they had acquired their goals and ideals, as well as their Americanized manners, language, and habits. In large measure they had grown away both from the customs of their parents and from their parents themselves.

Many of the *Niseis* came to the relocation center with burning feelings that "they can't do this to me!" They were quite bewildered and at sea as to what they should do and what to expect. They were not particularly troubled or concerned with the future of Japan. Rather their concerns revolved about a job, "three square meals," and what they would make of their lives. Although confused and suspicious, they still had faith in some American leaders. They came to the centers angry and discouraged, yet they were not without hope, "wanting to believe," "looking for a chance," and on the whole receptive to the ideas of community living entertained by the American officials. From among the *Niseis* came the active participants in community life.

On the whole, cooperation and accommodation were reflected among the evacuees in the development of self-government and liaison with the administration of the camp, in the maintenance of law and order, in obedience to regulations, in work on plans for community buildings, and, in short, in practically every aspect of daily living. Accommodation ranged from those who made outer and superficial adjustment to center life, making the best of a situation against which they internally rebelled, to those who, while preferring release from the camp, actively and willingly participated in the overall life of the camp. In addition, there were some instances of evacuees showing extreme dependence, and clinging to various American officials for support. Such evacuees were likely to agree to any proposal made by the American officials, even those that were ill advised, and would maintain that their food was satisfactory when by any normal standards it was inadequate.

Self-Conceptions

In order to enter into sustained social relationships with others, individuals must establish who they are. As discussed in chapter 4, people evolve identities in the course of social interaction. Probably no attitudes are more important than the attitudes people have about themselves. In everyday life people interact with others not so much on the basis of what they actually are but in terms of their conceptions of themselves and others. From the way others behave toward them, people discover the answers to the questions: "Who am I?" "What kind of person am I?" and "How valued am I?" A core aspect of personal identity has to do with our ethnic and racial membership.

Internalization of Accepting Attitudes

We have noted that some minority-group members *dislike* their disadvantaged status but become *resigned* to it. Others may go even further and *internalize* the attitudes associated with this status. They accept the existing order, neither questioning it nor doing anything about it. In essence they accept the dominant group's evaluation of themselves. They become indifferent to or even oblivious of their status. This sentiment is reflected in such statements as "I never think about it. I just take life as it comes, and go on from there." The attitude is typified by a black Birmingham mill worker during the 1930s:

> No telling what I would do if I had to set down to the table and eat a meal with a white man. I wouldn't enjoy it. I would be wondering what everybody that sees us would say. I tell you it would be hard. I would much rather wait until they finish if I had to eat at the same place with them. They would feel better, and I know I would (Johnson, 1943:256).

His attitude was reflected in his philosophy toward voting:

> I can't read and write, so I don't need to be voting just to be doing something. Ain't much need of these Negroes getting in that voting business, anyhow. The white folks running the country, and he [the Black] can't do no good. That's the way it looks like it is to me (Johnson, 1943:-256).

An older black lower-class woman in Harlem tells about her earlier life in the South:

> To tell the truth, I never had no trouble down there. I heard of people being treated bad but it never happened to me. The people I worked for, we got along fine. When you live there you know where you're supposed to go and what you're supposed to do and if you mind your own business you won't have any trouble. It's like that wherever you be. The world is like a bunch of bees. If you stir them up you get into trouble. If you let things be you won't have no trouble, but if you go looking for trouble, you'll get it (Kardiner and Ovesey, 1951:146).

In some instances, such accommodating attitudes were taken over from those of parents and grandparents who had accepted the unequal status of the races as natural and inevitable. Frazier (1940), in his study of blacks in Washington, D.C., and in Louisville, Kentucky, during the 1930s, found such patterns most prevalent among lower-class blacks. A twenty-year-old black youth of fifth-grade education had accommodating attitudes impressed upon him by his parents. When he lived in North Carolina his parents had taught him "to do as we were told, be as courteous as possible to white people, don't talk back to them, and do your work as well as possible. They said 'niggers' that are liked by white people are those who don't give any trouble and don't ask for much." The youth indicated he thought this advice was good and he had tried to "follow it to the letter." He had not given "white people any trouble," but he had not "bitten his tongue in asking for things." He had discovered that "if you can act big enough monkey [clown], you can get almost what you want" (Frazier, 1940:42–43).

Minority–Group Self-Hatred

Closely associated with the internalization of accepting attitudes is the phenomenon of **minority-group self-hatred**. The social psychologist Kurt Lewin (1948) suggests that a tendency exists among minority group members toward self-hatred—an attitude toward one's own group characterized by aversion and dislike. Feelings of negative identification or rejection may have any number of sources:

1. Minority-group individuals may accept a large number of dominant-group values by virtue of making the dominant group their reference group—the group that provides them with their standards for evaluating behavior. Included among these values may be the dominant group's evaluations and conceptions of the minority group. Accordingly, minority-group members may acquire the dominant group's appraisal, seeing themselves and their group through its eyes. This process often underlies assimilationist strivings and in some circumstances leads to the individual's absorption by the dominant group.

2. Since belonging to a minority group may produce disadvantages in meeting various social and psychic needs, some individuals attempt to disaffiliate themselves from the minority and move outward into the dominant society. Yet they are often blocked by the dominant group in this, and as a result build up frustration and finally aggression. Since the dominant group is seen as unusually powerful and possessing high status, this aggression may be turned inward upon the self and upon the minority group.

3. Learning that one is a member of a minority—a "black," a "Jew," or a "Mexican"—is part of the process of acquiring one's self-identity. Children learn their racial or ethnic roles in much the manner in which they learn their other roles. Yet their racial or ethnic roles are defined for them by the larger society as demeaning and inferior. Consequently, the self-image that they acquire may have many unfavorable properties and promote feelings of inferiority.

Self-hatred is seldom an open and uncomplicated reaction. Most of the time it takes the form of an indirect, unconscious self-hatred that may be accompanied by ambivalent feelings of superiority and chauvinism. Indeed, research suggests that blacks who show the greatest prejudice toward whites also exhibit the strongest rejection of their own group and themselves (Trent, 1957; Noel, 1964).

Self-hatred finds expression in anti-Semitism among some Jews. The individuals may expend considerable energy attempting to dissociate themselves from Jewish-group membership. Nathan W. Ackerman and Marie Jahoda (1950), in their study of anti-Semitism, encountered a number of anti-Semitic Jews. One individual changed his Jewish-sounding name and adopted Christianity, not because of religious conviction but in a desire to fortify himself against Jewish membership. He considered Jews inferior, disliked Jewish women, and sympathized with Hitler's program against the Jews. Several individuals planned conversion to Catholicism, and one woman underwent a nose operation to alter her appearance so that she might look more "Christian." To this end she wore a cross. She hoped to get married but never to a Jew—"Who wants to be a 'Mrs. Cohen'?"

Other minorities may experience similar feelings. A Japanese-American student at a midwestern university observes:

> I feel whites are superior—up here [gesturing with her hand] and Japanese down here. They're [Japanese] just an inferior bunch of people—just passive. They aren't aggressive enough. They're in a rut. They're too complacent. I've assimilated white ways—I'm aggressive in getting what I want. The only way to get away from Japanese is to associate with whites. I don't date Japanese or associate with them. I'm going to marry an American or else I will always be looked down upon.

A number of social scientists have hypothesized that by virtue of American racism, blacks suffer considerably in terms of self-esteem and have every incentive for self-hatred. In many respects even good performance is an irrelevant factor; blacks, regardless of what they do or what their merits are, often get a poor reflection of themselves from the behavior of whites. The notion that blacks suffer debilitating effects from the stresses associated with racism found wide support in the scholarly literature prior to the late 1960s (McCarthy and Yancey, 1971; Zirkel, 1971; Adam, 1978). Indeed, the Supreme Court assigned considerable importance to the argument that psychological damage results from segregation in reaching its 1954 school-desegregation ruling *(Brown* v. *Board of Education)*. This view was strongly influenced by the research of Kenneth and Mamie Clark (1939, 1947, 1950). They found that black preschool children preferred white dolls to black dolls and concluded that the selection of white dolls reflected racial self-hatred.

For more than a decade, this early research has been subjected to new scrutiny. The doll studies have been criticized for the methods that the researchers employed in testing children's racial self-attitudes (Katz and Zalk, 1974; Banks, 1976). Recent investigators have found that the dolls preferred by black children vary according to the social situation (Banks and Rompf, 1973); the tester's race (Katz and Zalk, 1974); and the cleanliness of the dolls (Epstein et al., 1976). Further, other research reveals that the levels of self-esteem among black children and adolescents are higher than among white youngsters, or at least that there are no differences between the two racial groups (Yancey et al., 1972; Rosenberg and Simmons, 1972; Paton et al., 1973; Cummings, 1975). Other research points to similar conclusions regarding Native American and Chicano children (Carter, 1968; DeBlaissie and Healy, 1970; Cockerham and Blevins, 1976).

Social scientists now recognize that a good many factors blunt the impact of the negative racist feedback minority groups receive (McCarthy and Yancey, 1971; Heiss and Owens, 1972). First, blacks do not necessarily judge themselves by the standards of the white group; assessment by the black group is much more relevant. Second, the situation that blacks confront (e.g., institutional racism) allows them to blame the system rather than themselves should they be unable to attain American success goals. And third, an increase in black militancy has contributed to enhanced feelings of black pride and unity.

In Search of a Positive Ethnic Identity: The Ramapoughs

For at least two centuries the Ramapo Mountains of northern New Jersey and southeastern New York have been the home of the Ramapoughs (Mayer and Frons, 1980; Hanley, 1980). They have earned their livelihood by hunting, fishing, and whatever jobs they could find. Few have finished high school and most have lived a meager existence. Neighboring groups have long scorned and distrusted these mountain people. The Ramapo people have faced discrimination in school and work and are called "Jackson whites," a much-hated racial slur.

According to legend, the people are descendants of black prostitutes and Hessian mercenaries and British soldiers garrisoned in Manhattan at the time of the Revolutionary War. Local accounts say that a British sea captain by the name of Jackson was orderd to procure 3,500 English prostitutes for the British forces but instead dispatched a ship to the West Indies and brought back 400 black women—whom the soldiers labeled "Jackson's whites." In time, the women made their way to the Ramapo area, which is thirty-five miles west of Manhattan. Here they are alleged to have interbred with freed blacks and runaway slaves, refugee Indians, Hessian deserters, and Dutch settlers. According to another account, preferred by some historians, freed blacks during the eighteenth century were known as "Jacks" and the derogatory term for blacks and whites who intermarried was "Jacks and whites." Eventually, the name became simply "Jackson whites."

The Ramapo people reject both these versions and insist that they are Indians. They say that they are descended from the Delaware and Tuscarora and consequently have organized into three clans. Recently they have incorporated themselves as the Ramapough Mountain Indians and embraced Indian culture with newfound pride. New Jersey has recognized the Ramapoughs as a legitimate Indian tribe. The Ramapoughs themselves have petitioned the U.S. Bureau of Indian Affairs for similar recognition. Should their petition be approved, the designation would make them eligible for federal grants that are available to Indian peoples.

Some historians dispute the claim of the Ramapoughs that they are Indians. Historian David S. Cohen, who lived among the people for a year and studied their roots, dismisses the claim as wishful thinking. He says that their ancestors were blacks and Dutch. Cohen notes that most of their folklore and customs are European in origin. Dutch surnames —Mann, DeGroat, Van Dunk, and DeFreese—predominate among them (Hanley, 1980:310). However, even should the Ramapoughs be unsuccessful in convincing the Bureau of Indian Affairs of the legitimacy of their claim, the people will continue to think of themselves as Indians. "So what if they're not?" asks New Jersey state Senator Matthew Feldman. "They've never had anything to be really proud of before. Why try to take this away from them?" (Mayer and Frons, 1980:32).

Variables Affecting the Response of Minority-Group Members

Being a member of a minority group does not mean the same thing to every person but, rather, operates psychologically within the context of many variables. Social scientists have repeatedly pointed to the fact that minority-group members react in different ways to their status. For instance, a lack of uniformity in black views on race relations has been the rule rather than the exception. However, social scientists are not necessarily in agreement on the role and relative importance of the variables that influence the selection of the varying responses. Further, the responses of minorities ebb and flow in accordance with historical conditions, so that attitudes and behavior frequently shift from one period to another (Turner and Wilson, 1976).

A particularly important variable is a person's socioeconomic-class membership. Prior to the 1960s, patterns of accommodation among blacks were most prevalent among lower-class individuals. By virtue of such factors as their poverty, their minimal formal schooling, their greater isolation from differing conceptions of the black's position in American society, and their frequent dependence upon whites, they were more inclined toward accommodation than were other socioeconomic groups (Matthews and Prothro, 1966; Scott, 1966).

Age is another factor of importance in influencing minority reaction. Hortense Powdermaker (1939) found in her pre-World War II study of a Mississippi community that the older generation of blacks were more inclined than younger generations to accept the doctrine of white supremacy and to display deference toward whites. The sociologists Judith R. Kramer and Seymour Leventman (1961) similarly point to generational differences in the responses of Jews in a midwestern community to the problems posed by minority status. The first generation —immigrants from Eastern Europe—experienced the problem of economic and social survival in an alien society. They responded economically through employment in the garment and retail trades, socially through the establishment of a ritualistically correct community in a segregated ghetto, and religiously through the acceptance of Orthodox Judaism and the acquisition of a secular ethic of self-improvement. The second generation's life situation was characterized by marginality, which resulted in tensions pressing individuals to improve their social position. Members sought upward mobility into middle-class occupations and professions. Socially the second generation sought to resolve its problems through the establishment of acculturated but separate ethnic communities, while religiously it adapted Judaism to modern American life, reflected in Conservative and Reform Judaism. The third generation accepted the economic and religious resolutions of the second generation but rejected its social resolutions, namely, its isolation from the larger society. The third generation sought appropriate social status and acceptance in the community-at-large through movement to the suburbs.

SUMMARY

1. Avoidance and assimilation constitute polar opposites on a continuum. Confronted with a potential intergroup situation, minority-group members may either avoid contact with the dominant group or attempt to merge themselves socially and culturally with it. Similarly, acceptance and aggression are opposites, each constituting a pole on a continuum. Confronted with an intergroup situation, minority-group individuals may either acquiesce in their disadvantaged and subordinate status or strike out against it. These two continua pose choices that confront minority individuals. First, they must allow intergroup contact to take place or they must avoid such contact. Second, once in the contact situation, they must acquiesce in their subordinate status or strike out against it.

2. Acceptance involves the renunciation of protest against the circumstances of minority status and the organization of responses so that instead accommodation appears. Resignation is one expression of acceptance. Some minority-group members feel that the wisest course is to accept what cannot be changed or avoided.

3. Within the rural areas of the South a social system of white dominance and black subordination survived the Civil War and the abolition of slavery. A black tenant population predominated, dependent upon white owners and planters. The tenants under the sharecropping system had no stake in the land and no voice in determining what or how much would be planted or when and where the crop would be sold. Where education was minimal and where there was little communication with the "outside" world, traditional patterns of accommodation tended to prevail.

4. Many sociologists have portrayed religion as a vehicle by which blacks sublimated their frustration into emotionalism and fixed their hopes on the afterworld. Yet, as the sociologist Gary T. Marx points out, the effect of religion on racial protest has by no means been only in one direction. Although many blacks did turn to religion as a solace during slavery, black preachers such as Denmark Vesey and Nat Turner and the religiously inspired abolitionists actively fought slavery. More recently, black religion made a significant contribution to the mobilization of the civil-rights movement identified with the leadership of Reverend Martin Luther King, Jr. A churchlike orientation associated with the established black denominations, especially with those that emphasize activism, increases militancy. In contrast, where membership is in a sectlike religious group, militancy is lowered.

5. In his studies of the black middle class during the 1920s and 1930s, Frazier found that a sizeable proportion of upper- and middle-class blacks had secured their positions by virtue of racially separate institutions. Behind the walls of segregation that barred blacks from full participation in American life, there had grown up institutions duplicating those in the white community. These institutions were largely the product of segregation. As a consequence of their stake in the separate institutions, many middle- and upper-class blacks had ambivalent feelings regarding desegregation.

6. The changes in American life following on the heels of the desegregation decision of the Supreme Court in 1954 in *Brown* v. *Board of Education* contributed to new patterns of black leadership. Earlier black leadership within the South was predominantly of the "accommodating" or "compromise" type. These compromise leaders held their position primarily because they were acceptable to white leaders. Blacks tended to go along with their leaders because accommodation appeared to be the most practical and effective type of adjustment within a setting where segregation had legal and exralegal sanction. Following 1954, militant black leaders, reflecting the protest motive, emerged on the

southern horizon and gained considerable recognition. The late Reverend Martin Luther King, Jr., symbolized this new type of leadership. Whereas compromise leadership had typically operated in a noncontroversial and often clandestine manner, miltant leadership has been characterized by its controversial, public, and activist techniques.

7. Some minority-group individuals internalize the atitudes associated with a disadvantaged status. They accept the existing order, neither questioning it nor doing anything about it. They become indifferent to or even oblivious of their status.

8. Lewin suggests that a tendency exists among minority-group members toward self-hatred. Feelings of negative identification or rejection may have any number of sources. First, minority-group individuals may take the dominant group as their reference group. Second, aggression felt toward the dominant group may be redirected inward upon the self and the minority group. And third, minority-group individuals in assuming a disadvantaged role also may take on the attitudes of disadvantage.

9. Being a member of a minority group does not mean the same thing to every person but, rather, operates within the context of many variables. Social scientists have repeatedly pointed to the fact that minority-group members react in different ways to their status. Further, the responses of minorities ebb and flow in accordance with historical conditions, so that attitudes and behavior frequently shift from one period to the next. A particularly important variable affecting individuals' response is their socioeconomic-class status.

GLOSSARY

Acceptance   Minority-group members may come to acquiesce in—to accommodate themselves to—their disadvantaged and subordinate status.

Aggression   Minority-group members may respond to dominance by striking out against—engaging in hostile acts against—a status that is subordinate and disadvantaged.

Assimilation   Minority-group members may attempt to become socially and culturally fused with the dominant group.

Avoidance   Minority-group members may attempt to shun—to escape from—situations in which they are likely to experience prejudice and discrimination.

Minority-group Self-hatred   An attitude toward one's own group characterized by aversion and dislike.

Responding by Aggression   12

Still another reaction to minority-group status is *aggression*. Some members of minority groups respond to dominance by striking out against—engaging in hostile acts against—a status that is subordinate and disadvantaged. Hostility represents an extremely common type of reaction to frustration. All individuals, not alone minorities, experience anger; they get "mad" from time to time. But the aggressive acting out of hostility is a potentially destructive and disruptive force within human interaction. Accordingly, societies undertake to regulate, suppress, and rechannel aggressive impulses. A major part of socialization is directed toward this end. It is easy to overlook the part that aggression plays in human life since it takes so many different forms. Not infrequently it becomes so well camouflaged as to be virtually unrecognizable.

The Expression of Hostility

Minority-group members generally find it the better part of wisdom to suppress and contain aggressive impulses toward members of the dominant group, by virtue of the greater retaliatory capabilities and resources commonly enjoyed by the latter. As a result, passive acceptance and resignation may ensue. Hostile protest is driven underground, bottled up within the individual. Yet it frequently remains a lurking and latent force. It is not unusual to hear minority-group members indicating to one another how infuriated they get from time to time over some discriminatory or insulting action on the part of dominant-group members. Occasionally some may really "get mad" and strike back in the fury of frustration.

The bitterness and resentment that some blacks feel regarding their subordinate and disadvantaged status is reflected in these statements by two Harlem blacks (Clark, 1965:2, 6):

The way the Man has us, he has us wanting to kill one another. Dog eat dog, amongst us! He has us, like we're so hungry up here, he has us up so tight! Like his rent is due, my rent is due. It's Friday. The Man wants sixty-five dollars. If you are three days over, or don't have the money; like that, he wants to give you a dispossess! Take you to court! . . . They say get the money and pay the Man, but they don't say how to get it. Now, if you use illegal means to obey his ruling to try to get it—which he's not going to let you do—if you use illegal means to pay your bills according to his ruling—he will put you in jail.

—Man, age thirty-one

The flag here in America is for the white man. The blue is for justice; the fifty white stars you see in the blue are for the fifty white states; and the white you see in it is the White House. It represents white folks, The red in it is the white man's blood—he doesn't even respect your blood, that's why he will lynch you, hang you, barbecue you and fry you.

—Man, age about thirty-five

Aggression against the Dominant Group

Outright aggression on the part of blacks against white persons tends to represent a point of considerable sensitivity in the United States, especially within the South. In fact, in wide areas of the South, direct aggression by a black against a white historically posed a grave threat to the black. The taboo against physical assault upon whites operated with its greatest severity in relation to adult black men. Much more open antagonism was tolerated from black women; they could often say and do things that would bring men a severe penalty.

Aggression may find many routes for expression. Although blacks have traditionally been taught to hide their hostility toward whites, one need not look far for examples of it. Hostility is attested to by a large number of derogatory words such as "crackers, rednecks, white trash, lynchers, paddies, pinks, ofays, grays, cotton tops, peckerwoods, devils, buckras, whitey, charley," and "honkeys." Hostility is more evident in the sporadic outpourings of violence toward whites and white-owned property, reflected in the form of gang attacks upon whites and in ghetto "rioting." It may also find expression through secretive acts including the slashing of tires, setting fire to property, poisoning a valued dog, or "shooting from the bush" (murdering a white man under cover of night or from ambush). Gossipy tales may be spread that sooner or later reach the ears of whites and endanger the reputation of a hated white.

A far safer form for the expression of hostility is vicarious aggression. A case in point is the black community's adulation of Joe Louis several decades ago:

In the ring he was the picture of fury. As he demolished foe after foe, every black man could vicariously taste his victory. If his victims were white, the pleasure was even greater. He symbolized assertiveness and unbridled aggression for the black man. In watching him or reading about him, an entire community could find expression through him of inhibited masculine drives. As others have entered professional sports in later years, the heroes have served a similar purpose. Educated and sophisticated Negroes also participate in this hero worship, since all black men swim in the same sea (Grier and Cobbs, 1968:57–58).

Hostility may find other channels for indirect expression. Automobiles may be used to this end. A black furnace worker in Texas said of his own experience:

> I drive in a way that makes it look like I'll run over them [whites] if they walk in front of me when I have the right. I act like I don't see them. I have had some of them to curse at me for this, but I just laugh at them and keep on driving (Johnson, 1943:303).

Politeness itself may be used as a weapon, as in the case of a black schoolteacher in Arkansas. Referring to white insurance agents, she said:

> Sometimes when they come here and act so smart—they always have some nasty joke to tell you—I make them stand out on the porch, and when it's cold it is not so comfortable. You know there is a way of being polite to white people that it is almost impolite. I say polite things, but I look at them hard and I don't smile, and while what I was saying is polite the way in which I say it isn't (Johnson, 1943:304).

Undercurrents of Hostility

In chapter 11 we observed that minority-group members may come to acquiesce in—to accommodate themselves to—their disadvantaged and subordinate status. Yet despite seeming accommodation to the racial structure, blacks have nonetheless harbored covert or latent aggressive impulses toward whites. The sociologist Guy B. Johnson (1939:-126) observes that

> no system of human adjustment which is based upon the subordination of one group or race to another and the restriction of free competition between them can operate with perfect smoothness. There may be mutual adjustment, good will, and a high degree of cooperation, but always beneath the surface there will be the subtle play of friction. . . .

In brief, the stifling and destruction of a people's self-pride and identity —termed by some "psychological castration"—tends to beget aggressive impulses.

Alvin F. Poussaint (1970), a distinguished black psychiatrist on the staff of the Harvard University Medical School, says that the psychological castration of black men, women, and children was inherent in the slave system and in the repressive racist order that followed the Civil War. During slavery black people were degraded as pieces of property and treated as nonpersons. The plantation system fostered helplessness and subserviency in black minds by making blacks dependent upon the good will and paternalism of whites. In white eyes a docile, nonassertive black was the only "good" black. Passivity became a necessary survival technique.

During the post-Civil War period, a color caste system ordained practices of "racial etiquette" (*see* chapter 4) that constantly reminded blacks that they were "castrated" human beings. Whites called blacks "boy" and "girl," while demanding that blacks address whites with courtesy titles. By being "uppity" blacks could endanger their lives. Black mothers, fearing for the safety of their children, taught their two- and three-year-olds to "behave" and say "yes, sir" and "no, sir" when conversing with whites.

Whites rewarded and encouraged attitudes and behavior in blacks that substantiated white stereotypes of blacks as happy-go-lucky, stupid, and lazy. The mass media reinforced these images with such characters as Amos and Andy, Stepin Fetchit, and Beulah. Blacks were brainwashed into thinking that only "white is right." Light-skinned blacks with straight hair were favored by the white world. Whites demanded that blacks relinquish their African heritage and deny their black identities. Even in the 1980s blacks who are "too outspoken" about racial injustices may lose their jobs or not gain promotions because they are viewed by white gatekeepers as "unreasonable" and "too sensitive."

The demands of being unwillingly subservient and self-denigrating are psychologically quite taxing. Frustration and anger are the byproducts of social arrangements that require people to suppress their self-respect, dignity, and pride. One technique for dealing with anger is to develop a chronic resentment and stubbornness toward whites, interpreted as a "chip on the shoulder." But when the force of rage is constrained through self-control to a simmer of chronic irritability, it always has the potential for becoming explosive.

Thus evidence points to the fact that there exist among blacks deep undercurrents of hostility and aggression toward whites. Simultaneously, blacks have been immersed in a cultural tradition calling for the suppression and repression of hostility and aggression toward whites. Consequently many blacks find themselves in a dilemma. They are placed in racial situations in which hostility is an inevitable product; life confronts them with circumstances that constantly stimulate aggressive thoughts and fantasies. Yet the expression of hostile and aggressive impulses is dangerous and defined as morally "sinful."

Within this setting, the program of nonviolent resistance to segregation offered a strong appeal to southern blacks. The program, closely identified with the leadership of the late Reverend Martin Luther King, Jr., had particular appeal in the early 1960s during the early phases of the "Black Revolution." King placed great stress upon nonviolent means such as boycotts and sit-ins and nonviolent reactions in the face of attack. He gave articulate and forceful expression to the crosscurrents we have noted—the feelings of hostility toward whites on the one hand, and the dictates requiring suppression of these impulses on the other—and posed a solution to the dilemma. Not untypical was his speech on December 1, 1957, to the National Committee for the Rural Schools, in New York City:

> And so we must rise up and protest courageously wherever we find segregation. Yet we must do it nonviolently. We cannot afford to use violence in this struggle. If the Negro succumbs to the temptation of using violence in this struggle, unborn generations will be the recipients of a long and desolate night of bitterness, and our chief legacy will be an endless reign of meaningless chaos. There is still a voice crying out through the vista of time saying to every potential Peter: "Put up your sword." History is replete with the bleached bones of nations and communities that failed to follow the command of Jesus on this point.

King told blacks that they had long been abused, insulted, and mistreated, that they had been "kicked about by the brutal feet of oppression." In essence, he repeatedly stressed to his black audiences, using such non-threatening terms as "protest," that it was permissible and legitimate to feel hostility and to engage in aggressive activities against the existing racial order. Indeed, he emphasized the theme that blacks have "a moral obligation" to fight segregation: "To accept passively an unjust system is to cooperate with that system; thereby the oppressed become as evil as the oppressor. Noncooperation with evil is as much a moral obligation as is cooperation with good." He thus defined the traditional pattern of acceptance and resignation as immoral.

Simultaneously, King and his followers paid extensive homage to nonhatred and Christian love: "Love must be our regulating ideal. Once again we must hear the words of Jesus echoing across the centuries: 'Love your enemies, bless them that curse you, and pray for them that despitefully use you.' " Hence, he called upon blacks to love whites and "to turn the other cheek" when attacked. In a sense, King's message appeared to say that blacks could protest but that they were motivated not by animosity but by love. He aided blacks to redefine as moral and acceptable what otherwise had been defined as immoral and unacceptable (i.e., the assault upon white institutions).

An incident at a Knoxville rally in support of the "Stay Away from Downtown" movement (part of a campaign to win the desegregation of that city's lunch counters) is illustrative. After a number of bitter and militant speeches, the chairman of the meeting came back to the microphone and reassuringly indicated, "We're making a lot of noise, but that doesn't mean we're angry at anybody. If you have no love in your heart, stay at home" (Proudfoot, 1962:118). The assembled blacks were permitted to vent their hostility but then, fittingly enough, were comforted, "We're really not angry." Indeed, anger constituted an appropriate reaction, yet it was felt necessary to deny it. As the "Black Revolution" gained momentum, blacks became more comfortable in expressing protest sentiment. The King appeal, then, mediated between the conflicting traditions of the accommodating black and the militant black. In some respects it marked a *transitional* phase in the civil-rights movement between accommodation and the more militantly aggressive tactics of the late 1960s and 1970s.

The Delinquent: Rebel Against Minority Status

For lower-class youth who have internalized the glittering goals of the "American Dream" involving the "good life," their racial or ethnic background may be a formidable obstacle. Television and the movies have taught that a luxurious style of life is within the grasp of every American. But as they get into their teens many young people learn that their prospects for "getting ahead" are poor. Poussaint says:

> Many lower-class blacks are continually primed for violent outbursts just by the problems of daily living. They are dirt poor in a society that rewards everyone else with affluence. They are black in a society that tells them black is bad. Unlike the middle-class people, they generally lack ways to defuse their rage, and they see ample evidence that society does not place the same value on crimes against blacks as it does against whites (Daniels, 1980:40).

Existing welfare and social programs have been unable to solve the deep-rooted miseries of the hard-core jobless. The welfare check is not a one-way ticket out of poverty but simply a claim check on a subsistence life. This situation has led Bayard Rustin, a black veteran of the civil-rights campaign, to observe that privatized guerrilla warfare is emerging among some black youth—"not rioting, but preying on the affluent by means of stealing, muggings, drug trafficking and violent assaults" (*U.S. News & World Report,* May 14, 1979:49).

In short, many lower-class minority youths find themselves trapped at the bottom of the socioeconomic heap. Their racial or ethnic membership offers one obstacle, but there are also others. Sent to school because the law requires it and because their mothers may be anxious to get them out from underfoot, they regard the classroom as a kind of prison. Parents and friends, in contrast with those in the middle and upper classes, tend to believe education will not really matter in their children's lives, and often they do not encourage strenuous efforts to learn. Consequently, lower-class minority youth often lack the incentive for academic achievement, regardless of their intellectual potentialities. In time, many of them find themselves retarded in basic skills such as reading, and, whether they are promoted, "left back," or shunted into "slow" programs, others frequently define them as "dumb." School becomes still more unpleasant, and disinterest increases. By adolescence, education no longer represents a realistic road to a higher standard of living.

Lower-class minority youth confront still other problems in school. Many of their teachers have conceptions of them that work against effective education. For instance, a study of teachers in ten public schools located in depressed areas of a large northern city revealed that

> ... while there were some outstanding exceptions ... the overwhelming majority of these teachers and their supervisors rejected these children and looked upon them as inherently inferior. For most, the teachers indicated that they considered these children to be incapable of profiting from a normal curriculum. The children were seen as intellectually inferior and therefore not capable of learning (Clark, 1963:148).

Thus it is not uncommon for many middle-class teachers to communicate to their lower-class students the attitude and feeling that they are somehow unacceptable. Most American teachers, regardless of their social class origins, fit into middle-class life and share its outlook on such things as thrift, cleanliness, punctuality, respect for property, ambition, sexual mores, and neatness. Judged by such standards, lower-class youth at times come up short. Yet teacher disgust, horror, and discomfort regarding them are not easily hidden. In turn, many children, especially minority-group children, turn out dull because their teachers *expect* them to be dull—a self-fulfilling prophecy (Crano and Mellon, 1978). Indeed, this is one of the institutional subtleties of racism.

With the educational route to a higher standard of living blocked by poor scholastic performance, minority youth may quit school. But those who leave school find that unskilled work as a stock clerk or dishwasher, or waiting tables, offers little chance for advancement. Difficulties with teachers may be carried over to supervisors, and employment is recurrently changed. Uncommitted to school or job, such youth may start "hanging out" on street corners with other unsuccessful boys. The gang sets up a heroic rather than an economic basis for self-respect. The individual must demonstrate that he is not "chicken," and to do this he must display a reckless willingness to steal, to fight, and to indicate rebellion against conventional values. As the sociologist Jackson Toby (1958:545–546) points out:

> He must repudiate the bourgeois virtues associated with school and job: diligence, neatness, truthfulness, thrift. He becomes known as a "loafer" and a "troublemaker" in the community. When family and neighbors add their condemnations to those of teachers and employers, all bridges to respectability are burned, and he becomes progressively more concerned with winning "rep" inside the gang.

The role of delinquents comes to represent rebellion against, and compensation for, permanent low status in the community-at-large. Since the larger society has clearly rejected them, they reject—or appear to reject—the values and norms of that society.

Ethnic groups differ in their attitudes toward academic achievement, a factor apparently related to the incidence of delinquency among them. Both Jews and Italians came to the United States in large numbers at the turn of the century and settled in urban areas. But the two groups differed in their attitudes toward intellectual accomplishment. Eastern European Jews regarded religious study as of immense importance for an adult male. Life in the United States gave a secular reinforcement to the Jewish reverence for learning. Immigrants from southern Italy, on the other hand, frequently viewed formal education as either a frill or the source of dangerous ideas. Children were encouraged in neglect of schoolwork and in truancy.

The Jews, through their emphasis upon academic achievement, tended to open a major route for the social ascent of their children. On the other hand, the Italian immigrants, with their conception of schools as of little worth, tended to deprive their children of the best opportunity for upward mobility. This factor may well be related to the disproportionately high incidence of delinquency among second-generation Italians and the low incidence of delinquency among second-generation Jews. Apparently, second-generation Jewish youths had less reason to become delinquents. As Toby (1958:549) observes, "Their parents kept legitimate channels of social ascent open for them by inculcating the traditional attitude of respect for education and by transmitting the business know-how gleaned from hundreds of years of urban life in Europe."

Ingroup Aggression

A repressive racist order compels minority-group members to contain and suppress a good many of their hostile impulses toward the dominant group. Some of the aggression that otherwise might be directed toward the dominant group is redirected, or displaced, against one's fellows. Studies of lower-class blacks point to a relatively high incidence of internal aggression. For instance, at least 60 to 70 percent of the victims of black crimes are black. It is quite likely that this aggression represents in some part hostility that is deflected from the white group. Since whites occupy a powerful position, it is dangerous to vent aggressive impulses directly against them. It is safer to divert the hostility from the white group and focus it instead upon the black group. But it should not be assumed that all the aggression found within a minority is displaced from the dominant group. A good deal of it is the product of interaction within the minority group itself.

One of the most important sources of black aggression against black derives from sexual jealousy. Charles S. Johnson (1934:51) wrote of the plantation area (where white repression was unusually severe):

> Jealousy and the violent expressions of this passion are manifested by both men and women during the courtship period, by legally married couples and by companions in a common-law relationship. Because Ben Mason began courting Alice Harris' daughter another woman shot him five times. But Ben Mason had not himself the best reputation. A few years earlier he had accidentally killed one girl while shooting at another who had spurned his attentions.

John Dollard (1957), in his study of Southerntown, also notes the prevalence of encounters deriving from sexual jealousy. Razor blades, ice picks, and knives were used as weapons by both men and women who felt themselves "wronged" by a lover.

Similar patterns prevail among lower-class blacks in large cities. The sociologists St. Claire Drake and Horace R. Cayton (1945:588) cite the case of a black night watchman who was employed at a Chicago junkyard. He would get home about seven o'clock in the morning and sleep during the day. One day, he woke earlier than usual and called his wife. Not finding her home, he dressed and went looking for her. He found her at her friend's house with two other men, consuming a bottle of whisky:

> We began to argue and a rap came to the door. A young man said, "Is this the place that ordered the beer?" My wife said, 'Yes, bring it in." She gave him a dollar bill and the boy was going to give her some change. She said, "It's on John"—meaning me. I got mad and I punched her. I chased the two men out and I grabbed her again. I told her to put her clothes on and get home. She was half drunk and she took a long time to get ready.
>
> When we got down in front of the house she began to call me dirty names. I hit her on the face and she fell. She began to bleed, but I didn't care. I was so mad I could've killed her.

Gambling also provides occasion for the expression of violence. So does a type of aggressive banter and boasting that occurs among groups of men gathered together. The banter takes the form of competition between men in which insulting remarks are exchanged about the other person's status, his performance, and even about the virtue of his wife, sweetheart, or mother. Although beginning in jest, the activity sometimes goes over into violent assault. Among some ghetto blacks personal violence is idealized. It is not dissimilar from the admiration felt during the frontier period for individuals who were capable of taking care of themselves. Under circumstances where the formal machinery of law takes care of blacks' grievances much less adequately than those of whites, it is necessary to have greater recourse to one's own competence in protecting and advancing one's interests.

Violence may be a frequent accompaniment of family and marital conflict. At times the outbreaks are expressions of rage deflected from problems in other areas of life. One South Side Chicago black machine operator, baffled and frustrated by problems brought on by the economy, says in exasperation, "You want to blame [the president]. You want to blame city officials. But instead you strike out at your wife or husband. And you drink more than you should" (Kaufman, 1980:25).

Deflection of Hostility to Other Minorities

Not only may hostility be deflected from the dominant group and focused upon one's fellows, it may also be displaced upon other minorities. As was noted in chapter 4, the social distance rankings of minority-group members are quite similar to those of dominant-group members. However, while the minority retains the standardized social-distance pattern, it moves its own ranking from one near the bottom of the scale to one at the top. Clearly social norms play an important role in influencing the attitudes and behavior of one minority toward another. Simultaneously, hostility that cannot find direct expression against the dominant group may in some instances be rechanneled toward a permissible target, another minority. Other minorities are also weak, sometimes weaker than one's own group. Further, through aggression directed against another minority, minority persons borrow some measure of dominant-group status.

Anti-Semitism among blacks in the United States is a relatively recent development and largely limited to urban settings. It has found fertile roots among black business owners who are competitors of Jewish merchants (Sheppard, 1947; Glazer and Moynihan, 1963). Traditionally a large proportion of the white merchants who solicited black trade and established their businesses in black ghettos were Jews. Similarly, there were other areas of friction with Jews. Many of the housewives who hired black domestic workers in large cities were Jews, and many of the property owners who were willing to rent or sell homes to blacks were Jews. A black owner of a small grocery store says:

> When we first opened up, we had just as good a stock as any of them whites. But then the colored did not come in and buy and we went back. We had a struggle. A Jew across the street tried to move us out. But he's gone now. He tried to undersell us. Jews are dirty. He told the cake man and vegetable man that if they sold to me they could not sell to him (Warner et al., 1941:115).

A study by the sociologist Gary T. Marx (1967a) suggests that 24 percent of those blacks who are anti-Semites are in positions where an economic explanation of the hostility they express toward Jews seems likely (and in another 42 percent of such cases, economic factors appear to be relevant).

Yet, contrary to popular opinion (and the expectations of the scapegoat theory of displacement), a good deal of black anti-Semitism is directed not at Jews as Jews but at Jews as whites. Indeed, Marx, in the survey referred to above, found that, to the extent blacks distinguish between Jewish and non-Jewish whites as merchants, landlords, and employers, they prefer Jews: Nationally, 20 percent said Jewish store owners were better than other white store owners; 7 percent said they were worse; and 68 percent said they were about the same; 34 percent said they were better to work for; 19 percent, they were worse; and 10 percent said that they were about the same (37 percent replied, "Don't know"); 24 percent said they were better landlords; 7 percent, they were worse; and 32 percent said that they were about the same (37 percent replied, "Don't know"); and 45 percent believed they were more in favor of civil rights than other whites, 3 percent, they were less in favor; and 35 percent said that they were about the same.

During the demonstrations, marches, sit-ins, and voter registration drives of the 1960s, Jewish students, professors, and rabbis were notable participants. But as black goals shifted to compensatory programs to close the gap between themselves and whites, many Jews felt threatened. The anti-Semitic slogans of some black militants and their denunciation of Israel as racist and imperialist deepened Jewish concerns. During the 1970s the alliance between Jewish and black organizations ruptured over the issue of affirmative-action programs to assist blacks in hiring, promotions, and college admissions. Whereas Jewish organizations have pressed for equality of opportunity, they have opposed programs that employ racial and ethnic quotas as dangerously retrogressive. Consequently, the same Jewish organizations that had submitted arguments for school desegregation in *Brown* v. *Board of Education* in 1954 supported Allen Bakke's court challenge to quotas in university admissions in 1978 (Goren, 1980). The divisions between blacks and Jews have carried over to the Democratic party; in Michigan, Miami, and Washington, D.C., disputes between the two groups have led to countercharges of "racism" and "anti-Semitism" (Clymer, 1981).

Protest

Our discussion of aggression has emphasized that oppressed peoples typically harbor aggressive impulses toward their oppressors. However, they may be compelled to suppress and contain their hostile feelings lest they be further penalized and victimized by members of the dominant group. Nonetheless, aggressive impulses may find alternative channels of expression, including aggression against members of the ingroup or other minorities. Aggression may also be directed into protest activities. The dominant group then becomes the target for the minority's anger.

Humor

One way of expressing hostility is through humor. When friction and antagonism are commonplace, joking and teasing may function to discourage overt aggression and violence. The following is an illustration of this principle:

> A factory hand in Cleveland, Mississippi, indicated that at the place where he worked the white foreman and the black workers often exchanged jokes. One morning the foreman told one of the blacks, "Hurry up there, you son-of-a-bitch. Your mammy must not have given you any breakfast." The black youth retorted, "You skinny bastard, look like your mammy never gives you anything to eat." Then all laughed (Johnson, 1943:308).

Aggressive impulses that otherwise might not be tolerated find a permissible outlet behind the veil of joking. Hostility is often rendered harmless, or so it seems, through jest. But many a true word is said, and many genuine feelings are expressed, by means of the "joke." Thus, joking and teasing provide an important outlet for hostility.

Humor may also be a mechanism for expressing aggression toward the dominant group in the latter's absence. Through ridicule and sarcasm, hostile impulses are released. At times the jokes are so bitter as almost to lack humor:

> It says in the white folks' newspaper that our women are trying to ruin the white folks' homes by quitting their jobs as maids.
> Yeah. A lot of white women are mad because they have to bring up their own children (Myrdal, 1944:961).

And this bitter joke in a message from H. Rap Brown:

> That whole nonviolence thing was nothing but a preparation for genocide. At one point, not so long ago, the Man could have sent a message to black people, saying meet me at such and such a concentration camp and black people would have been there—on time! (Stern, 1967:26–27).

Some of the jokes have a strong protest character, as did the following joke during the period of Jim Crow segregation in the South:

> I went into the store _____ to get some tobacco. I asked for "Prince Albert" and the clerk said "see the man on that can. He's white. Say 'Mister Prince Albert.' " I thought for a minute and then said "No thank you, sir; I believe I'll just take Bull Durham; I don't have to 'mister' him!" (Burma, 1946:713–714).

As Dollard (1957) points out, many jokes that blacks tell have a delicate suppressed quality, in which the hostility is hard to locate but in which the individual has the baffled general feeling that the whites have been lampooned without knowing quite how.

Protest in Art

Through poetry, prose, and songs, racial and ethnic minorities may find vehicles by which to voice protest. Some of the black spirituals suggest underlying symbolism with important elements of protest hidden in them. A number such as "Go Down, Moses," "The Lord Delivered Daniel," and "Good News, Member" were vehicles by which to report the success of an escaped slave's flight via the underground railroad. "Heaven" and "Paradise" were often symbolic representations of freedom and the North.

Opinions differ as to how much the spirituals represented a vehicle for black protest. A few authorities suggest that these elements were entirely lacking in the spirituals; others insist that they contained marked symbolic expressions of conscious protest; and still others are convinced that the spirituals represented a deep and profound sort of protest in which the meaning often was hidden from the singers themselves in an unconscious form. Whatever the case, the spirituals did represent a means by which blacks expressed their grim dissatisfaction with their worldly status. The emphasis upon otherworldliness was reflected in such songs as "Dere's a Great Camp Meetin' in de Promised Land," "Look Away in de Heaven, Lord," "Fo' My Soul's Goin' to Heaven Jes' Sho's Your Born," and "Heaven, Heaven, Everybody Talkin' 'Bout Heaven Ain't Goin' There." They typified the slaves' hope that life would be easier in the next world. In a sense they were "sorrow songs" molded by the hardships and suffering during slavery. "Nobody Knows" expressed such sentiment:

> Oh, nobody knows de trouble I've seen.
> Nobody knows but Jesus.
> Nobody knows de trouble I've seen.
> Glory hallelujah.
>
> Sometimes I'm up, sometimes I'm down,
> Oh, yes, Lord.
> Sometimes I'm almost to de groun',
> Oh, yes, Lord.
>
> Although you see me goin' 'long so,
> Oh, yes, Lord.
> I have my trials here below,
> Oh, yes, Lord.

The "blues" played a somewhat similar role during a later period, but they no longer appear to be in accord with the contemporary mood of blacks.

Literature may also represent a vehicle for expressing protest. Among a group of blacks during the decades between the First and

Second World Wars, a literary movement emerged that has been variously referred to as the "Harlem Renaissance," the "Black Renaissance," and the "New Negro Movement." For the most part, the work was the product of a race-conscious group. Poetry and prose became instruments for crying out against social and economic wrongs. The writers protested against segregation and lynching; demanded higher wages, shorter hours, and better working conditions; and insisted upon full social equality and first-class citizenship. Among them were Claude McKay, James Weldon Johnson, Jean Toomer, Countee Cullen, Langston Hughes, Walter White, W.E.B. Du Bois, and Richard Wright. Probably the best known of these was Richard Wright, whose *Uncle Tom's Children* (1938), *Native Son* (1940), and *Black Boy* (1945) depicted with stark, tragic realism the frustrations of many blacks (Franklin, 1952). More recently, Imamu Amiri Baraka, Eldridge Cleaver, Ralph Ellison, John Oliver Killens, and Bobby Seale, among others, have emerged as powerful protest writers.

Litigation

In those nations in which there is recourse to courts of law, minority groups may seek to advance their status through legal means. The dominant and minority groups then fight for their respective aspirations through legislation and litigation. The U.S. Constitution, especially since the adoption of the equality provisions of the Fourteenth Amendment, has provided an important weapon in the hands of racial and ethnic minorities.

A major part of the black attack upon the American caste system has been waged within the legal arena. The historic vulnerability of blacks (especially in the South, where various informal and economic controls have prevailed) served to limit the means by which the black minority might advance its position. Accordingly, for decades the National Association for the Advancement of Colored People (NAACP) focused its efforts primarily upon legal action. More recently, with the urbanization of large segments of the black population, new means such as the ballot, boycotts, and sit-ins have come to the forefront as weapons in the black arsenal.

The legal action that brought about the Supreme Court's school-desegregation ruling of May 17, 1954, in *Brown* v. *Board of Education* provides a good illustration of the NAACP's strategy. By virtue of the Supreme Court's unique position in the American governmental system, the NAACP was able to enlist its aid in unleashing vast forces of social change. The "separate but equal" doctrine formulated in 1896 in the famous case of *Plessy* v. *Ferguson* had provided legal sanction to the South's system of legalized segregation (Jim Crow). In the 1896 decision the Supreme Court had held that laws requiring the separation of the races did not violate the Fourteenth Amendment so long as equal facilities were provided for blacks. The Court denied that the enforced separation of the races stamped blacks with a badge of inferiority. "If this be so," the Court said, "it is not by reason of anything found in the act [of separation], but solely because the colored race chooses to put that construction upon it."

The *Plessy* v. *Ferguson* decision established a new equilibrium by granting blacks formal equality in principle and whites separation in fact, in this manner preserving the caste order (Borinski, 1958). But, in a dynamic, ever changing society such as that in the United States, a social equilibrium established in 1896 could not be expected to prevail endlessly into the future. Within the 1896 adjustment there were elements of latent legal and social conflict. Southern whites did not really accept the equality of blacks and blacks did not accept separation. As time progressed, circumstances altered. The May 17, 1954, ruling gave recognition to this fact and liquidated the old "separate but equal" doctrine.

The new Supreme Court ruling did not, however, provide for a sudden or immediate liquidation of the old arrangement, and hence cases of school desegregation are still being litigated during the 1980s. In its decree of May 31, 1955, implementing the desegregation ruling, the Court provided for the gradual realization of school desegregation. The 1955 decree in essence invited further litigation. Concrete plans for local desegregation were left in the hands of federal district judges. Furthermore, if desegregation were to be realized, unless communities would desegregate without judicial compulsion, separate legal action would have to be instituted in virtually every school district. The Supreme Court's approach was widely interpreted as allowing for the gradual institutionalization of social change without disrupting the social fabric through precipitous change.

Accordingly, the stage was set for acute legal conflict. Many southern states resorted to legal obstruction in hopes of frustrating desegregation. More than 200 new segregation laws were enacted. The strategy of the South was outlined in editorial candor in the influential and respected Richmond, Virginia, *News Leader* on June 1, 1955:

> To acknowledge the court's authority does not mean that the South is helpless. . . . Rather, it is to enter upon a long course of lawful resistance; it is to take advantage of every moment of the law's delays. . . . Litigate? Let us pledge ourselves to litigate this thing for 50 years. If one remedial law is ruled invalid, then let us try another; and if the second is ruled invalid, then let us enact a third.

For its part, the National Association for the Advancement of Colored People successfully organized to overturn through litigation these various legal devices. The courtroom thus became a major instrument of intergroup conflict. The Civil Rights acts of 1957, 1960, 1964, 1965, and

1968 gave blacks additional legal weapons with which to fight discrimination and segregation.

Sit-ins

As the black movement expanded during the early 1960s, additional weapons were introduced with which to wage the struggle. "Sit-ins" at Jim Crow lunch counters (later expanded to libraries and other facilities), "wade-ins" at segregated beaches and pools, "kneel-ins" at all-white churches, "stand-ins" at voter registration offices, and "freedom rides" to bus terminals with Jim Crow seating and eating facilities became new notes on the American scene.

The lunch-counter demonstrations appeared first and served as an inspiration for the later tactics, hence let us consider them at greater length. The movement was launched on February 1, 1960, when four black freshmen from North Carolina Agricultural and Technical College entered a Greensboro variety store and bought some merchandise. About 4:30 in the afternoon, they sat down at a lunch counter reserved for whites, but they had not been served by closing time an hour later. The movement did not take formal, organized shape until the next day, when some seventy-five A & T students inaugurated a "sit-in" at the same lunch counter. The movement quickly snowballed throughout the South, involving black youth from at least thirty-nine colleges and white youth from another nine. "You sell us pencils, paper, toothpaste, and clothes," was the students' argument, "therefore you are inconsistent not to serve us meals." Black students undertook to sit at lunch counters despite their failure to be served. In this manner facilities were tied up and the stores lost business. Success was not long in coming to the movement. Within a year and a half at least 126 southern cities had some eating facilities desegregated.

The sit-ins had a number of ingredients that offered special appeal to the participants. For one thing they presented an opportunity for individual participation and direct action. There was no need to go through the intermediary of a team of lawyers and a court. The issue was clear-cut, not bogged down in legal jargon. Furthermore, the activity had a flair for the dramatic; it was spectacular and quickly gained the attention of the mass media. The participants derived considerable satisfaction from their involvement in the movement. Feelings of rapport and solidarity flourished in the crowded atmosphere of the lunch counters and reinforced determination while providing a euphoric sense of strength and achievement. And, with the opposition economically vulnerable, victory promised to be immediate.

Although the sit-in movement is typically regarded as beginning with the 1960 Greensboro episode, civil rights activists had conducted less publicized sit-ins in at least fifteen other cities between 1957 and 1960 (Morris, 1981). The NAACP Youth Councils were involved in these sit-ins in nine of the fifteen cities while CORE (usually working with the NAACP) played a role in seven. These sit-ins received substantial backing from the black churches in their respective communities. The churches provided communication networks, organized parishioners, finances, and a safe environment in which to hold meetings. However, it was the Greensboro sit-in that provided the immediate impetus for the sit-in movement that developed at an incredible pace across the South. We shall consider the civil-rights movement at greater length in chapter 13.

Native American Militancy

Chapter 8 detailed the various changes that have occurred during the past two centuries in government policy toward Native Americans (Indians). During the colonial period a major response of Native Americans to the European invasion was the founding of tribal confederations. The Iroquois and, on a smaller scale, the Abnakis, the Wampanoags, and a number of other peoples formed political confederacies in the Northeast to resist white incursions. In the Southeast the Creeks and the Pamunkeys acted similarly. By the time of the American Revolution the Native Americans in the East had been overwhelmed and the confederacies destroyed.

Nonetheless, as the new government pursued separation, Native Americans intensified their efforts at unity. The Shawnee leader Tecumseh (1788–1813) organized an alliance among many displaced groups in the Northwest Territory and urged Native Americans to cease selling their lands, to hold on to them, and to resist white encroachments and pressures. In the war between Tecumseh's forces and the U.S. Army, the Native Americans were crushed and Tecumseh was killed (Spicer, 1980).

Native Americans also pursued other policies in defense of their people, territory, and rights. When President Andrew Jackson undertook to dispossess the tribes of the Southeast of their lands under the Removal Act, some of the Cherokee undertook lobbying actions in Washington, D.C., launched appeals for justice to the American public, and initiated action in the federal courts. However, these policies were unsuccessful. Native American peoples were driven from their lands while policies of genocide were directed against them. During the post-Civil War period, Native American resistance to assimilation and white dominance frequently found expression in religious movements like the Ghost Dance, which on occasion took on military aspects (*see* chapter 14).

The 1960s brought a new rise in Native American activism. In 1963, the National Indian Youth Council (primarily a group of younger college-trained Indians) led demonstrations in the Northwest to highlight the problem of Native American fishing rights. During the mid-1800s, several tribes in the state of Washington agreed to reside on reservations but retained by treaty their right to hunt and fish in their accustomed areas, especially the salmon runs of the territory's rivers. Nonetheless, during the course of the following century whites systematically interfered with Native American exercise of their rights. The emergence of sports fishing among whites and the commercially profitable canned-salmon industry undermined Native American interests. Game Department officers and white vigilantes in the Northwest harassed the Native Americans, destroying their boats, fishing nets, and gear. During the 1960s and 1970s the Native Americans launched a vigorous campaign to regain their treaty-guaranteed rights.

In other areas of the West Coast, Native American activism also made itself felt. In November 1969, the San Francisco Indian Center, which served bay-area Native Americans, burned down. Unable to secure government assistance in procuring another center, Native American activists took over the abandoned federal prison on Alcatraz Island in San Francisco Bay. The action functioned as a rallying point for Native Americans much in the fashion that Birmingham and Selma had for blacks in the civil-rights movement. Representatives from tribal groups throughout the United States converged on Alcatraz. However, the effort disintegrated in the face of internal factionalism. Nonetheless, activism has continued, finding additional avenues by which to promote Native American goals. In some instances, as in Maine, Native Americans have initiated court action to regain tribal lands.

During the 1960s, Native Americans also injected new activism into the National Congress of American Indians. And in Minneapolis, a number of younger and more militant Native Americans founded the American Indian Movement (AIM). The organization expanded its operations throughout much of the Midwest. In some centers AIM organized Indian patrols, which undertook surrveillance of police activities, checking out arrests that police officers attempted. In 1973 AIM took over the small community of Wounded Knee, South Dakota, and held it for seventy-one days. The occupation resulted in a white backlash and violence. Two years later two agents of the FBI were shot to death on the Pine Ridge Reservation. However, as a consequence of the Wounded Knee movement, the Oglala Sioux gained tribal control of law enforcement on the reservation.

Variables Affecting the Response of Minority-Group Members

Socioeconomic-class membership plays a crucial role in influencing patterns of reaction to dominance. Tendencies toward the direct expression of aggression among blacks are probably most prevalent in the lower class. The economic difficulties and frustrations of lower-class life often encourage an explosive resolution of intense hostile impulses.

Further, children see considerable violence within their communities and families, and some are also the object of the violent behavior of their parents and immediate associates.

By virtue of their relatively greater isolation, the product of their disadvantaged position and lower levels of education, lower-class blacks have traditionally been less involved in civil-rights activities and movements than have the other classes. The strength of the NAACP and Urban League has historically resided in the middle and upper classes. Covert expressions of hostility in the form of petty sabotage, quitting of jobs, gossip, and pseudo-ignorant malingering tend to be more prevalent among the lower class than among the middle and upper classes.

The sociologist Robert Johnson (1957), in his study of 150 blacks in an upstate New York community, found that aggression, as a response to dominance, was more prevalent among the less educated, the southern-born, youths and adults under age forty-five, females, and those whose interracial contact was minimal. Not infrequently, hostility was deflected toward other groups, especially the foreign-born, who were resented for enjoying privileges on their first day in America that were denied blacks who were lifetime residents. Hostility was most closely related to place of birth. Lifetime residents of the North were generally less hostile than the southern-born, a finding also confirmed by other studies. Buried racial antagonisms arising from southern experiences often came to the foreground in the more permissive setting of the North.

The readiness to employ violence as a way of gaining black rights is associated with age and sex (Campbell and Schuman, 1968; Turner and Wilson, 1976. *See also* Figure 12.1, p. 352). The disposition toward violence is also associated with those blacks who are intensely dissatisfied, feel powerless to change their position, and have a minimum commitment to the larger society. These blacks have lost faith in the leaders and institutions of the community and presumably have little hope for improvement through organized protest (Ransford, 1968; Turner and Wilson, 1976).

FIGURE 12.1 RELATIONSHIP OF AGE AND SEX TO
WILLINGNESS TO EMPLOY VIOLENCE.

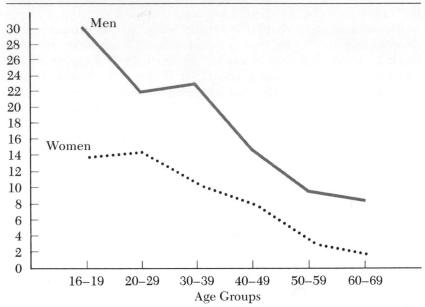

a. Percentage saying readiness to use violence is way to gain black rights

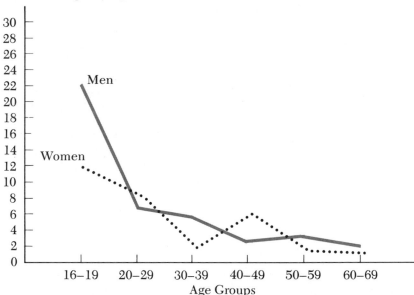

b. Percentage saying violence should be used against discriminatory
   shopkeeper if other methods fail

Data based on a survey of blacks in 15 major cities, conducted on
behalf of the National Advisory Board on Civil Disorders.
Source: Angus Campbell and Howard Schuman, *Racial Attitudes in Fifteen American
Cities* (Washington, D.C.: U.S. Government Printing Office, 1968), Figs. V-a and V-c,
p.56.

SUMMARY

1. Another reaction to minority-group status is aggression. Hostility represents an extremely common type of reaction to frustration. But the aggressive acting out of hostility is a potentially destructive and disruptive force within human interaction. Accordingly, societies undertake to regulate, suppress, and rechannel aggressive impulses. Minority-group members generally find it the better part of wisdom to suppress and contain aggressive impulses toward members of the dominant group. Consequently hostile protest is often driven underground, bottled up within the individual. Yet it frequently remains a lurking and latent force.

2. Although individuals may accommodate themselves to a disadvantaged and subordinate status, they may nonetheless harbor covert or latent aggressive impulses toward the dominant group. Beneath the surface there is the subtle play of friction. The stifling and destruction of a people's self-pride and identity—termed by some "psychological castration"—tends to beget aggressive impulses. Poussaint says that the psychological castration of black men, women, and children was inherent in the slave system and in the repressive racist order that followed the Civil War.

3. For lower-class youth who have internalized the glittering goals of the "American Dream" involving the "good life," their racial or ethnic background may be a formidable obstacle. Their prospects for "getting ahead" are poor. The educational route to a higher standard of living is often blocked by poor scholastic performance. For some the role of the hoodlum comes to represent rebellion against, and compensation for, permanent low status in the community-at-large.

4. A repressive racist order compels minority-group members to contain and suppress a good many of their hostile impulses toward the dominant group. Some of the aggression that otherwise might be directed toward the dominant group is redirected, or displaced, against one's fellows. Studies of lower-class black life point to a relatively high incidence of internal aggression.

5. Not only may hostility be deflected from the dominant group and focused upon one's fellows, it may also be displaced upon other minorities. Clearly social norms play an important role in influencing the attitudes and behavior of one minority toward another. Simultaneously, hostility that cannot find direct expression against the dominant group may in some instances be rechanneled toward a permissible target, another minority.

6. Aggression may be directed into protest activities. The dominant group then becomes the target for the minority's anger. One way of expressing hostility is through humor. Another vehicle is art. Still an-

other is irresponsible and awkward work. And litigation may be a mechanism by which minorities use legal institutions to advance their circumstances.

7. Socioeconomic-class membership plays a crucial role in influencing patterns of reaction to dominance. Tendencies toward the direct expression of aggression among blacks are probably most prevalent in the lower class. The economic difficulties and frustrations of lower-class life often encourage an explosive resolution of intense hostile impulses. Further, children see considerable violence within their communities and families, and some are also the object of the violent behavior of their parents and immediate associates.

Responding by Assimilation

13

A s pointed out in chapter 11, avoidance may be viewed as the polar opposite of assimilation, and aggression as the polar opposite of acceptance. These two continua pose choices that confront minority-group individuals within an intergroup situation. First, they must either allow intergroup contact to take place or they must avoid (or, at least minimize) such contact. Second, once in the contact situation, they must either acquiesce in their subordinate status or strike out against it. Thus far we have considered acceptance and aggression. In this chapter we shall consider assimilation as a reaction to dominance.

In chapter 10 we defined assimilation as those processes whereby groups with distinctive identities become culturally and socially fused together. But in contrast with our discussion in chapter 10, in which we considered assimilation as an *intergroup* process, in this chapter we shall treat assimilation more narrowly. Rather than focusing upon the interplay between dominant-group and minority-group individuals, we shall emphasize the responses of the minority. Hence, this chapter will examine an approach found among some minority-group individuals in which they undertake to lose their distinct minority-group identity and to fuse themselves socially and culturally with the dominant group.

European Immigrant Groups

Viewed over the long run, European immigrant groups within the United States have typically oriented themselves toward an assimilationist goal. Usually acculturation—alterations in a group's cultural practices in the direction of the dominant Anglo-American pattern—has proceeded more rapidly than integration—alterations in a group's network of formal and informal social relationships. Consequently, ingroup ties have tended to display greater strength than customs. Perhaps an illustration, that of the assimilation of southern Italians, may prove helpful. Of the "new immigrants"—those arriving after 1880— the Italians deserve special emphasis. They constitute the second-largest ethnic group within the United States, more than 5 million Italians having migrated to this nation since 1820. Their recorded immigration is exceeded only by that of the Germans. Today there are within the United States some 4.5 million individuals who were born in Italy or had at least one Italian-born parent. The peak years of the Italian immigration were 1907 and 1913. The pre-World War I migration, which had reached 300,000 in a single year, was reduced to 5,807 by the quota system of 1924 (although special laws often admitted more than twice as many nonquota immigrants). Prior to 1900, Italians from northern provinces represented more than two-thirds of the total migrants from Italy. By the time of the quota law, four-fifths of all the Italians within the United States were from southern Italy, a fourth of these being from Sicily. (Schermerhorn, 1949; Velikonja, 1967; Briggs, 1978).

Background of Southern Italian Immigrants

The Italians from southern Italy and Sicily came from an agrarian, small-village background. In their native land the lot of the peasants had been one of economic hardship. The soil was not especially fertile and rainfall was inadequate. Remnants of the feudal order persisted, and the peasant renter often received little to support his family. Onerous mortgage debts, usurious interest, exploitation by landlords, and unemployment were among the hardships that made America seem attractive by comparison. The people were largely illiterate. Christianity had been instituted by decree rather than conviction, and numerous ancient religious practices persisted, often taken over bodily into Catholic practice with little modification.

Individuals were closely and intimately linked with their families. The *famiglia,* the large "family," included both blood relatives and in-laws up to the fourth degree. Family allegiance, solidarity, and affection were stressed. The *famiglia* represented a world within a world, in which obligation to family members was absolute. Outside the family was a world of "strangers," and a benevolent act performed for a non-family member was often considered as a weak-headed deed. The individuals' responsibility was to their family rather than to the community, and friendships outside the family generally were not intimate. To southern Italians, the government and everyone else outside their little village was suspect. For the most part, the Italian family was patriarchal, the men exercising authority. Nevertheless, the mother enjoyed a powerful position (Glazer and Moynihan, 1963; Tomasi, 1972; Yans-McLaughlin, 1977).

Early Adjustments to American Life

By the turn of the twentieth century, the frontier and free lands had virtually vanished from the American scene. It was largely this fact that accounted for the settlement of the southern Italians within urban communities, especially those in the Northeast and on the Atlantic seaboard. New York City became the largest center of Italians in the United States, for that matter in the world, Rome not excluded. The original enclave was usually in or near the central business district. As the newcomers secured jobs, they tended to move out, making room for new arrivals.

The introduction of the Italians to American life took place under difficult circumstances. In the cities they suffered from low wages, irregular and unskilled employment, child labor, and poor housing in slum tenements. They were found in large numbers in the "sweatshops" of New York City; some earned their living as peddlers of vegetables and as pushcart vendors; and many others found work in the building trades and on the railroads, where they succeeded the Irish laborers.

During the earlier years of the immigration, males greatly predominated among the migrants. Lacking relatives or friends in the United States and unfamiliar with the language, money, and customs, the migrants frequently secured employment through an intermediary—the *padrone*. The *padrone* was usually an Italian who already "knew the ropes" and who found jobs for his fellow countrymen. Similarly he often made arrangements for room and board, banking, and other services. In some cases the *padrone* contracted for the labor of men in Italy and arranged for their passage to the United States. By virtue of the *padrone*'s position and the ignorance of the immigrants, exploitation was not unusual. (Glazer and Moynihan, 1963; Nelli, 1980).

Many of the men had expectations of returning to Italy once they had amassed sufficient funds for achieving a "comfortable" existence in their homeland. More than half did return to Italy (between 1899 and 1924, 3.8 million Italians landed in the United States, but some 2.1 million departed during the same interval). Some of the returnees stayed in Italy for a time and then repeated the process. Eventually many of these settled in the United States (Nelli, 1980). It became a common custom for those in America to send for other members of their families to have as many of them together as possible. With time, the Italian communities in American cities were characterized by polynucleated groups—with one street made up of villagers from a hamlet in Avellino, still another from a community in Basilicata, and so on.

In many cases, immigrants came from parts of Italy in which Italian nationalism had not yet taken firm hold. Many identified themselves in terms of a section, province, or town. But in America, their circle of friends from the old area was too small to be self-sustaining. Moreover, members of the dominant group, confused by the multiplicity of place names, and accustomed to thinking in national terms, referred to them not by region—the region being unfamiliar—but rather by nation (Italy). Within the Italian-American community, collective action of any sort—social club, burial society, politics—was more effective if undertaken not by the people from this or that province, but by "Italians." But the "sense" of being an Italian had been generated in the United States. Immigrants from provincial and rural areas became conscious of their "national origin" only after a few years in the United States. Indeed, Italian-American immigrant organizations sometimes used their influence to sponsor nationalistic movements in the old country (Nelli, 1980).

To a considerable degree, the immigrants were insulated from the larger American society. It was not unusual to find the dialect, cooking habits, and religious practices of the old country continuing without an appreciable break. "Little Italys" enabled the immigrants to cushion the shock of adjusting from a rural to an urban and from a foreign to an American society. By the same token the "Little Italys" afforded some shelter from the hostility and antagonism of the native-born Americans who viewed them as "wops," "dagos," and "guineas" (Schermerhorn, 1949). Yet it should not be overlooked that "Little Italys" seldom contained solidly Italian neighborhoods—indeed, it was unusual for the Italian population density to exceed 50 or 60 percent. This mixing of nationalities made inevitable innumerable contacts with non-Italian peoples. And as a result, neither the Italian community nor its institutions were fully Italian in character; nor were they fully American (Briggs, 1978; Nelli, 1980).

Mutual-aid societies, organized to reduce the ever-present risks of sickness, accident, and death, sprang up by the hundreds. In time their functions were broadened to include social activities. Group mergers designed to overcome financial weakness contributed to an increase in their size and a decrease in their number. The Order of Sons of Italy of America, the Venetian Fraternal Order, and the Italo-American National Union were among the better-known fraternal insurance organizations. Similarly, a considerable number of Italian newspapers grew up in the United States. As late as World War II, there were some 130 Italian newspapers in this country, most of them weeklies. The press served as a kind of crutch for immigrants having difficulties in adapting to their new surroundings or for those unable to break away from homeland traditions (Schermerhorn, 1949, Nelli, 1980).

Italian immigrants gained notoriety among Anglicized Americans (and the wrath of social workers) because their children were often not permitted to obtain adequate schooling. While complaining that their own lack of education kept them from getting better jobs, parents nonetheless sent their offspring out to work to supplement family income. Although in time most Italians complied with minimum requirements of compulsory education laws, they encouraged their children to take jobs after school hours. When Italian children reached the legal withdrawal age of fourteen, they were frequently withdrawn from school and put to work (Tomasi, 1977).

Yet despite dire predictions that Italians were caught in a "cycle of poverty," by the early 1900s they had begun progressing from unskilled labor into commercial, trade, and professional classes, working in printing, bricklaying, carpentering, import and export businesses, banking, law, and medicine. Notwithstanding the complaints of reformers and the laments of social workers, financial success at this time did not absolutely require education. Ambition and cunning could, and did, overcome the handicaps associated with illiteracy. Crime—one means of economic advancement independent of education, social background, or political connections—provided an avenue for quick and substantial monetary gain and at times social and political advancement as well. In time the "syndicate" (the Mafia), an illegal business operation reaping vast profits from the American community, offered almost limitless opportunities for a measure of upward social mobility. As a consequence, many Americans came to believe that Italians were "natural criminals" much in the same manner that the Irish were "natural politicians" (yet a comparison of Irish experiences in other parts of the world would have challenged this belief—Irish immigrants and their children, for instance, did not achieve political successes in London, Liverpool, or other English and Scotch cities comparable to their achievements in the United States). The prominence of Italians in crime was due primarily to availability of opportunity, much in the fashion of Irish preeminence in political life and Jewish prominence in the clothing industry. Thus the experience of Italian immigrants in Latin America has been substantially different in terms of their involvement in crime and political movements than that of Italians immigrants in the United States (Della-Cava, 1977).

The Children of Southern Italian Immigrants

For a large part of each day, the children of the immigrant Italians were immersed within the mainstream of American life by the public-school system. From their teachers and school companions they learned to value American ways and to look down upon Italian ways as "foreign" and "undesirable." They often developed contempt for their parents as stupid "greenhorns," unknowing of American ways. A conflict ensued within the families between two ways of life: the one American, the other Italian. Considerable misunderstanding and frustration existed between the parents and the children and threatened to destroy family stability. The children frequently expressed American values and expectations and attempted to transmit them to the family setting. On the other hand, the parents sought to reinforce the pattern of the old-country peasant family (Campisi, 1948).

The sociologist Irwin L. Child (1943), in a study of the Italian colony in New Haven prior to World War II, distinguished three types of reaction among American-born children of Italian parents to their situation: the *rebel,* the *ingroup,* and the *apathetic.* The *rebels* responded by revolting against their parents and the old traditions. They wished to be considered Americans and attempted to dissociate themselves from everything Italian. In contrast, the *ingroupers* strongly identified themselves with Italian symbols and traits and sought to shun American ways. They preferred membership in the Italian subcommunity to full participation in the larger American society. The *apathetic* group attempted to retreat from the stresses and strains deriving from the counterpulls of the two ways of life. They undertook to avoid situations where nationality would be emphasized, and they minimized their membership within the Italian group. They sought to get along with both the older generation and their American associates, but their dual status often posed problems for them.

Acculturation of Southern Italian Immigrants

Today the families of the American-born children of southern Italian immigrants typically resemble mainstream families. From the patriarchal, peasant-style family of the Italian countryside, they have shifted toward the democratic and highly individualized family. Family solidarity has been increasingly undermined, and the small-family system —as opposed to the *famiglia*—has come to prevail. Where previously the focus had been upon children "living for" their parents, among the American-born the situation has been reversed with the parents "living for" children. The age at marriage has risen; mates are no longer selected by parents; dowry rights are unrecognized; and a growing number of marriages are taking place outside Italian and Catholic groups. Few magical and superstitious notions persist in connection with pregnancy. During illness, increasing reliance is placed on physicians and specialists. Birth control is relatively common. The value of chastity has declined; chaperonage is no longer practiced; and divorce has become permissible (Campisi, 1948; Palisi, 1966; Lalli, 1969). Italian names are slowly being Anglicized, while a second-generation child named

Giuseppe by his parents introduces himself as Joseph and gives only the English name to his own son. A number of Italian patterns, however, have survived, the most visible being eating habits. Nonetheless, the food is milder and less spicy than that eaten by their parents.

In a like fashion, acculturation has occurred in the religious sphere. Italian newcomers found the Roman Catholic church in America to be a cold and puritanical organization, controlled and operated by Irish clergy. Many church leaders feared that the degree and prevalence of immigrant antagonism toward the church posed a serious threat to its future in the United States. This antagonism, however, has waned among the second and third generations. Indeed, the Italians of the second and third generations closely approximate the Irish in their attitudes toward parish priests and in their participation in parish activities. Unaccustomed to church donations and collections in Italy where the church was state-supported, the first generation contributed little to church support; the second generation, in contrast, seemingly has adopted the Irish pattern of generous support, a pattern continued by the third generation. Similarly, a considerable increase has occurred among third-generation Italians in Catholic school enrollment (Russo, 1969; Nelli, 1980). As regards religious practices among Italian-Americans, the evidence is in keeping with the general finding of Gerhard Lenski's (1963) Detroit study, namely, church attendance tends to increase among immigrant groups with increasing Americanization. Overall, then, acculturation has severely eroded Italian cultural patterns among the second generation, and continues to do so in the third generation (Gans, 1962). However, during the 1970s some Italian-Americans, especially in the East, undertook to proclaim their ethnicity and search for their roots. One result was the organization of a number of rallies and demonstrations to protest the negative image of Italians that is often projected by the mass media. Likewise, some Italian-Americans have opposed affirmative-action programs, which they believe unfairly favor blacks and Hispanics (Nelli, 1980).

Integration of Southern Italian Immigrants

Integration—the disappearance of the Italian social system—has proceeded much more slowly than acculturation. The sociologist Herbert J. Gans (1962:35), in a study of an Italian section in Boston, notes:

> Indeed, the social structure of the West End . . . is still quite similar to that of the first generation. Social relationships are almost entirely limited to other Italians, because much sociability is based on kinship, and because

most friendships are made in childhood, and are thus influenced by residential propinquity. Intermarriage with non-Italians is unusual among the second-generation, and is not favored by the third. As long as both parties are Catholic, however, disapproval is mild.

Nathan Glazer and Daniel P. Moynihan (1963:187), in their study of New York City ethnic groups, make a similar observation about that city's Italians:

> Nor are these old Italian neighborhoods only shells of their former selves, inhabited exclusively by the older people. Many of the married sons and daughters have stayed close to their parents. Even the trek to the suburbs, when it does occur among Italians, is very often a trek of families of two generations, rather than simply of the young. And it is striking how the old neighborhoods have been artfully adapted to a higher standard of living rather than simply deserted, as they would have been by other groups, in more American style.

This pattern—a lag of integration behind acculturation—has also been common among many other European immigrant groups.

Passing

Undoubtedly one of the most complete forms of assimilation is leaving the minority group and "passing" as a member of the dominant group. This adjustment is a feasible alternative for those minority-group members who physically and culturally resemble the dominant group. The task is not particularly difficult for German immigrants who decide to Anglicize their names and to become Episcopalians rather than Lutherans. Nevertheless, accents, cultural differences, and community knowledge of their family background may in part frustrate their efforts. Still, their attempt to identify themselves with the dominant group may meet with little resistance, in fact it may be actually welcomed by the larger community as part of a process of Americanization.

As the position of the racial or ethnic minority declines in relation to the social-distance scale of the larger community, the possibility of successful passing becomes more difficult, especially when physical or cultural differences are discernible. Nevertheless, some minority-group members may succeed, as in the following case:

> I was a Jew, until a few years ago. Now, I am not!
> Many of you, the Jews whom I address, as well as many gentiles, may scoff at the notion of a Jew ever becoming a non-Jew. And my former people may blame me bitterly for changing.
> Fortunately, I cannot be reached. I have changed my name. I have changed my work. I have moved into a strange region and started

afresh. My past is as finally sealed as though I had died and arisen with a new personality—for it is really necessary that a Jew change some important parts of his personality when he throws off his Jewishness (Forum, 1940).

This man changed his name and claimed to be descended from non-Jewish Adrianople Turks. He went west and "tried a variety of callings, but shunned the Jewish favorites." He later entered a western university and married. "I am now raising children who need never learn to endure snubs, who will never be tempted to retaliate against cruel discrimination. From this pleasant sunshine, I look back with horror at the somber world in which my race-proud kin persist on their ancient and unhappy course."

The sociologists Leonard Broom, Helen P. Beem, and Virginia Harris (1955) studied the characteristics of more than 1,000 persons in Los Angeles County who had petitioned to change their names. Although Jews constituted only 6 percent of the population, 46 percent of those petitioning to change their names were of Jewish origin. In comparison with non-Jewish petitioners, the Jewish group had a significantly higher percentage of foreign-born, married males, children included in the petition, older males, and residents in areas of high social rank and urbanization. The researchers concluded that the change in names most likely represented a change in self-definition and group identification, especially by those who regarded their membership in the Jewish group as a barrier to further upward mobility.

Where a sharp line is drawn on the basis of color, as in the case of blacks, passing is open to only a small proportion. For those possessing light skin coloring and relatively Caucasian hair texture and facial characteristics, it is a feasible alternative. How many blacks pass permanently into the white group? Estimates range from a few thousand to tens of thousands annually within the United States. But, since present methods of making such estimates are quite inadequate, the actual number is not known. Blacks and passers themselves are reluctant to give information about those who pass, and census data and vital statistics are too inaccurate to catch discrepancies from one period to another. As a result of recent movements emphasizing black pride, passing is probably less frequent today than it was several decades ago.

Seldom do people, regardless of the extent of their white features, grow up as black and then suddenly make an intellectual decision to pass. Rather it is a step-by-step process in which emotional ties to the black group are severed and new relationships with whites achieved. Initially passing may be unintentional, but the realization that one can pass for white may lead to more adventurous passing for convenience or employment. As intimate relationships are established with white friends and fellow workers, individuals gradually draw farther and farther away from their emotional attachments to the black community. The final break comes when the irritations of racism and the attractiveness of the white world outweigh the individual's inner agitation (Drake and Cayton, 1945).

The Black Protest—1955 to 1965: Aggression–Assimilation

As European immigrants to the United States became acculturated, they lost many of the identifying "marks" or "signs" that set them apart from the dominant group. By the second and third generations, their English was usually indistinguishable from that of other Americans, while their distinct ethnic mannerisms, dress, gestures, food habits, religious practices, and the like became less pronounced. In brief, their "visibility"—those conspicuous features differentiating them from the dominant group and so essential for maintaining ingroup and outgroup boundaries—became less apparent. Although integration generally proceeded less rapidly than acculturation, the slower pace of integration was in part the product of the immigrant group's own actions; many of its members simply preferred to make their own group the primary focus for their informal and formal social relationships.

American blacks have found themselves in somewhat different circumstances. Although for the most part culturally indistinguishable from dominant-group whites, blacks are visibly distinguishable from whites. Barriers premised upon race pose major obstacles to black integration. Yet despite the fact that blacks experience persistent racism, public opinion polls continue to show that a substantial majority of black Americans share an integrationist outlook—the goal of an open society.

Blocked in realizing their integrationist aspirations, many blacks responded with a social movement designed to break down the walls that barred them from full and equal participation in American life. These efforts found expression in the Niagara Movement in 1905 (which culminated in 1910 in the formation of the NAACP) and in the Southern Christian Leadership Conference (identified with the leadership of the late Reverend Martin Luther King, Jr.). They represented a combined *aggression-assimilation* response. The movements constituted a striking out against—a protest against—minority status. Yet they also represented an assimilationist response reflecting a strong integrationist orientation.

The Aims of the Black Protest—
1955 to 1965

The black protest movement that unfolded during the 1950s and the early 1960s was not so much directed against major deprivations inherent in the American social system as against major deprivations or inequalities that blacks experience as American citizens. One sociologist, writing in 1965 and prior to the emergence of the slogan "Black Power," observed of the movement:

> . . . its grand strategy is designed to achieve goals and effectuate values that are already acknowledged to be inherent in a political democracy and which are firmly established in our national culture. Consequently, Negro protest leaders do not advocate the overthrow of constitutional laws, changing the basic structure of our republican form of government, rearrangement of the American class structure, or the establishment of new political, economic, and ethical goals. Instead—except for a small extremist element—the Negro protest, itself, is a clear endorsement of the "American Creed" and a reaffirmation of the faith which the great majority of Negroes have in the essential goodness of the individual and in the democratic process (Thompson, 1965:20).

Yet in some respects, even during this early period, the black protest resembled more typical revolutions. It stressed direct action (demonstrations, sit-ins, boycotts, and the like); possessed broad objectives (the elimination of the segregated order); and entailed a genuine *mass* movement. And like revolutionary movements, it achieved a heightened militancy and urgency, a sense that "even yesterday was too late."

Nevertheless, in a technical sense, this black protest constituted a reform and not a revolutionary movement. As the sociologist Thomas F. Pettigrew (1964:193) noted at the time:

> It aims to modify, not to overturn, the society it confronts; it seeks to amend, not to ravage. Negro Americans are so firmly rooted in and shaped by their land that their . . . [movement] is attempting merely to guarantee full participation in the society as it otherwise exists. In short, they do not wish to deprecate or destroy that which they wish to join.

The "Old" and "New" Protests

A good many blacks have always resented the disadvantaged and subordinate status assigned them in American society. However, they have been unable to do much about it, at least until recently, because they have been virtually powerless. Hence, accommodation constituted the principal black reaction to dominance. Yet, even so, the decades have witnessed at least periodic ripples of black protest. During slavery, more than 200 antislavery plots and revolts were recorded (Aptheker,

1943; Genovese, 1974). The Civil War and Reconstruction brought new strivings among segments of the black population for equality, but these were crushed with the overthrow of the Reconstructionist regimes and by the evolution of a Jim Crow system in the 1890s (Woodward, 1966).

The twentieth century witnessed the formation of a number of civil-rights organizations, through which blacks worked toward participation in previously all-white institutions. The most important of these was the National Association for the Advancement of Colored People. The NAACP established a legal redress committee soon after its founding, and it won some important legal victories even in its early days—beginning with the Supreme Court decision against the "grandfather clauses" in 1915. It was this highly developed, selectively applied, legal-istic approach on the part of the NAACP that led to the Supreme Court's overthrow in 1954 of the legal foundation of segregation. Yet it was an approach that entailed "tokenism"—a small gain here, and a small gain there involving a white university, park, public facility, or railroad pullman car, gains chiefly realized by middle-class blacks *for* middle-class blacks and having little implications for the great mass of American blacks. For the most part, the great majority of blacks were merely spectators during the legal battle. Extensive support in the local community was not needed since one or a few plaintiffs were sufficient to enable the NAACP lawyers to launch their legal attack and to pursue their strategy until at least a token victory was won (Killian, 1975).

The black protest of the 1960s differed from these earlier protest activities in a number of respects: (1) the shift from primarily legal and educational means of protest to direct action (demonstrations, boycotts, sit-ins, wade-ins, and the like); (2) the shift in initiative from the hands of a relatively few professional desegregationists (NAACP lawyers and officials) to a large number of average citizens who were willing to confront the segregated system through direct action; (3) the broaden-ing of objectives from a narrow attack on a particular public facility to a full-scale attack against the entire segregated order; and (4) the expan-sion of the movement to assume a *mass* character that cut across divi-sions in the black community and reached from coast to coast.

The Montgomery Bus Boycott

The Montgomery bus boycott (1955–1956) marked a turning point in the black protest movement. Here the narrowly circumscribed bounda-ries of legalistic tactics were broken, and large numbers of blacks in Montgomery became active participants in the civil-rights struggle. The Montgomery movement constituted a spontaneous confrontation of the white community by an aggrieved and aroused black community. With Montgomery the black protest moved from selective attack to mass confrontation.

The Montgomery movement incorporated many specific tactics—mass meetings, nonviolent techniques, mass boycotts, and legal-judiciary measures—that became "standard operating procedures" for the civil-rights movement of the 1960s. The success of the Montgomery movement projected upon the national horizon a new group of militant black leaders represented by the late Reverend Martin Luther King, Jr.

The Montgomery movement was precipitated by an incident that occurred on December 1, 1955. Mrs. Rosa Parks, a forty-two-year-old black seamstress employed at a downtown department store, was returning home in the evening on a city bus. At one stop, several white passengers boarded the bus, whereupon the driver instructed four blacks to stand so that the whites might sit. The bus driver was acting within his rights as prescribed by Alabama law. Three of the blacks complied with the driver's instructions, but Mrs. Parks refused. The bus driver called a police officer, and Mrs. Parks was charged with violating the bus segregation law.

Word of Mrs. Parks's arrest spread throughout the black community. Talk was heard among some rowdy elements of initiating physical reprisals against Montgomery bus drivers. But a nonviolent direction was given to resentment by a group of black ministers who called a one-day boycott of the buses for the day of the trial. The protest plans received wide dissemination through announcements at black church services and through news stories carried in the Montgomery press. On December 5, the day of the trial, a very high percentage of blacks, perhaps as many as 75 percent of the usual riders, stayed off the buses. Since blacks represented about 70 percent of the company's passengers, the protest was noticeable.

Mrs. Parks was fined $10 and $4 in court costs. That evening a mass meeting was held in the local Holt Street Baptist Church. Some 5,000 blacks, including forty-seven ministers, and one white minister of a black congregation were present. The crowd engaged in hymn singing and listened to attacks upon the Jim Crow system. A resolution was adopted continuing the bus boycott until such time as city and bus-company officials would agree to (1) more courteous treatment of blacks, (2) seating on a first-come-first-serve basis, and (3) the employment of black bus drivers on predominantly black runs. The Montgomery Improvement Association was formed and Reverend Martin Luther King, Jr., was elected chairperson. Twenty-seven years of age, King had secured his doctorate in religion from Boston University prior to becoming pastor of Montgomery's Dexter Avenue Baptist Church.

The Montgomery Improvement Association set up a car pool to get blacks to work. Unsigned and unidentified schedules were posted on telephone poles and the sides of buildings. The city police responded to this challenge by becoming especially zealous in enforcing traffic laws, attempting in this manner to interfere with the operation through harassment.

Montgomery white leaders expected the movement to collapse. But the boycott continued into 1956 with considerable effectiveness— roughly 80 percent of the usual black riders stayed off the buses. Exasperated, Montgomery Mayor W.A. Gayle issued a statement on January 23 announcing that he and members of the city commission had joined the Citizens' Councils, the militant white segregationist group. He stated that Montgomery whites had "pussy-footed around on this boycott long enough."

Within a month of Mayor Gayle's announcement of his intention to take firm action, a grand jury returned indictments against some ninety blacks, including twenty-four ministers. The action was taken under an almost forgotten antilabor law enacted in 1921. Blacks were angered by this development, but King cautioned, "Even if we are arrested every day, let no man drag you so low as to hate."

Despite police harassment, the boycott continued. The NAACP, at the request of Montgomery blacks, undertook legal action challenging the legality of bus segregation in Alabama. During 1956 the case moved through the federal courts. On November 13, 1956, the U.S. Supreme Court upheld a lower federal court's ruling that invalidated the Alabama law and the city ordinance requiring bus segregation. The following evening some 2,000 Montgomery blacks held another mass meeting and voted to end the eleven-month-old boycott as soon as the Supreme Court's decree was delivered to Montgomery. This occurred on December 21, 1956. Once again blacks rode Montgomery buses, but no longer on a segregated basis.

After Montgomery

The sit-ins of 1960 (*see* chapter 12) unleashed black protest on a national scale. Cities across the nation—both North and South—became the scene for demonstrations, boycotts, sit-ins, and the like. During the course of these developments, the late Reverend Martin Luther King, Jr., and his associates evolved a fourfold set of tactics, which King (1965: 16) explained in these terms:

1. Nonviolent demonstrators go into the streets to exercise their constitutional rights.

2. Racists resist by unleashing violence against them.

3. Americans of conscience in the name of decency demand federal intervention and legislation.

4. The Administration, under mass pressure, initiates measures of immediate intervention and remedial legislation.

In brief, blacks needed "a crisis to bargain with"—and hence often had to create a crisis.

This fourfold strategy was effectively employed to secure passage of the Civil Rights acts of 1964 and 1965. In the spring of 1963, Reverend King took the civil-rights fight to Birmingham, Alabama, alleged to be the most segregated large city in the South, saying, "As Birmingham goes, so goes the whole South." He organized a "siege of demonstrations" against that city's segregation barriers (the first step). More than 3,000 Birmingham blacks were arrested, while newspapers, magazines, and television stations beamed to the nation pictures of blacks facing snarling police dogs and being bowled over by high-pressure fire hoses (the second step). Although little was accomplished in Birmingham itself, the civil-rights issue quickly became the number-one topic not just in the South, but throughout the entire nation (the third step). Demonstrations quickly spread across the nation, some 1,122 being recorded within a four-month period. The demonstrations culminated in August 28, 1963, in the "March on Washington" in which some 200,000 civil-rights marchers demonstrated "for jobs and freedom." The wave of demonstrations spurred the Kennedy administration to sponsor new civil-rights legislation, legislation that was passed by Congress the following year (the fourth step).

The same strategy was employed in 1965 when many black leaders became convinced that a much more stringent law was needed to protect black voting rights. This time King took his campaign to Selma, Alabama. On Sunday, March 7, some 520 blacks prepared to march from Selma to Montgomery, the state capital, to dramatize their case to the nation (the first step). Television cameras recorded this scene: as the blacks, marching two abreast, reached the Pettus Bridge crossing the Alabama River, Alabama state troopers unleashed a savage attack against the marchers with billy clubs and gas grenades (the second step). The nation was collectively outraged at this brutality. Soon thousands of sympathizers were bound for Selma, and the national spotlight was again focused upon the civil-rights issue (the third step). The Johnson administration responded with the Civil Rights Act of 1965 (the fourth step). Selma was the last of the classic southern nonviolent campaigns and was followed two months later by Watts (the 1965 Los Angeles ghetto riot).

In the Montgomery and post-Montgomery civil-rights movement, the late Reverend Martin Luther King, Jr., enjoyed a preeminent position among black leaders—in both 1963 and 1966, for instance, some 88 percent of blacks approved of his leadership (Brink and Harris, 1966). During this period he served as the symbol of the direct action movement. King's influence and popularity centered on the fact that he articulated the aspirations of blacks. They responded to the cadence of his addresses, his religious phraseology and manner of speaking, and the vision of his dream for them and America. He intuitively adopted the style of the old-fashioned black preacher and restored oratory to its place among the arts. Further, he effectively communicated black aspirations to white America. His religious terminology and use of Christian symbols of love and nonviolence were reassuring to white America. In many ways, King gave the feeling to whites that he was their good friend and posed no threat to them. He combined militancy with conservatism and caution and with a willingness to negotiate and bargain with White House emissaries. King, then, epitomized conservative militancy (Meier, 1965).

Factors Underlying the Black Protest

In Chapter 11 we pointed out that during the period between the overthrow of Reconstruction and the 1950s the principal response of blacks to their minority status was that of accommodation. This pattern changed during the 1950s and early 1960s as a number of forces were at work that made blacks susceptible to a protest or militant approach. Let us examine a few of these factors.

An Emergent, New Black Self-Image. Heightened black self-respect and identity acted as a powerful stimulus to the protest movement. This improved black self-image was partially fostered by an emergent redefinition of the black's status within American life. The Supreme Court in particular played an important role in this development. The net effect of the Supreme Court's desegregation decisions was to advance in an authoritative, formal, and official fashion a new definition of the black as a first-class citizen. In its 1954 school ruling in *Brown* v. *Board of Education,* the Supreme Court overturned the "separate but equal" doctrine formulated in 1896 in *Plessy* v. *Ferguson,* a decision that had relegated blacks to second-class citizenship and gave legal sanction to a segregated racial order. Presidential statements and congressional enactment of new civil-rights laws reinforced the effect of the Supreme Court's decisions.

These developments were closely associated with another important stimulus to an improved black self-image, the emergence of the new nations of Africa. Reverend Martin Luther King, Jr. (1956:26), observed: ". . . today he [the black] looks beyond the borders of his own land and sees the decolonization and liberation of Africa and Asia; he sees colored peoples, yellow, black and brown, ruling over their own new nations. He sees colored statesmen voting on vital issues at the United Nations. . . ." Such developments as these contributed to a new black self-image in which accommodation no longer constituted for many blacks an acceptable response to segregation. And the civil-rights movement itself, once it got under way, offered a further impetus to heightened black self-respect and identity.

The Anticipation of Victory. Until the late 1950s, strong feelings of defeatism tended to characterize many blacks. For those in the South in particular, the "road to a better life" appeared as an endless maze, with a mammoth white wall at every turn. Government officials, the police, and business and educational leaders—in a word, the entire power structure—were usually lily-white. Concentrated largely in lower socioeconomic-class positions many blacks felt virtually powerless. The segregated order seemed impregnable. Indeed, segregation appeared to be—and in truth was—the "law of the land." The U.S. Army still had all-white and all-black units at the time of the Korean War, *Plessy* v. *Ferguson* still had the force of law, and since the defeat of Reconstruction the nation had been more or less willing to allow the South a measure of sovereignty on the race issue. History reveals that movements for basic social change are unlikely to originate with people of despair. Demoralized people typically do not believe that an improved future is possible, and their sense of futility leads to apathy, not action, and to despair rather than demonstrations.

During the 1950s, however, especially with the Supreme Court's 1954 school ruling, this picture was altered. The machinery and resources of the federal government became decisively committed for the first time since Reconstruction to an antisegregation program. Where previously widespread despair and hopelessness prevailed, now the situation was progressively defined as one that could be altered. This prospect of victory created a climate conducive to struggle.

A Sense of Relative Deprivation. During World War II promotions were rapid and widespread in the Air Force and slow and piecemeal in the Military Police. Most of us probably would be inclined to predict that the men in the Air Force would be more satisfied with their chances for promotion than the men in the Military Police since in absolute terms they were moving ahead faster in their careers. Yet research has demonstrated that the men in the Air Force were considerably more frustrated over promotions than those in the Military Police. Among the men in the Air Force it was not so much the *absolute* level of attainment that made for poor morale but a sense of **relative deprivation**—the gap between what people actually have and what they have come to expect and feel to be their just due. In contrast, the Military Police did not expect rapid promotions and they learned to live with relatively few advances in rank (Merton and Kitt, 1950).

In hindsight it is surprising that social scientists did not anticipate the black protest. Yet at the time it was easy to conclude that blacks should be more satisfied than in any previous time in American history: Data revealed that employment opportunities for blacks had gradually expanded, their median annual family income had increased 73 percent between 1950 and 1960, and from 1940 to 1960 the number of blacks who attended college had more than doubled. Yet many blacks in 1960 found themselves in a position quite similar to the men in the Air Force. The prosperity of the World War II years and the 1950s gave blacks a taste of "the good life," a taste of the affluent society. Blacks had gained enough to hope realistically for more. Hence barriers blocking their further advancement were felt as severely frustrating. Any number of observers have noted that revolutions are not made by persons who are utterly dispossessed and despairing, but by those who have already gained something, who hope for more, and who believe their aspirations to be legitimate and realistic (Hoffer, 1951; Davies, 1962; Geschwender, 1964).

The mass media—radio, television, magazines, and the press—penetrate, indeed invade, the black ghettos with the values and aspirations of the larger white-dominated society. Some nine of ten black homes have a TV set, and a TV set that juts out an antenna that senses the white world and its ways as never before. Even a soap commercial can sow seeds of discontent if its setting is a modern suburban kitchen. Those who live in the congested black ghettos of large American cities are aware that others are not so disadvantaged. The black protest then arose not so much as a product of despair as a product of rising expectations.

Additional Factors.   We have examined a number of factors that made blacks increasingly susceptible to the protest orientation. Other factors were also at work. Among these factors were the "piling up" of blacks in urban ghettos where communication and social movements can spread rapidly; the assumption by the movement during Reverend King's leadership of a strong religious flavor having a revivalistic impact; the exposure of many blacks in the armed forces to a democratic and integrationist ideology; and the movement's early successes, which begot pressures for still more change.

Aftermath

The black protest subsided by the early 1970s. Not since Reverend King mobilized blacks during the 1960s has a black leader been able to rally a comparable national constituency. Indeed, no longer is there a national civil-rights movement on the scale that once existed. Black leadership has become more diffuse and the movement more fragmented. Of the "Big Five" civil-rights groups of the 1960s, only the NAACP and the National Urban League remain viable organizations. The Student Nonviolent Coordinating Committee (SNCC) has faded away. The Southern Christian Leadership Conference has been torn by internal feuds among Reverend King's family and associates. The Congress of Racial Equality (CORE), which led the Freedom Rides of 1961, is a shadow of what it used to be and has been caught up in leadership struggles that have brought charges of violence and corruption.

The nation has gone through more than a decade in which blacks have not had a sense of great progress in civil rights. White support on civil-rights issues has eroded and in many instances it has been replaced

by opposition. Moreover, today's issues are different and more complicated than those twenty-five years ago. No longer does one usually find
direct, blatant, formal segregation. Yet discrimination persists, having
taken new and subtler forms. For instance, legally segregated schools
have been barred but tests, unequal disciplinary practices (school sus-
pensions), and ability groupings frequently produce comparable outcomes.

Andrew Young, the former congressman and U.S. ambassador to the
United Nations who was one of Reverend King's top strategists, says
that the 1950s were "the days of the lawyer," when legalized segregation was first successfully challenged in court. With the 1960s came "the
time of the preachers," who organized demonstrations to achieve the
enactment of new civil-rights legislation. And the 1970s saw blacks
move into elective politics and into issues affecting the economy. "You
almost can't talk about civil rights anymore because it's all so wrapped
up in politics and business," Young asserts. "What we are seeing now
is the creation of a black movement aimed at business and jobs" (Maxwell, 1980:1).

Benjamin L. Hooks, executive director of the NAACP, says that in
the early days of the civil-rights movement

> we were fighting for elemental things, like being able to eat at Walgreen's
> or ride the bus. White folks in the North said, "Why the hell are they
> shooting fire hoses at those people just for that?" and they supported us.
> Now they know that what we really want is a job, and they are beginning
> to perceive that maybe it's *their* job (Maxwell, 1980:1).

Further, during the early 1960s, the chief civil-rights issues involved
blacks. Today the movement for social equality has expanded to encompass a great many new groups including women, gays, and the handicapped.

The black protest subsided for a number of reasons (Killian, 1975).
First, the existence of new laws and administrative policies, many of
them a response to the black protest, made it possible for blacks to
pursue their goals through existing institutional channels. Second, in
some respects American concern during the late 1960s and early 1970s
with the conduct of the Vietnam War preempted the controversy surrounding black demands. Third, on the local level the white power
structure was able to coopt and bring many young black militants into
"the system"—government and political organizations. Fourth, the
ranks of the more visible and aggressive black leaders (including Malcolm X, Reverend King, H. Rap Brown, Stokely Carmichael, Eldridge
Cleaver, Bobby Seale, and Huey Newton) were decimated by assassination, imprisonment, and emigration, thereby weakening the more militant organizations. White power demonstrated that open black
defiance was extremely dangerous and often suicidal. Huey Newton,
founder and leader of the Black Panther party, observed in an inter-

view in 1972, "We've rejected the rhetoric of the gun; it got about forty of us killed and sent hundreds of us to prison. Our goal now is to organize the black communities politically" (Peterson, 1972:1).

Although the black protest has subsided, the black cultural revival (with a strong emphasis on black standards of beauty and black pride and unity) has become so pervasive that all segments of the black population have been awakened by it. During the 1970s many blacks turned to the task of electing black office-seekers and organizing local self-help programs. They have concentrated on the nuts-and-bolts of winning elections—registering voters, setting up telephone banks with voter names, getting supporters to the polls, and establishing poll-watching operations to guard against vote-stealing. And they have concentrated on such community-level activities as securing mortgages for black homeowners, establishing and running businesses, and getting jobs for the poor and training young people.

The past decade or so has constituted something of a "holding pattern," with no one knowing what direction the black movement will take. On the whole blacks have continued their pursuit of integration. This option has entailed "working within the system" nonviolently and taking advantage of new civil-rights measures. Nonetheless, the feeling prevails that the racial crisis continues to smolder. Racism persists. The black movement has been plagued by confusion as to whether it should pursue an assimilationist (civil-rights) or a separatist (black-nationalist) program. In many respects the black population has been too large to integrate quickly within American life while simultaneously it has been too small and scattered to go it alone as an independent nation. Consequently, the black movement continues to waver between the two approaches and one feels that at any time forces could be ignited that would bring a return of coercive public protest rather than the course emphasizing conventional political action (Killian, 1975).

Variables Affecting The Response of Minority-Group Members

Generational differences play an important part in the responses of minority individuals to their subordinate and disadvantaged status. Among European immigrants, the second and third generations generally have displayed stronger assimilationist strivings, particularly with an integrationist emphasis, than the first generation. Further, the civil-rights movement among blacks in the early 1960s found particular strength among black youth. Fredric Solomon and Jacob R. Fishman (1964), in their study of student participants in civil-rights activities, noted:

Most of the young demonstrators whom we have been studying were at the threshold of their adolescence when the United States Supreme Court ruled unanimously that the segregated schools these youngsters had been attending were illegal. This public recognition of the desirability of desegregation and of its possible achievement in the near future was an experience in the adolescent development of these young people that was quite different from that of their parents and older siblings. Feeling that desegregation was now their right, the students experienced increasing frustration with the painful slowness of its implementation and with the seeming hypocrisy and helplessness of adults—white and Negro—who paid lip service to principles but took no risks for their realization.

Similarly, assimilationist strivings have been particularly strong among middle-class blacks and European immigrants. Psychologically, they have tended to identify with similarly situated dominant-group members. The sociologists Ruth Searles and J. Allen Williams, Jr. (1962), in a study of black college student participation in sit-ins during the early 1960s, concluded:

> Socialized to value respectability and achievement, educated to affirm their right of equal opportunity, legitimized in their expectations by civil rights legislation and an important body of opinion, living in a college environment where freedom from constraints and ease of communication facilitate the development of protest activity, these students have selected nonviolent protest as an acceptable means of demonstrating their anger at barriers to first-class citizenship. Far from being alienated, the students appear to be committed to the society and its middle-class leaders.

Indeed, for such youth, middle-class white society functioned as a key reference group.

The sociologist Gary T. Marx (1967), in his study of the collective mood of the black community in 1964, found that those blacks who were militant on civil-rights issues tended to be an elite within the black community: In comparison with nonmilitants they were better educated and more involved in voluntary organizations, more likely to vote, they had more friends, a more positive self-image, a higher morale, greater sophistication, and they were less hostile toward whites. He suggests that high social status produces militancy to the extent that status fosters hope, which in turn makes militancy seem realistic. Militancy calls for at least some degree of hope, a belief that a new tomorrow is possible. A sense of futility, more prevalent among the less advantaged, seems to work against the development of the morale and hope required for a militant vision. Further, those who enjoy social privilege generally have the energy, resources, and self-confidence needed to challenge an oppressive and powerful system.

SUMMARY

1. Assimilation involves those processes whereby groups with distinctive identities become culturally and socially fused together. It is a response by which some minority-group individuals undertake to lose their distinct minority-group identity and to fuse themselves socially and culturally with the dominant group.

2. Viewed over the long run, European immigrant groups within the United States have typically oriented themselves toward an assimilationist goal. Usually acculturation—alterations in a group's cultural practices in the direction of the dominant Anglo-American pattern—has proceeded more rapidly than integration—alterations in a group's network of formal and informal social relationships. Consequently, in-group ties have tended to display greater strength than customs. The adjustment of Italians to American life provides a good illustration of these patterns.

3. One of the most complete forms of assimilation is leaving the minority group and "passing" as a member of the dominant group. This adjustment is a feasible alternative for those minority-group members who physically and culturally resemble the dominant group.

4. The civil-rights movement during the early 1960s, led by Reverend Martin Luther King, Jr., represented a combined aggression-assimilation response. The movement was not so much directed against major deprivations inherent in the American social system as against relative deprivations or inequalities that blacks experience as American citizens. Strictly speaking, it constituted a reform and not a revolutionary movement.

5. The black protest of the 1960s differed from the earlier protests led by the NAACP in a number of respects: (a) the shift from primarily legal and educational means of protest to direct action; (b) the shift in initiative from the hands of a relatively few professional desegregationists (NAACP lawyers and officials) to a large number of average citizens who were willing to confront the segregated system through direct action; (c) the broadening of objectives from a narrow attack upon a particular public facility to a full-scale attack against the entire segregated order; and (d) the expansion of the movement to assume a mass character that cut across divisions in the black community and reached from coast to coast.

6. The Montgomery bus boycott (1955–1965) marked a turning point in the black protest movement. Here the narrowly circumscribed boundaries of legalistic tactics were broken, and large numbers of blacks in Montgomery became active participants in the civil-rights movement. Later, in 1960, the sit-ins unleashed the black protest on a national scale. Particularly important in winning the passage of new

civil-rights legislation was the Birmingham campaign in 1964 and the Selma campaign in 1965.

7. Among the factors underlying the black protest during the 1960s were the following: (a) the emergence of a new black self-image in which accommodation no longer constituted for many blacks an acceptable response to segregation; (b) the replacement of widespread feelings of despair and hopelessness with a feeling that victory was possible; (c) the development of a deepening sense of relative deprivation; and (d) the "piling up" of blacks in urban ghettos, where communication and social movements rapidly spread.

8. The black protest subsided by the early 1970s. A number of factors were responsible for this change. First, the existence of new laws and administrative policies, many of them a response to the black protest, made it possible for blacks to pursue their goals through existing institutional channels. Second, in some respects American concern during the late 1960s and early 1970s with the conduct of the Vietnam War preempted the controversy surrounding black demands. Third, on the local level the white power structure was able to coopt and bring many young black militants into the system. Fourth, the ranks of the more visible and aggressive black leaders were decimated by assassination, imprisonment, and emigration.

9. Generational differences play an important part in the responses of minority-group individuals to their subordinate and disadvantaged status. Among European immigrants, the second and third generations generally have displayed stronger assimilationist strivings, particularly with an integrationist emphasis, than the first generation. Further, the civil-rights movement among blacks during the early 1960s found particular strength among black youth.

GLOSSARY

Relative Deprivation   The gap between what people actually have and what they have come to expect and feel to be their just due.

Responding by Avoidance 14

*I*n chapter 13 we considered assimilation as a minority-group reaction to dominance. In this chapter we continue our discussion by focusing upon a response that is the polar opposite of assimilation—*avoidance*. In avoidance members of a minority group attempt to shun—to escape from—situations in which they are likely to encounter prejudice and discrimination.

Insulation

Experiencing a variety of rebuffs from the dominant group, minority-group members may respond with efforts directed at withdrawal and isolation from the stresses of intergroup contacts. Withdrawal and avoidance represent a relatively frequent type of response. The sociologist Robert Johnson (1957), for instance, in his study of black youth in Elmira, New York, during the 1950s, found sentiment favoring insulation from whites quite prevalent as represented by endorsement of the following statements:

> "Negroes should live around their own people." (27% agree.)
> "If I had a choice between an all-Negro club and a mixed club, I would join the all-Negro club." (50% agree.)
> "I would find it a little distasteful to:
>   Eat with a white person." (9% agree.)
>   Dance with a white person." (17% agree.)
>   Go to a party and find that most of the people there were white." (21% agree.)
>   Have a white person marry somebody in my family." (42% agree.)
> (Johnson, 1957: 202.)

Black adults in the same community (based on a sample of 150) showed similar patterns as reflected in their endorsement of the following statements:

"Negroes shouldn't go into business establishments where they think they're not wanted." (64% agree.)

"Suppose you were downtown with a group of your Negro friends, and they asked you to go with them into a restaurant that you were pretty sure didn't serve Negroes—would you go?" (71% would not go.) (Williams, 1964: 249).

The reluctance of some blacks to take advantage of desegregated facilities and the continuance of avoidance patterns often stems from an uneasiness and uncertainty about the new situation. Lingering fears from the past may lead some blacks to expect that they will be humiliated and mistreated even at officially desegregated facilities. This vicious circle is quite similar to what psychologists describe as "avoidance learning." If we construct an experimental setting in which subjects' fingers are repeatedly shocked electrically immediately after the flashing of a light, they quickly learn to avoid the painful shock by lifting their fingers when the light comes on. But what happens when the electric shock is no longer applied? How can the subjects acquire knowledge of the changed setting? As long as they lift their fingers at the light, they can never learn that the light is no longer associated with a shock. This outcome is a critical element in avoidance learning. Blacks, too, have learned to withdraw from painful interracial settings. Even when these situations change and the discomfort is removed, many blacks are reluctant to test them and discover the changes (Pettigrew, 1964).

Blacks cite a wide variety of factors as influencing their avoidance patterns. One of these is antipathy toward whites and white racism. This is how two black youths stated the matter in Mobile, Alabama (Fancher, 1970: 18–19):

> We know integration (I should say desegregation—the court always uses that word) desegregation has been going on for a long time now. That's why black folks have thirteen shades of color. But integration is playing out, it's played out. In Mobile integration just won't work because when we go to a white school they treat us like some dog. We never get to be the officers of the class so we'd rather just stay in our own schools.

> I think it's [integration] an impossibility at this time. How can you have integration when the white man is on the top of the pole? He controls everything, he's the head of everything and he owns the power structure and we're at the bottom. We aren't equal in the white man's eyesight.

Avoidance may take the form of developing towns or communities composed principally or entirely of minority-group members. Even when residential segregation is not initiated and enforced by the dominant group, minority-group members may prefer to live in their own communities. In this manner they endeavor to avoid the continuous harassment incident to living in the larger society. The sociologist Mozell

C. Hill (1944) reports on a number of all-black communities in Oklahoma in which there is a positive feeling and consensus that the common welfare is best served by shunning social relations with whites. Mound Bayou, an all-black community in Mississippi, has fostered a tradition of race consciousness and avoidance of whites (Hermann, 1981). Within the South at the present time, any number of black communities have undertaken incorporation, making them eligible for federal aid projects and opening the door to greater black control. A forty-two-year-old steelworker who plans to move from Attala, Alabama, to nearby Ridgedale, a black town, observes: "I can't make it in the white man's society, so I'm getting out. I can't be elected to anything. I can't serve on the white man's boards, and I'm sick of it. I'm going to where I can do anything I'm capable of doing" (Maxwell, 1968:1).

Migration

Minority-group members may seek to deal with their disadvantaged position through migration. The stimulus to move may come from conditions at home that they desire to escape or from conditions elsewhere that attract them. More frequently forces of both "push" and "pull" are present. These forces influenced the mass migration of blacks from rural communities of the South to northern and southern urban centers between 1915 and 1970. Except for the movement of some 40,000 southern blacks to Kansas shortly after the Civil War, there was no significant migration to the North or the West until the period immediately preceding World War I.

In 1910 some 90 percent of the nation's black population was located in the South and 77 percent in rural communities. About this time factors of both "push" and "pull" began to encourage out-migration. Within the South white "infiltration" into types of work formerly monopolized by blacks, the shift westward of cotton growing, the ravaging of cotton crops by the boll weevil, and the droughts of 1916 and 1917 provided the impetus to black population movement. World War I accelerated the trend. The draft of youths for military service moved large numbers of black men from their home communities. Simultaneously, the military induction of white workers, the shutting down of European immigration, and conditions of wartime prosperity forced northern industry to turn actively to blacks for new workers.

The migration of blacks has resulted primarily from economic motivation. Census data reveal that the mounting inability of southern agriculture to absorb black tenants and workers induced a net migration from the South of more than 700,000 blacks between 1920 and 1930. During the 1930s, when few urban job openings beckoned, net black migration out of the South fell below 350,000. During the decade of

World War II large numbers of job openings for unskilled workers at higher wages encouraged 1,200,000 blacks, an unprecedented number, to leave the South. The migration of southern blacks to the North continued at high levels during the 1950s and 1960s. During the 1970s, the migration patterns began to reverse. The economic difficulties of the auto, steel, and related industries in the North and the rapid expansion of the job market in the Sun Belt encouraged both black and white workers to seek employment in the South and the Southwest. In the eleven states of the Confederacy extending from Virginia to Texas, the number of blacks increased by almost 2 million from 1970 to 1980, and is now more than 12 million.

Separatism

A separatist approach to minority-group status is diametrically opposite to the assimilationist response. Whereas assimilation implies the absorption of the minority by the larger society, separatism has a contrary aim—secession. The minority seeks to maintain or secure a distinct identity that is typically linked with efforts to achieve territorial separation from the dominant group. Consequently, separatism is a form of withdrawal or avoidance. But it seldom involves simply avoidance. Separatist movements commonly have an aggressive component, and hence may most aptly be described as an *aggressive-avoidance* response.

Zionism

The Zionist movement, which arose during the nineteenth century among Jews and culminated in 1948 in the establishment of Israel, provides a classic example of a separatist movement. Zionism was a response to the persecution that the Jews had experienced since their dispersion from their ancient homeland in Palestine. Theodor Herzl, great pioneer of Zionism, expressed the despair felt by many of the world's Jews in 1896 in a book that became an ideological cornerstone of the Zionist movement, *Der Judenstaat (The Jewish State)*:

> The Jewish question still exists. It would be foolish to deny it. It is a remnant of the Middle Ages, which civilized nations do not even yet seem able to shake off, try as they will. . . . The Jewish question exists wherever Jews live in perceptible numbers. Where it does not exist, it is carried by Jews in the course of their migrations. We naturally move to those places where we are not persecuted, and there our presence produces persecution. This is the case in every country, and will remain so, even in those highly civilized—for instance, France—until the Jewish question finds a solution on a political basis. The unfortunate Jews are now carrying the

seeds of Anti-Semitism into England; they have already introduced it into America (Herzl, 1946:75).

For Zionists, assimilation was not the answer. In fact it was unwanted. Herzl wrote, "I referred previously to our 'assimilation.' I do not for a moment wish to imply that I desire such an end. Our national character is too historically famous, and, in spite of every degradation, too fine to make its annihilation desirable" (Herzl, 1946:91). Herzl's answer to the Jewish question was "Let the sovereignty be granted us over a portion of the globe large enough to satisfy the rightful requirements of a nation; the rest we shall manage for ourselves" (Herzl, 1946:92).

Many contemporary Jewish leaders are no less strong than Herzl in rejecting Jewish assimilation. Leaders of the World Zionist Organization have continued to insist that Jews intensify their opposition to assimilation and deepen their identification with Israel as the center of Jewish life:

> We have become part and parcel of the life of the other peoples and with that we have lost the main basis of our separate existence. . . . The result is that we live in a period where a very large part of our people, especially the young generation, is threatened by an anonymous process of erosion, of disintegration, not as a theory or as a conscientious ideology but by the fact of this day-to-day life. This process, if not halted and reversed, threatens Jewish survival more than persecution, inquisition, pogroms and mass murder of Jews did in the past (Dr. Nahum Goldmann, president of World Zionist Organization, 1965).

And American Jewish leaders have warned that "defense against assimilation" is even more urgent today than "defense against discrimination." Seeking to boost enrollment in religious schools, the New York Board of Jewish Education has run advertisements in New York City-area newspapers warning, "If You Are Jewish, Chances Are Your Grandchildren Won't Be."

The chief Zionist aim, as set forth by Herzl, was to secure "the survival of the Jewish people" and to solve "the Jewish problem" by establishing the Jews in Palestine with all the attributes of a modern nation: land, language (Hebrew), and sovereignty. The dispersion of the Jews throughout the world was seen as an intolerable condition that could be solved only by the establishment of a Jewish nation. Zionists saw the root of the Jewish problem as residing in the fact that the Jews lived as unwelcomed guests in lands occupied and ruled by others. If this were the case, then the solution seemed obvious. The Jews needed to establish themselves in a land not occupied and ruled by others, a land in which they themselves would be the hosts.

Zionists thought that the mere existence of the Jewish state would solve the Jewish problem. Anti-Semitism was viewed as a kind of ghost fear aroused among the Gentiles by the anomalous survival of the Jews despite their dispersion when, under similar circumstances, other peoples had become extinct or assimilated. In turn, anti-Semitism contributed to Jewish self-hatred and inferiority complexes. Zionists asserted that both types of problems would be solved by the creation of a Jewish nation to which world Jews would migrate. By the same token those Jews who continued to live in other nations would be benefited. Jewish rights would then be protected through international diplomatic channels. Since the Jews living in Palestine would enjoy status as a nation, the Jewish nation would occupy a position among the nations of the world and be in a position to advance the interests of world Jewry. In addition, Jews living outside Palestine might derive a new sense of self-respect from the existence of a Jewish nation.

Since the establishment of Israel in 1948, the world Zionist movement has found itself divided. Israeli Zionist leaders insist that, to be qualitatively a full Jew, a Jew must settle in Israel. They strongly argue that it is obligatory for all Zionists to migrate to Israel now that the doors of the Jewish state are open to them. On the other hand, Zionists from the free West find it quite unreasonable that they should be expected to go to Israel as a duty (only about one-fifth of the Jews of the world live in Israel). As a result many American Zionists find themselves suspended in a kind of limbo somewhere between the Israeli stand and the various non-Zionist positions. Israeli Zionists, in essence, are saying, "Come or you excommunicate yourself." Non-Zionists are urging, "Let us hoe our respective gardens." Many American Zionists find themselves trapped between the two positions.

Garveyism

Immediately following World War I, a mass movement emerged among American blacks with a strong separatist appeal (Cronon, 1955; Martin, 1976). It blossomed under the leadership of Marcus Garvey, a black West Indian, who possessed considerable gifts of leadership. His organization, the Universal Negro Improvement Association (UNIA), found a responsive setting for its appeal of black nationalism among large numbers of southern blacks who had migrated to northern cities during and following the war. Among the migrants, there existed considerable disillusionment with the city as a promised land and with race riots and racial discrimination in the North. The migrants had been uprooted from traditional patterns of life and found themselves confused and disoriented within their new surroundings. An old way of life had been displaced, but a new way of life had not as yet been realized. Migration had brought with it a destruction of old rural values, a disruption of social roots, and an isolation from many traditional personal ties.

The setting provided a fertile ground for a mass movement with a strong racial and nationalistic appeal. A central ingredient in Garvey's appeal was the glorification of blackness. He exalted everything black and exhorted blacks to be proud of their distinctive features and color. He told his listeners, "I am the equal of any white man. I want you to feel the same way." One enthusiastic delegate to the first UNIA convention, in 1920, served notice that "it takes 1,000 white men to lick one Negro." Garvey catered to the darker blacks. He laughed at the light-skinned blacks, who, he asserted, were always seeking "excuses to get out of the Negro Race," and he scornfully accused his light-colored opponents, such as W.E.B. Du Bois of the NAACP, of being "time-serving, bootlicking agencies of subserviency to the whites."

Garvey angrily accused white scholars of distorting black history to make it appear unfavorable to blacks. "Every student of history, of impartial mind," Garvey taught, "knows that the Negro once ruled the world, when white men were savages and barbarians living in caves; that thousands of Negro professors . . . taught in the Universities of Alexandria." He glorified blacks and told how whites were far below the darker race:

> When Europe was inhabited by a race of cannibals, a race of savages, naked men, heathens and pagans, Africa was peopled with a race of cultured black men, who were masters in art, science and literature; men who were cultured and refined; men, who, it was said, were like the gods. Even the great poets of old sang in beautiful sonnets of the delight it afforded the gods to be in companionship with the Ethiopians. Why, then, should we lose hope? Black men, you were once great; you shall be great again. Lose not courage, lose not faith, go forward. The thing to do is to get organized (Cronon, 1955:176).

Along with his efforts to build black pride went a reorientation in religion as well. Garvey insisted that blacks should end their subservience to the white man through the worship of a white God and worship instead a black God. For him Christ was a black (Cronon, 1955).

Garvey advocated an aggressive philosophy of racial purity and social separation. He demanded that racial amalgamation end at once and warned that any member of UNIA who married a white would be summarily expelled. Speaking to whites, he indicated, "We do not seek intermarriage, nor do we hanker after the impossible. We want the right to have a country of our own, and there foster and re-establish a culture and civilization exclusively ours." It was a program of separation from whites. He denounced other black leaders as being bent on cultural assimilation, which he vigorously opposed. He viewed the NAACP as the worst offender because it "wants us all to become white by amalgamation, but they are not honest enough to come out with the truth."

Garvey reassured whites that they need have no fears of the aims of the UNIA. He declared the organization was stoutly opposed to "miscegenation and race suicide" and believed strongly "in the purity of the Negro race and the purity of the white race." He sought to warn the white world of the dangers lurking in social equality. "Some Negroes believe in social equality," he cautioned. "They want to intermarry with the white women of this country, and it is going to cause trouble later on. Some Negroes want the same jobs you have. They want to be Presidents of the nation" (Cronon, 1955:191–193). Thus Garvey abandoned the fight for integration, a type of assimilationist appeal, and promoted racial compartmentalization, or separatism. His plans for the abdication of black rights in America brought him the open support of white supremacists and the Ku Klux Klan, which was reactivated following World War I.

An integral aspect of Garvey's separatism was his program to lead blacks back to their African homeland. With his customary flair for the dramatic he assured his followers that within a few years Africa would be as completely dominated by blacks as Europe was by whites. He believed a great independent African nation was essential for race redemption, and he was earnestly convinced that within Africa blacks would achieve their destiny as a great people. Garvey warned whites, "We say to the white man who now dominates Africa that it is to his interest to clear out of Africa now, because we are coming . . . 400,-000,000 strong." But it was never Garvey's intention that all New World blacks should return to Africa. Like many Zionists he felt that, once a strong African nation was established, blacks everywhere would realize new prestige, strength, and protection.

In 1921 he created the "Empire of Africa" and made himself provisional "president-general." To assist him he created the positions of "potentate" and "supreme deputy potentate," and a nobility consisting of "knights of the Nile," "knights of the Distinguished Service Order of Ethiopia," and "dukes of the Niger and of Uganda." Since the new nation needed a military arm, Garvey founded the Universal African Legion, the Universal Black Cross Nurses, the Universal African Motor Corps, and the Black Eagle Flying Corps—all with uniforms and officers. Great emphasis was placed upon ceremony, ritual, and pomp. He staged parades and consecrated a black, red, and green flag for his organization. Through the invention of social distinctions, honors, and pageantry, blacks were made to feel important in their thisworldly environments. While blacks had found a degree of self-magnification in fraternal orders and the church, these organizations did not give the support to their ego-consciousness that whites found in the Masons, Kiwanis, and especially the Klan (Frazier, 1926).

Although the vision of a great black nation in Africa thrilled many blacks, probably few of them were really interested in returning to Africa. The prospect of a great African nation served to give the newly arrived migrants from the rural South a sense of identity in the face of the disorientation of urban industrial life. It helped to answer the question as to who they were, and it answered the question in terms that served to build up self-respect and a feeling of being significant, meaningful, and worthwhile. It identified blacks as a people with a heritage and a promising future. In the transition from a rural to an urban way of life it provided a stopgap identity. And it simultaneously provided emotional escape and a release for protest feelings.

Garvey set up his organization in New York City, with local branches in Chicago, Philadelphia, Cincinnati, Detroit, Washington, and other cities. In 1924 he claimed 6 million members. This figure is undoubtedly exaggerated, although the UNIA may have had as many as 100 thousand dues-paying members. The number of blacks who, though not actual members, identified themselves with the Garvey program probably was considerable and gave the movement a mass character. He published the *Negro World* as the official newspaper of the movement. He organized cooperative enterprises including grocery stores, laundries, restaurants, hotels, and printing plants.

The movement collapsed after 1923, not because Garvey's followers were disaffected, but because Garvey became entangled in a series of long-drawn-out legal suits. He was imprisoned in 1925, following conviction on a federal charge of using the mails to defraud in connection with the sale of stock for his Black Star Line, a steamship company. After two years he was released and deported as an undesirable alien. As a consequence of these reverses, the movement declined and lost membership rapidly.

In many respects Garvey resembled Theodor Herzl, pioneer of Jewish Zionism. The sociologist Arnold M. Rose (1949) points out that, in their early years, neither Garvey nor Herzl had been exposed to very strong antiminority feelings. When they later came into contact with prejudice, their predilection was to escape to a land free of discrimination, rather than to protest and to try to change the existing order. Both adopted a chauvinistic, even a religious, nationalism, and both condemned amalgamation and assimilation. Both sought support from those groups most hostile to their own minority. There is no evidence, however, that Garvey was familiar with Herzl's *Judenstaat*. The similarity between the two reflects the frequent similarity in the reactions of minorities facing extremely difficult circumstances.

The Black Muslims

Sometime in the midsummer of 1930, a peddler—variously known as Mr. Farrad Mohammad, Mr. F. Mohammad Ali, Professor Ford, Mr. Wali Farrad, and W. D. Fard—made his appearance in the black community of Detroit. Apparently he was an Arab, but his racial and national identity remains undocumented. In addition to peddling his silks and artifacts, he expounded a doctrine that was a hodgepodge of Christianity, Mohammedanism, and his own personal prejudices. As time passed, his teaching took the form of increasingly bitter attacks against the white race and the Bible. A number of people experienced sudden conversions and became his followers. Soon house-to-house meetings no longer could accommodate all those who wished to hear Fard. A hall was hired and named the Temple of Islam. With this, the Black Muslim movement was launched. Fard described himself to his followers as having been sent to awaken the "Black Nation" (American blacks) to the full range of its possibilities in a world temporarily dominated by whites—"blue-eyed devils" (Lincoln, 1961).

One of Fard's earliest lieutenants was Elijah Muhammad (1897–1975), born Elijah Poole in Sandersville, Georgia, the son of a black sharecropper-minister. The family moved to Detroit early in Muhammad's life. Muhammad left school at the age of nine and took odd jobs around Detroit, later drifting around the country. When he returned to Detroit, he was attracted to Fard and his movement (Worthy, 1961). Sometime around June 1934, Fard mysteriously disappeared. Muhammad took over the leadership of "The Lost Nation of Islam," as the movement was known. In time Fard, no longer present, became identified with the god Allah. Muhammad assumed the title of Allah's "prophet" and, more often, the "messenger of Allah."

Factionalism developed within the movement, and Muhammad withdrew to Chicago, where the headquarters of the organization remains. Renewed factionalism in 1964 led Malcolm X, East Coast leader of the Black Muslims, to break with Muhammad. Intense hostility and feuding developed between the followers of Muhammad and those of Malcolm X, the latter attempting to provide the Muslims with a more adaptable ideology, a less rigidly separatist orientation, and a more political direction. On February 21, 1965, Malcolm X was shot to death while addressing a rally, apparently slain by followers of Muhammad.

The Black Muslims are not recognized as a legitimate Moslem group by any affiliate of the Federation of Islamic Associations in the United States and Canada nor by the world Islamic movement. Many of the teachings of the group are at variance with those of other Moslem groups.

The Black Muslims do not consider themselves "Negroes." They resent and reject the word as no more than "a label the white man placed on us to make his discrimination more convenient." They prefer to call themselves Black Men. They rarely use the word "Negro" without the qualifier "so-called." Black Muslims assert that blacks have been kept in mental slavery by whites even while their bodies were free. Systematically and diabolically, whites have estranged them from their heritage and from themselves. "They have been educated in ignorance," and their origin, history, true names, and religion have been kept secret from them. They have been "absolutely deaf, dumb and blind—brainwashed of all self-respect and knowledge of kind by the white Slavemaster." They are little more than "free slaves" (Lincoln, 1961).

In the Garvey spirit, the black past is extolled. In fact, blacks are depicted as the original humans from whom all other races were made. In their earlier years the Black Muslims preached a virulent hatred of all whites. As one Muslim minister stated: "A white man's head is made to be busted" (Worthy, 1961:104). By the late 1960s, however, the movement had toned down its anti-white racism and stressed instead the pro-black character of its program (Yinger, 1970).

The Black Muslims stress the pursuit of a "righteous life." Their stringent code of morality prohibits extramarital sexual relations; the use of alcohol, tobacco, and narcotics; indulging in gambling, dancing, movie-going, dating, sports, long vacations from work, sleeping more than is necessary to health, quarreling between husband and wife, lying, stealing, discourtesy (especially to women), and insubordination to civil authority (except on the ground of religious obligation); and maintaining unclean personal habits and homes. Also prohibited are the eating of pork, cornbread, and kale (and generally any stereotyped southern black food), hair straightening and dyeing, and loud laughter or singing (Essien-Udom, 1964). A number of observers (Laue, 1964; Tyler, 1966; Edwards, 1968) have noted that these puritanical ethical prescriptions have placed the Black Muslims in the mainstream of the dominant American middle-class value system. Ironically, the movement has functioned to socialize lower-class blacks in the value system of the rejected white world.

Historically, the Black Muslims have demanded the absolute separation of the white and black races. In his booklet *The Supreme Wisdom*, Muhammad condemned integration as a kind of social opiate:

> The Slavemaster's children are doing everything in their power to prevent the so-called Negroes from accepting their own God and salvation, by putting on a great show of false love and friendship.
>
> This is being done through "integration," as it is called; that is, so-called Negroes and whites mixing together such as in schools, churches, and even intermarriage. . . . The poor slaves really think they are entering a condition of heaven with their former slaveholders, but it will prove to be their doom (Lincoln, 1961:124).

The Black Muslims have adamantly rejected intermarriage. They are convinced of their "superior racial heritage" and believe that admixture with whites would only weaken the Black Nation physically and morally (Lincoln, 1961).

The Black Muslims have demanded an entirely separate black economy. They have argued that blacks cannot achieve genuine freedom until they are economically independent. They point out that the total annual income of American blacks exceeds the total annual income of Canada. If this money were spent exclusively among black businesses and invested in black enterprise, they have claimed that it would command the respect of every nation in the world. Their ideal would involve a complete economic withdrawal from the white community (Lincoln, 1961).

Black Muslim statements about their political goals are couched in mystical and vague terms. But they have periodically called for "a separate nation for ourselves, right here in America" or "some good earth, right here in America, where we can go off to ourselves." Some years ago Muhammad told a Washington audience,

> To integrate with evil is to be destroyed with evil. What we want— indeed, justice for us is to be set apart. We want, and must insist upon an area in this land that we can call our own, somewhere we can hold our heads with pride and dignity without the continued harassments and indignities of our oppressors (Lincoln, 1961:95).

Muhammad called for "four or five states in America" to be turned over to him. Yet it is extraordinary that this demand for a national homeland was never coupled with political program for its realization. Indeed, the Black Muslims have been an apolitical movement. And despite newspaper sensationalism, the Black Muslims have not been a violent group.

The size of the membership is not known, but estimates for its peak years during the 1960s ranged from 5,000 to 200,000. Public opinion polls taken during the 1960s revealed that support for or approval of the Black Muslims and their most important leaders, Elijah Muhammad and Malcolm X, held at about 5 percent of the black population. However, the impact of the Black Muslims (especially through Malcolm X) on later expressions of Black Power was great. The Black Muslims' chief temple is on Chicago's South Side, where Muhammad had also established a Muslim restaurant, cleaning business, barbershop, grocery, butcher shop, and department store. In nearly every city with a temple, the organization attempted to launch some business establishments. In addition, the Black Muslims once owned large farms in Michigan, Georgia, Alabama, Florida, Mississippi, and Texas, and have operated parochial schools (known as "Universities of Islam") in a number of cities.

Through the years the Black Muslims have recruited their members primarily from among urban low-income groups with little schooling, many of them migrants from the rural South. Black nationalism has its roots in the frustrations, anxieties, and disillusionments of contemporary urban life that are complicated by segregation, discrimination, and poverty—by life within black ghettos at the periphery of white society. Black Muslims are often strangers not only to the white society but also to the urbanized black community. The vast majority are the "unwanted from Dixie," who find themselves rejected by both the white society and upwardly mobile and middle-class blacks who resent the migrants as a threat to an improved "black image." The result is a dual alienation giving rise to a sense of apathy, futility, and loss of purpose.

The sociologist E. U. Essien-Udom (1964:354–355), a Nigerian who studied the movement, asserts:

> In a psychological sense, many are lonesome within and outside their own group. They are rootless and restless. They are without an identity, i.e., a sense of belonging and membership in society. In this situation, there is neither hope nor optimism. In fact, most lower-class Negroes in these large cities see little or no "future" for themselves and posterity. This is partly because they have no faith in themselves or in their potential as black men in America and especially because important decisions which shape their lives appear entirely beyond their control.

The Black Muslims historically offered their members a way out. Converts to the movement are no longer members of a despised minority. They belong, at least spiritually, to a people who are "dark, proud, unapologetic." The movement combines the attractions of religion and nationalism with a sense of belonging and pride (Essien-Udom, 1964; Kaplan, 1969).

Elijah Muhammad died in 1975 and his son, Wallace D. Muhammad, assumed leadership of the organization. The younger Muhammad changed the organization's name to the World Community of Al-Islam in the West and reshaped the movement's philosophy to one of working with whites to improve black conditions. He also disbanded the group's semimilitary arm (the Fruit of Islam) and relaxed its strict puritanical codes. In the process the movement has increasingly accommodated itself to mainstream society.

These developments contributed to a split in the movement and to intense ideological controversy. Orthodox followers of Elijah Muhammad oppose the liberalizing tendencies of his son and have established a rival organization led by Abdul Haleem Farrakhan. The factionalism of recent years has resulted in a sharp drop in the movement's membership and in its influence within black communities.

Black Power

The slogan "Black Power" was apparently coined by Stokely Carmichael of the Student Nonviolent Coordinating Committee (SNCC) in 1966 (Aberbach and Walker, 1973). However, the slogan's connotations of racial pride, self-respect, and unity can be traced back to Marcus Garvey and indeed even to Booker T. Washington, or for that matter on further to Frederick Douglass and other black abolitionists. The slogan never had a sharply defined or agreed-upon meaning. Whites saw it as an illegitimate, revengeful challenge. One study during the 1960s found that 57.2 percent of whites viewed "Black Power" as a synonym for violence and destruction, racism, or even black rule over whites (Aberbach and Walker, 1973). As Carmichael (1966:6) put it at the time, "To most whites, Black Power seems to mean that the Mau Mau are coming to the suburbs at night!"

The militant rhetoric of Carmichael fed white fears: "Wherever the honkies got injustice, we're going to tear their cities apart" (*St. Petersburg Times,* April 19, 1967:3). Likewise, while Reverend Martin Luther King, Jr., was still talking about the value of nonviolent confrontation, H. Rap Brown, another SNCC leader, was declaring, "If America don't come around, we're going to burn America down" (Killian, 1975:123). Among blacks, the slogan "Black Power" excited many different emotions and at times motivated blacks to express their loyalty or take action for almost contradictory reasons (Aberbach and Walker, 1973).

Black Interpretations of the Black Power Slogan.   No sooner did the slogan appear, then an acrimonious debate unfolded among black leaders as to its true meaning. Initially it was a blunt battle cry symbolizing a break with the past tactics of the civil-rights movement. Carmichael put it this way in one of his early speeches:

> The only way we gonna stop the white men from whippin' us is to take over. . . .
>   We've been saying freedom for six years and we ain't got nothin'. What we gonna start saying now is black power . . . from now on when they ask you what you want, you know to tell them; black power, black power, black power! (Brink and Harris, 1966:50).

But speeches of this kind were not only a challenge to the white community. They threatened established black civil-rights leaders as well. The NAACP's executive director Roy Wilkins responded swiftly, angrily, and negatively:

> No matter how endlessly they try to explain it, the term means anti-white power. . . . It has to mean going it alone. It has to mean separatism. Now separatism . . . offers a disadvantaged minority little except a chance to shrivel and die. . . . It is a reverse Mississippi, a reverse Hitler, a reverse Ku Klux Klan. . . . We of the NAACP will have none of this. We have fought it too long (*New York Times,* July 6, 1966:14).

Although the rhetoric of Black Power had faded by 1970, a decade later Kenneth B. Clark (1980:26), a distinguished black psychologist and leader, reiterated this view: "The black-separatist movement, which reached its zenith in the late 1960's and the early 70's, was a carbon copy of white supremacy."

The clash over the meanings of Black Power was partly fueled by a clash of personalities and ambitions, but more basically it reflected differences over the role of a black minority in a white-dominated society. Should the ultimate goal be complete assimilation, one in which a "color-blind" society would arise; or should blacks strive to build a cohesive, autonomous community, one unified along racial lines, in which blacks would be in a position to extract fundamental concessions from whites and perhaps even carve out politically separate enclaves? Whereas the NAACP, the National Urban League, and the Southern Christian Leadership Conference emphasized working within the system, the separatists rejected existing social arrangements as racist and frequently postulated the need to work outside the system. At times this latter approach contained either a covert or an unconcealed threat of violence (Franklin and Resnik, 1973).

The slogan "Black Power" came to be identified with black nationalism. During the late 1960s and early 1970s Black Nationalism found expression in a variety of forms: economic, cultural, and political. *Economic nationalists* said that the disadvantaged status of blacks derives from their lack of control over the economic resources of the black ghettos. Consequently, they saw the solution to black difficulties in the development of a distinct and separate economy along racial lines. Once blacks acquire a firm economic base, they can gain their freedom and control their own destinies. For a time the Congress of Racial Equality (CORE) championed a program of black capitalism.

Cultural nationalism resembles cultural pluralism. The emphasis falls upon a black cultural nation, since black people share a common past, a common present, and a common future based upon their blackness. Cultural nationalists highlight black connections with the nations of Africa. Blacks are encouraged to cultivate their distinctive heritage and their own identity as black persons. Usually cultural nationalists seek neither integration nor physical separation but the right to practice black cultural ways while coexisting with other groups. Some blacks undertake to affirm their identity by giving high visibility to their blackness through such symbols as Afro hair styles, corn-rolls, the wearing of dashikis, and other African-style attire (Blackwell, 1975). This stress upon black culture has found expression in the writings of Harold Cruse (1968) and among the participants in college black-studies programs and Afro-American cultural centers.

Political nationalism emphasizes the need for blacks to gain control of all institutions having to do with black life. Sometimes the approach has embraced black control of the "political" institutions of the black community including the police, schools, health facilities, and welfare programs. At other times political nationalism has taken on the rhetoric of revolutionary nationalism. During the late 1960s the young revolutionaries typically adopted some modified version of Marxist ideology as articulated by Mao, Guevara, and others and liberally interspersed their declarations with such terms as "colonalism," "imperialism," the "people's movement," and "racist exploitation." Revolutionary nationalists insisted that the only effective strategy for black liberation is the overthrow of the existing American social order and its replacement by a new and more just order. Although rather explicit in their criticisms of American society, their proposals for a new society were often viewed as "fuzzy" by the black masses (Himes, 1973; Hall, 1978). During its early phase in the 1960s, the Black Panther party (based in Oakland, California) espoused a revolutionary nationalist program. Later the group switched to a reformist thrust.

Factors Contributing to the Shift from "Freedom" to "Black Power." The decade of the 1960s opened with the sit-ins and freedom rides and continued through Birmingham, the March on Washington, and Selma with the battle cry "Freedom Now." Yet by 1964 and 1965, episodes of rioting began unfolding in the nation's black ghettos. The rhetoric of protest became increasingly demanding, blanket charges of pervasive white racism were more common, and some blacks began actively to discourage whites from participating in protest demonstrations and civil-rights organizations. Probably nothing better symbolized the changing mood and style of black protest than the change in the dominant slogan from "Freedom Now" to "Black Power." A number of factors produced this shift.

First, many blacks experienced considerable disappointment, disgust, and despair over the pace, scope, and quality of social change (Aberbach and Walker, 1973). The millennium so eloquently promised by President John F. Kennedy, if only a civil-rights program were enacted, did not come to pass. President Lyndon B. Johnson successfully steered the program through Congress—additionally calling for an "unconditional War on Poverty in America" and the building of a Great Society—yet the heritage of Jim Crow lived on. Probably the closest one can come to social dynamite is to promise people freedom and a Great Society and then deliver handouts.

For decades blacks have been the victims of inequality and low status. The handicaps associated with poverty, high fertility, an absence of skills, inadequate education, and low job seniority were left untouched by civil-rights legislation. Indeed, low status is self-perpetuating. President Johnson himself apparently came to recognize this fact, for, in a commencement address at Howard University in 1965, he asserted: "you do not take a person who for years has been hobbled by chains and liberate him, bring him up to the starting line of a race and . . . say, you're free to compete with all the others, and still justly believe that you have been completely fair."

Equality of opportunity could not get the job done for it does not produce equality of results: On the contrary, to the extent that winners imply losers, equality of opportunity ensures inequality of results. Hence, blacks became increasingly concerned not merely with removing the barriers to full *opportunity* but with achieving the fact of *equality of results,* and achieving them *now.* More recently Vernon Jordan of the National Urban League made a similar point in these words:

> The 70's [in comparison with the 1960s] are much more difficult because they deal with making real those things defined and conferred on black people in the 60's. White people never understand that the 60's were about checking into the hotel while the 70's are getting the wherewithal to check out of the hotel. . . . It is just not enough to pass a law, we now need the efforts that will give life and meaning to what we did back then (Wilkins, 1978:9).

However, despite its detractors, the civil-rights movement did open up genuine opportunities for a small minority of blacks who were already middle class, highly educated, and relatively well off. But it was as if the color computer had been programmed to extend to selected blacks of high accomplishment selected categories of privileges previously withheld from all blacks. Yet this was of little help to the vast majority of blacks who were, after all, not discriminated against merely as *individuals*, but as a *group*. As we have noted elsewhere in this book, they were excluded from the system in a systematic, self-perpetuating fashion. Under such circumstances, a new generation of leaders recognized that blacks would have to be brought into the system as a group, just as they had been excluded from it as a group. And thus the slogan of "Black Power" was born.

Second, the whole emphasis of the civil-rights movement had been one that stressed that whites should change *their* attitudes (the emphasis, for instance, of Reverend Martin Luther King's message being one of gaining white sympathy and appealing to the hearts and souls of whites) and open up avenues of access to opportunities under *white* control. Blacks were to enter the white world—be assimilated within it —but not the other way around. Yet some blacks found this a degrading, emasculating position. Stokely Carmichael (1966:6) put it this way:

> Integration today means the man who "makes it," leaving his black brothers behind in the ghetto as fast as his new sports car will take him. . . . Integration, moreover, speaks to the problem of blackness in a despicable way. As a goal, it has been based on complete acceptance of the fact that in order to have a decent house or education, blacks must move into a white neighborhood or send their children to a white school. This reinforces, among both black and white, the idea the "white" is automatically better and "black" is by definition inferior. This is why integration is a subterfuge for the maintenance of white supremacy.

Further, the white world had undertaken to deprive blacks of their own ethnic identity and to make them feel that they had no culture, no history, no roots, no art, no language—that they were merely a substandard version of general white American culture. And the role and contributions of blacks in American life were played down in the school texts on which white and black children were raised. The American educational system inculcated racism. The slogan, "Black Power," became a vehicle by which blacks could foster a sense of self-awareness, pride, and identity.

A third factor accounting for the shift in the direction of Black Power was the friction that developed between black and white civil-rights workers in the South. During the Summer Projects of 1964 and 1965, campaigns that brought many white students into southern civil rights work, it became apparent that a crisis in black-white relations was emerging. All civil-rights organizations (including the Congress of Racial Equality [CORE] and the Student Non-Violent Coordinating Committee [SNCC]) had initially championed black-white solidarity—indeed, the anthem of the movement, "We Shall Overcome," was rarely sung without including the stanza, *"Black and white together,* we shall overcome." Within the movement, idealistic young people tried to be exemplars of successful interracial living; most workers—both black and white—set out with dedication to be "color-blind" and to accept all people as "just human beings." For their part, local black people often went out of their way to accommodate the white students in their homes and their communities.

As the blacks and whites were drawn into working relationships, however, their latent feelings slowly began to emerge. They painfully learned that racism had affected their behavior in so many ways that normal human relations between the races were fraught with severe social and psychological difficulties. Blacks complained that in one way or another white volunteers acted as if they thought themselves superior to blacks: Within a week or so of their arrival, whites often behaved like "experts" and "authorities" (dubbed the "White African Queen Complex" [in women] and the "Tarzan Complex" [in men]), doing most of the "talking" and very little "listening"; whites were impatient and quickly began to "direct programs" and "run" the project offices, thus "taking over" from blacks; and, in some instances, some whites were anxious to show off how "free" they were around blacks, flouting the moral and social standards of the black community with unconventional behavior (as if to say "anything goes in the black community"). The antagonism was compounded by sociosexual conflicts (resulting from black male–white female and white male–black female relationships). Increasingly black workers became disenchanted and discouraged by the problems that an integrated movement had presented. Frustrated, they began to theorize that the movement was not "ready" for white workers, and, further, they launched a drive "to get the whites out!" This drive took many forms, but finally culminated in the slogan of "Black Power," which was widely interpreted as excluding whites automatically from work in the black community (Poussaint, 1966a, 1966b; Poussaint and Ladner, 1968).

Fourth, the slogan "Black Power" seemed to make white America pay heed to black demands. Whites for the most part found the slogan threatening, conjuring up images of black racism, violence, and destruction (Aberbach and Walker, 1973). Paraphrasing the *Communist Manifesto,* Jerry Talmer of the *New York Post* (June 19, 1967:33) aptly observed: "A specter is haunting America—the specter is Black Power." According to some social scientists, it is the *threat* of violence, not violence itself, that gets one what one wants. With a vivid enough imagination, especially on matters in which widespread ignorance prevails, it is possible to erect a creditably threatening facade of potential guerrilla warfare and violence, even though carrying out the threat might be self-defeating and hence irrational. Strictly speaking, this would constitute a black bluff. Yet none of this is sufficiently calculable or controllable to be so calmly dismissed. And if someone has a reputation for being quite angry already, who is to say how rational the person will be?

One black student summarized the matter in these terms:

> If you have something I want, okay. I can ask you for it; I can beg you for it; I can demonstrate around it; I can sit in it. But as long as it's yours, it's yours. And the only way I'm going to get you to listen to me is if you think I can destroy you (Mosher, 1970:12).

Similarly Malcolm X made the tactical observation to a middle-of-the-road black leader that without pressure from the extremists the moderates would get nowhere. The rhetoric of Black Power, then, offered the promise of extracting white concessions where the rhetoric of nonviolence had failed.

Nativistic Movements

When societies with different cultures are in continuous contact, it is not unusual to find a situation of inequality existing between them. Under conditions of dominance whereby the one society holds the other in a subordinate and disadvantaged state, *nativistic movements* have been known to emerge. **Nativistic movements** constitute a conscious, organized effort on the part of the members of the subordinate society to revive or perpetuate selected aspects of their culture. A notable ingredient of nativistic movements is the attempt to resist assimilation by the alien society that surrounds them. Strong undercurrents of withdrawal are present in which members of the subordinate society undertake to separate themselves from various elements and patterns of the dominant group's culture and to advance various current or remembered elements of their own culture. Simultaneously, strong overtones of aggressive behavior may be present (Linton, 1943).

Among the North American Indians, nativistic movements represented one type of reaction to conditions of widespread deprivation. Under the impact of the white culture, Indian societies were undermined and their members thrown out of adjustment with significant features of the social environment. Old sets of norms were weakened by contact with the white culture, and as a consequence there arose a prevailing sense of confusion and a loss of orientation. No longer did there exist a foundation for security (Carroll, 1975). The impact of the white culture not only deprived the Indians of their customary sense of direction and usual satisfactions, but it added to their sufferings by introducing the effects of new diseases and intoxicating liquor. Epidemics of measles, grippe, and whooping cough served to decimate their numbers (Barker, 1941; Thornton, 1981).

One of the fundamental myths of the Indian nativistic movements is the belief that a culture hero would one day appear and lead the tribal members to a terrestrial paradise. Through the intervention of the Great Spirit or his emissary, a "golden age" was to be ushered in within a short time. With its arrival there was to be no sickness or death, only eternal happiness. Some twenty such movements were recorded in the United States prior to 1890. In anticipation of the establishment of the millennium, believers were instructed to return to the aboriginal mode of life. Traits and customs symbolic of foreign influence were to be put away.

Probably the best known of these movements was the "Ghost Dance," which spread among the Plains tribes in 1890 (Berry, 1965; LaBarre, 1972; Mooney, 1973). The movement had gone through an earlier phase in 1870 but by 1875 had exhausted itself. Wovoka, a Paiute, who was known to the whites as Jack Wilson, played a key role in the revived movement. During an illness Wovoka had experienced a trance that led him to believe he had been chosen by departed ancestors to initiate a movement among the Indians. His teachings were a composite of various beliefs and traditions long present in Indian life plus ingredients acquired from Christianity. Wovoka urged the Indians to live morally, to love one another, to live at peace with the world, and to prepare for a day when all Indians living and dead would be reunited in a state of everlasting happiness. A Messiah would appear in the future and would bring with him in bodily form their deceased ancestors. A great whirlwind would arise and all whites would perish (whereas Wovoka believed that the cataclysm would be a natural disaster, the Sioux interpreted his prophecy as a call for military action against the whites). The buffalo and other game would be restored. It was essentially a doctrine of hope. The golden age would be a world without whites, in which once again Indians might attain stature. All this represented an effort to isolate the Indians from the disorganizing impact of white society.

Messengers went from tribe to tribe, bringing with them the new religion and teaching the dance. Some of the participants in the dance would wear a "ghost shirt," tailored in the Indian fashion and made of white cloth. The leader would carry red feathers, red cloth, and a "ghost stick" some six feet in length. Arrows with bone heads, bows, gaming wheels, and sticks found incorporation within the ritual. The dancers would shake with emotion and fall into hypnotic trances. During the trances, they would experience visions of departed Indians in the world beyond, who were engaged in dancing, playing games, gathering for war dances, preparing for the hunt, and joining together in traditional fraternal organizations. The magnitude of the movement frightened whites and resulted in the massacre of the Indians at Wounded Knee, South Dakota.

Variables Affecting the Response of Minority-Group Members

The sociologist Robert Johnson (1957), in his study of blacks in an upstate New York community during the 1950s, found the withdrawing or insulating response most prevalent among women, the southern-born, the less educated, and older people (the most significant variables associated with insulating attitudes were low education and southern origin). But these patterns appeared to have changed by the late 1960s. The 1960s had opened with blacks overwhelmingly supporting interracial cooperation and the goal of integration. On the whole blacks were highly optimistic about the effectiveness of protests against racial discrimination. But by the close of the 1960s, alienation and pessimism had eroded black support for interracial cooperation, and integration was being challenged by the competing philosophies of racial solidarity and separatism. Consequently, by the late 1960s it was black youths who were the most inclined of all age groups to favor "separatist" policies (Campbell and and Schuman, 1968; Turner and Wilson, 1976; *See also* Table 14.1). And one study of Milwaukee teen-agers (Jacobson, 1977) found that the blacks who were better students supported separatism, not integration. Further, research suggests that blacks who are race-conscious also tend to be separatist in their orientation (Turner and Wilson, 1976; Jacobson, 1977).

As we pointed out in this chapter, the slogan "Black Power" came to the forefront in the black community in 1966. It meant quite different things to various segments of the black community, although the most popular interpretations revolved about racial unity and a claim to a fair share of America's good things. Viewed in these terms, the appeal of Black Power cut across age and socioeconomic-class lines.

A study by the political scientists Aberbach and Walker (1973), based on an attitude survey in Detroit, found that the variable of age did not appreciably differentiate among members of the black community with reference to a favorable interpretation of Black Power. Differences existed, not so much between the young and the old, but between those who grew up in Michigan and those who were born and grew up in the South. The data suggested that the further blacks were from life in the South, and the sooner they experienced life in a city like Detroit, the more likely they were to approve of Black Power. Life in the northern city apparently brought to bear forces that led blacks to reject the traditional, accommodating attitudes of the South. They were away from the parochial, oppressive atmosphere of the South, while being

TABLE 14.1 PERCENTAGE IN EACH AGE CATEGORY SHOWING SEPARATIST THINKING ON FIVE QUESTIONS

	Black Men					
	16-19	**20-29**	**30-39**	**40-49**	**50-59**	**60-69***
Believe stores in "a Negro neighborhood should be owned and run by Negroes"	28	23	20	18	14	18
Believe school with mostly Negro children should have mostly Negro teachers	22	15	13	6	5	15
Agree that "Negroes should have nothing to do with whites if they can help it"	18	14	6	12	4	13
Believe whites should be discouraged from taking part in civil rights organizations	19	12	8	6	3	5
Agree that "there should be a separate black nation here"	11	10	5	5	4	10
	Black Women					
Believe stores in "a Negro neighborhood should be owned and run by Negroes"	18	16	16	15	13	8
Believe school with mostly Negro children should have mostly Negro teachers	11	9	6	5	5	12
Agree that "Negroes should have nothing to do with whites if they can help it"	11	7	7	8	5	7
Believe whites should be discouraged from taking part in civil rights organizations	11	7	7	5	7	3
Agree that "there should be a separate black nation here"	9	3	2	6	4	3

*Campbell and Schuman suspect that the relatively high percentage of males in the 60–69 age bracket involves an irrelevant artifact.

Source: Angus Campbell and Howard Schuman, *Racial Attitudes in Fifteen American Cities* (Washington, D.C.: U.S. Government Printing Office, 1968), Table II-f, p. 18.

exposed within the North to a cosmopolitan, secularized culture. The new life in the promised lands of Detroit, New York, and Chicago was experienced as exciting although simultaneously disillusioning. It brought new hopes and the promise of a better life, yet disappointments when achievements did not live up to expectations.

Similarly, support for Black Power cut across socioeconomic-class lines. For blacks with limited educations, however, approval of Black Power was strongly influenced by dissatisfaction with their lot and pessimism about the future. For blacks with higher levels of education, these factors proved of considerably less importance. Rather they were drawn to Black Power by their identification with the black community.

Jan E. Dizard (1970) likewise found in his study of black attitudes in Berkeley that a positive attachment to black identity cut across age and socioeconomic-class lines. Although occupational strata differed in attachment (*see* Figure 14.1), persons with a positive sense of black identity were nonetheless widely distributed throughout the social structure of the black community. Dizard contends that the growing attachment to black identity has helped to obscure the lines of stratification within the black community.

FIGURE 14.1   ATTACHMENT TO BLACK IDENTITY, BY OCCUPATIONAL STATUS.

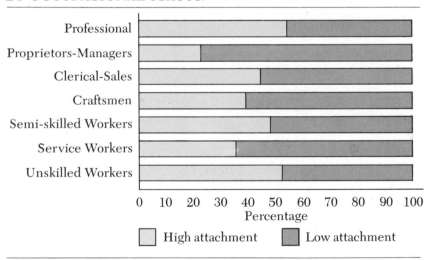

Source: Adapted from Jan E. Dizard, "Black identity, Social Class, and Black Power," *Psychiatry* 33 (1970), Table 2, p. 202.

SUMMARY

1. In avoidance members of a minority group attempt to shun—escape from—situations in which they are likely to encounter prejudice and

discrimination. Experiencing a variety of rebuffs from the dominant group, minority-group members may respond with efforts directed at withdrawal and isolation from the stresses of intergroup contacts. Avoidance may also take the form of developing towns or communities composed principally or entirely of minority-group members.

2. Minority-group members may seek to deal with their disadvantaged position through migration. The stimulus to move may come from conditions at home that they desire to escape or from conditions elsewhere that attract them. More frequently forces of both "push" and "pull" are present. These forces influenced the mass migration of blacks from rural communities of the South to northern and southern urban centers between 1915 and 1970.

3. A separatist approach to minority-group status is diametrically opposite to the assimilationalist response. Whereas assimilation implies the absorption of the minority by the larger society, separatism has a contrary aim—secession. The minority seeks to maintain or secure a distinct identity that is typically linked with efforts to achieve territorial separation from the dominant group. Consequently, separatism is a form of withdrawal or avoidance. But it seldom involves simply avoidance. Separatist movements commonly have an aggressive component and, hence, may most aptly be described as an aggressive-avoidance response. Zionism, Garveyism, and the Black Muslims are examples of separatist movements.

4. The slogan "Black Power" resulted in quite different meanings among different segments of the black population. The clash in meanings was partly fueled by a clash of personalities and ambitions, but more basically it reflected differences over the role of a black minority in a white-dominated society. Should the ultimate goal be complete assimilation, one in which a "color-blind" society would arise; or should blacks strive to build a cohesive, autonomous community, one unified along racial lines, in which blacks would be in a position to extract fundamental concessions from whites and perhaps even carve out politically separate enclaves? Whereas the NAACP, the National Urban League, and the Southern Christian Leadership Conference emphasized working within the system, the separatists rejected existing social arrangements as racist and frequently postulated the need to work outside the system.

5. The slogan "Black Power" came to be identified with black nationalism. During the late 1960s and early 1970s black nationalism found expression in a variety of forms. Economic nationalists said that the disadvantaged status of blacks derives from their lack of control over the economic resources of the black ghettos. Cultural nationalists stressed the components of a black cultural nation. Political nationalists emphasized the need for blacks to gain control of all institutions having to do with black life.

6. A number of factors contributed to the shift in emphasis from "Freedom Now" during the early 1960s to "Black Power" during the late 1960s. First, many blacks experienced considerable disappointment, disgust, and despair over the pace, scope, and quality of social change. Second, the whole emphasis of the civil-rights movements had been one in which whites should change their attitudes but failed to emphasize black pride and identity. Third, the friction that developed between black and white civil-rights workers during the 1964 and 1965 Summer Projects produced ill will and black disenchantment with black-white cooperation. And fourth, the slogan "Black Power" seemed to make white America pay heed to black demands.

7. When societies with different cultures are in continuous contact, it is not unusual to find a situation of inequality existing between them. Under conditions of dominance whereby the one society holds the other in a subordinate and disadvantaged state, nativistic movements have been known to emerge. A notable ingredient of nativistic movements is the attempt to resist assimilation by the alien society that surrounds them. Strong undercurrents of withdrawal are present in which members of the subordinate society undertake to separate themselves from various elements and patterns of the dominant group's culture and to advance various current or remembered elements of their own. The "Ghost Dance" movement, which spread among the Plains Indians in 1890, provides a good illustration of a nativistic movement.

8. During the 1950s the withdrawing or insulating response among blacks was most prevalent among women, the southern-born, the less educated, and older individuals. But these patterns appeared to have changed by the late 1960s. The 1960s had opened with blacks overwhelmingly supporting interracial cooperation and the goal of integration. On the whole blacks were highly optimistic about the effectiveness of protests against racial discrimination. But by the close of the 1960s, alienation and pessimism had eroded black support for interracial cooperation, and integration was being challenged by the competing philosophies of racial solidarity and separatism. Consequently, by the late 1960s it was black youths who were the most inclined of all age groups to favor "separatist" policies.

GLOSSARY

Nativistic Movement A conscious, organized effort on the part of the members of a subordinate society to revive or perpetuate selected aspects of their culture.

V
Social Change

Toward Lessening Racism **15**

*T*hrough the years American race and ethnic relations have undergone considerable change. Social institutions change not only because of various impersonal and nondeliberative forces but because people intentionally set out to change them. Such has been the case with the patterns governing American ethnic, racial, and religious interaction. Racism conflicts with the assumptions underlying the American democratic creed. The creed stresses the dignity and worth of each individual and the right of each to enjoy equality and the privileges of liberty. Accordingly, many Americans have sought to bring the nation's race and ethnic patterns in line with the democratic creed.

With the growing recognition that sociological and psychological findings can be applied to alter human behavior, social scientists have been called upon to contribute scientific knowledge that would be helpful in achieving democratic goals. A value premise is implicit, namely, that racism is undesirable and should be combated. In response to such demands, a body of scientific literature has emerged dealing with means by which democratic goals may be advanced. In this chapter we shall focus attention on a number of these findings.

Some Preliminary Considerations

Before proceeding with our consideration of techniques for combating racism, it would be well to recognize the existence of a number of controversies. First, individuals differ in the goals that they pursue. Some prefer a "melting pot" approach, in which the outcome would be the fusion of differing groups within one common American culture. Others favor an "Americanization" focus, in which ethnic and racial minorities would divest themselves of their distinctive traits and assume the ways of the dominant group. Still others prefer cultural pluralism, in which groups would conform to common standards in crucial areas but differences would be welcomed and tolerated in less essential areas. And finally there are those who prefer separation—not only some members of the dominant group but those "nationalists" among minorities who seek autonomy and self-determination. Science cannot answer the question as to which of these orientations is the most desirable—or, for that matter, if any of them are desirable. But it can shed light on the likely consequences of pursuing any one of them. This diversity in goals complicates the task of formulating an action approach for the lessening of prejudice and discrimination.

Second, as we observed in chapters 3, 4, and 5, the sources of racism are not a simple matter to untangle—racism feeds from many springs, all of which are interrelated and reinforce one another. By virtue of the great complexity that characterizes intergroup behavior and the multiplicity of factors involved, an attack upon racism must involve a many-sided approach. Moreover, social scientists are not in agreement as to the key factors that underlie racism. And, by virtue of their own predilections as well as the limited nature of our contemporary knowledge, they are often in disagreement on how best to tackle the problem. Furthermore, our knowledge of the causes of racism furnishes us merely with cues for action. These cues for lessening racism need to be evaluated in their actual application by research.

Third, prejudice and discrimination are not the same phenomenon. It will be recalled that prejudice involves a state of mind whereas discrimination entails overt behavior. Attitudes and behavior are not to be equated. A considerable gulf often exists between them. Accordingly, one technique may be quite effective in combating prejudice but may be of little value in combating discrimination, and vice versa. Education may be useful in altering attitudes, but the normative system dictating discrimination may continue to prevail. Or discriminatory behavior may be punished via legal sanctions, and thus be reduced, yet prejudice may persist. And all these matters are further reinforced and complicated by institutional racism—the fact that society itself is structured and saturated with built-in patterns that impose more burdens and give less benefits to the members of one racial or ethnic group than to another.

Fourth, racism is not a phenomenon, as is sometimes implicitly assumed, that can be dealt with by focusing exclusively upon the dominant group. While there is probably good foundation for placing emphasis upon changing the attitudes and behavior of dominant-group members, racial and ethnic patterns are in some measure reciprocal. The antagonism between various racial and ethnic groups is not a one-way street in which the dominant group has a monopoly in adverse and negative feelings, ideas, and actions. Consequently, rounded action programs need to deal with both sides of the racial or ethnic equation.

This chapter will focus attention upon a number of strategies commonly suggested for combating racism. We will be particularly interested in considering evidence dealing with the effectiveness of these strategies.

Propaganda

For many people propaganda has gained a sinister connotation. They frequently equate propaganda with lies, deceit, and fraud. This view became especially prevalent during World War II, when propaganda was commonly identified with the hate and racist appeals of Nazi Germany. More recently it has become associated with extremist and anti-American elements. However, as commonly used within the social sciences, the term has no necessary relation to truth or falsity. Defined sociologically **propaganda** refers to a deliberate attempt to influence opinions or behavior to some predetermined end. Symbols are the vehicles by which propaganda is transmitted, whether they are written, printed, spoken, pictorial, or musical.

Propaganda in Combating Prejudice

A major problem faced by those who would employ propaganda is the difficulty in reaching people who are not already in favor of the view it presents. Communications research reveals that people commonly avoid points of view that are at odds with their own by simply not exposing themselves to such views. Those whom the propagandist would most like to influence by certain communications are often the least likely to be reached by them. People tend to listen only to ideas that agree with their own opinions. It has been found, for example, that political propaganda within the United States that attempts to win support from those who ordinarily give their allegiance to another party is usually unsuccessful. For one thing, Republicans, by and large, listen only to Republican speakers; Democrats expose themselves to Democratic speakers. A similar problem exists in the area of race relations. During World War II the government sponsored a weekly radio program, *Immigrants All, Americans All.* Each week the program dealt with the contribution of a specific nationality group within American life. Public-opinion research revealed that, when the program dealt with Italians, the great majority of listeners were Italians; when the Poles were presented, mostly people of Polish descent listened. Similarly, antiprejudice propaganda is likely to reach a considerably smaller proportion of the prejudiced group than the nonprejudiced group.

Selective exposure influenced the television public's viewing of *Roots* and its sequel *Roots: The Next Generation (Roots II).* Both series were based on Alex Haley's partly biographical and partly fictional account of his family's experiences in Africa and the United States. *Roots* was concerned with the black struggle for freedom from slavery while *Roots II* focused on the family's post-Civil War experiences and their struggle for equality. Residents of some 32.0 million households viewed one or more episodes of *Roots;* 22.5 million households viewed

one or more episodes of *Roots II*. Egalitarianism (antiprejudiced sentiment) was systematically related to the number of nights Americans
watched *Roots* and *Roots II*. Those who scored higher on egalitarianism
watched more episodes than those who scored low on egalitarianism
(Hur and Robinson, 1978; Ball-Rokeach, Grube, and Rokeach, 1981).

With the increasing role that movies and television play in American
recreational life, the potentialities for mass influence have been greatly
enlarged. A number of studies have examined the impact that these
media have on racial and ethnic prejudice. The evidence suggests that
movies portraying an ethnic or racial group in negative terms increases
prejudice. In their pioneering study of the phenomenon, the psychologists Ruth C. Peterson and Louis Thurstone (1933) found that schoolchildren who saw *Birth of a Nation,* a film depicting Reconstruction
from a white southern view, exhibited a slight increase in prejudice
toward blacks. A number of studies have also revealed that movies with
an antiprejudice theme tend to reduce prejudice among these exposed
to them.

Illustrative of these latter studies is Russell Middleton's (1960) investigation of the impact of the movie *Gentleman's Agreement* upon the
attitudes of a group of university students. This film, which won the
1947 Academy Award, carries a strong message against anti-Semitic
prejudice and sets forth an appeal for brotherhood, equality, and democracy. Middleton selected an experimental group and a control
group of students, the latter of which did not see the movie. Both
groups completed an attitude questionnaire: the experimental group
before and again after the movie; the control group before and again
after the intervention of a comparable period. The control group was
introduced into the study to check for any attitude changes that might
result from the mere fact of taking the "test." It was conceivable that
any changes noted in the attitudes of the experimental group after they
had seen the film might be due not to the film but rather to the test
itself. Thus the differences between the before and after scores of the
experimental group might reflect not the influence of the movie but
that of the intervening variable, the questionnaire administered the
second time.

The results presented in Figure 15.1 reflect the wisdom of having
introduced the control group, as both the control and experimental
groups displayed attitude changes. Nevertheless, the evidence strongly
suggests that the film played a major role in reducing the expression of
anti-Semitic prejudice. Subjects in the experimental group were five
times more likely to display a reduction of eleven or more scale points
than those in the control group. Reductions of four to ten scale points
were also found to be more extensive among those in the experimental
group. Yet the fact should not be overlooked that some 50 percent of
the individuals in the experimental group did not show an appreciable

decline in expressed anti-Semitism. Some even displayed an increase.

In evaluating antiprejudice films, the question arises as to how well the effects of the film are retained over time. Our knowledge on this matter is still far from adequate. However, available evidence suggests that there is usually a regression in attitudes—after the intervention of time, opinions tend to slip back toward the original view, but not all the way. But such regression does not occur in all cases. The psychologists Carl I. Hovland, Arthur A. Lumsdaine, and Fred D. Sheffield (1949) show that some opinion changes in the direction of the propagandist's position are larger after the lapse of time than immediately after the communication. They refer to this as the "sleeper effect." They suggest that individuals may be suspicious of the motives of the propagandist and initially discount the position. Thus these individuals may give little or no evidence of an immediate change in their opinion. But with the passage of time they may remember and accept *what* was com-

FIGURE 15.1 CHANGE IN EXPRESSED ANTI-SEMITISM SCORES AFTER SHOWING OF MOVIE *GENTLEMAN'S AGREEMENT.*

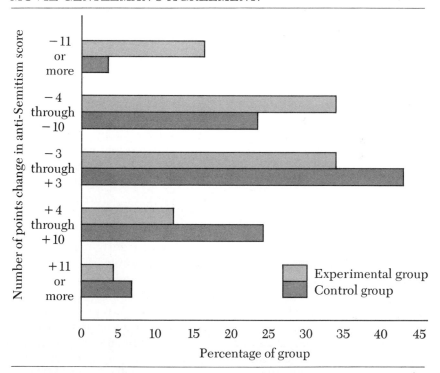

Source: Adapted from Russell Middleton, "Ethnic prejudice and susceptibility to persuasion." *American Sociological Review* 25 (1960),Table 2, p. 682.

municated although they may not remember *who* communicated it. Consequently they may be more inclined to agree with the position at a later date than immediately after it was presented.

The Evasion of Antiprejudice Propaganda

Antiprejudice propagandists face a major task in confronting prejudiced individuals with their point of view. As we have noted, people are inclined to avoid communications that are contrary to their established beliefs. But what happens when prejudiced people are involuntarily confronted with antiprejudice propaganda? It might be inferred that they would either fight the propaganda or give in to it. But often many people are unwilling to do either. They prefer to *evade* the implications of ideas opposed to their own. It is often much easier simply not to understand or to twist and to misinterpret a message than to defend oneself or to admit error. While educational level is related to the understanding of antiprejudice communications, more people who are prejudiced are apt to misunderstand the message than comparably educated unprejudiced people.

The psychologists Eunice Cooper and Marie Jahoda (1947) have identified a number of techniques that prejudiced individuals employ to avoid understanding antiprejudice messages:

1. *Identification avoided—understanding "derailed."* Individuals may avoid the implications of the message through misunderstanding the point of the communication. Although initially grasping the message, they then disassociate themselves from it, and in the process lose the original understanding that they had. The process is reflected in a number of typical reactions to a series of cartoons lampooning a character dubbed Mr. Biggott. The cartoons depict Mr. Biggott as a rather prudish figure with exaggerated antiminority feelings. In one cartoon, Mr. Biggott, lying sick in bed, says to a somewhat startled doctor, "In case I should need a transfusion, doctor, I want to make certain I don't get anything but blue, sixth-generation American blood!" In another cartoon, Mr. Biggott says to a humble American Indian, "I'm sorry, Mr. Eaglefeather, but our company's policy is to employ 100 percent Americans only!" The producers of the cartoons had hoped that the following process would occur: Prejudiced individuals would see that Mr. Biggott's ideas about minorities were similar to their own, that Mr. Biggott was an absurd character, and that to have antiminority ideas was to appear as ridiculous as Mr. Biggott. Presumably the individuals would then reject their own prejudice to avoid identification with Mr. Biggott.

Yet a study of reactions to the cartoons revealed a different outcome. Prejudiced individuals often initially identified themselves with Mr. Biggott, as did one respondent who indicated, "I imagine he's a sour old bachelor. [laughing] I'm an old bachelor myself." He also appeared to be aware of Mr. Biggott's prejudices. But this did not end the matter. Criticism and disapproval of prejudice were implicit in the cartoons; Mr. Biggott had been made to appear ridiculous for holding such beliefs. Thus it was not uncommon for individuals to invent means by which to disassociate themselves from Mr. Biggott without necessarily surrendering their prejudice. Some people accomplished this task by making Mr. Biggott appear to be an intellectual inferior, a Jew, a foreigner, or a member of the lower class. The net result was that they ended up losing the original understanding of the message. In the above illustration the "bachelor" finally concluded that the purpose of the cartoon was "to get the viewpoint of people to see if they coincide with the artist's idea of character and all." Clearly the issue of prejudice had been completely sidetracked.

2. *The message made invalid.* In other cases, individuals admitted understanding the message to a degree that did not permit their distortion of it. For them the process of disidentification often led to a more rationalized argument. They accepted the message on the surface but maintained the message was invalid for themselves. This result was accomplished in one of two ways. Individuals might admit the general principle but conclude that exceptions existed that entitled them to their prejudices. One cartoon in the Cooper-Jahoda study concluded with a variant of the Golden Rule, "Live and let live." Prejudiced persons frequently expressed acceptance of the Golden Rule but would add, "But it's the Jews that don't let you live; they put themselves outside the rule." The second type of distortion involved an admission that the message was convincing in itself, but with the qualification that it did not contain a correct picture of usual life situations involving the minority group discussed. A case in point was a radio dramatization entitled *The Belgian Village.* In the story a Jewish couple in a Nazi-occupied Belgian village were saved by the loyal support of the villagers who hid them from the Gestapo. The story was followed by an appeal for sympathy and tolerance toward the Jews. Many prejudiced individuals refused to admit the applicability of this dramatic story to other situations. They labeled it an "adventure story" or "a war story."

3. *Changing the frame of reference.* In some cases the perception of the prejudiced individuals was so colored by prejudice that the message of the cartoon escaped them. They saw the issues that the

cartoon presented in a frame of reference different from that which had been intended. One cartoon depicted a congressman who had extremist antiminority views. He was shown in his office, interviewing an applicant who had with him a letter of recommendation saying that he had been in jail, had started race riots, and had smashed windows. The congressman was pleased and said, "Of course I can use you in my new party." Some prejudiced individuals imposed on the cartoon their own ideology and made it appear that "bad politics" was the sole issue. One respondent observed, "It's about a strike . . . about trouble like strikes . . . He is starting a Communist party." Still another, "It's a Jewish party that would help Jews get more power."

4. *The message is too difficult.* At times the message may be poorly designed and thus miss its target. Some individuals state, "I haven't gotten the point." This outcome may result from a complicated, involved communication.

5. *Denial by discrediting the source.* Individuals often impugn the motives and credibility of a source as a way to disregard unpleasant facts that disrupt their existing image of social reality (Newman, 1973). For example, if the National Urban League or the National Association for the Advancement of Colored People releases new data on discrimination or institutional racism, the prejudiced response is frequently, "What did you expect them to say?"

Limits on the Effectiveness of Propaganda

It has been noted above that individuals may consciously or unconsciously modify the stimuli they perceive from propaganda according to their own predispositions. Consequently, they fail to understand the message contained in antiprejudice propaganda. For somewhat similar reasons propaganda may "boomerang"—it may produce a result directly opposite to that intended by the propagandist. Instead of lessening prejudice, antiprejudice propaganda may actually promote it. For instance, some psychologists suggest that there may be a boomerang effect in films showing cruelty against minority groups. Many prejudiced persons, far from being repelled, are attracted by cruelty. Films depicting the persecution of minority-group victims permit these prejudiced individuals to secure vicarious gratification for their sadistic impulses, and allow them to bring their hidden desires to the foreground.

The various television series featuring Archie Bunker have been the source of much controversy. Archie is depicted as a loveable bigot. Counterposed to Archie is a foil such as Mike (the "Meathead") and Murray Klein, individuals who represent a stereotyped liberal position on ethnic and racial issues. Archie's bigotry is made to appear foolish. Yet since Archie is at root a loveable "softy" and "average guy," his bigotry emerges as an individual quirk that is laughable but not particularly dangerous. Indeed, Archie's bigotry is employed to make him an "endearing" figure. We learn little or nothing from the various episodes about the operation of institutional bigotry and racism. Instead, Archie is portrayed as a decent "middle American guy" whose racism is as American as "football and apple pie." Consequently, many social scientists say that the program serves to legitimate racism. Moreover, the portrayal of blacks, Hispanics, and Jews in terms of modern-day stereotypes reinforces popular prejudices and patterns.

Another factor that limits the effectiveness of antiracist propaganda is the limited impact of a single program. Public-opinion experts stress that a single program may be relatively ineffective in reaching the public with a message. One program is not enough. A campaign is necessary. Several related programs are often capable of producing effects even greater than could be accounted for in terms of simple summation. Multiple exposure tends to produce a pyramiding stimulation.

Overall, it appears that propaganda has a very limited direct effect in combating prejudice. Dominant groups possess the power to define social reality through their control of the mass media and key institutions. Further, their members typically have little difficulty mentally warding off discrepant challenges to these definitions. However, we should not assume that there is no value in prodemocratic propaganda. Some social scientists say that its effectiveness cannot be counted only in terms of winning the prejudiced over to a nonprejudiced view. Propaganda may strengthen the attitudes of those who are unprejudiced and make them less susceptible to proprejudice propaganda. Antiprejudice propaganda may also give the impression to anti-Semites, segregationists, and others that public sentiment is against them. Accordingly, although continuing to hold their prejudiced attitudes, they may be less disposed to engage in discriminatory behavior.

Education

Underlying a good deal of the work in the area of intergroup relations is the assumption that prejudice will disappear if people are given the facts. The appeal to "education" as a cure-all for the most varied social problems is deeply rooted in the ideology of American life. Thus,

within the setting of racial and ethnic relations many intergroup workers believe that their primary task is to teach the facts about minority
groups, and prejudice will be reduced. This view assumes that (1) people are predominantly rational beings and (2) prejudice is the product
of ignorance. If people are rational and if prejudice is due to "distorted
stereotypes" and "warped social perception," then "correct" facts can
be expected to change their hostile feelings. The naïveté of this view
is apparent in terms of both the complexity of human behavior in
general and prejudice in particular.

"Give People the Facts!"

The assumption that education is a powerful cure-all for prejudice
was one of the first premises within the field of minority relations to be
subjected to the scrutiny of scientific investigation. Teachers of race
relations were especially anxious to measure the impact of their courses
upon their students' prejudices. The results were quite discouraging,
especially as many of the teachers were highly motivated to curb prejudice. On the whole the studies coming out during the late 1920s and
the 1930s revealed that education at best had negligible effects. By
1948, the sociologist Robert M. MacIver (1948:222) could conclude in
his survey of strategies useful in combating prejudice, "All we can claim
for instruction of a purely factual kind is that it tends to mitigate some
of the more extreme expressions of prejudice."

Today specialists in race relations tend to take a rather dim view of
the effectiveness of antiprejudice education. It suffers from many of the
same problems as does antiprejudice propaganda. Individuals selectively perceive and interpret "facts" and protect themselves against
facts they do not wish to believe.

Experimental evidence indicates that people most readily learn
materials with which they agree. When given the experimental task of
learning statements, individuals who favor segregation learn plausible
prosegregation statements and implausible antisegregation statements
much more readily than they do plausible antisegregation and implausible prosegregation statements. Individuals opposed to segregation reverse the process (Jones and Kohler, 1958).

Still another limitation of education is its failure to penetrate beyond
the level of verbal expression to overt conduct and become translated
into nondiscriminatory behavior. It is axiomatic that in learning situations rhetorical exhortations have little chance of success when they are
in battle against actual behavior patterns. For example, children will
not become honest simply because their parents so instruct them (although they may mouth honest platitudes) if the same parents are
constantly engaged in dishonest practices themselves.

Prejudice and Level of Education

Education is commonly looked upon in the United States as a source of liberation—as a means of freeing people from narrowness and provincialism. Since education stresses rational processes, it is often assumed that it causes people to control or reject the irrational and absurd. From this assumption some have concluded that education has value in and of itself as an instrument for eliminating prejudice. On the surface these surmises appear to be borne out by research. Researchers have consistently reported a negative correlation between prejudice of all kinds and the amount of a person's formal education (the higher the level of education, the less the prejudice). Illustrative are the findings of the sociologists Gertrude J. Selznick and Stephen Steinberg (1969), which are based on a national sample and are summarized in Figure 15.2. Moreover, Selznick and Steinberg interpret these and other findings of their study as supporting the view that education is an "enlightening" process and leads to a rejection of anti-Semitism, antidemocratic attitudes, and provincial orientations.

Yet any number of researchers have raised questions regarding such

FIGURE 15.2 ACCEPTANCE OF ANTI-SEMITIC BELIEFS, BY LEVEL OF FORMAL EDUCATION.

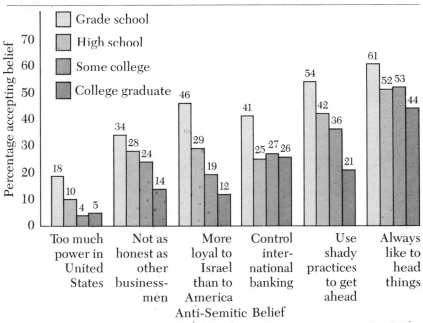

Source: Adapted from Gertrude J. Selznick and Stephen Steinberg, *The Tenacity of Prejudice* (New York: Harper & Row, 1969), Table 18, p. 71.

interpretations. For instance, the sociologist Charles H. Stember (1961) says that most studies understate the prevalence of prejudice among the educated. His research lends support to the critics of attitudinal studies on race issues who allege that educated groups, because of their intellectual sophistication, fail to state their prejudiced sentiment, which they realize runs contrary to the norms of the American democratic creed. Stember finds that the educated express their prejudices more subtly. When responding on attitude tests, they are capable of recognizing and avoiding a trap set with rather obviously biased clichés. Nevertheless, they may agree in substance with the prejudiced position (Orbell and Sherrill, 1969).

Stember assembled a number of prejudice studies and reanalyzed the data with appropriate controls. He found that the better educated different from the less educated in (1) their beliefs and perceptions concerning minorities, (2) their attitudes toward discrimination, and (3) their acceptance of personal relationships with minority groups. In terms of beliefs and perceptions of minorities, the better educated were more likely than the less educated to give credence to certain anti-Jewish stereotypes: that Jews are a threat to the country, that many of them are Communists and racketeers, and that they are less willing than non-Jews to serve in the armed forces. On the other hand, the better educated were less likely to believe that Jews are unscrupulous in business, dishonest in public office, and too powerful or too demanding. Thus, although the less educated appear more likely to hold *traditional* stereotypes, the better educated nonetheless may hold certain highly charged and derogatory stereotypes of minority groups.

Stember found that formal or official discrimination is less acceptable to the educated than to the less educated, particularly in terms of such issues as systematic job discrimination, school desegregation, desegregation of public transportation, admission of refugees to the United States, and acceptability of a Jewish candidate for the presidency. However, in terms of *informal* discrimination, it appears that the educated do not take as strong a position as they do on more formal discrimination. Stember found that a similar picture emerges on issues of personal acceptance. While the better educated are more inclined to accept casual relationships with minority-group members than are the less educated, they appear less willing than the less educated to accept contacts that verge on the more intimate aspects of life. Thus one study revealed that persons of the middle educational level are more likely than others to reject blacks as guests in their homes.

And Selznick and Steinberg, despite their conclusion that education has intrinsic value as an instrument for eliminating anti-Semitism, found that college graduates are the most likely of all educational groups to defend social club discrimination and that education is unrelated to attitudes toward intermarriage. They observe:

Considering their frequent acceptance of anti-Semitic beliefs, the uneducated are relatively tolerant in the private areas of intermarriage and social clubs. But this must be set against their greater tendency to express their anti-Semitism in the political realm. On the other hand, the failure of the college educated to be especially tolerant in private areas must be set against their greater rejection of traditional anti-Semitic beliefs and greater opposition to political discrimination and political anti-Semitism.

It would appear, then, that the issue is not so much one of which group —the better educated or the less educated—is the most anti-Semitic. Rather the matter might be more appropriately phrased in terms of the ways the two groups either converge or differ in anti-Semitic tendencies and behavior.

On the basis of his survey, Stember (1961:171) concludes that the impact of education is limited: "Its chief effect is to reduce traditional provincialism—to counteract the notion that members of minorities are strange creatures with exotic ways, and to diminish fear of casual personal contact. But the limits of acceptance are sharply drawn; while legal equality is supported, full social participation is not."

Robin M. Williams, Jr. (1964), in his summary of the findings of Cornell sociologists, came to somewhat similar conclusions as did Stember. He notes that the better educated tend to have more complex attitudes on issues since they have access to more facts, to divergent opinions, and to more subtle distinctions. Better educated people—in contrast with the less educated—tend to react to a more differentiated and varied social world. Moreover, their prejudice may be harder, colder, more polite, and more thoroughly buttressed by rationalizations. However, like other researchers, the Cornell sociologists find that some types of behavior are not related to education, for example, education is not associated with willingness to have a member of one's family marry a Jew. Hence, the relationships between education and prejudice and between education and discrimination are quite complex.

Intergroup Contact

"Bring differing racial and ethnic groups into contact and their prejudices will wither away." This counsel is manifest in a good many current activities to combat racism—indeed, an almost mystical faith resides in "getting to know one another" as a solvent of racial tensions. The view assumes that contact makes for intergroup friendliness. According to this perspective, people are basically good and seek understanding and mutual respect. If they had the opportunity to communicate with one another and appreciate each other's way of life, good will would come to prevail (Amir, 1969, 1976).

Prejudice and Segregation

The simplified argument of the contact approach to prejudice runs as follows: People in their daily lives are creatures of habit. They more or less continually follow a beaten path—a path that leads from home to work, then back home, then to a lodge meeting, back home, on Sundays to church and back, and occasionally a visit to relatives and friends. Consequently, people are exposed to few new social environments and few contacts with people of other racial and ethnic groups. Their lives are limited and they lack real experience with members of minority groups. But this lack of contact does not prevent them from forming stereotypes of these groups. If people with differing racial and ethnic origins are brought together, their stereotypes will be challenged. They will see that the minority groups are not in fact the people of the stereotypes. They will then give up their prejudices and engage in harmonious interaction (Dean and Rosen, 1955).

Proponents of this view go on to argue that segregation has the opposite effect because it promotes distance and racism. Whites observe blacks living under conditions in which the latter are assigned inferior positions. It is not too difficult for whites to conclude that blacks are indeed different and perhaps even inferior and undesirable. Segregation thus reinforces prejudice. By the same token, segregation limits white opportunities for interacting with blacks of similar status. The net effect is that it shields whites from having to check their prejudiced beliefs against reality. Racism, then, is institutionalized. It is *bred* by the way our society structures social relationships. In turn racism becomes self-perpetuating.

Racial isolation has still other consequences. It prevents each group from learning of the beliefs and values that they share. In chapter 3 we noted that people are attracted to others who hold beliefs and attitudes similar to their own. Further, they feel aversion toward people with dissimilar beliefs and attitudes. We reviewed Milton Rokeach's (1960) thesis that white Americans are motivated to reject blacks less by racial considerations than by assumed belief and value differences. And we further noted that a variety of studies reveal that whites typically accept in a social situation a black with beliefs that are similar to their own over a white with different beliefs (especially in more formal matters of general personal evaluation and social acceptance).

Segregationist patterns, then, whether of the de jure or de facto variety, bar those forms of interaction that might otherwise undermine a racist social order, enable blacks and whites to discover their shared attitudes, and provide a basis for mutual attraction. Hence, it is not surprising that the U. S. Commission on Civil Rights (1967), in its study of *Racial Isolation in the Public Schools,* found that both black and white adults who as children had attended interracial schools were more likely today to live in an interracial neighborhood and hold more positive racial attitudes than comparable adults who had known only segregated schools. And further, the Coleman report (see chapter 2) suggests that white students who attend public schools with blacks are the least likely to prefer all-white classrooms and all-white "close friends." This effect is strongest among those who began their interracial schooling in the early grades.

Selective Perception and Exemption

In and of itself, contact does not necessarily dispel prejudice. In fact, superficial contact is often a means by which prejudice is increased. Whites having casual contact with blacks typically come to the relationships possessing well-formulated sets of stereotypes. To a considerable extent the blacks they "see" are the blacks of their stereotypes. Stereotypes *sensitize* individuals to signs that confirm and reinforce the stereotyping process. The net result is that perception tends to be *selective*—indeed, even distorted. What in other relationships may be taken to be a normal lack of knowledge on a matter is taken by many a white in interaction with a black to be evidence of black "ignorance" and "inferiority." Similarly, what may be otherwise taken to be appropriate aggressiveness is taken by many a Gentile in interaction with a Jew to be evidence of Jewish "assertiveness" and "unbridled gall." Should a black or Jew engage in behavior remotely resembling the black or Jewish stereotype, the incident "registers."

When interacting with members of a racial or ethnic minority, people have a tendency to scrutinize the individuals for behavior conforming to the stereotypes of their group (they are sensitized to the traits). In interaction with ingroup members, the trait would be overlooked or dismissed as a trait unique to a particular individual. Casual interaction does not usually lead to a challenging of stereotypes, because the contact is not sufficiently intimate to permit people to assess other individuals in a genuine manner. Thus the character of the individual as a unique human does not penetrate the armor of the racial mythology.

Intergroup contact may fail to challenge stereotypes for another reason—*exemption*. Occasionally an individual meets a member of another racial or ethnic group who fails to fit that group's stereotype. But instead of altering or eliminating the stereotype, the person makes the individual an exception. For example, a black who is remarkably energetic, hard working, and self-disciplined may be excluded from the stereotype as an exception, as "not really" a "black." Through exemption, individuals retain their prejudice while circumventing discriminatory patterns for some purpose, for instance, accepting a particular black in a social clique.

There is also substantial agreement among social scientists that contact between members of groups holding very different social and economic status is likely to increase prejudice. In contrast, contact between groups having the same or a nearly equal status tends to reduce prejudice. When white middle-class individuals have contact with only lower-class blacks, the stereotype that blacks are "dirty," "dumb," and "shiftless" is reinforced. Class prejudices are readily activated in unequal-status contacts. Individuals' perceptions of an ethnic or racial group may be influenced by their class antagonisms. On the other hand, individuals possessing a common status tend to share common values and goals. Experiences along equal-status lines are more likely to contradict the stereotypes of prejudiced individuals than are those that run along unequal-status lines.

Evidence Relating to the Effects of Interracial Contact

With the growth of public housing since World War II, a particularly fruitful laboratory has been provided social scientists for examining the impact of interracial apartment living upon racial attitudes and behavior. Interracial housing affords an unusual opportunity for intimate and prolonged contact between individuals of differing racial groups. Two studies have been undertaken that have employed sophisticated methodological procedures and provided valuable insights on interracial residential contact. The first study, by the psychologists Morton Deutsch and Mary Evans Collins (1951), investigated four low-rent public-housing projects—two integrated interracial projects in New York City and two similar but segregated biracial projects in Newark—for the purpose of determining the social and psychological effects of the two occupancy patterns upon race relations and attitudes. In the two integrated housing projects, black and white families were assigned to apartment buildings regardless of race. In the two segregated biracial projects, blacks were assigned to buildings that were area-separated from those of the whites. Deutsch and Collins selected the projects in the two cities to match them in black-white ratios and other relevant variables. Some 100 white housewives were intensively interviewed in each of the four projects.

Deutsch and Collins found marked differences between the two types of projects in racial relations and attitudes. Compared with the segregated biracial projects, the integrated interracial projects were characterized by

1. a higher incidence of friendly, neighborly contacts between the two racial groups;

2. a social atmosphere more favorable to friendly interracial associations;

3. the ascription of a higher incidence of favorable stereotypes and a lower incidence of unfavorable stereotypes to blacks;

4. a higher rate of acceptance of the interracial character of the project and of recommendations for an integrated occupancy pattern for future projects; and

5. a far greater proportion of those who reported they had undergone favorable attitude change toward blacks as a consequence of living in the project.

The white residents in the integrated projects were much more likely than those in the area-segregated projects to view blacks with respect and as the equals of white people. Considerably more of the housewives in the integrated projects made such statements as: "They're very nice; they have beautiful homes"; "A lot of them are nicer than the white people; when I was sick the lady across the hall came in and cooked soup"; and "They're just the same as the white people here; except for color, there's no difference." On the other hand, many more women in the segregated projects made statements that implied that blacks were inferior.

A second study confirmed the major findings of the Deutsch and Collins research. Employing a comparable research design, Daniel M. Wilner, Rosabelle P. Walkley, and Stuart W. Cook (1955) were able to verify the findings in a setting beyond the metropolitan area of New York City. The authors concluded that, the more intimate the contact between blacks and whites, the more favorable the attitudes of the whites toward blacks. Similarly, the more favorable the perceived social climate surrounding interracial contact, the more favorable were the white attitudes. These studies suggest that contact, under the favorable conditions prevailing in these interracial public-housing projects, provides concrete experiences that test the white resident's preexisting stereotypes and encourage the development of friendly relations and feelings.

Whether black attitudes become more favorable toward whites in interracial public-housing projects is an unsettled question. The sociologist Ernest Works (1961) studied the attitudes of black tenants in a single housing project that was partly desegregated and partly segregated and found that anti-white prejudice is diminished through intimate contacts between status equals. However, another sociologist, W. Scott Ford (1973), did not find more favorable attitudes among blacks residing in integrated than in segregated public-housing projects in Lexington, Kentucky (although the attitudes of the white tenants residing in integrated housing were more favorable toward blacks than those of whites in segregated projects). Ford speculates that blacks entered relationships with white neighbors with caution and suspicion by virtue of their earlier life experiences. Consequently, the blacks were sensitive to condescending attitudes among their white counterparts.

Research of a somewhat different sort was undertaken by the psychologists David L. Hamilton and George D. Bishop (1976), who studied the effects on whites of the initial integration of their all-white suburban neighborhoods. Interviewers assessed residents' attitudes and behavior to new neighbors in eighteen suburbs. In eight neighborhoods the new residents were a black family and in ten neighborhoods a white family. The interviews were conducted one month, three months, and one year after the families had moved into their new homes. The initial interviews revealed that the racial factor did make a difference among white residents, who mostly disapproved of the entry of a black family into their neighborhoods. Whites commonly expressed fear that the financial value of their homes would be adversely affected by black neighbors.

The one-year interviews revealed a different picture. The concern and apprehension that the white residents had experienced regarding their black neighbors had largely disappeared. The whites no longer seemed worried about property values. But perhaps of greater interest, the whites living in integrated neighborhoods showed significantly less racism than those still living in all-white neighborhoods. However, this shift in attitudes did not appear to be the product of interracial contact (neighborhood interaction was low regardless of race). Rather, a disconfirmation of expectancies was at work. Over time the experience of having black neighbors served to disconfirm many of the whites' expectations—the appearance of the neighborhood had not changed, physical assault and violence had not occurred, and real-estate prices had continued to climb.

Some Limits to the Effectiveness of Interracial Contact

Like other techniques for combating racism, interracial contact is not a panacea. One of its limitations is that many individuals fail to generalize their favorable attitudes toward particular minority-group members so as to include the whole minority group. In this way the experiences acquired within one context are not carried over into other interracial situations. Some thirty years ago, John Harding and Russell Hogrefe (1952) investigated the attitudes of white department-store employees toward their black co-workers, for the purpose of determining whether the attitudes acquired within the one context would carry over into others. For purposes of the study, they secured the cooperation of two leading eastern department stores that had just begun to employ blacks in white-collar jobs. The study revealed that equal-status job contact produced a large increase in the willingness of the white employees to work with blacks on an equal basis. The white employees were also willing to continue this pattern in a new situation of the same type. But there was no significant change in their willingness to accept blacks in *other* relationships—in sitting next to blacks in buses or trains, sitting down with a black in a lunchroom or cafeteria, living in a new apartment building or housing project that contained both white and black families, and having a black for a personal friend. Thus the white employees tended to "compartmentalize" their experience of working with blacks and did not generalize the experience to other situations involving blacks.

A not too different kind of situation prevailed during the immediate post-World War II period in the coal fields of McDowell County, West Virginia (Minard, 1952). Within the coal mines the black and white miners worked together as equals in a spirit of general good will. In a number of instances, blacks worked in higher status positions as motormen on mine lorries or as company physicians without any friction. However, the community outside the mine constituted a quite different environment in which the spirit of integration dissolved and the white miners again became members of a superior caste. The boundary line between the two communities was the mouth of the mine. Here management assisted the miners in recognizing their entrance into the outside world by providing separate baths and locker rooms. About one-fifth of the white miners behaved in a consistently prejudiced fashion and another one-fifth in a consistently unprejudiced fashion both inside and outside the mine. The remaining three-fifths shifted their role and status upon passing from the mouth of the mine into the world-at-large. Thus, many white miners handled their dual role and status by "segmenting" their personalities . In this manner they escaped the need for reorienting their attitudes and behavior toward blacks in a fundamental fashion.

Deutsch and Collins and Winner, Walkley, and Cook, in their respective studies of the effects of interracial housing on interracial attitudes and behavior, found some evidence for the generalization of attitudes. Nevertheless, there was a considerable gulf between the favorableness of attitudes toward the specific blacks in the contact situation and the generalizing of favorable attitudes to blacks as a group. Generalization to other nonwhite minorities was not significant.

Personality factors also influence changes in prejudice in interracial situations. A number of psychologists (Cook, 1972; Foley, 1976) have compared the personality inventories of those individuals who show a decrease in prejudice with those who show no change in settings favoring positive interracial relations. Individuals who change their attitudes are characterized by more negative self-concepts and more positive attitudes toward people in general than are individuals whose attitudes do not change.

Research reveals that some contact situations are more favorable than others in changing the behavior and attitudes of prejudiced people:

1. The contact takes place between status equals (Cook, 1972; Amir, 1976; Rosenfield et al., 1981).

2. The behavior of the objects of prejudice is at variance with or does not conform to the beliefs of the prejudiced individuals; for instance, the blacks with whom the prejudiced whites have contact are "hard working," "bright," and "law abiding" (Deutsch and Collins, 1951; Cook, 1972).

3. The contact is of sufficient duration and intimacy to challenge sufficiently the stereotypes of the prejudiced individual (Brown and Albee, 1966; Amir, 1976).

4. The prevailing social norms dictate that prejudiced attitudes and behavior are inappropriate (Cook, 1972; Foley, 1976).

5. The members of the differing racial groups within the contact situation have a common interest, goal, or task that is the focus of the interaction (Brophy, 1949; Foley, 1976; Amir, 1976; Norvell and Worchel, 1981).

6. Positive support for change is forthcoming from reference groups outside the specific contact situation (Cook, 1972; Amir, 1976).

7. The contact is pleasant and rewarding (Amir, 1976).

When individuals are given a choice, they typically prefer to interact within rather than between racial groups. Consequently, encouraging people to interact across group lines poses a major difficulty. Further, more prejudiced individuals avoid intergroup situations more strongly than do the less prejudiced. When people do enter intergroup settings, their attitudes tend to shift in the direction of those sanctioned by group norms. Since contact between members of differing racial and ethnic groups often occurs under unfavorable conditions, intergroup contact frequently breeds hostility and prejudice (*see* chapter 3). Unfavorable conditions include intergroup competition, unpleasant, tension-laden contact, threats to the status of one of the parties, deep-seated frustrations arising from social or economic forces within one or both groups, unequal-status contacts, and starkly conflicting moral and ethical standards (Cook, 1972; Amir, 1976).

Psychological Techniques

Since prejudice is often deeply embedded in the functioning of the entire personality, some psychologists insist that an effective program for combating prejudice must aim at reducing or rechanneling those elements within the personality that feed racial and ethnic antipathies. Focusing their attention upon the deep-seated anxieties, insecurities, and fears that frequently underlie and accompany prejudiced personalities, these specialists take a rather dim view of efforts that fail to come to grips with an individual's basic personality structure. The authors of *The Authoritarian Personality* are representative of this orientation. They suggest that educational approaches that employ rational arguments cannot be expected to have deep or lasing effects upon a phenomenon that is as intrinsically irrational in nature as is prejudice. Similarly, appeals to sympathy may backfire when they are directed toward people who harbor a deep fear of being identified with weakness or suffering. Nor can closer contact with members of minority groups be expected to influence an individual when the basic personality organization impairs or even precludes the person from establishing a deep or meaningful relationship with anybody, regardless of racial or ethnic membership. What then can be done about prejudice? T. W. Adorno and his associates (1950) suggest that, ideally, psychological techniques need to be employed to change personality.

Individual Therapy

Individual therapy has as its goal the readjustment of individuals who are psychologically maladjusted. By means of therapy provided by a psychiatrist or trained counselor, individuals may come to terms with their problems—their feelings of insecurity, inadequacy, and anxiety—and find socially acceptable outlets for their needs. Clearly, individuals do not seek out a therapist for the express purpose of altering their attitudes toward minorities. However, as individuals gain self-insight, their emotional need for racial prejudice and discriminatory behavior may diminish. As they become capable of dealing with their problems and feelings on a mature, objective level, they will presumably have less need to find immature or inappropriate outlets.

Individuals who compensate for their inner feelings of weakness and inadequacy by power-seeking may clutch at their membership in the dominant group (the white race) to provide themselves with a sense of strength. To give themselves the power they otherwise lack, they may incessantly search out opportunities to vilify and humiliate Jews and blacks. In the process they seek to reassure themselves, "I am powerful." The minority, being weak and helpless, gives them a contrasting sense of strength. But the power they realize is not genuine because it is external and not rooted in the personality itself. They have to reassert and demonstrate their power continually to prove to themselves and the world that they really are powerful. Accordingly, their involvement in racist behavior becomes a preoccupation. Through therapy they may come to realize an inner sense of strength and adequacy. As a result they will have less need to find some external, artificial bulwark for their sense of well-being.

As a means of combating prejudice, individual therapy has a number of obvious limitations. First, therapy usually takes considerable time and arduous work, often encompassing more than 200 hours distributed over a number of years. Second, the number of trained therapists is small and even inadequate for dealing with the number of individuals who might benefit from their services. Third, highly prejudiced individuals are frequently characterized by personality types that are relatively unresponsive to psychotherapeutic methods. And finally, available evidence (Pearl, 1955) raises serious doubts whether short-term individual psychotherapy (i.e., therapy averaging three times weekly for nine weeks) contributes much in the way of prejudice reduction, while little is known about the impact of long-term individual psychotherapy.

Group Therapy

The goals of group therapy are similar to those of individual therapy. With the growing recognition of the role that groups play in the lives of human beings, increasing use has been made of therapy in a group situation. It offers a means by which individuals may overcome their feelings of isolation and rejection and gain a sense of acceptance by other persons. Within the group, patients can find helpful new experiences and new insights that enable them to cope better with their problems and difficulties. Through the free, uninhibited atmosphere fostered within the group by the psychiatrist or counselor, individuals are led to break down barriers and undergo corrective emotional experiences.

The psychologists Morris and Natalie Haimowitz (1950) studied the indirect effects of group therapy upon prejudice. As a part of a training program in counseling at the University of Chicago, twenty-four individuals participated over a six-week period in thirty-five hours of group therapy in which they discussed their personal problems. The individuals ranged in age from twenty-five to sixty, had a master's degree or its equivalent in psychology, and had at least three years of professional experience. Before and after the six-week training period, the members were administered the Bogardus social-distance test.

On the basis of the Bogardus test results, the researchers classified the individuals as "friendly," "mildly hostile," or "strongly hostile" in their attitudes toward minority groups. The study revealed that after the group-therapy experience, the number of individuals rated as "friendly" increased. The group designated "hostile" remained fairly constant. The changes that occurred took place among those who came to the therapy experience mildly hostile. There were no cases where a friendly individual became mildly or strongly hostile on the second test, and only one individual who had been strongly hostile on the first test displayed a shift on the second.

The psychologists suggest that the higher incidence of those classified as "friendly" after group therapy lends confirmation to the hypothesis that, with improved adjustment, hostility to minority groups frequently declines. Through therapy, individuals presumably become better able to cope directly and effectively with the source of their frustrations. They become less hostile in their reactions and have less need to displace whatever tensions do emerge. The authors conjecture that prejudice assumes a more salient and basic part of the personalities of strongly bigoted persons. Since the therapeutic experience was relatively brief, it was not of sufficient duration to have an impact upon more deeply rooted prejudices.

Two years later a follow-up study was made of seventeen of the twenty-four subjects in the study. The changes that had occurred between the pre- and post-therapy tests were maintained. Furthermore, there was a continued, though smaller, change during the succeeding two-year period toward greater friendliness toward minorities. Yet individuals who were classified as "friendly" on the pre-test were not necessarily "tolerant" personalities. Although friendly toward racial and ethnic minorities, some of them revealed marked hostility toward Ku Klux Klansmen, Nazis, and Fascists. For instance, one individual classed as "friendly" said that anyone associated with the Ku Klux Klan should be hung without trial. In some cases of friendliness toward minorities, deep-lying hostility is diverted into other channels.

The psychologist Irwin M. Rubin (1967) also found that participants in a two-week sensitivity training program (akin to group therapy) displayed significant increases in self-acceptance and decreases in prejudice. Further, he found a positive relationship between changes in self-acceptance and changes in prejudice.

The psychologist David Pearl (1955), in still another study, came to somewhat less optimistic conclusions regarding the value of group psychotherapy as an instrument for combating prejudice. He administered a series of attitude and personality scales (the same questionnaires utilized in *The Authoritarian Personality* studies) to twenty-one male, neurotic, hospitalized patients before and after psychotherapeutic treatment. A control group of seven randomly selected male tuberculous patients was given the same scales but not exposed to psychotherapeutic treatment. Pearl found no significant difference between the effectiveness of brief group therapy (twelve hours of treatment) and intensive group therapy (sixty hours of treatment) in reducing prejudice. But of even greater significance, the magnitude of the changes produced by group therapy were generally too small to be of great practical importance:

> Statistically significant shifts which yet leave highly ethnocentric individuals with strong ethnocentric ideology do not support the hope held by some that group psychotherapy may become a major technique for

combating group prejudice. It would appear rather, that while psychotherapeutic treatment may play a role in any program designed to reduce
ethnocentrism, it is not a panacea and must be utilized in conjunction
with other approaches (Pearl, 1955:229).

In view of the conflicting evidence, we may wish to reserve our judgment on the effectiveness of group psychotherapy until such time as
more research is available.

Prejudice Reduction Through Self-Insight

Daniel Katz and his psychological associates (Katz et al., 1956, 1957;
Sarnoff and Katz, 1954; Stotland et al., 1959) have undertaken experiments dealing with the reduction of prejudice through the arousal of
self-insight. They say that an individual's attitudes (including prejudice)
reflect deep motivational roots. Hence, to modify an individual's attitudes, it is necessary to produce self-insight into the associated underlying motivations. The experiments show that individuals holding
negative stereotypes toward blacks—and otherwise resistant to positive
information about blacks—modify their attitudes through materials
that give them insight into the dynamics of prejudice.

In the experiments, subjects read a case history designed to provide
them with self-insight into the psychodynamics of prejudice. This task
was followed by a threefold approach: (1) The subjects ordered statements about the psychodynamics of prejudice in a logical sequence; (2)
the subjects reworked the materials that they had read in a manner that
made the reading relevant to anti-black prejudice; and (3) the subjects
were encouraged to be rational and consistent in their attitudes. No
significant changes occurred immediately after the experiment but significant change did emerge several weeks later. This later change apparently resulted from a "sleeper effect" associated with internal
restructuring. Presumably, an incubation period was necessary for the
personality to integrate the new attitudes.

The Legal Approach

It is often said, "You cannot legislate against prejudice." The notion
that laws are ineffective weapons for combating racism is an argument
often used against the enactment of civil-rights measures. According to
this assumption laws must follow rather than precede social change and
cannot by themselves alter the norms of a society. The view was stated
in classic fashion at the turn of the twentieth century by the sociologist
William Graham Sumner (1906), who declared that "stateways [laws]

cannot change folkways." Sumner believed that when laws moved ahead of the customs or mores of the people they could not succeed because they were not enforceable. The dismal failure of Prohibition in barring the manufacture, transportation, and sale of alcoholic beverages is usually cited as proof of this position. Yet interestingly enough, many Americans believed that they *could* legislate inequality. And they proceeded to do so. Beginning in the late nineteenth century, one southern state after another enacted Jim Crow laws and revised suffrage provisions so as to disfranchise black voters (Smith, 1975).

Although the Sumner-type argument against legislation sounds plausible, it is based upon a misunderstanding of the nature of laws and fails to distinguish between prejudice and discrimination. Laws can have little direct effect upon prejudice, because a state of mind—attitudes and feelings—is involved. But laws can prove effective weapons against overt acts of discriminatioin. Similarly, laws against murder and theft do not attempt to root out the desire to kill or steal. They seek to prevent these desires from being translated into overt acts. Laws are effective to the degree to which they function as deterrents to certain kinds of behavior, and therefore to the extent to which they are enforced. The fact that laws against murder and theft do not always succeed is no more evidence for the uselessness of such laws than is discrimination in employment evidence against fair-employment-practice acts. Many people feel that the fight against discrimination and segregation is more important than the fight against prejudiced attitudes and feelings. The former affect the right of an ethnic or racial minority to achieve equality and freedom of opportunity. The latter may be considered a private matter so long as the sentiment remains unexpressed.

Evidence on the Effectiveness of Laws

Probably one of the clearest instances of the effectiveness of legal and administrative methods in combating discrimination and segregation is the undermining of southern Jim Crow institutions during the past three decades through legislative, executive, and judicial action. The federal government undertook a monumental project in the field of social engineering, and it is an unquestionable fact that it is succeeding. Although in some instances contributing to a higher incidence of interracial friction, federal action has compelled the South to alter its traditional patterns in the direction of desegregation. Similarly, desegregation in the nation's armed forces was realized through the authoritative intervention of a presidential executive order. Table 15.1 summarizes the major civil-rights legislation of the United States.

New York State passed one of the first laws directed against discrimination in job hiring. The law took effect during the immediate post-

TABLE 15.1   MAJOR CIVIL RIGHTS LAWS

Fourteenth Amendment.

This amendment to the Constitution, adopted in 1868, declares that all persons born or naturalized in the United States are citizens, and provides that, if Congress chooses, a state's representation in Congress may be reduced if some citizens are denied the right to vote.

Fifteenth Amendment.

This amendment, adopted in 1870, declares that "the right of the citizens of the United States to vote shall not be denied or abridged by the United States or by any state on account of race, color, or previous condition of servitude."

Legislation, 1865–1875.

Of the many laws passed during this decade, six major laws survive, the others either struck down by Supreme Court decisions or repealed by Congress. These six laws restate the right of all citizens to vote regardless of race. Attempts to deprive anyone of any constitutional right, interpreted as including voting, are made federal crimes, and guilty persons are also made liable for civil damage suits.

Hatch Act of 1939.

Although not strictly a civil-rights law, this act makes it a crime to threaten, intimidate, or coerce voters in a federal election.

Civil Rights Act of 1957.

This statute gives the Attorney General of the United States the power to enter court suits to protect the voting rights of any citizen in any election —federal, state, or local. A Civil Rights Commission was created and given subpoena powers to investigate violations of voting rights in any election.

Civil Rights Act of 1960.

This statute makes defiance of court orders in voting cases a federal crime, requires preservation of all voting records for twenty-two months to prevent local officials from destroying registration forms and applications (these records are then available for court cases), and authorizes federal courts to appoint referees to see that qualified blacks are allowed to register and vote should local registrars balk or resign to avoid complying with court orders.

Twenty-fourth Amendment.

This amendment to the Constitution, adopted in 1964, abolishes the payment of poll taxes as a requirement for voting in federal elections.

Civil Rights Act of 1964.

The voting rights section of this act applies to federal elections only. It provides that the same standards must be used in registering all voters; minor errors in applications cannot be used to disqualify registrants; a sixth-grade education is proof of literacy for voting purposes unless election officials can prove otherwise in court; literary tests must be given in writing, with copies available to applicants; and a three-judge federal court must be impaneled to hear any case in which the attorney general of the United States charges voting discrimination, with right of direct appeal to the U.S. Supreme Court.

The statute prohibits discrimination or refusal of service on account of race in hotels, motels, restaurants, gasoline stations, and places of amusement if their operations affect interstate commerce or if their discrimination "is supported by state action"; requires that blacks have equal access to, and treatment in, publicly owned or operated facilities such as parks, stadiums, and swimming pools; empowers the attorney general of the United States to bring school desegregation suits; and authorizes the use of federal technical and financial aid to assist school districts in desegregation.

The act further provides that no person shall be subjected to racial discrimination in any program receiving federal aid, and directs federal agencies to take steps against discrimination, including—as a last resort, and after hearings—withholding of federal funds from state or local agencies that discriminate. It bans discrimination by employers or unions with 100 or more employees or members the first year the act is effective, reducing over four years from 100 or more to 25 or more. And the statute permits the attorney general of the United States to intervene in suits filed by private persons complaining that they have been denied rights guaranteed to them by the Fourteenth Amendment.

Title VII of the act also bars discrimination based on sex but permits such discrimination where it involves "a bona fide occupational qualification reasonably necessary to the normal operation of the business enterprise." This portion of the act created the Equal Employment Opportunity Commission (EEOC) to administer the law and investigate alleged violations. However, the EEOC was given no enforcement powers of its own; its role was limited principally to conciliation.

Civil Rights Act of 1965.
This act extends some of the provisions of the 1964 statute to cover state and local as well as federal elections, and simplifies the intricate time-consuming judicial procedures required for enforcing present voting laws.

Civil Rights Act of 1968.
The act bars discrimination in the sale or rental of federally owned housing and multiunit dwellings whose mortgages are insured or underwritten by the Federal Housing Administration and the Veterans Administration; bars discrimination in multiunit housing, such as apartments and in real-estate developments; and bars discrimination in single-family houses sold or rented through real-estate brokers (owners selling their houses without the aid of brokers can discriminate but are not allowed to use discriminatory signs or other such advertisements).

The act also provides stiff federal penalties for individuals convicted of intimidating or injuring civil-rights workers and blacks engaged in schooling, housing, voting, registering to vote, jury duty, and the use of public facilities; makes it a federal crime to travel from one state to another with an intent to incite a riot; makes it a federal crime to manufacture, sell, or demonstrate the use of firearms, fire-bombs, or other explosive devices meant for use in a riot or other civil disorder; and extends broad rights to American Indians in their dealings with their tribal governments, the courts, and local, state, and federal governments.

The Equal Employment Opportunity Act of 1972.
The act extends coverage of Title VII of the Civil Rights Act of 1964 to include employers and unions with between fifteen and twenty-five employees or members, state and local governments, and educational institutions. It permits the EEOC to issue administrative "cease and desist" orders in certain types of cases and gives the EEOC power to go to court when conciliation efforts fail. Further, the act requires that federal employment be freed from discrimination on the basis of race, color, religion, sex, or national origin.

World War II period and prior to the Supreme Court's 1954 school-desegregation ruling in *Brown* v. *Board of Education* (and the controversy that ensued). Consequently, the experience of New York residents during these early years provided social scientists with an unusual opportunity for investigating the impact of legislation upon people's behavior. The social psychologists Gerhart Saenger and E. Gilbert (1950) fortunately undertook such an investigation. They studied the reaction of white customers to black sales personnel in establishments that had hired blacks in response to the law. Since the law did not apply to customers, they could withdraw their trade from the integrated stores if they so desired. Saenger and Gilbert compared the attitudes of white customers buying from black clerks with attitudes of white customers buying from white clerks in a large New York City department store. Trained interviewers were stationed near those sales counters where black and white clerks worked side-by-side. In this manner, customers who dealt with black clerks were distinguished from those dealing with neighboring white clerks. Both the customers of black clerks and those of white clerks were then followed out of the store and interviewed. Since the customers were not told that they had previously been observed, it was possible to compare their actual behavior with their attitudes.

In the interviews, the white customers were asked to express their sentiments on the employment of black clerks. At least 20 percent indicated that they would not buy in stores that hired them. Another 20 percent gave limited approval provided black saleswomen were not used in departments handling food or clothing. However, the study revealed that there was no relationship between what people said and what they did. No difference was found in prejudice between customers who had dealt with black clerks and customers who had dealt with white clerks. In both groups 38 percent either disapproved of black clerks or wanted them excluded from some of the departments within the store. In fact, a number of women who had insisted a short time previously that they would not buy from blacks were later observed buying from black clerks.

Saenger and Gilbert suggest that a number of factors contributed to the discrepancy between what white people said and how they acted in relation to the black clerks. First, prejudiced individuals were caught in a conflict between two contradictory motivations: their prejudice on the one hand and their desire to shop where they found it most comfortable and convenient on the other. The individuals in the study tended to resolve the dilemma through acting contrary to their prejudice and completing their shopping as quickly and expediently as possible. Second, prejudiced individuals were caught in still another conflict: whether to follow the dictates of prejudice or whether to live up to America's democratic ideals. Either of these attitudes may be activated, depending upon the prejudiced individual's definition of the situation. Third, a desire to conform with prevailing public opinion may be uppermost in the individual's mind. They may prefer to translate their prejudice into overt action but, nevertheless, yield to local custom. The fact that blacks were found in the stores as clerks suggested to many individuals that the public approved of their presence. Individuals who are strongly prejudiced are often insecure and, accordingly, frequently have a deep need to conform. Thus, where they have the impression that others do not share their thinking, they are less likely to defend their prejudices and less likely to translate them into discriminatory behavior.

The sociologist Lewis M. Killian (1952), in his study of the adjustment of southern white migrants to life in Chicago, came to similar conclusions. Evidence gathered from employers and the migrants themselves revealed that southern whites were able to make a peaceful accommodation to the norms governing interracial situations within Chicago. Not only did they work in plants with blacks, but they shared the same rest rooms and dressing rooms. The South continued as their principal reference group and they followed its practices of racial segregation when it was conveniently possible. When confronted with situations in which these ways could not be adhered to without personal sacrifice, they tended to make the necessary behavioral adjustments although attitude changes did not necessarily occur. There are also instances of verbal expressions of tolerance accompanied by discriminatory behavior, although they are not as well documented, including the flight of white, liberal, middle-class families from the cities to the suburbs.

Studies such as those we have cited show that what people do in intergroup situations seems to be almost independent of how they feel or what they think. The *social setting* appears to constitute the chief factor. As the social psychologist Gordon W. Allport (1962:123) observes, "Segregationists act like integrationists where social prescription requires; integrationists behave like segregationists when it is socially appropriate to do so." Hence laws may play an important part in defining the social setting for individuals.

Two types of individuals appear to be particularly susceptible to the influence of antidiscriminatory laws: first, those who are themselves not prejudiced but who find it expedient or profitable to stand by silently or to give passive support to discrimination; second, those who are prejudiced but who are not prepared to pay a significant price for translating their attitudes into behavior, preferring instead the easier course of conformity. For these two groups, laws against discrimination frequently provide an impetus for overcoming previous patterns and for instituting nondiscriminatory behavior; thus, the laws act as deterrents to discriminatory behavior. Taken together, these two groups probably make up a sizeable majority of the population (the militant integrationists and militant segregationists represent smaller segments of the total population).

In evaluating the effectiveness of laws, we have stressed that they can play an important part in combating discrimination—overt behavior. But what about prejudice—a state of mind? The matter is by no means simple. As we have noted, at least in the short run, laws may have relatively little impact upon prejudice. Indeed, legally mandated desegregation often intensifies intergroup tensions and antagonisms and hence for a time may increase prejudice (Marshall et al., 1978). However, over the long run prejudice in many cases decreases. Evidence suggests that specific attitudes shape themselves to overt behavior. In considering intergroup contact earlier in the chapter, we pointed out that whites who actually work with blacks, especially as equals, tend to develop favorable attitudes toward working with blacks. Although this sentiment may not generalize to other interracial situations, it nevertheless points to specific attitude change—to the lessening of prejudice in at least one sphere.

Some social scientists claim that law exerts a *direct* influence on attitudes, without necessarily changing overt behavior first. Arthur E. Bonfield (1965:108–109) argues: ". . . the mere existence of the law itself affects prejudice. People usually agree with the law and internalize its values. This is because considerable moral and symbolic weight is added to a principle when it is embedded in legislation." In brief, law sets the moral atmosphere in which society exists, and in its own right it is a powerful instrument of education. A case in point is physicians' attitudes toward Medicare. Seldom has a law been more bitterly opposed by any group than was Medicare by the medical profession. Yet the proportion of physicians in favor of Medicare jumped from 38 percent before the law was passed to 70 percent ten months after it was passed, and then to 81 percent six months after it was implemented. Hence, some laws may influence attitudes without first changing overt behavior (Colombotos, 1969).

Some Limits to the Effectiveness of Law

During recent years, sociologists have increasingly come to recognize that laws can be effective instruments for reducing discrimination. But law, especially in a nontotalitarian society, is not all-powerful. Moreover, informal, indirect, subtle discrimination is much less susceptible to legal remedies than formal, direct, and blatant discrimination (Marshall et al., 1978; Burstein, 1979).

Moreover, civil-rights legislation often functions as a tool with an essentially negative character—it prescribes "thou shall nots." At still other times it may contribute to at best a "grudging acceptance" of minorities. Hence, although realizing desegregation, integration may remain a still distant goal. Accordingly, positive measures designed to promote intergroup good will are also called for. For instance, the economist Ray Marshall and his associates (1978) concluded on the basis of case studies that litigation is a necessary but insufficient condition for promoting equal employment opportunity. It is necessary because litigation demonstrates and publicizes grievances over discrimination and because it stimulates federal action. It is insufficient because extensive supplementary action is required before long-term changes in black-white inequality are brought about.

Then too, laws are likely to be effective to the extent that they are enforced; and of course authorities within the United States—both North and South, locally and nationally—have not always been committed to enforcing fully civil-rights laws. Another problem is that law typically channels charges of discrimination into a burdensome, conciliation-oriented administrative arrangement, operating on a case-by-case basis, which depends on effective prosecution and a sympathetic judiciary for progress to be achieved. Still another problem is that the victims of discrimination are often ignorant of the laws or reluctant to make complaints under them, patterns most frequently encountered among those segments of minority groups most susceptible to discrimination, namely poorly educated, low-income groups. The New York City "fair housing" ordinance is a case in point. New York City was the first community to enact a "fair housing" or "open occupancy" ordinance banning discrimination in the sale or rental of housing. Yet, the effect of the law appear to have been limited. During the first three years of its operation, the New York City law adjusted slightly more than 200 complaints to the satisfaction of the black complainant. While this constituted a gain, it is small when viewed in the perspective of New York City's nearly 1 million blacks. Most of the black complainants were middle-class blacks in white-collar or professional occupations. Lower-class blacks, for whom the housing problem is perhaps most severe, hardly participated in the benefits of the open-occupancy law at all. And finally, nearly half of the complaints were from blacks who already were living in areas that were predominantly white (Goldblatt and Cromien, 1962). It is perhaps somewhat unfair, however, to view a law's effectiveness in terms of the number of complainants benefiting from it. Some landlords undoubtedly "fell into line" with the law once it appeared on the books. These types of gains are difficult to measure.

School Desegregation

During the past three decades the United States has undertaken a major program of social engineering involving desegregation of the nation's schools. Among the program's goals, the reduction of dominant-group prejudice is cited almost as frequently as the promotion of minority-group academic achievement. During the 1950s a rather naïve optimism pervaded the scientific community that school desegregation would almost automatically improve intergroup relations. Many of the social scientists who testified on behalf of the black plaintiffs in the 1954 Supreme Court case of *Brown* v. *Board of Education* believed that school desegregation would lead to more positive racial attitudes (Stephen and Rosenfield, 1978). However, the intervening decades have not entirely borne out this optimism. Numerous studies have shown that the changes produced by desegregation are complex.

Nearly three decades after the Supreme Court ruled mandatory school segregation unconstitutional, a fifth of the nation's black students still attend schools that are almost all black in enrollment and more than half still attend schools in which the majority of students are black. The biggest difficulty in achieving desegregation is that black children often far outnumber white children in big cities and each race is concentrated in different sections of the city. White children are outnumbered in twenty-one of the nation's twenty-nine largest school districts. In Atlanta, New Orleans, Chicago, Detroit, San Francisco, Baltimore, and Washington, D.C., minority-group children comprise 75 percent or more of the public-school enrollment.

Confronted with segregated schooling, the NAACP and the federal government have returned repeatedly to the courts to bar school officials from perpetuating racist patterns. For the courts to have power under the Constitution and to order a remedy, the minority litigants must prove intentional, purposeful segregation on the part of government officials. Because the violations have frequently been pervasive and sophisticated, the remedies have had to be exact and tailored to each community's situation. In some instances the courts have redrawn school-district boundaries, altered school locations, scrutinized transfer policies, and reassigned students. Busing has also been employed to cure extensive segregation.

The Civil Rights Commission says that areawide busing may be the only way to achieve racially balanced schools. However, the Supreme

Court has refused to uphold city-suburban plans unless both the cities and suburbs are proven guilty of past discrimination or unless there is a unified school district. Large-scale busing of students to school has occurred in the United States since 1919 because many children do not live within walking distance of a school. Today 44 percent of America's schoolchildren are taken to school on buses. Only 3 percent are transported for desegregation. Busing as a social issue seems to dissipate for many whites if their bused children end up at predominantly white schools.

Intergroup Attitudes and Behavior.   Experience demonstrates that merely creating desegregated classrooms does not necessarily improve interracial attitudes. Likewise, research has provided conflicting findings. Some studies suggest that school desegregation can have a positive impact on intergroup attitudes and behavior, others reveal no effect, and a few have demonstrated negative outcomes (Carithers, 1970; St. John, 1975; Cohen, 1975; Gerard and Miller, 1975; Pearce, 1980; Rosenfield et al., 1981). These mixed findings suggest that there is more to successful integration than simply placing children from different racial backgrounds together in the same schools. Rather than asking whether desegregation improves intergroup relations, social scientists are increasingly investigating the *conditions* that make desegregation effective. In so doing they distinguish between desegregation and integration.

Desegregation refers to the removal of structural barriers within a society, both legal and social, that are premised upon racial or ethnic membership. It results in the elimination of segregation in institutional functioning and the achievement of what is commonly termed "civil rights." Integration encompasses the idea of eliminating prejudice as well as discrimination. As such it implies much more than simply desegregation. Integration involves attitudinal changes and the removal of fears, hatreds, suspicions, and superstitions. It results in the acceptance of individuals without regard to their group membership within informal, personal, and voluntary relationships.

Children bring to school the same fears and prejudices that characterize their parents and neighbors (St. John and Lewis, 1975). Research conducted among black and white students in Indianapolis public high schools reveals that racial attitudes that predict negative interracial behavior are students' own preexisting unfavorable attitudes and those of their families and peers (Patchen et al., 1976, 1977). Favorable family and peer racial attitudes particularly influence positive interracial behaviors. This evidence suggests that when desegregation is opposed by parents and neighbors, powerful social norms discourage informal interracial contact. It is illogical and unreasonable to expect the schools to undo the racism that the larger society relentlessly creates in the course of its daily operation.

In contrast, interracial friendliness is promoted by policies that foster positive interracial contact at *early* ages in elementary schools and neighborhoods (Singleton and Asher, 1977). For this reason desegregation should begin at the earliest possible grade, including kindergarten, to be most effective. Racial and ethnic attitudes are formed early and adjusting to new environments and avoiding negative stereotypes is more difficult for older students than for young ones. Indeed, the junior high-school years may be the worst period in which to start desegregation (Kihss, 1981).

Diana Pearce (1980), the director of research at the Catholic University Center for National Policy Review, finds that busing between suburban and inner-city districts tends to encourage integrated housing. She notes that housing in Charlotte, North Carolina, one of the earliest metropolitan areas to inaugurate areawide busing under court order, is one-third more integrated now than in 1970, when busing began. By contrast, Richmond, Virginia, which has successfully resisted interdistrict busing suits, is currently only one-fifth more integrated than in 1970. Other research suggests that desegregating schools can promote housing desegregation because pressure for whites to move is eliminated when a school system has guaranteed racial stability and white children will not be the lone members of their race to be enrolled (Kihss, 1981).

The sociologist Cardell K. Jacobson (1978) investigated attitude shifts of Milwaukee residents based on a survey conducted before and after a school desegregation ruling. On the whole parents of children in the public schools became more supportive of integration and busing. By contrast, people without children in the schools became more resistant, and parents of children in parochial schools displayed the greatest negative attitude change.

Academic Achievement. In 1966 the voluminous Coleman report (*see* chapter 2) appeared and seemed to show that the academic performance of black students improved as the proportion of white students in a school increased. Social scientists assumed that this change was due to the higher levels of educational motivation and background present in predominantly white student bodies—the "lateral transmission of values" hypothesis. According to this notion, black students acquire the achievement-related values held by whites when immersed within schools with high white enrollments (Bradley and Bradley, 1977).

Although a substantial number of studies have examined the relationship between the racial composition of a school and the academic achievement of its students, the evidence is inconclusive and even contradictory. Based upon an examination of more than 120 studies, the sociologist Nancy St. John (1975) could only determine that desegregation rarely lowers academic achievement for either black or white pupils. Other researchers concur that academic achievement, as measured by the usual standardized academic tests, is typically not affected in a negative manner in desegregated schools (Crain and Mahard, 1977; Hawley, 1979; Kihss, 1981). Overall, the effect of desegregation on the achievement of black students is not uniform. Other factors like socioeconomic status, family background, degree of racial tension, and interracial acceptance within the schools play critical roles. Considerably more is necessary if desegregation is to succeed than simply sending children from different racial backgrounds to the same schools.

"White Flight." James S. Coleman, the senior author of the Coleman report, now claims that the results promised by the 1966 study have not been achieved. On the basis of his ongoing research, he says that school desegregation has contributed to "white flight" from big cities and is rapidly producing resegregation of central cities (Coleman, 1975, 1976; Coleman et al., 1975). He is convinced that the policies pursued by the nation's courts are counterproductive, defeating increased interracial contact within school districts.

Coleman's work and conclusions have provoked bitter attacks from those who favor desegregation and busing programs (Ravitch, 1978). These latter scholars lost no time in criticizing his findings. Some have objected that his conclusions are invalid because his sample of school districts was relatively small (Pettigrew and Green, 1976; Rossell, 1976; Sly and Pol, 1978). Others cite evidence that shows that white out-migration from central cities is a long-term trend predating school desegregation (Henderson and von Euler, 1979; Frey, 1980). And still others note that desegregation does not cause white out-migration because the same degree of movement is observed in cities whether they have implemented desegregation plans, have had large-scale civil-rights protests, or experienced severe riots (Marshall, 1979; Frey, 1979, 1980). The most general conclusion is that whites are drawn to the suburbs rather than pushed to them (Marshall, 1979).

Admittedly the data and arguments surrounding the white flight controversy are confusing. A more fruitful line of inquiry may be one that seeks to specify the conditions under which school desegregation might lead to white out-migration and under which it might lead to white enrollment stability. A survey of the literature suggests the following tentative conclusions:

1. School desegregation accelerates the long-term decline in white public-school enrollment in the year it is implemented if a school district is above 30 to 35 percent black or if it involves the reassignment of whites to formerly black schools (Rossell, 1976; Levine and Meyer, 1977; Giles, 1978; Hawley, 1979).

2. Metropolitan-area plans (linking a central city and its suburbs) contribute to less white out-migration than city-only plans (Henderson and von Euler, 1979; Hawley, 1979; Kihss, 1981).

3. Voluntary school desegregation plans (including arrangements employing magnet schools) typically produce little or no white out-migration because they result in little desegregation (Hawley, 1979; Kihss, 1981).

4. White reassignments to formerly predominantly black schools produce more than twice the white out-migration of black reassignments to predominantly white schools. White reassignments to Hispanic or Asian schools tend to be associated with less white out-migration than reassignment to black schools (Hawley, 1979).

Conclusion. An intriguing theme appears to run below the surface of virtually all school-desegregation research. Desegregation can work if people really want it to work. Too often individuals have ulterior motives for not really wanting it to succeed (Sage, 1978). Where community leaders including mayors and school board members strongly support desegregation, it does work. Where leaders oppose it or drag their feet in response to court orders, the failure of the program and of busing becomes a self-fulfilling prophecy. Moreover, we should abandon the simplistic question "Does desegregation work?" and move to develop and test theory specifying the conditions for effective desegregation and for maximizing its benefit to students (St. John, 1975).

Affirmative-Action Programs

To a considerable degree American life is premised on the liberal belief in *equality of opportunity.* The object of equality of opportunity has been to free individuals from discriminations based on some group attribute like race, family, gender, religion, class, or community so that they might rise in society according to their capabilities and merits. Equality of opportunity denies that birth, nepotism, or patronage should be used in the allocation of positions. Instead, it holds that positions should be open equally to all through fair competition based upon talent and ambition.

However, during the past three hundred years of American life various minorities have been excluded from many positions by virtue of discrimination and institutional arrangements. They have not enjoyed equality of opportunity. Nor, as pointed out in chapter 14, have recent civil-rights programs been able to close the gap and produce *equality of results* in income, status, and power. Civil-rights programs have as their aim the ending of discrimination and the inauguration of equality of opportunity. But antidiscriminatory programs do not guarantee that minorities will be found in employment and other areas of social life in numbers equal to their proportion in the population.

Affirmative-action programs are means designed to expedite the entry of minorities into positions from which they have been barred by the operation of discrimination and institutional arrangements. They typically "target" figures for blacks, Chicanos, women, and other groups that have historically been discriminated against by the dominant group. In practice this emphasis has meant the implementation of priorities in recruitment and hiring for persons from these groups and the setting of timetables for reaching given employment goals. Blacks, Chicanos, women, and others are then hired as a matter of right, in proportion to their numbers, and the requirements of professional qualification or individual achievement may in some instances be relaxed.

Affirmative-action programs are designed to right historic wrongs. Whereas discrimination is usually criticized because it denies a justly earned position to people based upon some attribute (Jew, black, woman, youth, welfare recipient, homosexual, mental patient), affirmative-action programs require that individuals be placed in part *because* of their membership in a particular group. In sum, the argument is advanced that since the members of a group were discriminated against in the past *because* they were members of the group, now they should be hired to bring them in to the system *because* they are members of the group. Proponents of affirmative action say that programs are needed to undo the consequences of a long history of racism. They insist that the cancer of white racism is eroding American society and that, unless firm steps are taken, the United States will become two separate societies, one black, one white—separate and unequal.

Critics of affirmative action claim that the programs entail "reverse discrimination" and victimize whites, especially white males. They say that the establishment of quotas violates American constitutional provisions that set forth a basic standard of equality and mandate color-blind procedures. Further, sociologists like Nathan Glazer (1976) and economists like Thomas Sowell (1981) insist that special efforts are unnecessary because very substantial progress is being made in the upgrading of black employment and income. And finally, critics question whether affirmative-action measures actually assist black people with employment problems. They argue that jobs gained through quota systems very often have large attrition rates and cause minorities to become bitter, bruised, and badly hurt by their experience.

The legal status of affirmative-action programs is somewhat confused. In 1971 the Supreme Court considered a case brought by a member of black workers against Duke Power Company challenging the company's requirement that employees have a high-school diploma or pass generalized intelligence tests before being hired or transferred to better jobs (the *Griggs* case). Chief Justice Warren Burger, writing for a unanimous Court, held that "good intent or absence of discriminatory intent does not redeem employment procedures or testing mechanisms that operate as 'built-in headwinds' for minority groups and are unrelated to measuring job capability." The nation's highest court said that once a plaintiff has shown that an employment practice has a discriminatory impact, the burden is on the employer to show that any given requirement has a "manifest relationship" to the jobs in question and represents a "business necessity." The decision was widely interpreted as calling for the vigorous enforcement of the 1964 Civil Rights Act and as providing a hint that the Court might view affirmative-actions programs favorably.

In 1978 the high court ruled on a case brought by Allan Bakke. Bakke is a white man who was twice rejected by the University of California Medical School at Davis, although the university had rated him as better qualified than some of the sixteen minority-group members admitted through a special program. In a five to four decision the justices held that Bakke had been improperly denied admission because of his race. However, the Supreme Court held that the method the medical school had used was an illegal classification of applicants by race. Simultaneously it approved the principle of affirmative action by holding that race could be taken into account in granting admission to colleges and universities. The decision added up to considerable uncertainty as to what the Supreme Court actually had in mind.

A year later the Supreme Court considered the case of Brian F. Weber, a white worker at the Kaiser Aluminum plant in Gramercy, Louisiana. He had been rejected by a training program while blacks with less seniority were accepted. The Court upheld the legality of the plant's affirmative-action plan. The justices treated the program as purely "voluntary" and, in the absence of "state action," did not believe it necessary to consider constitutional issues.

In 1980 the Supreme Court handed down a decision in the case of *Fullilove* v. *Klutznick* that was widely interpreted as a breakthrough on the affirmative-action issue. For the first time the Court endorsed the power of Congress to award federal benefits on the basis of race. It upheld a public works program that entitled various minorities to 10 percent of federal construction grants. Six justices in the majority opinion accepted the premise that the Constitution does not require strict color-blindness in the pursuit of equality of economic opportunity and that color-blindness is inadequate when disadvantaged groups have to catch up to compete equally.

SUMMARY

1. A major problem faced by those who would employ propaganda is the difficulty in reaching people who are not already in favor of the view it presents. Communications research reveals that people commonly avoid points of view that are at odds with their own by simply not exposing themselves to such views. Those whom the propagandist

would most like to influence by certain communications are often the least likely to be reached by them.

2. When prejudiced people are involuntarily confronted with anti-prejudice propaganda, they often prefer to evade its implications. It is often easier simply not to understand or to twist and to misinterpret a message than to defend oneself or to admit error. Among the techniques that people employ to avoid understanding antiprejudice messages are the following: (1) identification avoided—understanding "derailed"; (2) the message made invalid; (3) changing the frame of reference; (4) finding the message too difficult; and (5) denial by discrediting the source.

3. At times propaganda may boomerang and promote prejudice. Some psychologists suggest that there may be this sort of effect in films showing cruelty against minority groups. Many prejudiced persons, far from being repelled, are attracted by cruelty. Another problem with propaganda is that the impact of a single program is typically limited. A campaign is necessary. Overall, it appears that propaganda has a very limited effect in combating prejudice. Dominant groups possess the power to define social reality through their control of the mass media and key institutions.

4. Underlying a good deal of work in the area of intergroup relations is the assumption that prejudice will disappear if people are given the facts. This view assumes that (1) people are predominantly rational beings and (2) prejudice is the product of ignorance. However, social scientists find that instruction of a factual kind only serves to mitigate some of the more extreme expressions of prejudice. Education suffers from many of the same problems as does antiprejudice propaganda. Another limitation of education is its failure to penetrate beyond the level of verbal expression to overt conduct.

5. Education is commonly looked upon in the United States as a source of liberation—as a means of freeing people from narrowness and provincialism. Since education stresses rational processes, it is often assumed that it causes people to control or reject the irrational and absurd. Yet any number of researchers have raised questions regarding such interpretations. Educated individuals, because of their intellectual sophistication, fail to state their prejudiced sentiments, which they realize run counter to the norms of the American democratic creed.

6. Contact among members of differing racial and ethnic groups is assumed to undermine racial tensions. According to this view, people are basically good and seek understanding and mutual respect. If they had the opportunity to communicate with one another and appreciate each other's way of life, good will should come to prevail. Proponents say that segregation has the opposite effect because it promotes dis-

tance and racism. It also prevents people from learning of the beliefs and values that they share with the members of the other group.

7. In and of itself, contact does not necessarily dispel prejudice. In fact, superficial contact is often a means by which prejudice is increased. Stereotypes sensitize individuals to signs that confirm and reinforce the stereotyping process. The net result is that perception tends to be selective. Intergroup contact may fail to challenge stereotypes for another reason—exemption. Occasionally an individual meets a member of another racial or ethnic group who fails to fit that group's stereotype. But instead of altering or eliminating the stereotype, the person makes the individual an exception.

8. Like other techniques for combating racism, interracial contact is not a panacea. One of its limitations is that many individuals fail to generalize their favorable attitudes toward particular minority-group members so as to include the whole minority group. Personality factors also influence changes in interracial situations. Individuals who change their attitudes are characterized by more negative self-concepts and more positive attitudes toward people in general than are those who maintain their attitudes.

9. Research reveals that some contact situations are more favorable than others in changing the behavior and attitudes of prejudiced people: (a) The contact takes place between status equals; (b) the behavior of the objects of prejudice is at variance with or does not conform to the beliefs of the prejudiced individuals; (c) the contact is of sufficient duration and intimacy to challenge sufficiently the stereotypes of the prejudiced individuals; (d) the prevailing social norms dictate that prejudiced attitudes and behavior are inappropriate; (e) the members of the differing groups have a common goal that is the focus of the interaction; (f) positive support for change is forthcoming from reference groups outside the specific contact situation; and (g) the contact is pleasant and rewarding.

10. Since prejudice is often deeply embedded in the functioning of the entire personality, some psychologists insist that an effective program for combating prejudice must aim at reducing or rechanneling those elements within the personality that feed racial and ethnic antipathies. Individual therapy is one technique. However, it is not a particularly practical method for combating racism. Group therapy is another technique. The evidence concerning the effectiveness of group therapy is contradictory and we may wish to reserve judgment on its effectiveness until more research is available.

11. Laws can be an effective mechanism for combating racism. Studies suggest that what people do in intergroup situations seems to be almost independent of how they feel or what they think. The social setting

appears to constitute the chief factor. Laws can play an important part in defining the social setting for individuals. Further, specific attitudes shape themselves to overt behavior. By punishing racist acts, legal remedies can bring about nonracist behaviors and indirectly undermine prejudice.

12. Law is not all-powerful. Positive measures designed to promote intergroup good will are also called for. Further, laws are likely to be effective to the extent that they are enforced. Another problem is that law typically channels charges of discrimination into a burdensome, conciliation-oriented administrative arrangement, operating on a case-by-case basis, which depends on effective prosecution and a sympathetic judiciary for progress to be achieved. Still another problem is that the victims of discrimination are often ignorant of the laws.

13. Experience and research demonstrates that merely creating desegregated classrooms does not necessarily improve interracial attitudes. Children bring to school the same fears and prejudices that characterize their parents and neighbors. When desegregation is opposed by parents and neighbors, powerful social norms discourage informal interracial contact. It is illogical and unreasonable to expect the schools to undo the racism that the larger society relentlessly creates in the course of its daily operation. Desegregation can work if people really want it to work. Where leaders oppose desegregation or drag their feet in response to court orders, the failure of the program and of busing becomes a self-fulfilling prophecy.

14. To a considerable degree American life is premised upon the liberal belief in equality of opportunity. The object of equality of opportunity has been to free individuals from discriminations based on some group attribute like race, family, gender, religion, class, or community so that they might rise in society according to their capabilities and merits. However, during the past three hundred years of American life various minorities have been excluded from many positions by virtue of discrimination and institutional arrangements. They have not enjoyed equality of opportunity. Affirmative-action programs have been designed to right these historic wrongs. The argument is advanced that since the members of a group were discriminated against in the past because they were members of the group, now they should be hired to bring them into the system because they are members of the group.

GLOSSARY

Affirmative-Action Programs Means designed to expedite the entry of minorities into positions from which they have been barred by the operation of discrimination and institutional arrangements.

Desegregation The removal of structural barriers within a society, both legal and social, that are premised upon racial or ethnic membership.

Propaganda A deliberate attempt to influence opinions or behavior to some predetermined end.

References

Aberbach, J. D. and Walker, J. L. 1973. *Race in the City*. Boston: Little, Brown & Co.

Abramson, H. J. 1973. *Ethnic Diversity in Catholic America*. New York: John Wiley & Sons.

Ackerman, N. W. and Jahoda, M. 1950. *Anti-Semitism and Emotional Disorder*. New York: Harper & Row.

Acuña, R. 1972. *Occupied America: The Chicano's Struggle toward Liberation*. San Francisco: Canfield Press.

Adam, B. D. 1978. Inferiorization and "self-esteem." *Social Psychology*, 41:47–53.

Adorno, T. W. 1950. *The Authoritarian Personality*. New York: Harper & Row.

Alba, R. D. 1976. Social assimilation among American Catholic national-origin groups. *American Sociological Review*, 41:1030–1046.

——— and Kessler, R. C. 1979. Patterns of interethnic marriage among American Catholics. *Social Forces*, 57:1124–1140.

Allen, R. 1973. Black liberation and world revolution. In Chrisman, R. and Hare, N. (Eds.) *Contemporary Black Thought*. New York: Bobbs-Merrill.

———. 1975. *Reluctant Reformers*. Garden City, N.Y.: Doubleday & Co.

Allport, G. W. 1954. *The Nature of Prejudice*. Boston: Beacon Press.

———. 1962. Prejudice: Is it societal or personal? *Journal of Social Issues*, 18:120–134.

Amir, Y. 1969. Contact hypothesis in ethnic relations. *Psychological Bulletin*, 71:319–342.

———. 1976. The role of intergroup contact in change of prejudice and ethnic relations. In Katz, P.A. (Ed.) *Towards the Elimination of Racism*. New York: Pergamon Press.

Antonovsky, A. 1956. Toward a refinement of the "marginal man" concept. *Social Forces*, 35:57–62.

Aptheker, H. 1943. *American Negro Slave Revolts.* New York: Columbia University Press.

Asch, S. E. 1952. *Social Psychology.* Englewood Cliffs, N.J.: Prentice-Hall.

Back, K. W. and Simpson, I. H. 1964. The dilemma of the Negro professional. *The Journal of Social Issues,* 20:60–70.

Bagby, J. W. 1957. A cross-cultural study of perceptual predominance in binocular rivalry. *Journal of Abnormal and Social Psychology,* 54: 331–334.

Baker, D. G. 1978. Race and power: Comparative approaches to the analysis of race relations. *Ethnic and Racial Studies,* 1:316–335.

Ball-Rokeach, S. J., Grube, J. W., and Rokeach, M. 1981. "Roots: The Next Generation"—Who watched and with what effect? *Public Opinion Quarterly,* 45:58–68.

Banks, W. C. 1976. White preference in blacks: A paradigm in search of a phenomenon. *Psychological Bulletin,* 83:1179–1186.

——— and Rompf, W. J. 1973. Evaluative bias and preference behavior in black and white children. *Child Development,* 44:776–783.

Barber, B. 1941. Acculturation and messianic movements. *American Sociological Review,* 6:663–669.

Barden, J. C. 1981. The impact of poverty on black children cited. *New York Times,* January 7, p. 7.

Barrera, M. 1979. *Race and Class in the Southwest: A Theory of Racial Inequality.* Notre Dame, Ind.: University of Notre Dame Press.

Barth, E. A. T. and Noel, D. L. 1972. Conceptual frameworks for the analysis of race relations: An evaluation. *Social Forces,* 50:333–347.

Beck, E. M. 1980. Discrimination and white economic loss: A time series examination of the radical model. *Social Forces,* 59:148–168.

Beeghley, L. and Butler, E.W. 1974. The consequences of intelligence testing in the public schools before and after desegregation. *Social Problems,* 21:740–754.

Benedict, R. 1940. *Race: Science and Politics.* New York: Modern Age Books.

Berger, A. S. and Simon, W. 1974. Black families and the Moynihan Report: A research evaluation. *Social Problems,* 22:145–161.

Bergesen, A. J. 1977. Neo-ethnicity as defensive political protest. *American Sociological Review,* 42:823–825.

Berkowitz, L. 1962. *Aggression: A Social Psychological Analysis.* New York: McGraw-Hill.

Berreman, G. D. 1971. Speech to Council. *Newsletter of the American Anthropological Association,* 12 (January):19.

Berry, B. 1965. *Race and Ethnic Relations.* 3rd ed. Boston: Houghton Mifflin.

Bettelheim, B. and Janowitz, M. 1950. *Dynamics of Prejudice.* New York: Harper & Row.

Biblarz, A. 1969. On the question of objectivity in sociology. *Et Al,* 2:4.

Bierstedt, R. 1963. *The Social Order.* 2nd ed. New York: McGraw-Hill.

Billingsley, A. 1968. *Black Families in White America.* Englewood Cliffs, N.J.: Prentice-Hall.

Blackwell, J. E. 1975. *The Black Community Diversity and Unity.* New York: Dodd, Mead & Co.

Blair, W. G. 1982. Study finds an increase in anti-Semitic actions. *New York Times,* January 6, p. 9.

Blake, R. R. and Manton, J. S. 1961. Comprehension of own and outgroup positions under intergroup competition. *Journal of Conflict Resolution,* 5:301–309.

Blalock, H. M., Jr. 1967. *Toward a Theory of Minority-Group Relations.* New York: John Wiley & Sons.

Blau, P. M. and Duncan, O. D. 1967. *The American Occupational Structure.* New York: John Wiley & Sons.

———. 1972. *The American Occupational Structure.* 2nd ed. New York: John Wiley & Sons.

Blauner, R. 1969. Internal colonialism and ghetto revolt. *Social Problems,* 16:393–408.

———. 1972. *Racial Oppression in America.* New York: Harper & Row.

———. 1973. Black culture: Lower-class result or ethnic creation. In Rainwater, L. R. *The Black Experience.* New Brunswick, N.J.: Transaction Books.

Bloom, L. and Riemer, R. 1949. *Removal and Return.* Berkeley: University of California Press.

Blum, D. J. 1981. Cabrini-Green project, big ghetto in Chicago, fights a losing battle. *The Wall Street Journal,* May 5, p. 1, 15.

Blumer, H. 1961. Race prejudice as a sense of group position. In Masuoka, J. and Valien, P. (Eds.) *Race Relations.* Chapel Hill: University of North Carolina Press.

Bogardus, E. S. 1959. *Social Distance.* Yellow Springs, Ohio: Antioch Press.

———. 1968. Comparing racial distance in Ethiopia, South Africa, and the United States. *Sociology and Social Research,* 52:149–156.

Bogue, D. 1959. *The Population of the United States.* New York: The Free Press.

Bonacich, E. 1972. A theory of ethnic antagonism: The split-labor market. *American Sociological Review,* 37:547–559.

———. 1973. A theory of middleman minorities. *American Sociological Review,* 38:583–594.

———. 1975. Abolition, the extension of slavery, and the position of free blacks: A study of split-labor markets in the United States, 1830–1863. *American Journal of Sociology,* 81:601–628.

Bonfield, A. E. 1965. The role of legislation in eliminating racial discrimination. *Race,* 7:108–109.

Borinski, E. 1958. The litigation curve and the litigation filibuster in civil rights cases. *Social Forces,* 37:142–147.

Borrie, W. D. 1959. *The Cultural Integration of Immigrants.* Paris: UNESCO.

Boyd, W. C. 1950. *Genetics and the Races of Man.* Boston: Little, Brown & Co.

Bradley, L. A. and Bradley, G. W. 1977. The academic achievement of black students in desegregated schools: A critical review. *Review of Educational Research,* 47:399–449.

Brewer, M. B. and Campbell, D. T. 1976. *Ethnocentrism and Intergroup Attitudes: East African Evidence.* New York: Halsted Press.

Briggs, J. W. 1978. *An Italian Passage: Immigrants to Three American Cities, 1890–1930.* New Haven: Yale University Press.

Briggs, K. A. 1979. Change is found in Jewish views of intermarriage. *New York Times,* January 24, p. B3.

Brink, W. and Harris, L. 1966. *Black and White.* New York: Simon & Schuster.

Brinton, C. 1938. *The Anatomy of Revolution.* New York: W. W. Norton.

Broom, L., Beem, H. P., and Harris, V. 1955. Characteristics of 1,108 petitioners for change of name. *American Sociological Review,* 20:-33–39.

Brophy, I. N. 1949. The luxury of anti-Negro prejudice. *Public Opinion Quarterly,* 9:456–466.

Brown, B. S. and Albee, G. W. 1966. The effect of integrated hospital experiences on racial attitudes—A discordant note. *Social Problems,* 13:324–333.

Bruner, E. M. 1956. Primary group experience and the process of acculturation. *American Anthropologist,* 58:605–623.

Bugelski, B. R. 1961. Assimilation through intermarriage. *Social Forces,* 40:148–153.

Burma, J. H. 1946. Humor as a technique in race conflict. *American Sociological Review,* 11:713–714.

Burstein, P. 1979. Equal employment opportunity legislation and the income of women and nonwhites. *American Sociological Review,* 44:-367–391.

Byrne, D. and Wong, T. J. 1962. Racial prejudice, interpersonal attraction, and assumed dissimilarity of attitudes. *Journal of Abnormal and Social Psychology,* 65:246–253.

Campbell, A. and Schuman, H. 1968. *Racial Attitudes in Fifteen American Cities.* Washington, D.C.: Government Printing Office.

Campisi, P. J. 1948. Ethnic family patterns: The Italian family in the United States. *American Journal of Sociology,* 43:443–449.

Cantril, H. 1941. *The Psychology of Social Movements.* New York: John Wiley & Sons.

———. 1943. Educational and economic composition of religious groups: An analysis of poll data. *American Journal of Sociology,* 47:- 574–579.

Carithers, M. 1970. School desegregation and racial cleavage, 1954– 1970: A review of the literature. *Journal of Social Issues,* 26:25–47.

Carmichael, S. 1966. What we want. *The New York Review of Books,* September 22, p. 5+.

——— and Hamilton, C. V. 1967. *Black Power.* New York: Random House.

Carroll, M. P. 1975. Revitalization movements and social structure: Some quantitative tests. *American Sociological Review,* 40:389–401.

Carter, T. 1968. Negative self-concept of Mexican-American students. *School and Society,* 96:217–219.

Cash, W. J. 1954. *The Mind of the South.* New York: Doubleday & Co.

Catton, W. R., Jr., and Hong, S. C. 1962. Apparent minority ethnocentrism and majority antipathy. *American Sociological Review,* 27:178– 191.

Chambliss, W. and Nagasawa, R. 1969. On the validity of official statistics: A comparative study of white, black, and Japanese high school boys. *Journal of Research in Crime and Delinquency,* 6:71–77.

Chancellor, L. and Monahan, T. 1955. Religious preference and interreligious mixtures in marriages and divorces in Iowa. *American Journal of Sociology,* 60:232–237.

Cheng, D. T. 1948. *Acculturation of the Chinese in the United States.* Philadelphia: University of Pennsylvania Press.

Child, I. L. 1943. *Italian or American?* New Haven: Yale University Press.

Christensen, H. T. and Barber, K. E. 1967. Interfaith versus intrafaith marriage in Indiana. *Journal of Marriage and the Family,* 29:461–469.

Christie, R. and Jahoda, M. (Eds.) 1954. *Studies in the Scope and Method of "The Authoritarian Personality."* New York: The Free Press.

Clark, K. B. 1963. Educational stimulation of racially disadvantaged children. In Passow, A. H. (Ed.) *Education in Depressed Areas.* New York: Teachers College Bureau of Publications.

———. 1964. *Youth in the Ghetto.* New York: Haryou Associates.

———. 1965. *Dark Ghetto.* New York: Harper & Row.

———. 1967. The search for identity. *Ebony,* 22 (August):42.

———. 1978. No. No. Race, not class, is still at the wheel. *New York Times,* March 22, p. 22.

———. 1980. The role of race. *New York Times Magazine,* October 5, p. 24+.

——— and Clark, M. P. 1939. Development of consciousness of self and the emergence of racial identification in Negro preschool children. *Journal of Social Psychology,* 10:591–599.

—— and ——. 1947. Racial identification and preference in Negro children. In Newcomb, T. M. and Hartley, E. L. (Eds.) *Readings in Social Psychology.* New York: Holt.

—— and ——. 1950. Emotional factors in racial identification and preference in Negro children. In Grossack, M. (Ed.) *Mental Health and Segregation.* New York: Springer.

Clay, P. L. 1979. The process of black suburbanization. *Urban Affairs Quarterly,* 14:671–692.

Clymer, A. 1981. Growing disputes split black and Jewish Democrats. *New York Times,* March 30, p. 10.

Cockerham, W. C. and Blevins, A. L., Jr. 1976. Open school vs. traditional school: Self-identification among Native American and white adolescents. *Sociology of Education,* 49:164–169.

Cohen, E. 1975. The effects of desegregation on race relations. *Law and Contemporary Problems,* 39:271–299.

Coleman, J. S. 1966. *Equality of Educational Opportunity.* Washington, D.C.: Government Printing Office.

——. 1975. Racial segregation in the schools: New research with new policy implications. *Phi Delta Kappan,* 57:75–82.

——. 1976. Response to Professors Pettigrew and Green, *Harvard Educational Review,* 46:217–224.

——, Kelley, S. D., and Moore, J. 1975. *Trends in School Segregation.* Washington, D.C.: Urban Institute.

Coleman, R. D. and Rainwater, L. 1978. *Social Standing in America: New Dimensions of Class.* New York: Basic Books.

Collins, R. 1975. *Conflict Sociology.* New York: Academic Press.

Colombotos, J. 1969. Physicians and Medicare: A before-after study of the effects of legislation on attitudes. *American Sociological Review,* 34:319–334.

Columbus Dispatch. 1981. Group says Jewish position in U.S. is secure. April 27, p. A9.

Comas, J. 1951. *Racial Myths.* Paris: UNESCO.

Connor, W. 1978. A nation is a nation, is a state, is an ethnic group is a . . . *Ethnic and Racial Studies,* 1:377–400.

Cook, S. W. 1972. Motives in a conceptual analysis of attitude-related behavior. In Brigham, J. and Weissbach, T. (Eds.) *Racial Attitudes in America: Analyses and Findings of Social Psychology.* New York: Harper & Row.

Coon, C. S. 1962. *The Origin of Races.* New York: Alfred A. Knopf.

——. 1965. *The Living Races of Man.* New York: Alfred A. Knopf.

——. 1967. Reply to Buettner-Janusch. *American Journal of Physical Anthropology,* 26:359–360.

——, Garn, S. M., and Birdsell, J. B. 1950. *Races: A Study of the Problems of Race Formation in Man.* Springfield, Ill.: Charles C. Thomas.

Cooper, E. and Jahoda, M. 1947. The evasion of propaganda: How prejudiced people respond to anti-prejudice propaganda. *The Journal of Psychology*, 23:15–25.

—— and Dinerman, H. 1951. Analysis of the film "Don't Be a Sucker": A study in communication. *Public Opinion Quarterly*, 15:-243–264.

Coser, L. A. 1956. *The Functions of Social Conflict.* New York: The Free Press.

——. 1968. Conflict: Social aspects. In Sills, D. (Ed.) *International Encyclopedia of the Social Sciences.* New York: The Macmillan Co.

Coward, B. E., Williams, J. A., Jr., and Feagin, J. R. 1974. The culture of poverty debate: Some additional data. *Social Problems*, 21:621–634.

Cox, O. C. 1948. *Caste, Class, and Race.* New York: Doubleday & Co.

Crain, R. L. and Mahard, R. E. 1977. "Desegregation and Black Achievement." Durham, N.C.: Working paper, Institute of Policy Sciences and Public Affairs, Duke University.

Crano, W. D. and Mellon, P. M. 1978. Causal influence of teachers' expectations on children's academic performance: A cross-lagged panel analysis. *Journal of Educational Psychology*, 70:39–49.

Crewdson, J. M. 1979. Inquiry in Texas finds employers cheating aliens. *New York Times*, October 29, p. A16.

——. 1980a. Study suggests 6 million or fewer illegal aliens in U.S. *New York Times*, February 4, p. A12.

——. 1980b. Thousands of aliens held in virtual slavery in U.S. *New York Times*, October 19, pp. 1, 58.

——. 1980c. Illegal aliens are bypassing farms for higher pay of jobs in cities. *New York Times*, November 10, pp. A1, D9.

——. 1981. Hispanic voters in U.S. register gains as debate swirls about the rights act. *New York Times*, May 22, p. 6.

Cronon, E. D. 1955. *Black Moses.* Madison: University of Wisconsin Press.

Crosby, F., Bromley, S., and Saxe, L. 1980. Recent unobtrusive studies of black and white discrimination and prejudice: A literature review. *Psychological Bulletin*, 87:546–563.

Crouthamel, J. L. 1969. The Springfield, Illinois race riot of 1908. In Boskin, J. (Ed.) *Urban Racial Violence in the Twentieth Century.* New York: The Free Press.

Cruse, H. 1968. *Rebellion or Revolution?* New York: William Morrow & Co.

Cummings, S. 1975. An appraisal of some recent evidence dealing with the mental health of black children and adolescents, and its implications for school psychologists and guidance counselors. *Psychology in the Schools*, 12:234–238.

Daniels, L. A. 1980. Blacks pursue more active role in dealing with crime by blacks. *New York Times*, November 9, pp. 1, 40.

Davie, M. R. 1949. *Negroes in American Society.* New York: McGraw-Hill.

Davies, J. C. 1962. Toward a theory of revolution. *American Sociological Review,* 27:5–19.

Davis, A., Gardner, B. B., and Gardner, M. 1941. *Deep South.* Chicago: University of Chicago Press.

Dean, J. P. and Rosen, A. 1955. *A Manual of Intergroup Relations.* Chicago: University of Chicago Press.

DeBlaissie, R. R. and Healy, G. W. 1970. *Self-Concept: A Comparison of Spanish-American, Negro, and Anglo Adolescents across Ethnic, Sex, and Socioeconomic Variables.* Las Cruces, N.M.: ERIC Clearinghouse on Rural Education and Small Schools.

DeFleur, M. L. and Westie, F. R. 1958. Verbal attitudes and overt acts. *American Sociological Review,* 23:667–673.

Degler, C. N. 1959. Slavery and the genesis of American race prejudice. *Comparative Studies in Society and History,* 2:49–66.

Della-Cava, R. 1977. The Italian immigrant experience: Views of a Latinamericanist. In Tomasi, S. M. (Ed.) *Perspectives in Italian Immigration and Ethnicity.* New York: Center for Migration Studies.

Della-Fave, L. R. 1974. The culture of poverty revisited: A strategy for research. *Social Problems,* 21:609–621.

Deniker, J. 1912. *The Races of Man.* New York: Charles Scribner.

Dent, E. M. 1978. The salience of pro-white/antiblack bias. *Child Development,* 49:1280–1283.

Deutsch, M. and Collins, M. E. 1951. *Interracial Housing.* Minneapolis: University of Minnesota Press.

Dizard, J. E. 1970. Black identity, social class, and Black Power. *Psychiatry,* 33:195–207.

Dobzhansky, T. 1962. *Mankind Evolving.* New Haven: Yale University Press.

———. 1962. Comment on Livingstone's paper. *Current Anthropology,* 3:279–280

———. 1963. *Evolution, Genetics, and Man.* New York: John Wiley & Sons.

———. 1968. Introduction. In Mead, M., Dobzhansky, T., Tobach, E., and Light, R. E. (Eds.) *Science and the Concept of Race.* New York: Columbia University Press.

Doise, W. 1969. Intergroup relations and polarization of individual and collective judgments. *Journal of Personality and Social Psychology,* 12:136–143.

Dollard, J. 1939. *Frustration and Aggression.* New Haven: Yale University Press.

———. 1957. *Caste and Class in a Southern Town.* 3rd ed. New York: Doubleday & Co.

Dowd, D. 1964. Thorstein Veblen and C. Wright Mills: Social science and social criticism. In Horowitz, I. (Ed.) *The New Sociology.* New York: Oxford University Press.

Dowd, J. J. 1981. Age and inequality: A critique of the age stratification model. *Human Development,* 24:157–171.

Drake, S. C. and Cayton, H. R. 1945. *Black Metropolis.* New York: Harcourt Brace Jovanovich.

Duncan, O. D. 1969. Inheritance of poverty or inheritance of race? In Moynihan, D. P. (Ed.) *On Understanding Poverty.* New York: Basic Books.

Dynes, R. and Quarantelli, E. L. 1968. Looting in American cities: A new explanation. *Trans-action* (May):14.

Edwards, H. 1968. Black Muslim and Negro Christian family relationships. *Journal of Marriage and the Family,* 30:604–611.

———. 1979. Review of *The Declining Significance of Race* by William J. Wilson. *Social Forces,* 57:991–993.

Elder, G. H., Jr. 1970. Group orientations and strategies in racial change. *Social Forces,* 48:445–460.

Epstein, Y. M., Krupat, E., and Obudho, C. 1976. Clean is beautiful: Identification and preference as a function of race and cleanliness. *Journal of Social Issues,* 32:109–118.

Erbe, B. M. 1975. Race and socioeconomic segregation. *American Sociological Review,* 40:801–812.

Erickson, F. 1975. Gatekeeping and the melting pot: Interaction in counseling encounters. *Harvard Educational Review,* 45:44–70.

Essien-Udom, E. U. 1964. *Black Nationalism.* New York: Dell Publishing Co.

Etzioni, A. 1959. The ghetto: A re-evaluation. *Social Forces,* 37:255–262.

Fairchild, H. P. 1925. *Immigration.* New York: The Macmillan Co.

———. 1947. *Race and Nationality.* New York: The Ronald Press.

Fancher, B. 1970. *Voices from the South.* Atlanta: Southern Regional Council.

Fanon, F. 1966. *Black Skin, White Masks.* New York: Grove Press.

Farber, B., Gordon, L., and Mayer, A. J. 1979. Intermarriage and Jewish identity: The implications for pluralism and assimilation in American society. *Ethnic and Racial Studies,* 2:222–230.

Farley, R. 1980. The long road: Blacks and whites in America. *American Demographics,* 2:11–17.

———, Schuman, H., Bianchi, S., Colasanto, D., and Hatchett, S. 1978. Chocolate city, vanilla suburbs. *Social Science Research,* 7:319–344.

Featherman, D. L. 1971. The socioeconomic achievement of white religio-ethnic subgroups: Social and psychological explanations. *American Sociological Review,* 36:207–222.

——— and Hauser, R. M. 1976. Sexual inequalities and socioeconomic achievement in the U.S., 1962–1973. *American Sociological Review,* 41:462–483.

Feshbach, S. and Singer, R. 1957. The effects of personal and shared threats upon social prejudice. *Journal of Abnormal and Social Psychology,* 54:411–416.

Fly, J. W. and Reinhart, G. R. 1980. Racial separation during the 1970s: The case of Birmingham. *Social Forces,* 58:1255–1262.

Foley, L. A. 1976. Personality and situational influences on changes in prejudice: A replication of Coo's railroad game in a prison setting. *Journal of Personality and Social Psychology,* 34:846–856.

Ford, W. S. 1973. Interracial public housing in a border city: Another look at the contact hypothesis. *American Journal of Sociology,* 78:- 1426–1447.

Fortes, M. and Evans-Pritchard, E. E. 1940. *African Political Systems.* London: Oxford University Press.

Forum, 1940. I was a Jew. *103*:8–9.

Franklin, J. H. 1952. *From Slavery to Freedom.* New York: Alfred A. Knopf.

Franklin, R. S. 1971. The political economy of Black Power. In Geschwender, J. A. (Ed.) *The Black Revolt.* Englewood Cliffs, N.J.: Prentice-Hall.

———— and Resnik, S. 1973. *The Political Economy of Racism.* New York: Holt, Rinehart & Winston.

Frazier, E. F. 1926. The Garvey movement. *Opportunity,* 4 (November):346–348.

————. 1932. *The Negro Family in Chicago.* Chicago: University of Chicago Press.

————. 1940. *Negro Youth at the Crossways.* Washington, D.C.: American Council on Education.

————. 1951. The Negro's vested interest in segregation. In Rose, A. M. (Ed.) *Race Prejudice and Discrimination.* New York: Alfred A. Knopf.

————. 1957. *Black Bourgeoisie.* New York: The Free Press.

Freeman, R. B. 1977. *Black Elite: The New Market for Highly Educated Black Americans.* New York: McGraw-Hill.

Frenkel-Brunswik, E. 1948. A study of prejudice in children. *Human Relations,* 1:301–305.

Frey, W. H. 1979. Central city white flight: Racial and nonracial causes. *American Sociological Review,* 44:425–448.

————. 1980. Black in-migration, white flight, and the changing economic base of the central city. *American Journal of Sociology,* 85:- 1396–1417.

Friedman, S. 1969. How is racism maintained? *Et Al,* 2:19.

Friedrichs, R. W. 1968. Interpretation of black aggression. *The Yale Review,* 21:358–374.

Fritzpatrick, J. P. 1966. Intermarriage of Puerto Ricans in New York City. *American Journal of Sociology,* 71:395–406.

Gans, H. J. 1956. American Jewry: Present and future. *Commentary,* 21:422–430.

————. 1962. *The Urban Villagers.* New York: The Free Press.

————. 1979. Symbolic ethnicity: The future of ethnic groups and cultures in America. *Ethnic and Racial Studies,* 2:1–20.

Garn, S. M. 1963. Comment. *Current Anthropology,* 4:197–198.

————. 1964. Comment. *Current Anthropology,* 5:316.

————. 1965. *Human Races.* 2nd ed. Springfield, Ill.: Charles C. Thomas.

Geertz, C. 1963. *Old Societies and New States.* New York: The Free Press.

Genovese, E. D. 1974. *Roll, Jordan, Roll: The World the Slaves Made.* New York: Random House.

Gerard, H. B. and Miller, N. 1975. *School Desegregation.* New York: Plenum Press.

Gergen, K. J. 1967. The significance of skin color in human relations. *Daedalus,* 96 (Spring):145–158.

Gershman, C. 1980. A matter of class. *New York Times Magazine,* October 5, p. 24+.

Geschwender, J. A. 1964. Social structure and the Negro revolt. *Social Forces,* 43:248–256.

————. 1978. *Racial Stratification in America.* Dubuque, Iowa: William C. Brown.

Gilbert, G. M. 1951. Stereotype persistence and change among college students. *Journal of Abnormal and Social Psychology,* 46:245–254.

Giles, M. W. 1978. White enrollment stability and school desegregation: A two-level analysis. *American Sociological Review,* 43:848–864.

————, Gatlin, D. S., and Cataldo, E. F. 1976. Racial and class prejudice: Their relative effects on protest against school desegregation. *American Sociological Review,* 41:280–288.

Gillin, J. 1948. *The Ways of Men.* New York: Appleton-Century-Crofts.

Glazer, N. 1976. *Affirmative Discrimination: Ethnic Identity and Public Policy.* New York: Basic Books.

———— and Moynihan, D. P. 1963. *Beyond the Melting Pot.* Cambridge, Mass.: MIT Press.

Glenn, N. D. and Hyland, R. 1967. Religious preference and worldly success: Some evidence from national surveys. *American Sociological Review,* 32:73–85.

Goldblatt, H. and Cromien, F. 1962. The effective reach of the fair housing practices law of the City of New York. *Social Problems,* 9:365–370.

Goldman, Nahum. 1965. World Zionists Beset by Doubt. *New York Times,* January 12.

Goodman, M. E. 1952. *Race Awareness in Young Children.* Reading, Mass.: Addison-Wesley Publishing Co.

Goody, J. 1962. *Death, Property and the Ancestors.* Stanford, Calif.: Stanford University Press.

Gordon, M. M. 1958. *Social Class in American Sociology.* Durham, N.C.: Duke University Press.

―――. 1964. *Assimilation in American Life.* New York: Oxford University Press.

Goren, A. A. 1980. Jews. *Harvard Encyclopedia of American Ethnic Groups.* Cambridge, Mass.: Harvard University Press.

Gornick, V. and Moran, B. K. 1971. *Woman in Sexist Society.* New York: New American Library.

Gould, L. 1969. Who defines delinquency: A comparison of self-reported and officially-reported indices of delinquency for three racial groups. *Social Problems,* 16:325–336.

Grebler, L., Moore, J. W., and Guzman, R. C. 1970. *The Mexican-American People.* New York: The Free Press.

Greeley, A. M. 1970. Religious intermarriage in a denominational society. *American Journal of Sociology,* 75:949–952.

―――. 1971. *Why Can't They Be Like Us?* New York: E.P. Dutton.

―――. 1972. *The Most Distressful Nation.* Chicago: Quadrangle.

―――. 1974. *Ethnicity in the United States: A Preliminary Reconnaissance.* New York: John Wiley & Sons.

―――. 1976. The ethnic miracle. *The Public Interest,* 45:20–36.

―――. 1977. *The American Catholic: A Social Portrait.* New York: Basic Books.

Grier, W. H. and Cobbs, P. M. 1968. *Black Rage.* New York: Bantam Books.

Grimshaw, A. D. 1960. Urban racial violence in the United States. *American Journal of Sociology,* 64:109–119.

Guillemin, J. 1978. The politics of national integration: A comparison of United States and Canadian Indian administrations. *Social Problems,* 25:319–332.

Haimowitz, M. L. and Haimowitz, N. R. 1950. Reducing ethnic hostility through psychotherapy. *Journal of Social Psychology,* 31:231–241.

Hall, R. L. 1978. *Black Separatism in the United States.* Hanover, N.H.: University Press of New England.

Hallowell, A. I. 1951. Cultural factors in the structuralization of perception. In Rohrer, J. H. and Sherif, M. (Eds.) *Social Psychology at the Crossroads.* New York: Harper & Row.

Hamblin, R. J. 1962. The dynamics of racial discrimination. *Social Problems,* 10:103–120.

Hamilton, D. L. and Bishop, G. D. 1976. Attitudinal and behavioral effects of initial integration of white suburban neighborhoods. *Journal of Social Issues,* 32:47–67.

Hanley, R. 1980. Ramapo people seek recognition as Indians. *New York Times,* January 17, p. B1.

Hannerz, U. 1969. Roots of black manhood. *Trans-action* (October):13–21.

Hansen, M. L. 1952. The third generation in America. *Commentary,* 14:492–500.

Harbin, S. P. and Williams, J. E. 1966. Conditioning of color connotations. *Perceptual & Motor Skills,* 22:217–218.

Harding, J. and Hogrefe, R. 1952. Attitudes of white department store employees toward Negro co-workers. *Journal of Social Issues,* 8:18–28.

Hawley, A. H. 1963. Power as an attribute of social system. *American Journal of Sociology,* 68:422–431.

Hawley, W. D. 1979. Getting the facts straight about the effects of school desegregation. *Educational Leadership,* 36:314–321.

Hecht, P. K. and Cutright, P. 1979. Racial differences in infant mortality rates: United States, 1969. *Social Forces,* 57:1180–1193.

Heer, D. M. 1980. Intermarriage. *Harvard Encyclopedia of American Ethnic Groups.* Cambridge, Mass.: Harvard University Press.

Heiss, J. and Ownes, S. 1972. Self-evaluations of blacks and whites. *American Journal of Sociology,* 78:360–370.

Henderson, R. and von Euler, M. 1979. *What Research and Experience Teach Us About Desegregating Large Northern Cities.* Washington, D.C.: Clearinghouse for Civil Rights Research, Catholic University.

Hendrick, C., Bixenstine, V. E., and Hawkins, G. 1971. Race versus belief similarity as determinants of attraction. *Journal of Personality and Social Psychology,* 17:250–258.

Herbers, J. 1978. Black-white split persists a decade after warning. *New York Times,* February 26, p. 1ff.

Hermann, J. S. 1981. *The Pursuit of a Dream.* New York: Oxford University Press.

Hernton, C. C. 1965. *Sex and Racism in America.* New York: Doubleday & Co.

Herzl, T. 1946. *The Jewish State.* New York: American Zionist Emergency Council.

Hill, M. C. 1944. Basic racial attitudes toward whites in the Oklahoma all-Negro community. *American Journal of Sociology,* 39:519–523.

Hill, R. 1972. *The Strengths of Black Families.* New York: Emerson Hall Publishers.

Himes, J. S. 1973. *Racial Conflict in American Society.* Columbus, Ohio: Charles E. Merrill.

Hindelang, M. J. 1978. Race and involvement in common law personal crimes. *American Sociological Review,* 43:93–109.

———. 1981. Variations in sex-race-age-specific incidence rates of offending. *American Sociological Review,* 46:461–474.

Hoffer, E. 1951. *The True Believer.* New York: Harper & Row.

Hollingshead, A. B. 1952. Trends in social stratification. *American Sociological Review,* 18:679–686.

Hooton, E. A. 1946. *Up from the Ape.* Rev. ed. New York: The Macmillan Co.

——— and Dupertuis, C. W. 1955. *The Physical Anthropology of Ireland.* Cambridge, Mass.: Peabody Museum of Archaeology and Ethnology, Harvard University.

Horowitz, E. L. and Horowitz, R. E. 1938. Development of social attitudes in children. *Sociometry,* 1:301–338.

Hostetler, J. A. 1980. *Amish Society.* Baltimore: The Johns Hopkins University Press.

Hovland, C. I., Lumsdaine, A. A., and Sheffield, F. D. 1949. *Experiments on Mass Communication.* Princeton, N.J.: Princeton University Press.

Howard, D. H. 1966. An exploratory study of attitudes of Negro professionals toward competition with whites. *Social Forces,* 45:20–27.

Howell, F. M. and Frese, W. 1979. Race, sex, and aspirations: Evidence for the race convergence hypothesis. *Sociology of Education,* 52:34–46.

Howells, W. W. 1973. *Evolution of the Genus Homo.* Reading, Mass.: Addison-Wesley Publishing Co.

Huey, J. 1977. Police prisoner's death brings angry reaction by Houston minorities. *Wall Street Journal,* November 11, p. 1, 23.

Hunt, L. L. and Hunt, J. G. 1977. Black religion as both opiate and inspiration of civil rights militance: Putting Marx's data to the test. *Social Forces,* 56:1–14.

Hur, K. K. and Robinson, J. P. 1978. The social impact of "Roots." *Journalism Quarterly,* 55:19–21.

Hurvitz, N. 1958. Sources of middle-class values of American Jews. *Social Forces,* 37:117–123.

Hyman, H. H. and Sheatsley, P. B. 1954. The Authoritarian Personality—A methodological critique. In Christie, R. and Jahoda, M. (Eds.) *Studies in Scope and Method of "The Authoritarian Personality."* New York: The Free Press.

Jackman, M. R. 1973. Education and prejudice or education and response-set? *American Sociological Review,* 38:327–339.

Jacobson, C. K. 1977. Separatism, integrationism, and avoidance among black, white, and Latin adolescents. *Social Forces,* 55:1011–1027.

———. 1978. Desegregation rulings and public attitude changes: White resistance or resignation? *American Journal of Sociology,* 84:-698–705.

Jencks, C. 1979. *Who Gets Ahead? The Determinants of Economic Success in America.* New York: Basic Books.

Jenkins, W. S. 1935. *Pro-Slavery Thought in the Old South.* Chapel Hill: University of North Carolina Press.

Jensen, A. R. 1969. How much can we boost IQ and scholastic achievement? *Harvard Educational Review,* 39:1–123.

————. 1973. Race, intelligence and genetics: The differences are real. *Psychology Today*, 7 (December):80–86.

Johnson, C. S. 1934. *Shadow of the Plantation*. Chicago: University of Chicago Press.

————. 1939. Race relations and social change. In Thompson, E. T. (Ed.) *Race Relations and the Race Problem*. Durham, N.C.: Duke University Press.

————. 1941. *Growing Up in the Black Belt*. Washington, D.C.: American Council on Education.

————. 1943. *Patterns of Negro Segregation*. New York: Harper & Row.

Johnson, G. B. 1939. Patterns of race conflict. In Thompson, E. T. (Ed.) *Race Relations and the Race Problem*. Durham, N.C.: Duke University Press.

Johnson, M. P. and Sell, R. R. 1976. The cost of being black: A 1970 update. *American Journal of Sociology*, 82:183–190.

Johnson, R. 1957. Negro reactions to minority group status. In Barron, M. L. (Ed.) *American Minorities*. New York: Alfred A. Knopf.

Johnson, T. A. 1979. Two black leaders differ over split between poor and middle class. *New York Times*, May 17, p. B11.

Jones, E. E. and Kohler, R. 1958. The effects of plausibility on the learning of controversial statements. *Journal of Abnormal and Social Psychology*, 57:315–320.

Jordan, W. D. 1968. *White Over Black*. Chapel Hill: University of North Carolina Press.

Kamin, L. J. 1974. *The Science and Politics of IQ*. Potomac, Md.: Lawrence Erlbaum.

Kang-Ning, C. 1981. Education for Chinese and Indochinese. *Theory into Practice*, 20 (Winter):35–44.

Kaplan, H. M. 1969. The Black Muslims and the Negro quest for communion. *British Journal of Sociology*, 20:164–176.

Kardiner, A. and Ovesey, L. 1951. *The Mark of Oppression*. New York: W. W. Norton.

Karlins, M., Coffman, T. L., and Walters, G. 1969. On the fading of social stereotypes: Studies in three generations of college students. *Journal of Personality and Social Psychology*, 13:1–16.

Kass, D. and Lipset, S. M. 1980. America's new wave of Jewish immigrants. *New York Times Magazine*, December 7, p. 44+.

Katz, D. and Braley, K. W. 1933. Racial stereotypes of 100 college students. *Journal of Abnormal and Social Psychology*, 28:280–290.

————, McClintock, C., and Sarnoff, I. 1957. The measurement of ego defense as related to attitude change. *Journal of Personality*, 25:465–474.

————, Sarnoff, I., and McClintock, C. 1956. Ego-defense and attitude change, *Human Relations*, 9:27–45.

Katz, P. A. 1973. Perception of racial cues in preschool children: A new look. *Developmental Psychology,* 8:295–299.

———. 1976. The acquisition of racial attitudes in children. In Katz, P. A. (Ed.) *Towards the Elimination of Racism.* New York: Pergamon Press.

———, Sohn, M., and Zalk, S. R. 1975. Perceptual concomitants of racial attitudes in urban grade-school children. *Developmental Psychology,* 11:135–144.

——— and Zalk, S. R. 1974. Doll preferences: An index of racial attitudes? *Journal of Educational Psychology,* 66:663–668.

Katznelson, I. 1971. Power in the reformulation of race research. In Orleans, P. and Ellis, W. R., Jr. (Eds.) *Race, Change and Urban Society.* Beverly Hills, Calif.: Sage.

Kaufman, J. 1980. In big-city ghettos, life is often worse than in the '60s tumult. *Wall Street Journal,* May 23, pp. 1, 25.

Kaufman, W. C. 1957. Status, authoritarianism, and anti-Semitism. *American Journal of Sociology,* 62:379–382.

Kennedy, R. J. R. 1944. Single or triple melting-pot? Intermarriage trends in New Haven, 1870–1940. *American Journal of Sociology,* 49:-331–339.

Kerckhoff, A. C. and Campbell, R. T. 1977a. Black-white differences in the educational attainment process. *Sociology of Education,* 50:-15–27.

——— and ———. 1977b. Race and social status differences in the explanation of educational ambition. *Social Forces,* 55:701–714.

——— and McCormack, T. C. 1955. Marginal status and marginal personality, *Social Forces,* 50–67.

Kerner Commission. 1968. *Report of the National Advisory Commission on Civil Disorders.* New York: Bantam Books.

Key, V. O., Jr. 1950. *Southern Politics.* New York: Alfred A. Knopf.

Kibbe, P. R. 1946. *Latin Americans in Texas.* Albuquerque: University of New Mexico Press.

Kihss, P. 1980. Study finds Puerto Ricans in an 'awesome crisis.' *New York Times,* November 2, p. 53.

———. 1981. Study discerns desegregation benefit. *New York Times,* September 16, p. 12.

Killian, L. M. 1952. The effects of southern white workers on race relations in northern plants. *American Sociological Review,* 17:327–331.

———. 1953. The adjustment of southern white migrants to northern urban norms. *Social Forces,* 33:66–69.

———. 1975. *The Impossible Revolution, Phase II.* New York: Random House.

——— and Grigg, C. 1964. *Racial Crisis in America.* Englewood Cliffs, N.J.: Prentice-Hall.

Killian, L. M. and Smith, C. U. 1960. Negro protest leaders in a southern community. *Social Forces*, 38:253–257.

Kilson, M. 1981. Black social classes and intergenerational poverty. *The Public Interest*, 64:58–78.

Kim, H. C. 1977. The relationship of protestant ethic beliefs and values to achievement. *Journal for the Scientific Study of Religion*, 16:255–262.

Kinder, D. R. and Sears, D. O. 1981. Prejudice and politics: Symbolic racism versus racial threats to the good life. *Journal of Personality and Social Psychology*, 40:414–431.

King, M. L., Jr. 1958. *Stride Toward Freedom*. New York: Ballantine Books.

————. 1965a. Behind the Selma march. *Saturday Review of Literature* (April 3):15+.

————. 1965b. Civil Right No. 1—The right to vote. *New York Times Magazine*, March 14, p. 26+.

King, P. J. 1980. Black leadership? An 'anachronistic notion.' *New York Times*, July 6, p. E5.

King, W. 1980. The violent rebirth of the klan. *New York Times Magazine*, December 7, pp. 150–160.

Kirscht, J. P. and Dillehay, R. C. 1967. *Dimensions of Authoritarianism: A Review of Research and Theory*. Lexington: University of Kentucky Press.

Kitano, H. H. L. 1980. Japanese. *Harvard Encyclopedia of American Ethnic Groups*. Cambridge, Mass.: Harvard University Press.

Klineberg, O. 1935. *Negro Intelligence and Selective Migration*. New York: Columbia University Press.

————. 1951. *Race and Psychology*. Paris: UNESCO.

Kluckhohn, C. 1960. *Mirror for Man*. Greenwich, Conn.: Fawcett Publications.

———— and Kelly, W. H. 1945. The concept of culture. In Linton, R. (Ed.) *The Science of Man in the World Crisis*. New York: Columbia University Press.

Kluegel, J. R. 1978. The causes and cost of racial exclusion from job authority. *American Sociological Review*, 43:285–301.

Knight, M. 1979. Boston: City of culture—and unusual racial woes. *New York Times*, June 2, p. 6.

Kramer, J. R. and Leventman, S. 1961. *Children of the Gilded Ghetto*. New Haven: Yale University Press.

Kristol, I. 1969. Blacks are the last immigrant group. In Moynihan, D. P. (Ed.) *On Understanding Poverty: Perspectives from the Social Sciences*. New York: Basic Books.

LaBarre, W. 1972. *The Ghost Dance: Origins of Religion*. New York: Dell Publishing Co.

Labovitz, S. and Hagedorn, R. 1975. A structural-behavioral theory of intergroup antagonism. *Social Forces,* 53:444–448.

Ladd, E. C., Jr. 1966. *Negro Political Leadership in the South.* Ithaca, N.Y.: Cornell University Press.

LaFree, G. D. 1980. The effect of sexual stratification by race on official reactions to rape. *American Sociological Review,* 45:842–854.

Lalli, M. 1969. The Italian-American family: Assimilation and change, 1900–1965. *The Family Coordinator,* 18:44–48.

Langford, D. L. 1980. Ku Klux Klan bouncing back across U.S. *Columbus Dispatch,* December 31, p. A2.

LaPiere, R. T. 1934. Attitudes vs. actions. *Social Forces,* 13:230–237.

Laue, J. H. 1964. A contemporary revitalization movement in American race relations: The "Black Muslims." *Social Forces,* 42:315–324.

La Violette, F. E. 1946. *Americans of Japanese Ancestry.* Toronto: Canadian Institute of International Affairs.

Lazerwitz, B. and Harrison, M. 1979. American Jewish denominations: A social and religious profile. *American Sociological Review,* 44:-656–666.

Leach, E. R. 1954. *Political Systems of Highland Burma.* Cambridge, Mass.: Harvard University Press.

————. 1960. The Frontiers of "Burma." *Comparative Studies in Society and History,* 3:49.

Lee, A. M. and Humphrey, N. D. 1943. *Race Riot.* New York: Holt, Rinehart, & Winston.

Lee, E. S. 1951. Negro intelligence and selective migration: A Philadelphia test of the Klineberg hypothesis. *American Sociological Review,* 16:227–233.

Lee, R. H. 1949. The decline of Chinatowns in the United States. *American Journal of Sociology,* 54:422–432.

————. 1960. *The Chinese in the United States of America.* Hong Kong: Hong Kong University Press.

Lehman, F. K. 1967. Ethnic categories in Burma and the theory of social systems. In Kunstadter, P. (Ed.) *Southeast Asian Tribes, Minorities, and Nations.* Vol. 1. Princeton, N.J.: Princeton University Press.

Leighton, A. H. 1945. *The Governing of Men.* Princeton, N.J.: Princeton University Press.

Lenski, G. 1963. *The Religious Factor.* Rev. ed. Garden City, N.Y.: Doubleday & Co.

Levine, D. U. and Meyer, J. K. 1977. Level and rate of desegregation and white enrollment decline in a big city school district. *Social Problems,* 24:451–462.

LeVine, R. A. and LeVine, B. B. 1966. *Nyansogo, a Gusii Community in Kenya.* New York: John Wiley & Sons.

Lewin, K. 1948. *Resolving Social Conflicts.* New York: Harper & Row.

Lewis, O. 1965. *La Vida: A Puerto Rican Family in the Culture of San Juan and New York*. New York: Random House.

Lieberson, S. 1961. A societal theory of race and ethnic relations. *American Sociological Review,* 26:902–910.

————. 1970. Stratification and ethnic groups. *Sociological Inquiry,* 40:172–181.

———— and Silverman, A. R. 1965. Precipitants and conditions of race riots. *American Sociological Review,* 30:887–899.

Liebow, E. 1967. *Tally's Corner.* Boston: Little, Brown & Co.

Light, I. and Wong, C. C. 1975. Protest or work: Dilemmas of the tourist industry in American Chinatowns. *American Journal of Sociology,* 80:1342–1368.

Lincoln, C. E. 1961. *The Black Muslims in America.* Boston: Beacon Press.

Lindgren, E. J. 1938. An example of culture contact without conflict: Reindeer Tungus and Cossacks of Northwestern Manchuria. *American Anthropologist,* 40:605–621.

Lindsey, R. 1978. Study finds wage gap between races narrowing. *New York Times,* May 8, p. 1, 15.

Linton, R. 1937. One hundred per cent American. *American Mercury,* 40:427–429.

————. 1940. *Acculturation in Seven American Indian Tribes.* New York: Appleton-Century-Crofts.

————. 1943. Nativistic movements. *American Anthropologist,* 45:-230–240.

————. 1945. *The Cultural Background of Personality.* New York: Appleton-Century-Crofts.

Lippmann, W. 1922. *Public Opinion.* New York: Harcourt Brace Jovanovich.

Lipset, S. M. 1963. *The First New Nation.* New York: Basic Books.

Liska, A. E. 1974. Emergent issues in the attitude-behavior consistency controversy. *American Sociological Review,* 39:261–272.

Liu, W. T., Lamanna, M., and Murata. 1979. *Transition to Nowhere.* Nashville, Tenn.: Charter House Publishers.

Livingstone, F. B. 1962. On the non-existence of human races. *Current Anthropology,* 4:279–281.

Loehlin, J. C., Lindzey, G., and Spuhler, J. N. 1975. *Race Differences in Intelligence.* San Francisco: W. H. Freeman & Co.

Loewenstein, R. M. 1951. *Christians and Jews.* New York: International Universities Press.

Logan, J. R. and Stearns, L. B. 1981. Suburban racial segregation as a nonecological process. *Social Forces,* 60:61–73.

Lohman, J. D. and Reitzes, D. C. 1952. Note on race relations in a mass society. *American Journal of Sociology,* 58:242.

Lopez, D. E. 1976. The social consequences of Chicano home/school bilingualism. *Social Problems,* 24:234–246.

Lundborg, H. and Linders, F. J. 1926. *The Racial Character of the Swedish Nation.* Uppsala and Stockholm: Swedish State Institute for Race Biology.

Lyman, S. M. 1974. *Chinese Americans.* New York: Random House.

McCarthy, J. D. and Yancey, W. L. 1971. Uncle Tom and Mr. Charlies: Metaphysical pathos in the study of racism and personal disorganization. *American Journal of Sociology,* 76:648–672.

McConahay, J. B. and Hough, J. C., Jr. 1976. Symbolic racism. *Journal of Social Issues,* 32:23–45.

MacCrone, I. D. 1937. *Race Attitudes in South Africa.* London: Oxford University Press.

McFee, M. 1968. The 150% man, a product of Blackfeet acculturation. *American Anthropologist,* 70:1096–1107.

MacIver, R. M. 1948. *The More Perfect Union.* New York: The Macmillan Co.

McKenzie, R. D. 1928. *Oriental Exclusion.* Chicago: University of Chicago Press.

MacKinnon, W. J. and Centers, R. 1956. Authoritarianism and urban stratification. *American Journal of Sociology,* 61:610–620.

McLaughlin, S. D. 1978. Occupational sex identification and the assessment of male and female earnings inequality. *American Sociological Review,* 43:909–921.

McLemore, S. D. 1980. *Racial and Ethnic Relations in America.* Boston: Allyn & Bacon.

McWilliams, C. 1944. *Prejudice.* Boston: Little, Brown & Co.

————. 1949. *North from Mexico.* Philadelphia: J. B. Lippincott.

Marshall, H. 1979. White movement to the suburbs: A comparison of explanations. *American Sociological Review,* 44:975–994.

Marshall, R., Knapp, C. B., Ligget, M. H., and Glover, R. W. 1978. *Employment Discrimination: The Impact of Legal and Administrative Remedies.* New York: Praeger Publishers.

Martin, T. 1976. *Race First: The Ideological and Organizational Struggles of Marcus Garvey and the Universal Negro Improvement Association.* Westport, Conn.: Greenwood Press.

Matthews, D. R. and Prothro, J. W. 1966. *Negroes and the New Southern Politics.* New York: Harcourt Brace Jovanovich.

Marx, G. T. 1967a. *Protest and Prejudice.* New York: Harper & Row.

————. 1967b. Religion: Opiate or inspiration of civil rights militancy among Negroes? *American Sociological Review,* 32:64–72.

Masotti, L. H., Hadden, J. K., Seminatore, K. F., and Corsi, J. R. 1969. *A Time to Burn?* Chicago: Rand McNally.

Maxwell, N. 1968. Negroes in Dixie form separate municipalities in bid to improve lot. *Wall Street Journal,* November 11, p. 1.

————. 1980. Civil-rights groups face tough challenge in bid to regain power. *Wall Street Journal,* September 19, pp. 1, 19.

Mayer, A. J. and Frons, M. 1980. Is this tribe Indian? *Newsweek* (January 7):32.

―――― and Sharp, H. 1962. Religious preference and worldly success. *American Sociological Review,* 27:218–227.

Meier, A. 1965. On the role of Martin Luther King. *New Politics,* 4:52–59.

Mercer, J. R. 1972. IQ: The lethal label. *Psychology Today,* 6 (September):44–47ff.

Merton, R. K. 1957. *Social Theory and Social Structure.* Rev. ed. New York: The Free Press.

―――― and Kitt, A. S. 1950. Contributions to the theory of reference group behavior. In Merton, R. K. and Lazarsfeld, P. F. (Eds.) *Continuities in Social Research: Studies in the Scope and Method of "The American Soldier."* New York: The Free Press.

―――― and Nisbet, R. A. 1976. *Contemporary Social Problems,* 4th ed. New York: Harcourt Brace Jovanovich.

Meyers, G. 1960. *History of Bigotry in the United States.* New York: G.P. Putnam.

Mezei, L. 1971. Perceived social pressure as an explanation of shifts in the relative influence of race and belief on prejudice across social interactions. *Journal of Personality and Social Psychology,* 19:69–81.

Middleton, R. 1960. Ethnic prejudice and susceptibility to persuasion. *American Sociological Review,* 25:679–689.

Miller, N. E. and Bugelski, R. 1948. Minor studies of aggression: II. The influence of frustrations imposed by the in-group on attitudes expressed toward out-groups. *Journal of Psychology,* 25:437–442.

Miller, S. C. 1974. *The Unwelcome Immigrant: The American Image of the Chinese, 1785–1882.* Berkeley: University of California Press.

Mills, C. W., Senior, C., and Goldsen, R. K. 1950. *The Puerto Rican Journey.* New York: Harper & Row.

Minard, R. D. 1952. Race relationships in the Pocahontas coal fields. *Journal of Social Issues,* 8:29–44.

Mittelbach, F. G. and Moore, J. W. 1968. Ethnic endogamy—the case of Mexican Americans. *American Journal of Sociology,* 71:395–406.

Moe, J. L., Nacoste, R. W., and Insko, C. A. 1981. Belief versus race as determinants of discrimination. *Journal of Personality and Social Psychology,* 41:1031–1050.

Monahan, T. P. 1976. An overview of statistics on interracial marriage in the United States, with data on its extent from 1963–1970. *Journal of Marriage and the Family,* 38:223–231.

Montagu, A. 1942. *Man's Most Dangerous Myth: The Fallacy of Race.* New York: Columbia University Press.

――――. 1951. *Statement on Race.* New York: Abelard-Schuman.

――――. 1963. What is remarkable about varieties of man is likeness-es, not differences. *Current Anthropology,* 4:361–364.

――――. 1964. *The Concept of Race.* New York: The Free Press.

Montero, D. 1978. For Japanese-Americans, erosion. *New York Times,* December 4, p. A21.

―――. 1979. Vietnamese refugees in America: Toward a theory of spontaneous international migration. *International Migration Review,* 13:624–648.

Montgomery, P. 1981. For Cuban refugees, promise of U.S. fades. *New York Times,* April 19, pp. 1, 8.

Mooney, J. 1973. *The Ghost Dance Religion and Wounded Knee.* New York: Dover Publications.

Morland, J. K. 1958. Race recognition by nursery school children in Lynchburg, Virginia. *Social Forces,* 37:132–137.

Morris, A. 1981. Black southern student sit-in movement: An analysis of internal organization. *American Sociological Review,* 46:744–767.

Mosher, L. 1970. Why blacks turn backs to war protest. *National Observer* (June 29):12.

Myrdal, G. 1944. *An American Dilemma.* New York: Harper & Row.

Nadel, S. F. 1947. *The Nuba.* London: Oxford University Press.

―――. 1957. *The Foundation of Social Anthropology.* New York: The Free Press.

Nelli, H. S. 1980. Italians. *Harvard Encyclopedia of American Ethnic Groups.* Cambridge, Mass.: Harvard University Press.

Nelsen, H. M., Madron, T. W., and Yokley, R. L. 1975. Black religion's Promethean motif: Orthodoxy and militancy. *American Journal of Sociology,* 81:139–146.

Newcomb, T. M. 1954. Sociology and psychology. In Gillin J. (Ed.) *For a Social Science of Social Man.* New York: Macmillan.

Newman, M. T. 1963. Geographic and Microgeographic races. *Current Anthropology,* 4:189–192.

Newman, W. M. 1973. *American Pluralism.* New York: Harper & Row.

New York Times. 1981. Gallup Poll finds improved attitude toward Jews. April 16, p. 10.

Noel, D. L. 1964. Group identification among Negroes: An empirical analysis. *Journal of Social Issues,* 20:71–84.

―――. 1969. Minority responses to intergroup situations. *Phylon,* 30:367–374.

―――. 1972. *The Origins of American Slavery and Racism.* Columbus, Ohio: Charles E. Merrill.

Novak, M. 1971. *The Rise of the Unmeltable Ethnics.* New York: Macmillan.

Novell, N. and Worchel, S. 1981. A reexamination of the relations between equal status contact and intergroup attraction. *Journal of Personality and Social Psychology,* 41:902–908.

Oberschall, A. 1973. *Social Conflict and Social Movements.* Englewood Cliffs, N.J.: Prentice-Hall.

Office of Policy Planning and Research. 1965. *The Negro Family.* Washington, D.C.: U.S. Department of Labor.

Okimoto, D. I. 1971. *From American in Disguise.* New York: John Weatherhill.

Orbell, J. M. 1967. Protest participation among southern Negro college students. *American Political Science Review,* 61:446–456.

———— and Sherrill, K. S. 1969. Racial attitudes and the metropolitan context. *Public Opinion Quarterly,* 33:46–54.

Palisi, B. J. 1966. Ethnic generation and family structure. *Journal of Marriage and the Family,* 28:49–50.

Parcel, T. L. 1979. Race, regional labor markets and earnings. *American Sociological Review,* 44:262–279.

Park, R. E. 1928. Human migration and the marginal man. *American Journal of Sociology,* 33:881–893.

————. 1949. *Race and Culture.* New York: The Free Press.

Patchen, M., Davidson, J. D., Hofmann, G., and Brown, W. R. 1977. Determinants of students' interracial behavior and opinion change. *Sociology of Education,* 50:55–75.

————, Hofmann, G., and Davidson, J. D. 1976. Interracial perceptions among high school students. *Sociometry,* 39:341–354.

Paton, S. M., Walberg, H. J., and Yeh, E. G. 1973. Ethnicity, environmental control, and academic self-concept in Chicago. *American Educational Research Journal,* 10:85–99.

Patterson, O. 1977. *Ethnic Chauvinism: The Reactionary Impulse.* New York: Stein & Day.

Peach, C. 1980. Which triple melting pot? A re-examination of ethnic intermarriage in New Haven, 1900–1950. *Ethnic and Racial Studies,* 3:1–16.

Pearce, D. M. 1979. Gatekeepers and homeseekers: Institutional patterns in racial steering. *Social Problems,* 26:325–342.

————. 1980. *Breaking Down Barriers: New Evidence on the Impact of Metropolitan School Desegregation on Housing Patterns.* Washington, D.C.: Center for National Policy Review, Catholic University.

Pearl, D. 1955. Psychotherapy and ethnocentrism. *Journal of Abnormal and Social Psychology,* 50:227–229.

Pearlin, L. I. 1954. Shifting group attachments and attitudes toward Negroes. *Social Forces,* 33:47–50.

Peñalosa, F. 1979. *Chicano Sociolinguistics: A Brief Introduction.* Rowley, Mass.: Newbury House Publishers.

Pérez, L. 1980. Cubans. *Harvard Encyclopedia of American Ethnic Groups.* Cambridge, Mass.: Harvard University Press.

Petersen, W. 1958. A general typology of migration. *American Sociological Review,* 23:256–266.

————. 1966. Success story, Japanese-American style. *New York Times Magazine,* January 9, p. 20+.

————. 1971. *Japanese Americans.* New York: Random House.

Peterson, J. 1972. Huey Newton. *National Observer,* 7 (February 12):1.

Peterson, R. C. and Thurstone, L. I. 1933. *Motion Pictures and the Social Attitudes of Children.* New York: The Macmillan Co.

Pettigrew, T. F. 1958. Personality and sociocultural factors in intergroup attitudes: A cross-national comparison. *Journal of Conflict Resolution,* 2:29–42.

―――. 1959. Regional differences in anti-Negro prejudice. *The Journal of Abnormal and Social Psychology,* 59:28–36.

―――. 1964. *A Profile of the Negro American.* New York: Van Nostrand Reinhold Co.

―――. 1980. The changing—not declining—significance of race. *Contemporary Sociology,* 9:19–21.

――― and Green, R. L. 1976. School desegregation in large cities: A critique of the Coleman "white flight" thesis. *Harvard Educational Review,* 46:1–53.

Pfautz, H. W., Huguley, H. C., and McClain, J. W. 1975. Changes in reputed black community leadership, 1962–1972: A case study. *Social Forces,* 53:460–467.

Pinard, M., Kirk, J., and Von Eschen, D. 1969. Processes of recruitment in the sit-in movement. *Public Opinion Quarterly,* 33:355–369.

Porter, B. and Dunn, M. 1981. A year after the Miami riot embers still glow. *New York Times,* May 17, p. 25EY.

Porter, J. 1971. *Black Child, White Child: The Development of Racial Attitudes.* Cambridge, Mass.: Harvard University Press.

Portes, A. and Wilson, K. L., 1976. Black-white differentials in educational attainment. *American Sociological Review,* 41:414–431.

Porterfield, E. 1978. *Black and White Mixed Marriages.* Chicago: Nelson-Hall.

Poussaint, A. F. 1966a. The stresses of the white female worker in the civil rights movement in the South. *American Journal of Psychiatry,* 123:401–407.

―――. 1966b. Problems of white civil rights workers in the South. *Psychiatric Opinion,* 3:18–24.

―――. 1970. Minority group psychology: Implications for social action. In Pascal, A. (Ed.) *Thinking About Cities.* New York: Dickenson.

――― and Ladner, J. 1968. "Black Power": A failure for racial integration within the civil rights movement. *Archives of General Psychiatry,* 18:385–391.

Powdermaker, H. 1939. *After Freedom.* New York: Viking Press.

Price, A. G. 1950. *White Settlers and Native Peoples.* Melbourne, Australia: Georgian House.

Proudfoot, M. 1962. *Diary of a Sit-In.* Chapel Hill: University of North Carolina Press.

Quinn, O. W. 1954. The transmission of racial attitudes among white Southerners. *Social Forces,* 33:41–47.

Rabbie, J. M. and Horowitz, M. 1969. Arousal of ingroup-outgroup bias by a chance win or loss. *Journal of Personality and Social Psychology*, 13:269–277.

Radke, M. J., Sutherland, J., and Rosenberg, P. 1950. Racial attitudes of children. *Sociometry*, 13:151–171.

Raines, H. 1978. Revolution in South: Blacks at the polls and in office. *New York Times*, April 3, pp. 1, 16.

―――. 1979. Whites grow reluctant to back integration steps. *New York Times*, December 2, pp. 1, 68.

Rainwater, L. and Yancey, W. L. 1967. *The Moynihan Report and the Politics of Controversy*. Cambridge, Mass: The M.I.T. Press.

Ramirez, A. 1980. Miami Cubans prosper by sticking together, aiding later refugees. *Wall Street Journal*, May 20, pp. 1, 21.

Rand, C. 1958. *The Puerto Ricans*. New York: Oxford University Press.

Ransford, H. E. 1968. Isolation, powerlessness, and violence: A study of attitudes and participation in the Watts riot. *American Journal of Sociology*, 73:581–591.

Ravitch, D. 1978. The "white flight" controversy. *The Public Interest*, 51:135–149.

Razran, G. 1950. Ethnic dislike and stereotypes: A laboratory study. *Journal of Abnormal and Social Psychology*, 45:7–27.

Record, W. 1980. Review of *The Declining Significance of Race* by William J. Wilson. *American Journal of Sociology*, 85:965–968.

Redekop, C. 1969. *The Old Colony Mennonites*. Baltimore: The Johns Hopkins University Press.

Reich, M. 1972. Economic theories of racism. In Carnoy, M. (Ed.) *Schooling in a Corporate Society*. New York: David McKay.

Reinhold, R. 1979. Job programs for black youths need coordination, experts say. *New York Times*, March 14, pp. 1, 8.

Riley, M. W., Johnson, M., and Foner, A. 1972. *Aging and Society: A Sociology of Age Stratification*. Vol. 3. New York: Russell Sage Foundation.

Ripley, W. Z. 1899. *The Races of Europe*. New York: Appleton-Century-Crofts.

Roberts, A. H. and Rokeach, M. 1956. Anomie, authoritarianism, and prejudice: A replication. *American Journal of Sociology*, 61:355–358.

Robertson, H. M. 1933. *Aspects of the Rise of Economic Individualism*. London: Cambridge University Press.

Rodman, H. 1963. The lower class value stretch. *Social Forces*, 42:205–215.

Rohrer, J. H. 1942. The test intelligence of Osage Indians. *Journal of Social Psychology*, 16:99–105.

Rokeach, M. 1960. *The Open and Closed Mind*. New York: Basic Books.

――― and Mezei, L. 1966. Race and shared belief as factors in social choice. *Science*, 151 (January 14):167–172.

Roof, W. C. 1979. Socioeconomic differentials among white socioreligious groups in the United States. *Social Forces,* 58:280–289.

———. 1981. Unresolved issues in the study of religion and the national elite: Response to Greeley. *Social Forces,* 59:831–836.

Rose, A. M. 1944. Anti-Semitism's root in city-hatred. *Commentary,* 6:374–378.

———. 1949. *The Negro's Morale.* Minneapolis: University of Minnesota Press.

Rosen, B. C. 1959. Race, ethnicity and the achievement syndrome. *American Sociological Review,* 24:47–60.

Rosenberg, M. and Simmons, R. G. 1972. *Black and White Self-Esteem: The Urban School Child.* Washington, D.C.: American Sociological Association.

Rosenfield, D., Sheehan, D. S., Marcus, M. M., and Stephan, W. G. 1981. Classroom structure and prejudice in desegregated schools. *Journal of Educational Psychology,* 73:17–26.

Ross, J. M., Vanneman, R. D., and Pettigrew, T. F. 1976. Patterns of support for George Wallace: Implications for racial change. *Journal of Social Issues,* 32:69–91.

Rossell, C. 1976. School desegregation and white flight. *Political Science Quarterly,* 90:675–698.

Rubin, I. M. 1967. Increased self-acceptance: A means of reducing prejudice. *Journal of Personality and Social Psychology,* 5:233–238.

Rubovits, P. C. and Maehr, M. L. 1973. Pygmalion black and white. *Journal of Personality and Social Psychology,* 25:210–218.

Russo, N. J. 1969. Three generations of Italians in New York City: Their religious acculturation. *International Migration Review,* 3:3–17.

Saenger, G. and Flowerman, S. 1954. Stereotypes and prejudicial attitudes. *Human Relations,* 7:217–238.

——— and Gilbert, E. 1950. Customer reactions to the integration of Negro sales personnel. *International Journal of Opinion and Attitude Research,* 4:57–76.

Sage, W. 1978. Social scientists have some answers about the busing controversy. What are they? To find out you just pay your money and take your choice. *Human Behavior,* 7:18–23.

St. John, N. 1975. *School Desegregation: Outcomes for Children.* New York: John Wiley & Sons.

——— and Lewis, R. G. 1975. Race and the social structure of the elementary classroom. *Sociology of Education,* 48:346–368.

Samuelsson, K. 1961. *Religion and Economic Action: A Critique of Max Weber.* New York: Harper Torchbooks.

Sarnoff, I. and Katz, D. 1954. The motivational basis of attitude change. *Journal of Abnormal and Social Psychology,* 49:115–124.

Scarr-Salapatek, S. and Weinberg, R. A. 1975. When black children grow up in white homes. *Psychology Today,* 9 (December):80–83.

—— and Weinberg, R. A. 1976. IQ test performance of black children adopted by white families. *American Psychologist,* 31:726–739.

Schermerhorn, R. A. 1949. *These Our People.* Boston: D.C. Heath & Co.

Schlesinger, L. E. 1955. The influence of exposure to peer group opinions on the expression of attitudes toward a minority group. Ph.D. dissertation, Boston University.

Schrieke, B. 1936. *Alien Americans.* New York: Viking Press.

Schulman, G. I. 1974. Race, sex, and violence: A laboratory test of the sexual threat of the black male hypothesis. *American Journal of Sociology,* 79:1260–1277.

Scott, J. L. 1966. Social class factors underlying the civil rights movement. *Phylon,* 27:132–144.

Scully, M. G. 1978. Is race less important than class? *The Chronicle of Higher Education* (September 18):7–8.

Searles, R. and Williams, J. A., Jr. 1962. Negro college students' participation in sit-ins. *Social Forces,* 40:215–219.

Seidenberg, R. 1952. The sexual basis of social prejudice. *Psychoanalytic Review,* 39:90–95.

Selznick, G. J. and Steinberg, S. 1969. *The Tenacity of Prejudice.* New York: Harper & Row.

Sewell, W. H. and Hauser, R. M. 1976. Causes and consequences of higher education: Models of the status attainment process. In Sewell, W. H., Hauser, R. M., and Featherman, D. L. (Eds.) *Schooling and Achievement in American Society.* New York: Academic Press.

Sheppard, H. L. 1947. The Negro merchant: A study of Negro anti-Semitism. *American Journal of Sociology,* 43:96–99.

Sherif, M. 1949. The problem of inconsistency in intergroup relations. *Journal of Social Issues,* 5:32–37.

——, Harvey, O. J., White, B. J., Hood, W. R., and Sherif, C. W. 1961. *Intergroup Conflict and Cooperation: The Robbers Cave Experiment.* Norman: Institute of Group Relations, University of Oklahoma.

Shibutani, T. and Kwan, K. M. 1965. *Ethnic Stratification.* New York: The Macmillan Co.

Singleton, L. C. and Asher, S. R. 1977. Peer preferences and social interaction among third-grade children in an integrated school district. *Journal of Educational Psychology,* 69:330–336.

Sly, D. F. and Pol, L. G. 1978. The demographic context of school segregation and desegregation. *Social Forces,* 56:1072–1086.

Smedley, J. W. and Bayton, J. A. 1978. Evaluative race-class stereotypes by race and perceived class of subjects. *Journal of Personality and Social Psychology,* 36:530–535.

Smith, A. W. 1981. Racial tolerance as a function of group position. *American Sociological Review,* 46:558–573.

Smith, C. U. 1975. Public school desegregation and the law. *Social Forces,* 54:317–327.

Smothers, R. 1981. Puerto Rican family income found to be half U.S. median. *New York Times,* July 10, p. 7.

Solomon, F. and Fishman, J. R. 1964. The psychosocial meaning of nonviolence in student civil rights activities. *Psychiatry,* 27:91–99.

Sorce, J. F. 1979. The role of physiognomy in the development of racial awareness. *Journal of Genetic Psychology,* 134:33–41.

Sorkin, A. L. 1978. *The Urban American Indian.* Lexington, Mass.: D.C. Heath & Co.

Southern Commission on the Study of Lynching. 1931. *Lynchings and What They Mean.* Atlanta, Ga.: Southern Commission on the Study of Lynching.

Sowell, T. 1975. *Race and Economics.* New York: David McKay Co.

————. 1980. Ethnic groups, prejudice and economic progress. *Wall Street Journal,* December 4, p. 22.

————. 1981. *Ethnic America: A History.* New York: Basic Books.

Speier, H. 1941. The social types of war. *American Journal of Sociology,* 46:441–448.

Spicer, E. H. 1980. Federal policy toward American Indians. *Harvard Encyclopedia of American Ethnic Groups.* Cambridge, Mass.: Harvard University Press.

Spilerman, S. 1970. The causes of racial disturbances: A comparison of alternative explanations. *American Sociological Review,* 35:627–649.

Stampp, K. 1956. *The Peculiar Institution.* New York: Alfred A. Knopf.

Stein, B. N. 1979. Occupational adjustment of refugees: the Vietnamese in the United States. *International Migration Review,* 13:25–45.

Stein, H. F. and Hill, R. F. 1977. *The Ethnic Imperative: Examining the New White Ethnic Movement.* University Park: Pennsylvania State University Press.

Steinberg, J. A. and Hall, V. C. 1981. Effects of social behavior on interracial acceptance. *Journal of Educational Psychology,* 73:51–56.

Stember, C. H. 1961. *Education and Attitude Change.* New York: Institute of Human Relations Press.

————. 1976. *Sexual Racism.* New York: Elsevier.

Stephan, W. G. and Rosenfield, D. 1978. Effects of desegregation on race relations and self-esteem. *Journal of Educational Psychology,* 70:-670–679.

Sterba, J. P. 1977a. Where they come, what awaits them. *New York Times,* May 1, p. E3.

————. 1977b. Mexicans living illegally in U.S. "sneak" back home for holiday. *New York Times,* December 23, p. 14.

Stern, S. 1967. America's Black Guerillas. *Ramparts,* 6 (September):26–27.

Stevens, W. K. 1979. Millions of Mexicans view illegal entry to U.S. as door to opportunity. *New York Times,* February 19, pp. 1, 10.

Stokes, R. G. 1975. Afrikaner Calvinism and economic action: The Weberian thesis in South Africa. *American Journal of Sociology,* 81:-62–81.

Stonequist, E. V. 1937. *The Marginal Man.* New York: Charles Scribner.

Stotland, E., Katz, D., and Patchen, M. 1959. The reduction of prejudice through the arousal of self-insight. *Journal of Personality,* 27:-507–531.

Strodtbeck, F. L., McDonald, M. M., and Rosen, B. C. 1957. Evaluation of occupations: A reflection of Jewish and Italian mobility differences. *American Sociological Review,* 22:546–553.

Strong, E. K., Jr. 1933. *Japanese in California.* Stanford, Calif.: Stanford University Press.

Stryker, R. 1981. Religio-ethnic effects on attainments in the early career. *American Sociological Review,* 46:212–231.

Stuart, R. 1981. Black businesses still facing an uphill battle. *New York Times,* July 26, pp. 1, 13.

Sumner, W. G. 1906. *Folkways.* Boston: Ginn & Co.

Svensson, F. 1978. The final crisis of tribalism: Comparative ethnic policy on the American and Russian frontiers. *Ethnic and Racial Studies,* 1:100–123.

Szymaski, A. 1976. Racial discrimination and white gain. *American Sociological Review,* 41:403–414.

———. 1978. White workers' loss from racial discrimination. *American Sociological Review,* 43:776–782.

Taylor, D. G., Sheatsley, P. B., and Greeley, A. M. 1978. Attitudes toward racial integration. *Scientific American,* 238 (June):42–49.

Taylor, R. L. 1979. Black ethnicity and the persistence of ethnogenesis. *American Journal of Sociology,* 84:1401–1423.

Thomas, D. S. and Nichimoto, R. S. 1946. *The Spoilage.* Berkeley: University of California Press.

Thomas, J. L. 1951. The factor of religion in the selection of marriage mates. *American Sociological Review,* 16:487–491.

Thomas, W. I. 1931. The relation of research to the social process. In *Essays on Research in the Social Sciences.* Washington, D.C.: The Brookings Institution.

Thompson, D. C. 1963. *The Negro Leadership Class.* Englewood Cliffs, N.J.: Prentice-Hall.

———. 1965. The rise of the Negro protest. *The Annals of the American Academy of Political and Social Science,* 357:18–30.

Thornton, R. 1981. Demographic antecedents of a revitalization movement: Population change, population size, and the 1890 Ghost Dance. *American Sociological Review,* 46:88–96.

Toby, J. 1958. Hoodlum or business man: An American dilemma. In Sklare, M. (Ed.) *The Jews.* New York: The Free Press.

Tomasi, L. F. 1972. *The Italian American Family.* New York: Center for Migration Studies.

Tomasi, S. M. 1977. *Perspectives in Italian Immigration and Ethnicity.* New York: Center for Migration Studies.

Tomlinson, T. M. 1968. The development of a riot ideology among urban Negroes. *American Behavioral Scientist,* 2:27–31.

Trent, R. D. 1957. The relation between expressed self-acceptance and expressed attitudes toward Negroes and whites among Negro children. *Journal of Genetic Psychology,* 91:25–31.

Tumin, M. M. 1963. *Race and Intelligence.* New York: Anti-Defamation League of B'nai B'rith.

Turnbull, C. M. 1961. *The Forest People.* New York: Simon & Schuster.

———. 1965. *Wayward Servants.* Garden City, N.Y.: The Natural History Press.

Turner, C. B. and Wilson, W. J. 1976. Dimensions of racial ideology: A study of urban black attitudes. *Journal of Social Issues,* 32:-139–152.

Tyler, L. L. 1966. The Protestant ethnic among the Black Muslims. *Phylon,* 27:5–14.

U.S. Commission on Civil Rights. 1967. *Racial Isolation in the Public Schools.* Washington, D.C.: Government Printing Office.

Valentine, C. A. 1968. *Culture and Poverty: Critique and Counter-Proposals.* Chicago: University of Chicago Press.

van den Berghe, P. L. 1964. Toward a sociology of Africa. *Social Forces,* 43:11–18.

———. 1967. *Race and Racism.* New York: John Wiley & Sons.

———. 1974. Bringing beasts back in. *American Sociological Review,* 39:777–788.

———. 1976. The African diaspora in Mexico, Brazil, and the United States. *Social Forces,* 54:530–545.

Vander Zanden, J. W. 1965. *Race Relations in Transition.* New York: Random House.

———. 1981a. *Human Development,* 2nd ed. New York: Alfred A. Knopf.

———. 1981b. *Social Psychology.* 2nd ed. New York: Random House.

Velikonja, J. 1967. Italian immigrants in the United States in the mid-sixties. *International Migration Review,* 1:25–37.

Vidal, D. 1980a. Hispanic newcomers in city cling to values of homeland. *New York Times,* May 11, pp. 1, 42.

———. 1980b. Hispanic residents find some gains amid woes. *New York Times,* May 12, pp. 1, B6.

———. 1980c. Study shows Hispanic residents in favor of bilingual way of life. *New York Times,* May 13, pp. 1, B8.

————. 1980d. For Hispanic migrants, 'home' is elusive. *New York Times,* May 14, pp. 1, B4.

Villemez, W. J. 1978. Black subordination and white economic well-being. *American Sociological Review,* 43:772–776.

————. 1980. Race, class, and neighborhood: Differences in the residential return on individual resources. *Social Forces,* 59:414–430.

von Eickstedt, E. 1934. *Rassenkunde und Rassengeschechte der Menschheit.* Stuttgart: Gustav Fisher Verlag.

Wagley, C. and Harris, M. 1964. *Minorities in the New World.* New York: Columbia University Press.

Wang, J. 1981. Periling Chinatown. *New York Times,* May 15, p. 27.

Warner, L. G. and DeFleur, M. L. 1969. Attitude as an interactional concept: Social constraint and social distance as intervening variables between attitudes and action. *American Sociological Review,* 34:153–169.

Warner, W. L. 1949. *Democracy in Jonesville.* New York: Harper & Row.

————, Junker, B. H., and Adams, W. A. 1941. *Color and Human Nature.* Washington, D.C.: American Council on Education.

———— and Lunt, P. S. 1941. *The Social Life of a Modern Community.* New Haven: Yale University Press.

———— and Lunt, P. S. 1942. *The Status System of a Modern Community.* New Haven: Yale University Press.

————, Meeker, M., and Eells, K. 1949. *Social Class in America.* Chicago: Science Research Associates.

———— and Srole, L. 1945. *The Social System of American Ethnic Groups.* New Haven: Yale University Press.

Washburn, S. L. 1963. The study of race. In Tumin, M. M. *Race and Intelligence.* New York: Anti-Defamation League of B'nai B'rith.

Weber, M. 1905/1930. *The Protestant Ethic and the Spirit of Capitalism.* Trans. by Parsons, T. New York: Charles Scribner.

————. 1946. *From Max Weber: Essays in Sociology.* Trans. by Gerth, H. H. and Mills, C. W. New York: Oxford University Press.

————. 1947. *The Theory of Social and Economic Organization.* Trans. by Henderson, A. M. and Parsons, T. New York: Oxford University Press.

Weinstock, S. A. 1964. Some factors that retard or accelerate the rate of acculturation. *Human Relations,* 17:321–340.

Weiss, A. 1958. Jews need not apply. In Belth, N. C. (Ed.) *Barriers.* New York: Friendly House.

Wessel, B. B. 1931. *An Ethnic Survey of Woonsocket, Rhode Island.* Chicago: University of Chicago Press.

West, L. J.1965.On racial violence.*Northwest Medicine,* 64:679–682.

Westie, F. R. 1964. Race and ethnic relations. In Faris, R. E. L. (Ed.) *Handbook of Modern Sociology.* Chicago: Rand McNally.

Willhelm, S. M. 1971. *Who Needs the Negro?* Garden City, N.Y.: Doubleday Anchor.

————. 1980. Can Marxism explain America's racism? *Social Problems,* 28:98–112.

Williams, J. E. 1964. Connotations of color names among Negroes and Caucasians. *Perceptual & Motor Skills,* 18:721–731.

————. 1966. Connotations of racial concepts and color names. *Journal of Personality and Social Psychology,* 3:531–540.

———— and Morland, J. K. 1976. *Race, Color, and the Young Child.* Chapel Hill: University of North Carolina Press.

————, Tucker, R. D., and Dunham, F. Y. 1971. Changes in the connotations of color names among Negroes and Caucasians: 1963–1969. *Journal of Personality and Social Psychology,* 19:222–228.

Williams, J. R. and Gold, M. 1972. From delinquent behavior to official delinquency. *Social Problems,* 20:209–229.

Williams, R. M., Jr. 1947. *The Reduction of Intergroup Tensions.* New York: Social Science Research Council.

————. 1964. *Strangers Next Door.* Englewood Cliffs, N.J.: Prentice-Hall.

Willie, C. V. 1979. *Caste and Class Controversy.* New York: General Hall.

Wilner, D. M., Walkley, R. P., and Cook, S. W. 1955. *Human Relations in Interracial Housing.* Minneapolis: University of Minnesota Press.

Wilson, B. R. 1973. *Magic and the Millennium.* London: Heinemann.

Wilson, K. L. and Portes, A. 1980. Immigrant enclaves: An analysis of the labor market experiences of Cubans in Miami. *American Journal of Sociology,* 86:295–319.

Wilson, W. J. 1978. *The Declining Significance of Race.* Chicago: University of Chicago Press.

Wirth, L. 1928. *The Ghetto.* Chicago: University of Chicago Press.

————. 1945. The problem of minority groups. In Linton, R. (Ed.) *The Science of Man in the World Crisis.* New York: Columbia University Press.

Wolf, W. C. and Fligstein, N. D. 1979. Sex and authority in the workplace: The causes of sexual inequality. *American Sociological Review,* 44:235–252.

Wong, W. 1977. San Francisco killings jolt nationwide myth of carefree Chinatown. *Wall Street Journal,* November 16, pp. 1, 15.

Woodrum, E. 1981. An assessment of Japanese-American assimilation, pluralism, and subordination. *American Journal of Sociology,* 87:157–169.

Woodward, C. V. 1951. *Origins of the New South, 1877–1913.* Baton Rouge: Louisiana State University Press.

————. 1966. *The Strange Career of Jim Crow.* 2nd rev. ed. New York: Oxford University Press.

Works, E. 1961. The prejudice-interaction hypothesis from the point of view of the Negro minority group. *American Journal of Sociology*, 67:47–52.

Worthy, W. 1961. The angriest Negroes. *Esquire*, 55:101ff.

Wright, M. B. 1980. Indochinese. *Harvard Encyclopedia of American Ethnic Groups*. Cambridge, Mass.: Harvard University Press.

Yancey, W. L., Ericksen, E. P., and Juliani, R. N. 1976. Emergent ethnicity: A review and reformulation. *American Sociological Review*, 41:391–403.

———, Rigsby, L., and McCarthy, J. D. 1972. Social position and self-evaluation: The relative importance of race. *American Journal of Sociology*, 78:338–359.

Yankelovich, D. 1979. Who gets ahead in America. *Psychology Today* 13 (July):28–34+.

Yans-McLaughlin, V. 1977. *Family and Community: Italian Immigrants in Buffalo, 1880–1930*. Ithaca, N.Y.: Cornell University Press.

Yerkes, R. M. 1921. Psychological examining in the United States Army. *National Academy of Sciences*, Memoir 15.

Yinger, J. M. 1970. *The Scientific Study of Religion*. New York: The Macmillan Co.

Young, D. 1937. *Research Memorandum on Minority Peoples in the Depression*. New York: Social Science Research Council.

Yuan, D. Y. 1963. Voluntary segregation: A study of new Chinatown. *Phylon*, 24:260–262.

Yutzy, D. 1968. The decline of orthodoxy among the Amish. *Sociological Focus*, 2:19–26.

Zangwill, I. 1921. *The Melting Pot: Drama in Four Acts*. New York: The Macmillan Co.

Zirkel, P. A. 1971. Self-concept and the "disadvantage" of ethnic group membership and mixture. *Review of Educational Research*, 41:-211–225.

Author Index

Subject Index

About the Author

James W. Vander Zanden is a professor in the College of Social and Behavioral Sciences at The Ohio State University and previously taught at Duke University. His Ph.D. degree is from the University of North Carolina. Professor Vander Zanden's published works include more than twenty professional articles, primarily in the area of race relations, as well as books on social psychology, education, and human development.

A Note on the Type

The text of this book is set in Gael, a CRT/Videocomp version of Caledonia, a linotype face designed by W. A. Dwiggins. It belongs to the family of printing types called "modern face" by printers—a term used to mark the change in style of type-letters that occurred about 1800. Caledonia borders on the general design of Scotch Modern, but is more freely drawn than that letter.